Lecture Notes in Computer Science 15934

Founding Editors

Gerhard Goos
Juris Hartmanis

AF166660

The series Lecture Notes in Computer Science (LNCS), including its subseries Lecture Notes in Artificial Intelligence (LNAI) and Lecture Notes in Bioinformatics (LNBI), has established itself as a medium for the publication of new developments in computer science and information technology research, teaching, and education.

LNCS enjoys close cooperation with the computer science R & D community, the series counts many renowned academics among its volume editors and paper authors, and collaborates with prestigious societies. Its mission is to serve this international community by providing an invaluable service, mainly focused on the publication of conference and workshop proceedings and postproceedings. LNCS commenced publication in 1973.

Ruzica Piskac · Zvonimir Rakamarić
Editors

Computer Aided Verification

37th International Conference, CAV 2025
Zagreb, Croatia, July 23–25, 2025
Proceedings, Part IV

 Springer

Editors
Ruzica Piskac
Yale University
New Haven, CT, USA

Zvonimir Rakamarić
Amazon (United States)
Seattle, WA, USA

ISSN 0302-9743   ISSN 1611-3349 (electronic)
Lecture Notes in Computer Science
ISBN 978-3-031-98684-0   ISBN 978-3-031-98685-7 (eBook)
https://doi.org/10.1007/978-3-031-98685-7

This Springer imprint is published by the registered company Springer Nature Switzerland AG
The registered company address is: Gewerbestrasse 11, 6330 Cham, Switzerland

If disposing of this product, please recycle the paper.

Preface

It was our privilege to serve as the program chairs for CAV 2025, the 37th International Conference on Computer-Aided Verification. CAV 2025 was held in Zagreb, Croatia, on July 23–25, 2025, and the pre-conference workshops were held on July 21–22, 2025.

CAV is an annual conference dedicated to the advancement of the theory and practice of computer-aided formal analysis methods for hardware and software systems. The primary focus of CAV is to extend the frontiers of verification techniques by expanding to new domains such as security, quantum computing, and machine learning. This puts CAV at the cutting edge of formal methods research. This year's program is a reflection of this commitment.

CAV 2025 received 305 submissions. We accepted 24 tool papers, 4 case-study papers, and 51 regular papers, which amounts to an acceptance rate of roughly 25.9% overall. The accepted papers cover a wide spectrum of topics, from theoretical results to applications of formal methods. These papers apply or extend formal methods to a wide range of domains such as concurrency, machine learning and neural networks, quantum systems, as well as hybrid and stochastic systems. The program featured keynote talks by Corina Păsăreanu (Carnegie Mellon University, USA), Emina Torlak (Amazon Web Services and University of Washington, USA), and Roderick Bloem (Graz University of Technology, Austria). In addition to the contributed talks, CAV 2025 also hosted the CAV Award ceremony, and a report from the Synthesis Competition (SYNTCOMP) chairs. Furthermore, we continued the tradition of Logic Lounge, a series of discussions on computer science topics targeting a general audience. This year's Logic Lounge speakers were Moshe Y. Vardi (Rice University) and Henry Shevlin (University of Cambridge) who invited us to examine the nature of mind itself and whether artificial intelligence met its defining criteria.

In addition to the main conference, CAV 2025 hosted the following workshops: Verification Mentoring Workshop (VMW), Workshop on Synthesis (SYNT), Workshop on Verification of Quantum Computing (VQC), Workshop on Automated Reasoning for Tensor Compilers (AR4TC), International Workshop on Trustworthy Cyber-Physical Systems (TACPS), Workshop on Hyperproperties: Advances in Theory and Applications (HYPER), Symposium on AI Verification (SAIV), Meeting on String Constraints and Applications (MOSCA), Workshop on Horn Clauses for Verification and Synthesis (HCVS), and Workshop on Verification of Probabilistic Programs (VeriProP). Furthermore, CAV 2025 also included the following events dedicated to two prominent members of the CAV community: Ken McMillan Celebration and Allen Emerson Memorial.

Organizing a flagship conference like CAV requires a great deal of effort from the community. The Program Committee for CAV 2025 consisted of 122 members and two co-chairs—a committee of this size ensures that each member has to review only a reasonable number of papers in the allotted time. In all, the committee members wrote 958 reviews while investing significant effort to maintain and ensure the high quality of the conference program. We are grateful to the CAV 2025 Program Committee for their outstanding efforts in evaluating the submissions and making sure that each paper got a fair chance.

Like recent years in CAV, we made artifact evaluation mandatory for tool paper submissions, but optional for the rest of the accepted papers. This year we received 68 artifact submissions, all of which received at least one badge. We rejected 5 tool papers because the associated artifacts did not meet the functional badge criteria. The Artifact Evaluation Committee consisted of 83 members and two co-chairs, who put in significant effort to evaluate each artifact. The goal of this process was to provide constructive feedback to tool developers and help make the research published in CAV more reproducible. We are also very grateful to the Artifact Evaluation Committee for their hard work and dedication in evaluating the submitted artifacts.

CAV 2025 would not have been possible without the tremendous help we received from a number of individuals, and we would like to thank everyone who helped make CAV 2025 a success. First, we would like to thank our area chairs Anthony Widjaja Lin, Azadeh Farzan, Erika Ábrahám, Eva Darulova, Guy Katz, Peter Müller, Philipp Rümmer, and Roderick Bloem. Moreover, we would like to thank Matthias Heizmann and Tanja Schindler for chairing the Artifact Evaluation Committee. We also thank Grigory Fedyukovich for chairing the workshop organization. Ferhat Erata and Hadar Frenkel for leading publicity efforts, Ning Luo as the fellowship chair, Borzoo Bonakdarpour and Jana Hofmann as sponsorship chairs, and Jordan Schmerge as the website chair. Steve Siegel helped prepare the proceedings, while Alan Jović spearheaded the local organization. We also thank Grigory Fedyukovich, Mukund Raghothaman, Elizabeth Polgreen, Kaushik Mallik, and Thom Badings for organizing the Verification Mentoring Workshop. Last but not least, we would like to thank the members of the CAV Steering Committee (Kenneth McMillan, Aarti Gupta, Orna Grumberg, and Daniel Kroening) for helping us with several important aspects of organizing CAV 2025.

We hope that you will find the proceedings of CAV 2025 scientifically interesting and thought-provoking!

June 2025

Ruzica Piskac
Zvonimir Rakamarić

Organization

Steering Committee

Orna Grumberg	Technion, Israel
Aarti Gupta	Princeton University, USA
Daniel Kroening	Amazon, USA
Kenneth McMillan	University of Texas at Austin, USA

Conference Co-chairs

Ruzica Piskac	Yale University, USA
Zvonimir Rakamarić	Amazon Web Services, USA

Artifact Evaluation Co-chairs

Matthias Heizmann	University of Stuttgart, Germany
Tanja Schindler	University of Basel, Switzerland

Local Chair

Alan Jović	University of Zagreb, Croatia

Area Chairs

Anthony Widjaja Lin	Technical University of Kaiserslautern, Germany
Azadeh Farzan	University of Toronto, Canada
Erika Ábrahám	RWTH Aachen University, Germany
Eva Darulova	Uppsala University, Sweden
Guy Katz	Hebrew University of Jerusalem, Israel
Peter Müller	ETH Zurich, Switzerland
Philipp Rümmer	University of Regensburg, Germany
Roderick Bloem	Graz University of Technology, Austria

Workshop Chair

Grigory Fedyukovich   Florida State University, USA

Fellowship Chair

Ning Luo   University of Illinois Urbana-Champaign, USA

Publicity Chairs

Ferhat Erata   Yale University, USA
Hadar Frenkel   Bar Ilan University, Israel

Publication Chair

Stephen Siegel   University of Delaware, USA

Website Chair

Jordan Schmerge   Yale University, USA

Program Committee

Aarti Gupta   Princeton University, USA
Ahmed Bouajjani   Université Paris Cité, France
Aina Niemetz   Stanford University, USA
Alan J. Hu   University of British Columbia, Canada
Alberto Griggio   Fondazione Bruno Kessler, Italy
Alessandro Cimatti   Fondazione Bruno Kessler, Italy
Alexander J. Summers   University of British Columbia, Canada
Alexander Nadel   Technion & Intel, Israel
Alfons Laarman   Leiden University, Netherlands
Aman Goel   Amazon Web Services, USA
Anastasia Isychev   TU Wien, Austria
Anastasia Mavridou   KBR/NASA Ames Research Center, USA
Anca Muscholl   LaBRI, Université Bordeaux, France

Andreas Pavlogiannis	Aarhus University, Denmark
Andreas Podelski	University of Freiburg, Germany
Anna Lukina	TU Delft, Netherlands
Anne-Kathrin Schmuck	Max Planck Institute for Software Systems, Germany
Anthony Widjaja Lin	TU Kaiserslautern, Germany
Anton Wijs	Eindhoven University of Technology, Netherlands
Arie Gurfinkel	University of Waterloo, Canada
Armin Biere	University of Freiburg, Germany
Azadeh Farzan	University of Toronto, Canada
Barbara Jobstmann	Cadence Design Systems, Switzerland
Benjamin Kaminski	Saarland University, Germany
Bernd Finkbeiner	CISPA Helmholtz Center for Information Security, Germany
Bettina Könighofer	Graz University of Technology, Austria
Borzoo Bonakdarpour	Michigan State University, USA
Burcu Kulahcioglu Ozkan	Delft University of Technology, Netherlands
Cesar Sanchez	IMDEA Software Institute, Spain
Christoph M. Wintersteiger	Imandra, UK
Christoph Matheja	University of Oldenburg, Germany
Clark Barrett	Stanford University, USA
Claudia Cauli	Huawei Ireland Research Center, Ireland
Corina Pasareanu	NASA Ames Research Center, USA
Cristina David	University of Bristol, UK
Damien Zufferey	NVIDIA, Switzerland
Daniel Kröning	Amazon, USA
Daniel Stan	LRE EPITA Research Laboratory, France
Dirk Beyer	LMU Munich, Germany
Dominik Winterer	ETH Zurich, Switzerland
Đorđj e Žikelić	Singapore Management University, Singapore
Dorra Ben Khalifa	ENAC – University of Toulouse, France
Duc-Hiep Chu	Google Research, USA
Elizabeth Polgreen	University of Edinburgh, UK
Elvira Albert	Complutense University of Madrid, Spain
Enrico Magnago	Amazon Web Services, Germany
Erika Ábrahám	RWTH Aachen University, Germany
Eva Darulova	Uppsala University, Sweden
Gidon Ernst	LMU Munich, Germany
Guowen Xu	University of Electronic Science and Technology of China, China
Guy Amir	Cornell University, USA
Guy Katz	Hebrew University of Jerusalem, Israel

Hadar Frenkel	Bar Ilan University, Israel
Haoze (Andrew) Wu	Amherst College, USA
Harald Ruess	SRI International, USA
Hari Govind Vediramana Krishnan	University of Waterloo, Canada
Hazem Torfah	Chalmers University of Technology, Sweden
He Zhu	Rutgers University, USA
Hossein Hojjat	Tehran Institute of Advanced Studies, Iran
Ichiro Hasuo	National Institute of Informatics, Japan
Jana Hofmann	Max Planck Institute for Security and Privacy, Germany
Ji Guan	Institute of Software, Chinese Academy of Sciences, China
Jianan Yao	Amazon Web Services, USA
Jingbo Wang	Purdue University, USA
Jocelyn (Qiaochu) Chen	New York University, USA
Joey Dodds	Amazon Web Services, USA
Joost-Pieter Katoen	RWTH-Aachen University, Germany
Jorge A. Pérez	University of Groningen, Netherlands
Junkil Park	Aptos Labs, USA
Kaushik Mallik	IMDEA Software Institute, Spain
Kedar Namjoshi	Bell Labs, Nokia, USA
Kshitij Bansal	Google, USA
Kyungmin Bae	POSTECH, South Korea
Laura Kovacs	TU Wien, Austria
Magnus Myreen	Chalmers University of Technology, Sweden
Marco Faella	University of Naples Federico II, Italy
Marieke Huisman	University of Twente, Netherlands
Mark Santolucito	Barnard College, Columbia University, USA
Michael Emmi	Amazon Web Services, USA
Mihaela Sighireanu	University Paris-Saclay, France
Mirco Giacobbe	University of Birmingham, UK
Natasha Sharygina	University of Lugano, Switzerland
Nian-Ze Lee	National Taiwan University, Taiwan
Ning Luo	University of Illinois Urbana-Champaign, USA
Ondřej Lengál	Brno University of Technology, Czech Republic
Pablo Castro	Universidad Nacional de Río Cuarto - CONICET, Argentina
Pavithra Prabhakar	Kansas State University, USA
Peter Müller	ETH Zurich, Switzerland
Philipp Ruemmer	University of Regensburg, Germany
Qinxiang Cao	Shanghai Jiao Tong University, China
Ravi Mangal	Colorado State University, USA

Rayna Dimitrova	CISPA Helmholtz Center for Information Security, Germany
Roderick Bloem	Graz University of Technology, Austria
S. Akshay	Indian Institute of Technology Bombay, India
S. Krishna	Indian Institute of Technology Bombay, India
Shaobo He	Amazon Web Services, USA
Shibashis Guha	Tata Institute of Fundamental Research, India
Soham Chakraborty	TU Delft, Netherlands
Stefan Leue	University of Konstanz, Germany
Stefan Zetzsche	Amazon Web Services, UK
Stephen F. Siegel	University of Delaware, USA
Subhajit Roy	Indian Institute of Technology Kanpur, India
Sylvie Putot	Ecole Polytechnique, France
Sébastien Bardin	CEA List, Université Paris Saclay, France
Tachio Terauchi	Waseda University, Japan
Tatjana Petrov	University of Trieste, Italy
Thomas Wahl	Trusted Science and Technology, Inc., USA
Tim King	Amazon Web Services, USA
Timos Antonopoulos	Yale University, USA
Tom van Dijk	University of Twente, Netherlands
Tomas Vojnar	Masaryk University, Czech Republic
Vijay Ganesh	Georgia Tech, USA
Viktor Kunčak	EPFL, Switzerland
Wenxi Wang	University of Virginia, USA
William Hallahan	Binghamton University, USA
Xi (James) Zheng	Macquarie University, Australia
Yakir Vizel	Technion, Israel
Yedi Zhang	National University of Singapore, Singapore
Yu-Fang Chen	Academia Sinica, Taiwan
Yuting Wang	Shanghai Jiao Tong University, China
Yuxin Deng	East China Normal University, China
Yuyang Sang	Alibaba Cloud, USA

Artifact Evaluation Committee

Abdalrhman Mohamed	Stanford University, USA
Abhishek Kr Singh	National University of Singapore, Singapore
Adwait Godbole	UC Berkeley, USA
Akshatha Shenoy	Università della Svizzera italiana, Switzerland
Alejandro Hernández-Cerezo	Complutense University of Madrid, Spain
Ameer Hamza	Florida State University, USA

Amit Samanta	University of Utah, USA
Anna Becchi	Fondazione Bruno Kessler, Italy
Annelot Bosman	Universiteit Leiden, Netherlands
Avaljot Singh	University of Illinois Urbana-Champaign, USA
Avraham Raviv	Bar Ilan University, Israel
Benjamin F. Jones	Amazon Web Services, USA
Bruno Andreotti	Federal University of Minas Gerais, Brazil
Calvin Chau	Technische Universität Dresden, Germany
Cayden Codel	Carnegie Mellon University, USA
Chenyu Zhou	University of Southern California, USA
Christoph Weinhuber	University of Oxford, UK
Clara Rodríguez-Núñez	Universidad Complutense de Madrid, Spain
Daniel Ajeleye	University of Colorado, Boulder, USA
Diptarko Roy	University of Birmingham, UK
Ehsan Kafshdar Goharshady	Institute of Science and Technology, Austria
Enrico Magnago	Amazon Web Services, Germany
Filip Cano	Graz University of Technology, Austria
Filip Macák	Brno University of Technology, Czech Republic
Filipe de Arruda	Universidade Federal de Pernambuco, Brazil
Florian Sextl	TU Wien, Austria
Frédéric Recoules	CEA LIST, France
Geunyeol Yu	Pohang University of Science and Technology, South Korea
Guangyu Hu	Hong Kong University of Science and Technology, China
Hichem Rami Ait-El-Hara	Université Paris-Saclay, France
Idan Refaeli	Hebrew University of Jerusalem, Israel
Jacqueline Mitchell	University of Southern California, USA
Jaime Arias	CNRS, LIPN, Université Sorbonne Paris Nord, France
Jiong Yang	Georgia Institute of Technology, USA
Joseph Tafese	University of Waterloo, Canada
Kadiray Karakaya	Paderborn University, Germany
Konstantin Britikov	University of Lugano, Switzerland
Konstantin Kueffner	Institute of Science and Technology, Austria
Leni Aniva	Stanford University, USA
Lutz Klinkenberg	RWTH Aachen University, Germany
Mahboubeh Samadi	Tehran Institute for Advanced Studies, Iran
Mahyar Karimi	Institute of Science and Technology, Austria
Marek Chalupa	Institute of Science and Technology, Austria
Mário Pereira	NOVA School of Science and Technology, Portugal

Mathias Fleury	University of Freiburg, Germany
Mehrdad Karrabi	Institute of Science and Technology, Austria
Miguel Isabel	Complutense University of Madrid, Spain
Mihai Nicola	Stevens Institute of Technology, USA
Mihály Dobos-Kovács	Budapest University of Technology and Economics, Hungary
Mikael Mayer	Amazon Web Services, USA
Muqsit Azeem	Technical University of Munich, Germany
N. Ege Saraç	Institute of Science and Technology, Austria
Neea Rusch	Augusta University, USA
Nicolas Koh	Princeton University, USA
Omar Inverso	Gran Sasso Science Institute, Italy
Omkar Tuppe	IIT Bombay, India
Omri Isac	Hebrew University of Jerusalem, Israel
Oyendrila Dobe	Amazon Web Services, USA
Pablo Gordillo	Complutense University of Madrid, Spain
Patrick Trentin	Amazon Web Services, USA
Pei-Wei Chen	UC Berkeley, USA
Peixin Wang	Nanyang Technological University, Singapore
Philipp Kern	Karlsruhe Institute of Technology, Germany
Pinhan Zhao	University of Michigan, USA
Po-Chun Chien	LMU Munich, Germany
Rajarshi Roy	University of Oxford, UK
Sankalp Gambhir	EPFL, Switzerland
Sascha Klüppelholz	Technische Universität Dresden, Germany
Shantanu Kulkarni	IIT Bombay, India
Simon Guilloud	EPFL, Switzerland
Stefan Zetzsche	Amazon Web Services, UK
Timo Lang	Huawei Ireland Research Center, Ireland
Xuan Xie	University of Alberta, Canada
Yanju Chen	University of California, Santa Barbara, USA
Yannik Schnitzer	University of Oxford, UK
Yibo Dong	East China Normal University, China
Yizhak Elboher	Hebrew University of Jerusalem, Israel
Yogev Shalmon	Technion, Israel
Yuning Wang	Rutgers University, USA
Yusen Su	University of Waterloo, Canada
Zhengyang John Lu	University of Waterloo, Canada
Zhiyang Chen	University of Toronto, Canada
Zunchen Huang	CWI, Netherlands

Additional Reviewers

Abha Chaudhary
Adam Husted Kjelstrøm
Adam Rogalewicz
Alejandro Luque-Cerpa
Alejandro Villoria Gonzalez
Alex Ozdemir
Alexander Bork
Alexander C. Wilton
Alexander Stekelenburg
Andoni Rodriguez
Andrew Reynolds
Anja Petkovic Komel
Anton Varonka
Antonina Skurka
Antonio Casares
Arend-Jan Quist
Áron Ricardo Perez-Lopez
Arshia Rafieioskouei
Ashwani Anand
Benedikt Maderbacher
Benjamin Monmege
Che Cheng
Chia-Hsuan Su
Christian Lidström
Christina Gehnen
Christophe Chareton
Christopher Brix
Christopher Watson
Corto Mascle
Cruise Song
Daniela Kaufman
David Boetius
Dimitrios Thanos
Fabio Mogavero
Faezeh Labbaf
Felix Stutz
Filip Cano
Gianluca Redondi
Grigory Fedyukovich
Grégoire Menguy
Hangcheng Cao
Henrik Wachowitz
Igor Walukiewicz

Irmak Saglam
Iwo Kurzidem
Jan Martens
Jannick Strobel
Jasper Nalbach
Jia Hu
Jingyi Mei
Jinhua Wu
Johannes Haring
Joonhwan Yoo
Konstantin Britikov
Ling Zhang
Lutz Klinkenberg
Marc Farreras I Bartra
Marek Jankola
Marian Lingsch-Rosenfeld
Marvin Brieger
Massimo Benerecetti
Mathias Preiner
Matthew Davis
Matthias Kettl
Matthieu Bovel
Matthieu Lemerre
Michal Hečko
Milad Rabizadeh
Min Wu
Mingyu Huang
Muhammad Mahmoud
Pengzhi Xing
Pierre Ganty
Piyush Jha
Po-Chun Chien
Pranshu Gaba
Prithwish Jana
Rachel Cleaveland
Rafael Dewes
Raffael Senn
Ritam Raha
Robert Mensing
Roy Hermanns
Satya Prakash Nayak
Simon Guilloud
Steef Hegeman

Stefan Pranger
Subhajit Bandopadhyay
Thomas Hader
Thomas Lemberger
Tian-Fu Chen
Timm Spork
Tobias Winkler
Tomas Kolarik
Tomáš Dacík
Tzu-Han Hsu

Valentin Promies
Xieting Chu
Xin Hong
Xinyuan Qian
Yanis Sellami
Yicheng Ni
Yizhou Mao
Zhengyang Lu
Zhengyu Li
Zihao Li

Keynote Talks

Through the Looking Glass: Semantic Analysis of Neural Networks

Corina Păsăreanu

Carnegie Mellon University, USA

Abstract. Neural networks are known for their lack of transparency, making them difficult to understand and analyze. In this talk, we explore methods designed to interpret, formally analyze, and even shape the internal representations of neural networks using human-understandable abstractions. We review recent techniques including the use of vision-language models to investigate perception modules, the application of probing and steering vectors to identify vulnerabilities in code models, and an axiomatic approach for validating mechanistic interpretation of transformer models.

Bio. Corina Păsăreanu is an ACM Fellow working at NASA Ames. She is affiliated with KBR and Carnegie Mellon University's CyLab. Her research interests include model checking, symbolic execution, compositional verification, AI safety, autonomy, and security. She is the recipient of several awards, including an ETAPS Test of Time Award and an ACM Impact Paper Award. She has served as Program/General Chair for several conferences, including CAV in 2015, and more recently ICSE in 2025. More information can be found on her website: https://www.andrew.cmu.edu/user/pcorina/.

Cedar: A New Language for Expressive, Fast, Safe, and Analyzable Authorization

Emina Torlak

Amazon Web Services and University of Washington, USA

Abstract. Authorization is the problem of deciding who has access to what in a multi-user system. Every cloud-based application has to solve this problem, from photo sharing to online banking to health care. This talk presents Cedar, a new language for authorization that is designed to be ergonomic, fast, safe, and analyzable by reduction to SMT. Cedar's simple and intuitive syntax supports common authorization use-cases with readable policies, naturally expressing concepts from role-based, attribute-based, and relation-based access control models. Cedar's policy structure enables authorization requests to be decided quickly. Its policy validator uses optional typing to help policy writers avoid mistakes, but not get in their way. Cedar's design has been finely balanced to allow for a sound, complete, and decidable logical encoding, which enables precise policy analysis, e.g., to ensure that policy refactoring preserves existing permissions. We have implemented Cedar in Rust and used Lean to formally verify important properties of its design. Cedar is used at scale in Amazon Verified Permissions and Amazon Verified Access, and it is freely available at https://github.com/cedar-policy.

Bio. Emina Torlak is a Senior Principal Scientist at Amazon Web Services and an Affiliate Professor at the University of Washington. Emina works on new languages and tools for program verification and synthesis. She received her Bachelors (2003), Masters (2004), and Ph.D. (2009) degrees from MIT. Emina is the creator of Rosette and Kodkod, and leads the development of Cedar. Rosette is a solver-aided language that powers verification and synthesis tools for all kinds of systems, from radiation therapy control to Linux JIT compilers. Kodkod is a solver for relational logic, used widely in tools for software analysis and design. Cedar is an expressive, fast, and analysable language for authorization, used at scale at Amazon Web Services and beyond. Emina is a recipient of the Robin Milner Young Researcher Award (2021), NSF Career Award (2017), Sloan Research Fellowship (2016), and the AITO Dahl-Nygaard Junior Prize (2016).

Side Channel Secure Software: A Hardware Question

Roderick Bloem

Graz University of Technology, Austria

Abstract. We will present a method to prove the absence of power side channels in systems that are protected using masking. Power side channels may allow attackers to discover secret information by measuring electromagnetic emanations from a chip. Masking is a countermeasure to hide secrets by duplication and addition of randomness. We will discuss how to formally prove security against power side channel techniques for circuits. We will then move on to software running on a CPU, where hardware details can have surprising effects. We will present some vulnerabilities on a small CPU and how to fix them, and we will talk about contracts that take side channels into account.

Bio. Roderick Bloem is a professor at Graz University of Technology. He received his M.Sc. degree in Computer Science from Leiden University, the Netherlands, in 1996, and his Ph.D. degree in Computer Science from the University of Colorado at Boulder in 2001. From 2002 until 2008, he was an Assistant at Graz University of Technology, Graz, Austria. From 2008, he has been a full professor of Computer Science at the same university. He is a co-editor of the *Handbook of Model Checking* and has published over 140 peer reviewed papers in formal verification, reactive synthesis, Safe AI, and security.

References

1. Bloem, R., Gigerl, B., Gourjon, M., Hadzic, V., Mangard, S., Primas, R.: Power contracts: provably complete power leakage models for processors. In: Yin, H., Stavrou, A., Cremers, C., Shi, E. (eds.) Proceedings of the 2022 ACM SIGSAC Conference on Computer and Communications Security, CCS 2022, Los Angeles, CA, USA, 7–11 November 2022. pp. 381–395. ACM (2022). https://doi.org/10.1145/3548606.3560600
2. Bloem, R., Gross, H., Iusupov, R., Könighofer, B., Mangard, S., Winter, J.: Formal verification of masked hardware implementations in the presence of glitches. In: Nielsen, J., Rijmen, V. (eds.) EUROCRYPT 2018. LNCS, vol. 10821, pp. 321–353. Springer, Cham (2018). https://doi.org/10.1007/978-3-319-78375-8_11

3. Hadzic, V., Bloem, R.: COCOALMA: a versatile masking verifier. In: Formal Methods in Computer Aided Design, FMCAD 2021, New Haven, CT, USA, 19–22 October 2021, pp. 1–10. IEEE (2021). https://doi.org/10.34727/2021/ISBN.978-3-85448-046-4_9

4. Haring, J., Hadzic, V., Bloem, R.: Closing the gap: Leakage contracts for processors with transitions and glitches. IACR Trans. Cryptogr. Hardw. Embed. Syst. 2024(4), 110–132 (2024). https://doi.org/10.46586/TCHES.V2024.I4.110-132

Contents – Part IV

Applications

Quantum Computing

Verifying Fault-Tolerance of Quantum Error Correction Codes

Kean Chen[1]($^{(\boxtimes)}$) , Yuhao Liu[1] , Wang Fang[2] , Jennifer Paykin[3],
Xin-Chuan Wu[4], Albert Schmitz[3], Steve Zdancewic[1]($^{(\boxtimes)}$) , and Gushu Li[1]($^{(\boxtimes)}$)

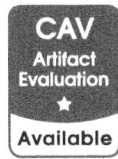

[1] University of Pennsylvania, Philadelphia, USA
{keanchen,stevez,gushuli}@seas.upenn.edu
[2] University of Edinburgh, Edinburgh, UK
[3] Intel Corporation, Hillsboro, USA
[4] Intel Corporation, Santa Clara, USA

Abstract. Quantum computers have advanced rapidly in qubit count and gate fidelity. However, large-scale fault-tolerant quantum computing still relies on quantum error correction code (QECC) to suppress noise. Manually or experimentally verifying the fault-tolerance property of complex QECC implementation is impractical due to the vast error combinations. This paper formalizes the fault-tolerance of QECC implementations within the language of quantum programs. By incorporating the techniques of quantum symbolic execution, we provide an automatic verification tool for quantum fault-tolerance. We evaluate and demonstrate the effectiveness of our tool on a universal set of logical operations across different QECCs.

1 Introduction

Quantum computers have the potential to address many significant problems that are hard to tackle on classical computers [38,43]. However, real-world quantum computers suffer from noise, and practical quantum computation relies on the quantum error correction codes (QECCs) [20,22] to correct the errors caused by the noises and protect the quantum information. Recently, prototyping QECCs have been experimentally demonstrated on various devices of different quantum computing technologies [2,3,6,44].

A critical property that a QECC must satisfy is *fault-tolerance*. That is, a QECC should be able to correct a certain amount of errors even if the physical operations to implement the QECC are themselves noisy. Proving fault-tolerance is required for every newly designed QECC. However, hand-written proofs [22,23] are only feasible for low-distance and few-qubit codes by propagating the state under combinations of errors. Such proofs soon become overwhelming as more advanced and sophisticated QECCs [10,33,52] involving more physical qubits and physical operations are proposed.

Computer-aided techniques are well-suited for verifying the fault-tolerance of QECCs. However, current verification tools on quantum programs either 1)

© The Author(s) 2025
R. Piskac and Z. Rakamarić (Eds.): CAV 2025, LNCS 15934, pp. 3–27, 2025.
https://doi.org/10.1007/978-3-031-98685-7_1

fail to capture the stabilizer formalism of QECCs [14,24,28,48,53,54], leading to significant scalability issues, or 2) do not consider execution faults [4,16,17,36], making it hard for them to accommodate verification for fault-tolerance.

In particular, we identify several key challenges for mechanically proving the fault-tolerance of a QECC. (1) Quantum computing is intrinsically analog with *continuous errors*, which are hard to reason about on digital classical computers. (2) The implementations of QECC often involve complex control flow, such as *loops*, which introduce non-monotonicity in the transitions, making both semantics and error analysis less tractable. (3) QECCs contain non-Clifford logical operations for universality, which usually cannot benefit from the stabilizer formalism for efficient processing.

In this paper, we overcome these challenges and propose an automated verification tool for QECC fault-tolerance. **First,** we extend the semantics of classical-quantum programming language [57,58] under the presence of quantum errors, where we can describe and formalize the criterion of fault-tolerance for QECC components. **Second,** we show that the continuous errors in the input quantum states and during the execution can both be *discretized* to certain input states and Pauli errors. This allows us to develop a symbolic execution engine to prove QECC fault-tolerance via stabilizer formalism. **Third,** we observe that the loops in typical QECCs have unique properties, *memory-less/conservative*, which can enable new symbolic transition rules to overcome the complexity caused by loops. **Fourth,** to handle the non-Clifford components, we propose a two-party framework that absorbs non-Clifford components in the inputs. Then, we show that the execution with only Clifford components is fault-tolerant for arbitrary inputs and thus prove the overall fault-tolerance.

We have implemented a symbolic execution framework to prove the fault-tolerance of QECCs and used it to check the fault-tolerance of the essential functional components (i.e., state preparation, gate, measurement, error correction) of various QECCs of different sizes. For example, we are able to prove the fault-tolerance of a two-logical-qubit gate in Toric code with up to 100 physical qubits in about 3 h and the fault-tolerance of sophisticated state preparation protocol in surface code with 49 physical qubits in about 70 h. When the checking fails, our framework can show the error propagation path that violates the fault-tolerance criterion to help debug the QECC implementation.

The major contributions of this paper can be summarized as follows:

1. We extend and define the semantics of quantum programs with faulty executions to reason about the influence of faults and formalize the fault-tolerance properties of QECCs.
2. We overcome the challenges of mechanically proving the QECC fault-tolerance by introducing a series of theorems to discretize the continuous errors, designing new transition rules by leveraging the unique properties of loops in QECCs, and a two-party framework to handle non-Clifford components.

3. We implement a symbolic execution framework based on our theories and show that it can prove the fault-tolerance of various QECCs or indicate the error propagation path that violates the fault-tolerance criterion.

2 Background

2.1 Quantum Computing Basics

The state space of a quantum system is described by a d-dimensional complex Hilbert space $\mathcal{H}^d$. A **pure state** of such a system is a unit vector $|\psi\rangle \in \mathcal{H}^d$. A **mixed state** is a statistical ensemble of pure states $\{|\psi_i\rangle\}$ with probability p_i, described by the **partial density operator** $\rho = \sum_i p_i |\psi_i\rangle\langle\psi_i|$. If $\sum_i p_i = 1$, then ρ is also called a **density operator**. A pure state $|\psi\rangle$ can also be regarded as the density operator $\rho = |\psi\rangle\langle\psi|$. Suppose $\rho = \sum_i \lambda_i |\psi_i\rangle\langle\psi_i|$ is the spectral decomposition of a density operator ρ such that $\lambda_i > 0$, then the **support** of ρ is defined as $\mathrm{supp}(\rho) = \mathrm{span}(\{|\psi_i\rangle\}_i)$ and is denoted as $\mathbf{supp}(\rho)$.

We use **quantum channel** to describe a general quantum evolution, which is mathematically a completely positive [15,30,38] trace-preserving map $\mathcal{E}$ on density operators. Specifically, $\mathcal{E}$ has the non-unique form $\mathcal{E}(\rho) = \sum_i E_i \rho E_i^\dagger$ such that $\sum_i E_i^\dagger E_i = I$. The operators $\{E_i\}$ are called Kraus operators. In particular, a **quantum gate** corresponds to a unitary quantum evolution that can be described by a unitary channel: $\mathcal{E}(\rho) = U\rho U^\dagger$, where U is a unitary matrix (i.e., $U^\dagger U = I$). **Qubit** (quantum bit) has a 2-dimensional Hilbert space $\mathcal{H}^2$ as its state space and $\{|0\rangle, |1\rangle\}$ as the **computational basis**. The state space of n qubits is the tensor product of all state spaces of each qubit.

A **quantum measurement** is described by a set of linear operators $\{M_i\}$ such that $\sum_i M_i^\dagger M_i = I$. When measuring a state ρ, the probability of outcome i is $p_i = \mathrm{tr}(M_i \rho M_i^\dagger)$, after which the state collapses to $\rho' = M_i \rho M_i^\dagger / p_i$.

2.2 Pauli Operator and Stabilizer Formalism

The following unitaries are called the Pauli matrices: $X = \left(\begin{smallmatrix} 0 & 1 \\ 1 & 0 \end{smallmatrix}\right), Y = \left(\begin{smallmatrix} 0 & -i \\ i & 0 \end{smallmatrix}\right), Z = \left(\begin{smallmatrix} 1 & 0 \\ 0 & -1 \end{smallmatrix}\right)$. An **$n$-qubit Pauli operator** P is a tensor product of n Pauli matrices $\sigma_i \in \{I = \left(\begin{smallmatrix} 1 & 0 \\ 0 & 1 \end{smallmatrix}\right), X, Y, Z\}$ with a global phase $c \in \{1, -1, i, -i\}$: $P = c \cdot \sigma_1 \otimes \cdots \otimes \sigma_n$. The **weight of the Pauli operator** P is the number of indices i such that $\sigma_i \neq I$. Note that the set of all n-qubit Pauli operators forms a group $\mathcal{P}_n$ under matrix multiplication. The **vector representation** [1,38] of the unsigned Pauli operator $\sigma_1 \otimes \cdots \otimes \sigma_n$ is a $2n$-length vector $[x_1, \ldots, x_n, z_1, \ldots, z_n]$ where $x_i, z_i \in \{0, 1\}$ and the pair (x_i, z_i) corresponds to $(0,0), (0,1), (1,0), (1,1)$ representing $\sigma_i = I, Z, X, Y$, respectively.

A state $|\psi\rangle$ is stabilized by a unitary U if $U|\psi\rangle = |\psi\rangle$ and U is called the stabilizer of $|\psi\rangle$. Suppose $\{P_1, \ldots, P_m\}$ is a set of m commuting and independent[1] n-qubit Pauli operators such that $P_i \neq \pm I$ and $P_i^2 \neq -I$. These Pauli

---

[1] Each P_j cannot be written as a product of others.

operators generate a group $\mathcal{G} = \langle P_1, \ldots, P_m \rangle$ by matrix multiplication. Suppose V is the subspace containing the states stabilized by elements in $\mathcal{G}$, i.e., $V := \{|\psi\rangle \mid \forall P \in \mathcal{G}, P|\psi\rangle = |\psi\rangle\}$, then $\mathcal{G}$ is called the **stabilizer group** of V, and the group elements $P \in \mathcal{G}$ are called the **stabilizers** of V. Particularly, $P_1, \ldots, P_m$ are called the **generators**. Note that V is a 2^{n-m}-dimensional subspace. In particular, if $m = n$, then V is a one-dimensional subspace.

An n-qubit unitary U is called an **Clifford** unitary if it maps Pauli operators to Pauli operators under conjugation, i.e., $\forall P \in \mathcal{P}_n$, $UPU^\dagger \in \mathcal{P}_n$. All n-qubit Clifford unitaries can be generated by the H, S, and CNOT gates [1,38]. There is a special type of quantum circuit called the **stabilizer circuits**, which contains only the following elements: 1) preparing qubits into the computational basis; 2) applying Clifford gates; 3) measuring qubits in the computational basis. Stabilizer circuits are vastly utilized in quantum error correction and can be simulated efficiently by classical computers [21].

2.3   Quantum Error Correction

Quantum computers in the real world suffer errors that will significantly impact the outcome. Due to the no-cloning theorem [38], it is impossible to duplicate quantum states to resist errors. Instead, we employ quantum error correction codes to encode quantum information, which can detect and correct errors. A **quantum error correction code** (QECC) $\mathcal{C}$ uses n physical qubits ($\mathcal{H}^{2^n}$) to encode k logical qubits ($\mathcal{H}^{2^k}$). Specifically, it assigns a 2^k-dimensional subspace $\mathcal{H}' \subseteq \mathcal{H}^{2^n}$, called the **code space**, and an isomorphism between $\mathcal{H}'$ and $\mathcal{H}^{2^k}$. If it is clear from the context, we will use $\mathcal{C}$ to refer to both the QECC and its code space. The error correction process of a QECC consists of the following steps:

- **Syndrome measurement**: applying a list of measurements on physical qubits to detect potential errors.
- **Recovery**: performing recovery operations based on the outcome of the syndrome measurement.

The vast majority of QECC are **stabilizer codes**. For a stabilizer code $\mathcal{C}$, its code space is the subspace stabilized by a stabilizer group $\mathcal{G} = \langle P_1, \ldots, P_m \rangle$, where $P_1, \ldots, P_m$ are Pauli operators. Note that the code space is of dimension 2^{n-m}. Therefore, it encodes $k = n - m$ logical qubits. The error syndromes can be obtained by performing Pauli measurement of the generators $P_1, \ldots, P_m$. A Pauli error E that anticommutes with a generator can be detected by the measurement of this generator. The code distance d is defined as the smallest integer t such that there exists a Pauli operator of weight t acting as a non-trivial logical operation on the code space $\mathcal{C}$.

Throughout this paper, the **code parameters** of stabilizer codes are denoted as $[[n, k, d]]$, where n, k and d stand for the number of physical qubits, number of encoded logical qubits and code distance, respectively.

2.4 Error Propagation and Fault-Tolerance

We first introduce the following definition.

Definition 1. *The* **r-error space surrounding** $|\psi\rangle$ *is defined as*

$$\mathcal{S}_r(|\psi\rangle) := \mathrm{span}(\{P|\psi\rangle \mid P \text{ is a Pauli operator of weight at most } r\}).$$

We say that a quantum state ρ has at most **r errors w.r.t.** $|\psi\rangle$ if $\mathrm{supp}(\rho) \subseteq \mathcal{S}_r(|\psi\rangle)$. We may ignore $|\psi\rangle$ if it is clear from the context. We can further generalize the notion of error space for any pure state $|\psi\rangle \in \mathcal{H}_1 \otimes \cdots \otimes \mathcal{H}_m$ in a composite system by defining:

$$\mathcal{S}_{r_1,\ldots,r_m}(|\psi\rangle) := \mathrm{span}(\{P|\psi\rangle \mid P \text{ is a Pauli of weight at most } r_i \text{ on block } \mathcal{H}_i\}).$$

We say ρ has at most r_i **errors on block** $\mathcal{H}_i$ **w.r.t.** $|\psi\rangle$ if $\mathrm{supp}(\rho) \subseteq \mathcal{S}_{r_1,\ldots,r_m}(|\psi\rangle)$.

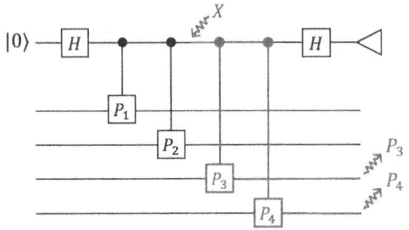

(a) Multi-qubit Pauli measurement using a single ancilla, in which a Pauli-X error on the ancilla qubit will propagate to two Pauli errors P_3, P_4 on the data qubits.

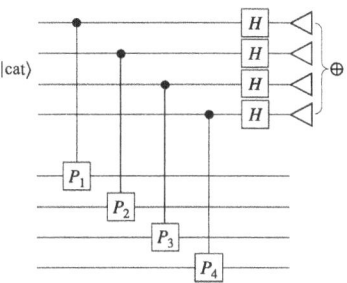

(b) Multi-qubit Pauli measurement using the cat state.

Fig. 1. Two implementations of multi-qubit Pauli measurement $P_1 \otimes P_2 \otimes P_3 \otimes P_4$.

While QECCs effectively detect existing errors on quantum states, the error correction process and logical operations can introduce new errors during executions. Even worse, errors may propagate among the qubits. For example, Fig. 1a shows an error propagation in an implementation of a multi-qubit Pauli measurement (which corresponds to a logical Pauli measurement). In contrast, Fig. 1b shows a "transversal" implementation, where the ancilla qubits are initialized to the cat state $|cat\rangle = (|0000\rangle + |1111\rangle)/\sqrt{2}$. Here, a single error will not propagate to two or more errors, which, roughly speaking, is called **fault-tolerance**[2]. However, being entangled, the cat state itself cannot be prepared transversally, requiring a more elaborate design (see Sect. 8.1) for fault-tolerance. This leads to a fundamental question:

---

[2] The formal definition of fault-tolerance is given in Sect. 4.

> *Given a QECC and an implementation of a logical operation on it, how can we tell if it is fault-tolerant?*

It turns out that manually checking the fault-tolerance of QECC implementation is highly non-trivial because the prover needs to iterate over all possible error combinations and propagation paths. In the rest of this paper, we will introduce our new theory and tools to formalize and verify the fault-tolerance of QEC code implementations.

3   Related Work

Formal Logic for Quantum Computing. There are extensive works on building formal logic to reason quantum programs, including quantum assertions [34], quantum Hoare logic [18,35,56], the logic for erroneous quantum programs [28,53], ZX-calculus [41,42], mechanized verification [25,35,40,47,60], etc. However, most of these works require human interaction, and none focus on fault-tolerance. In contrast, our work formally characterizes QEC fault-tolerance and provides an automated verification tool.

Automatic Testing and Verification of Quantum Programs. Other works focus on proving properties of quantum programs based on certain automatic techniques, including quantum symbolic execution [4,16,17,36], equivalence checking of quantum programs [11,12,26,55], program invariance generation [29,59], automatic testing and verification [14,24,48,54], etc. However, these tools are not designed to target the fault-tolerance of QECCs.

4   Formalism of Quantum Fault-Tolerance

Before verifying the fault-tolerance, we first formalize the quantum fault-tolerance by extending the language of classical-quantum programs [57,58] with faulty transitions and then formalizing the QEC fault-tolerance criteria.

4.1   Classical-Quantum Program (*cq-prog*)

Note that QEC protocols contain not only unitary circuits but also include mid-circuit measurements with sophisticated classical control flows (e.g., classical oracles, branches, and repeat-until-success). Therefore, it is necessary to adapt a language with classical components. In this paper, we select the classical-quantum program [16,56–58].

Definition 2 (Syntax of Classical-Quantum Programs (*cq-prog*)). *A classical-quantum program (cq-prog) on qubits $q_1, \ldots, q_n$ with classical variables and repeat-until-success structure is defined by the following syntax:*

$$
\begin{aligned}
S ::= \ & S_1; S_2 & (sequence) \quad & | \ q := |0\rangle & (initialization) \\
& | \ U(\overline{q}) & (unitary) \quad & | \ x := \texttt{measure } q & (measurement) \\
& | \ x := e & (assign) \quad & | \ \texttt{if } b \texttt{ then } S_1 \texttt{ else } S_2 & (conditionals) \\
& | \ y := f(x) & (classical\ oracle) \quad & | \ \texttt{repeat } S \texttt{ until } b & (repeat\text{-}until)
\end{aligned}
$$

The notations used in Definition 2 are explained as follows: q is a qubit, x and y are classical variables, e is an expression on classical variables, f is a classical oracle, $\bar{q} = q_i, \ldots, q_j$ is an arbitrary list of distinct qubits; $U(\bar{q})$ performs a unitary gate U on a list of qubits $\bar{q}$; $x :=$ measure q performs a computational-basis measurement $\{|0\rangle\langle 0|, |1\rangle\langle 1|\}$ on the qubit q and stores the result (0 or 1) in the classical variable x; repeat S until b performs the quantum program S until the Boolean expression b is evaluated as true.

Then, the execution of a classical-quantum program can be described in terms of the transition between the classical-quantum configurations.

Definition 3 (Classical-Quantum Configuration). *A classical-quantum configuration is a triple $\langle S, \sigma, \rho \rangle$, where S is a cq-prog, $\sigma : x \mapsto v$ is a map from classical variables to classical values, and ρ is a partial density operator describing the (sub-normalized) quantum state of the qubits.*

$$(\text{IN}) \quad \langle q := |0\rangle, \sigma, \rho \rangle \to \langle \downarrow, \sigma, \rho_{q:=|0\rangle} \rangle \qquad (\text{UT}) \quad \langle U(\bar{q}), \sigma, \rho \rangle \to \langle \downarrow, \sigma, U_{\bar{q}} \rho U_{\bar{q}}^\dagger \rangle$$

$$(\text{M0}) \quad \langle x := \text{measure } q, \sigma, \rho \rangle \to \langle \downarrow, \sigma[0/x], |0\rangle_q \langle 0|\rho|0\rangle_q \langle 0| \rangle$$

$$(\text{M1}) \quad \langle x := \text{measure } q, \sigma, \rho \rangle \to \langle \downarrow, \sigma[1/x], |1\rangle_q \langle 1|\rho|1\rangle_q \langle 1| \rangle$$

$$(\text{AS}) \quad \langle x := e, \sigma, \rho \rangle \to \langle \downarrow, \sigma[\sigma(e)/x], \rho \rangle \qquad (\text{CO}) \quad \langle y := f(x), \sigma, \rho \rangle \to \langle \downarrow, \sigma[f(x)/y], \rho \rangle$$

$$(\text{SC}) \quad \frac{\langle S_1, \sigma, \rho \rangle \to \langle S_1', \sigma', \rho' \rangle}{\langle S_1; S_2, \sigma, \rho \rangle \to \langle S_1'; S_2, \sigma', \rho' \rangle}$$

$$(\text{CT}) \quad \frac{\sigma \models b}{\langle \text{if } b \text{ then } S_1 \text{ else } S_2, \sigma, \rho \rangle \to \langle S_1, \sigma, \rho \rangle}$$

$$(\text{CF}) \quad \frac{\sigma \models \neg b}{\langle \text{if } b \text{ then } S_1 \text{ else } S_2, \sigma, \rho \rangle \to \langle S_2, \sigma, \rho \rangle}$$

$$(\text{RU}) \quad \langle \text{repeat } S \text{ until } b, \sigma, \rho \rangle \to \langle S; \text{if } b \text{ then } \downarrow \text{ else } \{\text{repeat } S \text{ until } b\}, \sigma, \rho \rangle$$

Fig. 2. Rules for the ideal transition relation. In rule (IN), $\rho_{q:=|0\rangle} = |0\rangle_q \langle 0|\rho|0\rangle_q \langle 0| + |0\rangle_q \langle 1|\rho|1\rangle_q \langle 0|$ where we use $|i\rangle_q$ to denote the pure state $|i\rangle$ at qubit q and $|i\rangle_q \langle j|$ is the abbreviation of product of $|i\rangle_q$ and $_q\langle j|$; in rule (UT), $U_{\bar{q}}$ means a unitary that acts as U on $\bar{q} = q_i \ldots q_j$, and acts trivially on other qubits.

We can now define the operational semantics of a *cq-prog* by specifying the transition relationship between the classical-quantum configurations. The rules in Fig. 2 define the ideal transition relation "$\to$" between classical-quantum configurations.

4.2 Execution with Faults

We now inject faults into ideal executions. We assume that all the classical operations (i.e., (AS), (CO), (CT), (CF), and (RU)) are flawless, and only quantum operations (i.e., (IN), (UT), (M0), and (M1)) can be faulty. When a fault happens, the original quantum operation is replaced by an arbitrary quantum operation acting on the same qubits. The corresponding transition is called faulty transition.

Definition 4 (Faulty Transition). *The following rules define the faulty transition "$\rightsquigarrow$" between classical-quantum configurations when faults occur during the execution of a quantum program:*

(F-IN) $\langle q := |0\rangle, \sigma, \rho\rangle \rightsquigarrow \langle\downarrow, \sigma, \mathcal{E}_q(\rho)\rangle$ (F-UT) $\langle U(\overline{q}), \sigma, \rho\rangle \rightsquigarrow \langle\downarrow, \sigma, \mathcal{E}_{\overline{q}}(\rho)\rangle$

(F-M0) $\langle x := \mathtt{measure}\ q, \sigma, \rho\rangle \rightsquigarrow \langle\downarrow, \sigma[0/x], \mathcal{E}_{0,q}(\rho)\rangle$

(F-M1) $\langle x := \mathtt{measure}\ q, \sigma, \rho\rangle \rightsquigarrow \langle\downarrow, \sigma[1/x], \mathcal{E}_{1,q}(\rho)\rangle$

where in rules (F-IN) and (F-UT), $\mathcal{E}_q$ and $\mathcal{E}_{\overline{q}}$ can be arbitrary trace-preserving quantum operations that act non-trivially only on q and $\overline{q}$, respectively; in rules (F-M0) and (F-M1), $\mathcal{E}_{0,q}$ and $\mathcal{E}_{1,q}$ can be arbitrary (non-trace-preserving) quantum operations[3] acting non-trivially only on q. We omit the rule (F-SC) here as it is simply analogous to the rule (SC) in Fig. 2.

Now, we can describe the execution of a *cq-prog* with faults using the following faulty transition tree.

Definition 5 (Transition Tree with Faults). *Let S_0 be a cq-prog, σ_0 be a classical state and $r \geq 0$ be an integer. An r-fault transition tree $\mathcal{T}$ starting with (S_0, σ_0) is a (possibly infinite) tree with classical-quantum configurations as nodes and satisfies the following conditions:*

1. *The root is $\langle S_0, \sigma_0, \widetilde{\rho}\rangle$, where $\widetilde{\rho}$ is an indeterminate quantum state.*
2. *A node is of the form $\langle\downarrow, \sigma, \rho\rangle$ iff it is a leaf node.*
3. *A node is of the form $\langle x := \mathtt{measure}\ q; S, \sigma, \rho\rangle$ iff it has two children, either generated by (M0) and (M1), or generated by (F-M0) and (F-M1). Furthermore, for the latter case, the quantum operations $\mathcal{E}_{0,q}$ and $\mathcal{E}_{1,q}$ in the transition rules satisfy that $\mathcal{E}_{0,q} + \mathcal{E}_{1,q}$ is trace-preserving.*
4. *If a node v is not of the form $\langle\downarrow, \sigma, \rho\rangle$ or $\langle x := \mathtt{measure}\ q; S, \sigma, \rho\rangle$, then it has only one child v' such that $v \rightarrow v'$ or $v \rightsquigarrow v'$ (cf. Figure 2 and Definition 4).*
5. *Each path contains at most r faulty transitions "$\rightsquigarrow$".*

Let ρ_0 be a concrete quantum state. We use $\mathcal{T}(\rho_0)$ to denote the tree obtained by replacing the indeterminate quantum state $\widetilde{\rho}$ with ρ_0 in the root node.

If we fix a *cq-prog* S and a classical state σ_0, then any r-fault transition tree $\mathcal{T}$ starting with (S_0, σ_0) corresponds to a well-defined quantum channel.

Proposition 1. *Let S_0 be a quantum program, σ_0 be a classical state and $r \geq 0$. If $\mathcal{T}$ is an r-fault transition tree starting with (S_0, σ_0), then the map $\mathcal{E}_{\mathcal{T}}$: $\rho \mapsto \sum_{\langle\downarrow, \sigma, \rho'\rangle \in \mathcal{T}(\rho)} \rho'$ is a quantum channel (not necessarily trace-preserving).*

---

[3] It is worth noting that (F-M0) and (F-M1) also cover the case of bit-flip error on the measurement outcome, since it is equivalent to letting $\mathcal{E}_{0,q}(\rho) = |1\rangle_q\langle 1|\rho|1\rangle_q\langle 1|$ and $\mathcal{E}_{1,q} = |0\rangle_q\langle 0|\rho|0\rangle_q\langle 0|$.

The proof can be found in [13, Appendix C].

Note that the semantics of a *cq-prog* in the presence of faults is nondeterministic. This is because there can be infinite many r-fault transition trees starting with (S_0, σ_0), where each transition tree corresponds to a valid semantics with r faults. In this context, each tree T is also referred to as an **r-fault instantiation** of (S_0, σ_0), or simply an instantiation of S_0 with r faults, if $\sigma_0 = \emptyset$.

4.3 Formalization of Quantum Fault-Tolerance

Given the definition of quantum gadgets and *cq-prog*, we can formally define quantum fault-tolerance developed in previous QEC theory [22,23]. Different from their definitions, we separate the fault-tolerance property of a QEC program from its semantical correctness in the ideal case, and we further assume that a QEC program always produces the correct semantics in the ideal case.

A QECC usually consists of four types of **gadgets**: (1). **Preparation**: prepare a logical state, e.g., the logical state $|\bar{0}\rangle$. (2). **Measurement**: measure on a logical basis, e.g., the logical Z-basis measurement $\{|\bar{0}\rangle\langle\bar{0}|, |\bar{1}\rangle\langle\bar{1}|\}$.[4] (3). **Gate**: perform a logical quantum gate, e.g., the logical CNOT gate. (4). **Error correction**: detect and correct physical errors in the logical state. We provide some circuit implementation examples of the gadgets in [13, Appendix K].

In the rest this section, we fix a QECC C with distance d and set $t := \lfloor \frac{d-1}{2} \rfloor$ as the **number of correctable errors**. The following symbols will be used:

- "$=$" stands for a logical block of C formed by physical qubits.
- $|\psi\rangle\!=\!\langle r\rangle\!=$ stands for an arbitrary quantum mixed state having at most r errors w.r.t. $|\psi\rangle$ (see Definition 1). When multiple $\langle r_i\rangle$ are applied on multiple blocks, they together denote a quantum mixed state having at most r_i errors on the i-th block, respectively.
- $\mathbb{C}$, $\mathbb{D}$, $\overline{\mathbb{U}}$ and $=\boxed{EC}=$ stand for the preparation, measurement, (two-qubit) gate, and error correction gadgets, respectively.
- "s" near a gadget indicates s faults appear in the execution of the gadget. The gadget is ideal (fault-free) if no number is present near it.

Then, we introduce the formalization of fault-tolerance. We only present the two-qubit case for gate gadgets, which can be easily extended to n-qubit cases.

Definition 6 (Fault-Tolerance of QECC Gadgets)

1. A **state preparation gadget** is fault-tolerant if the following holds:

$$\text{whenever } s \le t, \qquad \mathbb{C}^{s}\!= \quad = \quad \mathbb{C}\!=\!\langle s\rangle\!= \; . \tag{1}$$

That is, a *cq-prog* S is a FT preparation gadget if for any s-fault instantiation of S, s.t. $s \le t$, the prepared state has at most s errors.

---

[4] A bar on a ket (pure state) denotes the corresponding logical state w.r.t. a QECC.

2. A **two-qubit logical gate gadget** is fault-tolerant if the following holds:

$$\text{whenever } r_1 + r_2 + s \le t, \qquad |\overline{\psi}\rangle \overset{r_1}{\underset{r_2}{\diamond}} \!\!\boxed{U}^{\,s} = |\overline{\psi}\rangle \boxed{U} \overset{e_1}{\underset{e_2}{\diamond}}, \tag{2}$$

where $e_1, e_2 = r_1 + r_2 + s$. That is, a *cq-prog* S is a FT gate gadget if for any input logical state $|\overline{\psi}\rangle$ with r_1 and r_2 errors on each logical block and any s-fault instantiation of S, s.t. $r_1 + r_2 + s \le t$, the output state has at most $r_1 + r_2 + s$ errors on each block.

3. A **measurement gadget** is fault-tolerant if the following holds:

$$\text{whenever } r + s \le t, \qquad |\overline{\psi}\rangle \overset{r}{\Longrightarrow} \diamond\!\!\!D^{\,s} = |\overline{\psi}\rangle \Longrightarrow\!\!\!D. \tag{3}$$

That is, a *cq-prog* S is a FT measurement gadget if for any input logical state $|\overline{\psi}\rangle$ with r errors and any s-fault instantiation of S, s.t. $r + s \le t$, the measurement outcomes are the same (in distribution) as those in the ideal case.

4. An **error correction gadget** is fault-tolerant if the following holds:

$$\text{whenever } r + s \le t, \qquad |\overline{\psi}\rangle \overset{r}{\diamond}\!\!\boxed{\text{EC}}^{\,s} = |\overline{\psi}\rangle \overset{s}{\diamond}. \tag{4}$$

That is, a *cq-prog* S is a fault-tolerant error correction gadget if for any input logical state $|\overline{\psi}\rangle$ with r errors and any s-fault instantiation of S, s.t. $r + s \le t$, the output state has at most s errors.

5   Discretization

Because physical quantum errors are analog (e.g., small imprecisions in rotation angle), the fault-tolerance conditions formalized above are defined over continuous error channels and logical states that are difficult to reason about using computer-aided techniques. It is essential to break these formulations into discrete yet equivalent forms. In this section, we introduce two new discretization theorems that allow us to analyze and verify quantum fault-tolerance on *cq-prog* in a systematic way.

5.1   Discretization of Input Space

We show that, for fault-tolerance verification, the input space can be discretized from continuous code space into discrete logical basis states. A similar result of input space discretization was given in [16] for verifying *fault-free* QEC programs. Our result is a further refinement that uses fewer inputs and applies to fault-tolerance verification of various types of gadgets.

Theorem 1 (Discretization of Input Space)

1. *A gate or error correction gadget is fault-tolerant if and only if it satisfies the corresponding fault-tolerance properties (c.f. Eqs (2), (4)) on both the logical computational basis $\{|\overline{i}\rangle\}_{i=0}^{2^k-1}$ and the logical state $|\overline{+}\rangle := \sum_{i=0}^{2^k-1} |\overline{i}\rangle / \sqrt{2^k}$, where k is the number of logical qubits.*
2. *A Z-basis measurement gadget is fault-tolerant if and only if it satisfies the corresponding fault-tolerance properties (c.f. Eq. (3)) on the logical computational basis $\{|\overline{i}\rangle\}_{i=0}^{2^k-1}$, where k is the number of logical qubits.*

The proof can be found in [13, Appendix E].

5.2   Discretization of Faults

Since a general *cq-prog* contains complicated control flows that can also be affected by quantum faults (e.g., through outcomes of mid-circuit measurements), the discretization theorem in conventional QEC theory [22,23] does not fit our *cq-prog* framework. We provide our discretization result for *cq-prog*, showing that faults can be discretized from arbitrary quantum channels into Pauli channels.

Definition 7 (Transition Tree with Pauli Faults). *Let S_0 be a quantum program, σ_0 be a classical state and $r \geq 0$ be an integer. An **r-Pauli-fault** transition tree $\mathcal{T}$ starting with (S_0, σ_0) is a transition tree (c.f. Definition 5), such that all faulty transitions in it satisfy the following rules instead:*

$$(\text{PF-IN}) \quad \langle q := |0\rangle, \sigma, \rho \rangle \rightsquigarrow \langle \downarrow, \sigma, P_q \rho_{q:=|0\rangle} P_q \rangle$$

$$(\text{PF-UT}) \quad \langle U(\overline{q}), \sigma, \rho \rangle \rightsquigarrow \langle \downarrow, \sigma, P_{\overline{q}} U_{\overline{q}} \rho U_{\overline{q}}^\dagger P_{\overline{q}} \rangle$$

$$(\text{PF-M0}) \quad \langle x := \texttt{measure } q, \sigma, \rho \rangle \rightsquigarrow \langle \downarrow, \sigma[0/x], P_{0,q}|0\rangle_q \langle 0| Q_q \rho Q_q |0\rangle_q \langle 0| P_{0,q} \rangle$$

$$(\text{PF-M1}) \quad \langle x := \texttt{measure } q, \sigma, \rho \rangle \rightsquigarrow \langle \downarrow, \sigma[1/x], P_{1,q}|1\rangle_q \langle 1| Q_q \rho Q_q |1\rangle_q \langle 1| P_{1,q} \rangle$$

where in rules (PF-IN) and (PF-UT), P_q and $P_{\overline{q}}$ are arbitrary Pauli operators acting on q and $\overline{q}$, respectively. In rules (PF-M0) and (PF-M1), $P_{0,q}, P_{1,q}, Q_q$ are arbitrary Pauli operators acting on q.[5] Furthermore, if a node is $\langle x := \texttt{measure} q; S, \sigma, \rho \rangle$ and its two children are generated by (PF-M0) and (PF-M1), then both transitions share the same Pauli error Q_q.

We call such tree $\mathcal{T}$ an *r-Pauli-fault instantiation* of (S_0, σ_0) and if $\sigma_0 = \emptyset$, we call it an *r-Pauli-fault instantiation* of S_0. Then, we have the following theorem.

Theorem 2 (Discretization of Faults). *A gadget is fault-tolerant if and only if it satisfies the corresponding fault-tolerance properties (c.f. Eqs. (1), (2), (3), (4)) with the Pauli fault instantiation (see Definition 7).*

The proof can be found in [13, Appendix F].

---

[5] Rules (PF-M0) and (PF-M1) introduce both pre- and post-measurement Pauli errors, aiming to account for all possible error patterns of a measurement operation.

6   Symbolic Execution with Quantum Faults

Having discretized the inputs and errors, we can now establish a symbolic execution framework based on the quantum stabilizer formalism to reason about fault-tolerance of QECC implementations. Specifically, we maintain a symbolic configuration $\langle S, \widetilde{\sigma}, \widetilde{\rho}, p, \varphi, \widetilde{F} \rangle$, where

- S is the quantum program to be executed,
- $\widetilde{\sigma}$ is a symbolic classical state,
- $\widetilde{\rho}$ is a symbolic quantum stabilizer state, parameterized by a set of symbols, and is equipped with a set of stabilizer operations (see Sect. 6.1).
- p is the probability corresponding to the current execution path, which is, in fact, a concrete number instead of a symbolic expression.
- φ is the path condition, expressing the assumptions introduced in an execution path of the *cq-prog*.
- $\widetilde{F}$ is a symbolic expression that records the number of faults occurring during the execution of faulty transitions.

6.1   Symbolic Stabilizer States and Error Injection

Definition 8 (Symbolic Stabilizer States). *For any commuting and independent set* $\{P_1, \ldots, P_n | P_i \neq \pm I, P_i^2 \neq -I\}$ *of n-qubit Pauli operators and Boolean functions* $g_1, \ldots, g_n$ *over* m *Boolean variables, the symbolic stabilizer state* $\widetilde{\rho}(s_1, \ldots, s_m)$ *over symbols* $s_1, \ldots, s_m$ *is a stabilizer state of*

$$\langle (-1)^{g_1(s_1,\ldots,s_m)} P_1, \ldots, (-1)^{g_n(s_1,\ldots,s_m)} P_n \rangle,$$

where $\langle A_1, \ldots, A_n \rangle$ *denotes the group generated by* $A_1, \ldots, A_n$.

When it is clear from the context, we will omit the symbols $s_1, \ldots, s_m$ using $\widetilde{\rho}$ to denote $\widetilde{\rho}(s_1, \ldots, s_m)$, and directly use $\langle A_1, \ldots, A_n \rangle$ to denote the stabilizer state of the group generated by $A_1, \ldots, A_n$.

There are four types of symbolic stabilizer operations:

1. A symbolic function $\mathrm{IN}(q_i, \widetilde{\rho})$ for the initialization statement $q_i := |0\rangle$.
2. A symbolic function $\mathrm{UT}(U, \overline{q}, \widetilde{\rho})$ for the Clifford unitary transform statement $U(\overline{q})$.
3. A symbolic function $\mathrm{M}(q_i, \widetilde{\rho})$ for the measurement statement $x := \mathtt{measure}\ q_i$.
4. A symbolic error injection function $\mathrm{EI}(\overline{q}, \widetilde{\rho})$ for the faulty transitions.

The symbolic functions $\mathrm{IN}(q_i, \widetilde{\rho})$, $\mathrm{UT}(U, \overline{q}, \widetilde{\rho})$ return the symbolic quantum states resulting from the corresponding quantum operations and $\mathrm{M}(q_i, \widetilde{\rho})$ returns a triplet comprising the measurement outcome, probability and post-measurement state. They are similarly to those in [16] and are available in [13, Appendix A]. Here we introduce our new symbolic error injection function $\mathrm{EI}(\overline{q}, \widetilde{\rho})$. Suppose $\widetilde{\rho}$ is a symbolic stabilizer state:

$$\widetilde{\rho} = \langle (-1)^{g_1(s_1,\ldots,s_m)} P_1, \ldots, (-1)^{g_n(s_1,\ldots,s_m)} P_n \rangle. \tag{5}$$

The symbolic error injection function acts on $\widetilde{\rho}$ by injecting symbolic Pauli errors. It returns a symbol recording the activation of those Pauli errors and the symbolic state $\widetilde{\rho}$ after error injection. Specifically, it is defined as follows.

Definition 9 (Symbolic Error Injection). *The symbolic Pauli error injection function* $\mathrm{EI}(q_i, \widetilde{\rho})$ *is defined as*

$$\mathrm{EI}(q_i, \widetilde{\rho}) = (e_X \vee e_Z, \langle (-1)^{g_1 \oplus e_X \cdot c_1^X \oplus e_Z \cdot c_1^Z} P_1, \ldots, (-1)^{g_n \oplus e_X \cdot c_n^X \oplus e_Z \cdot c_n^Z} P_n \rangle),$$

where e_X *and* e_Z *are newly introduced symbols recording the inserted Pauli* X *and* Z *errors;* $c_i^X = 0$ *if* P_i *commutes with* X_i *and* $c_i^X = 1$ *otherwise (similarly for* c_i^Z*).*

If the symbolic Pauli error injection function is applied on a sequence of qubit variables $\overline{q} = q_{j_1}, \ldots, q_{j_a}$, *then* $\mathrm{EI}(\overline{q}, \widetilde{\rho})$ *is defined as*

$$\mathrm{EI}(\overline{q}, \widetilde{\rho}) = (e_1 \vee \cdots \vee e_a, \widetilde{\rho}^{(a)}),$$

where $(e_i, \widetilde{\rho}^{(i)}) = \mathrm{EI}(q_{j_i}, \widetilde{\rho}^{(i-1)})$ *for* $i = 1, \ldots, a$ *and* $\widetilde{\rho}^{(0)} := \widetilde{\rho}$.

Note that in the definition of error injection on a sequence of qubits, we set the fault counter as $e_1 \vee \cdots \vee e_a$ rather than $e_1 + \cdots + e_a$. This is because a single faulty multi-qubit operation may introduce errors on multiple qubits but we count it as only one fault.

6.2   Symbolic Faulty Transitions

With the new error injection rule, we can define the symbolic faulty transitions, which are a symbolization of the faulty transitions in Definition 7.

Definition 10 (Symbolic Faulty Transitions). *The following are the symbolic faulty transition rules on the symbolic configurations*:

$$(\text{SF-IN}) \quad \langle q_i := |0\rangle, \widetilde{\sigma}, \widetilde{\rho}, p, \varphi, \widetilde{F} \rangle \twoheadrightarrow \langle \downarrow, \widetilde{\sigma}, \widetilde{\rho}', p, \varphi, \widetilde{F} + e \rangle$$
$$\text{where} \quad (e, \widetilde{\rho}') = \mathrm{EI}(q_i, \mathrm{IN}(q_i, \widetilde{\rho}))$$

$$(\text{SF-UT}) \quad \langle U(\overline{q}), \widetilde{\sigma}, \widetilde{\rho}, p, \varphi, \widetilde{F} \rangle \twoheadrightarrow \langle \downarrow, \widetilde{\sigma}, \widetilde{\rho}', p, \varphi, \widetilde{F} + e \rangle$$
$$\text{where} \quad (e, \widetilde{\rho}') = \mathrm{EI}(\overline{q}, \mathrm{UT}(U, \overline{q}, \widetilde{\rho}))$$

$$(\text{SF-M}) \quad \langle x := \mathtt{measure} \ q_i, \widetilde{\sigma}, \widetilde{\rho}, p, \varphi, \widetilde{F} \rangle \twoheadrightarrow \langle \downarrow, \widetilde{\sigma}[s/x], \widetilde{\rho}^{(3)}, pp', \varphi, \widetilde{F} + e_1 \vee e_2 \rangle$$
$$\text{where} \ (e_2, \widetilde{\rho}^{(3)}) = \mathrm{EI}(q_i, \widetilde{\rho}^{(2)}), \ (s, p', \widetilde{\rho}^{(2)}) = \mathrm{M}(q_i, \widetilde{\rho}^{(1)}), \ (e_1, \widetilde{\rho}^{(1)}) = \mathrm{EI}(q_i, \widetilde{\rho})$$

$$(\text{SF-AS}) \quad \langle x := e, \widetilde{\sigma}, \widetilde{\rho}, p, \varphi, \widetilde{F} \rangle \twoheadrightarrow \langle \downarrow, \widetilde{\sigma}[\widetilde{\sigma}(e)/x], \widetilde{\rho}, p, \varphi, \widetilde{F} \rangle$$

$$(\text{SF-CO}) \quad \langle y := f(x), \widetilde{\sigma}, \widetilde{\rho}, p, \varphi, \widetilde{F} \rangle \twoheadrightarrow \langle \downarrow, \widetilde{\sigma}[s/y], \widetilde{\rho}, p, \varphi \wedge C_f(\widetilde{\sigma}(x), s), \widetilde{F} \rangle$$

$$(\text{SF-CT}) \quad \langle \mathtt{if} \ b \ \mathtt{then} \ S_1 \ \mathtt{else} \ S_2, \widetilde{\sigma}, \widetilde{\rho}, p, \varphi, \widetilde{F} \rangle \twoheadrightarrow \langle S_1, \widetilde{\sigma}, \widetilde{\rho}, p, \varphi \wedge \widetilde{\sigma}(b), \widetilde{F} \rangle$$

$$(\text{SF-CF}) \quad \langle \mathtt{if} \ b \ \mathtt{then} \ S_1 \ \mathtt{else} \ S_2, \widetilde{\sigma}, \widetilde{\rho}, p, \varphi, \widetilde{F} \rangle \twoheadrightarrow \langle S_2, \widetilde{\sigma}, \widetilde{\rho}, p, \varphi \wedge \neg\widetilde{\sigma}(b), \widetilde{F} \rangle$$

$$(\text{SF-RU}) \quad \langle \mathtt{repeat} \ S \ \mathtt{until} \ b, \widetilde{\sigma}, \widetilde{\rho}, p, \varphi, \widetilde{F} \rangle \twoheadrightarrow \langle S; S', \widetilde{\sigma}, \widetilde{\rho}, p, \varphi, \widetilde{F} \rangle$$
$$\text{where} \ S' = \mathtt{if} \ b \ \mathtt{then} \ \downarrow \ \mathtt{else} \ \{\mathtt{repeat} \ S \ \mathtt{until} \ b\}$$

where in rules (SF-IN), (SF-UT) *and* (SF-M), e, e_1 *and* e_2 *are newly introduced bit symbols recording the inserted faults and in rule* (SF-CO), *s is a newly introduced symbol and* C_f *is a logical formula asserting the behavior of* f. *We omit the rule* (SF-SC) *here as it is simply analogous to the rule* (SC) *in Fig. 2.*

Note that in rule (SF-CO), we do not actually run the classical oracle $f(x)$, but instead add an assertion C_f for the output of $f(x)$ to the path condition. This is beneficial when the behavior of the classical oracle can be abstracted into a logical formula, such as the decoding algorithms for stabilizer codes. More details about the assertion of the decoding algorithm can be found in [13, Appendix B].

6.3 Repeat-Until-Success

Analyzing the repeat-until-success loop, also known as the do-while loop, presents significant challenges. The symbolic transition rule (SF-RU) shown in Definition 10 does not perform well in practice since it can lead to numerous execution paths or even render the symbolic execution non-terminable.

To circumvent this issue, we observe that loops employed in QEC gadgets typically adhere to specific patterns. By leveraging these patterns, we propose the following symbolic transition rule in place of (SF-RU):

$$\text{(SF-RU}') \quad \frac{\langle S, \widetilde{\sigma}, \widetilde{\rho}, p, \varphi, \widetilde{F} \rangle \twoheadrightarrow^* \langle \downarrow, \widetilde{\sigma}', \widetilde{\rho}', p', \varphi', \widetilde{F}' \rangle}{\langle \texttt{repeat } S \texttt{ until } b, \widetilde{\sigma}, \widetilde{\rho}, p, \varphi, \widetilde{F} \rangle \twoheadrightarrow \langle \downarrow, \widetilde{\sigma}', \widetilde{\rho}', p', \varphi' \wedge \widetilde{\sigma}'(b), \widetilde{F}' \rangle}$$

where $\twoheadrightarrow^*$ stands for the transitive closure of $\twoheadrightarrow$. Notably, it executes the loop body only once and then post-selects on success by adding the success condition to the path condition.

We will explain its conditional validity in the following and then conclude the overall soundness and completeness in Sect. 6.5.

The first pattern is from the fault-tolerant cat state preparation gadget. Here, a repeat-until-success structure is used to test the prepared state, where in each iteration, all quantum and classical variables are reset before being used again. This pattern is recognized as the *memory-less repeat-until-success*.

Definition 11 (Memory-Less Repeat-Until-Success). *A repeat-until-success loop* "repeat S until b" *is memory-less if all classical and quantum variables used in the loop body S are reset before being used in each iteration.*

For the memory-less repeat-until-success structure, it suffices only to consider the last iteration. The intuition is straightforward: suppose t errors are injected into the loop. Errors injected in iteration other than the last one have no effect beyond that iteration. Therefore, the worst case is when all errors are injected into the final iteration. If the fault-tolerance property holds in the worst-case scenario, it also holds in the general case.

The second pattern witnesses the applicability of (SF-RU') in a more general scenario, where qubits are not reset across iterations. Our observation is based on Shor's error correction. Here, syndrome measurements are repeated until consecutive all-agree syndrome results of length $\lfloor \frac{d-1}{2} \rfloor + 1$ are observed. Therefore, qubits are not reset, meaning errors in one iteration can affect subsequent iterations. Nevertheless, through closer examination, we observe that syndrome measurements are implemented "transversally" upon proper cat state preparation. This means the errors will not propagate. As a result, any errors injected in an early iteration can be commuted to the last iteration without increasing the total number of errors. Additionally, in the fault-free case, the stabilizer syndrome measurements exhibit idempotent semantics, meaning a single iteration suffices to capture all possible quantum state outputs that would arise from multiple iterations. We refer to this type of loop as a *conservative* repeat-until-success.

Definition 12 (Conservative Repeat-Until-Success). *A repeat-until-success loop* "repeat S until b" *is conservative if*

1. *the classical variables in S are reset before used in each iteration,*
2. *in the fault-free case, the loop always terminates after a single iteration, and the fault-free semantics of the loop body S is non-adaptive and idempotent (see [13, Appendix G] for more details).*

Consequently, for a conservative loop, the rule (SF-RU′) remains valid provided that an additional condition is met: errors do not propagate uncontrollably within the loop body S. Fortunately, this can again be verified inside the loop body S recursively, using our symbolic execution.

6.4   Verification of Fault-Tolerance

Here, we present the overall pipeline of our verification tool for FT properties (i.e., Eqs. 1, 2, 3 and 4). For simplicity, we only demonstrate the verification of a gate gadget for a logical gate $\overline{U}$. Other types of gadgets can be handled similarly.

By Theorem 1, it suffices to check whether Eq. (2) holds for the following two cases: $|\overline{\psi}\rangle = |\overline{i}\rangle$ for all i and $|\overline{\psi}\rangle = \sum_{i=0}^{2^k-1} |\overline{i}\rangle / \sqrt{2^k}$. Therefore, we construct two symbolic stabilizer states respectively:

$$
\begin{aligned}
\widetilde{\rho}_Z &= \langle P_1, \ldots, P_{n-k}, (-1)^{s_1}\overline{Z}_1, \ldots, (-1)^{s_k}\overline{Z}_k \rangle, \\
\widetilde{\rho}_X &= \langle P_1, \ldots, P_{n-k}, \overline{X}_1, \ldots, \overline{X}_k \rangle,
\end{aligned}
\tag{6}
$$

where $P_1, \ldots, P_{n-k}$ are the Pauli stabilizers of the QECC $\mathcal{C}$ and $\overline{Z}_i, \overline{X}_i$ are the Pauli operators corresponding to the logical Z_i and logical X_i in $\mathcal{C}$, respectively. We will only deal with the state $\widetilde{\rho}_Z$, and the state $\widetilde{\rho}_X$ can be handled analogously.

Let $\widetilde{\rho}_0 = \widetilde{\rho}_Z$. We apply the Pauli error injection function EI on $\widetilde{\rho}_0$ recursively for all physical qubits, i.e., $(e_i, \widetilde{\rho}_i) = \text{EI}(q_i, \widetilde{\rho}_{i-1})$ for $i = 1, \ldots, n$. Then we define $\widetilde{\rho}_{\text{in}} := \widetilde{\rho}_n$ and $\widetilde{F}_{\text{in}} := \sum_{i=1}^n e_i$, which records the number of errors injected in the symbolic state $\widetilde{\rho}_{\text{in}}$. The initial symbolic configuration is set to $\langle S, \emptyset, \widetilde{\rho}_{\text{in}}, 1, \text{True}, \widetilde{F}_{\text{in}} \rangle$, where S is the cq-prog implementing the gate gadget. By applying our symbolic faulty transitions (see Definition 10) recursively on the initial configuration, we obtain a set of output configurations cfgs = $\{\text{cfg}_i\}_i$, where the indices i refer to different execution paths and each cfg$_i$ is of the form $\langle \downarrow, \widetilde{\sigma}, \widetilde{\rho}, p, \varphi, \widetilde{F} \rangle$, in which $p > 0$ is a concrete positive number.

Then, the gadget is fault-tolerant if and only if each symbolic configuration in cfgs describes a set of noisy states that are not "too far" from the error-free output state. Specifically, for each $\langle \downarrow, \widetilde{\sigma}, \widetilde{\rho}, p, \varphi, \widetilde{F} \rangle \in$ cfgs, let $\{s_1, \ldots, s_m\}$ be the set of symbols involved in this configuration (i.e., all symbols occurring in $\widetilde{\sigma}, \widetilde{\rho}, \varphi$ and $\widetilde{F}$). Then, we need to check whether the following holds

$$\forall s_1, \ldots, s_m, \ (\varphi \wedge \widetilde{F} \leq t) \rightarrow D(\widetilde{\rho}, \widetilde{\rho}_{\text{ideal}}) \leq \widetilde{F}, \tag{7}$$

where $\widetilde{\rho}_{\text{ideal}}$ is the symbolic state obtained by applying the (concrete) ideal unitary transform $\overline{U}$ on $\widetilde{\rho}_0$, and $D(\widetilde{\rho}, \widetilde{\rho}_{\text{ideal}})$ represents the Pauli distance between $\widetilde{\rho}$ and $\widetilde{\rho}_{\text{ideal}}$, i.e., the minimal weight of a Pauli operator that can transform $\widetilde{\rho}$ to $\widetilde{\rho}_{\text{ideal}}$. Note that the computation of $D(\widetilde{\rho}, \widetilde{\rho}_{\text{ideal}})$ is not straightforward but can still be formulated in a first-order formula. Specifically, let $P_1, \ldots, P_n$ be the unsigned stabilizers of $\widetilde{\rho}$, which should also be the unsigned stabilizers of $\widetilde{\rho}_{\text{ideal}}$ (otherwise we can direct conclude that the gadget is not fault-tolerant). Suppose

$$\widetilde{\rho} = \langle (-1)^{g_1} P_1, \ldots, (-1)^{g_n} P_n \rangle, \quad \widetilde{\rho}_{\text{ideal}} = \langle (-1)^{h_1} P_1, \ldots, (-1)^{h_n} P_n \rangle,$$

where g_i and h_i are functions taking symbols $s_1, \ldots, s_m$ as inputs. Therefore, $D(\widetilde{\rho}, \widetilde{\rho}_{\text{ideal}}) \leq \widetilde{F}$ can be expressed as

$$\exists P, \text{wt}(P) \leq \widetilde{F} \wedge \bigwedge_{i=1}^{n} h_i \oplus c(P, P_i) = g_i, \tag{8}$$

where P is a symbolic Pauli represented by a symbolic vector of length $2n$ (c.f. the vector representation in Sect. 2.2), wt(P) is the weight of P and $c(P, P_i) = 0$ if P and P_i commutes and 1 otherwise.

Note that the existence quantifier is, in fact, applied on $2n$ variables. We can further reduce it to n variables. To see this, note that the computation of $c(P, P_i)$ for $i = 1, \ldots, m$ involves multiplication (over GF(2)) of the matrix representing the stabilizers with the vector representing P. Specifically, let M be the $n \times 2n$ matrix, in which each row represents a stabilizer, and let v be the $2n$-length vector representing the symbolic Pauli P. Then, $c(P, P_i) = (M\Lambda v)_i$, where $\Lambda = \left(\begin{smallmatrix} 0 & I \\ I & 0 \end{smallmatrix} \right)$ is a $2n \times 2n$ matrix with $n \times n$ identity matrices as its off-diagonal blocks (see Sect. 10.5.1 in [38]). By solving the linear system over $GF(2)$, Eq. (8) is equivalent to

$$\exists w, \text{wt}(Nw \oplus p) \leq \widetilde{F}, \tag{9}$$

where w is an n-length vector, N is a $2n \times n$ matrix with columns spanning the null space of $M\Lambda$, p is a particular solution of the linear equation $M\Lambda p = g \oplus h$, in which g and h are the n-length vectors with entries g_i and h_i, respectively. As a result, we can reduce the number of quantified variables from $2n$ to n.

Interpreting $D(\widetilde{\rho}, \widetilde{\rho}_{\text{ideal}}) \leq \widetilde{F}$ by Eq. (9), we can use the SMT solver to check the validity of Eq. (7). The same method is also applied on $\widetilde{\rho}_X$ (see Eq. (6)), and "fault-tolerant" is claimed if both checks on $\widetilde{\rho}_Z$ and $\widetilde{\rho}_X$ pass.

6.5 Soundness and Completeness

Here, we state our main theorem about the soundness and completeness of our verification tool.

Definition 13 (Soundness and Completeness). *Suppose* Alg *is an algorithm taking a cq-prog S as input. Then, for the task of verifying quantum fault-tolerance, we define the soundness and completeness of* Alg *as follows.*

- **Soundness**: Alg(S) *returns "fault-tolerant"* $\implies S$ *is fault-tolerant.*
- **Completeness**: S *is fault-tolerant* $\implies$ Alg(S) *returns "fault-tolerant".*

Theorem 3. *Suppose S is a cq-prog implementing a quantum gadget with stabilizer quantum operations.*

- *If the repeat-until-success statements in S are memory-less, then our fault-tolerance verification is both sound and complete.*
- *If the repeat-until-success statements in S are conservative, then our fault-tolerance verification is sound.*

The proof can be found in [13, Appendix G]. Notably, when S is non-fault-tolerant, our quantum symbolic execution will always return a fault instantiation that witnesses the failure of fault-tolerance.

7 Verifying Magic State Distillation

We have applied our verification tools on QEC gadgets with Clifford circuits. We still need one more non-Clifford QEC gadget for universal quantum computing [37,46]. A widely used approach for universal fault-tolerant quantum computing is using the gate teleportation [23,38] with magic state distillation [9,32] to implement non-Clifford gates. Since the teleportation circuit is already a stabilizer circuit, the remaining problem is verifying the fault-tolerance of a magic state distillation protocol.

Typically, a magic state distillation protocol employs a distillation code $\mathcal{D}$. It performs the error correction (or error detection) process of $\mathcal{D}$ on multiple noisy magic states to yield a high-quality magic state encoded in $\mathcal{D}$, followed by the decoding. The code $\mathcal{D}$ must exhibit desirable properties for magic state distillation, such as the transversality of the logical T-gate [50].

In the context of quantum fault-tolerance, we instead use a concatenated code with $\mathcal{D}$ as an outer code and a QECC $\mathcal{C}$ (used for fault-tolerance) as an inner code (i.e., each qubit of $\mathcal{D}$ is encoded in $\mathcal{C}$). To better illustrate the idea of fault-tolerant magic state distillation, we reformulate it in a **two-party framework** in Fig. 3.

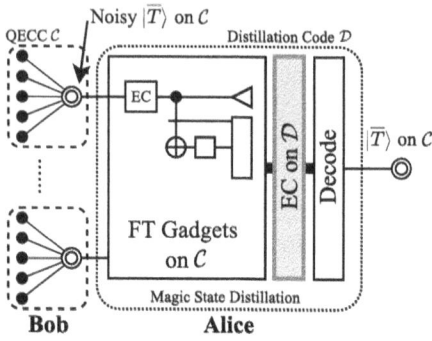

- Bob works on physical qubits and produces logical qubits encoded in $\mathcal{C}$ equipped with fault-tolerant stabilizer operations and non-fault-tolerant magic state preparation.
- Alice works on the encoded qubits produced by Bob and performs a magic state distillation protocol using a distillation code $\mathcal{D}$.

Fig. 3. Two-party magic state distillation framework with a QECC $\mathcal{C}$ on Bob and a distillation code $\mathcal{D}$ on Alice.

Specifically, Alice makes use of the logical operations of $\mathcal{C}$ provided by Bob and performs magic state distillation as follows:

1. Call the non-FT magic preparation to produce noisy magic states on $\mathcal{C}$.
2. Call error correction process of $\mathcal{C}$ on each noisy magic state.
3. Prepare logical state $|\overline{+}\rangle$ encoded in $\mathcal{D}$.
4. Implement logical-T gate of $\mathcal{D}$ by gate teleportation with noisy magic states.
5. Perform error correction of $\mathcal{D}$.

All the steps except step 1 contain only stabilizer operations of $\mathcal{C}$, which can be verified for fault-tolerance. Therefore, we only need to investigate how the errors from the noisy magic states propagate through the distillation process. Intuitively, step 2 ensures that the physical errors (in Bob's perspective) are suppressed, and only physical errors (in Alice's perspective), which are logical errors in Bob's view, can further propagate. Fortunately, in Alice's perspective, the gate teleportation is transversal, so errors do not propagate between qubits. Therefore, it suffices to check whether Alice's error correction (i.e., step 5) can correct the errors on the magic state encoded in $\mathcal{D}$.

Our quantum symbolic execution is not directly applicable for this case since the magic state encoded in $\mathcal{D}$ is not a stabilizer state. Nevertheless, we can circumvent it by generalizing the input. That is, we instead verify a **stronger** statement: Alice's error correction can correct errors on an arbitrary state, not only on the magic state. Then, we can use a discretization lemma like Theorem 1 to reduce it back to a verification task on stabilizer states. We remark that Alice's error correction itself is not required to be fault-tolerant but only needs to be able to correct errors on the input assuming no faults occur during its execution, which we call **ideal-case correct**. Formally, the magic state distillation gadget is fault-tolerant if

1. Bob's stabilizer operations are fault-tolerant,
2. Alice's error correction process is ideal-case correct.

Our tool verifies the fault-tolerance of Bob's stabilizer operations. For the ideal-case correctness of Alice's EC process, we can use similar techniques where error injections are only applied on inputs and are disabled in symbolic transitions. Consequently, we have:

Theorem 4. *If the magic state preparation is implemented within the two-party distillation framework and the repeat-until-success statements are either memory-less or conservative, then our fault-tolerance verification is sound.*

The proof can be found in [13, Appendix H].

8   Case Study

We implemented our verification tool[6] based on the Julia [5] package QuantumSE.jl [16] and use Bitwuzla [39] 0.7.0 as the SMT solver. Our experiments are executed on a desktop with AMD Ryzen 9 7950X and 64GB of RAM.

8.1   Bug Finding Example: Cat State Preparation

Cat state preparation is a crucial module in fault-tolerant (FT) quantum computing, extensively used in various FT gadgets such as FT Pauli measurement and Shor's error correction [49]. A fault-tolerant[7] cat state preparation can be implemented through the following steps: **1)** Prepare the cat state non-fault-tolerantly; **2)** Perform a check on the cat state; **3)** If the check fails, discard the state and start over. For the second step, a parity check on pairs of qubits of the cat state is performed. However, the pairs must be selected carefully.

For example, we found with our tool that the 4-qubit cat state preparation with the check on the second and third qubits, as shown in Fig. 4a, turns out to be non-FT, and the corresponding error propagation path found by our tool is marked in Fig. 4a. In contrast, our tool proves that when checking the third and fourth qubits (Fig. 4b), the cat state preparation is FT.

---

[6] The code is available at: https://github.com/vftqc/vftqecc.
[7] Although the cat state itself is not encoded in any QECC with positive code distance, we can still define its fault-tolerance up to t faults as follows: for any $s \leq t$, if s faults occur during the cat state preparation, the output contains at most s errors.

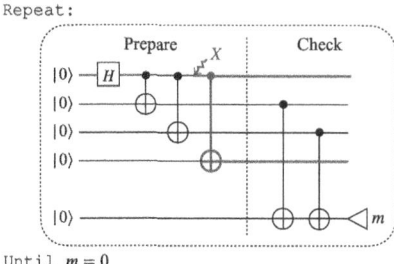

(a) Non-FT cat state preparation.

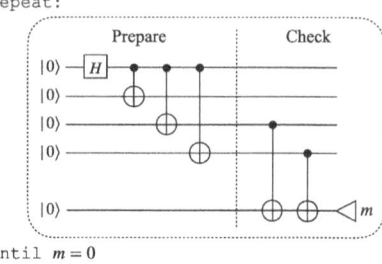

(b) FT cat state preparation.

Fig. 4. Comparison of 4-qubit cat state preparations with different checks. By our verification tool, we found that the first is non-FT and the second is FT.

The implementation of cat state preparation also depends on the number of faults it needs to tolerate. For example, consider the cat state preparation in Fig. 5 with checks on pairs of consecutive qubits. This implementation is only fault-tolerant up to 2 faults but fails to be fault-tolerant for 3 faults. The error pattern violating the fault-tolerance of Fig. 5 reported by our tool is marked in red (Pauli-X error, failed measurement, failed CNOT). Note that all the checks passed since the first and sixth checks failed to detect the errors. Consequently, these 3 faults cause 4 errors in the output state, which violates the

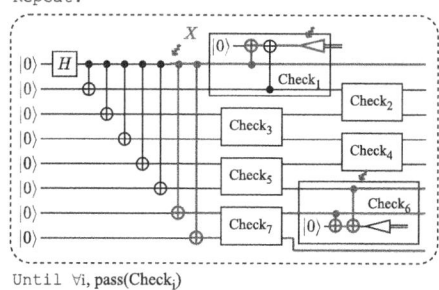

Fig. 5. An implementation of 8-qubit cat state preparation. By our verification tool, it is proved to be FT up to 2 faults but disproved to be FT for 3 faults.

fault-tolerance condition. Two additional examples of fault-tolerance bugs are provided in [13, Appendix I].

8.2   Verification of Fault-Tolerance

We perform our verification tool on the fault-tolerant quantum gadgets over the color code [8,45], rotated surface code [7,27], and the toric code [31]. The verification time is shown in Table 1. The preparation (Prep.) gadgets prepare the logical state $|\bar{0}\rangle$, ($|\overline{00}\rangle$ for toric code), the measurement (Meas.) gadgets perform the logical-Z measurement (logical-Z_1 for toric code) and the error correction (EC) gadgets implements the Shor's error correction [49]. We also perform our verification on the magic state distillation protocol in Sect. 7 with quantum Reed-Muller code [50] as the distillation code. Other single-qubit Clifford gates, such as the phase gate and Hadamard gate, can be either implemented transversally or via fault-tolerant state preparation of specific "magic" states (see Theorem 13.2 in [23]. These preparations are analogous to the preparation gadgets verified in Table 1, and the results are provided in [13, Appendix J]. We remark that the time cost mostly comes from the SMT solver, which is a typical challenge faced by most symbolic execution frameworks. For example, for the 121-qubit rotated surface code, our symbolic execution (excluding the SMT solver stage) uses only 54.72 s to generate the FT constraints of the EC gadget.

Table 1. Verification time of fault-tolerant gadgets over different QECCs. The quantum Reed-Muller code is used as distillation code for magic state distillation and only the error correction (EC) gadget is reported.

QECC	$[[n, k, d]]$	Time (s)			
		Prep.	CNOT	Meas.	EC
Color Code [8,45]	$[[7,1,3]]$	2.81	1.36	3.65	3.15
	$[[17,1,5]]$	13.91	30.29	27.92	20.98
Rotated Surface Code [7,27]	$[[9,1,3]]$	2.96	1.27	3.91	3.10
	$[[25,1,5]]$	22.38	181.72	42.79	52.15
	$[[49,1,7]]$	250818	Out of Time	82319	435011
Toric Code [31]	$[[18,2,3]]$	4.42	2.37	5.53	4.51
	$[[50,2,5]]$	818.34	12168.51	916.51	1918.95
Quantum Reed-Muller Code [50]	$[[15,1,3]]$	N.A.	N.A.	N.A.	4.89

9   Conclusion and Future Work

In this paper, we presented a novel framework for the verification for fault-tolerance of QECCs. By extending the semantics of classical-quantum programs to model faulty executions and developing discretization theorems for both quantum states and faults, we enabled the use of quantum symbolic execution to verify fault-tolerance of quantum programs. Our approach is both sound and complete under certain structural assumptions on loops and has been implemented into a practical tool capable of verifying real-world QECC implementations across a range of codes and gadgets. For future work, we believe the scalability can be significantly enhanced by incorporating interactive strategies [56,57,60] and human-assisted annotations and assertions [34]. In addition, we believe our framework could be extended to accommodate leakage errors [19,51] by introducing new language primitives, such as qubit loss detection and qubit refilling.

Acknowledgement. We thank the anonymous reviewers for their careful and constructive feedback. The work was supported in part by the U.S. National Science Foundation CAREER Award No. 2338773 and the U.S. Department of Energy, Office of Science, Office of Advanced Scientific Computing Research through the Accelerated Research in Quantum Computing Program MACH-Q project. WF was supported by the Engineering and Physical Sciences Research Council grant EP/X025551/1. GL was also supported in part by the Intel Rising Star Faculty Award.

References

1. Aaronson, S., Gottesman, D.: Improved simulation of stabilizer circuits. Phys. Rev. A **70**, 052328 (2004)
2. Acharya, R., et al.: Quantum error correction below the surface code threshold. arXiv preprint arXiv:2408.13687 (2024)
3. Acharya, R., et al.: Suppressing quantum errors by scaling a surface code logical qubit. Nature **614**(7949), 676–681 (2023)
4. Bauer-Marquart, F., Leue, S., Schilling, C.: symqv: automated symbolic verification of quantum programs. In: International Symposium on Formal Methods, pp. 181–198. Springer (2023)
5. Bezanson, J., Edelman, A., Karpinski, S., Shah, V.B.: Julia: a fresh approach to numerical computing. SIAM Rev. **59**(1), 65–98 (2017)
6. Bluvstein, D., et al.: Logical quantum processor based on reconfigurable atom arrays. Nature **626**(7997), 58–65 (2023)
7. Bombín, H., Martin-Delgado, M.A.: Optimal resources for topological two-dimensional stabilizer codes: Comparative study. Phys. Rev. A-Atomic, Mol. Opt. Phys. **76**(1), 012305 (2007)
8. Bombin, H., Martin-Delgado, M.A.: Topological quantum distillation. Phys. Rev. Lett. **97**(18), 180501 (2006)
9. Bravyi, S., Kitaev, A.: Universal quantum computation with ideal clifford gates and noisy ancillas. Phys. Rev. A-Atomic Mol. Opt. Phys. **71**(2), 022316 (2005)
10. Breuckmann, N.P., Eberhardt, J.N.: Quantum low-density parity-check codes. PRX Quant. **2**(4) (2021)
11. Burgholzer, L., Wille, R.: Advanced equivalence checking for quantum circuits. IEEE Trans. Comput. Aided Des. Integr. Circuits Syst. **40**(9), 1810–1824 (2021)
12. Burgholzer, L., Wille, R.: Handling non-unitaries in quantum circuit equivalence checking. In: Proceedings of the 59th ACM/IEEE Design Automation Conference, DAC 2022, ACM (2022)
13. Chen, K., et al.: Verifying fault-tolerance of quantum error correction codes (extended version). arXiv preprint arXiv:2501.14380 (2025)
14. Chen, K., Ying, M.: Automatic test pattern generation for robust quantum circuit testing. ACM Trans. Des. Autom. Electron. Syst. **29**(6), 1–36 (2024)
15. Choi, M.D.: Completely positive linear maps on complex matrices. Linear Algebra Appl. **10**(3), 285–290 (1975)
16. Fang, W., Ying, M.: Symbolic execution for quantum error correction programs. Proc. ACM Program. Lang. **8**(PLDI), 1040–1065 (2024)
17. Fang, W., Ying, M.: Symphase: phase symbolization for fast simulation of stabilizer circuits. In: Proceedings of the 61st ACM/IEEE Design Automation Conference, pp. 1–6 (2024)

18. Feng, Y., Ying, M.: Quantum hoare logic with classical variables. ACM Trans. Quant. Comput. **2**(4), 1–43 (2021)
19. Ghosh, J., Fowler, A.G., Martinis, J.M., Geller, M.R.: Understanding the effects of leakage in superconducting quantum-error-detection circuits. Phys. Rev. A **88**(6), 062329 (2013)
20. Gottesman, D.: Stabilizer Codes and Quantum Error Correction. California Institute of Technology (1997)
21. Gottesman, D.: The heisenberg representation of quantum computers. arXiv preprint quant-ph/9807006 (1998)
22. Gottesman, D.: An introduction to quantum error correction and fault-tolerant quantum computation. In: Quantum Information Science and Its Contributions to Mathematics, Proceedings of Symposia in Applied Mathematics, vol. 68 (2010)
23. Gottesman, D.: Surviving as a quantum computer in a classical world. Textbook manuscript preprint (2024)
24. Guan, J., Feng, Y., Turrini, A., Ying, M.: Measurement-based verification of quantum markov chains. In: International Conference on Computer Aided Verification, pp. 533–554. Springer (2024)
25. Hietala, K., Rand, R., Hung, S.H., Li, L., Hicks, M.: Proving quantum programs correct. arXiv preprint arXiv:2010.01240 (2020)
26. Hong, X., Ying, M., Feng, Y., Zhou, X., Li, S.: Approximate equivalence checking of noisy quantum circuits. In: 2021 58th ACM/IEEE Design Automation Conference (DAC), pp. 637–642. IEEE (2021)
27. Horsman, D., Fowler, A.G., Devitt, S., Van Meter, R.: Surface code quantum computing by lattice surgery. New J. Phys. **14**(12), 123011 (2012)
28. Hung, S.H., Hietala, K., Zhu, S., Ying, M., Hicks, M., Wu, X.: Quantitative robustness analysis of quantum programs. Proc. ACM Program. Lang. **3**(POPL), 1–29 (2019)
29. Hung, S.H., Peng, Y., Wang, X., Zhu, S., Wu, X.: On the theory and practice of invariant-based verification of quantum programs (2019), https://api.semanticscholar.org/CorpusID:208634831
30. Jamiołkowski, A.: Linear transformations which preserve trace and positive semidefiniteness of operators. Rep. Math. Phys. **3**(4) (1972)
31. Kitaev, A.: Fault-tolerant quantum computation by anyons. Ann. Phys. **303**(1), 2–30 (2003)
32. Knill, E.: Fault-tolerant postselected quantum computation: Schemes. arXiv preprint quant-ph/0402171 (2004)
33. Leverrier, A., Zémor, G.: Quantum tanner codes. In: 2022 IEEE 63rd Annual Symposium on Foundations of Computer Science (FOCS), pp. 872–883. IEEE (2022)
34. Li, G., Zhou, L., Yu, N., Ding, Y., Ying, M., Xie, Y.: Projection-based runtime assertions for testing and debugging quantum programs. Proc. ACM Program. Lang. **4**(OOPSLA), 1–29 (2020)
35. Liu, J., et al.: Formal verification of quantum algorithms using quantum hoare logic, pp. 187–207. Computer Aided Verification (2019)
36. Nan, J., Zichen, W., Jian, W.: Quantum symbolic execution. Quant. Inf. Process. **22**(10), 389 (2023)
37. Nebe, G., Rains, E.M., Sloane, N.J.: The invariants of the clifford groups. Des. Codes Crypt. **24**(1), 99–122 (2001)
38. Nielsen, M.A., Chuang, I.L.: Quantum Computation and Quantum Information: 10th Anniversary Edition. Cambridge University Press (2010)

39. Niemetz, A., Preiner, M.: Bitwuzla. In: Enea, C., Lal, A. (eds.) Computer Aided Verification - 35th International Conference, CAV 2023, Paris, France, July 17-22, 2023, Proceedings, Part II. Lecture Notes in Computer Science, vol. 13965, pp. 3–17. Springer (2023). https://doi.org/10.1007/978-3-031-37703-7_1, https://doi.org/10.1007/978-3-031-37703-7_1

40. Paykin, J., Rand, R., Zdancewic, S.: Qwire: a core language for quantum circuits. ACM SIGPLAN Notices **52**(1), 846–858 (2017)

41. Peham, T., Burgholzer, L., Wille, R.: Equivalence checking of quantum circuits with the zx-calculus. IEEE J. Emerg. Sel. Top. Circ. Syst. **12**(3), 662–675 (2022)

42. Peham, T., Burgholzer, L., Wille, R.: Equivalence checking of parameterized quantum circuits: verifying the compilation of variational quantum algorithms. In: Proceedings of the 28th Asia and South Pacific Design Automation Conference, ASP-DAC 2023, pp. 702–708. ACM, New York, NY, USA (2023)

43. Preskill, J.: Quantum computing 40 years later. In: Feynman Lectures on Computation, pp. 193–244. CRC Press (2023)

44. Reichardt, B.W., et al.: Logical computation demonstrated with a neutral atom quantum processor. arXiv preprint arXiv:2411.11822 (2024)

45. Rodriguez, P.S., et al.: Experimental demonstration of logical magic state distillation. arXiv preprint arXiv:2412.15165 (2024)

46. Sawicki, A., Karnas, K.: Universality of single-qudit gates. In: Annales Henri Poincaré, vol. 18, pp. 3515–3552. Springer (2017)

47. Shi, W.J., Cao, Q.X., Deng, Y.X., Jiang, H.R., Feng, Y.: Symbolic reasoning about quantum circuits in Coq. J. Comput. Sci. Technol. **36**, 1291–1306 (2021)

48. Shi, Y., et al.: Certiq: a mostly-automated verification of a realistic quantum compiler. arXiv preprint arXiv:1908.08963 (2019)

49. Shor, P.W.: Fault-tolerant quantum computation. In: Proceedings of 37th Conference on Foundations of Computer Science, pp. 56–65. IEEE (1996)

50. Steane, A.M.: Quantum reed-muller codes. IEEE Trans. Inf. Theory **45**(5), 1701–1703 (1999)

51. Suchara, M., Cross, A.W., Gambetta, J.M.: Leakage suppression in the toric code. In: 2015 IEEE International Symposium on Information Theory (ISIT), pp. 1119–1123. IEEE (2015)

52. Tamiya, S., Koashi, M., Yamasaki, H.: Polylog-time-and constant-space-overhead fault-tolerant quantum computation with quantum low-density parity-check codes. arXiv preprint arXiv:2411.03683 (2024)

53. Tao, R., Shi, Y., Yao, J., Hui, J., Chong, F.T., Gu, R.: Gleipnir: toward practical error analysis for quantum programs. In: Proceedings of the 42nd ACM SIGPLAN International Conference on Programming Language Design and Implementation, PLDI 2021, pp. 48–64. ACM, New York, NY, USA (2021)

54. Tao, R., et al.: Giallar: push-button verification for the qiskit quantum compiler. In: Proceedings of the 43rd ACM SIGPLAN International Conference on Programming Language Design and Implementation, PLDI 2022, pp. 641–656. ACM, New York, NY, USA (2022)

55. Wang, Q., Li, R., Ying, M.: Equivalence checking of sequential quantum circuits. IEEE Trans. Comput. Aided Des. Integr. Circuits Syst. **41**(9), 3143–3156 (2022)

56. Ying, M.: Floyd-hoare logic for quantum programs. ACM Trans. Program. Lang. Syst. (TOPLAS) **33**(6), 1–49 (2012)

57. Ying, M.: A practical quantum hoare logic with classical variables, i. arXiv preprint arXiv:2412.09869 (2024)

58. Ying, M., Feng, Y.: A flowchart language for quantum programming. IEEE Trans. Softw. Eng. **37**(4), 466–485 (2010)

59. Ying, M., Ying, S., Wu, X.: Invariants of quantum programs: characterisations and generation. In: Proceedings of the 44th ACM SIGPLAN Symposium on Principles of Programming Languages, POPL 2017, pp. 818–832. ACM, New York, NY, USA (2017)
60. Zhou, L., Barthe, G., Strub, P.Y., Liu, J., Ying, M.: CoqQ: foundational verification of quantum programs. Proc. ACM Program. Lang. **7**(POPL) (2023)

FeynmanDD: Quantum Circuit Analysis with Classical Decision Diagrams

Ziyuan Wang[1], Bin Cheng[2], Longxiang Yuan[1], and Zhengfeng Ji[1,3(✉)]

[1] Department of Computer Science and Technology, Tsinghua University,
Beijing, China
[2] Centre for Quantum Technologies, National University of Singapore,
Singapore, Singapore
[3] Zhongguancun Laboratory, Beijing, China
jizhengfeng@tsinghua.edu.cn

Abstract. Applications of decision diagrams in quantum circuit analysis have been an active research area. Our work introduces FeynmanDD, a new method utilizing standard and multi-terminal decision diagrams for quantum circuit simulation and equivalence checking. Unlike previous approaches that exploit patterns in quantum states and operators, our method explores useful structures in the path integral formulation, essentially transforming the analysis into a counting problem. The method then employs efficient counting algorithms using decision diagrams as its underlying computational engine. Through comprehensive theoretical analysis and numerical experiments, we demonstrate FeynmanDD's capabilities and limitations in quantum circuit analysis, highlighting the value of this new BDD-based approach.

Keywords: Decision Diagrams · Quantum Computing · Classical Simulation of Quantum Circuits · Quantum Circuit Equivalence

1 Introduction

Binary Decision Diagrams (BDDs) are widely regarded as one of the most influential data structures for representing, analyzing, and simulating classical circuits [11,38]. Since their introduction in the 1980s [10], BDDs have found applications in various domains, including circuit synthesis, formal verification, and model checking. In one of his video lectures given in the 2000s on trees and BDDs, Donald Knuth described them as "one of the few truly fundamental data structures that came out in the last twenty-five years". In his seminal book series, *The Art of Computer Programming*, he dedicated an entire section to BDDs [31].

Given their success in classical circuit design and analysis, it is natural to explore how BDDs can be extended to the representation and simulation of quantum circuits. The core idea of decision diagrams is to exploit repeated patterns

---

Z. Wang and B. Cheng—First authors.

© The Author(s) 2025
R. Piskac and Z. Rakamarić (Eds.): CAV 2025, LNCS 15934, pp. 28–52, 2025.
https://doi.org/10.1007/978-3-031-98685-7_2

in truth tables, enabling compact data representations. Quantum states and operations, like truth tables, scale exponentially yet may also exhibit repetitive patterns. For example, directly representing an n-qubit state requires storing 2^n complex numbers, known as amplitudes. Several existing works in quantum computing adopt this approach to identify patterns in quantum states and operations [3,12,26,30,35,41,51,52,56,61–63]. Some studies, like those in [29,32], combine tensor network methods with decision diagrams to enhance computational efficiency. Others, such as [47], incorporate additional compression techniques based on context-free languages. These methods, inspired by BDDs, extend beyond traditional BDDs and are better described as *BDD-motivated* techniques.

In BDD-motivated approaches, entirely new implementations of the data structure are often required. Additionally, to capture more intricate patterns, non-trivial labels may need to be assigned to the diagram's links [29,41,62,63]. In contrast, a less-explored approach uses classical BDD data structures and decision diagram packages, such as CUDD [49], to directly represent and manipulate quantum states. For example, Ref. [50] proposed a bit-slicing method to represent quantum amplitudes of states generated by the Clifford and T gate set using BDDs. We refer to this as a *BDD-based* method, as it utilizes classical BDDs as the underlying engine. Given the limited research on BDD-based methods for quantum circuits, a natural question arises: *Are there other BDD-based methods that can significantly enhance the analysis and simulation of quantum circuits?*

Key Contributions. We answer this question in the affirmative by proposing a new BDD-based method.

The first key contribution is the novel integration of the counting capabilities of decision diagrams in quantum circuit analysis. The profound connection between counting and quantum computing [1,21,57] is well-established, with counting complexity classes providing natural upper bounds for BQP [57] and underpinning quantum supremacy schemes [1]. While the counting perspective has been explored in quantum circuit analysis [37], this work uniquely combines quantum circuits' counting nature with BDDs' efficient counting algorithms. When decision diagrams have bounded size, counting solutions becomes efficient—a key advantage of BDDs highlighted in Knuth's book [31]. This counting algorithm then serves as the computational engine in our method. Unlike traditional Schrödinger-style simulators that use specialized BDD variants for state vector evolution [29,41,50,62,63], our method explores structures in the Feynman-type exponential sums. To emphasize its foundations in Feynman path integral, we name our method *FeynmanDD* (Feynman Decision Diagrams).

The second contribution encompasses efficiency-enhancing techniques. We present a binary synthesis method for constructing FeynmanDD's underlying decision diagram, carefully transforming low-degree multilinear polynomials to BDDs through strategic term ordering. This approach reduces both intermediate representation sizes and computational complexity. We also emphasize the importance of variable ordering for BDDs, providing various ordering heuristics for different circuit families. The combined consideration of term orders and variable orders proves crucial for the overall efficiency of our method. Furthermore, we introduce a sum-of-powers framework that is both flexible—supporting multiple gate sets within a unified approach—and efficient, as it delays conversion to BDDs, further optimizing performance.

Finally, extensive numerical experiments demonstrate the superior performance of FeynmanDD compared to existing decision diagram tools like DDSIM and SliQSim in amplitude computation while showing advantageous performance in sampling tasks for many families of circuit types even though our sampling efficiency does not match that for amplitude estimation. FeynmanDD also proves effective for circuit equivalence checking for certain families of circuits, with performance comparable to its simulation capabilities. These results confirm that FeynmanDD represents a promising new direction in quantum circuit analysis that is worthy of further investigation. In a follow-up work, we will provide a characterization of the complexity of the FeynmanDD method, showing provable efficiency advantages over tensor network methods for certain families of circuits.

Outline. We develop a sum-of-powers (SOP) framework to handle diverse quantum gate sets in Sect. 3, consistently mapping circuits of different discrete quantum gate sets into SOP forms. As special cases of tensor networks, SOPs can be manipulated and simplified using tensor techniques, which we explain in Sect. 4. Converting a quantum circuit to its SOP representation is straightforward. The challenge lies in representing the SOP function f as a BDD (or multi-terminal BDD [9]), which is carefully discussed in Sect. 5. After constructing the BDD for f_C, we demonstrate in Sect. 6 how FeynmanDD enables quantum circuit analysis and simulation, including amplitude computation, measurement outcome sampling, and circuit equivalence checking. To initiate a rigorous understanding of FeynmanDD's capabilities, we construct circuits using the linear network construction in [31] (Fig. 23), which FeynmanDD can simulate efficiently, while tensor network and Clifford methods face provably high complexity. Extensive numerical experiments on quantum circuit simulation and equivalence checking are conducted and discussed in Sect. 7 and Sect. 8 respectively.

2   Preliminaries

2.1   Basics of Quantum Circuits

This work focuses on pure quantum states and does not consider noise and mixed states. An n-qubit pure quantum state is a normalized vector in the Hilbert space $\mathbb{C}^{2^n}$, denoted as $|\psi\rangle = \sum_{x \in \{0,1\}^n} c_x |x\rangle$, where $|x\rangle$ represents the computational basis. Quantum circuits describe the evolution of quantum states through sequences of unitary operators, typically acting on one, two, or three qubits. Important quantum gates include the Hadamard gate $H = \frac{1}{\sqrt{2}} \begin{pmatrix} 1 & 1 \\ 1 & -1 \end{pmatrix}$, the Pauli-Z gate $Z = \begin{pmatrix} 1 & 0 \\ 0 & -1 \end{pmatrix}$, the controlled-Z gate (CZ), and the controlled-controlled-Z gate (CCZ). These gates form a weak universal set capable of approximating any (real) unitary operator to arbitrary precision and sufficient to simulate all quantum computation. Other gates are also considered in this work and are discussed in Sect. 3. Our analysis considers quantum circuits acting on initial state $|0^n\rangle$ without loss of generality. With U denoting the circuit's unitary operator, the final measurement in the computational basis yields a classical string $x \in \{0,1\}^n$ with probability $|\langle x|U|0^n\rangle|^2$.

2.2   Quantum Circuit Analysis

There are several types of quantum circuit analysis tasks widely considered in the literature, including circuit simulation, equivalence checking, circuit synthesis and optimization. Our method is currently applicable to the simulation and equivalence-checking tasks.

As our equivalence checking method is reduced to a variant of circuit simulation in the end, we will focus on the discussion of quantum circuit simulation here. There are two notions for classical simulation of quantum circuits: the strong simulation and the weak simulation. The strong simulation requires computing the output amplitude $\langle x|U|0^n\rangle$ (or the output probability) given x and U. The weak simulation requires sampling from the output distribution of the quantum circuit, i.e., returning a string x with probability $|\langle x|U|0^n\rangle|^2$.

A straightforward way to simulate quantum circuits is to use the Schrödinger method, where the quantum state is stored as a 2^n-dimensional vector [33]. The quantum gates are represented by $2^n \times 2^n$ matrices, and the quantum state is updated by matrix-vector multiplication. Since the quantum state is stored, both the strong and weak simulations can be performed. The Schrödinger method requires exponential space and time complexity, which quickly becomes infeasible for large quantum circuits.

Another classical simulation technique is based on the Feynman path integral [23]. Suppose U consists of m gates, $U = U_m \cdots U_2 U_1$. Then, the idea of Feynman path integral is to insert identity operators in between, transforming the output amplitude into an exponential sum of products:

$$\langle x|U|0^n\rangle = \sum_{y_1,\ldots,y_{m-1}\in\{0,1\}^n} \langle x|U_m|y_{m-1}\rangle \cdots \langle y_2|U_2|y_1\rangle\langle y_1|U_1|0^n\rangle. \qquad (1)$$

Note that each matrix element in the summation can be directly obtained from the specification of the corresponding gate. For some universal gate sets, these matrix elements can be represented by a particularly simple form, giving a sum-of-powers representation as detailed in Sect. 3. This simulation method has polynomial space complexity but the time complexity is exponential in the *number of gates*, which is even worse than the Schrödinger method.

Instead of directly computing the summation in Eq. (1), one can also compute it by tensor network contraction, one of the state-of-the-art classical simulation techniques [36,42]. A rank-k tensor with bond dimension two can be represented by a 2^k-dimensional array, $f_{i_1,\ldots,i_k}$, where $i_1,\ldots,i_k \in \{0,1\}$. In this way, a single-

or two-qubit gate can be represented by a rank-2 or rank-4 tensor, respectively. A tensor network is a collection of tensors, where each index may appear in one or two tensors. The contraction of a tensor network is to sum over all indices that shared by two tensors. For tensor network representation of the amplitude $\langle x|U|0^n\rangle$, no open wires remain and all indices appearing in the tensor network are summed over, giving a scalar of interest. In this work, we explore BDD-based techniques for Feynman-type simulation. We briefly mention that other families of techniques beyond decision diagrams have also been studied in the literature including, for example, phase polynomials [5,40], tensor-based techniques [36,42], ZX calculus [15,16,59], and tree automata [4,14].

2.3   Binary Decision Diagrams

A binary decision diagram is a rooted, directed acyclic graph that succinctly represents Boolean functions. It contains two node types: decision nodes and terminal nodes. Each decision node carries a variable label, such as x_i, with two outgoing links to child nodes. The dashed link represents the branch for $x_i = 0$, while the solid link represents $x_i = 1$. The terminal nodes, valued as 0 and 1, represent the function's output values. Any path from the root to a terminal node corresponds to a specific variable assignment, with the terminal node indicating the Boolean function's value for that assignment. An example of a BDD is shown in Fig. 2.

Two additional properties of BDDs are important: being ordered and reduced. An *ordered* BDD ensures that variables appear in a consistent order along all paths from the root to terminal nodes. A *reduced* BDD contains no isomorphic subgraphs and no node has identical children. In the literature, BDDs typically refer to reduced ordered BDDs (ROBDDs), which provide a canonical representation of Boolean functions. This work employs multi-terminal BDDs (MTBDDs), also known as Algebraic Decision Diagrams (ADDs) [9], a generalized version where terminal nodes can take multiple values rather than just binary values.

For a Boolean function f, we denote $B(f)$ as the number of nodes in its BDD representation. Once a compact BDD representation is found for f, many problems related to the function become tractable, with time complexity polynomial in $B(f)$, even if they were computationally hard originally. Notably, counting solutions for $f(x) = 1$ using BDD requires time linear in $B(f)$ [31,58]. Therefore, when $B(f)$ remains polynomially bounded, such counting operations can be performed efficiently. It is well-known that the variable ordering significantly impacts the BDD size, and that finding the optimal ordering is known to be NP-hard [58]. Most BDD packages provide dynamic variable ordering heuristics [45] which is useful for our purpose.

3   Sum-of-Powers Representation for Quantum Circuits

We begin our exposition by introducing the sum-of-powers (SOP) representation, derived from the Feynman path integral formalism, which emerges as a flexible framework for quantum circuit analysis; see, e.g., [6,7,13,19,53–55]. The SOP approach utilizes the fact that there exist universal gate sets consisting of unitary gates with particularly simple forms—so simple that all non-zero entries of the unitary matrix have values proportional to the *power* $\omega^{f(x_1,x_2,\ldots,x_k)}$, where ω is some root of unity and $x_1, x_2, \ldots, x_k$ are variables labeling the input and output wires discussed later. This method has been explored in several quantum computing works, initially by [18] and subsequently by [39]. Here, we review and slightly extend this approach within the SOP framework.

3.1   Gate Set $\mathcal{Z}$

First, consider quantum circuits over the gate set $\mathcal{Z} = \{H, Z, CZ, CCZ\}$. As in [39], we will label the wires of the circuit using the following method. Initially, we introduce a new variable for each qubit to label its corresponding wire. Subsequently, each Hadamard gate creates an additional variable to label its output wire, which is the only way a new variable can be generated. For a circuit with n qubits and h Hadamard gates, the total number of variables will be $n + h$. A labeling example is given in the left part in Fig. 1, where the circuit consists of four H gates, one Z gate, one CZ gate, and two CCZ gates. In this circuit, seven variables $x_1, x_2, \ldots, x_7$ label the circuit wires where x_1, x_2, x_3 represent the initial three qubits and $x_4, \ldots, x_7$ are introduced by the four H gates.

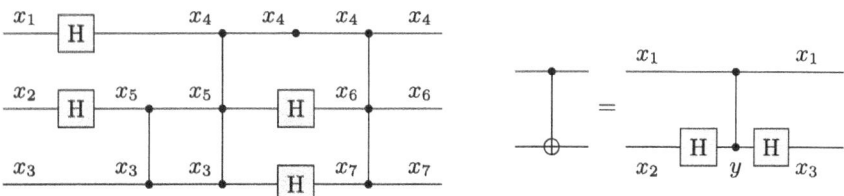

Fig. 1. Left: Variable labeling for a quantum circuit of gates from gate set $\mathcal{Z}$. Right: A decomposition that derives a power-of-sum representation for CNOT.

The H gate has matrix entries $(-1)^{xy}/\sqrt{2}$ where x and y are the variables for the input and output wires respectively. The CCZ gate has diagonal entries of $(-1)^{x_1 x_2 x_3}$ with 0 entries elsewhere, using the same set of variables for the input and output to indicate its diagonal nature. In the example of Fig. 1, the top qubit's H gate is represented as the power $(-1)^{x_1 x_4}/\sqrt{2}$ and the final CCZ gate is represented by $(-1)^{x_4 x_6 x_7}$. The gates CZ and Z can be discussed similarly with fewer variables. Notice that, in this example, all gates in $\mathcal{Z}$ are represented by powers of -1 up to a normalization factor (for H).

The power forms of the gates in the set $\mathcal{Z}$ can be identified as a special tensor. For H, it is a tensor of two legs labeled by variables x, y, and for given values $x, y \in \{0, 1\}$, the tensor takes value $(-1)^{xy}/\sqrt{2}$. The gate CCZ is a tensor of six legs where three of them x_1, x_2, x_3 are input and other three y_1, y_2, y_3 are output. This tensor takes value zero if input variables (x_1, x_2, x_3) and output variables (y_1, y_2, y_3) differ, and $(-1)^{x_1 x_2 x_3}$ when they are identical. This explains the reason we use the same set of variables for CCZ in the labeling which enforces the input-output variable equality. Consequently, each gate in $\mathcal{Z}$ is mapped to a tensor of the power form, and each variable represents either the external (input and output) variables or internal variables that are summed over by the tensor network contraction operation. For example, the circuit in the left of Fig. 1 corresponds to a tensor $\frac{1}{\sqrt{2^4}} \sum_{x_5} (-1)^{f_C(x_1, x_2, \ldots, x_7)}$ where

$$
\begin{aligned}
f_C(x_1, x_2, \ldots, x_7) &= x_1 x_4 + x_2 x_5 + x_3 x_5 \\
&+ x_3 x_4 x_5 + x_4 + x_5 x_6 + x_3 x_7 + x_4 x_6 x_7.
\end{aligned}
$$

We call this summation the *sum-of-powers* form for the circuit. In this example, x_5 is the only variable summed over in the expression.

Generally, for a circuit using gates from set $\mathcal{Z}$, the sum-of-powers form is $\frac{1}{\sqrt{2^h}} \sum_y (-1)^{f_C(x,y)}$, where h is the number of H gates and y stands for the internal variables. We define -1 as the *base* of the sum-of-powers forms above and *modulus* as the smallest positive integer exponent that brings the base to identity. The function f_C is a multilinear polynomial of degree at most three. For each H gate, the product of the input and output variables gives the term. While for Z, CZ, or CCZ gates, the product of the input variables gives the term.

3.2 Complex Gates

Not all elementary gates have the power form, but fortunately, there are different ways to work with them in the sum-of-powers framework. Consider the CNOT gate as an example, where CNOT : $|x_1, x_2\rangle \mapsto |x_1, x_1 \oplus x_2\rangle$. By definition, CNOT is a tensor that evaluates to 1 if the input variables x_1, x_2 and output variables y_1, y_2 satisfy $y_1 = x_1$ and $y_2 = x_1 \oplus x_2$ and to 0 otherwise. So one way to work with the CNOT gate is to label the wires with not just variables, but linear functions of variables. This approach was taken in [18], one of the early papers that used the wire labeling variables to analyze quantum circuits.

We take a different approach and use the fact that gates in $\mathcal{Z}$ are universal so one can decompose CNOT as $(I \otimes H) \, CZ \, (I \otimes H)$. See the right part of Fig. 1 for an illustration. A sum-of-powers form for CNOT is, therefore, $\frac{1}{2} \sum_y (-1)^{x_1 y + x_2 y + x_3 y}$. It is easy to verify directly that if $x_3 = x_1 \oplus x_2$, the summation evaluates to 1 and otherwise evaluates to 0, which is consistent with the definition of CNOT. So the CNOT gate in the sum-of-powers form is represented by input variables x_1 and x_2, output variables x_1 and x_3, internal variable y and normalization factor 2. In this approach, gates obtained by such decompositions as the CNOT gate are called complex gates, whereas gates of the power form are called simple gates. The complex gates can be treated easily as the "syntactic sugar" of a sequence of simple gates in implementation.

We prefer this method because it is flexible and is much easier to implement. For example, it works with Toffoli gates as well where the Toffoli gate has input variables x_1, x_2, x_3, output variables x_1, x_2, x_4, and one internal variable y. The sum-of-powers form for Toffoli is $\frac{1}{2} \sum_y (-1)^{x_1 x_2 y + x_3 y + x_4 y}$. If we choose the first method using functions of variables as wire labels, multiple Toffoli gates will induce high-degree polynomials in the general case, which may be even more difficult to implement.

3.3 Gate Set $\mathcal{T}$

All the sum-of-powers forms we have considered so far have modulus 2 and the functions f_C are effectively modulo 2. We emphasize that the modulus pertains to a sum-of-powers form of a gate, not the gate itself, as a single gate may admit multiple sum-of-powers representations with varying moduli.

We now expand our scope to the gate set $\mathcal{T} = \{\text{CNOT}, \text{H}, \text{T}\}$ and introduce sum-of-powers forms of base other than -1. Let ω_8 be the 8-th root of unity $\omega_8 = e^{i\pi/4}$. The T gate is a diagonal matrix $\begin{pmatrix} 1 & 0 \\ 0 & \omega_8 \end{pmatrix}$. So in the sum-of-powers form, the input and output wire will have the same variable x and the T gate is represented as the power ω_8^x. The H gate has input and output variables x and y, respectively, as before, and has a power form $\omega_8^{4xy}/\sqrt{2}$. The CNOT gate has input x_1, x_2 and output variables x_1, x_3 as before and take the form $\frac{1}{2} \sum_y \omega_8^{4(x_1 + x_2 + x_3)y}$. In sum-of-powers representations, we work with the same base for all gates in the gate set. This is always possible to achieve by choosing the least common multiple of all the moduli of the gates as the common modulus, as we have done for the gate set $\mathcal{T}$.

3.4 Gate Set $\mathcal{G}$

In addition to the gate sets $\mathcal{Z}$ and $\mathcal{T}$, the sum-of-powers framework is flexible enough to natively represent the gate set used in the Google supremacy experiment as well [8]. There, the gate set employed is $\mathcal{G}$ which includes the single-qubit gates $\sqrt{X} = \frac{1}{\sqrt{2}} \begin{pmatrix} 1 & -i \\ -i & 1 \end{pmatrix}$, $\sqrt{Y} = \frac{1}{\sqrt{2}} \begin{pmatrix} 1 & -1 \\ 1 & 1 \end{pmatrix}$, $\sqrt{W} = \frac{1}{\sqrt{2}} \begin{pmatrix} 1 & -\sqrt{i} \\ \sqrt{-i} & 1 \end{pmatrix}$, and two-qubit gates

$$\text{fSim}(\pi/2, \pi/6) = \begin{pmatrix} 1 & & & \\ & 0 & -i & \\ & -i & 0 & \\ & & & e^{-i\pi/6} \end{pmatrix}, \quad \text{iSWAP} = \begin{pmatrix} 1 & & & \\ & 0 & -i & \\ & -i & 0 & \\ & & & 1 \end{pmatrix}.$$

The iSWAP is a simplified version of fSim($\pi/2, \pi/6$) often used in benchmarking BDD simulation methods. All these gates have the power form shown in Tab. 1, and the common modulus is 24.

We have introduced three distinct gate sets—$\mathcal{Z}$, $\mathcal{T}$, and $\mathcal{G}$—each characterized by its native gates. We summarize the discussion in the following theorem.

Table 1. Sum-of-powers representation for the Google supremacy gate set.

Gate	Input	Output	Representation	Factor
$\sqrt{X}$	x_0	x_1	$\omega_{24}^{18x_0+18x_1+12x_0x_1}$	$1/\sqrt{2}$
$\sqrt{Y}$	x_0	x_1	$\omega_{24}^{12x_0+12x_0x_1}$	$1/\sqrt{2}$
$\sqrt{W}$	x_0	x_1	$\omega_{24}^{15x_0+21x_1+12x_0x_1}$	$1/\sqrt{2}$
fSim$(\pi/2,\pi/6)$	x_0,x_1	x_1,x_0	$\omega_{24}^{18x_0+18x_1+10x_0x_1}$	1
iSWAP	x_0,x_1	x_1,x_0	$\omega_{24}^{18x_0+18x_1+12x_0x_1}$	1

Theorem 1. *For any quantum circuit C of n qubits and m gates in universal gate sets $\mathcal{Z}$, $\mathcal{T}$, or $\mathcal{G}$, one can efficiently derive an SOP form $\frac{1}{\sqrt{R}}\sum_y \omega^{f(x,y)}$, representing the tensor of the circuit. In the representation, $f(x,y)$ is a multi-linear polynomial of $\mathcal{O}(m)$ terms and degree at most three, and x corresponds to external variables assigned to the input and output wires of C.*

A key advantage of our method is its remarkable flexibility: the approach can be readily extended to new gate sets without requiring customized implementation, in contrast to previous methods like [50]. Supporting a new gate set becomes a simple matter of creating a configuration file that defines the coefficients, monomial terms, and other characteristics of the sum-of-powers representation for each gate in the set.

4 Tensor Contraction and Substitution on Sum-of-Powers

In the circuit simulation and equivalence checking problems discussed below, it is convenient to work with the sum-of-powers representations not only for circuits, but for other derived quantities such as $\langle a|U_C|0^n\rangle$ as well. These quantities are easy to formulate in the sum-of-powers framework given the following two operations of SOPs.

In tensor networks, the most important procedure for manipulating tensors is the tensor contraction operation, where two indices are identified and summed over [36]. For a sum-of-powers tensor $\sum_y \omega^{f(x,y)}$ and two external variables x_1 and x'_1 in x, it is natural to consider the *contraction* of variables x_1 and x'_1. The resulting form is still a sum-of-powers tensor having the form $\sum_{x_1,y} \omega^{f[x_1/x'_1](x,y)}$, where $f[x_1/x'_1]$ is a function obtained by substituting all the variable x'_1 in f with x_1. More generally, let $x_1,x_2,\ldots,x_k$ and $x'_1,x'_2,\ldots,x'_k$ be the different external variables that are contracted respectively, then the resulting sum-of-powers tensor is

$$\sum_{x_1,\ldots,x_k,y} \omega^{f[x_1/x'_1,\,\ldots,\,x_k/x'_k](x,y)},$$

where $f[x_1/x'_1,\ldots,x_k/x'_k]$ is the function obtained by substituting $x'_1,x'_2,\ldots,x'_k$ with $x_1,x_2,\ldots,x_k$ respectively. Note that even though we write $f[x_1/x'_1,\ldots,x_k/x'_k](x,y)$ but $f[x_1/x'_1,\ldots,x_k/x'_k]$ is a function independent of $x'_1,x'_2,\ldots,x'_k$.

Another procedure we need is variable *substitution*. Let $\sum_y \omega^{f(x,y)}$ be a sum-of-powers tensor, and let $x_1, x_2, \ldots, x_k$ be external variables in x. For any values $a_1, a_2, \ldots, a_k \in \{0, 1\}$, the substitution of x_i with a_i for $i = 1, 2, \ldots, k$ results in a sum-of-powers tensor $\sum_y \omega^{f[a_1/x_1, \ldots, a_k/x_k](x,y)}$. This operation naturally arises when the wire corresponding to variable x_j is contracted with a basis state $|a_j\rangle$. The above discussions establish the following simple claim.

Theorem 2. *The contraction and substitution of an SOP result in another SOP.*

With the contraction and substitution operations established, we can now efficiently compute the sum-of-powers forms for the two quantities we require below. The first is the amplitude $\langle a|U_C|0^n\rangle$ where U_C is the unitary matrix for circuit C and $a \in \{0, 1\}^n$ is a computation basis. Let $\frac{1}{R}\sum_y \omega^{f_C(x,y)}$ be the sum-of-powers tensor for circuit C. From Theorem 1, we know that f_C is a summation of $\mathcal{O}(m)$ monomial terms where m is the number of gates in the circuit.

Let $x^{\text{in}} = (x_1^{\text{in}}, x_2^{\text{in}}, \ldots, x_n^{\text{in}})$ and $x^{\text{out}} = (x_1^{\text{out}}, x_2^{\text{out}}, \ldots, x_n^{\text{out}})$ be the variables corresponding to the input and output qubits respectively. Each consists of n different variables, but they may share some common variables. This could happen, for example, when all gates acting on a qubit are diagonal, and the labeling strategy discussed in Sect. 3 will not introduce new variables for the qubit. Suppose there are $s \geq 0$ common variables in x^{in} and x^{out} and there are qubit indices $j_1, \ldots, j_s$ and $k_1, \ldots, k_s$ such that $x_{j_i}^{\text{in}} = x_{k_i}^{\text{out}}$ for all $i = 1, \ldots, s$. Let $k_{s+1}, \ldots, k_n$ be the output qubit indices assigned non-common variables (that is, they are not in $\{k_1, \ldots, k_s\}$). The sum-of-powers tensor for $\langle a|U_C|0^n\rangle$ is then 0 if there is an $i \in \{1, 2, \ldots, s\}$ such that $a_{k_i} \neq 0$ (in other words, this constitutes a contradictory substitution, as a variable cannot simultaneously be substituted with both 0 and 1), or $\frac{1}{R}\sum_y \omega^{f_C'(y)}$ where

$$f_C'(y) = f_C[a_{k_{s+1}}/x_{k_{s+1}}^{\text{out}}, \ldots, a_{k_n}/x_{k_n}^{\text{out}}, 0/x_1^{\text{in}}, \ldots, 0/x_n^{\text{in}}](y).$$

This finishes the discussion on how to represent $\langle a|U_C|0^n\rangle$ as a sum-of-powers tensor network.

Next, we consider the representation for $\text{tr}\, U_C$. The basic idea is quite simple; we only need to perform a contraction of the input and output variables. Since an input variable may become an output variable on another qubit (e.g., the iSWAP gate in the gate set $\mathcal{G}$), we must ensure consistent substitution of each original variable during the contraction. Continuing with the above setup, consider the case that there are s common variables. Define a graph G of n vertices containing s edges (or self-loops) specified by $\{j_i, k_i\}$. Consider partitioning of the graph into t connected components $G_1, G_2, \ldots, G_t$. Define a new variable z_j for each G_j where $j = 1, 2, \ldots, t$. Suppose circuit C has the sum-of-powers form $\frac{1}{\sqrt{R}}\sum_y \omega^{f(x,y)}$. It is easy to convince oneself that the sum-of-powers form for $\text{tr}\, U_C$ is $\frac{1}{\sqrt{R}}\sum_{z,y} \omega^{f_C'(z,y)}$ where f' is the function obtained by substituting all external variables x in f_C using the following method. For each input variable x_i^{in} and output variable x_i^{out}, let G_{j_i} be the connected component to which vertex i belongs, and we substitute x_i^{in} and x_i^{out} with z_{j_i}.

5 FeynmanDD: Decision Diagram for Sum-of-Powers

In Sects. 3 and 4, we presented methods for deriving sum-of-powers representations for circuit and quantities related to the circuit $\frac{1}{\sqrt{R}}\sum_y \omega^{f(x,y)}$, where R is a normalization factor, ω is the r-th root of unity, and $f : \{0,1\}^k \to \{0, 1, \ldots, r-1\}$ is a multilinear polynomial with values modulo r. The next step of the FeynmanDD method is to represent the function f using a variant of BDD called multi-terminal binary decision diagram (MTBDD).

As discussed in Sect. 1, FeynmanDD departs from most existing BDD-motivated approaches by utilizing classical decision diagrams as its underlying data structure. This strategy facilitates the immediate use of robust and efficient implementations developed over decades, including CUDD [49], BuDDy [34], Sylvan [20], and adiar [48]. Moreover, it seamlessly incorporates powerful variable ordering heuristics. CUDD and Sylvan offer multi-terminal support, rendering them suitable MTBDD engines for gate sets of any modulus. BuDDy and adiar currently support only standard BDDs and are consequently limited to gate sets with a modulus of 2. Our current implementation exclusively employs CUDD, leaving support for additional packages reserved for future development.

In many applications, it is possible to first represent the function f for the circuit C as an MTBDD and then try to compute the MTBDD for function f' for the derived quantities such as $\langle a|U_C|0^n\rangle$ or $\operatorname{tr} U_C$. But the substitution and contraction usually help to simplify the multilinear polynomial significantly in the sum-of-powers and thereby also simplify its MTBDD representation. It is therefore preferred first to try to use methods in Theorem 2 to transform f at the polynomial representation level and delay the creation of the MTBDD as late as possible.

For instance, in the example circuit on the left part of Fig. 1, the function f_C has 7 variables and 8 terms. When representing it as a BDD, it has 28 nodes, including the constants 0 and 1. However, when enforcing the initial state condition, variables x_1, x_2, x_3 are set to 0, and the function reduces to one with 4 variables and 3 terms: $x_4 + x_5x_6 + x_4x_6x_7$. Its BDD is much smaller, containing only 10 nodes as shown in Fig. 2.

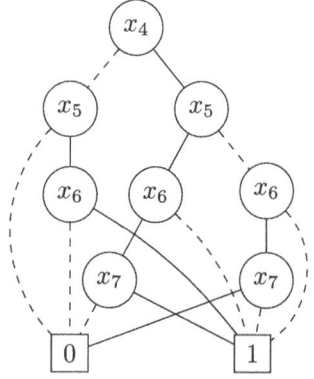

Given a function $f : \{0,1\}^n \to [r]$ representing a multilinear polynomial of m terms

$$f(x) = \sum_{k=1}^{m} a_k\, x_1^{i_{k,1}} x_2^{i_{k,2}} \cdots x_n^{i_{k,n}},$$

Fig. 2. BDD for the reduced function $x_4 + x_5x_6 + x_4x_6x_7$.

for $i_{k,j} \in \{0,1\}$, we need to build the BDD representation of it from scratch. This represents the most computationally expensive step in our method. While the summation is commutative, the order of term addition can lead to dramatically different computational costs. To illustrate this phenomenon, consider a sequence of Hadamard gates. The polynomial f takes the form $\frac{r}{2}\sum_{j=0}^{k-1} x_j x_{j+1}$.

When variables are ordered sequentially, the final BDD has a size of $\mathcal{O}(k)$. However, naive sequential term addition can result in a quadratic $\Omega(k^2)$ runtime, becoming inefficient for large k. The quadratic scaling emerges from the computational complexity of adding each term. Specifically, the time cost for combining the partial sum with the current term scales linearly with the MTBDD size of the partial sum. This linear scaling leads to a quadratic overall runtime through recursive addition. To address this efficiency challenge, we employ a *binary synthesis method*. This approach, utilizing the commutativity of addition modulo r, partitions terms into two groups of approximately equal size, first computes results within each group and then combines them. For the Hadamard sequence example, this reduces time complexity to $\mathcal{O}(k \log k)$. Numerical simulations suggest this binary synthesis method performs effectively across more generalized scenarios.

For the construction of a MTBDD, the second order that deserves careful consideration is the order of the variables in the decision diagram data structure as it may significantly impact the final size. Consider again the Hadamard sequence example: ordering the odd variables $x_1, x_3, \ldots$ first will cause the BDD size to grow exponentially. A well-know dynamic variable reordering heuristic is called sifting [45], which is supported by CUDD and is sometimes useful in the circuit classes used in Sect. 7. In our numerical experiments, we explore several other variable ordering heuristics to mitigate this challenge. For low-depth circuits, a pragmatic approach involves sequential qubit-based ordering. This method prioritizes variables by qubit, ordering all variables for the first qubit, then the second, and so on. We term this the *qubit order* strategy. For circuits with a small number of qubits, the *gate order* heuristics offer an effective variable ordering strategy. This approach ranks variables based on the first gate that employs them, providing a temporally informed sequence. An alternative method leverages standard tensor contraction optimization tools like *cotengra* to determine an optimal term order. Once this order is established, variables are arranged according to their appearance in the ordered terms. This approach, which we call the *tensor order* can sometimes be advantageous for random circuits. The concept of using tensor contraction complexity to bound BDD size has precedent in classical verification, where researchers previously explored the treewidth of CNF formulas [22]. Our approach diverges by focusing on the treewidth of XOR formulas. By employing these sophisticated ordering strategies, we can significantly optimize the efficiency of the MTBDD creation step.

The intuition behind the tensor contraction based heuristics is as follows. A fundamental fact about the size of a Boolean function f given variable order $x_1, x_2, \ldots, x_n$ is that the number of nodes with label x_i is the different number of functions $f[a_1/x_1, \ldots, a_{i-1}/x_{i-1}]$ that essentially depends on x_i. This number is upper bounded by $O(2^{N_i})$ where N_i is the number of external wires in the process of contracting the sum-of-powers tensor network. While it is a useful ordering heuristics, its performance on linear-network circuits is poor, indicating that the tensor contraction complexity bound is an upper bound that may be very loose in certain cases.

Another useful technique for improving the efficiency of FeynmanDD is to use the counting identity $\sum_x (-1)^{xy+xz} = 2\delta_{y,z}$ to simplify the function f in the SOP. More specifically, when a variable x appears exactly twice in the terms having form $\frac{r}{2}xx_0$ and $\frac{r}{2}xx_1$, we have

$$\frac{1}{\sqrt{R}} \sum_{x,x_0,x_1,y} \omega^{f(x,x_0,x_1,y)} = \frac{1}{\sqrt{R}} \sum_{x_0,x_1,y} \sum_{x} (-1)^{x(x_0+x_1)} \omega^{f_{\text{rem}}(x_0,x_1,y)},$$

which simplifies to $\frac{2}{\sqrt{R}} \sum_{x_0,y} \omega^{f_{\text{rem}}[x_0/x_1](x_0,y)}$. This technique reduces the number of variables and therefore the size of the MTBDD and is most useful for simulating simple structured circuits.

On the technical level, CUDD does not support addition modulo r by default, and we implement a custom-made function for this and use CUDD's API `Cudd_addApply` to perform the operation on the data structure it maintains. Another technical issue worth mentioning is the requirement to handle high precision integers, as the counters involved for large circuits is huge. We implement a high precision counting algorithm for CUDD using the *GNU multiple precision arithmetic library*.

6   Quantum Circuit Analysis Using FeynmanDD

6.1   Simulation of Quantum Circuits

In quantum circuit simulation, a fundamental problem is computing the amplitude $\langle a|C|0\rangle$ for a given $a \in \{0,1\}^n$. This single amplitude simulation problem, which appears straightforward, is actually BQP-complete even for an approximation and $a = 0^n$. Considering a multilinear polynomial f representing the sum-of-powers representation of $\langle a|C|0\rangle$ with size $B(f)$, our simulation algorithm achieves runtime linear in $B(f)$. Consequently, when the multi-terminal binary decision diagram (MTBDD) representing f is small, we can effectively solve this problem.

The core algorithm reduces the evaluation of the sum-of-powers form to a finite number of counting problems on the MTBDD. By rewriting the amplitude SOP representation, we can express it as

$$\frac{1}{\sqrt{R}} \sum_{y} \omega^{f(y)} = \frac{1}{\sqrt{R}} \sum_{j=0}^{r-1} N_j \omega^j,$$

where $N_j = \left|\{y \mid f(y) \equiv j \pmod{r}\}\right|$ represents the number of inputs to f that evaluate to $j \in \{0,1,\ldots,r-1\}$. Given the MTBDD representing f, there are algorithms that can count the numbers N_j in time $\mathcal{O}(mB(f))$ where m is the bit length of the counting result [31,58]. The number m is bounded by the number of gates, but usually much smaller and can often be considered constant in practice.

In quantum circuit simulation, another common task is computing the acceptance probability for a quantum circuit. Consider a circuit C acting on the initial state $|0^n\rangle$, with its sum-of-powers representation expressed as $\frac{1}{\sqrt{R}}\sum_y \omega^{f(x,y)}$, where x represents variables labeling the output qubits, the task is to estimate the probability of observing 1 when measuring the first qubit. We introduce a derived function $F(x,y,y') = f(x,y) - f(x,y')$ that operates on variables x, y, y', with y' being a new set of variables matching y's size. By defining x_1 as the variable of the qubit to be measured and $x_{>1}$ as the remaining variables, the acceptance probability can be formulated as:

$$\Pr(C \text{ accepts}) = \langle 0^n|C^\dagger\big(|1\rangle\langle 1| \otimes I\big)C|0^n\rangle$$

$$= \frac{1}{R}\sum_{x_{>1},y,y'} \omega^{f[1/x_1](x_{>1},y)-f[1/x_1](x_{>1},y')}$$

$$= \frac{1}{R}\sum_{x_{>1},y,y'} \omega^{F[1/x_1](x_{>1},y,y')},$$

where the contraction and substitution operations of SOPs are employed. Hence, the probability can be represented as $\frac{1}{R}\sum_z \omega^{F[1/x_1](z)}$ for $z = (x_{>1}, y, y')$. Notice that $\mathrm{B}(F[1/x_1]) \leq \mathrm{B}(F) \leq \mathcal{O}(\mathrm{B}(f)^2)$, the algorithm has a quadratic complexity in terms of $\mathrm{B}(f)$. In practice, we indeed observe that it is much less efficient compared with the linear complexity of the amplitude computation task. Yet, its performance is still comparably well for many circuit families.

Using a similar technique, we can estimate joint probabilities of measuring output qubits corresponding to variables $x_1, \ldots, x_j$ as

$$\Pr[x_1 = a_1, \ldots, x_j = a_j] = \frac{1}{R}\sum_{x_{>j},y,y'} \omega^{F[a_1/x_1,\ldots,a_j/x_j](x_{>j},y,y')},$$

where $x_{>j}$ are the remaining variables in x excluding $x_1, \ldots, x_j$. This allows us to compute the conditional probabilities using the conditional probability formula

$$\Pr[x_j = a_j \,|\, x_1 = a_1, \ldots, x_{j-1} = a_{j-1}] = \frac{\Pr[x_1 = a_1, \ldots, x_j = a_j]}{\Pr[x_1 = a_1, \ldots, x_{j-1} = a_{j-1}]}.$$

for all j and $a_1, a_2, \ldots, a_j \in \{0, 1\}$. We can leverage this method to sample from the output distribution of $C|0^n\rangle$ using a simple sequential sampling algorithm. The process begins by computing the probability $p_1 = \Pr[x_1 = 0]$ and sampling the first bit with probabilities p_1 and $1 - p_1$. For subsequent bits, we compute $p_j = \Pr[x_j = 0 \,|\, x_1 = a_1, \ldots, x_{j-1} = a_{j-1}]$ and sample accordingly. By repeating this process for $j = 2, 3, \ldots, n$, we complete the sampling of all n output bits.

We remark that even though our simulation method requires a discrete universal gate set and cannot deal with arbitrary single-qubit rotations directly, it is possible to work with such circuits by expanding the rotations using Solovay-Kitaev theorem [17] or methods in [24,44] to a sequence of, for example, H and T gates. As H will create a new variable and T gates will not, the gate sequence will introduce terms of the form $\frac{r}{2}\sum_{j=1} x_j x_{j+1} + \ell(x)$ where $x_2, x_3, \ldots$ are new variables introduced by the H gates and $\ell(x)$ is a linear function. By ordering $x_2, x_3, \ldots$ after x_1, the resulting BDD will have a size not very sensitive to the length of the gate sequence.

6.2   Circuit Equivalence Checking

Circuit equivalence checking is another important task for quantum circuit analysis and optimization [27, 28, 43]. Usually, BDD-based methods are ideal for such a task thanks to the uniqueness of BDD representations, and the circuit equivalence checking problem is reduced to check whether the BDDs for two circuits are identical. In our case, however, the BDD's for equivalent circuits may be dramatically different as it is based on the classical syntactical description of the circuit, not the semantic meaning (the unitary operator) of the circuit.

Fortunately, however, we are still able to use FeynmanDD to compute the trace of the unitary operator $\operatorname{tr} U_C$ for circuit C. Given two circuits C_0, C_1 of n qubits, $\operatorname{tr}(U_{C_0}^\dagger U_{C_1}) = 2^n \omega^j$ for some j, if and only if C_0 and C_1 are equivalent. This is a fact that was utilized in many previous works on circuit equivalence checking [28, 43]. Our method is then to first obtain the sum-of-powers form for $\frac{1}{2^n} \operatorname{tr}(U_{C_0}^\dagger U_{C_1})$ and build the corresponding FeynmanDD for it as explained in Sect. 5. And the counting based method as in Sect. 6.1 is used for circuit simulation to evaluate the sum-of-powers form. We know that the two circuits are equivalent (up to a global phase) if the value has a unit norm. By using the multiple precision arithmetic library, the computation is performed exactly which is crucial for the equivalence checking application. Numerical experiments on using FeynmanDD for equivalence checking are discussed in Sect. 8.

7   Circuit Simulation Experiments and Comparisons

To evaluate the performance of FeynmanDD, we conducted a series of experiments comparing it with (a) three state-of-the-art quantum circuit simulators, DDSIM [62, 63], SliQSim [50], and WCFLOBDD [46, 47] and (b) MQT-QCEC (https://github.com/cda-tum/qcec) for the task of equivalence checking, a widely used tool that integrates multiple equivalence checking techniques. The experiments were performed on a server equipped with two Intel (R) Xeon (R) Platinum 8358P CPUs @ 2.60 GHz (64 cores, 128 threads in total) and 512 GB of memory. However, as CUDD does not support parallel computing, each simulation is performed using a single thread and our method barely uses more than 1 GB of memory.

Our numerical experiments cover three types of computational tasks: (1) the calculation of the amplitude $\langle 0|U|0 \rangle$, (2) the simulation of sampling a full computational-basis measurement outcome, and (3) the equivalence checking of two given circuits. Furthermore, in the amplitude and sampling tasks, we measured the runtime and peak memory usage during the execution of these tasks by the program. Each simulation was limited to 3600 s (1 h). For simplicity, we use qubit order to arrange the variables in all our experiments.

We tested four different families of circuits for quantum circuit simulation tasks: Google supremacy circuits, GHZ circuits, BV circuits, and a specially constructed family called linear-network circuits. The results are summarized in Tables 2 to 6. We present the comparison of circuit equivalence checking experiments in Sect. 8.

7.1 Google Supremacy Circuits

We used benchmarks from the GRCS repository[1]: `cz_v2` and `is_v1` circuits. The gate sets are $\{H, \sqrt{X}, \sqrt{Y}, T, CZ\}$ and $\{H, \sqrt{X}, \sqrt{Y}, T, iSWAP\}$ respectively. Since SliQSim does not natively support iSWAP, the corresponding results in Tables 2 and 3 were obtained via the decomposition

$$iSWAP = (S \otimes S)(H \otimes I)CNOT_{0,1}CNOT_{1,0}(I \otimes H).$$

For WCFLOBDD, since it does not natively support $Rx(\frac{\pi}{2})$ and $Ry(\frac{\pi}{2})$, we decomposed them as $Rx(\frac{\pi}{2}) = HSH$ and $Ry(\frac{\pi}{2}) = HZ$. Moreover, since WCFLOBDD provides only an interface for computing probabilities rather than amplitudes, and this interface did not function correctly in our tests, we conducted only the `Single Sample Output` test for WCFLOBDD. Each benchmark consists of ten circuits, and the table reports the average time and memory usage across these ten circuits.

FeynmanDD significantly outperformed DDSIM, SliQSim, and WCFLOBDD in runtime and memory usage. For `cz_v2` circuits, FeynmanDD was much faster and consumed less memory. Larger `cz/5x5_10` circuits timed out for DDSIM, SliQSim, and WCFLOBDD, while FeynmanDD completed within 0.05 s for amplitude estimation and 95 s for sampling. Due to excessive memory consumption, WCFLOBDD was severely limited in this test. Similar results were observed for `is_v1` circuits.

7.2 GHZ and BV Circuits

We tested two types of circuits in this part: GHZ circuits and BV circuits. GHZ circuits generate n-qubit GHZ states, while BV circuits implement the Bernstein-Vazirani algorithm with the all-ones secret string. These circuits were chosen as they generate simple yet highly entangled states.

As shown in Tables 4 and 5, FeynmanDD performed better than DDSIM and SliQSim in terms of both time and memory usage. The results confirm that FeynmanDD is capable of efficiently simulating these relatively simple circuits and can handle larger sizes of GHZ and BV circuits with little additional cost. In these tests, WCFLOBDD achieves the fastest runtime, while its memory usage is significantly higher than that of FeynmanDD.

7.3 Linear Network Circuits

These are IQP circuits based on degree-3 polynomials [39] $f : \{0,1\}^n \to \{0,1\}$ as follows:

$$f(x) = A(x) \sum_{i=1}^{n} x_i + \sum_{i=1}^{n-k+1} C_{i:i+k-1}, \qquad (2)$$

---

[1] https://github.com/sboixo/GRCS.

Table 2. Quantum circuit simulation benchmarks on Google supremacy circuits for the task of zero to zero amplitude computation. In this and the following tables, n stands for the number of qubits, m is the number of gates, time is in seconds (s), memory is in MB, TO means timeout.

Circuit	n	m	Zero to Zero Amplitude					
			DDSIM		SliQSim		Ours	
			Time	Mem	Time	Mem	Time	Mem
cz/4x4_10	16	115	0.64	48.0	5.8	81.3	0.01	12.1
cz/4x5_10	20	145	67.6	362.3	666.9	255.5	0.03	12.2
cz/5x5_10	25	184	TO		TO		0.04	12.2
is/4x4_10	16	115	1.0	55.7	10.6	128.1	0.03	12.3
is/4x5_10	20	145	158.2	477.5	976.9	245.4	0.1	15.1
is/5x5_10	25	184	TO		TO		0.2	20.9

Table 3. Quantum circuit simulation benchmarks on Google supremacy circuits for the task of sampling. The (x) mark indicates that x tests timeout among the ten circuits tested in the group, and the shown value is derived from the average of the remaining $10 - x$ test results.

Circuit	n	m	Single Output Sample							
			DDSIM		SliQSim		WCFLOBDD		Ours	
			Time	Mem	Time	Mem	Time	Mem	Time	Mem
cz/4x4_10	16	115	0.53	48.00	6.10	153.53	184.32	18160.96	4.94	42.76
cz/4x5_10	20	145	71.65	362.31	785.91	355.38	TO		34.66	101.94
cz/5x5_10	25	184	TO		TO		TO		94.63	132.98
is/4x4_10	16	115	1.05	55.72	12.74	163.16	259.91	22349.67	7.62	76.02
is/4x5_10	20	145	178.52	477.57	1020.1	378.28	TO		25.36	116.72
is/5x5_10	25	184	TO		TO		TO		153.20(1)	156.15

Table 4. Quantum circuit simulation benchmarks on BV circuits. Time is measured in seconds (s), memory usage is meausred in MB.

Qubits	Gates	Zero to Zero Amplitude						Single Output Sample							
		DDSIM		SliQSim		Ours		DDSIM		SliQSim		WCFLOBDD		Ours	
		Time	Mem	Time	Mem	Time	Mem	Time	Mem	Time	Mem	Time	Mem	Time	Mem
100	299	0.002	71.4	0.05	14.5	0.005	12.2			0.05	14.62	0.04	480.02	0.007	14.54
500	1499	0.04	272.2	3.7	66.0	0.06	12.1			3.96	66.15	0.12	487.08	0.12	13.98
1000	2999	0.35	31.7	104.6	116.1	0.2	13.4	Error		118.02	116.53	0.23	496.66	0.47	13.98
5000	14999	19.5	2540	506.0	234.1	5.8	65.9			520.05	234.93	1.21	592.82	10.27	17.39
10000	29999	138.7	5051	394.3	396.4	24.2	98.0			367.66	398.11	2.37	717.26	42.74	28.49

Table 5. Quantum circuit simulation benchmarks on GHZ circuits. Time is measured in seconds (s), memory usage is meausred in MB.

Qubits	Gates	Zero to Zero Amplitude						Single Output Sample							
		DDSIM		SliQSim		Ours		DDSIM		SliQSim		WCFLOBDD		Ours	
		Time	Mem	Time	Mem	Time	Mem	Time	Mem	Time	Mem	Time	Mem	Time	Mem
100	100	0.0019	71.2	0.01	12.5	0.0023	12.2	0.002	71.29	0.009	14.19	0.03	478.84	0.005	13.98
500	500	0.04	271.8	0.07	23.9	0.01	12.3	0.04	271.72	0.06	24.36	0.04	479.87	0.05	13.98
1000	1000	0.3	530.3	0.9	48.2	0.04	12.8	0.26	530.34	0.91	48.93	0.06	481.52	0.18	13.98
5000	5000	19.9	2535	17.2	192.4	1.4	64.5	19.58	2535.00	18.73	193.14	0.22	495.71	4.14	13.98
10000	10000	142.1	5041	74.9	324.6	6.2	66.7	144.98	5041.17	78.12	326.00	0.43	512.53	16.68	18.71

where $A(x) := \sum_{i=1}^{n} \alpha_i x_i$, with α_i randomly selected from $\{0,1\}$ and $k = \mathcal{O}(\log n)$ $C_{i:j}$ consists exclusively of degree-3 terms involving variables $x_i, \ldots, x_j$. The design purposefully ensures that the second term $C_{i:i+k-1}$ involves k consecutive variables, guaranteeing that the number of forward signals for each module in Fig. 23 of [31] remains bounded by $k + 1$. An important reason to include the $C_{i:i+k-1}$ terms in this construction is that they are implemented using CCZ gates, which are non-Clifford and prevent the use of the Gottesman-Knill algorithm [2, 25]. For each (n, k) pair, ten circuits were generated. The values (including the number of gates) in Table 6 are the average values.

Table 6 demonstrates FeynmanDD's strength in simulating linear-network circuits. For fixed n, increasing k moderately increased FeynmanDD's runtime, but still much faster than DDSIM. For instance, when $n = 30$, $k = 7$ in amplitude task, FeynmanDD took 0.003s and 12MB, while DDSIM required approximately 1065s and 662MB on average. For the simulation task, FeynmanDD took 1s and 26MB while DDSIM used 1428s and 722MB on average. In contrast, WCFLOBDD was unable to complete the computation within one hour.

Table 6. Quantum circuit simulation benchmarks on linear-network circuits. In the table n is the number of qubits, k is a constant measuring gate locality. Time is measured in seconds (s), memory usage is meausred in MB. SliQSim is not compared as it currently does not support CCZ gates.

n	k	Gates	Zero to Zero Amplitude				Single Output Sample					
			DDSIM		Ours		DDSIM		WCFLOBDD		Ours	
			Time	Mem	Time	Mem	Time	Mem	Time	Mem	Time	Mem
20	5	162.0	0.20	34.17	0.002	12.15	0.19	34.21	187.06	12466.84	0.14	13.79
20	7	163.0	0.30	38.20	0.003	12.13	0.29	38.23	464.12	21069.78	0.64	16.74
30	5	319.8	459.07 (1)	157.49	0.003	12.13	460.53 (1)	157.56	TO		0.34	13.92
30	7	321.1	1065.42 (4)	662.17	0.003	12.14	1428.32 (3)	721.57	TO		1.00	26.06
40	5	527.3	TO		0.004	12.17	TO		TO		0.75	26.63
40	7	531.7	TO		0.005	12.13	TO		TO		1.60	35.47

8   Circuit Equivalence Checking Experiments and Results

We evaluated the performance of FeynmanDD for the task of equivalence checking by comparing it with MQT-QCEC (https://github.com/cda-tum/qcec) a

Table 7. Quantum circuit equivalence check benchmarks. n stands for the number of qubits, m is the number of gates of original circuit, m' is the number of gates of transformed circuit, time is in seconds (s), TO means timeout.

Circuit	n	m	m'	Equivalent		Missing		Reverse	
				MQT-QCEC	Ours	MQT-QCEC	Ours	MQT-QCEC	Ours
0410184_169	14	46	46	1.73	0.08	1.51	0.32	1.25	0.43
4gt11-v1_85	5	8	8	0.45	0.02	0.32	0.02	0.45	0.02
alu-v0_27	5	11	11	0.49	0.02	0.48	0.01	0.46	0.01
alu-v1_29	5	12	12	0.54	0.02	0.44	0.02	0.37	0.003
alu-v2_33	5	12	12	0.08	0.002	0.06	0.002	0.06	0.002
alu-v3_35	5	12	12	0.08	0.002	0.07	0.002	0.07	0.002
alu-v4_37	5	12	12	0.18	0.002	0.16	0.003	0.12	0.003
apex2_289	498	1785	1779	38.13	TO	36.36	TO	137.44	TO
avg16_324	576	3996	3996	57.39	TO	TO	TO	TO	TO
avg8_325	320	2013	2013	27.39	TO	TO	TO	TO	TO
bw_291	87	312	312	0.90	2.33	0.96	3.39	TO	6.80
c2_181	35	116	116	2.87	TO	0.56	81.36	2.60	TO
cps_292	923	2787	2779	35.76	TO	27.50	TO	TO	TO
cycle10_293	39	90	88	3.13	0.03	3.21	0.02	5.04	0.06
e64-bdd_295	195	452	452	13.78	0.41	28.31	0.20	13.22	0.18
ham7_106	7	32	32	1.92	4.15	2.28	2.53	1.80	4.02
ham7_299	21	68	62	0.59	0.01	0.77	0.005	0.69	0.005
pdc_307	619	2096	2096	11.52	TO	11.60	TO	412.45	TO
spla_315	489	1725	1725	34.94	TO	21.39	TO	27.96	TO
sym6_316	14	35	35	1.08	0.02	0.98	0.03	0.98	0.03
sym9_317	27	71	71	3.05	0.12	1.87	0.27	3.17	0.38
GHZ_100	100	100	100	4.88	0.01	4.96	0.01	5.00	0.01
GHZ_500	500	500	500	13.22	0.35	13.47	0.32	13.29	0.47
GHZ_1000	1000	1000	1000	15.16	1.35	15.04	1.49	15.29	1.21
GHZ_5000	5000	5000	5000	311.40	26.10	354.13	26.36	320.29	25.71
GHZ_10000	10000	10000	10000	TO	91.53	TO	91.72	TO	89.18
BV100	100	299	299	4.03	0.04	4.22	0.08	4.58	0.04
BV500	500	1499	1499	13.27	0.79	13.57	0.88	13.88	0.78
linear_20_5_1_0	20	208	184	1.96	0.01	1.76	0.01	No CNOT	
linear_20_7_1_0	20	205	181	1.99	0.005	3.71	0.004		
linear_30_5_1_0	30	380	346	2.58	0.03	2.76	0.02		
linear_30_7_1_0	30	407	369	2.05	0.01	5.15	0.03		
linear_40_5_1_0	40	645	601	2.48	0.02	2.01	0.02		
linear_40_7_1_0	40	596	540	3.39	0.01	4.06	0.01		
cz_v2/4x4_10	16	115	181	1.24	0.29	1.34	0.42	No CNOT	
cz_v2/4x5_10	20	145	229	0.73	0.93	0.74	0.91		
cz_v2/5x5_10	25	184	289	0.78	1.01	0.46	1.34		
cz_v2/4x4_5	16	61	100	0.83	0.005	0.58	0.01		
cz_v2/4x5_5	20	79	132	0.92	0.01	1.03	0.01		
cz_v2/5x5_5	25	99	164	1.37	0.01	1.34	0.01		
cz_v2/5x6_5	30	120	199	1.42	0.04	1.45	0.06		
cz_v2/6x6_5	36	144	238	1.50	0.24	1.52	0.22		

widely used tool that integrates multiple equivalence checking techniques. To conduct the tests, both input circuits needed to use discrete gate sets supported by FeynmanDD. Specifically, we selected (1) a subset of quantum circuits from RevLib [60] that FeynmanDD can process and (2) some quantum circuits used in Sect. 7. The experimental setup followed the same configuration as described in Sect. 7. The time limit for each check was set to 600 s (10 min).

Following convention in the literature, we considered three types of equivalence checking tasks:

1. *Equivalent*: Confirming equivalence between the original and transformed circuits. We used the `transpile` function in Qiskit with an optimization level of *O3* to generate transformed circuits. For Google supremacy circuits, the transformed basic gate set was specified as $\{H, Z, Rz, CZ\}$, which sometimes led to an increased gate count compared to the original.
2. *Missing*: Randomly removing one gate from the transformed circuit obtained in (1) and checking its difference with the original circuit.
3. *Reverse*: For transformed circuits containing CNOT gates after (1), we randomly selected one CNOT gate and swapped its control and target qubits, then checked for differences between the modified and original circuits. If no CNOT gates were present, this task was not performed.

The results are summarized in Table 7, which reports execution times for both programs. They demonstrate that FeynmanDD generally outperforms in equivalence checking tasks when applied to the quantum circuits from Sect. 7. For instance, in tests with GHZ circuits, FeynmanDD runs significantly faster than MQT-QCEC. When evaluating circuits from RevLib, FeynmanDD also shows superior performance in some cases. However, for certain RevLib circuits, particularly those with numerous gates, FeynmanDD's performance is less satisfactory.

9   Summary

In summary, FeynmanDD represents a new method for quantum circuit analysis, building upon the Feynman path integral concept and decision diagram-based counting algorithms. The approach transforms circuits with a supported gate set into specialized tensor networks—proposed as sum-of-powers forms—effectively reducing many quantum circuit simulation tasks to counting problems. The method converts quantum circuits to multi-terminal BDDs and computes quantities of interest by counting function values modulo a constant. Experimental results demonstrate superior performance in single amplitude computation compared to existing decision diagram methods. FeynmanDD also delivers competitive performance in multi-qubit measurement string sampling and equivalence checking, successfully completing certain computations that remain intractable for other approaches.

This research reveals several promising future directions. First, it would be interesting to explore approximation techniques to complement the current exact computation approach, potentially enabling scaling to larger systems. Second, alternative methods for handling complex gates like CNOT could be investigated, such as using linear function labels for variables instead of introducing additional variables. Third, further improvements might be achieved through more comprehensive circuit simplification techniques, which were minimally utilized in our implementation. Fourth, the implementation could expand beyond CUDD, potentially adopting Sylvan as an alternative support package to leverage parallel computing capabilities. Given that memory usage is not currently the bottleneck, such a transition may yield significant performance improvements for large circuits. Finally, this technique shows promise for broader quantum computing applications, including quantum device validation, performance benchmarking, quantum circuit simplification, and verifiable quantum advantage.

Acknowledgments. The work is supported by National Key Research and Development Program of China (Grant No. 2023YFA1009403), National Natural Science Foundation of China (Grant No. 12347104), Beijing Natural Science Foundation (Grant No. Z220002), Zhongguancun Laboratory, and Tsinghua University. BC acknowledges the support by the National Research Foundation, Singapore, and A*STAR under its CQT Bridging Grant and its Quantum Engineering Programme under grant NRF2021-QEP2-02-P05.

References

1. Aaronson, S., Arkhipov, A.: The computational complexity of linear optics. Theory Comput. **9**(1), 143–252 (2013). https://doi.org/10.4086/toc.2013.v009a004
2. Aaronson, S., Gottesman, D.: Improved simulation of stabilizer circuits. Phys. Rev. A **70**(5), 052328 (2004). https://doi.org/10.1103/PhysRevA.70.052328
3. Abdollahi, A., Pedram, M.: Analysis and synthesis of quantum circuits by using quantum decision diagrams. In: Proceedings of the Design Automation & Test in Europe Conference, pp. 1–6. IEEE, Munich, Germany (2006). https://doi.org/10.1109/date.2006.244176
4. Abdulla, P.A., et al.: Verifying quantum circuits with level-synchronized tree automata. Verifying Quantum Circuits Level-Synchronized Tree Autom. **9**(POPL), 32:923–32:953 (2025). https://doi.org/10.1145/3704868
5. Amy, M.: Formal Methods in Quantum Circuit Design. Ph.D. thesis, University of Waterloo (2019)
6. Amy, M.: Towards large-scale functional verification of universal quantum circuits. Electron. Proc. Theoret. Comput. Sci. **287**, 1–21 (2019). https://doi.org/10.4204/EPTCS.287.1
7. Amy, M.: Complete equational theories for the sum-over-paths with unbalanced amplitudes. Electron. Proc. Theoret. Comput. Sci. **384**, 127–141 (2023). https://doi.org/10.4204/eptcs.384.8
8. Arute, F., et al.: Quantum supremacy using a programmable superconducting processor. Nature **574**(7779), 505–510 (2019). https://doi.org/10.1038/s41586-019-1666-5
9. Bahar, R., Frohm, E., Gaona, C., Hachtel, G., Macii, E., Pardo, A., Somenzi, F.: Algebraic decision diagrams and their applications. In: Proceedings of 1993

International Conference on Computer Aided Design (ICCAD), pp. 188–191. IEEE Comput. Soc. Press, Santa Clara, CA, USA (1993). https://doi.org/10.1109/iccad.1993.580054

10. Bryant, R.E.: Graph-based algorithms for boolean function manipulation. IEEE Trans. Comput. **C-35**(8), 677–691 (1986). https://doi.org/10.1109/tc.1986.1676819

11. Bryant, R.: Binary decision diagrams and beyond: enabling technologies for formal verification. In: Proceedings of IEEE International Conference on Computer Aided Design (ICCAD), pp. 236–243. IEEE Comput. Soc. Press, San Jose, CA, USA (1995). https://doi.org/10.1109/iccad.1995.480018

12. Burgholzer, L., Bauer, H., Wille, R.: Hybrid Schrödinger-feynman simulation of quantum circuits with decision diagrams. In: 2021 IEEE International Conference on Quantum Computing and Engineering (QCE), pp. 199–206. IEEE, Broomfield, CO, USA (2021). https://doi.org/10.1109/QCE52317.2021.00037

13. Chareton, C., Bardin, S., Bobot, F., Perrelle, V., Valiron, B.: An automated deductive verification framework for circuit-building quantum programs. In: Programming Languages and Systems: 30th European Symposium on Programming, ESOP 2021, Held as Part of the European Joint Conferences on Theory and Practice of Software, ETAPS 2021, Luxembourg City, Luxembourg, March 27 - April 1, 2021, Proceedings, pp. 148–177. Springer-Verlag, Berlin, Heidelberg (2021). https://doi.org/10.1007/978-3-030-72019-3_6

14. Chen, Y.F., Chung, K.M., Lengál, O., Lin, J.A., Tsai, W.L.: AutoQ: an automata-based quantum circuit verifier. In: Enea, C., Lal, A. (eds.) Computer Aided Verification, pp. 139–153. Springer Nature Switzerland, Cham (2023). https://doi.org/10.1007/978-3-031-37709-9_7

15. Coecke, B., Duncan, R.: Interacting quantum observables. In: Aceto, L., Damgård, I., Goldberg, L.A., Halldórsson, M.M., Ingólfsdóttir, A., Walukiewicz, I. (eds.) Automata, Languages and Programming, pp. 298–310. Springer, Berlin, Heidelberg (2008). https://doi.org/10.1007/978-3-540-70583-3_25

16. Coecke, B., Horsman, D., Kissinger, A., Wang, Q.: Kindergarden quantum mechanics graduates ...or how I learned to stop gluing LEGO together and love the ZX-calculus. Theoret. Comput. Sci. **897**, 1–22 (2022). https://doi.org/10.1016/j.tcs.2021.07.024

17. Dawson, C.: Solovay Kitaev algorithm (2019)

18. Dawson, C.M., Hines, A.P., Mortimer, D., Haselgrove, H.L., Nielsen, M.A., Osborne, T.J.: Quantum computing and polynomial equations over the finite field Z2. Quantum Info. Comput. **5**(2), 102–112 (2005)

19. Deng, H., Tao, R., Peng, Y., Wu, X.: A case for synthesis of recursive quantum unitary programs. Proc. ACM Program. Lang. **8**(POPL) (2024). https://doi.org/10.1145/3632901

20. van Dijk, T.: Sylvan: multi-core decision diagrams. PhD, University of Twente, Enschede, The Netherlands (2016). https://doi.org/10.3990/1.9789036541602

21. Fenner, S., Green, F., Homer, S., Pruim, R.: Determining acceptance possibility for a quantum computation is hard for the polynomial hierarchy. Proc. R. Soc. London. Series A: Math. Phys. Eng. Sci. **455**(1991), 3953–3966 (1999). https://doi.org/10.1098/rspa.1999.0485

22. Ferrara, A., Pan, G., Vardi, M.Y.: Treewidth in verification: local vs. global. In: Sutcliffe, G., Voronkov, A. (eds.) Logic for Programming, Artificial Intelligence, and Reasoning, pp. 489–503. Lecture Notes in Computer Science, Springer, Berlin, Heidelberg (2005). https://doi.org/10.1007/11591191_34

23. Feynman, R., Hibbs, A.: Quantum Mechanics and Path Integrals. International series in pure and applied physic, McGraw-Hill (1965)
24. Giles, B., Selinger, P.: Exact synthesis of multiqubit Clifford+ T circuits. Phys. Rev. A **87**(3), 032332 (2013). https://doi.org/10.1103/physreva.87.032332
25. Gottesman, D.: The Heisenberg Representation of Quantum Computers. arXiv:quant-ph/9807006 (1998)
26. Hillmich, S., Zulehner, A., Kueng, R., Markov, I.L., Wille, R.: Approximating decision diagrams for quantum circuit simulation. ACM Trans. Quantum Comput. **3**(4), 22:1–22:21 (2022). https://doi.org/10.1145/3530776
27. Hong, X., Feng, Y., Li, S., Ying, M.: Equivalence checking of dynamic quantum circuits. In: 2022 IEEE/ACM International Conference On Computer Aided Design (ICCAD), pp. 1–8 (2022)
28. Hong, X., Ying, M., Feng, Y., Zhou, X., Li, S.: Approximate equivalence checking of noisy quantum circuits. In: 2021 58th ACM/IEEE Design Automation Conference (DAC), pp. 637–642 (2021). https://doi.org/10.1109/DAC18074.2021.9586214
29. Hong, X., Zhou, X., Li, S., Feng, Y., Ying, M.: A tensor network based decision diagram for representation of quantum circuits. ACM Trans. Des. Autom. Electron. Syst. **27**(6), 60:1–60:30 (2022). https://doi.org/10.1145/3514355
30. Jiang, S., Fu, R., Burgholzer, L., Wille, R., Ho, T.Y., Huang, T.W.: FlatDD: a high-performance quantum circuit simulator using decision diagram and flat array. In: Proceedings of the 53rd International Conference on Parallel Processing, pp. 388–399. ICPP '24, Association for Computing Machinery, New York, NY, USA (2024). https://doi.org/10.1145/3673038.3673073
31. Knuth, D.E.: The Art of Computer Programming, Volume 4, Fascicle 1 (Bitwise Tricks & Techniques; Binary Decision Diagrams). AddisonWesley Professional, Upper Saddle River, NJ, 1 edition edn. (2009)
32. Larsen, C.B., Olsen, S.B., Larsen, K.G., Schilling, C.: Contraction heuristics for tensor decision diagrams. Entropy **26**(12), 1058 (2024). https://doi.org/10.3390/e26121058
33. Li, R., Wu, B., Ying, M., Sun, X., Yang, G.: Quantum supremacy circuit simulation on sunway Taihulight. IEEE Trans. Parallel Distrib. Syst. **31**(4), 805–816 (2020). https://doi.org/10.1109/TPDS.2019.2947511
34. Lind-Nielsen, J.: Buddy : A binary decision diagram package (1999)
35. Lu, C.Y., Wang, S.A., Kuo, S.Y.: An extended XQDD representation for multiple-valued quantum logic. IEEE Trans. Comput. **60**(10), 1377–1389 (2011). https://doi.org/10.1109/TC.2011.114
36. Markov, I.L., Shi, Y.: Simulating quantum computation by contracting tensor networks. SIAM J. Comput. **38**(3), 963–981 (2008). https://doi.org/10.1137/050644756
37. Mei, J., Bonsangue, M., Laarman, A.: Simulating Quantum Circuits by Model Counting (2024). https://doi.org/10.48550/arXiv.2403.07197
38. Molitor, P., Mohnke, J., Becker, B., Scholl, C.: Equivalence Checking of Digital Circuits: Fundamentals, Principles. Methods. Springer, New York, NY (2004)
39. Montanaro, A.: Quantum circuits and low-degree polynomials over F2. J. Phys. A: Math. Theor. **50**(8), 084002 (2017). https://doi.org/10.1088/1751-8121/aa565f
40. Nam, Y., Ross, N.J., Su, Y., Childs, A.M., Maslov, D.: Automated optimization of large quantum circuits with continuous parameters. NPJ Quantum Inf. **4**(1), 1–12 (2018). https://doi.org/10.1038/s41534-018-0072-4
41. Niemann, P., Wille, R., Miller, D.M., Thornton, M.A., Drechsler, R.: QMDDs: efficient quantum function representation and manipulation. IEEE Trans. Comput.

Aided Des. Integr. Circuits Syst. **35**(1), 86–99 (2016). https://doi.org/10.1109/tcad.2015.2459034

42. Pan, F., Zhang, P.: Simulation of quantum circuits using the big-batch tensor network method. Phys. Rev. Lett. **128**(3), 030501 (2022). https://doi.org/10.1103/PhysRevLett.128.030501

43. Peham, T., Burgholzer, L., Wille, R.: Equivalence checking of quantum circuits with the ZX-calculus. IEEE J. Emerg. Sel. Top. Circ. Syst. **12**(3), 662–675 (2022). https://doi.org/10.1109/JETCAS.2022.3202204

44. Ross, N.J., Selinger, P.: Optimal ancilla-free Clifford+T approximation of z-rotations. arXiv:1403.2975 [quant-ph] (2016)

45. Rudell, R.: Dynamic variable ordering for ordered binary decision diagrams. In: Proceedings of 1993 International Conference on Computer Aided Design (ICCAD), pp. 42–47 (1993). https://doi.org/10.1109/ICCAD.1993.580029

46. Sistla, M., Chaudhuri, S., Reps, T.: Symbolic quantum simulation with quasimodo. In: Computer Aided Verification: 35th International Conference, CAV 2023, Paris, France, July 17–22, 2023, Proceedings, Part III, pp. 213–225. Springer-Verlag, Berlin, Heidelberg (2023). https://doi.org/10.1007/978-3-031-37709-9_11

47. Sistla, M., Chaudhuri, S., Reps, T.: Weighted context-free-language ordered binary decision diagrams. Weighted CFLOBDDs **8**(OOPSLA2), 320:1390–320:1419 (2024). https://doi.org/10.1145/3689760

48. Sølvsten, S.C., van de Pol, J., Jakobsen, A.B., Thomasen, M.W.B.: Efficient Binary Decision Diagram Manipulation in External Memory. arXiv:2104.12101 [cs] (2021)

49. Somenzi, F.: CUDD: CU decision diagram package (release 3.0.0). University of Colorado at Boulder (2005)

50. Tsai, Y.H., Jiang, J.H.R., Jhang, C.S.: Bit-slicing the Hilbert space: scaling up accurate quantum circuit simulation. In: 2021 58th ACM/IEEE Design Automation Conference (DAC), pp. 439–444 (2021). https://doi.org/10.1109/DAC18074.2021.9586191

51. Viamontes, G.F., Markov, I.L., Hayes, J.P.: Improving gate-level simulation of quantum circuits. Quantum Inf. Process. **2**(5), 347–380 (2003). https://doi.org/10.1023/b:qinp.0000022725.70000.4a

52. Viamontes, G.F., Markov, I.L., Hayes, J.P.: Checking equivalence of quantum circuits and states. In: 2007 IEEE/ACM International Conference on Computer-Aided Design, pp. 69–74. IEEE, San Jose, CA, USA (2007). https://doi.org/10.1109/iccad.2007.4397246

53. Vilmart, R.: The structure of sum-over-paths, its consequences, and completeness for Clifford (2020)

54. Vilmart, R.: Completeness of sum-over-paths for Toffoli-Hadamard and the dyadic fragments of quantum computation (2022)

55. Vilmart, R.: Rewriting and completeness of sum-over-paths in dyadic fragments of quantum computing. Logical Methods Comput. Sci. **20**(1) (2024). https://doi.org/10.46298/lmcs-20(1:20)2024

56. Vinkhuijzen, L., Grurl, T., Hillmich, S., Brand, S., Wille, R., Laarman, A.: Efficient implementation of LIMDDs for quantum circuit simulation. In: Caltais, G., Schilling, C. (eds.) Model Checking Software, pp. 3–21. Springer Nature Switzerland, Cham (2023). https://doi.org/10.1007/978-3-031-32157-3_1

57. Watrous, J.: Quantum computational complexity. In: Meyers, R.A. (ed.) Encyclopedia of Complexity and Systems Science, pp. 7174–7201. Springer, New York, NY (2009). https://doi.org/10.1007/978-0-387-30440-3_428

58. Wegener, I.: Branching programs and binary decision diagrams: theory and applications. Society for Industrial and Applied Mathematics, Philadelphia, SIAM monographs on discrete mathematics and applications (2000)
59. van de Wetering, J.: ZX-calculus for the working quantum computer scientist. arXiv:2012.13966 [quant-ph] (2020)
60. Wille, R., Große, D., Teuber, L., Dueck, G.W., Drechsler, R.: RevLib: an online resource for reversible functions and reversible circuits. In: Int'l Symp. on Multi-Valued Logic, pp. 220–225 (2008)
61. Wille, R., Hillmich, S., Burgholzer, L.: Tools for quantum computing based on decision diagrams. ACM Trans. Quantum Comput. **3**(3), 13:1–13:17 (2022). https://doi.org/10.1145/3491246
62. Zulehner, A., Hillmich, S., Wille, R.: How to Efficiently Handle Complex Values? Implementing Decision Diagrams for Quantum Computing. arXiv:1911.12691 [quant-ph] (2019)
63. Zulehner, A., Wille, R.: Advanced simulation of quantum computations. IEEE Trans. Comput. Aided Des. Integr. Circuits Syst. **38**(5), 848–859 (2019). https://doi.org/10.1109/tcad.2018.2834427

D-Hammer: Efficient Equational Reasoning for Labelled Dirac Notation

Yingte Xu[1], Li Zhou[2], and Gilles Barthe[1,3](✉)

[1] MPI-SP, Bochum, Germany
{yingte.xu,gilles.barthe}@mpi-sp.org
[2] Key Laboratory of System Software (Chinese Academy of Sciences) and State Key Laboratory of Computer Science, Institute of Software, Chinese Academy of Sciences, Beijing, China
zhouli@ios.ac.cn
[3] IMDEA Software Institute, Pozuelo de Alarcón, Spain

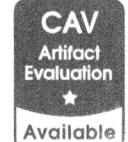

CAV
Artifact
Evaluation
★
Available

Abstract. Labelled Dirac notation is a formalism commonly used by physicists to represent many-body quantum systems and by computer scientists to assert properties of quantum programs. It is supported by a rich equational theory for proving equality between expressions in the language. These proofs are typically carried on pen-and-paper, and can be exceedingly long and error-prone. We introduce D-Hammer, the first tool to support automated equational proof for labelled Dirac notation. The salient features of D-Hammer include: an expressive, higher-order, dependently-typed language for labelled Dirac notation; an efficient normalization algorithm; and an optimized C++ implementation. We evaluate the implementation on representative examples from both plain and labelled Dirac notation. In the case of plain Dirac notation, we show that our implementation significantly outperforms DiracDec (Xu et al., POPL'25).

1 Introduction

Dirac notation [17], also known as bra-ket notation, is a mathematical formalism for representing quantum states using linear algebra notation. For example, Dirac notation uses the linear combination $a\,|\psi\rangle + b\,|\phi\rangle$ to represent the superposition of the quantum states $|\psi\rangle$ and $|\phi\rangle$. Another essential ingredient of Dirac notation is the tensor product $\otimes$, which is used to describe composite states. For instance, the tensor expression $|\psi\rangle \otimes |\phi\rangle$ denotes the composition of the two quantum states $|\psi\rangle$ and $|\phi\rangle$. A variant of Dirac notation, called labelled Dirac notation, is often used to describe composite quantum states. In labelled Dirac notation, bras and kets are tagged with labels to identify the subsystems they operate on. For example, the labelled tensor $|\psi\rangle_{S'} \otimes |\phi\rangle_S$ indicates that $|\psi\rangle_S$ and $|\phi\rangle_{S'}$ describe two quantum states over subsystem S and S', respectively. By considering the relationship between S and S', one can obtain identities for free, e.g.

$$|\phi\rangle_S \otimes |\psi\rangle_T = |\psi\rangle_T \otimes |\phi\rangle_S \quad \text{if } S \cap S' = \emptyset$$

© The Author(s) 2025
R. Piskac and Z. Rakamarić (Eds.): CAV 2025, LNCS 15934, pp. 53–76, 2025.
https://doi.org/10.1007/978-3-031-98685-7_3

In turn, commutativity of the tensor product ensures that one can reason locally about quantum systems, and contributes to making labelled Dirac notation a convenient, compositional formalism for reasoning about quantum states, akin to how bunched logics support compositional reasoning about mutable states.

Labelled Dirac notation is also widely used to express assertions in quantum programs. Specifically, many quantum Hoare logics rely on labelled Dirac notation and its variants to express program assertions (see, for example, [23,25,30,34–37]). These logics also employ implicit equational reasoning between labelled Dirac expressions to glue applications of proof rule–similar to the rule of consequence in the setting of classical program verification. Consequently, it is essential for the verification of quantum programs to have automated means of proving equality of two complex expressions based on labelled Dirac notation.

Contributions. This paper presents D-Hammer, an automated tool for reasoning about labelled Dirac notation. D-Hammer uses a rich, dependently typed language to formalize labelled Dirac notation and supports common idioms for describing quantum systems, including big operators of the form $\sum_{i \in I} a_i |\phi_i\rangle_S$ to represent indexed superpositions of states. The semantics of typable expressions are given in terms of Hilbert spaces, tailored to interpret the tensor product as an AC symbol. We leverage this interpretation to define a rich equational theory for labelled Dirac notation and prove its soundness with respect to our denotational semantics. Finally, we define an efficient normalization procedure to prove equivalence between two expressions. We then evaluate our procedure with respect to examples from the literature. Our evaluation covers examples in plain and labelled Dirac notation. The main conclusions are that our approach outperforms DiracDec [33] to reason about plain Dirac notation and is able of proving complex examples from the literature on labelled Dirac notation, including examples from prior work on quantum separation logic [36]. For completeness, we also evaluate D-Hammer on examples from the literature on equivalence checking of (parametrized) quantum circuits.

2   Motivation and Preliminaries

2.1   Plain Dirac Notation

Dirac notation, also known as bra-ket notation, provides an intuitive and concise mathematical framework for describing quantum states and operations in quantum mechanics. We write $\mathcal{H}$ for a Hilbert space, i.e., a vector space equipped with an standard inner product $\langle \mathbf{u}, \mathbf{v} \rangle \in \mathbb{C}$ for $\mathbf{u}, \mathbf{v} \in \mathcal{H}$. Dirac notation consists of the following components that reflect the basic postulates of quantum mechanics:

– Ket $|u\rangle$ is a column vector that denotes a quantum state $\mathbf{u}$ in the state Hilbert space $\mathcal{H}$. For example, the computational bases of qubit system are commonly written as $|0\rangle = \begin{bmatrix} 1 \\ 0 \end{bmatrix}$ and $|1\rangle = \begin{bmatrix} 0 \\ 1 \end{bmatrix}$.

- Bra $\langle u|$ is a row vector, the conjugate transpose of $|u\rangle$, that denotes the dual state of $|u\rangle$. For example, $\langle 0| = \begin{bmatrix} 1 & 0 \end{bmatrix}$ and $\langle 1| = \begin{bmatrix} 0 & 1 \end{bmatrix}$.
- Inner product $\langle u|v\rangle \triangleq \langle \mathbf{u}, \mathbf{v} \rangle$ which indicates the probability amplitude for $|u\rangle$ to collapse into $|v\rangle$. By convention, it is computed by matrix multiplication of two states, e.g., $\langle 0|1\rangle = \begin{bmatrix} 1 & 0 \end{bmatrix} \begin{bmatrix} 0 \\ 1 \end{bmatrix} = 0$.
- Outer product $|u\rangle\langle v| \triangleq |w\rangle \mapsto (\langle v|w\rangle)|u\rangle$. Any linear map, such as unitary tranformation, measurement operator, etc., can be decomposed as the sum of outer products. It is also computed by matrix multiplication, e.g., $|1\rangle\langle 0| = \begin{bmatrix} 0 \\ 1 \end{bmatrix} \begin{bmatrix} 1 & 0 \end{bmatrix} = \begin{bmatrix} 0 & 0 \\ 1 & 0 \end{bmatrix}$.
- Tensor product $|u\rangle \otimes |v\rangle$ (or simply $|u\rangle|v\rangle$ or $|uv\rangle$), $\langle u| \otimes \langle v|$ (or simply $\langle u|\langle v|$ or $\langle uv|$) for describing the state, dual state and linear map of composite systems respectively. It is computed by the the Kronecker product of matrices, e.g., $\langle 0|\langle 1| = \begin{bmatrix} 1 & 0 \end{bmatrix} \otimes \begin{bmatrix} 1 & 0 \end{bmatrix} = \begin{bmatrix} (1*1) & (1*0) & (0*1) & (0*0) \end{bmatrix} = \begin{bmatrix} 1 & 0 & 0 & 0 \end{bmatrix}$.

2.2   Labelled Dirac Notation and Motivating Example

Labelled Dirac notation is a generalization of Dirac notation for describing many-body quantum systems. The following example shows the necessity of labels:

Example 1. Let p, q, r be three qubits and initially in the (unnormalized) GHZ state $|\text{GHZ}\rangle \triangleq |000\rangle + |111\rangle$. Applying the 3-qubit Toffoli gate (CCNOT) with control qubits p, r and target qubit q to GHZ is equivalent to applying 2-qubit CNOT gate with control qubit r or p and target qubit q. Using Dirac notation, the identity is written as:

$$\text{CCNOT}|\text{GHZ}\rangle = (I \otimes \text{CNOT})|\text{GHZ}\rangle$$
$$= (\text{SWAP} \otimes I)(I \otimes \text{CNOT})(\text{SWAP} \otimes I)|\text{GHZ}\rangle,$$

which might be illustrated by the following circuit models.

Formalizing the statement in Dirac notation requires the following steps: 1. Arrange the qubits in a conventional order, here we choose p, r, q to simplify the representation of CCNOT; 2. Lift the local operation CNOT to the global system. When CNOT acts on r, q, it is straightforward, as r and q are consistent with the chosen order. We only need to tensor it with an identity operator I on p, i.e., $(I \otimes \text{CNOT})$. For CNOT acting on p, q, note that p, q are not adjacent in the chosen order. Thus, we additionally need the SWAP gate to temporarily exchange the qubits p and r, i.e., globally, we apply $(\text{SWAP} \otimes I)$ before and after $(I \otimes \text{CNOT})$ to lift CNOT on r, q.

Roughly speaking, encoding in plain Dirac notation requires tensoring identity operators and using additional SWAP gates, since the conventional order does not generally guarantee the following: 1. the order of all local operations is consistent with it, 2. the local operations only involve adjacent qubits in the conventional order.

To address the limitations of Dirac notations, physicists routinely use labels (or subscripts) to indicate the systems on which quantum states or operations are applied, thereby avoiding unnecessary lifting and swap gates. For example, rewriting the previous example using labels, we obtain:

$$\mathsf{CCNOT}_{prq}|\mathrm{GHZ}\rangle_{pqr} = \mathsf{CNOT}_{rq}|\mathrm{GHZ}\rangle_{pqr} = \mathsf{CNOT}_{pq}|\mathrm{GHZ}\rangle_{pqr}$$

This formalization avoids determining and maintaining the conventional order of qubits, nor lifting using additional I and SWAPs. In this setting, the tensor products become associative and commutative, allowing us to rearrange qubits as needed for calculations. For our example, we can perform the calculation as follows:

$$\mathsf{CCNOT}_{prq}|\mathrm{GHZ}\rangle_{pqr} = (\mathsf{CCNOT}|000\rangle + \mathsf{CCNOT}|111\rangle)_{prq} = (|000\rangle + |110\rangle)_{prq}$$
$$\mathsf{CNOT}_{rq}|\mathrm{GHZ}\rangle_{pqr} = (\mathsf{CNOT}|00\rangle)_{rq}|0\rangle_p + (\mathsf{CNOT}|11\rangle)_{rq}|1\rangle_p = (|000\rangle + |101\rangle)_{rqp}$$
$$\mathsf{CNOT}_{pq}|\mathrm{GHZ}\rangle_{pqr} = (\mathsf{CNOT}|00\rangle)_{pq}|0\rangle_r + (\mathsf{CNOT}|11\rangle)_{pq}|1\rangle_r = (|000\rangle + |101\rangle)_{pqr}$$

The right-hand side (RHS) of each line is equivalent, as shown. In addition, labelled Dirac notation can conveniently describe local measurements, partial traces (representing the state or evolution of subsystems in many-body systems), and partial inner products (which correspond to partial traces in pure states). These capabilities are sufficient for handling the mathematical formulas of quantum mechanics in many-body systems.

Labelled Dirac notation is not only pervasive in the description of many-body systems but also plays a crucial role in quantum program logic. Just as classical program logic uses variable names to construct logical formulas, avoiding the need for global memory functions, quantum program logic similarly uses variable names to label the subsystems on which quantum gates act, rather than lifting them to the global system. Actually, lifting operations would lead to an exponential increase in formula length relative to the number of variables, as discussed in [23].

In the following, we will use this motivating example as the primary focus in our demonstrations. Instead of GHZ states, we use a simpler example involving Bell states:

Example 2. Let q and r represent two quantum systems in the Hilbert space $\mathcal{H}_T$. Let M be a quantum operation acting on $\mathcal{H}_T$, and let $|\Phi\rangle = \sum_{i \in T} |i\rangle \otimes |i\rangle$ be the maximally entangled state. Then, it holds that

$$M_q |\Phi\rangle_{(q,r)} = M_r^T |\Phi\rangle_{(q,r)}.$$

As explained earlier regarding labels, we can consider the global system (q, r) and transform the equation above into the plain Dirac notation:

$$(M \otimes I) |\Phi\rangle = (I \otimes M^T) |\Phi\rangle . \tag{1}$$

The following sections introduce the formal language and labelled Dirac notation, and present a systematic approach for reducing labels. We will also demonstrate how an automated system can be built and used to solve similar equalities.

3   Dirac Notation

This section introduces the language of Dirac notation, its denotational and axiomatic semantics, and describes D-Hammer approach to equational reasoning. Three main ingredients of our language are:

- a rich typing discipline that distinguishes between scalars, kets, bras and operators, but supports sufficient overloading to remain close to standard Dirac notation;
- higher-order, indexed (a.k.a. weakly dependent) types. It allows to formally encode defined symbols like transpose or trace, which are usually used to represent the term in an abstract manner;
- operators with indefinite arities. Indefinite arities are instrumental for reasoning efficiently about associative and commutative (AC) symbols have indefinite arities, as they enable normalization by sorting.

3.1   Language

Since a Hilbert space $\mathcal{H}_V$ is dependent on the basis set V, types for Dirac notation also depends on the type V index. Therefore, the language is organized into three layers: the index, the type, and the term. Terms represent concrete instances such as kets, bras, and operators, which will be typed and checked. The index represents classical data types and appears in type expressions to differentiate between various Hilbert spaces and sets.

Definition 1 (Index Syntax). *The syntax for type indices is:*

$$\sigma ::= x \mid \sigma_1 \times \sigma_2.$$

Here, x is a variable, and $\sigma_1 \times \sigma_2$ represents the product type for tensor product spaces or Cartesian product sets.

Definition 2 (Type Syntax). *The syntax for Dirac notation types is:*

$$T ::= \mathsf{Basis}(\sigma) \mid \mathcal{S} \mid \mathcal{K}(\sigma) \mid \mathcal{B}(\sigma) \mid \mathcal{O}(\sigma_1, \sigma_2) \mid T_1 \to T_2 \mid \forall x.T \mid \mathsf{Set}(\sigma).$$

Basis(σ) denotes the type for basis elements in the index σ. $\mathcal{S}$ represents scalars, while $\mathcal{K}(\sigma)$ and $\mathcal{B}(\sigma)$ refer to ket and bra types in the Hilbert space σ, respectively. $\mathcal{O}(\sigma_1, \sigma_2)$ represents linear operators with σ_2 as the domain and σ_1 as the codomain. Set(σ) refers to the type of subsets of σ, used to denote the values of bound variables in summations. The remaining two constructs define function types: $T_1 \to T_2$ represent the set of functions that take a T_1-type argument and return a T_2-type term, while $\forall x.T$ represents the dependently typed functions that take an index argument x : Index and produce a T-type term, where T may depend on x. Index functions are essential for defining polymorphic transformations over Hilbert spaces.

Definition 3 (Term Syntax). *The syntax for Dirac notation terms is:*

$$
\begin{aligned}
e ::= \ & x \mid \lambda x : T.e \mid \lambda x : \mathsf{Index}.e \mid e_1 \ e_2 \mid (e_1, e_2) \\
& \mid 0 \mid 1 \mid e_1 \times \cdots \times e_n \mid e^* \mid \delta_{e_1, e_2} \\
& \mid \mathbf{0}_{\mathcal{K}}(\sigma) \mid \mathbf{0}_{\mathcal{B}}(\sigma) \mid \mathbf{0}_{\mathcal{O}}(\sigma_1, \sigma_2) \mid \mathbf{1}_{\mathcal{O}}(\sigma) \\
& \mid |e\rangle \mid \langle t| \mid e^\dagger \mid e_1.e_2 \mid e_1 + \cdots + e_n \mid e_1 \otimes e_2 \mid e_1 \cdot e_2 \\
& \mid \mathbf{U}(\sigma) \mid e_1 \star e_2 \mid \sum_{e_1} e_2.
\end{aligned}
$$

The terms above are explained in five lines.

1. **function and basis**: $\lambda x : T.e$ represents the abstraction for normal functions, and $\lambda x : \mathsf{Index}.e$ represents the abstraction for index functions. $e_1 \ e_2$ denotes function application. (e_1, e_2) is the basis pair for product types.
2. **scalar**: 0, 1, $e_1 \times \cdots \times e_n$ and e^* are symbols for scalars. δ_{e_1, e_2} compares whether two basis are the same and evaluates to 1 or 0 accordingly.
3. **Dirac constant**: zero ket, zero bra, zero operator and identity operator.
4. **Dirac function**: $|e\rangle$ is a ket, $\langle t|$ is a bra, and $e^\dagger$ denotes the conjugate transpose of e. $e_1.e_2$ represents scaling the term e_2 by scalar e_1. $e_1 + \cdots + e_n$ is the addition. $e_1 \otimes e_2$ represents tensor product, and $e_1 \cdot e_2$ represents the multiplication.
5. **summation**: $\mathbf{U}(\sigma)$ denotes the universal set with index σ. $e_1 \star e_2$ represents the Cartesian product of e_1 and e_2. $\sum_{e_1} e_2$ is the big operator sum, modeled by folding the function e_2 over the value set e_1. Typically, the sum's body is given by an abstraction. For convenience, we also use the notation $\sum_{x \in s} X$ to represent $\sum_s \lambda x : T.X$.

The scalar multiplication $\times$ and addition $+$ are AC symbols, and they have indefinite arity. We use letters like a, b, c to represent scalar variables, K and B to represent ket and bra variables, and O for operators. Therefore, $O \cdot K$ is interpreted as the operator-ket multiplication, and scalars can also be constructed from inner products $B \cdot K$.

3.2   Typing System

The typing system is responsible for classifying terms within a proof system, according to the types of variables and definitions. We use a context Γ to preserve the assumptions $x : T$ and definitions $x := t : T$.

Definition 4 (Context). *The syntax for context Γ is:*

$$\Gamma ::= [] \mid \Gamma; x : \mathsf{Index} \mid \Gamma; x : T \mid \Gamma; x := t : T.$$

Definitions refer to symbols that can be expanded or unfolded, and typically represent abstract concepts. such as transpose or trace in Dirac notation. Assumptions, on the other hand, define the types of variables. We say an expression t has type X in context Γ if the typing judgment $\Gamma \vdash t : X$ can be proven through the rules in Appendix A. These are two instances:

$$\frac{\Gamma \vdash t : \mathsf{Basis}(\sigma)}{\Gamma \vdash |t\rangle : \mathcal{K}(\sigma)} \, , \qquad \frac{\Gamma \vdash B : \mathcal{B}(\sigma) \qquad \Gamma \vdash K : \mathcal{K}(\sigma)}{\Gamma \vdash B \cdot K : \mathcal{S}} \, .$$

The ket $|t\rangle$ will have the type $\mathcal{K}(\sigma)$ if t is a basis term of index σ. Similarly, the inner product between a bra and a ket of the same index σ is typed as a scalar. It corresponds to the constraint of inner product that vectors should be from the same Hilbert space. Especially, the big operator sum is modeled by folding a function over a set, with the typing rule as follows:

$$\frac{\Gamma \vdash s : \mathsf{Set}(\sigma) \qquad \Gamma \vdash f : \mathsf{Basis}(\sigma) \to \mathcal{K}(\tau)}{\Gamma \vdash \sum_s f : \mathcal{K}(\tau)} \, .$$

3.3   Semantics

The semantics of a language define the meaning of its expressions. In this context, the objective of our algorithm is to determine whether two expressions are semantically equivalent. We define the semantics in a denotational manner, mapping syntax to set-theoretic objects.

Denotational Semantics. Denotational semantics maps types to sets, and expressions and indices to values in the interpretation of types and indices, respectively. As in other dependently typed systems, all interpretations are parametrized by a valuation mapping v, which assigns values to variables and indices. We let $[\![e]\!]_v$ denote the interpretation of an expression e w.r.t. a valuation v, and use similar notations for types and indices. As usual, we say that a valuation v is valid w.r.t. a context Γ if for every variable declaration $x : T$, we have $[\![x]\!]_v \in [\![T]\!]_v$ and for every definition $x := t : T$, we have $[\![x]\!]_v = [\![t]\!]_v$.

In more detail, variables typed with Index are interpreted as finite sets, and the product of two indices $[\![\sigma_1 \times \sigma_2]\!]$ is defined as the Cartesian product of the sets $[\![\sigma_1]\!]$ and $[\![\sigma_2]\!]$. More generally, each type is interpreted as a set. For example, the scalar type $[\![\mathcal{S}]\!]$ is interpreted as the set of complex numbers $\mathbb{C}$, and the ket and bra types $[\![\mathcal{K}(\sigma)]\!]$ and $[\![\mathcal{B}(\sigma)]\!]$ are interpreted as the Hilbert space $\mathcal{H}_{[\![\sigma]\!]}$ and its dual $\mathcal{H}^*_{[\![\sigma]\!]}$, respectively. Terms are explained as the set elements. For example, the semantics of ket tensor product $[\![K_1 \otimes K_2]\!] \equiv [\![K_1]\!] \otimes [\![K_2]\!]$, is obtained by first calculating the semantics $[\![K_1]\!]$ and $[\![K_2]\!]$ as vectors, and then take the vector tensor product as result. The complete interpretation of terms and types is provided in Appendix B.

The type system is sound w.r.t. the denotational semantics of expressions. Specifically, for a well-formed context Γ, term t, and type T, if $\Gamma \vdash t : T$, then for any valuation v that is valid for Γ, the interpretation of t w.r.t. v is an element of the interpretation of T w.r.t. v.

Lemma 1 (Soundness of type system). *If $\Gamma \vdash t : T$, then for all valuations v valid w.r.t. Γ, we have $[\![t]\!]_v \in [\![T]\!]_v$.*

This interpretation formalizes the standard understanding of Dirac notation and provides the foundation for the algorithm. However, computers cannot directly reason about equivalence through mathematical interpretations. We proceed by defining a proof system that abstracts these concepts.

Axiomatic Semantics. The proof system for equivalence is based on equational logic, together with axioms that describe the properties of Dirac notation. A full list of these axioms can be found in Appendix C. The axioms cover fundamental aspects of linear spaces, as well as other structures like the tensor and inner products. For example, we have the absorption law for zero symbols: $X \cdot \mathbf{0} = \mathbf{0}$, and the bilinearity of the dot product:

$$(a.X) \cdot Y = a \cdot (X \cdot Y), \quad X \cdot (Y_1 + Y_2) = X \cdot Y_1 + X \cdot Y_2,$$
$$X \cdot (a.Y) = a \cdot (X \cdot Y), \quad (X_1 + X_2) \cdot Y = X_1 \cdot Y + X_2 \cdot Y.$$

The entire axioms are separated into two sets R and E. R contains the axioms normalized by term rewriting. Other axioms requiring special algorithms, which are collected in the set E.

Definition 5 (axiom set E).

(AC-equivalence) *e.g.,* $X + Y = Y + X, \quad (X + Y) + Z = X + (Y + Z),$

(α-equivalence) $\lambda x.A = \lambda y.A\{x/y\}, \quad$ (SUM-SWAP) $\displaystyle\sum_{i \in s_1} \sum_{j \in s_2} A = \sum_{j \in s_2} \sum_{i \in s_1} A,$

(scalar theories) *e.g.,* $a + 0 = a, \quad a \times (b + c) = a \times b + a \times c.$

We say an equation $e_1 = e_2$ is provable, denoted as $\Gamma \vdash e_1 = e_2 : T$, if $\Gamma \vdash e_1 : T$ and $\Gamma \vdash e_2 : T$ are provable, and $e_1 = e_2$ can be deduced in Γ using the axioms and equational logic. An equation $e_1 = e_2$ is valid in context Γ, written as $\Gamma \vDash e_1 = e_2$, if $[\![e_1]\!]_v = [\![e_2]\!]_v$ for all valuations v that are valid w.r.t. Γ.

Theorem 1 (Soundness of equational theory). *If $\Gamma \vdash e_1 = e_2 : T$ then* $\Gamma \vDash e_1 = e_2$.

The proof of soundess is standard: we prove that all axioms are sound, and that all proof rules are sound.

Next, we formalize the motivating example Example 2 in Dirac notation.

Example 3 (Motivating Example Formalization). Definitions and assumptions in the context Γ are formalized as follows:

$$
\text{TPO} \quad := \lambda T_1 : \mathsf{Index}.\lambda T_2 : \mathsf{Index}.\lambda O : \mathcal{O}(T_1, T_2). \sum_{i \in \mathbf{U}(T_1)} \sum_{j \in \mathbf{U}(T_2)} \langle i| \, O \, |j\rangle \, . \, |j\rangle \, \langle i|
$$

$$
: \forall T_1.\forall T_2.\mathcal{O}(T_1, T_2) \rightarrow \mathcal{O}(T_2, T_1);
$$

$$
\text{phi} \quad := \lambda T : \mathsf{Index}. \sum_{i \in \mathbf{U}(T)} \sum_{j \in \mathbf{U}(T)} |(i, j)\rangle : \forall T.\mathcal{K}(T \times T);
$$

$$
T \quad : \mathsf{Index}; \qquad\qquad\qquad M \quad : \mathcal{O}(T, T).
$$

Notice how the functions and higher-order typing helps to formalize the abstract concepts here. The symbol TPO represents the transpose of an operator, polymorphic on the Hilbert spaces T_1 and T_2. The symbol phi takes the index T and defines the maximally entangled states, summing over all basis elements in T, as indicated by the universal set $\mathbf{U}(T)$. With the assumption of the index T and operator M, we can express the equivalence in the plain Dirac notation as:

$$
(\text{M} \otimes \mathbf{1}_{\mathcal{O}}(\text{T})) \cdot (\text{phi T}) = (\mathbf{1}_{\mathcal{O}}(\text{T}) \otimes (\text{TPO T T M})) \cdot (\text{phi T}).
$$

3.4   Normalization

The equivalence of Dirac notations is established through normalization, which transforms equivalent expressions into the same syntax under a set of axioms. We employ an efficient algorithm to perform the normalization fully on $R \cup E$.

1. **Rule based term rewriting**: Expand definitions and simplify expressions.
2. **Variable expansion**: Convert to abstract element-wise representation.
3. **Rule based term rewriting**: Normalize terms on R modulo E.
4. **Sorting without bound variables**: Normalize AC-equivalence.
5. **Swapping successive summations**: Normalize SUM-SWAP equivalence.
6. **Use de Bruijn index**: Normalize α-equivalence.

Step 1 through 3 involve term rewriting for R. Term rewriting is the process of repeatedly reducing a term using a set of rules in the form of $l \, \triangleright \, r$. The reduction works by matching the subterms with the left-hand side of a rule and replacing it with the right-hand side. For example, the term $(x \times y).|t\rangle + |t\rangle$ is matched by the rule $a.K + K \, \triangleright \, (a + 1).K$, and is rewritten into $(x \times y + 1).|t\rangle$. Step 1 and 3 use the same set of rewriting rules in Appendix D. Step 2 expands variables to their abstract element-wise representation, e.g., $K \, \triangleright \, \sum_i (\langle i| \cdot K).|i\rangle$, which is useful when reasoning about sums.

Steps 4 through 6 are specialized algorithms designed to further normalize the axiom set E. The main challenge here is the coexistence of AC-equivalence and SUM-SWAP, which means that naive sorting cannot alwasy convert equivalent terms into the same form. For step 4 and 5, the key observation is that in a successive sum expression $\sum_{i\in s_1}\cdots\sum_{j\in s_n} A$, the names and order of the bound variables $i,\ldots,j$ can be freely permuted. Therefore we first ignore bound variables and normalize AC-equivalence by sorting. Afterward, the order of summation can be established accordingly. The final step uses de Bruijn indices [16] to resolve α-equivalence. For further details, refer to Appendix E.

Figure 1 shows the normalization outline for $(M \otimes \mathbf{1}_{\mathcal{O}}(T)) \cdot (\mathrm{phi}\ T)$.

In contrast, previous work performs normalization only partially on R, and proves equivalence by checking all possible permutations according to E. Our algorithm fully normalize the term, as illustrated below, and is more efficient as a result.

$$\text{(partial)}\qquad e_1 \overset{R}{\twoheadrightarrow} e_1' \overset{E}{=} e_2' \overset{R}{\twoheadleftarrow} e_2 \qquad\qquad \text{(full)}\qquad e_1 \overset{R\cup E}{\twoheadrightarrow} e \equiv e \overset{R\cup E}{\twoheadleftarrow} e_2$$

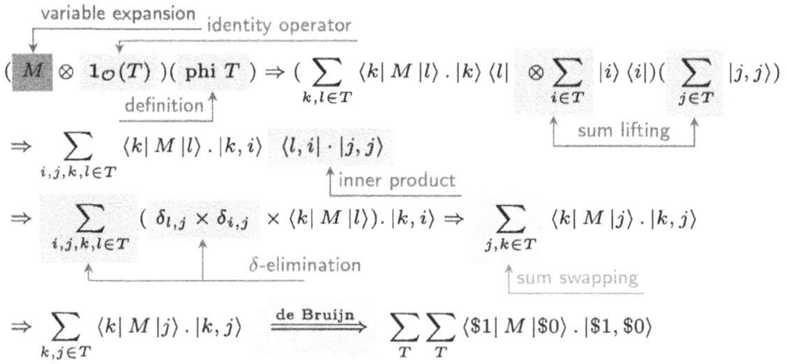

Fig. 1. A normalization outline for the left-hand side of Eq. (1). Matched subterms are marked with colors. Blue marking represents variable expansion, red marking represents rule applications, and brown marking represents normalization step 4–6.

4   Labelled Dirac Notation

In this section, we extend the language by allowing quantum variables to indicate the quantum system on which vectors and operators act. As discussed, this enables us to express and reason about the states and operations locally, without referring to the entire system. We further demonstrate how to transform the equivalence problem into one involving the plain Dirac notation studied earlier.

4.1   Syntax, Typing and Semantics

We begin by introducing the notation of quantum registers for structured variable combinations. This is necessary because, unlike assignments for classical variables, unitary transformations on composite systems–a quantum version of assignments–cannot generally be decomposed into separate unitary transformations on individual subsystems. Let $\mathcal{R}$ be the set of quantum variables.

Definition 6 (Quantum Register). *Register R is inductively generated by*

$$R ::= r \in \mathcal{R} \mid (R, R).$$

For simplicity, we restrict register formation to pairings, which corresponds to the structure of tensor product. In this context, $\mathcal{H}_{(R_1, R_2)}$ is isomorphic to $\mathcal{H}_{R_1} \otimes \mathcal{H}_{R_2}$, which allows us to view the tensor product space as the space of paired registers.

The no-cloning theorem, a fundamental property of quantum computing, prevents us from copying an unknown quantum state. This requires an additional check on the valid registers–they should not include repeated quantum variables–which is often handled in programming languages via linear types. As such, we define the *order-free* variable set of a register as all quantum variables appearing in the register; we let $\mathsf{var}(R)$ denote the variable set of register R. We use the variable set to establish side conditions of typing valid registers and employ it as the type parameter for annotating labelled Dirac terms.

Now, we are ready to extend the type syntax and term syntax as follows:

Definition 7 (Labelled Dirac Notation). *The **labelled Dirac notation** includes all plain Dirac notation symbols and the generators defined below. Here, $s \subseteq \mathcal{R}$ is a quantum variable set.*

$$T ::= \mathcal{D}(s, s) \mid \mathsf{Reg}(\sigma)$$
$$e ::= R \mid |i\rangle_r \mid {}_r\langle i| \mid e_R \mid e_{R;R} \mid e \otimes e \otimes \cdots \otimes e \mid e \cdot e.$$

$\mathcal{D}(s_1, s_2)$ is the unified type for all labelled Dirac notation, where s_1 indicates the codomain systems and s_2 indicates the domain systems. Roughly speaking, we define Hilbert space $\mathcal{H}_s \triangleq \bigotimes_{r \in s} \mathcal{H}_r$ for each set s, so that $\mathcal{H}_\emptyset$ is a one-dimensional space isomorphic to complex numbers. Then the function view of ket and bra [37] provides an alternative way, i.e., a ket on subsystem s as a linear map from $\mathcal{H}_\emptyset$ to $\mathcal{H}_s$, a bra as a linear map from $\mathcal{H}_s$ to $\mathcal{H}_\emptyset$, to unify the type of kets, bras, and operators. For instance, labelled ket $|i\rangle_r$ has type $\mathcal{D}(\{r\}, \emptyset)$, and labelled bra ${}_r\langle i|$ has type $\mathcal{D}(\emptyset, \{r\})$. $\mathsf{Reg}(\sigma)$ are types for registers R, and the index σ indicates the type of Hilbert space represented by the register. It is allowed to lift a plain Dirac notation associate with corresponding quantum variables or registers, e.g., $|i\rangle_r$ and ${}_r\langle i|$ are labelled basis, e_R for bra, ket, and $e_{R;R'}$ for operators which additionally allows different domain R' and codomain R. We further introduce new $\cdot$ for generalized composition (unified for all kinds of multiplications between kets, bras and operators) and $\otimes$ for labelled tensor product since they do not share the same properties v.s. its counterpart in plain

Dirac notation, i.e., generalized composition is not associative and labelled tensor is indeed an AC symbol.

Typing Rules. There are various rules for computing types and checking vadility of registers and labelled terms. Here we display some of the rules and refer the reader to Appendix A for the full set of rules.

$$\frac{\Gamma \vdash R : \mathsf{Reg}(\sigma) \quad \Gamma \vdash Q : \mathsf{Reg}(\tau) \quad \mathsf{var}(R) \cap \mathsf{var}(Q) = \emptyset}{\Gamma \vdash (R, Q) : \mathsf{Reg}(\sigma \times \tau)}$$

$$\frac{\Gamma \vdash r : \mathsf{Reg}(\sigma) \quad \Gamma \vdash i : \mathsf{Basis}(\sigma)}{\Gamma \vdash |i\rangle_r : \mathcal{D}(\{r\}, \emptyset)} \qquad \frac{\Gamma \vdash R : \mathsf{Reg}(\sigma) \quad \Gamma \vdash K : \mathcal{K}(\sigma)}{\Gamma \vdash K_R : \mathcal{D}(\mathsf{var}(R), \emptyset)}$$

$$\frac{\Gamma \vdash D_i : \mathcal{D}(s_i, s_i') \quad \forall i \neq j.\ s_i \cap s_j = \emptyset \quad \forall i \neq j.\ s_i' \cap s_j' = \emptyset}{\Gamma \vdash D_1 \otimes \cdots \otimes D_i : \mathcal{D}(\bigcup_i s_i, \bigcup_i s_i')}.$$

The first rule states that a paired register is of the product type and its components must be disjoint. To lift a plain Dirac notation into the labelled version (line 2), we enforce that the term and register share the same indices, reflecting the fact the state should be consistant to the corresponding subsystems. The third line provides the typing of labelled tensor product, with a check to ensure that the component subsystems are disjoint from each other.

Semantics. The labelled Dirac notation handles lifting and ordering for us, and its semantics accurately capture these details. The key points are: 1. cylindrical extension, which lift a ket or bra or operator to larger domain and codomain; 2. general composition, which further employs cylindrical extension that obeys the principle of "localizing objects as much as possible" [37]. Since $\mathcal{R}$ is given, we let $\sigma_r : \mathsf{Index}$ denote type of r, i.e., $\Gamma \vdash r : \mathsf{Reg}(\sigma_r)$, for simplicity.

Definition 8 (Cylindrical Extension). *For any $D : \mathcal{D}(s_1, s_2)$ and s that disjoint with both s_1 and s_2, we define $cl(D, s) \triangleq D \otimes \mathbf{1}_s$ of type $\mathcal{D}(s_1 \cup s, s_2 \cup s)$.*

Formally, we equip $\mathcal{R}$ with a default order, such as the alphabetical order of names. For any valid register R, there exists the operator SWAP_R that sorts R; for example, $\mathsf{SWAP}_{(q,p)} \triangleq \sum_{i \in \mathbf{U}(\sigma_p)} \sum_{j \in \mathbf{U}(\sigma_q)} |i\rangle\langle j| \otimes |j\rangle\langle i|$. We can further define $\mathsf{SWAP}_{s_1, s_2, \cdots}$ for merging disjoint sets orderly. See Appendix B for details.

For given context Γ and any valuation v, we interpret

$$[\![\mathcal{D}(s, s')]\!]_v \triangleq \mathcal{L}(\bigotimes_j \mathcal{H}_{[\![\sigma_{r_j'}]\!]_v}, \bigotimes_i \mathcal{H}_{[\![\sigma_{r_i}]\!]_v})$$

where $\mathcal{L}$ denotes the set of linear maps, $s = \{r_1, \cdots, r_n\}$ and $s' = \{r_1', \cdots, r_m'\}$ (r_i and r_j' are sorted). We interpret labelled Dirac notations inductively as (assume $\Gamma \vdash D_i : \mathcal{D}(s_i, s_i')$) :

- $[\![|i\rangle_r]\!]_v = |[\![i]\!]_v\rangle; \quad [\![\langle i|_r]\!]_v = \langle[\![i]\!]_v|; \quad [\![K_R]\!]_v = [\![\mathsf{SWAP}_R]\!]_v \cdot [\![K]\!]_v;$
  $[\![B_R]\!]_v = [\![B]\!]_v \cdot [\![\mathsf{SWAP}_R]\!]_v^\dagger; \quad [\![O_{R_1,R_2}]\!]_v = [\![\mathsf{SWAP}_{R_1}]\!]_v \cdot [\![O]\!]_v \cdot [\![\mathsf{SWAP}_{R_2}]\!]_v^\dagger;$
- $[\![D_1 \otimes \cdots \otimes D_n]\!]_v = [\![\mathsf{SWAP}_{s_1, \cdots, s_n}]\!]_v \cdot ([\![D_1]\!]_v \otimes \cdots \otimes [\![D_1]\!]_v) \cdot [\![\mathsf{SWAP}_{s_1', \cdots, s_n'}]\!]_v^\dagger;$

– $\llbracket D_1 \cdot D_2 \rrbracket_v = \llbracket cl(D_1, s_2 \backslash s_1') \rrbracket_v \cdot \llbracket cl(D_2, s_1' \backslash s_2) \rrbracket_v$. Note that $s_2 \backslash s_1'$ and $s_1' \backslash s_2$ are the minimal extension that make it interpretable. E.g., to interpret $_p\langle i| \cdot |j\rangle_{p,q}$, we at least need to extend $_p\langle i|$ to $_p\langle i| \otimes I_q$.

It can be shown that Lemma 1 also holds for labelled terms, i.e., $\llbracket D \rrbracket_v \in \llbracket \mathcal{D}(s, s') \rrbracket_v$ given $\Gamma \vdash D : \mathcal{D}(s, s')$. Following the semantics, labelled tensor is independent of its order, i.e., $\llbracket D_1 \otimes D_2 \rrbracket_v = \llbracket D_2 \otimes D_1 \rrbracket_v$ and $\llbracket D_1 \otimes (D_2 \otimes D_3) \rrbracket_v = \llbracket (D_1 \otimes D_2) \otimes D_3 \rrbracket_v$, which ensures the soundness of treating labelled tensor as an AC symbol.

4.2 Elimination of Labels

It is possible to eliminate labels from labelled Dirac expressions and thus to transform any equation in Labelled Dirac notation into an equation in plain Dirac notation. This is achieved by the following three steps:

1. Elimination of e_R or $e_{R;R}$. We decompose all e_R or $e_{R;R}$ to the labelled basis with scalar coefficients. Take operator as an example:

$$O_{R,R'} \vartriangleright \sum_{i_{r_1} \in \mathbf{U}(\sigma_{r_1})} \cdots \sum_{i_{r_n} \in \mathbf{U}(\sigma_{r_n})} \sum_{i_{r_1'} \in \mathbf{U}(\sigma_{r_1'})} \cdots \sum_{i_{r_{n'}'} \in \mathbf{U}(\sigma_{r_{n'}'})}$$

$$(\langle i_R| \cdot O \cdot |i_{R'}\rangle).(|i_{r_1}\rangle_{r_1} \otimes \cdots \otimes |i_{r_n}\rangle_{r_n} \otimes {}_{r_1'}\langle i_{r_1'}| \otimes \cdots \otimes {}_{r_{n'}'}\langle i_{r_{n'}'}|).$$

where $|i_R\rangle$ and $\langle i_{R'}|$ are constructed by tensoring the basis according to the structure of R (see Appendix B). The rules for e_R (ket and bra) are similar.

2. Rewriting to normal form. We add three types of rules for dealing with operators on labelled terms, 1) recursively applying them to subterms, 2) pushing big operators out and 3) eliminating generalized composition and bra-ket pairs. Take the rule for conjugate $(D_1 \cdot D_2)^\dagger \vartriangleright D_2^\dagger \cdot D_1^\dagger$ as an example of 1). For 2), we use distributivity rules for scaling, labelled tensor and generalized composition. For example, rule

$$X_1 \otimes \cdots (\sum_{i \in M} D) \cdots \otimes X_2 \vartriangleright \sum_{i \in M} (X_1 \otimes \cdots D \cdots \otimes X_n)$$

will lift summation to the outside. Extra rules for 3) are established including:

(R-L-SORT0) $A : \mathcal{D}(s_1, s_2), B : \mathcal{D}(s_1', s_2'), s_2 \cap s_1' = \emptyset \Rightarrow A \cdot B \vartriangleright A \otimes B$

(R-L-SORT1) $_r\langle i| \cdot |j\rangle_r \vartriangleright \delta_{i,j}$

(R-L-SORT2) $_r\langle i| \cdot (Y_1 \otimes \cdots \otimes |j\rangle_r \otimes \cdots \otimes Y_m) \vartriangleright \delta_{i,j}.(Y_1 \otimes \cdots \otimes Y_m)$

Assuming no variables of $\mathcal{D}(s_1, s_2)$, repeating the application of the above rules yield the normal form of both sides of the equality–the addition of big operators:

$$\sum_i \cdots \sum_j a_1.(|i\rangle_p \otimes \cdots \otimes \langle j|_q) + \cdots + \sum_k \cdots \sum_l a_m.(|k\rangle_r \otimes \cdots \otimes \langle l|_s) \quad (2)$$

where each sum body is a tensor of labelled basis with scalar coefficients in plain Dirac notation.

3. Ordering and elimination of quantum variables. We further sort tensors of labelled basis in every sum body of Eqn. (2) by 1. ket first and 2. the default order of variables. This yield the same shape of every subterm on both sides of the equality, e.g.,

$$\sum_i \cdots \sum_j \cdots \sum_{i'} \cdots \sum_{j'} a_1.((|i\rangle_p \otimes \cdots \otimes |j\rangle_q) \otimes (\langle i'|_{p'} \otimes \cdots \otimes \langle j'|_{q'})) \quad (3)$$

and thus it is equivalent to prove the equivalence of additions of subterms of:

$$\sum_i \cdots \sum_j \cdots \sum_{i'} \cdots \sum_{j'} a_1.((|i\rangle \otimes \cdots \otimes |j\rangle) \cdot (\langle i'| \otimes \cdots \otimes \langle j'|)) \quad (4)$$

which do not involve any labels.

The procedure to eliminate labels is sound and complete, in the sense that expressions in Labelled Dirac notation are equivalent iff their translations to plain Dirac notation are equivalent.

Theorem 2 (Label Elimination). *Assume* $\Gamma \vdash D_1 : \mathcal{D}(s, s')$, $\Gamma \vdash D_2 : \mathcal{D}(s, s')$ *and no variables of* $\mathcal{D}(\cdot, \cdot)$ *appear in* D_1, D_2. *Let* $e_1 = e_2$ *be obtained by above normalization procedure on* $D_1 = D_2$. *Then* $e_1 = e_2$ *is an equation in plain Dirac notation and* $\Gamma \vDash D_1 = D_2$ *if and only if* $\Gamma \vDash e_1 = e_2$.

The idea of the proof is as follows: first, we define a set of proof rules to rewrite every labelled Dirac notation into the form of Eqn. (1). We prove that each rule is sound w.r.t. semantics, and that every labelled Dirac expression can be rewritten to an expression of the form of Eqn. (1); the proof is by induction on the structure of the expression. Next, we show that reordering of labelled basis preserves the type and semantics and thus yield expressions of the form of Eqn. (4), as desired. Details appear in Appendix D.1.

5   Implementation and Case Study

We present **D-Hammer**, an open-source and publicly available[1] implementation of our approach. **D-Hammer** is an equational prover for Labelled Dirac notation written in C++. It features a parser built using ANTLR4, and scalar reasoning is powered by the Mathematica Engine. Users can use commands to make definitions and assumptions in the maintained context, conduct the normalization and equivalence checking, and obtain the rewriting trace output. D-Hammer can be run interactively from the command line or integrated into other C++ projects as a library.

---

[1] https://github.com/LucianoXu/D-Hammer.

Structure and Mechanism. The project consists of the following components:

- `antlr4`: A third-party library for building the parser.
- `WSTP interface`: A wrapper to link with Mathematica Engine.
- `ualg`: The framework module for universal algebra, defining basic concepts like terms and substitutions.
- `dhammer`: The main module containing symbols definitions, type checking, rewriting rules, normalization algorithm and the prover.
- `example`: An example benchmark for evaluation.
- `toplevel`: The command line application.

The internal data structure for terms follows a pointer-based syntax tree, using the function application style:

$$\text{term} ::= \text{ID} \mid \text{ID} [\text{term} (, \text{term})*].$$

The syntax tree can either be an identifier, or an application with an identifier as the function head, and several syntax trees as arguments. Below are several examples of Dirac notation terms and their corresponding syntax trees.

$X_1 + X_2 + X_3$ `ADD[X1, X2, X3]`

$\lambda x : \mathcal{O}(T_1, T_2).x^\dagger$ `FUN[x, OTYPE[T1, T2], ADJ[x]]`

$\sum_{i \in \mathbf{U}(T)} |i\rangle \langle i|$ `SUM[USET[T], FUN[i, BASIS[T], OUTER[KET[i], BRA[i]]]]`

To improve usability, D-Hammer also supports many special notations for terms, and most Dirac notation terms is encoded in the natural, intuitive way. Here are some examples for the parsing syntax.

syntax	parsing result	explanation
|e>	KET[e]	the ket basis
e1 + ... + en	ADD[e1, ..., en]	the addition
e1 e2	COMPO[e1, e2]	composition in Dirac notation
e1^*	CONJ[e1]	scalar conjugation
fun i : T => X	FUN[i, T, X]	lambda abstraction

Finally, D-Hammer uses a prover to host the computation. The prover maintains a well-formed context Γ, and processes commands to modify the context and conduct calculations. The commands are listed below.

- `Def ID :=` term. It defines the `ID` as the `term`, using the **W-Def** typing rule.
- `Var ID :=` term. It make an assumption of `ID` with the `term` as type, using the **W-Assume** typing rules.
- `Check` term. Type checking the `term` and output the result.
- `Normalize` term. Normalize the `term` using the algorithm in Appendix E.
- `CheckEq` term `with` term. Check the equivalence of the two terms calculating and comparing their normal forms.

The prover will type check the terms for each command. We can also use `Normalize` term `with trace.` to output the proof trace during normalization. The proof trace is a sequence of records, including the rule or transformation appied, the position of application, and the pre- and post-transformation terms. The record helps understand the normalization procedure better, and can be turned into verified proofs in theorem provers in the future.

Use Case. As a tutorial, we encode the motivating Example 2, examine and explain how to check it using D-Hammer. The encoding is shown below.

```
Var T : INDEX. Var M : OTYPE[T, T].
Def phi := idx T => Sum nv in USET[T], |(nv, nv)>.
Var r1 : REG[T]. Var r2 : REG[T].
CheckEq M_r1 (phi T)_(r1, r2) with (TPO T T M)_r2 (phi T)_(r1, r2).
```

The first three lines use the `Var` and `Def` commands to set up the context for the Dirac notation. `T` is a type index, representing arbitrary Hilbert space types. `M` is assumed to be an operator in the Hilbert space with type `T`. `phi` is defined as the maximally entangled state, depending on the bound variable `T` as index. `r1` and `r2` are register names for the two subsystems.

In the left-hand side of `CheckEq` command, `M_r1` denotes the labelled notation M_{r_1}, and `(phi T)_(r1, r2)` denotes the entangled state $|\Phi\rangle_{(r_1,r_2)}$. They are connected by a white space, which is parsed into the composition of Dirac notation, and will be reduced into the operator-ket multiplication after typing. The right hand side is interpreted similarly, except the defined symbol `TPO` in the context:

```
Def TPO := idx sigma => idx tau => fun O : OTYPE[sigma, tau] => Sum i in
    USET[sigma], Sum j in USET[tau], (<i| O |j>).(|j> <i|).
```

The `TPO` symbol represents the transpose of operators, and encodes the formalization in Example 3. Other commonly used concepts in Dirac notation are encoded and provided as defined symbols in D-Hammer.

Within one second, the prover reports the result of equivalence with their common normal form:

```
The two terms are equal.
[Normalized Term] SUM[USET[T], FUN[BASIS[T], SUM[USET[T], FUN[BASIS[T],
    SCR[DOT[BRA[$1], MULK[M, KET[$0]]], LTSR[LKET[$1, r1], LKET[$0, r2
    ]]]]]]] : DTYPE[RSET[r1, r2], RSET]
```

The normal form is in the internal syntax tree format mentioned above. A more readable interpretation is:

$$\sum_{\mathbf{U}(T)} \sum_{\mathbf{U}(T)} \langle \$1 | \, M \, | \$0 \rangle \cdot | \$1 \rangle_{r_1} \otimes | \$0 \rangle_{r_2} : \mathcal{D}(\{r_1, r_2\}, \emptyset).$$

Here $\$0$ and $\$1$ are de Bruijn indices. The result is a ket on the $\{r_1, r_2\}$ system as expected, and follows pattern proposed in Sect. 4.

6 Evaluation

We evaluate D-Hammer on several example sets, and make a comparison with the previous tool DiracDec [33]. The experiments are carried out using a MacBook Pro with M3 Max chip. Results are summarized as follows, which indicates significant performance improvements.

source	DiracDec			D-Hammer		
	expressable	success	time(s)	expressable	success	time(s)
textbook(QCQI)	18	18	1.02	18	18	0.82
CoqQ	162	156	48.69	158	158	9.74

Textbook (QCQI). As a warm-up, we consider 18 examples from Nielsen and Chuang's classic texbook [26]. All examples can be encoded in DiracDec and D-Hammer and are solved very efficiently.

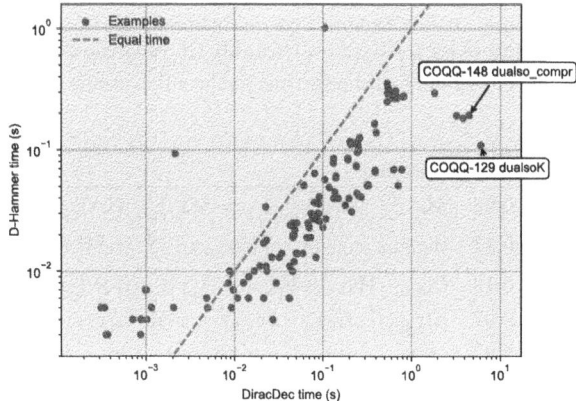

Fig. 2. Time comparison between DiracDec and D-Hammer on the CoqQ benchmark.

CoqQ. As a more substantial example, we consider the examples from CoqQ [37], an extensive formalization of quantum information theory and quantum programming languages in the Coq proof assistant.

CoqQ has been used as the main benchmark for evaluating DiracDec. Specifically, [33] isolates 162 statements in CoqQ that are in scope of the DiracDec language.

We have ported 158 out of 162 examples to D-Hammer. The remaining 4 examples uses projectors `fst` and `snd` on basis pairs, where $fst(s,t) = s$ and $snd(s,t) = t$. However, we found that this feature is rarely used and removed the support in D-Hammer. Note that the omission of the projection rules has a limited influence on the performance evaluation, because the efficiency of the 158 examples is not affected by projection rules.

D-Hammer verifies the whole 158 examples in less than 10 s, whereas DiracDec verifies 156/162 examples in more than 45 s. Figure 2 shows a direct comparison of the efficiency of the two tools. We observe that D-Hammer is slower than DiracDec on small examples, due to marginal overhead, but becomes faster by an average factor of 2 to 40 times as the running time of examples increases. This non-linear growth suggests that efficiency gains result from algorithmic improvements rather than the shift to a C++ implementation. Furthermore, examples with great improvements, e.g. COQQ-129 and COQQ-148 shown in Fig. 2, tend to use deeply nested sums, for which our algorithm is more efficient.

Labelled Dirac Notation. We present a new set of examples for labelled Dirac notation (LDN), as illustrated in Fig. 3. These examples include six representative cases drawn from various sources, such as well-established theorems, research paper results and quantum circuit equivalence. D-Hammer successfully normalizes these examples and checks their equivalence using the algorithm outlined in Sect. 4. Among the examples, LDN-16 is a generalization of Example 1 and LDN-4 for Example 2. LDN-12 shows the flexibility in combining labelled Dirac notations. LDN-14 shows how to calculate controlled-not gate in different ways.

A particularly noteworthy result is D-Hammer's solution to LDN-10, a highly complex and lengthy example. It is a theorem on quantum separation logic from [36], and proving it is challenging even for experts. Notably, it involves 7 registers, making it practically impossible to organize and referring to the subsystems without using labels.

example	source	time(s)	equation
LDN-4	theorem	0.03	$M_{r_1} \sum_i |(i,i)\rangle_{(r_1,r_2)} = M_{r_2}^T \sum_i |(i,i)\rangle_{(r_1,r_2)}$
LDN-10	paper [37]	5.17	$\mathrm{tr}_{((a',(b,b')),c')}\left[\mathrm{tr}_r\left(U_{(r,(a,b))} \cdot \left(|s\rangle_r\langle s| \otimes \left[V_{((a',(b,b')),c')} \cdots\right.\right.\right.$
LDN-11	paper [27]	0.12	$U_{(a,b)} \cdot W_{(b,c)} \cdot V_{(a,c)} = \sum_i |i\rangle_a\langle i| \otimes ((P_i)_c \cdot W_{(b,c)} \cdot (Q_i)_c)$
LDN-12	circuit	0.07	$|i\rangle_{a;b}\langle j| \cdot C_{(b,c)} \cdot D_{(c,d)} = {}_b\langle j| \cdot C_{(b,c)} \cdot D_{(c,d)} \cdot |i\rangle_a$
LDN-14	circuit	7.37	$\mathsf{CNOT}_{r_q} |\mathrm{GHZ}\rangle_{pqr} = (\mathsf{CNOT}\, |00\rangle)_{rq} |0\rangle_p + (\mathsf{CNOT}\, |11\rangle)_{rq} |1\rangle_p$
LDN-16	theorem	0.08	$M_{prq} |\mathrm{GHZ}\rangle_{prq} = N_{rq} |\mathrm{GHZ}\rangle_{pqr}, M \triangleq \sum_{ij} |ij\rangle\langle ij| \otimes U_{ij} \cdots$

Fig. 3. Part of examples for labelled Dirac notations. See Appendix F for the full list.

Quantum Circuits. Quantum circuits is a prominent model of quantum computation. This model is adopted by numerous tools, which can evaluate, optimize, or prove equivalence of quantum circuits. These tools are based on a variety of approaches, based on ZX-calculus [27], or decision diagrams [7], or other formalisms discussed in Sect. 7. In general, these tools are aggressively optimized to achieve scalability.

example	D-Hammer	ZX-Calculus [28]	Decision Diagrams (simulation) [7]
QC-1	0.029	0.0	0.0
QC-2	0.16	0.00039	0.0038
QC-3	0.29	5.7e-5	0.0057
QC-4	0.013	4.3e-5	0.0017
QC-5	15	6.4e-5	0.0044
QC-6	timeout	0.00014	0.016

Fig. 4. Time consumptions (in seconds) for quantum circuit equivalence checking using different tools.

Quantum circuits can also be described as unitary operators in Dirac notation. Therefore, D-Hammer can check the equivalence of quantum circuits through their Dirac notation representations. Although it is not the intended application of D-Hammer, we include an evaluation of D-Hammer on some simple examples. An evaluation of some examples is given in Fig. 4, and Fig. 5 shows one of them. As expected, D-Hammer does not perform well in comparison with specialized tools: it is always outperformed, often by several order of magnitude, on small quantum circuit examples, and it always times out on larger quantum circuit examples. In the future it would be of interest to make D-Hammer more competitive on quantum circuits by adopting some of the aggressive optimizations for other works.

(circuit)

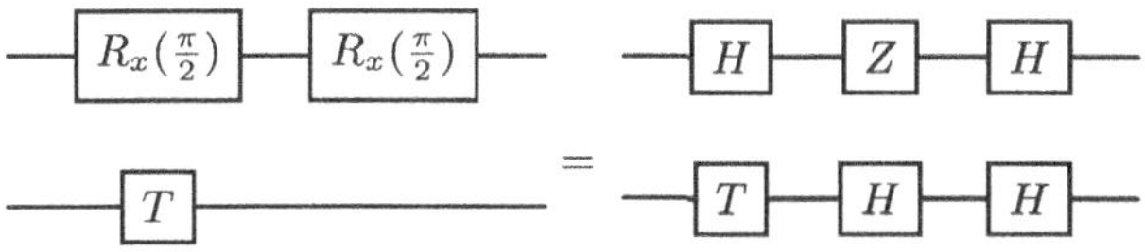

(notation)
$$(\mathsf{Rx}(\pi/2) \otimes \mathbf{1}_\mathcal{O}) \cdot (\mathbf{1}_\mathcal{O} \otimes \mathsf{T}) \cdot (\mathsf{Rx}(\pi/2) \otimes \mathbf{1}_\mathcal{O})$$
$$=(\mathbf{1}_\mathcal{O} \otimes \mathsf{H}) \cdot (\mathbf{1}_\mathcal{O} \otimes \mathsf{H}) \cdot (\mathsf{H} \otimes \mathbf{1}_\mathcal{O}) \cdot (\mathsf{Z} \otimes \mathbf{1}_\mathcal{O}) \cdot (\mathsf{H} \otimes \mathbf{1}_\mathcal{O}) \cdot (\mathbf{1}_\mathcal{O} \otimes \mathsf{T})$$

Fig. 5. The quantum circuit and Dirac notation encoding for example QC-5.

7 Related Work

Comparison with DiracDec. Xu *et al.* [33] define a language and an associate and commutative rewriting system for Dirac notation, and implement their language and rewriting system in Mathematica. Our approach follows a similar pattern. However, there are significant differences in terms of scope, expressiveness, and efficiency.

The most obvious difference is that D-Hammer targets labelled Dirac notation, whereas DiracDec targets plain Dirac notation. As already mentioned, the use of labelled Dirac notation is essential in many applications; in particular, labelled Dirac notation can simplify notation and proofs, and is in general better suited for writing and reasoning about complex, many-body, quantum states. However, there are several other important differences. First, our language leverages higher-order functions to provide a compact and expressive representation of big operators. Second, our language adopts AC symbols with indefinite arities, which leads to compact representation of terms, and eases AC reasoning. Third, the relation with Mathematica is fundamentally different. DiracDec is implemented in Mathematica; as a consequence, its behavior, and in particular, its typing rules are constrained by the lack of typing in Mathematica. In contrast, D-Hammer is designed as a separate tool; as a consequence, it benefits from an improved representation of terms (e.g. AC operators with indefinite arity), a more expressive type system (e.g. dependent types), and a more efficient rewriting engine. D-Hammer still relies on Mathematica to reason about functions that are not natively supported by rewriting rules, but these interactions are constrained and do not have negative effects on the overall efficiency of the system. This is reflected in our experimental comparison of D-Hammer and DiracDec, which shows how the former outperforms the latter.

Comparison with ZX Calculus. The ZX calculus [14,15] is a graphical calculus for quantum states. A main appeal of the ZX calculus is that its foundations are grounded in categorical quantum mechanics [2], a powerful framework for modeling quantum physics. Another main appeal of the ZX calculus is that it has a natural operational interpretation based on graph rewriting. There is a large body of work that defines rewriting systems for fragments/extensions/variants of the ZX calculus, and studies their theoretical properties, in particular completeness (a set of rules is complete if it can prove all valid identities) and minimality (a complete set of rules is minimal if removing a rule leads to incompleteness). Two main proof techniques for completeness are via termination, or via interpretation. In the first case, one shows that a rewriting system has unique normal forms and that two expressions are semantically equivalent iff they have the same normal form—there exists many relaxations of this result—whereas in the second case one shows completeness by exhibiting a well-behaved translation to another system for which completeness holds. Both proof techniques have been used to prove completeness for multiple settings, including the Clifford fragment [5], the Toffoli+Hadamard fragment [18], the Clifford+T fragment [20] and the (qubit) universal fragment [19,21]. Subsequent works generalize completeness to qudits [29], quantum circuits [13] or optical quantum circuits [12]. We refer the interested reader to [31] for a historical and technical account of completeness results up to 2020.

There are many similarities between the ZX calculus and our formalism for Labelled Dirac notation. However, there are also some differences between our formalism and the ones used in ZX calculus. In particular, our language supports big operators, tensors, and various operations on Hilbert spaces. These features are typically not considered in prior work on the ZX calculus, and as a consequence many examples handled by D-Hammer lack an immediate translation into ZX-calculus. This additional generality comes with a price. On the one hand, our theoretical results are weaker: we do not claim completeness or minimality. Similarly, practical implementations of the ZX-calculus [22, 27] outperform D-Hammer on examples that can be handled by both tools, as shown in Sect. 6.

Comparison with Other Tools. Beyond ZX calculus, there exists many other tools for simplifying and proving equivalence of quantum circuits; we refer the reader to recent surveys [8,24] for detailed accounts. Notable works include [4], which uses the path-sums formalism to check circuits with 1,000 of T gates, and [1,9,10], which uses automata-based approaches to verify quantum circuits at scale—their tool AUTOQ is able to verify circuits with over 100,00 gates, and was recently extended to support parametrized verification.

Canonical Forms in Multi-body Quantum Physics. Canonical forms play a fundamental role in quantum physics. For instance, [3,11,28] discuss canonical forms of Matrix Product States (MPS) and Tensor Networks respectively. An exciting direction for further work is to further develop automated deduction techniques for quantum physics.

Comparison with Egraphs. Our algorithm is based on term rewriting. However, it is a challenge to device well-behaved and efficient term rewriting for (labelled) Dirac notation. An alternative to term rewriting would be to use equality saturation [32], a powerful equational reasoning technique that does not require existence of normal forms. Equality saturation may be particularly useful when considering further extensions of labelled Dirac notation.

8   Conclusion and Future Work

We have designed and implemented D-Hammer, a dependently typed higher-order language and proof system for labelled Dirac notation. D-Hammer benefits from an optimized implementation in C++ and a tight integration with Mathematica to reason about a broad range of mathematical functions, including trigonometric and exponential functions, that are commonly used in quantum physics. There are two important directions for future work. The first direction is to extend D-Hammer with a mechanism to generate independently verifiable certificates. There is a large body of work on producing certificates for automated tools, in particular SMT solvers; see e.g. [6] for a recent overview. One potential option would be to integrate D-Hammer with the Coq or Lean proof assistants; in the first case, one would benefit from the formalization of labelled Dirac notation in CoqQ [37], whereas in the second case, one would benefit from powerful mechanisms to integrate rewriting procedures into the Lean proof assistant. The second direction is to connect D-Hammer with quantum program verifiers. Two potential applications are automating equational proofs for tools that already use Dirac notation, and to substitute numerical methods for tools that use matrices instead of symbolic assertions.

Acknowledgements. We thank the anonymous reviewers for their constructive feedback that helped improve this paper. We also extend our gratitude to Jam Kabeer Ali Khan and Ivan Ariel Renison for their work of testing of D-Hammer.

Disclosure of Interests. This research was supported by the National Key R&D Program of China under Grant No. 2023YFA1009403.

References

1. Abdulla, P.A., et al.: Verifying quantum circuits with level-synchronized tree automata. Proc. ACM Program. Lang. **9**(POPL) (2025). https://doi.org/10.1145/3704868
2. Abramsky, S., Coecke, B.: A categorical semantics of quantum protocols. In: 19th IEEE Symposium on Logic in Computer Science (LICS 2004), 14–17 July 2004, Turku, Finland, Proceedings, pp. 415–425. IEEE Computer Society (2004). https://doi.org/10.1109/LICS.2004.1319636
3. Acuaviva, A., et al.: The minimal canonical form of a tensor network. In: 2023 IEEE 64th Annual Symposium on Foundations of Computer Science (FOCS), pp. 328–362. IEEE, November 2023. https://doi.org/10.1109/focs57990.2023.00027, http://dx.doi.org/10.1109/FOCS57990.2023.00027
4. Amy, M.: Towards large-scale functional verification of universal quantum circuits. Electron. Proc. Theor. Comput. Sci. **287**, 1–21 (2019)
5. Backens, M.: The zx-calculus is complete for stabilizer quantum mechanics. New J. Phys. **16**(9), 093021 (2014)
6. Barbosa, H., Barrett, C.W., Cook, B., Dutertre, B., Kremer, G., Lachnitt, H., Niemetz, A., Nötzli, A., Ozdemir, A., Preiner, M., Reynolds, A., Tinelli, C., Zohar, Y.: Generating and exploiting automated reasoning proof certificates. Commun. ACM **66**(10), 86–95 (2023). https://doi.org/10.1145/3587692
7. Burgholzer, L., Kueng, R., Wille, R.: Random stimuli generation for the verification of quantum circuits. In: Proceedings of the 26th Asia and South Pacific Design Automation Conference, ASPDAC 2021, pp. 767–772. ACM, New York, NY, USA (2021). https://doi.org/10.1145/3394885.3431590

8. Chareton, C., Lee, D., Valiron, B., Vilmart, R., Bardin, S., Xu, Z.: Formal methods for quantum algorithms. In: Akleylek, S., Dundua, B. (eds.) Handbook of Formal Analysis and Verification in Cryptography, pp. 319–422. CRC Press (2023). https://doi.org/10.1201/9781003090052-7

9. Chen, Y.F., Chung, K.M., Lengál, O., Lin, J.A., Tsai, W.L.: Autoq: an automata-based quantum circuit verifier. In: Enea, C., Lal, A. (eds.) Computer Aided Verification, pp. 139–153. Springer, Cham (2023)

10. Chen, Y.F., Chung, K.M., Lengál, O., Lin, J.A., Tsai, W.L., Yen, D.D.: An automata-based framework for verification and bug hunting in quantum circuits. Proc. ACM Program. Lang. **7**(PLDI) (2023). https://doi.org/10.1145/3591270

11. Cirac, J.I., Pérez-García, D., Schuch, N., Verstraete, F.: Matrix product states and projected entangled pair states: Concepts, symmetries, theorems. Rev. Mod. Phys. **93**, 045003 (2021)

12. Clément, A., Heurtel, N., Mansfield, S., Perdrix, S., Valiron, B.: LO_v-calculus: a graphical language for linear optical quantum circuits. In: Szeider, S., Ganian, R., Silva, A. (eds.) 47th International Symposium on Mathematical Foundations of Computer Science (MFCS 2022). Leibniz International Proceedings in Informatics (LIPIcs), vol. 241, pp. 35:1–35:16. Schloss Dagstuhl – Leibniz-Zentrum für Informatik, Dagstuhl, Germany (2022). https://doi.org/10.4230/LIPIcs.MFCS.2022.35, https://drops.dagstuhl.de/entities/document/10.4230/LIPIcs.MFCS.2022.35

13. Clément, A., Heurtel, N., Mansfield, S., Perdrix, S., Valiron, B.: A complete equational theory for quantum circuits. In: 38th Annual ACM/IEEE Symposium on Logic in Computer Science, LICS 2023, Boston, MA, USA, 26–29 June 2023, pp. 1–13. IEEE (2023). https://doi.org/10.1109/LICS56636.2023.10175801

14. Coecke, B., Duncan, R.: Interacting quantum observables. In: Aceto, L., Damgård, I., Goldberg, L.A., Halldórsson, M.M., Ingólfsdóttir, A., Walukiewicz, I. (eds.) ICALP 2008. LNCS, vol. 5126, pp. 298–310. Springer, Heidelberg (2008). https://doi.org/10.1007/978-3-540-70583-3_25

15. Coecke, B., Duncan, R.: Interacting quantum observables: categorical algebra and diagrammatics. New J. Phys. **13**(4), 043016 (2011)

16. de Bruijn, N.: Lambda calculus notation with nameless dummies, a tool for automatic formula manipulation, with application to the church-rosser theorem. Indagationes Math. (Proceedings) **75**(5), 381–392 (1972)

17. Dirac, P.A.M.: A new notation for quantum mechanics. In: Mathematical Proceedings of the Cambridge Philosophical Society, vol. 35, pp. 416–418. Cambridge University Press (1939). https://doi.org/10.1017/S0305004100021162

18. Hadzihasanovic, A.: A diagrammatic axiomatisation for qubit entanglement. In: 2015 30th Annual ACM/IEEE Symposium on Logic in Computer Science, pp. 573–584 (2015). https://doi.org/10.1109/LICS.2015.59

19. Hadzihasanovic, A., Ng, K.F., Wang, Q.: Two complete axiomatisations of pure-state qubit quantum computing. In: Proceedings of the 33rd Annual ACM/IEEE Symposium on Logic in Computer Science, pp. 502–511. Association for Computing Machinery (2018). https://doi.org/10.1145/3209108.3209128

20. Jeandel, E., Perdrix, S., Vilmart, R.: A complete axiomatisation of the zx-calculus for clifford+t quantum mechanics. In: Proceedings of the 33rd Annual ACM/IEEE Symposium on Logic in Computer Science, pp. 559–568. ACM (2018). https://doi.org/10.1145/3209108.3209131

21. Jeandel, E., Perdrix, S., Vilmart, R.: Diagrammatic reasoning beyond clifford+t quantum mechanics. In: Dawar, A., Grädel, E. (eds.) Proceedings of the 33rd Annual ACM/IEEE Symposium on Logic in Computer Science, LICS 2018, Oxford,

UK, 09–12 July 2018, pp. 569–578. ACM (2018). https://doi.org/10.1145/3209108. 3209139

22. Kissinger, A., van de Wetering, J.: PyZX: large scale automated diagrammatic reasoning. In: Coecke, B., Leifer, M. (eds.) Proceedings 16th International Conference on Quantum Physics and Logic, Chapman University, Orange, CA, USA., 10–14 June 2019. Electronic Proceedings in Theoretical Computer Science, vol. 318, pp. 229–241. Open Publishing Association (2020). https://doi.org/10.4204/EPTCS. 318.14

23. Le, X.B., Lin, S.W., Sun, J., Sanan, D.: A quantum interpretation of separating conjunction for local reasoning of quantum programs based on separation logic. Proc. ACM Program. Lang. **6**(POPL) (2022). https://doi.org/10.1145/3498697

24. Lewis, M., Soudjani, S., Zuliani, P.: Formal verification of quantum programs: theory, tools and challenges. CoRR **abs/2110.01320** (2021), https://arxiv.org/ abs/2110.01320

25. Li, L., et al.: Qafny: a quantum-program verifier (2024). https://arxiv.org/abs/ 2211.06411

26. Nielsen, M.A., Chuang, I.L.: Quantum Computation and Quantum Information. Cambridge University Press (2010)

27. Peham, T., Burgholzer, L., Wille, R.: Equivalence checking of quantum circuits with the zx-calculus. IEEE J. Emerg. Sel. Top. Circ. Syst. **12**(3), 662–675 (2022). https://doi.org/10.1109/JETCAS.2022.3202204

28. Perez-Garcia, D., Verstraete, F., Wolf, M.M., Cirac, J.I.: Matrix product state representations (2007), https://arxiv.org/abs/quant-ph/0608197

29. Poór, B., Wang, Q., Shaikh, R.A., Yeh, L., Yeung, R., Coecke, B.: Completeness for arbitrary finite dimensions of zxw-calculus, a unifying calculus. In: 2023 38th Annual ACM/IEEE Symposium on Logic in Computer Science (LICS), pp. 1–14 (2023). https://doi.org/10.1109/LICS56636.2023.10175672

30. Unruh, D.: Quantum relational hoare logic. Proc. ACM Program. Lang. **3**(POPL) (2019). https://doi.org/10.1145/3290346

31. van de Wetering, J.: Zx-calculus for the working quantum computer scientist (2020), https://arxiv.org/abs/2012.13966

32. Willsey, M., Nandi, C., Wang, Y.R., Flatt, O., Tatlock, Z., Panchekha, P.: Egg: fast and extensible equality saturation. Proc. ACM Program. Lang. **5**(POPL), 1–29 (2021). https://doi.org/10.1145/3434304

33. Xu, Y., Barthe, G., Zhou, L.: Automating equational proofs in dirac notation. Proc. ACM Program. Lang. **9**(POPL) (2025). https://doi.org/10.1145/3704878

34. Yan, P., Jiang, H., Yu, N.: On incorrectness logic for quantum programs. Proc. ACM Program. Lang. **6**(OOPSLA1) (2022). https://doi.org/10.1145/3527316

35. Zhong, S.: Birkhoff-von neumann quantum logic enriched with entanglement quantifiers: coincidence theorem and semantic consequence. Acta Informatica **62**(1), 7 (2024)

36. Zhou, L., Barthe, G., Hsu, J., Ying, M., Yu, N.: A quantum interpretation of bunched logic & quantum separation logic. In: 36th Annual ACM/IEEE Symposium on Logic in Computer Science, LICS 2021, Rome, Italy, June 29 - July 2, 2021, pp. 1–14. IEEE (2021). https://doi.org/10.1109/LICS52264.2021.9470673

37. Zhou, L., Barthe, G., Strub, P.Y., Liu, J., Ying, M.: CoqQ: foundational verification of quantum programs. Proc. ACM Program. Lang. **7**(POPL) (2023). https://doi. org/10.1145/3571222

Synthesis and Learning

Deductive Synthesis of Reinforcement Learning Agents for Infinite Horizon Tasks

Yuning Wang and He Zhu

Rutgers University, New Brunswick, NJ, USA
{yw895,hz375}@cs.rutgers.edu

Abstract. We propose a deductive synthesis framework for constructing reinforcement learning (RL) agents that provably satisfy temporal reach-avoid specifications over infinite horizons. Our approach decomposes these temporal specifications into a sequence of finite-horizon subtasks, for which we synthesize individual RL policies. Using formal verification techniques, we ensure that the composition of a finite number of subtask policies guarantees satisfaction of the overall specification over infinite horizons. Experimental results on a suite of benchmarks show that our synthesized agents outperform standard RL methods in both task performance and compliance with safety and temporal requirements.

Keywords: Controller Synthesis · Deductive Synthesis · Reinforcement Learning · Temporal Property Verification

1 Introduction

Reinforcement learning (RL) has emerged as a powerful framework for autonomous decision-making in dynamic environments [16,33,45]. Its ability to learn complex behaviors through interaction with the environment makes it an attractive choice for a wide range of applications. However, in many safety-critical domains, it is not sufficient for RL agents to merely optimize rewards. These systems must also adhere to strict safety and liveness constraints that can often be described by temporal logic properties. One widely studied class of such constraints is linear temporal logic (LTL) properties, which express rich behaviors over infinite horizons, such as ensuring safety ("something bad never happens") or liveness ("something good eventually happens") conditions.

Several existing approaches have investigated using *fragments* of LTL to define learning objectives for complex tasks, such as truncated LTL [32], logic formulas combining sequences and Boolean operations over subtasks [26,27], and reward machines [20,21]. These methods typically generate a reward function based on a given specification, which an RL algorithm then utilizes to learn a policy. Some deep RL approaches attempt to optimize a lower bound on the

This work is supported by the National Science Foundation under grants CCF-2007799 and CCF-2124155.

R. Piskac and Z. Rakamarić (Eds.): CAV 2025, LNCS 15934, pp. 79–103, 2025.
https://doi.org/10.1007/978-3-031-98685-7_4

probability of satisfying *general* LTL formulas [4,5,18,46,47,54]. However, a key challenge with these approaches lies in how rewards are assigned: since success or failure is determined at the trajectory level for temporal logic properties, it is difficult to attribute rewards to specific actions. This exacerbates the credit assignment problem, making it harder for RL algorithms to learn effectively. More importantly, they do not provide formal guarantees for the satisfaction of the specified objectives.

In the domain of formal verification for RL controllers, existing work focuses on ensuring that a controller, when composed with system dynamics and an environment model, remains safe or reaches target regions within a finite task horizon. However, approaches [11,13,22,49,51] based on reachability analysis become intractable for long task horizons due to the need for highly precise abstractions to mitigate approximation errors in reachable state set computations, making them scalable only for short-horizon tasks. Alternative methods reduce the infinite-horizon verification problem to single-step verification by inferring the inductive invariant of a closed-loop system, in the form of Lyapunov functions [9,50] or control barrier functions [1,39]. While effective for simple reach-avoid problems, they are not easily generalized to temporal tasks—such as those involving *repeating* subroutines that must traverse a sequence of subgoals *infinitely* (Fig. 1).

We propose a deductive synthesis framework, VEL-∞ (**VE**rification-based **L**earning for Infinite Horizon Tasks), that synthesizes RL agents with formal guarantees of satisfying temporal reach-avoid specifications over *infinite horizons* (formalized in Sect. 2). Given a temporal reach-avoid property Ψ expressed in our specification language, VEL-∞ decomposes the global task into a sequence of finite-horizon subtasks, each characterized by well-defined preconditions and postconditions. These subtask controllers are independently learned and formally verified, and

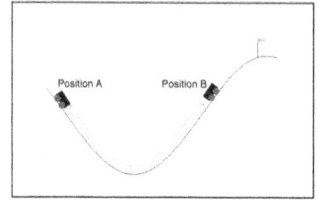

Fig. 1. A shuttle mountain car task where the car is tasked to repeatedly travel back and forth between two positions.

their composition is provably correct with respect to satisfying Ψ over an infinite execution. As an example, consider a shuttle mountain car problem, where the task is to repeatedly drive the car between Position A and Position B. VEL-∞ breaks this task into subtasks: moving from Position A to Position B (red arrow) and then back (blue arrow). Each subtask is defined by a precondition (e.g., starting at Position A with some velocity constraints) and a postcondition (e.g., reaching Position B with some other velocity constraints). Notably, the postcondition of one subtask serves as the precondition of the other, creating a cyclic dependency between the two. VEL-∞ verifies each subtask with its pre- and postconditions, ensuring that when subtasks are composed, they are always invoked in states that satisfy their preconditions—an invariant that guarantees the task can be executed indefinitely.

The key contributions of our work are as follows:

- Deductive Synthesis for RL: We introduce a framework that integrates deductive reasoning with reinforcement learning to synthesize control policies satisfying temporal reach-avoid properties over infinite horizons.
- Modular Sub-task Decomposition: Our method decomposes infinite-horizon specifications into sub-tasks, enabling efficient learning using off-the-shelf RL algorithms, and then composes the solutions to ensure global correctness.
- Experimental Validation: We demonstrate the effectiveness of our approach through experiments on a suite of benchmark tasks with continuous state and action space, showing that it outperforms existing RL-based methods in both performance and adherence to formal task specifications.

2 Problem Setup

Environment Model. We model the environment of an RL agent as a discrete-time dynamical system given by the tuple $M[\cdot] = (S, A, F, R, S_0, \cdot)$. Here, $S \subseteq \mathbb{R}^n$ is the state space, $A \subseteq \mathbb{R}^m$ is the action space. The system's dynamics are defined by the equation

$$s_{t+1} \sim F(s_t, a_t) = f(s_t, a_t, w_t) \qquad w_t \in W$$

where $t \in \mathbb{N}_0$ is a time step, $s_t \in S$ is a state of the system, $a_t \in A$ is a control action, and ω_t is a random time-varying disturbance vector from the disturbance space $W \subseteq \mathbb{R}^p$ at time step t. $R : S \times A \to \mathbb{R}$ is a reward function and $R(s, a)$ defines the immediate reward after the transition from an environment state $s \in S$ with action $a \in A$. S_0 is the set of initial states. We explicitly model the deployment of a control policy π in $M[\cdot]$ as a closed-loop system $M[\pi]$. The system dynamics of $M[\pi]$ are defined by the dynamics function $F : S \times A \to S$ and the control policy $\pi : S \to A$, which maps states to actions, i.e., $a_t = \pi(s_t)$.

Given an initial state s_0, we denote $\zeta \sim M[\pi](s_0)$ as a trajectory (or rollout) of $M[\pi]$ sampled from s_0, i.e. $\zeta = s_0 \xrightarrow{a_0} s_1 \xrightarrow{a_1} s_2 \cdots$ where each $a_t = \pi(s_t)$, each $s_{t+1} \sim F(s_t, a_t)$. We use $\zeta \sim M[\pi]$ for any trajectory of $M[\pi]$ sampled from an initial state $s_0 \in S_0$.

Key Assumptions. We assume that the dynamics f and policy π are Lipschitz continuous functions. The dynamics function f is *known* and is composed of standard trigonometric and polynomial terms, combined with arithmetic operations. Furthermore, we assume a *bounded* disturbance set W, i.e. the system's uncertainty is bounded within a specific range. For example, the disturbance vector ω_t is drawn from a triangular noise distribution at each time step t.

Example 1. Consider the 9Rooms environment in Fig. 2a. The agent (green dot) starts in the bottom left room $(1, 1)$ and is governed by the dynamics function, $s_{t+1} = s_t + 0.1 \min \big(\max(a_t, -1), 1 \big) + \omega_t$, where ω_t is drawn from a triangular noise distribution. The state space of the environment is defined as $[0, 3] \times [0, 3] \subset \mathbb{R}^2$. The set of initial states is $[0.4, 0.6] \times [0.4, 0.6]$. The state space contains unsafe areas that should be avoided, i.e., the red wall segments.

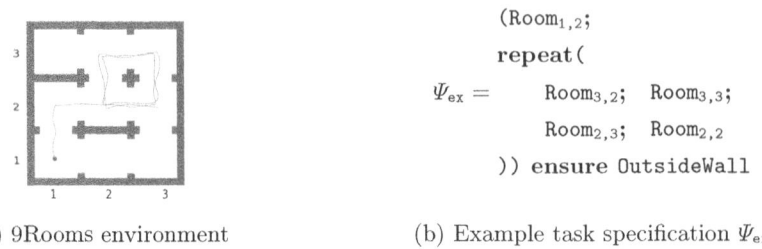

(a) 9Rooms environment   (b) Example task specification Ψ_{ex}

Fig. 2. A 9Rooms environment with specification Ψ_{ex} and a satisfying trajectory.

Temporal Reach-Avoid Specifications. We define a high-level specification language that concisely expresses desired RL agent behaviors for infinite-horizon reach-avoid tasks. Inspired by recent specification languages for RL tasks [20, 21, 26, 27], our language restricts classic LTL properties to enable reward shaping for efficient learning. The syntax of our specification language extends the SPECTRL language [26].

Definition 1 (Predicate). *A predicate φ is a quantifier-free Boolean combination of linear inequalities over the environment state variables x:*

$$\varphi :: = P \mid \varphi \wedge \varphi \mid \varphi \vee \varphi$$
$$P :: = \mathcal{A} \cdot x \leq b \text{ where } \mathcal{A} \in \mathbb{R}^{|x|}, b \in \mathbb{R}$$

A state $s \in S$ satisfies a predicate φ, denoted as $s \models \varphi$, iff $\varphi(s)$ is true.

Definition 2 (Task Specification). *A task specification Ψ is either a non-repetitive task specification ψ or a repetitive task specification ψ_R.*

$$\Psi :: = \psi \mid \psi_R$$

The syntax of ψ and ψ_R defined as:

$$
\begin{array}{ll}
\psi ::= \textbf{achieve } \varphi & \psi_R ::= \textbf{repeat } \psi \\
\quad \mid \psi \textbf{ ensure } \varphi & \quad \mid \psi_R \textbf{ ensure } \varphi \\
\quad \mid \psi_1; \psi_2 & \quad \mid \psi; \psi_{R1} \\
\quad \mid \psi_1 \textbf{ or } \psi_2 & \quad \mid \psi_{R1} \textbf{ or } \psi_{R2}
\end{array}
$$

Intuitively, a specification Ψ in our language is defined over trajectories with a finite prefix ψ and a possibly infinite suffix ψ_R. An infinite trajectory ζ satisfies ψ if there exists a finite prefix of ζ that satisfies ψ. In the definition for ψ, the first clause means that the prefix trajectory should eventually reach a state that satisfies the predicate φ. The second clause says that the prefix trajectory should satisfy specification ψ while always staying in states that satisfy a *safety constraint* φ. The third clause states that the prefix trajectory should sequentially satisfy ψ_1 followed by ψ_2. The fourth clause means that the prefix trajectory should satisfy either ψ_1 or ψ_2. An infinite trajectory ζ satisfies a repetitive task ψ_R if, beyond some time step i, the suffix of the trajectory $\zeta_{i:\infty}$ conforms to a temporal property **repeat** ψ, indicating a repeated execution of the task ψ to achieve its goal states infinitely often.

Example 2. The task specification Ψ_{ex} (Fig. 2b) for the 9Rooms environment requires the agent to first reach room $(1, 2)$ and then repeatedly traverse four rooms in a circular way infinitely, while avoiding collision with any red wall segments. $\text{Room}_{x,y}$ is the abbreviation for **achieve** $\texttt{Center(x,y)}$ where the predicate $\texttt{Center(x,y)}$ is true for states where the agent locates at the center of the room indexed by $\texttt{(x,y)}$. The $\texttt{OutsideWall}$ predicate is true for states where the agent stays away from any wall segments. The green curve in Fig. 2b shows an agent trajectory that satisfies Ψ_{ex}.

We formalize the semantics of task specification satisfaction in Ψ as follows.

Definition 3 (Task Specification Satisfaction). *Given an infinite trajectory* $\zeta = s_0 \xrightarrow{a_0} s_1 \xrightarrow{a_1} s_2 \cdots$, ζ *satisfies a non-repetitive task specification* ψ, *denoted as* $\zeta \models \psi$ *if and only if there exists a time step* i *such that the finite prefix trajectory* $\zeta_{0:i}$ *satisfies* ψ. *The satisfaction of* ψ *by* $\zeta_{0:i}$, *namely* $\zeta_{0:i} \models \psi$, *is defined inductively as follows:*

$$
\begin{aligned}
\zeta_{0:i} &\models \textbf{\textit{achieve }} \varphi & &\Leftrightarrow \exists\, 0 \le j \le i \text{ s.t. } s_j \models \varphi \\
\zeta_{0:i} &\models \psi \textbf{\textit{ ensure }} \varphi & &\Leftrightarrow \zeta_{0:i} \models \psi \text{ and } \forall\, 0 \le j < i, s_j \models \varphi \\
\zeta_{0:i} &\models \psi_1; \psi_2 & &\Leftrightarrow \exists\, 0 \le j < i \text{ s.t. } \zeta_{0:j} \models \psi_1 \text{ and } \zeta_{j+1:i} \models \psi_2 \\
\zeta_{0:i} &\models \psi_1 \textbf{\textit{ or }} \psi_2 & &\Leftrightarrow \zeta_{0:i} \models \psi_1 \text{ or } \zeta_{0:i} \models \psi_2
\end{aligned}
\tag{1}
$$

The satisfaction of a repetitive task specification ψ_R *by an infinite trajectory* ζ, *denoted as* $\zeta \models \psi_R$, *is defined inductively as follows:*

$$
\begin{aligned}
\zeta &\models \textbf{\textit{repeat }} \psi & &\Leftrightarrow \exists\, i \text{ s.t. } \zeta_{0:i} \models \psi \text{ and } \zeta_{i+1:\infty} \models \textbf{\textit{repeat }} \psi \\
\zeta &\models \psi_R \textbf{\textit{ ensure }} \varphi & &\Leftrightarrow \zeta \models \psi_R \text{ and } \forall i, s_i \models \varphi \\
\zeta &\models \psi; \psi_R & &\Leftrightarrow \exists\, i \text{ s.t. } \zeta_{0:i} \models \psi \text{ and } \zeta_{i+1:\infty} \models \psi_R \\
\zeta &\models \psi_{R1} \textbf{\textit{ or }} \psi_{R2} & &\Leftrightarrow \zeta \models \psi_{R1} \text{ or } \zeta \models \psi_{R2}
\end{aligned}
\tag{2}
$$

Finally, ζ *satisfies* Ψ, *denoted as* $\zeta \models \Psi$, *if and only if* ζ *satisfies the underlying* ψ *or* ψ_R.

Comparison with LTL. Compared to declarative LTL properties, our language Ψ is operationally direct, task-oriented, and tailored for RL agents. Notably, our language encodes a restricted fragment of LTL properties, disallowing temporal dependencies that combine temporal operators and Boolean connectives arbitrarily. The exact fragment of LTL that our specification language ψ_R supports is characterized as follows, where φ is a quantifier-free predicate over state variables:

$$
\begin{aligned}
\psi &::= \varphi \mid \mathbf{F}(\varphi \wedge \mathbf{X}\psi) \wedge \mathbf{G}\varphi \mid \psi \vee \psi \\
\psi_R &::= \psi \mid \psi \wedge \mathbf{G}\psi
\end{aligned}
\tag{3}
$$

This fragment focuses on task execution order. It captures task sequencing as $\mathbf{F}(\varphi_1 \wedge \mathbf{XF}\varphi_2)$, where the agent must first reach a state satisfying φ_1 and then proceed to a state satisfying φ_2. It also enforces safety constraints through $\mathbf{F}(\varphi_1 \wedge \mathbf{XF}\varphi_2) \wedge \mathbf{G}\varphi_3$, ensuring that the agent adheres to the safety condition φ_3 at all times. Additionally, it supports infinite repetition with $\mathbf{GF}(\varphi_1 \wedge \mathbf{XF}\varphi_2)$, requiring the agent to repeatedly visit states satisfying φ_1 and φ_2 indefinitely. Our specification language employs the **achieve**, **ensure**, and **repeat** operators to naturally capture eventual satisfaction, safety constraints, and global invariance, making it well-suited for expressing this fragment. Our language does not adopt classical LTL syntax in order to improve accessibility for RL practitioners who may not have a formal methods background. Instead, it uses an intuitive structure that aligns with common RL problem formulations, allowing users to specify infinite sequences of subtasks compositionally. This restricted fragment, as demonstrated below, enables an efficient verification procedure.

Relation to SPECTRL. Our specification language is based on the SPECTRL language [26]. VEL-∞ is part of the recent research trend in RL for LTL, leveraging RL techniques to optimize LTL objectives directly in continuous state and action spaces. Existing work SPECTRL [26] and DiRL [27] in this direction has developed efficient algorithms for handling temporal reach-avoid specifications defined over a finite number of subtasks. However, there remains a significant gap in developing a general RL algorithm capable of handling infinite-horizon LTL specifications, such as those requiring infinite oscillation between key subgoals. Formally, the SPECTRL and DiRL approaches support ψ (finite reach-avoid tasks) but do not generalize to ψ_R, which encompasses temporal reach-avoid objectives over infinite horizons. VEL-∞ fills this gap by introducing a novel framework that extends RL capabilities to the setting in ψ_R, and provide formal correctness guarantees for this extension using formal methods.

Problem Formulation. Given an environment model $M[\cdot]$ and a specification Ψ, our goal is to find a control policy π such that for all $\zeta \sim M[\pi]$, $\zeta \models \Psi$.

3   Verification-Based Learning over Infinite Horizons

Main Framework. Our approach, **V**erification-**B**ased **L**earning for Infinite horizon properties (VEL-∞), leverages the compositional property of a task specification Ψ in our language to construct an abstract reachability graph for the task. We use a graph search algorithm similar to the Dijkstra's algorithm to train formally verified policies for edge subtasks within the abstract reachability graph and construct a final policy that satisfies the overall task specification by strategically combining edge policies.

3.1   Abstract Reachability Graph Construction

Our approach builds on [27] to convert a task specification Ψ into an abstract reachability graph G_Ψ, but unlike [27], we do not require G_Ψ to be acyclic.

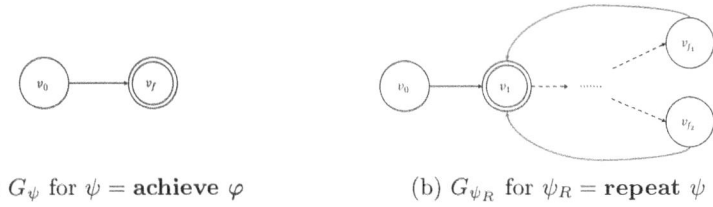

(a) G_ψ for $\psi = $ **achieve** φ (b) G_{ψ_R} for $\psi_R = $ **repeat** ψ

Fig. 3. Visualization of abstract reachability graph construction

We define $G_\Psi = (V_\Psi, E_\Psi, V_{F_\Psi}, \mu_\Psi, \beta_\Psi, v_{0_\Psi})$ where each vertex $v \in V_\Psi$ represents a region in the state space captured by some predicate φ_v (Definition 1). The predicate labeling function $\mu_\Psi(v)$ maps each vertex $v \in V_\Psi$ to its corresponding predicate φ_v. The initial vertex $v_{0_\Psi} \in V_\Psi$ encodes the initial state region S_0 of the environment model. The set V_{F_Ψ} includes all final vertices that may induce cycles (introduced by the *repeat* operator) defining recurring patterns in infinite trajectories. Each edge $e = (u \to v) \in E_\Psi$ corresponds to a goal-directed subtask with precondition $\mu_\Psi(u)$ and postcondition $\mu_\Psi(v)$:

$$\mathcal{T}_e : \ \mu_\Psi(u) \rightsquigarrow \mu_\Psi(v) \mid \beta_\Psi(e)$$

that transitions the agent from subregion $\mu_\Psi(u)$ to subregion $\mu_\Psi(v)$. The safety constraint labeling function $\beta_\Psi(e)$ maps each edge e to a predicate φ_e (enforced by the *ensure* operator) that must hold true on all states during the subtask represented by e. Intuitively, a trajectory that satisfies the specification Ψ should transition through a sequence of subgoal regions in V_Ψ, starting from the initial vertex and possibly cycling at some final vertex in V_{F_Ψ}, while adhering to the safety constraints associated with the edges in E_Ψ along the path.

We provide a high-level description of the algorithm used to construct the abstract reachability graph G_Ψ for a task specification Ψ. For more details, we refer interested readers to the extended version [58]. The abstract reachability graph G_ψ for a specification in the form of $\psi = $ **achieve** φ is shown in Fig. 3a. It consists of two vertices: the initial vertex v_0 with a predicate φ_{v_0} encoding the initial state space S_0 and the final vertex v_f with the predicate φ. The directed edge $(v_0 \to v_f)$ represents the subtask $S_0 \rightsquigarrow \varphi$ of transitioning from the initial region S_0 to the target region defined by φ. The graph for $\psi = \psi_1$ **ensure** φ can be obtained by updating the safety constraint $\beta(e)$ of each edge e within G_{ψ_1} (recursively constructed) through a conjunction $\beta(e) \wedge \varphi$. The graph for $\psi = \psi_1; \psi_2$ is constructed by adding edges in the form of $(v_{f_i} \to v_j)$, where v_{f_i} is any final vertex of G_{ψ_1} and v_j is any neighbor vertex of the initial vertex $v_{0_{\psi_2}}$ in G_{ψ_2}. Then $v_{0_{\psi_2}}$ and all its edges are removed. This construction ensures that the subtask for ψ_2 begins after that of ψ_1 completes. The graph for G_ψ for $\psi = \psi_1$ **or** ψ_2 is derived by merging the initial vertices $v_{0_{\psi_1}}$ and $v_{0_{\psi_2}}$ into a single initial vertex, allowing the agent to choose which task to complete.

For a repetitive task specification $\psi_R = $ **repeat** ψ, the graph G_{ψ_R} is obtained by adding edges that connect all the final vertices of G_ψ to the neighbors of the

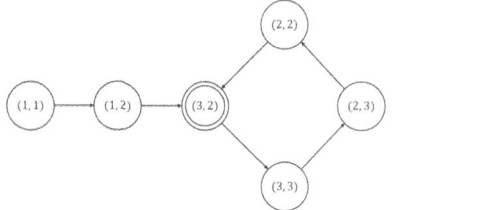
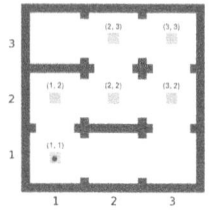

(a) Abstract reachability graph for $G_{\psi_{ex}}$ (b) Subregions for Each Vertex

Fig. 4. The abstract reachability graph for specification Ψ_{ex} in Fig. 2

initial vertex v_0, allowing the task ψ to be repeated. We then set these neighbors as the final vertices of G_{ψ_R}, marking the start and end of a cycle. The added edges are shown in blue in Fig. 3b. The graphs for other types of repetitive task specifications can be recursively constructed similarly to their counterparts in ψ.

Example 3 Consider the task specification Ψ_{ex} for 9Rooms in Fig. 2b, its abstract reachability graph $G_{\Psi_{ex}}$ is shown in Fig. 4a. Subregions represented by the predicates are marked in Fig. 4b. The safety constraint for each edge (no collision with red walls) is not shown.

After construction, the abstract reachability graph G_Ψ serves as a structured representation of the task specification Ψ. With subtasks encoded in the edges in G_Ψ, the completion of the full specification can be viewed as visiting vertices in G_Ψ in a specific order. Definition 4 shows how to validate if an agent trajectory accomplishes the task Ψ using the abstract reachability graph G_Ψ.

Definition 4 (Abstract Reachability Graph Satisfaction). *Given an infinite trajectory* $\zeta = s_0 \xrightarrow{a_0} s_1 \xrightarrow{a_1} s_2 \cdots$, ζ *satisfies the abstract reachability graph* G_ψ *of a non-repetitive task specification* ψ, *denoted as* $\zeta \models G_\psi$, *if and only if there exists a finite sequence of indices* $i_0 \leq i_1 \leq \cdots \leq i_n$ *and a path* $\rho = v_0 \to v_1 \to \cdots \to v_n$ *in* G_ψ *such that:*

- $v_n \in V_{F_\psi}$
- $\forall\, 0 \leq j \leq n,\ s_{i_j} \models \mu_\psi(v_j)$
- $\forall\, 0 \leq j < n,\ \zeta_{i_j:i_{j+1}} \models \beta_\psi(v_j \to v_{j+1})$

Given the abstract reachability graph G_{ψ_R} *of a repetitive specification* ψ_R, ζ *satisfies* G_{ψ_R}, *denoted as* $\zeta \models G_{\psi_R}$, *if and only if there exists an infinite sequence of indices* $i_0 \leq i_1 \leq \cdots \leq i_n \cdots$ *and an infinite path* $\rho = v_0 \to v_1 \to \cdots \to v_n \cdots$ *in* G_{ψ_R} *such that:*

- $v_n \in V_{F_{\psi_R}}$ *occurs infinite number of times in* ρ
- $\forall\, j \geq 0,\ s_{i_j} \models \mu_{\psi_R}(v_j)$
- $\forall\, j \geq 0,\ \zeta_{i_j:i_{j+1}} \models \beta_{\psi_R}(v_j \to v_{j+1})$

Theorem 1. *Given a task specification Ψ and its abstract reachability graph G_Ψ, for any infinite trajectory ζ, we have $\zeta \models \Psi$ if and only if $\zeta \models G_\Psi$.*

Proof. The theorem follows from a straightforward induction on Ψ.

Hereafter, we often omit the suffix Ψ for simplicity, such as referring to G_Ψ as G when the context is clear.

3.2 Dijkstra-Style Abstract Reachability Graph Search

After converting a task specification Ψ into an abstract reachability graph G, where subtasks are modeled as directed edges, a practical learning strategy [27] exploits this graph structure by decomposing the learning problem into goal-reaching subtasks. Individual edge policies are trained for the subtasks associated with the edges and subsequently composed to form a solution for the full specification Ψ^1. Since the edges of G represent smaller, localized subtasks, this approach avoids the complexity of satisfying the entire specification with a single RL algorithm. However, applying this decomposition strategy to infinite-horizon temporal reach-avoid problems is challenging, as it requires ensuring that the composition of finite subtasks can be executed over infinite horizons. VEL-∞ proceeds in the following three steps to tackle this challenge:

- Step 1: For each edge $e = u \to v$ in G, learn an edge policy π_e that aims to transition the system from any state $s \in \mu(u)$ to some state $s' \in \mu(v)$, while avoiding states that violate the safety constraint $\beta(e)$.
- Step 2: Formally verify that π_e can transition the system from $\mu(u)$ to $\mu(v)$ within c_e timesteps (where c_e is a parameter learned during training) while ensuring compliance with $\beta(e)$.
- Step 3: Use a graph search algorithm in conjunction with the edge costs c_e to compute a path $\rho = v_0 \to v_1 \to \cdots \to (v_k \to v_{k+1} \to \cdots \to v_{k+l})^\omega$ with a cyclic structure labeled with ω where $v_k = v_{k+l}$ and $v_k \in V_F$ is a final vertex in G. The path ρ minimizes $c(\rho) = \langle \sum_{j=k}^{k+l-1} c_{e_j}, \sum_{j=0}^{k-1} c_{e_j} \rangle$ by *lexicographic ordering*, where $e_j = v_j \to v_{j+1}$ corresponds to an edge policy $\pi_j = \pi_{e_j}$.

Our key idea is to establish a formally verified inductive invariant ensuring that, for any searched graph path ρ containing a cyclic structure $(v_k \to v_{k+1} \to \cdots \to v_{k+l})^\omega$ at step three, the set of states reachable at the end of the cycle on v_{k+l} is a subset of the states in $\mu(v_{k+l})$. Since $v_{k+l} = v_k$, we have shown that the set of states reachable at the end of the cycle is contained within the states at the beginning of the cycle, $\mu(v_k)$. This inductive property guarantees the infinite execution of the cycle along ρ.

Finally, we construct the overall controller as a *stateful* path policy:

Definition 5 (Path Policy). *Given the edge policies along with a path $\rho = v_0 \to v_1 \to \cdots \to (v_k \to v_{k+1} \to \cdots \to v_{k+l})^\omega$ where $v_k = v_{k+l}$ and $v_k \in V_F$*

---

[1] This is feasible because we assume access to a simulator with known dynamics.

in G, we define the overall controller as a path policy $\pi_\rho = \pi_0 \circ \cdots \circ \pi_{k-1} \circ (\pi_k \circ \ldots \circ \pi_{k+l-1})^\omega$ designed to achieve the sequence of edges in ρ. It navigates from $\mu(v_0)$ to $\mu(v_k)$, and then infinitely visits $\mu(v_k)$ through the cycle from v_k. It executes each policy π_j until it reaches $\mu(v_{j+1})$, and then switch to π_{j+1} unless $j = k + l - 1$ in which case j is reset to k. Note that π_ρ is stateful since it internally keeps track of the index j of the current policy.

We explain controller verification and the graph search algorithm in detail below. Specifically, VEL-∞ decomposes the verification of a path policy to the verification of its edge policies. VEL-∞ verifies an edge policy π_e against an environment model $M[\cdot]$ and a specification $\mathcal{T}_e$ using abstract interpretation.

Definition 6 (Symbolic Rollouts for Edge Policies). *Given an environment model $M[\cdot]$, an edge policy π_e, a subtask specification $\mathcal{T}_e : \mu(u) \rightsquigarrow \mu(v) \mid \beta(e)$, an abstract domain $\mathcal{D}$ with abstraction function α and concretization function γ, an abstract transformer $F^{\mathcal{D}}$ for the state transition function F of M, and abstract transformer $\pi_e^{\mathcal{D}}$ for the policy, a symbolic rollout of $M[\pi_e]$ over $\mathcal{D}$ constructs an H-step sequence of symbolic states $\zeta^{\mathcal{D}} = S_0^{\mathcal{D}}, S_1^{\mathcal{D}}, \ldots, S_H^{\mathcal{D}}$ where $S_0^{\mathcal{D}} = \alpha(\{s \mid s \models \mu(u)\})$, the abstraction of the initial subtask states. The symbolic state $S_{t+1}^{\mathcal{D}}$ that overapproximates the set of reachable states from the initial subtask states at time step $t + 1$ is computed as:*

$$S_{t+1}^{\mathcal{D}} = F^{\mathcal{D}}(S_t^{\mathcal{D}}, A_t^{\mathcal{D}})$$

where $A_t^{\mathcal{D}} = \pi_e^{\mathcal{D}}(S_t^{\mathcal{D}})$ is an overapproximation of the set of possible actions at t.

Edge Policy Verification. Our edge policy verification procedure leverages the concretization operator γ of the abstract domain $\mathcal{D}$. The concretization $\gamma(S_t^{\mathcal{D}})$ is defined as the set of concrete states represented by the abstract state $S_t^{\mathcal{D}}$. To balance precision and verification efficiency, we assume that this concretization can be approximated using a tight interval $\gamma_I(S_t^{\mathcal{D}})$, which represents the most precise interval enclosing all concrete states of $S_t^{\mathcal{D}}$. The edge policy π_e satisfies the subtask specification $\mathcal{T}_e : \mu(u) \rightsquigarrow \mu(v) \mid \beta(e)$, denoted as $\pi_e \models \mathcal{T}_e$, if the following conditions hold on the symbolic rollout of $M[\pi_e]$, $\zeta^{\mathcal{D}} = S_0^{\mathcal{D}}, S_1^{\mathcal{D}}, \ldots, S_H^{\mathcal{D}}$. First, every reachable state satisfies the safety constraint $\beta(e)$:

$$\forall 0 \leq t < H, \ \forall s \in \gamma_I(S_t^{\mathcal{D}}), \ s \models \beta(e)$$

Second, the reachable states at the final step H satisfy the subtask's goal condition,

$$\forall s \in \gamma_I(S_H^{\mathcal{D}}), \ s \models \mu(v)$$

Path Policy Verification. A path policy π_ρ is formally verified $\pi_\rho \models G$ if and only if each edge policy π_e on ρ is formally verified i.e. $\pi_e \models \mathcal{T}_e$.

Example 4 Fig. 5 illustrates the symbolic rollouts of the edge policies within a verified path policy for the 9Room environment. The abstract domain $\mathcal{D}$ used for edge policy verification is Taylor Model (TM) flowpipes, which we discuss further in Sect. 3.3. Each box represents the interval concretization of a symbolic state, with colors distinguishing different edge policies.

Theorem 2 (Path Policy Verification Soundness). *Given an environment model $M[\cdot]$, an abstract reachability graph G, a path policy $\pi_\rho = \pi_0 \circ \cdots \circ \pi_{k-1} \circ (\pi_k \circ \ldots \circ \pi_{k+l-1})^\omega$ along with a path $\rho = v_0 \to v_1 \to \cdots \to (v_k \to v_{k+1} \to \cdots \to v_{k+l})^\omega$ in G where $v_k = v_{k+l}$ and $v_k \in V_F$ is a final vertex, if $\pi_\rho \models G$, then for any $\zeta \sim M[\pi_\rho]$, $\zeta \models G$.*

Proof. For any infinite trajectory $\zeta = s_0 \xrightarrow{a_0} s_1 \xrightarrow{a_1} s_2 \cdots \sim M[\pi_\rho]$, by construction according to Definition 5, there exists an infinite sequence of indices $i_0 \leq \cdots \leq i_k \leq \cdots i_{k+l} \leq \cdots \leq i_{k+2l} \leq \cdots$, such that for all $0 \leq j < k$, $\zeta_{i_j:i_{j+1}} \sim M[\pi_j](s_{i_j})$ is produced by a policy π_j on the prefix of π_ρ, and for all $j \geq k$, $\zeta_{i_j:i_{j+1}} \sim M[\pi_{j \bmod l}](s_{i_j})$ is produced by a policy $\pi_{j \bmod l}$ on the cyclic structure of π_ρ. According to Definition 6, the verification procedure guarantees that for all $0 \leq j < k$, we have $s_{i_j} \models \mu(v_j)$ and $\zeta_{i_j:i_{j+1}} \models \beta(v_j \to v_{j+1})$. Similarly, for all $j \geq k$, we have $s_{i_j} \models \mu(v_{j \bmod l})$ and $\zeta_{i_j:i_{j+1}} \models \beta(v_{j \bmod l} \to v_{j \bmod l+1})$. As such, ζ visits states in $\mu(v_k)$ at i_k, i_{k+l}, i_{k+2l}, ..., etc., which means that ζ visits v_k infinitely often. Based on Definition 4, we have $\zeta \models G$ by construction.

Theorems 1 and 2 jointly demonstrate that, given an environment model $M[\cdot]$ and a specification Ψ, any trajectory $\zeta \sim M[\pi_\rho]$ generated by a formally verified path policy π_ρ satisfies $\zeta \models \Psi$.

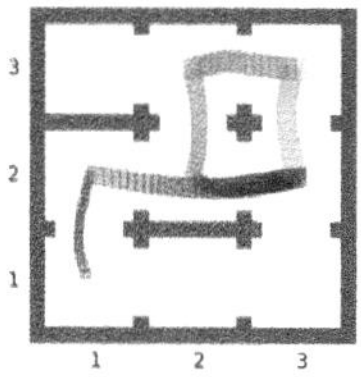

Fig. 5. A symbolic rollout for the 9Rooms environment.

Invariants at Final Vertices. The proof of Theorem 2 explains why VEL-∞ effectively handles infinite-horizon properties. It ensures that when the path policy π_ρ completes a cycle traversal at timestep $k + l$, the reached states remain within $\mu(v_{k+l})$. Since $v_k = v_{k+l}$, this means the states at the end of the cycle on v_{k+l} belong to the set of states $\mu(v_k)$ at the cycle's starting point at timestep k, where v_k is a final vertex. For example, at the center of Room$_{3,2}$ in Fig. 5, the last symbolic state for the edge policy in dark blue is fully enclosed within the initial yellow symbolic state, indicating cyclic behaviors.

Edge Cost and Path Cost. We measure the cost c_e of each edge e within an abstract reachability graph G as the horizon H of the symbolic rollout constructed to verify the subtask $\mathcal{T}_e$ of e (Definition 6). The cost c_ρ of a path $\rho = v_0 \to v_1 \to \cdots \to (v_k \to v_{k+1} \to \cdots \to v_{k+l})^\omega$ where $v_k = v_{k+l}$ and $v_k \in V_F$ is a tuple $\langle \sum_{j=k}^{k+l-1} c_{e_j}, \sum_{j=0}^{k-1} c_{e_j} \rangle$ where $e_j = v_j \to v_{j+1}$ corresponds to an edge on ρ. The first element measures the sum of the edge costs within the cyclic structure of ρ, and the second measures the sum of the edge costs on the prefix that leads to the cycle. VEL-∞ compares path costs using *lexicographic ordering*, meaning that we prefer the final vertex that has the least cost cycle back to itself for infinite visits. This is reasonable because, as the cycle is traversed infinitely, its cost dominates the cost of the prefix. VEL-∞ aims to learn the optimal path policy corresponding to the path in G with the least path cost.

Algorithm 1. VEL-∞ Policy Search Algorithm

1: **procedure** VEL-∞ $(M[\cdot], G = (V, E, V_F, \mu, \beta, v_0))$
2:     **for each** $v_f \in V_F$ **do**
3:         $\langle c^\omega_{v_f}, c^{v_0}_{v_f} \rangle, \pi_{v_f} \leftarrow$ LEARN$(M[\cdot], G, v_0, v_f)$
4:     **return** π_{v_f} with the least cost $\langle c^\omega_{v_f}, c^{v_0}_{v_f} \rangle$ by *lexicographic ordering*

5:
6: **procedure** LEARN $(M[\cdot], G, v_0, v_f, \text{Rec} = \text{True})$
7:     Initialize priority queue Q with $\{(0, v_0)\}$
8:     Initialize visited set $S \leftarrow \emptyset$
9:     **while** $Q \neq \emptyset$ **do**
10:         $c_u, u \leftarrow$ Dequeue the vertex with the least cost in Q
11:         **if** $u \notin S$ **then**
12:             **for each** outgoing edge $e = (u, v) \in G.E$ of u **do**
13:                 ▷ Learn an edge policy $\pi_e \models \mathcal{T}_e$ with TRAINVERIFY (Algorithm 2)
14:                 $\pi_e, H, S^\mathcal{D}_H \leftarrow$ TRAINVERIFY $(M[\cdot], \mathcal{T}_e : \mu(u) \rightsquigarrow \mu(v) \mid \beta(e))$
15:                 $c_e \leftarrow H$
16:                 ▷ Strengthen $\mu(v)$ by the *(verified)* set of states reachable at v
17:                 **if** $v \notin S$ **then** $\mu(v) \leftarrow \mu(v) \wedge \gamma_I(S^\mathcal{D}_H)$
18:                 **if** $v = v_f \wedge \text{Rec} \wedge v_f$ has outgoing edges **then**
19:                     ▷ Find the least-cost cycle from v_f
20:                     $\langle \_, c_\omega \rangle, \pi_\omega \leftarrow$ LEARN$(M[\cdot], G, v_f, v_f, \text{Rec} = \text{False})$
21:                     $\pi_{v_f} \leftarrow$ Path policy from v_0 to v_f followed by π_ω
22:                     **return** $\langle c_\omega, c_u + c_e \rangle, \pi_{v_f}$
23:                 **else if** $v = v_f$ **then**
24:                     $\pi_{v_f} \leftarrow$ Path policy from v_0 to v_f
25:                     **return** $\langle 0, c_u + c_e \rangle, \pi_{v_f}$
26:                 **else**
27:                   Enqueue $(c_u + c_e, v)$ into Q
28:         $S \leftarrow S \cup \{u\}$

Main Search Algorithm. The outline of our learning algorithm VEL-∞ is shown in Algorithm 1, which takes as input an environment model $M[\cdot]$ and an abstract reachability graph G that encodes a task specification Ψ. The algorithm is built on top of the Dijkstra's algorithm to traverse the reachability graph G. For each final vertex $v_f \in V_F$, the algorithm invokes the LEARN procedure at line 3 to learn edge policies that can be used to reach v_f.

In LEARN, a priority queue Q is maintained to store pairs (c, v), where c represents the path cost along the shortest path from the initial vertex v_0 to vertex v. Q is initialized to $\{(0, v_0)\}$ at line 7. Iteratively at line 9, LEARN handles an unprocessed vertex u closest to the initial vertex v_0 from Q. For each edge $e = u \rightarrow v$ in G, we learn an edge policy π_e for the subtask $\mathcal{T}_e : \mu(u) \rightsquigarrow \mu(v) \mid \beta(e)$ that transitions the system from any state $s \in \mu(u)$ to $s' \in \mu(v)$ safely with respect to the safety constraint $\beta(e)$. We invoke the TRAINVERIFY algorithm (given in Sect. 3.3) at line 14 to synthesize a formally verified policy π_e for the subtask: $\pi_e \models \mathcal{T}_e$. TRAINVERIFY also returns H as the horizon of the symbolic rollout constructed to verify the subtask $\mathcal{T}_e$ of e (Definition 6). We use H as the edge cost c_e of e (line 15). Importantly, TRAINVERIFY also returns the symbolic state $S_H^{\mathcal{D}}$ verified at timestep H and, at line 17, we strengthen $\mu(v)$, the set of reachable states represented by v, as the set of concrete states in $\gamma_I(S_H^{\mathcal{D}})$, which provides a tighter bound on the initial states for the subtasks represented by the outgoing edges from v. If v is the final vertex v_f and v has outgoing edges that induce a cycle (via the **repeat** operator), we launch a separate round of Dijkstra's algorithm to find the least-cost cycle back to v_f within the strongly connected component of G that includes v_f at line 20. We construct the path policy that satisfies the full task specification at line 21 by first reaching v_f using policies along the shortest path from v_0 to v_f and then combining policies along the shortest cycle back to v_f. The algorithm returns the policy and its cost in line 22. Similarly, for non-repetitive specifications, when v is the final vertex, we simply return the path policy from v_0 to v_f (line 25).

3.3   Provably Correct Edge Policy Synthesis

We introduce the TRAINVERIFY procedure to train an edge policy π_e that is formally verified with respect to the subtask specification $\mathcal{T}_e : \mu(u) \rightsquigarrow \mu(v) \mid \beta(e)$ for an abstract reachability graph edge $e : u \to v$, where $\mu(u)$ and $\mu(v)$ define the initial and target state space regions and $\beta(e)$ represents a safety constraint. TRAINVERIFY is outlined in Algorithm 2.

We first employ an arbitrary deep RL algorithm to train a neural network policy, π_{NN}, for task $\mathcal{T}_e$ using a reward function derived from the specification of $\mathcal{T}_e$. Intuitively, trajectories that satisfy the given specification will receive higher rewards than those that do not, steering the policy toward behaviors that effectively fulfill the task requirements. The following definition introduces a standard approach to quantitatively evaluate the predicates defined in Definition 1, allowing for a continuous predicate evaluation:

Definition 7 (State Correctness Loss Function). *For a predicate φ (Definition 1) over states $s \in S$, we define a non-negative loss function $\mathcal{L}(s, \varphi)$ such that $\mathcal{L}(s, \varphi) = 0$ iff s satisfies φ, i.e. $s \models \varphi$. We define $\mathcal{L}(s, \varphi)$ recursively, based on the possible shapes of φ:*

- $\mathcal{L}(s, \mathcal{A} \cdot x \leq b) := \max(\mathcal{A} \cdot s - b, 0)$
- $\mathcal{L}(s, \varphi_1 \wedge \varphi_2) := \max(\mathcal{L}(s, \varphi_1), \mathcal{L}(s, \varphi_2))$
- $\mathcal{L}(s, \varphi_1 \vee \varphi_2) := \min(\mathcal{L}(s, \varphi_1), \mathcal{L}(s, \varphi_2))$

Notice that $\mathcal{L}(s, \varphi_1 \wedge \varphi_2) = 0$ iff $\mathcal{L}(s, \varphi_1) = 0$ and $\mathcal{L}(s, \varphi_2) = 0$, and similarly $\mathcal{L}(\varphi_1 \vee \varphi_2) = 0$ iff $\mathcal{L}(\varphi_1) = 0$ or $\mathcal{L}(\varphi_2) = 0$.

The non-negative loss function $\mathcal{L}(s, \varphi)$ quantifies how much the state s violates the predicate φ. A larger loss indicates that the state is farther from the region defined by the predicate in the state space. The reward function for $\mathcal{T}_e$ is defined as:

$$R(s, a) = c_1 \cdot \mathcal{L}(s, \mu(v)) + c_2 \cdot \mathcal{L}(s, \beta(e))$$

for any state $s \in S$ and action $a \in A$. Here, c_1 and c_2 are negative constants. We train π_{NN} to maximize the discounted cumulative reward[2]:

$$\pi_{NN} = \arg\max_{\pi} \mathbb{E}_{s_0 \models \mu(u), s_0, a_0, s_1, \dots \sim M[s_0, \pi]} \left[\sum_{t=0}^{T} \kappa^t R(s_t, a_t) \right] \tag{4}$$

where $\kappa \in [0, 1]$ is the discount factor. Once training converges, the horizon H for the subtask $\mathcal{T}_e$, which ensures a safe rollout from any state in $\mu(u)$ to a state in $\mu(v)$, can be estimated based on evaluation episodes using the policy π_{NN}.

Principally, we can verify $M[\pi_{NN}]$ against the specification $\mathcal{T}_e$ with rollout length H using Definition 6. However, reachability analysis for closed-loop systems controlled by neural networks remains a major challenge [25], and neural network policies trained merely from reward signals often fail to satisfy formal specifications. For example, in Fig. 6a, in the 9Rooms environment, a trained π_{NN} agent for the edge policy from Room$_{2,2}$ to Room$_{3,2}$ fails to complete the loop and instead collides with the wall. To address this, following prior work [56,57], we distill π_{NN} to a time-varying linear policy that is as similar as possible to π_{NN}. Importantly, this process ensures that the time-varying linear policy can be formally verified concerning the subtask $\mathcal{T}_e$. A time-varying linear policy can provide an accurate local approximation of a neural controller at each timestep (if the timestep is small) and incur a much-reduced verification cost owing to the linearity of the representation. A time-varying policy $\pi_\theta(s, t)$ with trainable parameters θ for a time horizon H ($0 \le t < H$) can be expressed mathematically as

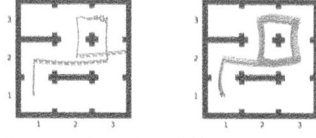

(a) π_{NN} trajectories   (b) π_θ trajectories

Fig. 6. Policy behavior in 9Rooms. π_θ is a verified distillation of π_{NN}.

$$\pi_\theta(s, t) = \theta_w(t)^T \cdot s + \theta_b(t) \tag{5}$$

where $\theta_w(t)$ and $\theta_b(t)$ are the time-varying gain matrix and bias. During execution within the time horizon H, the policy $\pi_\theta(s, t)$ iteratively generates the control input at timestep t when observing the current state s at t. The objective of distilling π_{NN} into a time-varying linear policy π_θ is

$$\theta^* = \arg\min_{\theta} \mathbb{E}_{s_0, s_1, \dots, s_H \sim M[\pi_{NN}]} ||\pi_\theta(s_t, t) - \pi_{NN}(s_t)||_2$$
$$\text{subject to } Verify(\pi_\theta, \mathcal{T}_e) \text{ is true} \tag{6}$$

where $|| \cdot ||_2$ is L_2 norm and the VERIFY procedure returns true if and only if π_θ satisfies the subtask specification $\mathcal{T}_e$ according to Definition 6. In our implementation of the VERIFY procedure, per Definition 6, the abstract interpreter $F^{\mathcal{D}}$ uses Taylor Model (TM) flowpipes as the abstract domain $\mathcal{D}$. For reachability analysis of $M[\pi_\theta]$, at each timestep t (where $t > 0$), we get the TM flowpipe $S_t^{\mathcal{D}}$

---

[2] By constraining the predicate $\mu(u)$ on each vertex u to a verified interval of reachable states (line 17 in Algorithm 1), edge policy training for outgoing edges from u can uniformly sample initial states s_0 from this interval.

Algorithm 2. Train a verified edge policy π_θ for an abstract reachability graph edge $e : u \to v$ such that $\pi_\theta \models \mathcal{T}_e : \mu(u) \rightsquigarrow \mu(v) \mid \beta(e)$.

1: **procedure** TRAINVERIFY$(M[\cdot], \mathcal{T}_e : \mu(u) \rightsquigarrow \mu(v) \mid \beta(e))$
2:    Train a neural network controller π_{NN} for $\mathcal{T}_e$ via Equation 4
3:    Estimate the horizon H for task $\mathcal{T}_e$ through sampling
4:    Initialize a time-varying linear policy π_θ over H timesteps via Equation 5
5:    Learn a *formally verified* π_θ for $\mathcal{T}_e$ that approximates π_{NN} via Equation 6
6:    $S_0^{\mathcal{D}}, \ldots, S_H^{\mathcal{D}} \leftarrow \text{REACHSET}(\pi_\theta, \mu(u), H)$ ▷ Definition 6
7:    **return** $\pi_\theta, H, S_H^{\mathcal{D}}$

---

for the reachable set of states of $M[\pi_\theta]$ at timestep $t - 1$. To obtain a TM representation for the output set of the time-varying linear policy π_θ at timestep t, we use TM arithmetic to evaluate a TM flowpipe $A_t^{\mathcal{D}}$ for $\pi_\theta(s, t) = \theta_w(t)^T \cdot s + \theta_b(t)$ for all states $s \in \gamma(S_t^{\mathcal{D}})$. The resulting TM representation $A_t^{\mathcal{D}}$ can be viewed as an overapproximation of the policy's output at timestep t. Finally, we construct the TM flowpipe overapproximation $S_{t+1}^{\mathcal{D}}$ for all reachable states at timestep t by reachability analysis over the state transition function $F^{\mathcal{D}}(S_t^{\mathcal{D}}, A_t^{\mathcal{D}})$. We use existing work [57] to solve the optimization task in Eq. 6. Intuitively, this method employs Lagrangian optimization to integrate the verification constraint into the distillation objective, effectively minimizing both the L^2 loss for distillation and the violation of the verification constraint. The latter quantifies the violation of the safety or reachability property in the worst case across all concrete states subsumed by a symbolic state $S_t^{\mathcal{D}}$. For completeness, we provide a detailed explanation of this procedure based on [57] in the extended version [58]. For example, in Fig. 6, the distilled policy π_θ from π_{NN} can be formally verified to navigate the four rooms in an infinite circular sequence.

Corollary 1 (Algorithm 2 Soundness). *Given an environment model $M[\cdot]$, an edge policy specification $\mathcal{T}_e : \mu(u) \rightsquigarrow \mu(v) \mid \beta(e)$, if TRAINVERIFY returns $(\pi_\theta, H, S_H^{\mathcal{D}})$, we have $\pi_\theta \models \mathcal{T}_e$. On the symbolic rollout $\zeta^{\mathcal{D}} = S_0^{\mathcal{D}}, S_1^{\mathcal{D}}, \ldots, S_H^{\mathcal{D}}$ of $M[\pi_\theta]$, we have $\forall 0 \le t < H \wedge s \in \gamma_I(S_t^{\mathcal{D}}), \; s \models \beta(e)$, and $\forall s \in \gamma_I(S_H^{\mathcal{D}}), \; s \models \mu(v)$.*

4   Experiments

We provide an implementation of our framework, VEL-∞[3], and evaluate it on a set of challenging environments with continuous state and action spaces and infinite-horizon specifications. For neural network policy learning, we use Soft Actor-Critic (SAC) [16], a state-of-the-art deep RL algorithm. We implemented the abstract interpreter for verifying time-varying linear policies on top of Flow* [7], which uses Taylor-Model flowpipes as the abstract domain.

Baselines. We compare VEL-∞ with five baselines: DIRL [27], LCER [54], CyclER [46], TLTL [32], and BHNR [2]. Similar to our approach, DIRL uses the

---
[3] VEL-∞ is available at https://github.com/RU-Automated-Reasoning-Group/VEL-inf.

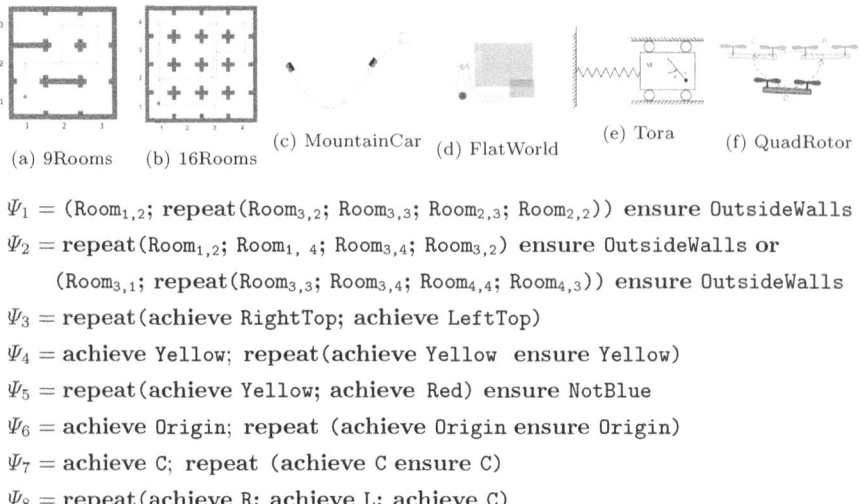

(a) 9Rooms   (b) 16Rooms   (c) MountainCar   (d) FlatWorld   (e) Tora   (f) QuadRotor

$\Psi_1 = $ (Room$_{1,2}$; repeat(Room$_{3,2}$; Room$_{3,3}$; Room$_{2,3}$; Room$_{2,2}$)) ensure OutsideWalls

$\Psi_2 = $ repeat(Room$_{1,2}$; Room$_{1,4}$; Room$_{3,4}$; Room$_{3,2}$) ensure OutsideWalls or

    (Room$_{3,1}$; repeat(Room$_{3,3}$; Room$_{3,4}$; Room$_{4,4}$; Room$_{4,3}$)) ensure OutsideWalls

$\Psi_3 = $ repeat(achieve RightTop; achieve LeftTop)

$\Psi_4 = $ achieve Yellow; repeat(achieve Yellow ensure Yellow)

$\Psi_5 = $ repeat(achieve Yellow; achieve Red) ensure NotBlue

$\Psi_6 = $ achieve Origin; repeat (achieve Origin ensure Origin)

$\Psi_7 = $ achieve C; repeat (achieve C ensure C)

$\Psi_8 = $ repeat(achieve R; achieve L; achieve C)

Fig. 7. Environments and Task Specifications. The predicates Room$_{x,y}$ and OutsideWalls are defined in Example 2. LeftTop and RightTop represent states at the left and right peaks of the mountain, respectively. The predicates Yellow, Red, and NotBlue correspond to regions that are yellow, red, and any color other than blue. Origin denotes the equilibrium state in the TORA environment. For the QuadRotor benchmark, L, R, and C specify three designated positions.

abstract reachability graph to decompose the specification and train the edge policies for each subtask. These edge policies are combined to address the full specification. However, DIRL does not provide any formal guarantee regarding the quality of generated controllers and it does not support infinite-horizon task specifications. In our experiments, we unroll repetitive specifications using the **repeat** operator five times for DIRL and reuse the edge policies as needed beyond this limit during evaluation. Another baseline, LCER, is a state-of-the-art RL algorithm for LTL specifications. LCER uses eventual discounting [54] to optimize a proxy value function that approximates the probability of satisfying a specified LTL formula and uses counterfactual experience replay to improve sample efficiency. We translate our specifications to LTL for LCER in our experiments. CyclER is a novel reward shaping technique that exploits the underlying structure of the LTL constraint to guide policy learning and combine it with quantitative semantics (QS) [32] in LTL reward shaping. TLTL and BHNR also use quantitative semantics for reward shaping and are computable for infinite-horizon LTL tasks.

Benchmarks. We use benchmarks considered in related works, visualized in Fig. 7. The 9Rooms environment and task specification Ψ_1, adapted from [61], were introduced in Example 2 and illustrated in Fig. 2. To explore more complex specifications, we designed a 16Rooms environment, where task Ψ_2 requires the

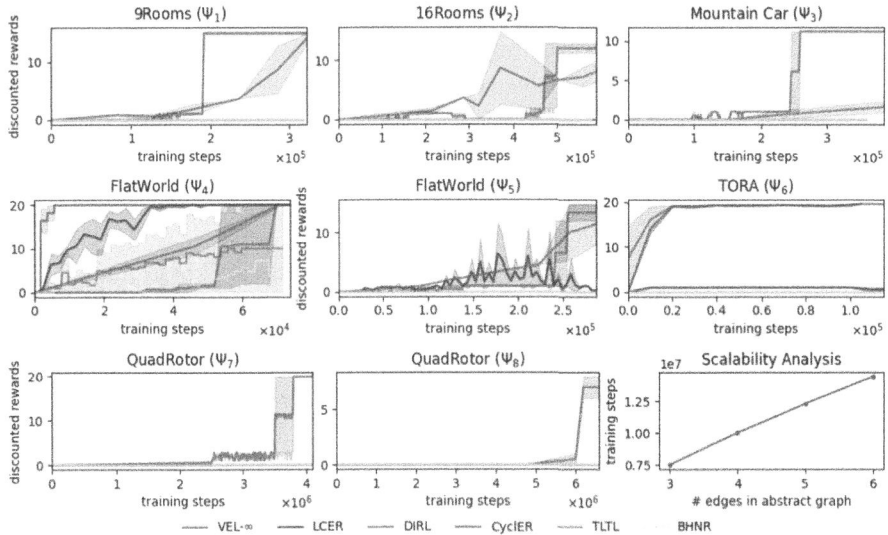

Fig. 8. Cumulative rewards under eventual discounting [54] *evaluated* over 5 seeds. A reward of 1 is given for each visit to final vertices or accepting states.

agent to traverse a circular path indefinitely via one of two possible routes, represented by dashed arrows in Fig. 7b. The MountainCar environment, a classic nonlinear control problem from [35], follows task specification Ψ_3, where the agent must repeatedly drive back and forth in the valley. In the FlatWorld environment, adapted from [54], tasks Ψ_4 and Ψ_5 involve stabilizing in the yellow region and oscillating between the yellow and red regions, respectively, while avoiding the blue region. The TORA environment [23] simulates a cart connected to a wall by a spring, with the task specification Ψ_6 requiring stabilization around the origin infinitely. The QuadRotor benchmark, adapted from [60], tasks a simulated 2D quadrotor with stabilizing at the equilibrium state $[x, y, \theta, \dot{x}, \dot{y}, \dot{\theta}] = 0$ in Ψ_7 and continuously navigating between three locations in a triangular pattern in Ψ_8. MountainCar, TORA and QuadRotor are nonlinear environments.

Results. Fig. 8 illustrates the learning performance throughout training for each benchmark, comparing VEL-∞ and the baselines. The x-axis shows environment steps, and the y-axis represents mean cumulative rewards under eventual discounting [54] for the intermediate policies evaluated. The shaded region indicates the standard deviation. VEL-∞ learned policies that are guaranteed correct for all these tasks. Computing the exact satisfaction probability (for the baseline models) over infinite horizons is an open problem. Eventually discounted return provides a proxy to the likelihood of task satisfaction [54]. It counts visits to final vertices in VEL-∞ and DIRL, and accepting states in the limit-deterministic Büchi automata of LTL formulas in the other baselines, assigning a reward of 1 per visit, with future visits discounted by $\gamma = 0.95$. We remark that this discounting schema is solely used for *evaluation* in VEL-∞. VEL-∞ demonstrates the highest sample efficiency across all benchmarks, except for FlatWorld (Ψ_4). Notably, in Fig. 8, VEL-∞'s training curve remains flat until the final edge policy is trained, after which its performance rapidly surpasses all other approaches to completely solve the tasks. DIRL is significantly less sample-efficient on our benchmarks, requiring an order of magnitude more samples during training compared to VEL-∞. Recall that repetitive specifications using the **repeat** operator are unrolled in DIRL. It must repeatedly learn new policies for similar tasks, whereas VEL-∞'s "train-and-verify" approach enables policy reuse with formal guarantees. LCER's low performance in our benchmarks may stem from its limited ability to utilize the structure of temporal logic properties during training. This challenge is particularly evident in the 9Rooms and 16Rooms environments, where the agent must accomplish several intermediate tasks before receiving any reward. Methods that do not account for task structures may find it harder to make steady progress in such settings. CyclER, TLTL, and BHNR show limited progress in our benchmarks, even though they utilize shaped rewards derived from the quantitative semantics of the given LTL formulas. These methods struggle with infinite-horizon tasks that involve multiple unordered subgoals, often leading to behaviors that optimize their respective QS-shaped LTL rewards without ensuring task completion. In contrast, VEL-∞ successfully achieves task satisfaction by explicitly decomposing temporal logic properties and synthesizing edge policies that guarantee correct composition for execution over infinite horizons. The strong performance of VEL-∞ in these benchmarks highlights the importance of synthesizing formally verified policies (with inductive invariants) within our framework. In the extended version of the paper [58], we report the average number of visits to final vertices (or accepting states) by trained policies at convergence for each benchmark. These results highlight that, unlike VEL-∞, the baselines lack formal correctness guarantees and often fail to produce policies that ensure infinite execution required by temporal reach-avoid specifications.

Scalability Analysis. We conduct a case study using QuadRotor to explore how VEL-∞ scales with increasing task specification complexity. We define specifications that require varying numbers of edge policies based on the QuadRotor configurations shown in Fig. 9. For a specification involving x edges in the repeat cycle, the quadrotor starts at state A, moves counterclockwise for $x - 1$ hops, and returns to A in the final edge. For example, when $x = 4$, the task specification

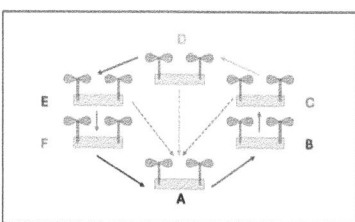

Fig. 9. Quadrotor configuration for the scalability case study.

is: **repeat** (**achieve** A; **achieve** B; **achieve** C; **achieve** D). The bottom-right plot in Fig. 8 shows the training timesteps required for each specification for $x = 3, 4, 5, 6$ *resp.* Our results show that the number of environment steps required for convergence by VEL-∞ increases linearly with the number of edge policies in the abstract reachability graph for a given specification.

5   Related Work

Verification in RL. RL has shown great potential in automatically acquiring new intelligent skills. However, verifying policies trained with RL algorithms to ensure their correctness and other desired properties is crucial before deployment, especially in safety-critical domains [17,48]. Some prior works, such as NNV, ReachNN*, and Verisig, have conducted reachability analysis to verify neural network-controlled systems [11,13,22,49,51]. However, these approaches verify the policies only after training is complete and do not use the verification results to improve the policy. Other works interleave policy training and verification by employing the idea of counterexample-guided abstraction and refinement or by optimizing for worst-case specification violation loss [24,56]. Policies learned together with reach-avoid supermartingales provide probabilistic guarantees of satisfying specifications [10,61]. In contrast, VEL-∞ supports synthesizing formally verified policies for temporal reach-avoid tasks.

RL for Temporal Logic Specifications. Linear Temporal Logic (LTL) has been widely adopted for specifying complex user behaviors [54]. A range of methods based on Q-learning have been developed to synthesize policies that satisfy LTL specifications, particularly in environments with discrete action spaces [4,47]. Other approaches aim to directly optimize the probability of satisfying LTL formulas [5,6,18,46,54], typically by guiding the agent toward accepting states in corresponding Büchi automata. To address the sparse reward issue that often arises in this setting, some of these methods incorporate experience replay to improve sample efficiency [54,55]. VEL-∞ takes a different approach by using abstract reachability graphs (Sect. 3.1) instead of Büchi automata for encoding specifications. Abstract reachability graphs provide a more structured and compositional representation at the subtask level, where each edge corresponds to a meaningful subtask from a precondition (source node) to a postcondition (target node). In contrast, Büchi automata operate at a lower level. For example, consider the LTL formula $F(\varphi_1 \wedge XF\varphi_2)$, which implies two sequential subtasks: first, reaching states that satisfy φ_1, and then proceeding to states that satisfy φ_2. In a Büchi automaton, the system often remains in the state corresponding to the satisfaction of φ_1 while attempting to reach φ_2, without explicitly encoding the completion of the first subtask or the initiation of the second. This makes it difficult to infer clear subtask boundaries and their associated preconditions and postconditions. VEL-∞ overcomes this limitation by organizing specifications through abstract reachability graphs, which naturally align with subtask-based reasoning and support more tractable verification and synthesis procedures. Truncated Linear Temporal Logic (TLTL) [32] and Bounded Horizon Nominal Robustness (BHNR) [2] use the quantitative semantics of temporal logic to define a reward function that encodes the intended agent behavior, enabling RL algorithms to learn policies from it [2,32]. Such reward functions can be challenging for RL algorithms to maximize in complex, long-horizon task specifications. There exists work that instructs agents in multi-task settings to follow instructions in the LTL task space [40,53]. These methods do not provide formal guarantees for temporal property satisfaction.

Controller Synthesis for LTL Objectives. Traditional controller synthesis algorithms, particularly those grounded in formal methods and temporal logic, often rely on automata-based approaches [12,14,15,28,30,36,38,52,59]. These techniques require abstraction and discretization [3,19,29,31,34,41–44], approximating continuous state and action spaces using finite-state models or grid-based representations. Once a discrete abstraction is constructed, standard synthesis algorithms for discrete systems can be applied. While such methods provide formal correctness guarantees, they face significant scalability challenges in high-dimensional or complex robotic systems due to issues like state explosion introduced by discretization. There are other LTL fragments, such as GR(1) [37] and GXW [8] that have been considered in the literature with favorable computational properties. Both GR(1) and GXW synthesis are formulated for discrete state and action spaces, typically in reactive synthesis for controllers. When applied to continuous systems, they require a finite abstraction step [59]. The LTL fragment VEL-∞ supports (for infinite-horizon temporal reach-avoid objectives) and GR(1)/GXW are incomparable. Based on RL, VEL-∞ is a controller learning algorithm that operates directly in continuous environments, avoiding the need for state discretization. This enables improved scalability in high-dimensional settings. Although RL methods generally lack formal guarantees of correctness, VEL-∞ addresses this limitation by incorporating verification mechanisms to formally certify the correctness of learned controllers.

6   Conclusion

We introduced VEL-∞, a deductive synthesis framework for RL agents that guarantees satisfaction of temporal reach-avoid properties over infinite horizons. VEL-∞ systematically decomposes these temporal objectives into finite subtasks while ensuring they can be composed and executed reliably over infinite time. Experimental results demonstrate that by combining the strengths of deductive reasoning with RL, VEL-∞ outperforms existing RL-based methods in both learning efficiency and adherence to formal specifications.

Limitations. VEL-∞ supports a limited fragment of LTL focused on temporal reach-avoid properties (Sect. 2), which can be naturally translated into abstract reachability graphs (Sect. 3.1) for efficient controller synthesis and verification. Extending VEL-∞ to handle general infinite-horizon LTL specifications remains an important direction for future work. Another main limitation of VEL-∞ is its reliance on an explicit environment model and sure property satisfaction. It requires a known model of the environment for reachability analysis, which may not scale to complex dynamics. Future work should focus on relaxing these assumptions by incorporating learned models and using probabilistic analysis to evaluate edge policies and their composition.

References

1. Alur, R.: Formal verification of hybrid systems. In: Chakraborty, S., Jerraya, A., Baruah, S.K., Fischmeister, S. (eds.) Proceedings of the 11th International Conference on Embedded Software, EMSOFT 2011, part of the Seventh Embedded Systems Week, ESWeek 2011, Taipei, Taiwan, October 9-14, 2011, pp. 273–278. ACM (2011)
2. Balakrishnan, A., Deshmukh, J.V.: Structured reward shaping using signal temporal logic specifications. In: 2019 IEEE/RSJ International Conference on Intelligent Robots and Systems (IROS), pp. 3481–3486 (2019)
3. Belta, C., Sadraddini, S.: Formal methods for control synthesis: an optimization perspective. Annu. Rev. Control. Robotics Auton. Syst. **2**, 115–140 (2019)
4. Bozkurt, A.K., Wang, Y., Zavlanos, M.M., Pajic, M.: Control synthesis from linear temporal logic specifications using model-free reinforcement learning. In: 2020 IEEE International Conference on Robotics and Automation, ICRA 2020, Paris, France, May 31 - August 31, 2020, pp. 10349–10355. IEEE (2020)
5. Cai, M., Hasanbeig, M., Xiao, S., Abate, A., Kan, Z.: Modular deep reinforcement learning for continuous motion planning with temporal logic. IEEE Robot. Autom. Lett. **6**(4), 7973–7980 (2021)
6. Camacho, A., Icarte, R.T., Klassen, T.Q., Valenzano, R., McIlraith, S.A.: LTL and beyond: Formal languages for reward function specification in reinforcement learning. In: Proceedings of the Twenty-Eighth International Joint Conference on Artificial Intelligence (IJCAI-19), pp. 6065–6073. International Joint Conferences on Artificial Intelligence Organization (2019)
7. Chen, X., Ábrahám, E., Sankaranarayanan, S.: Flow*: an analyzer for non-linear hybrid systems. In: Sharygina, N., Veith, H. (eds.) CAV 2013. LNCS, vol. 8044, pp. 258–263. Springer, Heidelberg (2013). https://doi.org/10.1007/978-3-642-39799-8_18
8. Cheng, C.-H., Hamza, Y., Ruess, H.: Structural synthesis for GXW specifications. In: Chaudhuri, S., Farzan, A. (eds.) CAV 2016. LNCS, vol. 9779, pp. 95–117. Springer, Cham (2016). https://doi.org/10.1007/978-3-319-41528-4_6
9. Daafouz, J., Riedinger, P., Iung, C.: Stability analysis and control synthesis for switched systems: a switched Lyapunov function approach. IEEE Trans. Autom. Control **47**(11), 1883–1887 (2002)
10. Delgrange, F., Avni, G., Lukina, A., Schilling, C., Nowé, A., Pérez, G.A.: Synthesis of hierarchical controllers based on deep reinforcement learning policies. CoRR abs/2402.13785 (2024)
11. Dutta, S., Chen, X., Sankaranarayanan, S.: Reachability analysis for neural feedback systems using regressive polynomial rule inference. In: Ozay, N., Prabhakar, P. (eds.) Proceedings of the 22nd ACM International Conference on Hybrid Systems: Computation and Control, HSCC 2019, Montreal, QC, Canada, April 16-18, 2019, pp. 157–168. ACM (2019)
12. Fainekos, G.E., Girard, A., Kress-Gazit, H., Pappas, G.J.: Temporal logic motion planning for dynamic robots. Autom. **45**(2), 343–352 (2009)
13. Fan, J., Huang, C., Chen, X., Li, W., Zhu, Q.: ReachNN*: a tool for reachability analysis of neural-network controlled systems. In: Hung, D.V., Sokolsky, O. (eds.) ATVA 2020. LNCS, vol. 12302, pp. 537–542. Springer, Cham (2020). https://doi.org/10.1007/978-3-030-59152-6_30
14. Girard, A.: Controller synthesis for safety and reachability via approximate bisimulation. CoRR abs/1010.4672 (2010)

15. Girard, A., Pappas, G.J.: Approximation metrics for discrete and continuous systems. IEEE Trans. Autom. Control **52**(5), 782–798 (2007)
16. Haarnoja, T., Zhou, A., Abbeel, P., Levine, S.: Soft actor-critic: off-policy maximum entropy deep reinforcement learning with a stochastic actor (2018). https://arxiv.org/abs/1801.01290
17. Hasanbeig, M., Kroening, D., Abate, A.: Towards verifiable and safe model-free reinforcement learning. In: CEUR Workshop Proceedings, vol. 2509 (2020)
18. Hasanbeig, M., Kroening, D., Abate, A.: Deep reinforcement learning with temporal logics. In: Bertrand, N., Jansen, N. (eds.) FORMATS 2020. LNCS, vol. 12288, pp. 1–22. Springer, Cham (2020). https://doi.org/10.1007/978-3-030-57628-8_1
19. Hsu, K., Majumdar, R., Mallik, K., Schmuck, A.: Lazy abstraction-based control for safety specifications. In: 57th IEEE Conference on Decision and Control, CDC 2018, Miami, FL, USA, December 17-19, 2018, pp. 4902–4907. IEEE (2018)
20. Icarte, R.T., Klassen, T.Q., Valenzano, R., McIlraith, S.A.: Reward machines: exploiting reward function structure in reinforcement learning. J. Artif. Intell. Res. **73**, 173–208 (2022)
21. Icarte, R.T., Klassen, T.Q., Valenzano, R.A., McIlraith, S.A.: Using reward machines for high-level task specification and decomposition in reinforcement learning. In: Dy, J.G., Krause, A. (eds.) Proceedings of the 35th International Conference on Machine Learning, ICML 2018, Stockholmsmässan, Stockholm, Sweden, July 10-15, 2018. Proceedings of Machine Learning Research, vol. 80, pp. 2112–2121. PMLR (2018)
22. Ivanov, R., Weimer, J., Alur, R., Pappas, G.J., Lee, I.: Verisig: verifying safety properties of hybrid systems with neural network controllers. In: Ozay, N., Prabhakar, P. (eds.) Proceedings of the 22nd ACM International Conference on Hybrid Systems: Computation and Control, HSCC 2019, Montreal, QC, Canada, April 16-18, 2019, pp. 169–178. ACM (2019)
23. Jankovic, M., Fontaine, D., Kokotovic, P.V.: Tora example: cascade- and passivity-based control designs. IEEE Trans. Control Syst. Technol. **4**(3), 292–297 (1996)
24. Jin, P., Tian, J., Zhi, D., Wen, X., Zhang, M.: TRAINIFY: A CEGAR-driven training and verification framework for safe deep reinforcement learning. In: Shoham, S., Vizel, Y. (eds.) Computer Aided Verification, pp. 193–218. Springer International Publishing, Cham (2022). https://doi.org/10.1007/978-3-031-13185-1_10
25. Johnson, T.T., et al.: ARCH-COMP21 category report: Artificial intelligence and neural network control systems (AINNCS) for continuous and hybrid systems plants. In: Frehse, G., Althoff, M. (eds.) 8th International Workshop on Applied Verification of Continuous and Hybrid Systems (ARCH21), Brussels, Belgium, July 9, 2021. EPiC Series in Computing, vol. 80, pp. 90–119. EasyChair (2021)
26. Jothimurugan, K., Alur, R., Bastani, O.: A Composable Specification Language for Reinforcement Learning Tasks. Curran Associates Inc., Red Hook, NY, USA (2019)
27. Jothimurugan, K., Bansal, S., Bastani, O., Alur, R.: Compositional reinforcement learning from logical specifications. In: Proceedings of the 35th International Conference on Neural Information Processing Systems. NIPS 2021, Curran Associates Inc., Red Hook, NY, USA (2024)
28. Mazo, M., Davitian, A., Tabuada, P.: PESSOA: a tool for embedded controller synthesis. In: Touili, T., Cook, B., Jackson, P. (eds.) CAV 2010. LNCS, vol. 6174, pp. 566–569. Springer, Heidelberg (2010). https://doi.org/10.1007/978-3-642-14295-6_49
29. Kim, E.S., Arcak, M., Seshia, S.A.: Symbolic control design for monotone systems with directed specifications. Autom. **83**, 10–19 (2017)

30. Kress-Gazit, H., Fainekos, G.E., Pappas, G.J.: Temporal-logic-based reactive mission and motion planning. IEEE Trans. Robot. **25**(6), 1370–1381 (2009)

31. Kurtz, V., Lin, H.: Temporal logic motion planning with convex optimization via graphs of convex sets. IEEE Trans. Robot. **39**(5), 3791–3804 (2023)

32. Li, X., Vasile, C.I., Belta, C.: Reinforcement learning with temporal logic rewards. In: 2017 IEEE/RSJ International Conference on Intelligent Robots and Systems (IROS), pp. 3834–3839 (2017)

33. Mania, H., Guy, A., Recht, B.: Simple random search provides a competitive approach to reinforcement learning (2018). https://arxiv.org/abs/1803.07055

34. Meyer, P., Dimarogonas, D.V.: Hierarchical decomposition of LTL synthesis problem for nonlinear control systems. IEEE Trans. Autom. Control **64**(11), 4676–4683 (2019)

35. Moore, A.W.: Efficient Memory-Based Learning for Robot Control. University of Cambridge, Tech. rep. (1990)

36. Mouelhi, S., Girard, A., Gößler, G.: CoSyMA: a tool for controller synthesis using multi-scale abstractions. In: Belta, C., Ivancic, F. (eds.) Proceedings of the 16th international conference on Hybrid systems: computation and control, HSCC 2013, April 8-11, 2013, Philadelphia, PA, USA, pp. 83–88. ACM (2013)

37. Piterman, N., Pnueli, A., Sa'ar, Y.: Synthesis of reactive(1) designs. In: Emerson, E.A., Namjoshi, K.S. (eds.) VMCAI 2006. LNCS, vol. 3855, pp. 364–380. Springer, Heidelberg (2005). https://doi.org/10.1007/11609773_24

38. Pola, G., Girard, A., Tabuada, P.: Approximately bisimilar symbolic models for nonlinear control systems. Autom. **44**(10), 2508–2516 (2008)

39. Prajna, S., Jadbabaie, A.: Safety verification of hybrid systems using barrier certificates. In: Alur, R., Pappas, G.J. (eds.) HSCC 2004. LNCS, vol. 2993, pp. 477–492. Springer, Heidelberg (2004). https://doi.org/10.1007/978-3-540-24743-2_32

40. Qiu, W., Mao, W., Zhu, H.: Instructing goal-conditioned reinforcement learning agents with temporal logic objectives. In: Thirty-seventh Conference on Neural Information Processing Systems (2023)

41. Reissig, G., Weber, A., Rungger, M.: Feedback refinement relations for the synthesis of symbolic controllers. IEEE Trans. Autom. Control **62**(4), 1781–1796 (2017)

42. Ren, W., Dimarogonas, D.V.: Logarithmic quantization based symbolic abstractions for nonlinear control systems. In: 17th European Control Conference, ECC 2019, Naples, Italy, June 25-28, 2019, pp. 1312–1317. IEEE (2019)

43. Ren, W., Jungers, R.M., Dimarogonas, D.V.: Zonotope-based symbolic controller synthesis for linear temporal logic specifications. IEEE Trans. Autom. Control **69**(11), 7630–7645 (2024)

44. Rungger, M., Zamani, M.: SCOTS: A tool for the synthesis of symbolic controllers. In: Abate, A., Fainekos, G. (eds.) Proceedings of the 19th International Conference on Hybrid Systems: Computation and Control, HSCC 2016, Vienna, Austria, April 12-14, 2016, pp. 99–104. ACM (2016)

45. Schulman, J., Wolski, F., Dhariwal, P., Radford, A., Klimov, O.: Proximal policy optimization algorithms (2017). https://arxiv.org/abs/1707.06347

46. Shah, A., Voloshin, C., Yang, C., Verma, A., Chaudhuri, S., Seshia, S.A.: LTL-constrained policy optimization with cycle experience replay (2024). https://arxiv.org/abs/2404.11578

47. Shao, D., Kwiatkowska, M.: Sample efficient model-free reinforcement learning from LTL specifications with optimality guarantees. In: Proceedings of the Thirty-Second International Joint Conference on Artificial Intelligence, IJCAI 2023, 19th-25th August 2023, Macao, SAR, China pp. 4180–4189. ijcai.org (2023)

48. Srinivasan, K., Eysenbach, B., Ha, S., Tan, J., Finn, C.: Learning to be safe: deep RL with a safety critic (2020). https://arxiv.org/abs/2010.14603
49. Sun, X., Khedr, H., Shoukry, Y.: Formal verification of neural network controlled autonomous systems. In: Ozay, N., Prabhakar, P. (eds.) Proceedings of the 22nd ACM International Conference on Hybrid Systems: Computation and Control, HSCC 2019, Montreal, QC, Canada, April 16-18, 2019 pp. 147–156. ACM (2019)
50. Tedrake, R., Manchester, I.R., Tobenkin, M.M., Roberts, J.W.: LQR-trees: feedback motion planning via sums-of-squares verification. Int. J. Robot. Res. **29**(8), 1038–1052 (2010)
51. Tran, H.-D., et al.: NNV: the neural network verification tool for deep neural networks and learning-enabled cyber-physical systems. In: Lahiri, S.K., Wang, C. (eds.) CAV 2020. LNCS, vol. 12224, pp. 3–17. Springer, Cham (2020). https://doi.org/10.1007/978-3-030-53288-8_1
52. Tumova, J., Yordanov, B., Belta, C., Cerna, I., Barnat, J.: A symbolic approach to controlling piecewise affine systems. In: Proceedings of the 49th IEEE Conference on Decision and Control, CDC 2010, December 15-17, 2010, Atlanta, Georgia, USA, pp. 4230–4235. IEEE (2010)
53. Vaezipoor, P., Li, A.C., Icarte, R.T., McIlraith, S.A.: Ltl2action: Generalizing LTL instructions for multi-task RL. In: Proceedings of the 38th International Conference on Machine Learning (ICML), vol. 139, pp. 10497–10508. Proceedings of Machine Learning Research (2021)
54. Voloshin, C., Verma, A., Yue, Y.: Eventual discounting temporal logic counterfactual experience replay. In: Krause, A., Brunskill, E., Cho, K., Engelhardt, B., Sabato, S., Scarlett, J. (eds.) International Conference on Machine Learning, ICML 2023, 23-29 July 2023, Honolulu, Hawaii, USA. Proceedings of Machine Learning Research, vol. 202, pp. 35137–35150. PMLR (2023)
55. Wang, C., Li, Y., Smith, S.L., Liu, J.: Continuous motion planning with temporal logic specifications using deep neural networks (2020). https://arxiv.org/abs/2004.02610
56. Wang, Y., Zhu, H.: Verification-guided programmatic controller synthesis. In: Sankaranarayanan, S., Sharygina, N. (eds.) Tools and Algorithms for the Construction and Analysis of Systems, pp. 229–250. Springer Nature Switzerland, Cham (2023). https://doi.org/10.1007/978-3-031-30820-8_16
57. Wang, Y., Zhu, H.: Safe exploration in reinforcement learning by reachability analysis over learned models. In: Gurfinkel, A., Ganesh, V. (eds.) Computer Aided Verification, pp. 232–255. Springer Nature Switzerland, Cham (2024). https://doi.org/10.1007/978-3-031-65633-0_11
58. Wang, Y., Zhu, H.: Deductive synthesis of reinforcement learning agents for ω-regular properties (extended version) (2025). https://github.com/RU-Automated-Reasoning-Group/VEL-inf/blob/main/VEL-inf_extended.pdf
59. Wongpiromsarn, T., Topcu, U., Ozay, N., Xu, H., Murray, R.M.: Tulip: a software toolbox for receding horizon temporal logic planning. In: Caccamo, M., Frazzoli, E., Grosu, R. (eds.) Proceedings of the 14th ACM International Conference on Hybrid Systems: Computation and Control, HSCC 2011, Chicago, IL, USA, April 12-14, 2011, pp. 313–314. ACM (2011)
60. Yang, L., Dai, H., Shi, Z., Hsieh, C.J., Tedrake, R., Zhang, H.: Lyapunov-stable neural control for state and output feedback: a novel formulation. In: Proceedings of the 41st International Conference on Machine Learning. ICML2024, JMLR.org (2024)

61. Žikelić, Ð., Lechner, M., Verma, A., Chatterjee, K., Henzinger, T.A.: Compositional policy learning in stochastic control systems with formal guarantees. In: Thirty-seventh Conference on Neural Information Processing Systems (2023)

Automata Learning from Preference and Equivalence Queries

Eric Hsiung$^{(\boxtimes)}$, Joydeep Biswas , and Swarat Chaudhuri

University of Texas at Austin, Austin, TX 78712, USA
{ehsiung,joydeepb,swarat}@cs.utexas.edu

Abstract. Active automata learning from membership and equivalence queries is a foundational problem with numerous applications. We propose a novel variant of the active automata learning problem: actively learn finite automata using *preference queries*—i.e., queries about the relative position of two sequences in a total preorder—instead of membership queries. Our solution is REMAP, a novel algorithm which leverages a symbolic observation table along with unification and constraint solving to navigate a space of symbolic hypotheses (each representing a set of automata), and uses satisfiability-solving to construct a concrete automaton (specifically a Moore machine) from a symbolic hypothesis. REMAP is guaranteed to correctly infer the minimal automaton with polynomial query complexity under exact equivalence queries, and achieves PAC–identification (ε-approximate, with high probability) of the minimal automaton using sampling-based equivalence queries. Our empirical evaluations of REMAP on the task of learning reward machines for two reinforcement learning domains indicate REMAP scales to large automata and is effective at learning correct automata from consistent teachers, under both exact and sampling-based equivalence queries.

1 Introduction

Active automata learning has applications from software engineering [1,37] and verification [29] to interpretable machine learning [44] and learning reward machines [16,20,39,46]. The classical problem formulation involves a teacher with access to a regular language and a learner which asks *membership* and *equivalence* queries to infer a finite automaton describing the regular language [5,22].

Consider an alternative formulation: *learning a finite automaton from preference and equivalence queries.*[1] A preference query resolves the relative position of two sequences in a total preorder available to the teacher. The motivation for learning from preferences stems from leveraging human preferences as a rich source of information. In fact, comparative feedback, such as preferences, is a modality which humans are apt at providing in comparison to giving specific

---

[1] Shah et al. [38] investigates choosing between membership and preference queries.

Supplementary Information The online version contains supplementary material available at https://doi.org/10.1007/978-3-031-98685-7_5.

R. Piskac and Z. Rakamarić (Eds.): CAV 2025, LNCS 15934, pp. 104–126, 2025.
https://doi.org/10.1007/978-3-031-98685-7_5

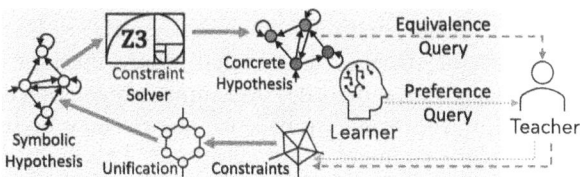

Fig. 1. REMAP Algorithm Overview.

numerical values, as shown by MacGlashan et al. [30] and Christiano et al. [12], likely due to *choice overload* [26]. But preferences need not be directly obtained from individual humans: preferences can also be obtained from automated systems in a frequency-based sense. For example, consider an obstacle avoidance scenario of a vehicle avoiding large debris in the middle of a roadway. Consider a dataset of a population of driver responses (vehicle trajectories) to such a scenario, procured from dashcam or traffic camera footage. The population preference of a given driving response can be automatically determined by ranking each response by the frequency of occurrence in the dataset. In fact, learning from human preference data has applications in fine-tuning language models [34], learning conditional preference networks [23,28], inferring reinforcement learning policies [13], and learning Markovian reward functions [10,11,27,36]. Possible applications for learning finite automata from preferences over sequences include inferring sequence classifications (e.g. program executions [21], vehicle maneuvers, human-robot interactions) using ordered classes (e.g. *safe, risky, dangerous, fatal*) with each automaton state labeled by a class, distilling interpretable preference models [44], and inferring reward machines. However, no method currently exists for learning finite automata from preferences with the termination and correctness guarantees enjoyed by classical automata learning algorithms such as L^* [5].

Unfortunately, adapting L^* to the preference-based setting is challenging. Preference queries do not directly provide the concrete observations available from membership queries, as required by L^*, so our solution REMAP addresses this challenge through a *symbolic approach* to L^*.

REMAP[2] (Fig. 1) features termination and correctness guarantees for *exact* and *probably approximately correct* [43] (PAC) *identification* [6] of the desired automaton, with a strong learner capable of symbolic reasoning and constraint-solving to offset the weaker preference-based signals from the teacher. While approximate learners have been proposed to learn from a combination of membership and preference queries [38], REMAP is the first exact learner with formal guarantees of minimalism, correctness, and query complexity. By using unification[3] to navigate the symbolic space of hypotheses, and constraint-solving

---

[2] Code available at https://eric-hsiung.github.io/remap/, as well as supplementary material.

[3] Symbolically obtaining sets of equivalent variables from sets of equations, and substituting variables in the equations with their representatives. See Sect. 4.2.

to construct a concrete automaton from a symbolic hypothesis, REMAP identifies, in a polynomial number of queries, the minimal Moore machine isomorphic to one describing the teacher's total preorder over input sequences when using *exact* equivalence queries. However, exact equivalence queries may be infeasible if the learner and teacher lack a common representation.[4] This motivates *sampling-based* equivalence queries under REMAP, which achieves *PAC–identification*.[5] Our empirical evaluations apply REMAP to learn reward machines for sequential-decision making domains in the reward machine literature. We measure query complexity for the exact and PAC–identification settings, and measure empirical correctness for the PAC–identification setting.

We contribute (a) REMAP, a novel L* style algorithm for learning Moore machines using preference and equivalence queries; under *exact* and *PAC-identifica-tion* settings we provide (b) theoretical analysis of query complexity, correctness, and minimalism, and (c) supporting empirical results, demonstrating the efficacy of the algorithm's ability to learn reward machines from preference and equivalence queries.

2 Background

Prior to introducing REMAP, we provide preliminaries on orders and finite automata, followed by a discussion of Angluin's L* algorithm in order to highlight how REMAP differs from L*.

Definition 1 (Total Preorder). *The binary relation $\precsim$ on a set A is a* total preorder *if $\precsim$ satisfies: $a \precsim a$ for all $a \in A$ (reflexivity); $a \precsim b \wedge b \precsim c \implies a \prec c$ for all $a, b, c \in A$ (transitivity); and $a \precsim b \vee b \precsim a$ for all $a, b \in A$ (total).*

Definition 2 (Total Order). *The binary relation $\precsim$ on a set A is a* total order *if $\precsim$ satisfies: total preorder conditions; and $a \precsim b \wedge b \precsim a \implies a = b$ for all $a, b \in A$ (antisymmetric); $a = b$ means a and b are the same element from A.*

Finite Automata. Automata describe sets of sequences. An *alphabet* Σ is a set whose elements can be used to construct sequences; Σ^* represents the set of sequences of any length created from elements of Σ. A sequence $s \in \Sigma^*$ has integer length $|s| \geq 0$; if $|s| = 0$, then s is the empty sequence ε. An element $\sigma \in \Sigma$ has length 1; if $s, t \in \Sigma^*$, then $s \cdot t$ represents s concatenated with t, with length $|s| + |t|$. Different types of finite automata have different semantics. Deterministic automata feature a deterministic transition function δ defined over a set of states Q and an input alphabet Σ^I. An output alphabet Σ^O may be present to label states or transitions using a labeling function L. The tuple $\langle Q, q_0, \Sigma^I, \Sigma^O, \delta, L \rangle$ is a *Moore machine* [33], where $q_0 \in Q$ is the initial state, $\delta : Q \times \Sigma^I \to Q$ describes transitions, and $L : Q \to \Sigma^O$ associates outputs with states. Extended, $\delta : Q \times (\Sigma^I)^* \to Q$, where $\delta(q, \varepsilon) = q$ and $\delta(q, \sigma \cdot s) =$

---

[4] Either a pair of identical representations, or between which a translation exists.
[5] See Definition 10 for PAC–identification and related Theorems 4 and 5.

$\delta(\delta(q, \sigma), s)$. In *Mealy machines* [32], outputs are associated with transitions instead, so $L : Q \times \Sigma^I \to \Sigma^O$. Mealy and Moore machines are equivalent [19] and can be converted between one another. Reward machines are an application of Mealy machines in reinforcement learning and are used to express a class of non-Markovian reward functions.

Active Automaton Learning. Consider the problem of actively learning a Moore machine $\langle Q, q_0, \Sigma^I, \Sigma^O, \delta, L \rangle$ to exactly model a function $f : (\Sigma^I)^* \to \Sigma^O$, where Σ^I and Σ^O are input and output alphabets of finite size known to both teacher and learner. We desire a learner which learns a model $\hat{f}$ of f exactly; that is for all $s \in (\Sigma^I)^*$, we require $\hat{f}(s) = f(s)$, where $\hat{f}(s) = L(\delta(q_0, s))$, with the assistance of a teacher $\mathcal{T}$ that can answer questions about f.

In Angluin's seminal active learning algorithm, L^* [5], the learner learns $\hat{f}$ as a binary classifier, where $|\Sigma^O| = 2$, to determine sequence membership of a regular language by querying $\mathcal{T}$ with: *(i) membership queries*, where the learner asks $\mathcal{T}$ for the value of $f(s)$ for a particular sequence s, and *(ii) equivalence queries*, where the learner asks $\mathcal{T}$ to evaluate whether for all $s \in (\Sigma^I)^*$, $\hat{f}(s) = f(s)$. For the latter query, $\mathcal{T}$ returns True if the statement holds; otherwise a counterexample c for which $\hat{f}(c) \neq f(c)$ is returned. An *observation table* $\langle S, E, T \rangle$ records the concrete observations acquired by the learner's queries (see Fig. 2). Here, S is a set of prefixes, E is a set of suffixes, and T is the empirical observation function that maps sequences to output values—$T : (S \cup (S \cdot \Sigma^I)) \cdot E \to \Sigma^O$. The observation table is a two-dimensional array; $s \in (S \cup (S \cdot \Sigma^I))$ indexes rows, and $e \in E$ indexes columns, with entries given by $T(s \cdot e)$. Any proposed hypothesis $\hat{f}$ must be consistent with T. The algorithm operates by construction: a deterministic transition function must be found exhibiting consistency (deterministic transitions) and operates in a closed manner over the set of states. If the consistency or closure requirements are violated, then membership queries are executed to expand the observation table. Once a suitable transition function is found, a hypothesis $\hat{f}$ can be made and checked via the equivalence query. The algorithm terminates if $\hat{f}(s) = f(s)$ for all $s \in (\Sigma^I)^*$; otherwise L^* continues on by adding counterexample c and all its prefixes to the table, and finds another transition function satisfying the consistency and closure requirements.

Consequently, we consider how L^*-style learning can be used to learn Moore machines from *preference queries* over sequences, as a foray into understanding how finite automaton structure can be learned from comparison information.

3   Problem Statement

We consider how a Moore machine $\langle Q, q_0, \Sigma^I, \Sigma^O, \delta, L \rangle$ can be actively learned from *preference queries* over $(\Sigma^I)^*$. We focus on the case of a finite sized Σ^I and Σ^O known to both teacher and learner. With a *preference query*, the learner asks the teacher $\mathcal{T}$ which of two sequences s_1 and s_2 is preferred, or if both are equally preferable. This requires a preference model, which we assume represents a total preordering over $(\Sigma^I)^*$; we also assume Σ^O is totally ordered. Thus, we consider a preference model for $\mathcal{T}$ where $f : (\Sigma^I)^* \to \Sigma^O$ is consistent with

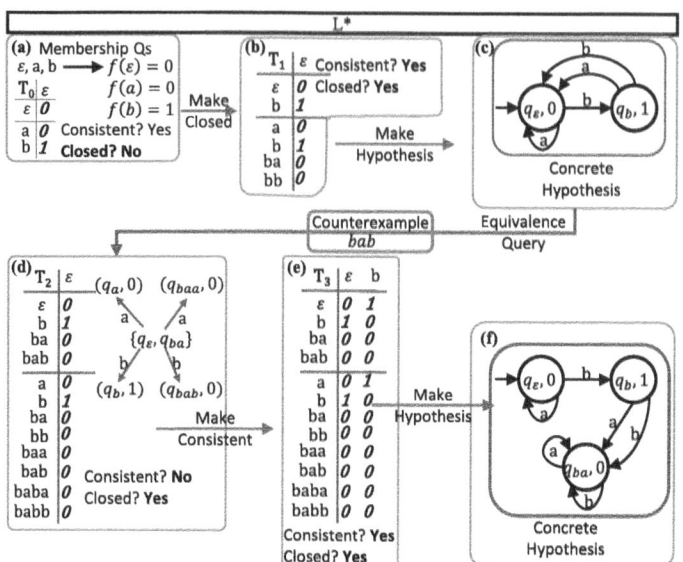

Fig. 2. L* example. Figure 3 illustrates REMAP. L* records concrete values from membership queries in observation table. Green symbolizes new information. Colors in *(d)* visually highlight transition inconsistencies.

both orderings, i.e., $\mathcal{T}$ prefers s_1 over s_2 if $f(s_1) > f(s_2)$, or otherwise has equal preference if $f(s_1) = f(s_2)$.

Several options for evaluating hypothesis equivalence (is $\hat{f} \equiv f$?) can be defined for this problem formulation. We first review the definition of exact equivalence, followed by an alternative notion of equivalence which respects ordering:

Definition 3 (Exact Equivalence). *Given a hypothesis $\hat{f}$ and a reference f, $\hat{f}$ is exactly equivalent to f if $\hat{f}(s) = f(s)$ for all s in $(\Sigma^I)^*$.*

Definition 4 (Order-Respecting Equivalence). *Given a hypothesis $\hat{f}$ and a reference f, $\hat{f}$ is order-respecting equivalent to f if, for all s,t in $(\Sigma^I)^*$, there exists a relation $\mathbf{R}_{s,t} \in \{=, >, <\}$ such that $\hat{f}(s)\mathbf{R}_{s,t}\hat{f}(t) \iff f(s)\mathbf{R}_{s,t}f(t)$.*

Since a hypothesis $\hat{f}$ satisfying exact equivalence is also always order-respecting, we focus on exact equivalence queries where $\mathcal{T}$ returns feedback along with counterexample c.

Definition 5 (Exact Equivalence Query with Feedback). *Given a hypothesis $\hat{f}$ and a reference f, an exact equivalence query EQ returns the following triple:*

$$EQ(\hat{f}) = \langle \forall s \in (\Sigma^I)^* : \hat{f}(s) = f(s), c : \exists c \text{ s.t. } \hat{f}(c) \neq f(c), \phi(c) \rangle$$

where c is a counterexample if one exists, and $\phi(c)$ is feedback associated with the counterexample, interpreted as a constraint.

The strength of feedback ϕ directly impacts how many hypotheses per counterexample can be eliminated by the learner: returning $\phi(c) := \hat{f}(c) \neq f(c)$, which means the value $f(c)$ is not $\hat{f}(c)$, is weak feedback compared to returning $\phi(c) := \hat{f}(c) = f(c)$, which means the value of $\hat{f}(c)$ should be $f(c)$, or returning $\phi(c) := \hat{f}(c) \in X$ (where $X \subset \Sigma^O$, which means the value of $\hat{f}(c)$ should be in a subset of Σ^O). Although REMAP outputs a concrete Moore machine, REMAP navigates symbolic Moore machine[6] space using solely preference information, while concrete information assists in selecting the concrete hypothesis. Thus, our theoretical analysis considers equivalence queries that provide counterexamples with strong feedback: $\phi(c) := \hat{f}(c) = f(c)$.

4   The REMAP Algorithm

REMAP is a L*-based algorithm employing preference and equivalence queries to gather constraints. By first leveraging unification to navigate the symbolic hypothesis space of Moore machines, solving the constraints yields a concrete Moore machine. In particular, REMAP (Algorithm 1) learns a Moore machine $\langle \hat{Q}, \hat{q}_0, \Sigma^I, \Sigma^O, \hat{\delta}, \hat{L} \rangle$, representing a multiclass classifier $\hat{f}(s) = \hat{L}(\hat{\delta}(\hat{q}_0, s))$.

Central to REMAP are four core components: **(1)** a new construct called a *symbolic observation table* (Sect. 4.1), shown in Fig. 3a, 3b, 3d, and 3e; **(2)** as well as an associated algorithm for *unification* [35] (Sect. 4.2) inspired by Martelli and Montanari [31] to contain the fresh variable explosion; both enable the learner to **(3)** generate symbolic hypotheses (Sect. 4.3) purely from observed symbolic constraints, along with **(4)** a constraint solver for obtaining a concrete hypothesis (Sect. 4.4). We first discuss the four components and how they fit together into REMAP (Sect. 4.5). Afterwards, we illustrate the correctness and termination guarantees.

4.1   Symbolic Observation Tables

Recall that in classic L*, the observation table entries are concrete values obtained from membership queries (Fig. 2a). However, observations obtained from *preference queries* are constraints, rather than concrete values, indicating that for a pair of sequences s_1 and s_2, one of $f(s_1) > f(s_2)$, $f(s_1) < f(s_2)$, or $f(s_1) = f(s_2)$ holds. We therefore introduce the **symbolic observation table** $\langle S, E, T; \mathcal{C}, \Gamma \rangle$, where S is a set of prefixes, E is a set of suffixes, $\mathcal{C}$ is the set of known constraints, Γ is a **context** which uniquely maps sequences to variables, with the set of variables $\mathcal{V}$ in the context Γ given by $\mathcal{V} = \{\Gamma[s \cdot e] | s \cdot e \in (S \cup (S \cdot \Sigma^I)) \cdot E\}$, and $T : (S \cup (S \cdot \Sigma^I)) \cdot E \to \mathcal{V}$ maps queried sequences to variables. Thus, in a symbolic observation table, the entry for each prefix-suffix pair

---

[6] i.e., a Moore machine with symbolic values as outputs.

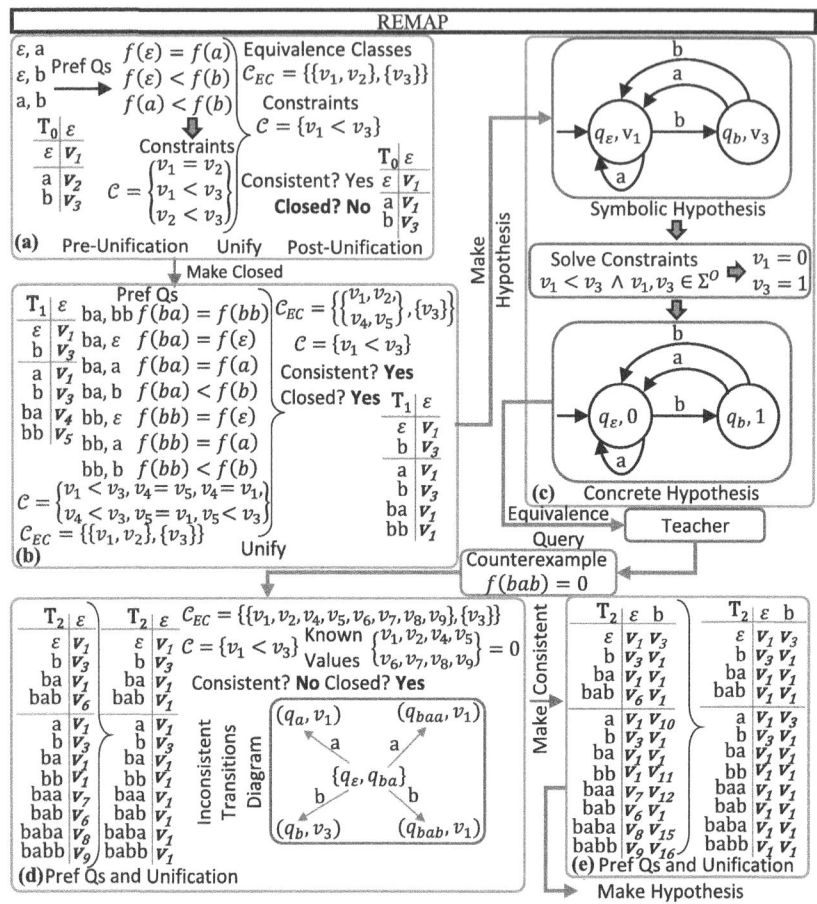

Fig. 3. REMAP example. Figure 2 illustrates L*. REMAP performs preference queries and records variables in symbolic observation table $\langle S, E, T; \mathcal{C}, \Gamma \rangle$ within a SYMBOLICFILL. *(a)* initializes $\langle S, E, T; \mathcal{C}, \Gamma \rangle$; *(b)* expands S with sequence b, followed by SYMBOLICFILL; yields unified, closed, and consistent $\langle S, E, T; \mathcal{C}, \Gamma \rangle$; *(c)* MAKEHYPOTHESIS yields concrete hypothesis h_1 from symbolic hypothesis and constraints in $\mathcal{C}$; *(d)* submits h_1 via equivalence query; receives and processes counterexample bab with feedback $f(bab) = 0$, adding bab, ba, and b to S, performs a SYMBOLICFILL, sets the value of equivalence class for $T(bab)$ to $f(bab)$; yields an inconsistent table. *(e)* shows resulting consistent table. Figure 2f shows ground truth Moore machine with $\Sigma^I = \{a, b\}$, $\Sigma^O = \{0, 1\}$. Green symbolizes new information. Colors in *(d)* visually highlight transition inconsistencies. (Color figure online)

is a variable, rather than a concrete value; and the constraints over those variables are stored in $\mathcal{C}$ (Fig. 3a, 3b, 3d, 3e). The constraints from the preferences of $\mathcal{T}$ over f about s_1 and s_2 correspond with $T(s_1) > T(s_2)$, $T(s_1) < T(s_2)$, or $T(s_1) = T(s_2)$, respectively.

Definition 6. *An **equivalence class** $\mathbb{C}$ of variables is a set with the property that all members of $\mathbb{C}$ are equivalent to each other. The **representative** $[\![\mathbb{C}]\!]$ of $\mathbb{C}$ is a deterministically elected member of $\mathbb{C}$. The set of variables $\mathcal{V}$ can be partitioned into disjoint equivalence classes. The set of equivalence classes $\mathcal{C}_{EC}$ corresponds with the partitioning of $\mathcal{V}$ into the smallest possible number of equivalence classes consistent with equality constraints. Let $\mathcal{R} = \{[\![\mathbb{C}]\!] | \mathbb{C} \in \mathcal{C}_{EC}\}$ be the set of representatives.*

4.2   Unification and Constraints

Since *preference queries* return observations comparing the values of two sequences, we leverage a simple unification algorithm to ensure the number of unique variables in the table remains bounded by $|\Sigma^O|$. As a reminder, unification involves symbolically solving for representatives and rewriting all constraints and variables in terms of those representatives. Whenever we observe the constraint $f(s_1) = f(s_2)$, this implies $T(s_1) = T(s_2)$, so we add $\Gamma[s_1]$ and $\Gamma[s_2]$ to an **equivalence class** $\mathbb{C}$, and elect a **representative** from $\mathbb{C}$. The unification algorithm is presented in Appendix.

If $\Gamma[s_1]$ already belongs to an equivalence class $\mathbb{C} \in \mathcal{C}_{EC}$, but $\Gamma[s_2]$ is an *orphan variable*—belonging to no class in $\mathcal{C}_{EC}$—then $\Gamma[s_2]$ is merged into $\mathbb{C}$. Swap s_1 and s_2 for the other case. If $\Gamma[s_1]$ and $\Gamma[s_2]$ belong to separate classes $\mathbb{C}_1$ and $\mathbb{C}_2$, with $\mathbb{C}_1 \neq \mathbb{C}_2$, then $\mathbb{C}_1$ and $\mathbb{C}_2$ are merged into one via $\mathbb{C} \leftarrow \mathbb{C}_1 \cup \mathbb{C}_2$, and one of $[\![\mathbb{C}_1]\!]$ and $[\![\mathbb{C}_2]\!]$ is deterministically elected as the representative $[\![\mathbb{C}]\!]$.

When this unification process is applied to a symbolic observation table $\langle S, E, T; \mathcal{C}, \Gamma \rangle$, we are unifying $\mathcal{V}$ (the set of variables in the context Γ) according to the set of known equivalence constraints $\mathcal{C}_{EQ}$ and equivalence classes $\mathcal{C}_{EC}$ available in $\mathcal{C}$; and each variable in the table is replaced with its equivalence class representative (see Fig. 3abde after the large right curly brace). That is, for all s in $(S \cup S \cdot \Sigma^I) \cdot E$, we substitute $T(s) \leftarrow [\![\mathbb{C}]\!]$ if $T(s) \in \mathbb{C}$. In the resulting *unified* symbolic observation table, T maps queried sequences to the set of representatives $\mathcal{R}$. Note $|\mathcal{R}| = |\mathcal{C}_{EC}| \leq |\Sigma^O|$.

Besides constraints from preferences queries, the learner obtains constraints about the value of $T(c)$ from *equivalence queries* (Fig. 3c to 3d) and adds them to $\mathcal{C}$. When first obtained, these constraints may possibly be expressed in terms of orphan variables, but during the process of unification, each orphan variable joins an equivalence class and is then replaced by its equivalence class representative in the constraint. Thus, after unification, all constraints in $\mathcal{C}$ are expressed in terms of equivalence class representatives.

Finally, unifying the symbolic observation table is critical for making a symbolic hypothesis without knowledge of concrete value assignments: unification permits $\langle S, E, T; \mathcal{C}, \Gamma \rangle$ to become *closed* and *consistent*—prerequisites for generating a symbolic hypothesis.

Definition 7. *Let $\mathbf{rows}(S) - \{\mathbf{row}(s) | s \in S\}$, where the row in $\langle S, E, T; \mathcal{C}, \Gamma \rangle$ indexed by s is $\mathbf{row}(s)$. $\langle S, E, T; \mathcal{C}, \Gamma \rangle$ is **closed** if $\mathbf{rows}(S \cdot \Sigma^I) \subseteq \mathbf{rows}(S)$.*

Algorithm 1. REMAP

Input: Alphabets Σ^I (input) and Σ^O (output), teacher $\mathcal{T}$
Output: Moore Machine $\mathcal{H} = \langle \hat{Q}, \Sigma^I, \Sigma^O, \hat{q}_0, \hat{\delta}, \hat{L} \rangle$

1: Initialize $\mathcal{O} = \langle S, E, T; \mathcal{C}, \Gamma \rangle$ with $S = \{\varepsilon\}$, $E = \{\varepsilon\}$, $\mathcal{C} = \{\}$, $\Gamma = \emptyset$
2: $\mathcal{O} \longleftarrow$ SYMBOLICFILL$(\mathcal{O}|\mathcal{T})$
3: **repeat**
4:     $\mathcal{O} \longleftarrow$ MAKECLOSEDANDCONSISTENT$(\mathcal{O}|\mathcal{T})$
5:     $\mathcal{H} \longleftarrow$ MAKEHYPOTHESIS$(\mathcal{O}, \Sigma^I, \Sigma^O)$
6:     $result \longleftarrow$ EQUIVALENCEQUERY$(\mathcal{H}|\mathcal{T})$
7:     $\mathcal{O} \longleftarrow$ PROCESSCEX$(\mathcal{O}, result)$ **if** $result \neq correct$
8: **until** $result = correct$
9: **return** $\mathcal{H}$

Definition 8. $\langle S, E, T; \mathcal{C}, \Gamma \rangle$ is **consistent** *if for all sequence pairs* s_1 *and* s_2 *where* $\boldsymbol{row}(s_1) \equiv \boldsymbol{row}(s_2)$, *all their transitions also remain equivalent with each other:* $\boldsymbol{row}(s_1 \cdot \sigma) \equiv \boldsymbol{row}(s_2 \cdot \sigma)$ *for all* $\sigma \in \Sigma^I$.

Definition 9. *Table* $\langle S, E, T; \mathcal{C}, \Gamma \rangle$ *is **unified** if* $T(s \cdot e) \in \mathcal{R}$ *for all* $s \cdot e \in (S \cup (S \cdot \Sigma^I)) \cdot E$.

4.3 Making a Symbolic Hypothesis

If symbolic observation table $\langle S, E, T; \mathcal{C}, \Gamma \rangle$ is *unified, closed,* and *consistent*, a symbolic hypothesis can be made (Fig. 3c). This construction is identical to L*, except that the outputs are symbolic:

$$\hat{Q} = \{\boldsymbol{row}(s) | \forall s \in S\} \text{ is the set of states}$$
$$\hat{q}_0 = \boldsymbol{row}(\varepsilon) \text{ is the initial state}$$
$$\hat{\delta}(\boldsymbol{row}(s), \sigma) = \boldsymbol{row}(s \cdot \sigma) \text{ for all } s \in S \text{ and } \sigma \in \Sigma^I$$
$$\hat{L}(\boldsymbol{row}(s)) = T(s \cdot \varepsilon) \text{ is the sequence to output function}$$
$$\langle \hat{Q}, \hat{q}_0, \Sigma^I, \Sigma^O, \hat{\delta}, \hat{L} \rangle \text{ is a symbolic hypothesis.}$$

4.4 Making a Concrete Hypothesis

The learner finds a satisfying solution Λ to the set of constraints $\mathcal{C}$, while subject to the global constraint requiring the value of each representative to be in Σ^O (Fig. 3c). Thus, $\hat{L}$ becomes concrete.

$$\Lambda \longleftarrow \text{FINDSOLUTION}(\langle S, E, T; \mathcal{C}, \Gamma \rangle, \Sigma^O) \tag{1}$$
$$\hat{L}(\boldsymbol{row}(s)) = \Lambda[T(s \cdot \varepsilon)] \tag{2}$$

In particular, Λ finds satisfying values for each member of $\mathcal{R}$, the set of equivalence class representatives. Since $\langle S, E, T; \mathcal{C}, \Gamma \rangle$ is unified, we are guaranteed that T maps from queried sequences to $\mathcal{R}$; hence $\Lambda[T(s \cdot \varepsilon)]$ is guaranteed to resolve to a concrete value as long as the teacher provides consistent preferences.

Algorithm 2. A Query Efficient Symbolic Fill Procedure

---

procedure SYMBOLICFILL($\langle S, E, T; C, \Gamma \rangle | T$)

1: $seqs = \{\}$; Let $\mathcal{O} = \langle S, E, T; C, \Gamma \rangle$; let *oldsortedseqs* be a sorted list of sequences.
2: $seqs = $ POPULATEMISSINGFRESHVARS($\mathcal{O}$)
3: $\mathcal{O} \longleftarrow$ PREFQSBYRANDOMIZEDQUICKSORTFOLLOWEDBYLINEARMERGE(*seqs*, *oldsortedseqs*, $\mathcal{O}|T$)
4: $\mathcal{O} \longleftarrow$ UNIFICATION($\mathcal{O}$)
5: **return** $\mathcal{O}$

4.5 REMAP

We now describe REMAP (Algorithm 1) in terms of the previously discussed components. In order to make a symbolic hypothesis, REMAP must first obtain a *unified, closed, and consistent* $\langle S, E, T; C, \Gamma \rangle$. To perform closed and consistency checks, the table must be unified. Therefore, REMAP must *symbolically fill*

$\langle S, E, T; C, \Gamma \rangle$ by asking preference queries and performing unification to obtain a unified table. If the unified table is not closed or not consistent, then the table is alternately expanded and symbolically filled until the table becomes unified, closed, and consistent.

SYMBOLICFILL. A symbolic fill (Algorithm 2 and Appendix) (*i*) creates fresh variables for empty entries in the table, (*ii*) asks preference queries, and (*iii*) performs unification. If a sequence $s \cdot e \in (S \cup (S \cdot \Sigma^I)) \cdot E$ does not have an associated variable in the context Γ, then a fresh variable $\Gamma[s \cdot e]$ is created. Preference queries are executed to obtain the total preordering of $(S \cup (S \cdot \Sigma^I)) \cdot E$. In our implementation, we use preference queries in place of comparisons in randomized quicksort and linear merge. Once every sequence in $(S \cup (S \cdot \Sigma^I)) \cdot E$ has a variable, and once the preference queries have been completed, unification is performed. SYMBOLICFILL is called on lines 2, 4 (in MAKECLOSEDANDCONSISTENT), and 7 (in PROCESSCEX.). Unification is shown in Appendix.

Ensuring Consistency. If the unified table is not consistent, then there exists a pair $s_1, s_2 \in S$ and $\sigma \in \Sigma^I$ for which $\boldsymbol{row}(s_1) \equiv \boldsymbol{row}(s_2)$ and $\boldsymbol{row}(s_1 \cdot \sigma) \not\equiv \boldsymbol{row}(s_2 \cdot \sigma)$, implying there is an $e \in E$ such that $T(s_1 \cdot \sigma \cdot e) \not\equiv T(s_2 \cdot \sigma \cdot e)$. To attempt to make the table consistent, add $\sigma \cdot e$ to E, and then perform a symbolic fill. Figure 3d shows inconsistency, and Fig. 3e shows a table made consistent through expansion of the suffix set.

Ensuring Closedness. If the unified table is not closed, then $\boldsymbol{rows}(S \cdot \Sigma^I) \not\subseteq \boldsymbol{rows}(S)$. To attempt to make the table closed, find a row $\boldsymbol{row}(s')$ in $\boldsymbol{rows}(S \cdot \Sigma^I)$ but not in $\boldsymbol{rows}(S)$. Add s' to S, update $S \cdot \Sigma^I$, then fill symbolically. Figure 3a to 3b shows a closure process.

The closed and consistency checks occur in a loop (consistency first, closed second) inside MAKECLOSEDANDCONSISTENT until the table becomes unified, closed, and consistent. Then hypothesis $h = \langle \hat{Q}, \hat{q}_0, \Sigma^I, \Sigma^O, \hat{\delta}, \hat{L} \rangle$ is generated by

MAKEHYPOTHESIS (Fig. 3c) and is sent to the teacher via EQUIVALENCEQUERY (Fig. 3c to 3d). If h is wrong, then a counterexample c is returned, as well as feedback $\phi(c)$ which is interpreted as a new constraint on the value of $\hat{f}(c)$. The counterexample c and all its prefixes are added to S, and then a symbolic fill is performed. Then the constraint on the value of $\hat{f}(c)$ is added to $\mathcal{C}$ as a constraint on the value of the representative at $T(c)$.

5   Theoretical Guarantees of REMAP

We now cover the algorithmic guarantees of REMAP when $\mathcal{T}$ uses exact equivalence queries, and show how sampling-based equivalence queries achieves PAC–identification. We first detail how REMAP guarantees termination and yields a correct, minimal Moore machine that classifies sequence equivalently to f. If REMAP terminates, then the final hypothesis must be correct, since termination occurs only if no counterexamples exist for the final hypothesis. Therefore, if the hypothesized Moore machine classifies all sequences correctly according to the teacher, it must be correct. Thus, proving termination implies correctness. See Appendix for sketches and proofs. Here, we assume the teacher provides feedback $\hat{f}(c) = f(c)$ with counterexample c.

Theorem 1. *If $\langle S, E, T; \mathcal{C}, \Gamma \rangle$ is unified, closed, and consistent, and the range of MAKEHYPOTHESIS($\langle S, E, T; \mathcal{C}, \Gamma \rangle$) is $\mathcal{H}$, then every hypothesis $h \in \mathcal{H}$ is consistent with constraints $\mathcal{C}$. Any other hypothesis consistent with $\mathcal{C}$, but not contained in $\mathcal{H}$, must have more states.*

Proof. (Sketch) A given unified, closed, and consistent symbolic observation table $\langle S, E, T; \mathcal{C}, \Gamma \rangle$ corresponds to $(\mathcal{S}, \mathcal{R}, \mathcal{C})$, where $\mathcal{S}$ is a symbolic hypothesis, $\mathcal{R}$ is the set of representatives used in the table, and $\mathcal{C}$ are the constraints expressed over $\mathcal{R}$. All hypotheses in $\mathcal{H}$ have states and transitions identical to $\mathcal{S}$. Each satisfying solution Λ to $\mathcal{C}$ corresponds to a unique concrete hypothesis in $\mathcal{H}$. Therefore every concrete hypothesis in $\mathcal{H}$ is consistent with $\mathcal{C}$. Let $|h|$ represent the number of states in h. We know for all $h \in \mathcal{H}$, $|h| = |\mathcal{S}|$. Let $\overline{\mathcal{H}}$ be the set of concrete hypotheses *not in* $\mathcal{H}$. Note $\overline{\mathcal{H}}$ can be partitioned into three sets—concrete hypotheses with (a) fewer states than $\mathcal{S}$, (b) more states than $\mathcal{S}$, and (c) same number of states as $\mathcal{S}$ but inconsistent with $\mathcal{C}$. We ignore (c) because we care only about hypotheses consistent with $\mathcal{C}$. Consider any concrete hypothesis h in $\mathcal{H}$ and its corresponding satisfying solution Λ. Suppose we desire another hypothesis h' to be consistent with h. If $|h'| < |h|$, then h' cannot be consistent with h because at least one sequence will be misclassified. Therefore, if h' must be consistent with h, then we require $|h'| \geq |h|$. Thus, any other hypothesis consistent with $\mathcal{C}$, but not in $\mathcal{H}$, must have more states. $\qquad\square$

Theorem 1 establishes that the output of REMAP will be the smallest Moore machine consistent with all the constraints in $\mathcal{C}$. This is necessary to prove termination.

Lemma 1. *Whenever a counterexample c is processed, either 0 or 1 additional representative values becomes known.*

Theorem 2. *Suppose $\langle S, E, T; \mathcal{C}, \Gamma \rangle$ is unified, closed, and consistent. Let $\hat{h} = \text{MAKEHYPOTHESIS}(\langle S, E, T; \mathcal{C}, \Gamma \rangle)$ be the hypothesis induced by Λ, a satisfying solution to $\mathcal{C}$. If the teacher returns a counterexample c as the result of an equivalence query on $\hat{h}$, then at least one of the following is true about $\hat{h}$: (a) $\hat{h}$ contains too few states, or (b) the satisfying solution Λ inducing $\hat{h}$ is either incomplete or incorrect.*

Corollary 1. REMAP *must terminate when the number of states and number of known representative values in a concrete hypothesis reach their respective upper bounds.*

Proof. (Sketch) This sketch applies to the above lemma, theorem, and corollary about termination. Consider the sequence $\dots, h_{k-1}, h_k, \dots$ of hypotheses that REMAP makes. For a given pair of consecutive hypotheses (h_{k-1}, h_k), consider how the number of states n, and the number of *known* representative values $n_\bullet$ changes. Let n^* be the number of states of the minimal Moore machine correctly classifying all sequences. Let $V^* \leq |\Sigma^O|$ be the upper bound on $|\mathcal{R}|$. Note that $0 \leq n_\bullet \leq |\mathcal{R}| \leq V^* \leq |\Sigma^O|$ always holds. Through detailed case analysis on returned counterexamples, we can show that the change in $n_\bullet$, denoted by $\Delta n_\bullet$, must always be either 0 or 1, and furthermore, if $\Delta n_\bullet = 0$, then we must have $\Delta n \geq 1$. By the case analysis and tracking n and $n_\bullet$, observe that if a counterexample c is received from the teacher due to hypothesis h, then *at least one of* (a) $n < n^*$ or (b) $n_\bullet < V^*$ must be true. Since $\Delta n_\bullet$ and Δn cannot simultaneously be 0, whenever a new hypothesis is made, progress must be made towards the upper bound of (n^*, V^*). If the upper bound is reached, then the algorithm must terminate, since it is impossible to progress from the point (n^*, V^*). □

Theorem 3 (Query Complexity). *If n is the number of states of the minimal automaton isomorphic to the target automaton, and m is the maximum length of any counterexample sequence that the teacher returns, then (a) REMAP executes at most $n + |\Sigma^O| - 1$ equivalence queries, and (b) the preference query complexity is $\mathcal{O}(mn^2 \ln(mn^2))$, which is polynomial in the number of unique sequences queried.*

Proof. Based on Theorem 2, we know that the maximum number of equivalence queries is the taxi distance from the point $(1, 0)$ to $(n, |\Sigma^O|)$, which is $n + |\Sigma^O| - 1$. From counterexample processing, we know there will be at most $m(n + |\Sigma^O| - 1)$ sequences added to the prefix set S, since a counterexample c of length m results in at most m sequences added to the prefix set S. The maximum number of times the table can be found inconsistent is at most $n - 1$ times, since there can be at most n states, and the learner starts with 1 state. Whenever a sequence is added to the suffix set E, the maximum length of sequences in E increases by at most 1, implying the maximum sequence length in E is $n - 1$. Similarly, closure operations can be performed at most $n-1$ times, so the total number of sequences in E is at most n; the maximum number of sequences in S is $n+m(n+|\Sigma^O|-1)$. The maximum number of unique sequences queried in the table is the maximum cardinality of $(S \cup S \cdot \Sigma^I) \cdot E$, which is

$$(n + m(n + |\Sigma^O| - 1))(1 + |\Sigma^I|)n = \mathcal{O}(mn^2).$$

Therefore, the preference query complexity of REMAP is $\mathcal{O}(mn^2 \ln(mn^2))$ due to randomized quicksort. □

Lemma 1, Theorem 2, and Corollary 1 imply REMAP makes progress towards termination with every hypothesis, and termination occurs when specific conditions are satisfied; therefore its output must be correct. Theorem 3 indicates that REMAP learns the correct minimal automaton isomorphic to the target automaton in polynomial time. Next, we show how REMAP achieves PAC–identification when sampling-based equivalence queries are used.

Definition 10 (Probably Approximately Correct Identification). *Given Moore machine $M = \langle Q, q_0, \Sigma^I, \Sigma^O, \delta, L \rangle$, let the classification function $f : (\Sigma^I)^* \to \Sigma^O$ be represented by $f(s) = L(\delta(q_0, s))$ for all $s \in (\Sigma^I)^*$. Let $\mathcal{D}$ be any probability distribution over $(\Sigma^I)^*$. An algorithm $\mathcal{A}$ probably approximately correctly identifies f if and only if for any choice of $0 < \epsilon \leq 1$ and $0 < d < 1$, $\mathcal{A}$ always terminates and outputs an ϵ-approximate sequence classifier $\hat{f} : (\Sigma^I)^* \to \Sigma^O$, such that with probability at least $1 - d$, the probability of misclassification is $P(\hat{f}(s) \neq f(s)) \leq \epsilon$ when s is drawn according to the distribution $\mathcal{D}$.*

Theorem 4. REMAP *achieves probably approximately correct identification of any Moore machine when the teacher $\mathcal{T}$ uses sampling-based equivalence queries with at least $m_k \geq \lceil \frac{1}{\epsilon} \left(\ln \frac{1}{d} + k \ln 2 \right) \rceil$ samples drawn i.i.d. from $\mathcal{D}$ for the kth equivalence query.*

Proof. (Sketch) The probability $1 - \epsilon_k$ of a sequence sampled from an arbitrary distribution $\mathcal{D}$ over $(\Sigma^I)^*$ depends upon the distribution and the intersections of sets of sequences of the teacher and the learner's kth hypothesis with the same classification values. The probability that the kth hypothesis misclassifies a sequence is ϵ_k. If the teacher samples m_k samples for the kth equivalence query, then an upper bound can be established for the case when $\epsilon_k \leq \epsilon$ for a given ϵ. Since we know REMAP executes at most $n + |\Sigma^O| - 1$ equivalence queries, one can upper bound the probability that REMAP terminates with an error by summing all probabilities of events that the teacher does not detect an error in at most $n + |\Sigma^O| - 1$ equivalence queries. An exponential decaying upper bound can be found, and a lower bound for m_k can be found in terms of ϵ, d, and k. □

Theorem 5. *To achieve PAC-identification under* REMAP, *given parameters ϵ and d, and if f can be represented by a minimal Moore machine with n states and $|\Sigma^O|$ classes, then teacher $\mathcal{T}$ needs to sample at least*

$$\mathcal{O}\left(n + |\Sigma^O| + \frac{1}{\epsilon} \left((n + |\Sigma^O|) \ln \frac{1}{d} + (n + |\Sigma^O|)^2 \right) \right)$$

sequences i.i.d. from $\mathcal{D}$ over the entire run of REMAP.

Proof. Since for the kth equivalence query, the teacher must sample at least $m_k \geq \lceil \frac{1}{\epsilon}(\ln\frac{1}{d} + k\ln 2)\rceil$ sequences in order to achieve PAC-identification, if the total number of samples is to be minimized while still achieving PAC-identification, then the teacher can just sample a quantity of sequences i.i.d. from $\mathcal{D}$ equal to the following total

$$\sum_{k=1}^{n+|\Sigma^O|-1} \left[\frac{1}{\epsilon}(\ln\frac{1}{d} + k\ln 2) + 1\right]$$

$$= n + |\Sigma^O| - 1 + \frac{1}{\epsilon}\left[(\ln\frac{1}{d})(n + |\Sigma^O| - 1) + \ln 2 \sum_{k=1}^{n+|\Sigma^O|-1} k\right]$$

$$= \mathcal{O}\left((n + |\Sigma^O|) + \frac{1}{\epsilon}((n + |\Sigma^O|)\ln\frac{1}{d} + (n + |\Sigma^O|)^2)\right)$$

$\square$

Theorem 4 and Theorem 5 imply REMAP achieves PAC–identification for a choice of ϵ and d as long as the teacher samples sufficient sequences per equivalence query. In particular, Theorem 5 indicates the total quantity of sequences sampled by the teacher to achieve PAC-identification depends on both n the number of states, and $|\Sigma^O|$ the number of output classes. This contrasts with the result for PAC-identification of DFAs (Theorem 7 [5]), which depends only on n. Finally, since REMAP outputs a Moore machine, one can leverage Moore and Mealy machine equivalence in order to convert the final hypothesis into a reward machine, as defined and covered in the next section.

6   Learning Reward Machines from Preferences

We consider applying REMAP to learn reward machines from preferences. Reward machines are Mealy machines with propositional and reward semantics. Equivalence between Mealy and Moore machines allows the output of REMAP to be converted to a reward machine. We first review reinforcement learning and reward machine semantics.

Markov Decision Processes. Decision making problems are often modeled by a Markov Decision Process (MDP), which is a tuple $\langle \mathcal{S}, \mathcal{A}, P, R, \gamma \rangle$ where $\mathcal{S}$ is the set of states, $\mathcal{A}$ is the set of actions, $P : \mathcal{S} \times \mathcal{A} \times \mathcal{S} \to [0, 1]$ represents the transition probability from state s to s' via action a. The reward function $R : \mathcal{S} \times \mathcal{A} \times \mathcal{S} \to \mathbb{R}$ provides the associated scalar reward, and $0 \leq \gamma \leq 1$ is a discount factor. In MDPs, the Markovian assumption is that transitions and rewards depend only upon the current state-action pair and the next state. However, not all tasks are expressible using Markovian reward [2].

Non-markovian Reward. Non-Markovian Reward Decision Processes are identical to MDPs, except that $R : (\mathcal{S} \times \mathcal{A})^* \to \mathbb{R}$ is non-Markovian a reward function that depends on state-action history. This allows reward machines to model a class of non-Markovian reward functions.

Reward Machines.   A reward machine (RM) is a Mealy machine where $\Sigma^I = 2^{\mathcal{P}}$, Σ^O is a set of reward emitting objects, and $\mathcal{P}$ is a set of propositions describing states and actions. A *labeling* function $\mathbb{L} : \mathcal{S} \times \mathcal{A} \times \mathcal{S} \to 2^{\mathcal{P}}$ with $\mathbb{L}(s_{k-1}, a_k, s_k) = l_k$ labels a state-action sequence $s_0 a_1 s_1 a_2 s_2 \ldots a_n s_n$ with label sequence $l_1 l_2 \ldots l_n$. Thus, reward machines operate over label sequences.

A single disjunctive normal formula (DNF) labeled transition can summarize multiple transitions with identical Σ^O labels (connecting a pair of states), since the elements of $2^{\mathcal{P}}$ are sets of propositions. Reward machines map label sequences to reward outputs and can be represented as $f : (2^{\mathcal{P}})^* \to \Sigma^O$, so REMAP learns a reward machine by converting the output Moore machine to a reward machine.

Sequential Tasks in OfficeWorld and CraftWorld.   Icarte et al. [25] and Andreas et al. [4] introduced the OfficeWorld and CraftWorld gridworld domains, respectively, and feature sequential tasks encoded as reward machines. Office-World features 4 sequential tasks across several rooms with various objects available for an agent to interact with. Example tasks include (1) picking up coffee and mail and delivering them to a certain room, or (2) continuously patrolling between a set of rooms. CraftWorld is a 2D version of MineCraft, where the 10 sequential tasks involve the agent collecting materials and constructing tools or objects in a certain order while avoiding hazards.

7   Empirical Results

We evaluate the exact and PAC–identification (PAC-ID) versions of REMAP and consider: first, *how often is PAC-ID REMAP correct?* (Exact REMAP is guaranteed to be correct). To answer this, we run experiments by applying PAC-ID REMAP to learn reward machines (RMs), by converting the Moore machine into a RM. We measure empirical correctness with *empirical probability of isomorphism* and *average regret*. Second, *how do exact and PAC-ID REMAP scale*? We measure preference query complexity as a function of the number of unique sequences queried, and present an example phase diagram of algorithm execution. We use Z3 [15] for the constraint solver.

Setup.   We investigate these questions on 14 sequential tasks in the Office-World and CraftWorld domains. The Appendix contains domain specific details. We implement exact equivalence queries (Definition 5) using a variant of the Hopcroft-Karp algorithm [3,24]. We implement i.i.d. sequence sampling in sampling-based equivalence queries with the following process per sample: sample a length L from a geometric distribution; then, construct an L-length sequence by drawing L elements i.i.d. from a uniform distribution over Σ^I. In both the exact and sampling-based equivalence queries, strong feedback is used.

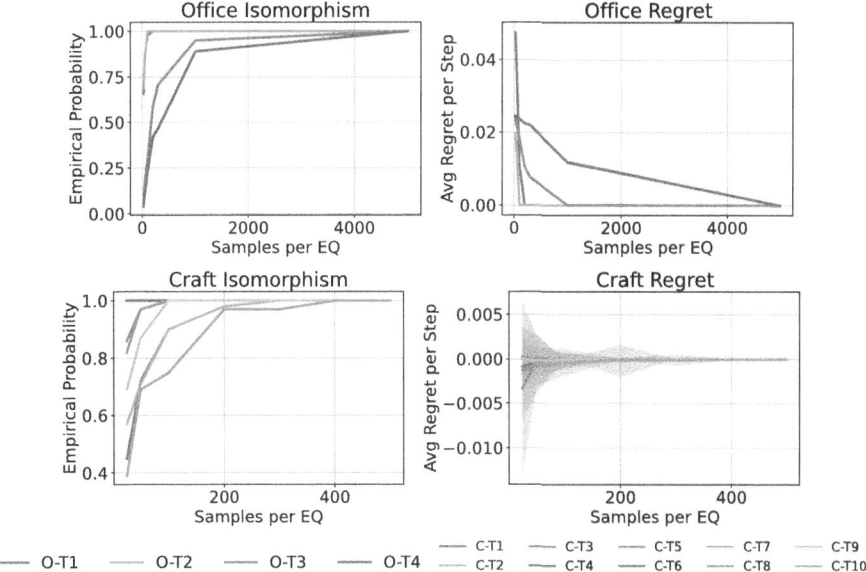

Fig. 4. PAC–identification REMAP: (*left*) empirical isomorphism probability, (*right*) average regret as functions of the number of samples per equivalence query for 4 Office-World tasks (O-T1-4) and 10 CraftWorld tasks (C-T1-10).

7.1   PAC–Identification Correctness Experiments

Reproducibility. PAC-ID REMAP was run 100 times per ground truth reward machine. We measure correctness based on (1) empirical probability that the learned RM is isomorphic to the ground truth RM, based on classification accuracy, and (2) average policy regret between the learned RM policy and the ground truth RM policy.

Empirical Probability of Isomorphism is the *fraction of learned RMs with 100% classification accuracy.* As the number of sample sequences tested by the teacher per equivalence query increases, the probability that the learner outputs a RM isomorphic to the ground truth RM upon termination goes to 1 (Fig. 4, left column). Classification accuracy is defined as the *fraction of a test set of sequences that are identically classified* by the learned and ground truth RMs. The Appendix describes the distribution over $(\Sigma^I)^*$ that the test set is drawn from.

Average Policy Regret. We employ *Q-learning with counterfactual experiences for reward machines* (CRM) [41] to obtain optimal policies for ground truth and learned RMs. We measured the empirical expected return of optimal policies learned from each type of RM. Average regret for a given task was measured as the *difference between the empirical return under the ground truth RM for that task* (averaged over 100 CRM trials) *and the empirical return under the learned RM* (with 10 CRM trials per learned RM, then averaging all

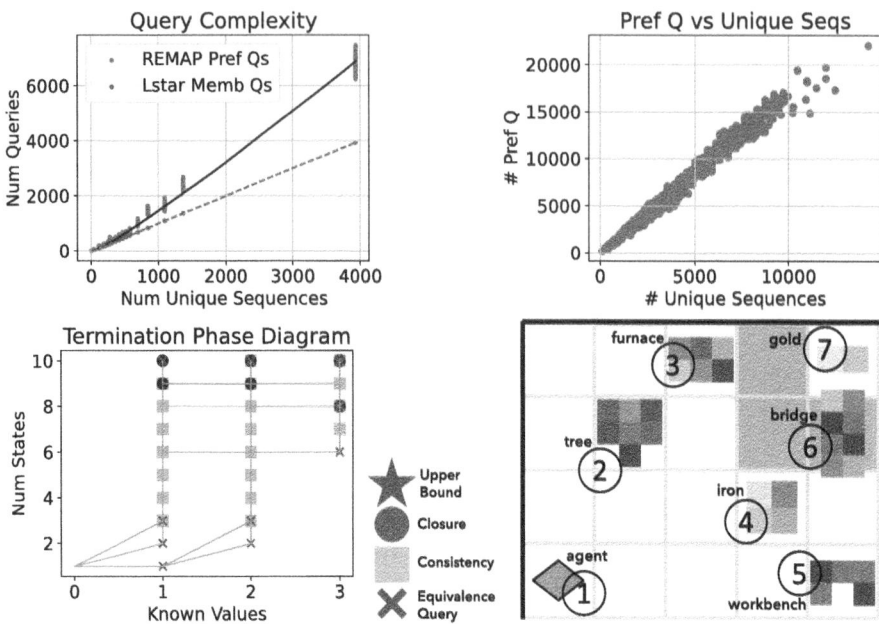

Fig. 5. Query Complexity. *Top left*: Exact REMAP preference query complexity. Mean of 100 trials per ground truth reward machine (blue dots) ±1 standard deviation (orange, grey bars). *Top right*: PAC-ID REMAP, preference query complexity is $\mathcal{O}(n \ln n)$ in the number of unique sequences in the table. *Bottom left*: Example termination phase diagram. *Bottom right*: CraftWorld environment depiction. (Color figure online)

$100 \times 10 = 1000$ trials). Regret goes to 0 as the number of samples tested by the teacher per equivalence query increases (Fig. 4, right column). The Appendix describes regret computation details.

Correctness Conclusion. Exact REMAP learns the correct automaton 100% of the time. Additionally, PAC-ID REMAP is more likely to be correct as the number of samples per equivalence query increases: isomorphism probability goes to 1 and regret goes to 0 for all tasks in both domains.

7.2   Scaling Experiments

Figure 5 shows query complexity results. We measure preference query complexity of exact and PAC-ID REMAP, as a function of the number of unique sequences stored in the table upon termination. Exact REMAP (upper left) displays a trendline of $C = 0.2114N \ln N$ with $R^2 = 0.99268$, where C is the number of queries, and N is the number of unique sequences in the observation table. PAC-ID REMAP (upper right) tends to make significantly more preference queries about unique sequences compared to exact REMAP due to the sampling process. However, the number of preference queries is still $\mathcal{O}(N \ln N)$ due to randomized quicksort and linear merge comparison complexity. In comparison, an L^*-based approach would use exactly N membership queries (exactly linear in N with a coefficient of 1).

The maximum number of equivalence queries REMAP makes (Theorem 3) is the taxi distance from $(0, 1)$ to $(|\Sigma^O|, n)$ in the termination phase diagram of Fig. 5. Progress (Lemma 1 and Theorem 2) towards termination (Corollary 1) occurs whenever a new hypothesis is made. REMAP can terminate early when all variables have correct values and the required number of states is reached.

8   Related Work

Active approaches for learning automata are variations or improvements of Angluin's seminal L^* algorithm [5], featuring *membership* and *equivalence queries*. We consider an alternative formulation: *actively learning automata from preference and equivalence queries* featuring feedback. We first discuss adaptations of L^* for learning variants of finite automata, including reward machine variants.

Learning Finite Automata. Angluin [5] introduced L^* to learn deterministic finite automata (DFAs). REMAP has similar theoretical guarantees as L^*, but utilizes a symbolic observation table, rather than an evidence-based one. Other algorithms adopt the evidence-based table of L^* to learn: symbolic automata [7,17], where Boolean predicates summarize state transitions; weighted automata [8,9] which feature valuation semantics for sequences on nondeterministic automata; probabilistic DFAs [44], a weighted automata that models distributions of sequences. None of these approaches uses preference queries.

However, Shah et al. [38] considers active, cost-based selection between membership and preference queries to learn DFAs, relying on a satisfiability encoding of the problem. They assume a *fixed hypothesis space* and have *probabilistic* guarantees for termination and correctness. REMAP, through unification, *navigates a sequence of hypothesis spaces*, each guaranteed to contain a concrete hypothesis satisfying current constraints, and has theoretical guarantees of correctness, minimalism, and termination under *exact* and *PAC–identification* settings.

Furthermore, learning finite automata from preference information relates to the novel problem of *learning reward machines* [25] *from preferences*. Learning Markovian reward functions from preferences has be studied extensively using neural [11,36] and interpretable decision tree [10,27] representations, but approaches for learning reward machines primarily adapt evidence-based finite automata learning approaches.

Reward Machine Variants. Several reward machine (RM) variants have been proposed. Classical RMs [25,42] have deterministic transitions and rewards; probabilistic RMs [16] model probabilistic transitions and deterministic rewards; and stochastic RMs [14] pair deterministic transitions with stochastic rewards. Symbolic RMs [47] are deterministic like classical RMs, but feature symbolic reward values in place of concrete values. Zhou and Li [47] apply Bayesian inverse reinforcement learning (BIRL) to infer optimal reward values and actualize symbolic RMs into classical RMs, and require a symbolic RM sketch. REMAP requires no sketch, since it navigates over a hypothesis space of symbolic RMs and outputs a concrete classical RM upon termination.

Learning Reward Machines. Many RM learning algorithms assume access to explicit reward samples via environment interaction. Given a maximum RM size, Toro Icarte et al. [42] apply discrete optimization to arrive at a perfect classical RM. Xu et al. [45] learn a minimal classical RM by combining regular positive negative inference [18] with Q-learning for RMs [25], and apply constraint solving to ensure each hypothesis RM is consistent with observed reward samples. Corazza et al. [14] extended the method to learn stochastic RMs. Topper et al. [40] extends BIRL to learn classical RMs using simulated annealing, but needs the number of states to be supplied, and requires empirical tuning of hyperparameters. L* based approaches have also been used to learn classical [20,39,46] and probabilistic [16] RMs, relying on concrete observation tables. Gaon and Brafman [20] and Xu et al. [46] use a binary observation table, while Tappler et al. [39] and Dohmen et al. [16] record empirical reward distribution table entries.

In contrast, REMAP uses a symbolic observation table, and uses preferences information in place of explicit reward values. REMAP navigates symbolic hypothesis space, with constraint solving enabling a concrete classical RM.

9   Conclusion

We introduce the problem of learning Moore machines from preferences and propose REMAP, an L* based algorithm, wherein a strong learner with access to a constraint solver is paired with a weak teacher capable of answering preference queries and providing counterexample feedback in the form of a constraint. Unification applied to a symbolic observation table permits symbolic hypothesis space navigation; the constraint solver enables concrete hypotheses. REMAP has theoretical guarantees for correctness, termination, and minimalism under both exact and PAC–identification settings, and it has been empirically verified under both settings when applied to learning reward machines. Future work will expound on more realistic preference models, variable strength feedback, and inconsistency.

Acknowledgments. This work is supported in part by the National Science Foundation (DGE-2125858, IIS-2416461), the Defense Advanced Research Projects Agency (HR00112320018, HR00112490431), and the Army Research Office (W911NF2110009). Any opinions, findings, and conclusions expressed in this material are those of the authors and do not necessarily reflect the views of the sponsors.

Disclosure of Interests. The authors have no competing interests to declare that are relevant to the content of this article.

References

1. Aarts, F., Kuppens, H., Tretmans, J., Vaandrager, F.W., Verwer, S.: Learning and testing the bounded retransmission protocol. In: International Conference on Graphics and Interaction (2012). https://api.semanticscholar.org/CorpusID:2641499

2. Abel, D., et al.: On the expressivity of Markov reward. In: Ranzato, M., Beygelzimer, A., Dauphin, Y., Liang, P., Vaughan, J.W. (eds.) Advances in Neural Information Processing Systems, vol. 34, pp. 7799–7812, Curran Associates, Inc. (2021). https://proceedings.neurips.cc/paper_files/paper/2021/file/4079016d940210b4ae9ae7d41c4a2065-Paper.pdf

3. Almeida, M., Moreira, N., Reis, R.: Testing the equivalence of regular languages. In: Workshop on Descriptional Complexity of Formal Systems (2009). https://api.semanticscholar.org/CorpusID:9014414

4. Andreas, J., Klein, D., Levine, S.: Modular multitask reinforcement learning with policy sketches. In: Precup, D., Teh, Y.W. (eds.) Proceedings of the 34th International Conference on Machine Learning, Proceedings of Machine Learning Research, vol. 70, pp. 166–175, PMLR (2017). https://proceedings.mlr.press/v70/andreas17a.html

5. Angluin, D.: Learning regular sets from queries and counterexamples. Inf. Comput. **75**(2), 87–106 (1987). https://doi.org/10.1016/0890-5401(87)90052-6

6. Angluin, D.: Queries and concept learning. Mach. Learn. **2**, 319–342 (1988)

7. Argyros, G., D'antoni, L.: The learnability of symbolic automata. In: International Conference on Computer Aided Verification (2018)

8. Balle, B., Mohri, M.: Learning weighted automata. In: Conference on Algebraic Informatics (2015)

9. Bergadano, F., Varricchio, S.: Learning behaviors of automata from multiplicity and equivalence queries. SIAM J. Comput. **25**, 1268–1280 (1994)

10. Bewley, T., Lécué, F.: Interpretable preference-based reinforcement learning with tree-structured reward functions. arXiv:abs/2112.11230 (2021). https://api.semanticscholar.org/CorpusID:245353680

11. Bıyık, E., Talati, A., Sadigh, D.: APReL: A library for active preference-based reward learning algorithms (2022)

12. Christiano, P.F., Leike, J., Brown, T., Martic, M., Legg, S., Amodei, D.: Deep reinforcement learning from human preferences. In: Guyon, I., Luxburg, U.V., Bengio, S., Wallach, H., Fergus, R., Vishwanathan, S., Garnett, R. (eds.) Advances in Neural Information Processing Systems, vol. 30, Curran Associates, Inc. (2017). https://proceedings.neurips.cc/paper_files/paper/2017/file/d5e2c0adad503c91f91df240d0cd4e49-Paper.pdf

13. Christiano, P.F., Leike, J., Brown, T.B., Martic, M., Legg, S., Amodei, D.: Deep reinforcement learning from human preferences. arXiv:abs/1706.03741 (2017). https://api.semanticscholar.org/CorpusID:4787508

14. Corazza, J., Gavran, I., Neider, D.: Reinforcement learning with stochastic reward machines. In: Thirty-Sixth AAAI Conference on Artificial Intelligence, AAAI 2022, Thirty-Fourth Conference on Innovative Applications of Artificial Intelligence, IAAI 2022, The Twelveth Symposium on Educational Advances in Artificial Intelligence, EAAI 2022 Virtual Event, February 22 - March 1, 2022, pp. 6429–6436, AAAI Press (2022). https://ojs.aaai.org/index.php/AAAI/article/view/20594

15. De Moura, L., Bjørner, N.: Z3: an efficient SMT solver. In: Proceedings of the Theory and Practice of Software, 14th International Conference on Tools and Algorithms for the Construction and Analysis of Systems, pp. 337–340, TACAS'08/ETAPS'08, Springer-Verlag, Berlin, Heidelberg (2008). ISBN 3540787992

16. Dohmen, T., Topper, N., Atia, G.K., Beckus, A., Trivedi, A., Velasquez, A.: Inferring probabilistic reward machines from non-markovian reward signals for reinforcement learning. In: Kumar, A., Thiébaux, S., Varakantham, P., Yeoh, W. (eds.) Proceedings of the Thirty-Second International Conference on Automated Planning and Scheduling, ICAPS 2022, Singapore (virtual), June 13-24, 2022, pp. 574–582, AAAI Press (2022). https://ojs.aaai.org/index.php/ICAPS/article/view/19844

17. Drews, S., D'antoni, L.: Learning symbolic automata. In: International Conference on Tools and Algorithms for Construction and Analysis of Systems (2017)

18. Dupont, P.: Regular grammatical inference from positive and negative samples by genetic search: the GIG method. In: Carrasco, R.C., Oncina, J. (eds.) Grammatical Inference and Applications, Second International Colloquium, ICGI-94, Alicante, Spain, September 21-23, 1994, Proceedings, Lecture Notes in Computer Science, vol. 862, pp. 236–245, Springer (1994), https://doi.org/10.1007/3-540-58473-0_152

19. Fleischner, H.: On the equivalence of mealy-type and Moore-type automata and a relation between reducibility and Moore-reducibility. J. Comput. Syst. Sci. 14(1), 1–16 (1977). ISSN 0022-0000, https://doi.org/10.1016/S0022-0000(77)80038-X, URL https://www.sciencedirect.com/science/article/pii/S002200007780038X

20. Gaon, M., Brafman, R.I.: Reinforcement learning with non-markovian rewards. In: The Thirty-Fourth AAAI Conference on Artificial Intelligence, AAAI 2020, The Thirty-Second Innovative Applications of Artificial Intelligence Conference, IAAI 2020, The Tenth AAAI Symposium on Educational Advances in Artificial Intelligence, EAAI 2020, New York, NY, USA, February 7-12, 2020, pp. 3980–3987, AAAI Press (2020)

21. Giannakopoulou, D., Rakamaric, Z., Raman, V.: Symbolic learning of component interfaces. In: Sensors Applications Symposium (2012). https://api.semanticscholar.org/CorpusID:1449946

22. Gold, E.M.: Complexity of automaton identification from given data. Inf. Control. 37, 302–320 (1978). https://api.semanticscholar.org/CorpusID:8943792

23. Guerin, J.T., Allen, T.E., Goldsmith, J.: Learning CP-net preferences online from user queries. In: AAAI Conference on Artificial Intelligence (2013). https://api.semanticscholar.org/CorpusID:15976671

24. Hopcroft, J.E., Karp, R.M.: A linear algorithm for testing equivalence of finite automata. (1971). https://api.semanticscholar.org/CorpusID:120207847

25. Icarte, R.T., Klassen, T., Valenzano, R., McIlraith, S.: Using reward machines for high-level task specification and decomposition in reinforcement learning. In: Dy, J., Krause, A. (eds.) Proceedings of the 35th International Conference on Machine Learning, Proceedings of Machine Learning Research, vol. 80, pp. 2107–2116, PMLR (2018). https://proceedings.mlr.press/v80/icarte18a.html

26. Iyengar, S.S., Lepper, M.R.: When choice is demotivating: can one desire too much of a good thing? J. Pers. Soc. Psychol. 79(6), 995 (2000)

27. Kalra, A., Brown, D.S.: Can differentiable decision trees learn interpretable reward functions? arXiv:abs/2306.13004 (2023). https://api.semanticscholar.org/CorpusID:259224487

28. Koriche, F., Zanuttini, B.: Learning conditional preference networks with queries. Artif. Intell. **174**, 685–703 (2009). https://api.semanticscholar.org/CorpusID: 3060370
29. Lin, S.W., Étienne André, Liu, Y., Sun, J., Dong, J.S.: Learning assumptions for compositional verification of timed systems. IEEE Trans. Softw. Eng. **40**(2), 137–153 (2014)
30. MacGlashan, J., et al.: Interactive learning from policy-dependent human feedback. In: Precup, D., Teh, Y.W. (eds.) Proceedings of the 34th International Conference on Machine Learning, Proceedings of Machine Learning Research, vol. 70, pp. 2285–2294, PMLR (2017). https://proceedings.mlr.press/v70/macglashan17a.html
31. Martelli, A., Montanari, U.: Unification in linear time and space: a structured presentation. Tech. rep, Istituto di Elaborazione della Informazione, Pisa (1976)
32. Mealy, G.H.: A method for synthesizing sequential circuits. Bell Syst. Tech. J. **34**(5), 1045–1079 (1955). https://doi.org/10.1002/j.1538-7305.1955.tb03788.x
33. Moore, E.F.: Gedanken-experiments on sequential machines. In: Shannon, C., McCarthy, J. (eds.) Automata Studies, pp. 129–153. Princeton University Press, Princeton, NJ (1956)
34. Ouyang, L., et al.: Training language models to follow instructions with human feedback. arXiv:abs/2203.02155 (2022). https://api.semanticscholar.org/ CorpusID:246426909
35. Robinson, J.A.: A machine-oriented logic based on the resolution principle. J. ACM **12**, 23–41 (1965)
36. Sadigh, D., Dragan, A.D., Sastry, S., Seshia, S.A.: Active preference-based learning of reward functions. In: Robotics: Science and Systems (2017)
37. Schuts, M., Hooman, J., Vaandrager, F.: Refactoring of Legacy Software Using Model Learning and Equivalence Checking: An Industrial Experience Report. Springer International Publishing (2016)
38. Shah, A., Vazquez-Chanlatte, M., Junges, S., Seshia, S.A.: Learning formal specifications from membership and preference queries (2023)
39. Tappler, M., Aichernig, B.K., Bacci, G., Eichlseder, M., Larsen, K.G.: L*-based learning of Markov decision processes. In: International Symposium on Formal Methods, pp. 651–669, Springer (2019)
40. Topper, N., Velasquez, A., Atia, G.: Bayesian inverse reinforcement learning for non-markovian rewards (2024)
41. Toro Icarte, R., Klassen, T.Q., Valenzano, R.A., McIlraith, S.A.: Reward machines: exploiting reward function structure in reinforcement learning. J. Artif. Intell. Res. (JAIR) **73**, 173–208 (2022). https://doi.org/10.1613/jair.1.12440
42. Toro Icarte, R., Waldie, E., Klassen, T., Valenzano, R., Castro, M., McIlraith, S.: Learning reward machines for partially observable reinforcement learning. In: Wallach, H., Larochelle, H., Beygelzimer, A., d'Alché-Buc, F., Fox, E., Garnett, R. (eds.) Advances in Neural Information Processing Systems, vol. 32, Curran Associates, Inc. (2019). https://proceedings.neurips.cc/paper/2019/file/ 532435c44bec236b471a47a88d63513d-Paper.pdf
43. Valiant, L.G.: A theory of the learnable. Commun. ACM **27**(11), 1134–1142 (1984). ISSN 0001-0782, https://doi.org/10.1145/1968.1972
44. Weiss, G., Goldberg, Y., Yahav, E.: Learning deterministic weighted automata with queries and counterexamples. In: Wallach, H., Larochelle, H., Beygelzimer, A., d'Alché-Buc, F., Fox, E., Garnett, R. (eds.) Advances in Neural Information Processing Systems, vol. 32, Curran Associates, Inc. (2019). https://proceedings. neurips.cc/paper_files/paper/2019/file/d3f93e7766e8e1b7ef66dfdd9a8be93b-Paper.pdf

45. Xu, Z., Gavran, I., Ahmad, Y., Majumdar, R., Neider, D., Topcu, U.,Wu, B.: Joint inference of reward machines and policies for reinforcement learning. Proc. Int. Conf. Autom. Plann. Sched. **30**(1), 590–598 (2020). https://doi.org/10.1609/icaps.v30i1.6756, https://ojs.aaai.org/index.php/ICAPS/article/view/6756

46. Xu, Z., Wu, B., Ojha, A., Neider, D., Topcu, U.: Active finite reward automaton inference and reinforcement learning using queries and counterexamples. In: Machine Learning and Knowledge Extraction: 5th IFIP TC 5, TC 12, WG 8.4, WG 8.9, WG 12.9 International Cross-Domain Conference, CD-MAKE 2021, Virtual Event, August 17–20, 2021, Proceedings, pp. 115–135, Springer-Verlag, Berlin, Heidelberg (2021). ISBN 978-3-030-84059-4, https://doi.org/10.1007/978-3-030-84060-0_8

47. Zhou, W., Li, W.: A hierarchical Bayesian approach to inverse reinforcement learning with symbolic reward machines. In: Chaudhuri, K., Jegelka, S., Song, L., Szepesvari, C., Niu, G., Sabato, S. (eds.) Proceedings of the 39th International Conference on Machine Learning, Proceedings of Machine Learning Research, vol. 162, pp. 27159–27178, PMLR (2022). https://proceedings.mlr.press/v162/zhou22b.html

Extending AALpy with Passive Learning:
A Generalized State-Merging Approach

Benjamin von Berg[1]($\boxtimes$) and Bernhard K. Aichernig[1,2]

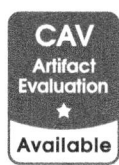

[1] Institute of Software Engineering and Artificial
Intelligence, Graz University of Technology, Graz, Austria
benjamin.vonberg@tugraz.at,
bernhard.aichernig@jku.at
[2] Institute for Formal Models and Verification,
Johannes Kepler University Linz, Linz, Austria

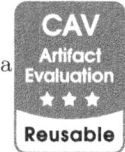

Abstract. AALpy is a well-established open-source automata learning library written in Python with a focus on active learning of systems with IO behavior. It provides a wide range of state-of-the-art algorithms for different automaton types ranging from fully deterministic to probabilistic automata. In this work, we present the recent addition of a generalized implementation of an important method from the domain of passive automata learning: state-merging in the red-blue framework. Using a common internal representation for different automaton types allows for a general and highly configurable implementation of the red-blue framework. We describe how to define and execute state-merging algorithms using AALpy, which reduces the implementation effort for state-merging algorithms mainly to the definition of compatibility criteria and scoring. This aids the implementation of both existing and novel algorithms. In particular, defining some existing state-merging algorithms from the literature with AALpy only takes a few lines of code.

Keywords: automata learning · model inference · passive learning · state merging · red-blue framework

1 Introduction

AALpy [19] is an active automata learning library written in Python with a focus on systems that show IO behavior, i.e. reactive systems. Automata learning algorithms extract a finite-state model from observations of a system-under-learning. They form the basis for black-box checking [2, 22].

AALpy is open-source and published on github[1]. It is well-established in the community and has been used in various domains. This includes reinforcement learning [27, 28], analysis of communication protocols [23, 24] and neural networks [20], black-box checking [15, 26], anomaly detection [18], software testing [10], process mining [6, 14] and reuse in other learning algorithms [3, 13].

---

[1] https://github.com/DES-Lab/AALpy

© The Author(s) 2025
R. Piskac and Z. Rakamarić (Eds.): CAV 2025, LNCS 15934, pp. 127–140, 2025.
https://doi.org/10.1007/978-3-031-98685-7_6

Passive learning algorithms use existing training data, like system logs, while active learning queries the system during learning. So far, AALpy has been mainly concerned with active automata learning. In this paper, we extend AALpy with a passive automata learning library for state-merging algorithms based on the red-blue framework [16]. This encompasses (1) algorithms already implemented in AALpy, such as RPNI [21] and IOAlergia [17], (2) existing algorithms that were not originally designed for the IO setting, such as the likelihood-ratio method by Verwer et al. [30] or EDSM [16] and (3) new approaches based on state-merging, be it completely novel methods or adaptations of existing methods in order to account for domain knowledge, such as additional constraints.

The rest of the paper is structured as follows. Section 2 gives some background and discusses how we generalized state merging. Section 3 demonstrates the usage of the new library. Section 4 draws the conclusions, relates AALpy to other tools and gives an outlook of further possible extensions. Further examples are provided in the appendix of the extended version of this paper [4].

2   Principles of Operation

2.1   Universal Internal Formalism

The tool presented in this work covers several types of finite-state automata with IO behavior. These automaton types share a small set of common assumptions: (1) There is a unique initial state from which execution starts. (2) Applying an input to an automaton triggers a state change and the emission of an output. (3) For each transition, the reached state is uniquely determined by the combination of current state, applied input and observed output. The following definition of automata covers Assumption 1 and 2 above and can be extended to more specific types of automata.

Definition 1. *An **IO automaton** is a tuple $\mathcal{M} = \langle Q, q_0, I, O, T \rangle$, where Q is the set of states, $q_0 \in Q$ is the initial state, I and O are the sets of input and output symbols respectively and $T \subseteq Q \times I \times O \times Q$ is a set of transitions.*

A transition $\langle q, i, o, q' \rangle \in T$ implies that applying input i in state q may cause $\mathcal{M}$ to emit the output o and switch to state q'. In other words, the automaton might behave nondeterministically. We discern between different forms of determinism.

Definition 2. *An automaton $\mathcal{M} = \langle Q, q_0, I, O, T \rangle$ is **deterministic** iff*

$$\forall \langle q_1, i_1, o_1, q'_1 \rangle, \langle q_2, i_2, o_2, q'_2 \rangle \in T : q_1 = q_2 \wedge i_1 = i_2 \Rightarrow o_1 = o_2 \wedge q'_1 = q'_2$$

*It is **observably nondeterministic** iff*

$$\forall \langle q_1, i_1, o_1, q'_1 \rangle, \langle q_2, i_2, o_2, q'_2 \rangle \in T : q_1 = q_2 \wedge i_1 = i_2 \wedge o_1 = o_2 \Rightarrow q'_1 = q'_2$$

Note that observable nondeterminism is equivalent to Assumption 3 above. Deterministic and observably nondeterministic automata allow writing the set of transitions as a (partial) transition function δ of the set of transitions with $\delta : Q \times I \rightharpoonup O \times Q$ and $\delta : Q \times I \times O \rightharpoonup Q$ respectively.

The definition of IO automata follows the behavior of Mealy machines, where the output of a transition depends on the source state, the target state and the provided input symbol. This is in contrast to Moore behavior, where the output depends on the target state alone:

Definition 3. *An IO automaton $\mathcal{M} = \langle Q, q_0, I, O, T \rangle$ has **Moore behavior** iff*

$$\forall \langle q_1, i_1, o_1, q_1' \rangle, \langle q_2, i_2, o_2, q_2' \rangle \in T : q_1' = q_2' \Rightarrow o_1 = o_2$$

A Moore machine can thus be seen as a deterministic IO automaton $\mathcal{M} = \langle Q, q_0, I, O, T \rangle$ with Moore behavior that emits the output o_0 associated with q_0 prior to handling the first input. Informally, we treat the emission of the initial output as the result of a transition $\langle \epsilon, \epsilon, o_0, q_0 \rangle \in T$.

When learning probabilistic automaton types, not only the possibility of a transition happening needs to be considered, but also its probability. This prompts the use of IO Frequency Automata (IOFA), which augment IOA with an observation count for transitions.

Definition 4. *An **IO frequency automaton** is a tuple $\mathcal{M} = \langle Q, q_0, I, O, \delta, \nu \rangle$, where $\langle Q, q_0, I, O, \delta \rangle$ is an observably nondeterministic IO automaton and $\nu : Q \times I \times O \to \mathbb{N}$ is the frequency function.*

The intuition behind $\nu(q, i, o) = n$ is that the transition from q on input i emitting o has been observed n times. We use IOFA as the common internal representation from which all supported automaton types can be extracted. This allows us to use a single implementation which is shared across all supported automaton types. Additional restrictions are required during the merging process to enforce the structural form of those automaton types and are covered in Sect. 2.3.

2.2   State Merging in the Red-Blue Framework

This section gives a brief overview over state merging algorithms and the red-blue framework. For a more detailed account consider [11,16] respectively.

State-merging algorithms are one of the main categories of passive automata learning algorithms. The input is given as a collection of traces, where each trace is a sequence of input-output pairs. The basic structure of state-merging algorithms consists of the following steps. First, a simple automaton representation of the provided traces is created, commonly using a so-called Prefix Tree Automaton (PTA). The PTA contains a state for every prefix in the input data. Grouping the behavior of traces with shared prefixes is admissible because we assume observable nondeterminism and results in a tree-shaped IOFA that describes exactly the observed traces and no other behavior. In the main loop of the algorithm, the automaton is generalized by iteratively merging pairs of states until no more merges are possible. We use the term *merge candidate* to refer to a pair of states that is considered for merging. Merging two states q_1 and q_2 results in a state that exhibits the behavior of both states. If both q_1 and q_2 have a transition with input i and output o leading to states q_1' and q_2' respectively, the assumption of observable nondeterminism implies that q_1' and q_2' must be the same state. Therefore, merging q_1 and q_2 also requires merging q_1' and q_2'. This is called an *implied merge*. Together, the initial merging of q_1 and q_2 and its implied merges results in a *partitioning* of the state space into sets of (transitively) merged states. The criteria for selecting potential merge candidates and evaluating their compatibility and quality are specific to the used algorithm.

Example 1 (PTAs and Merging). The left side of Fig. 1 shows the PTA for the three traces $\langle\langle x, a\rangle, \langle x, a\rangle, \langle x, a\rangle\rangle$, $\langle\langle x, a\rangle, \langle x, a\rangle, \langle y, b\rangle\rangle$ and $\langle\langle y, b\rangle\rangle$. Trying to merge q_1 and q_2 (dashed line) will lead to the implied merge of q_2 and q_4 (dotted line), which in turn requires merging not only q_4 and q_5 but also q_3 and q_6 since q_1 and q_4 are in the same partition. Applying the merge results in the automaton shown on the right where $p_1 = \{q_1, q_2, q_4, q_5\}$ and $p_2 = \{q_3, q_6\}$.

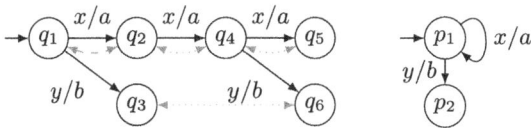

Fig. 1. Example of a PTA without frequencies (left) and the partitioning resulting from merging states q_1 and q_2 (right).

Algorithm 1 gives a high level description of the red-blue framework. The algorithm is parameterized by a scoring function *score* and an order relation over states $<$. The red-blue framework restricts which pairs of states are considered for merging in each iteration of the algorithm in order to reduce the number of compatibility calculations. This is achieved by dynamically dividing the nodes into three categories throughout the execution of the algorithm. The set of red states contains states that are considered mutually distinct. It is initialized to consist only of the root node of the PTA. The set of blue states is defined as the set of all states reachable from red states in a single transition that are not themselves red. The set of white states consists of all states that are neither red nor blue. In each iteration of the algorithm, only pairs consisting of a red and a blue state are considered for merging. If a blue state is incompatible with all red states, it is promoted to a red state. Otherwise the merge candidate with the best performing score according to an algorithm-specific function is chosen as the next intermediate model. For both promotion and merging, if there are several eligible candidates, ties are broken using a specified node order[2]. When all states are red, no more merges are possible and the final model is returned.

---

[2] Omitted in line 12 for brevity.

Algorithm 1. State Merging in the Red-Blue Framework.

Input: Collection of traces $\mathcal{TR}$
Parameters: Scoring function $score$, state order $<$
Output: Automaton model $\mathcal{M}$
Algorithm:

1: $\mathcal{M} \leftarrow$ PTA created from $\mathcal{TR}$
2: $Q_r \leftarrow \{q_0^{\mathcal{M}}\}$ ▷ Initialize red states to initial state
3: **loop**
4:       $Q_b \leftarrow$ set of blue states derived from Q_r
5:       **if** $Q_b = \emptyset$ **then**
6:            **return** $\mathcal{M}$ ▷ Terminate if no more merge candidates are available
7:       **end if**
8:       $S \leftarrow \{b \in Q_b \mid \forall r \in Q_r : score(\mathcal{M}, r, b) = -\infty\}$ ▷ Unmergeable blue states
9:       **if** $S \neq \emptyset$ **then**
10:          $Q_r \leftarrow Q_r \cup \{\min_< S\}$ ▷ Promote minimal unmergeable blue state
11:       **else**
12:          $\langle r, b \rangle \leftarrow \mathrm{argmax}_{\langle r,b \rangle \in Q_r \times Q_b} score(\mathcal{M}, r, b)$ ▷ Select best merge wrt. $score()$
13:          $\mathcal{M} \leftarrow merge(\mathcal{M}, r, b)$ ▷ Update model
14:       **end if**
15: **end loop**

Example 2 (Red-Blue Framework). Consider a slightly modified PTA compared to Example 1, where the transition from q_4 to q_6 on input y emits a instead of b. Figure 2 shows the progression from the PTA (left) to the final automaton (right) when applying the red-blue framework for learning a deterministic Mealy machine from the provided data. Nodes are ordered according to the shortlex order of their prefixes and labeled q_1 to q_6 accordingly. States q_1 and q_2 can not be merged due to the transitions on input y from states q_1 and q_4 emitting different outputs. The state q_2 is promoted since it is the minimal blue node and incompatible with the only red state q_1. Due to the order of nodes, q_1 and q_3 are merged before merging q_2 and q_4. As a result of the latter merge, q_6 becomes a child of q_2 and is finally merged with q_1.

2.3 Enforcing Automaton Structure

In this section, we describe how the automaton structure of the different supported automaton types is enforced in the internal representation. We categorize the automaton types supported by AALpy in two different ways: (1) output behavior and (2) transition behavior. The output behavior of states may depend on both inputs and the current state, like in Mealy machines, or on states alone, like in Moore machines. Transition behavior may be deterministic, nondeterministic or probabilistic. Taking the product of these two categorization schemes (1 and 2) results in six different automaton types also supported in AALpy. AALpy also supports two additional types for DFAs and discrete time Markov chains. However, these two types are subsumed by the other types. DFAs can be seen

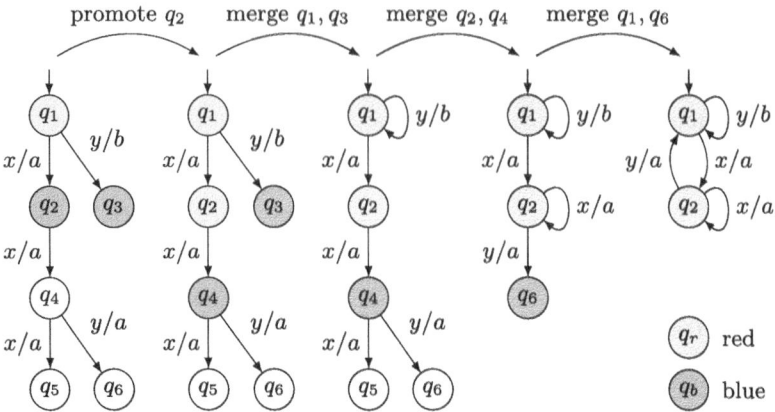

Fig. 2. Intermediate steps of state merging in the red-blue framework. (Color figure online)

as (deterministic) Moore machines with binary output, representing accept and reject. Markov chains have the same semantics as probabilistic Moore machines with a single input that represents the passage of time. Table 1 shows the different combination of behavior types and the respective classes in AALpy.

Table 1. Combination of output behavior (rows) and transition behavior (columns) and the respective automaton classes in AALpy.

	Deterministic	Nondeterministic	Probabilistic
Moore	MooreMachine, Dfa	NDMooreMachine	Mdp, MarkovChain
Mealy	MealyMachine	Onfsm	StochasticMealyMachine

Output Behavior. Mealy output behavior is the default for IOFAs and thus does not need to be enforced. This is not the case for Moore behavior. However, since each PTA state has only one predecessor, Moore behavior (Definition 3) is ensured at the beginning of the state-merging algorithm. The Moore property can be turned into an invariant of state-merging by strengthening the local compatibility criterion during merging such that merges which lead to a violation of the Moore property are rejected. Consequently, Moore behavior of the final automaton is ensured.

Transition Behavior. If deterministic transition behavior is given for a PTA, we can enforce it in the final automaton analogously to Moore behavior by rejecting merge candidates that lead to nondeterministic behavior (Definition 2). Similar to Mealy behavior, nondeterministic transition behavior is the default for

IOFA. To extract an automaton with probabilistic transition behavior from an IOFA $\langle Q, q_0, I, O, \delta, \nu \rangle$, the frequency function needs to be normalized. The probability distribution $p_{q,i}(o, q')$ describing the transitions originating from state q on input i to state q' emitting output o is given as

$$p_{q,i}(o, q') = \begin{cases} \nu(q, i, o) / \sum_{o' \in O} \nu(q, i, o') & \text{if } \delta(q, i, o) = q' \\ 0 & \text{otherwise} \end{cases}$$

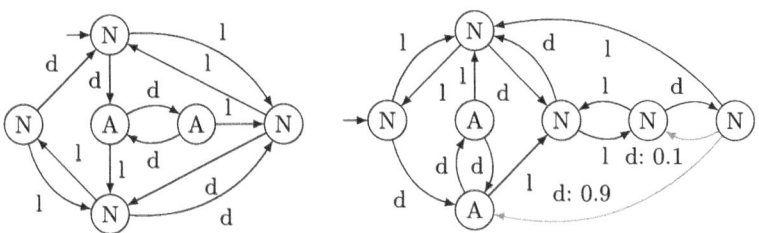

(a) Correct car alarm system.   (b) Faulty car alarm system.

Fig. 3. Car alarm systems with deterministic (a) and probabilistic (b) behavior.

3 Usage

3.1 Defining and Running State-Merging Algorithms

To define a state-merging algorithm, the `GeneralizedStateMerging` class is instantiated. Its most important parameters are:

`output_behavior`: Defines whether an automaton with Moore or Mealy behavior should be learned and adds corresponding restrictions for local compatibility. Possible values are `"moore"` and `"mealy"`.

`transition_behavior`: Defines whether the learned automaton is assumed to be deterministic, nondeterministic or probabilistic and adds corresponding restrictions for local compatibility. The values are `"deterministic"`, `"nondeterministic"` and `"stochastic"` respectively.

`score_calc`: An object of type `ScoreCalculation`, which governs the details of local compatibility and score calculation.

The defined algorithm can be executed using the object's `run` method, which requires a single argument representing the collection of available traces. Each trace is expected to be a sequence of input-output pairs. Algorithms with Moore behavior also expect the traces to be prepended with the initial output. Other input formats are discussed below. Depending on the combination of the arguments `output_behavior` and `transition_behavior`, the `run` method determines what kind of automaton is extracted from the internal representation.

Example 3. Consider a car which can be locked/unlocked (l) and its doors opened/ closed (d). The car also has an alarm, which triggers when the car is opened in a locked state and can only be disabled by unlocking the car. Figure 3a shows a Moore machine that models such a car alarm system. Depending on its state, its output is either alarm (A) or no alarm (N). Assume we do not know the real model and want to extract a model from recorded execution traces using RPNI [21], a well-known automata learning algorithm for DFAs which has been extended to Moore and Mealy machines in learning frameworks such as Learn-Lib [12] and AALpy. Assuming the variable `data` contains known traces from the car alarm system, a Moore machine can be learned using the following code.

```
1  data = [["N", ("d","A"), ("d","A"), ("l","N"), ("d","N")], ...]
2
3  alg = GeneralizedStateMerging(output_behavior="moore",
4      transition_behavior="deterministic")
5  model = alg.run(data)
```

No `ScoreCalculation` is provided, since RPNI greedily accepts possible merges without scoring and determinism is automatically enforced when specifying deterministic transition behavior. Mealy machines can be learned simply by setting `output_behavior="mealy"`, assuming `data` has the correct format.

The `ScoreCalculation` class can be instantiated with two parameters, which control local compatibility criteria and scoring. Those parameters are functions operating on the `GsmNode` class, which represents automaton states of IOFA.

`local_compatibility` is a function that takes two `GsmNode` objects and returns whether they are locally compatible. The first argument corresponds to the partition created up to that point and the second argument to the state to be added to the partition. Incompatibility of any two tested nodes leads to immediate rejection of the merge candidate.

`score_function` is a function that takes a dictionary mapping states prior to merging to the state describing the behavior of their associated partition. The function should return some form of score. The values `True` and `False` correspond to a score of positive and negative infinity and leads to immediate acceptance and rejection of the merge respectively.

Example 4. The Evidence Driven State Merging (EDSM) algorithm [16] is similar to RPNI, except that it also uses scoring in order to make better informed decisions. The score of a merge candidate depends on the amount of evidence available supporting the merge. This is quantified as the number of local compatibility checks triggered by merging the two states.

```
1  def EDSM_score(part : Dict[GsmNode, GsmNode]):
2      nr_partitions = len(set(part.values()))
3      nr_merged = len(part)
```

```
4        return nr_merged - nr_partitions
5
6  score = ScoreCalculation(score_function=EDSM_score)
7  alg = GeneralizedStateMerging(score_calc=score)
```

An example implementing the IOAlergia algorithm [17] for probabilistic systems such as the faulty car alarm depicted in Fig. 3b using a local compatibility criterion can be found in the appendix of the extended version of this paper [4].

The `ScoreCalculation` class can also be subclassed to create stateful score functions, which accumulate information from the local compatibility checks as the partitioning is created. In addition to the two methods described above, stateful implementations may override the method `reset` which is used to reset the internal state between score calculations. An example is provided in the appendix of the extended version of this paper [4].

Apart from the options listed above, `GeneralizedStateMerging` also has some minor parameters that change details in the red-blue framework. The options `pta_processing` and `postprocessing` allow to manipulate the internal representation before and after state merging. They can be set to arbitrary functions mapping one `GsmNode` to another and are applied to the initial state. Setting the flags `eval_compat_on_pta` and `eval_compat_on_futures` changes the way how local compatibility is evaluated, which is required e.g. to implement IOAlergia. Using the former causes the algorithm to use the original PTA for evaluating compatibility rather than the current automaton. The latter restricts compatibility checks to common futures, rather than computing it with respect to the partition implied by the merge candidate. The parameter `node_order` allows to specify the order in which merge candidates are evaluated. This is especially relevant for algorithms which greedily accept the first feasible merge without the use of scores. The default is the shortlex order of the prefix. The flag `consider_only_min_blue` further restricts the set of merge candidates to pairs of red states with the minimal blue node according to the node order. Finally, setting the flag `depth_first` causes the algorithm to search for violations of the local compatibility criterion in a depth first manner rather than breath first.

3.2 Utilities

The `run` method of the `GeneralizedStateMerging` class also has optional parameters that facilitate the analysis of algorithms. They can be used when experimenting with new algorithms or to better understand under which circumstances existing algorithms fail.

The parameter `convert` can be set to `False` to avoid converting the internal representation to the specific automaton type and causes `run` to return a `GsmNode` object.

The parameter `instrumentation` can be used to instrument the red-blue framework using an `Instrumentation` object that provides the option for callbacks at important points (merging, promotion, etc.).

Apart from the input format of input-output traces, other input formats are supported depending on the setting. In DFA inference, the training data is usually not prefix-closed. In this case, the input data can be represented as a set of labeled input sequences, where each element is a tuple consisting of an input sequence and a single output corresponding to the observation after applying the input sequence. For probabilistic models without input-output behavior, we support data specified as sequences of observations only. While the data format is usually detected automatically, it can be explicitly specified using the data_format argument of the run method.

The visualize method of the GsmNode class provides highly customizable visualization of automata based on the dot format of GraphViz [9]. For example, this could be used to highlight specific aspects of a model such as states that are locally deterministic, or to visualize incorrect merges during the design phase of new algorithms for debugging purposes.

4 Concluding Remarks

There are several software packages for automata learning. LearnLib [12] is very similar to AALpy in general. It mainly provides active automata learning for deterministic IO automata with a few passive algorithms. While its focus is more narrow, LearnLib provides more algorithms in its domain. The same holds true for jajapy [25], which is mainly concerned with passive learning of probabilistic models. The library libalf [7] falls in a similar category, but seems to be no longer actively developed. FlexFringe [29] is a C++ implementation of the red-blue framework and thus closely related to the presented extension of AALpy. A major difference is that FlexFringe does not support IO behavior out of the box. Supporting IO behavior requires a workaround, especially in the case of observably nondeterministic systems. On the other hand, FlexFringe offers more configuration options. A particularly noteworthy feature is the option to attach custom data to states which is exposed to the compatibility and scoring functions. The tools RALib [8], Tomte [1] and Mint [31] all deal with learning of Extended Finite State Machines in some form, which is not covered in AALpy.

We extended the passive automata learning capabilities of AALpy by adding a general implementation of the red-blue framework [16]. This implementation is general enough to cover state-merging algorithms for various types of IO automata which may exhibit deterministic, (observably) nondeterministic or probabilistic transition behavior and Mealy- or Moore-style output behavior. While the main focus was to provide a method that is general yet simple to use rather than performance, the provided implementation is sufficiently fast for practical applications. For example, we learned DFAs with well over thousand states from several hundred thousand traces in only a few minutes using the pypy interpreter on an ordinary laptop. Still, when comparing the RPNI implementations of LearnLib and our framework using the training data from the Abbadingo competition [16], our implementation is slower than LearnLib by a factor of 7.24. For the more complex (i.e. time consuming) Abbadingo tasks, the difference is less pronounced with a factor of 6.3. This constitutes a significant but not prohibitive difference. We assume the main causes for the difference to be (1) the lower performance of Python compared to Java and (2) our more general implementation supporting nondeterministic transitions, which is not required for RPNI and thus overhead. If performance is an issue, a dedicated implementation in a low level language is of course preferable. This is not our intention for AALpy and this extension. In some cases, the implementation abstracts the algorithm based on the parameters to reduce the overhead due to the generality of the red-blue framework. All in all, this results in a versatile state-merging tool which we expect to be useful to both researchers and industry.

In the future, we want to us the new capabilities of AALpy to explore combinations of active and passive algorithms. This can be particularly interesting when domain knowledge is available that can be used to efficiently generate traces with interesting (e.g. safety critical) behavior. We also aim to use the provided framework to explore how domain knowledge about systems can be injected into existing algorithms, which can be helpful in low data scenarios [5].

Acknowledgements. This work has received funding from the AIDOaRt project (grant agreement No 101007350) from the ECSEL Joint Undertaking (JU). The JU receives support from the European Union's Horizon 2020 research and innovation programs and Sweden, Austria, Czech Republic, Finland, France, Italy, and Spain.

The research leading to these results has received funding from the Transformative AI-Assisted Testing in Industrial Mobile Robotics (TASTE) project (project number FO999911053) from the ICT of the Future program. ICT of the Future is a research, technology and innovation funding program of the Republic of Austria, Ministry of Climate Action.

Disclosure of Interests. The authors have no competing interests to declare that are relevant to the content of this article.

References

1. Aarts, F., Heidarian, F., Kuppens, H., Olsen, P., Vaandrager, F.W.: Automata learning through counterexample guided abstraction refinement. In: Giannakopoulou, D., Méry, D. (eds.) FM 2012: Formal Methods - 18th International Symposium, Paris, France, August 27-31, 2012. Proceedings. Lecture Notes in Computer Science, vol. 7436, pp. 10–27. Springer (2012). https://doi.org/10.1007/978-3-642-32759-9_4
2. Aichernig, B.K., Tappler, M.: Probabilistic black-box reachability checking (extended version). Formal Methods Syst. Des. **54**(3), 416–448 (2019). https://doi.org/10.1007/S10703-019-00333-0
3. Ayoughi, N., Nejati, S., Sabetzadeh, M., Saavedra, P.: Enhancing automata learning with statistical machine learning: a network security case study. In: Egyed, A., Wimmer, M., Chechik, M., Combemale, B. (eds.) Proceedings of the ACM/IEEE 27th International Conference on Model Driven Engineering Languages and Systems, MODELS 2024, Linz, Austria, September 22-27, 2024, pp. 172–182. ACM (2024). https://doi.org/10.1145/3640310.3674087

4. von Berg, B., Aichernig, B.: Extending AALpy with passive learning: A generalized state-merging approach (2025). https://doi.org/10.5281/zenodo.15573752
5. von Berg, B., Aichernig, B.K., Rindler, M., Stern, D., Tappler, M.: Hierarchical learning of generative automaton models from sequential data. In: Madeira, A., Knapp, A. (eds.) Software Engineering and Formal Methods - 22nd International Conference, SEFM 2024, Aveiro, Portugal, November 6-8, 2024, Proceedings. Lecture Notes in Computer Science, vol. 15280, pp. 215–233. Springer (2024). https://doi.org/10.1007/978-3-031-77382-2_13
6. Bollig, B., Függer, M., Nowak, T.: A framework for streaming event-log prediction in business processes. CoRR arxiv:abs/2412.16032 (2024). https://doi.org/10.48550/ARXIV.2412.16032
7. Bollig, B., Katoen, J., Kern, C., Leucker, M., Neider, D., Piegdon, D.R.: libalf: the automata learning framework. In: Touili, T., Cook, B., Jackson, P.B. (eds.) Computer Aided Verification, 22nd International Conference, CAV 2010, Edinburgh, UK, July 15-19, 2010. Proceedings. Lecture Notes in Computer Science, vol. 6174, pp. 360–364. Springer (2010). https://doi.org/10.1007/978-3-642-14295-6_32
8. Cassel, S., Falk, H., Jonsson, B.: RALib: a LearnLib extension for inferring EFSMs. In: International Workshop on Design and Implementation of Formal Tools and Systems, DIFTS 2015, Austin, TX, USA, September 26-27 (2015). https://api.semanticscholar.org/CorpusID:12915995
9. Ellson, J., Gansner, E.R., Koutsofios, E., North, S.C., Woodhull, G.: Graphviz - open source graph drawing tools. In: Mutzel, P., Jünger, M., Leipert, S. (eds.) Graph Drawing, 9th International Symposium, GD 2001 Vienna, Austria, September 23-26, 2001, Revised Papers. Lecture Notes in Computer Science, vol. 2265, pp. 483–484. Springer (2001). https://doi.org/10.1007/3-540-45848-4_57
10. Ganty, P.: Learning the state machine behind a modal text editor: the (neo)vim case study. In: Neele, T., Wijs, A. (eds.) Model Checking Software - 30th International Symposium, SPIN 2024, Luxembourg City, Luxembourg, April 8-9, 2024, Proceedings. Lecture Notes in Computer Science, vol. 14624, pp. 167–175. Springer (2024). https://doi.org/10.1007/978-3-031-66149-5_9
11. de la Higuera, C.: Grammatical Inference: Learning Automata and Grammars. Cambridge University Press (2010). https://doi.org/10.1017/CBO9781139194655
12. Isberner, M., Howar, F., Steffen, B.: The open-source learnlib - a framework for active automata learning. In: Kroening, D., Pasareanu, C.S. (eds.) Computer Aided Verification - 27th International Conference, CAV 2015, San Francisco, CA, USA, July 18-24, 2015, Proceedings, Part I. Lecture Notes in Computer Science, vol. 9206, pp. 487–495. Springer (2015). https://doi.org/10.1007/978-3-319-21690-4_32
13. Junges, S., Rot, J.: Learning language intersections. In: Jansen, N., Stoelinga, M., van den Bos, P. (eds.) A Journey from Process Algebra via Timed Automata to Model Learning - Essays Dedicated to Frits Vaandrager on the Occasion of His 60th Birthday. Lecture Notes in Computer Science, vol. 13560, pp. 371–381. Springer (2022). https://doi.org/10.1007/978-3-031-15629-8_20
14. Kobialka, P., Pferscher, A., Bergersen, G.R., Johnsen, E.B., Tarifa, S.L.T.: Stochastic games for user journeys. In: Platzer, A., Rozier, K.Y., Pradella, M., Rossi, M. (eds.) Formal Methods - 26th International Symposium, FM 2024, Milan, Italy, September 9-13, 2024, Proceedings, Part II. Lecture Notes in Computer Science, vol. 14934, pp. 167–186. Springer (2024). https://doi.org/10.1007/978-3-031-71177-0_12

15. Kuze, N., Seno, K., Ushio, T.: Learning-based black box checking for k-safety hyperproperties. Eng. Appl. Artif. Intell. **126**, 107029 (2023). https://doi.org/10.1016/J.ENGAPPAI.2023.107029

16. Lang, K.J., Pearlmutter, B.A., Price, R.A.: Results of the Abbadingo One DFA learning competition and a new evidence-driven state merging algorithm. In: Honavar, V.G., Slutzki, G. (eds.) Grammatical Inference, 4th International Colloquium, ICGI-98, Ames, Iowa, USA, July 12-14, 1998, Proceedings. Lecture Notes in Computer Science, vol. 1433, pp. 1–12. Springer (1998). https://doi.org/10.1007/BFB0054059

17. Mao, H., Chen, Y., Jaeger, M., Nielsen, T.D., Larsen, K.G., Nielsen, B.: Learning deterministic probabilistic automata from a model checking perspective. Mach. Learn. **105**(2), 255–299 (2016). https://doi.org/10.1007/s10994-016-5565-9

18. Moddemann, L., Steude, H.S., Diedrich, A., Pill, I., Niggemann, O.: Extracting knowledge using machine learning for anomaly detection and root-cause diagnosis. In: 29th IEEE International Conference on Emerging Technologies and Factory Automation, ETFA 2024, Padova, Italy, September 10-13, 2024. pp. 1–8. IEEE (2024). https://doi.org/10.1109/ETFA61755.2024.10710647

19. Muskardin, E., Aichernig, B.K., Pill, I., Pferscher, A., Tappler, M.: AALpy: an active automata learning library. Innov. Syst. Softw. Eng. **18**(3), 417–426 (2022). https://doi.org/10.1007/S11334-022-00449-3

20. Muskardin, E., Aichernig, B.K., Pill, I., Tappler, M.: Learning finite state models from recurrent neural networks. In: ter Beek, M.H., Monahan, R. (eds.) Integrated Formal Methods - 17th International Conference, IFM 2022, Lugano, Switzerland, June 7-10, 2022, Proceedings. Lecture Notes in Computer Science, vol. 13274, pp. 229–248. Springer (2022). https://doi.org/10.1007/978-3-031-07727-2_13

21. Oncina, J., García, P.: Identifying regular languages in polynomial time. In: Bunke, H. (ed.) Advances in Structural and Syntactic Pattern Recognition. Series in Machine Perception and Artificial Intelligence, vol. 5, pp. 99–108. World Scientific (1993). https://doi.org/10.1142/9789812797919_0007

22. Peled, D., Vardi, M.Y., Yannakakis, M.: Black box checking. In: International Conference on Protocol Specification, Testing and Verification, pp. 225–240. Springer (1999). https://doi.org/10.1007/978-0-387-35578-8_13

23. Pferscher, A., Aichernig, B.K.: Fingerprinting bluetooth low energy devices via active automata learning. In: Huisman, M., Pasareanu, C.S., Zhan, N. (eds.) Formal Methods - 24th International Symposium, FM 2021, Virtual Event, November 20-26, 2021, Proceedings. Lecture Notes in Computer Science, vol. 13047, pp. 524–542. Springer (2021).https://doi.org/10.1007/978-3-030-90870-6_28

24. Pferscher, A., Aichernig, B.K.: Stateful black-box fuzzing of Bluetooth devices using automata learning. In: Deshmukh, J.V., Havelund, K., Perez, I. (eds.) NASA Formal Methods - 14th International Symposium, NFM 2022, Pasadena, CA, USA, May 24-27, 2022, Proceedings. Lecture Notes in Computer Science, vol. 13260, pp. 373–392. Springer (2022). https://doi.org/10.1007/978-3-031-06773-0_20

25. Reynouard, R., Ingólfsdóttir, A., Bacci, G.: Jajapy: a learning library for stochastic models. In: Jansen, N., Tribastone, M. (eds.) Quantitative Evaluation of Systems - 20th International Conference, QEST 2023, Antwerp, Belgium, September 20-22, 2023, Proceedings. Lecture Notes in Computer Science, vol. 14287, pp. 30–46. Springer (2023). https://doi.org/10.1007/978-3-031-43835-6_3

26. Shijubo, J., Waga, M., Suenaga, K.: Probabilistic black-box checking via active MDP learning. ACM Trans. Embed. Comput. Syst. **22**(5s), 148:1–148:26 (2023). https://doi.org/10.1145/3609127

27. Tappler, M., Pferscher, A., Aichernig, B.K., Könighofer, B.: Learning and repair of deep reinforcement learning policies from fuzz-testing data. In: Proceedings of the 46th IEEE/ACM International Conference on Software Engineering, ICSE 2024, Lisbon, Portugal, April 14-20, 2024, pp. 6:1–6:13. ACM (2024). https://doi.org/10.1145/3597503.3623311

28. Tappler, M., Pranger, S., Könighofer, B., Muskardin, E., Bloem, R., Larsen, K.G.: Automata learning meets shielding. In: Margaria, T., Steffen, B. (eds.) Leveraging Applications of Formal Methods, Verification and Validation. Verification Principles - 11th International Symposium, ISoLA 2022, Rhodes, Greece, October 22-30, 2022, Proceedings, Part I. Lecture Notes in Computer Science, vol. 13701, pp. 335–359. Springer (2022). https://doi.org/10.1007/978-3-031-19849-6_20

29. Verwer, S., Hammerschmidt, C.A.: FlexFringe: Modeling software behavior by learning probabilistic automata. CoRR arxiv:abs/2203.16331 (2022). https://doi.org/10.48550/ARXIV.2203.16331

30. Verwer, S., de Weerdt, M., Witteveen, C.: A likelihood-ratio test for identifying probabilistic deterministic real-time automata from positive data. In: Sempere, J.M., García, P. (eds.) Grammatical Inference: Theoretical Results and Applications, 10th International Colloquium, ICGI 2010, Valencia, Spain, September 13-16, 2010. Proceedings. Lecture Notes in Computer Science, vol. 6339, pp. 203–216. Springer (2010). https://doi.org/10.1007/978-3-642-15488-1_17

31. Walkinshaw, N., Taylor, R., Derrick, J.: Inferring extended finite state machine models from software executions. Empir. Softw. Eng. **21**(3), 811–853 (2016). https://doi.org/10.1007/S10664-015-9367-7

LearnLib: 10 years later

Markus Frohme[1] (✉), Falk Howar[1,2], and Bernhard Steffen[1]

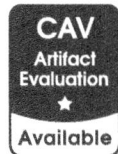

[1] TU Dortmund University, Dortmund, Germany
{markus.frohme,falk.howar,
bernhard.steffen}@cs.tu-dortmund.de
[2] Fraunhofer ISST, Dortmund, Germany

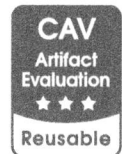

Abstract. In 2015, LearnLib, the open-source framework for active automata learning, received the prestigious CAV artifact award. This paper presents the advancements made since then, highlighting significant additions to LearnLib, including state-of-the-art algorithms, novel learning paradigms, and increasingly expressive models. Our efforts to mature and maintain LearnLib have resulted in its widespread use among researchers and practitioners alike. A key factor in its success is the achieved compositionality which allows users to effortlessly construct thousands of customized learning processes tailored to their specific requirements. This paper illustrates these features through the development of a learning process for the life-long learning of procedural systems. This development can be easily replicated and modified using the latest public release of LearnLib.

Keywords: (Active) Automata Learning · Monitoring · Refinement · Open-Source · Library · Java

1 Introduction

Active automata learning describes the process of inferring an automaton-based model from a hardware or software system by means of actively querying it. What originally started as a theoretical concept for language inference [9] has in recent decades gained a lot of interest from practitioners due to the role of automata learning as the key enabler of practical model-based quality assurance. There exist several success stories that underline its practical relevance [67, 47, 3, 20, 2, 4, 72, 32, 64].

Tools are of paramount importance when applying these theoretical concepts to practical scenarios. Unfortunately, by being mostly research-driven, many tools are no longer developed or even maintained once the main researcher or research group leaves the project. Specifically for active automata learning, we have observed this trend with tools such as *libALF* [16] (last release in 2011), *RALT* [70] (never published, internal use at France Telecom until 2014), *AIDE* [49] (development ceased in 2015), *Sp2Learn* [11] (development ceased in 2016), *Tomte* [1] (latest release in 2016), *SymbolicAutomata* [25] (no major contributions since 2019), or *ROLL* [53] (somewhat regular contributions, but no stable releases). Currently, we are only aware of *AALpy* [59] that is being actively developed and maintained.

© The Author(s) 2025
R. Piskac and Z. Rakamarić (Eds.): CAV 2025, LNCS 15934, pp. 141–160, 2025.
https://doi.org/10.1007/978-3-031-98685-7_7

This paper highlights the significant advancements of LearnLib a decade after receiving the CAV artifact award in 2015 [45]. These advancements include not only new paradigms for addressing the challenges of practical automata learning and the evolution of automata learning towards more expressive formalisms such as procedural systems, but also enhanced compositionality. We demonstrate how users can now easily construct thousands of customized learning processes tailored to their specific needs. In particular, researchers can easily benchmark their new learning algorithms against the state of the art by simply replacing components in established learning processes, while application developers can seamlessly compose tailored learning processes to evaluate their suitability for specific requirements. This paper showcases this potential through the development of a learning process for the life-long learning of procedural systems.

The open structure of LearnLib has inspired numerous researchers to contribute by providing case studies and algorithms which can now be seamlessly integrated as illustrated in this paper. We aim to further establish LearnLib as a comprehensive resource for automata learning.

LearnLib is written in Java, open-source[3], and released under the Apache 2.0 license[4]. It is deployed to Maven Central, the de-facto standard for various build tools in the Java ecosystem, and therefore can be directly used in many projects. Consequently, the developments presented in this paper can be easily replicated and modified.

Outline We continue in Section 2 with an overview of the current features of LearnLib and highlight the major additions of the last decade. Section 3 showcases the flexibility of LearnLib to easily configure a requirements-based learning process. In Section 4, we summarize our efforts to improve the development process of LearnLib and the impact it had on the research community. Section 5 concludes the paper and gives an outlook on the future of LearnLib.

2   New Features in LearnLib

Active automata learning usually operates within the *minimally adequate teacher* framework as proposed by Angluin [9]. During the exploration phase, a *learning algorithm* (or learner) queries the *system under learning* (SUL) for its behavior through a *membership oracle* to construct a tentative hypothesis model of the SUL. After hypothesis stabilization, an *equivalence oracle* then checks in the verification phase whether the hypothesis model and the SUL are equivalent and, if not, returns a counterexample (a witness for in-equivalence). This counterexample is used by the learner to refine the current hypothesis model, which triggers a subsequent exploration phase. The two phases alternate until the equivalence oracle no longer finds any counterexamples. For details, see [74].

Figure 1 sketches the current features of LearnLib for the involved concepts *learning processes* are composed of. For instantiating a learning process, the user

---

[3] https://github.com/LearnLib/learnlib
[4] https://www.apache.org/licenses/LICENSE-2.0

only needs to define the symbolic interactions with the system (`Symbols`) and provide a means to access it (`SUL`). All remaining parts are provided by LearnLib and can be combined depending on the requirements of the user. In the following, we highlight the novel additions to LearnLib.

Active Learning Algorithms Experiments [43] show that one bottleneck of active automata learning typically lies in the performance of the SUL for answering queries. As a result, many learners aim at reducing the number of queries that they pose and the length thereof. We have developed the concept of *lazy partition refinement* [41] which distills the idea of the TTT algorithm [46] to represent hypothesis states with a redundancy-free, prefix-closed set of access sequence while simultaneously distinguishing between them with a redundancy-free, suffix-closed set of discriminators. LearnLib provides two incarnations of this concept in the form of the L^λ algorithm (based on the L^* algorithm [9]) and the TTT^λ algorithm (based on the TTT algorithm [46]).

A different approach to pursue this goal concerns refining the way in which learners communicate with the SUL. The ADT learner [33] and the $L^\#$ learner [78] utilize adaptive distinguishing sequences to separate between hypothesis states. By adaptively deciding which inputs to query next, they can discriminate between more states, thus reducing the number of queries needed. The implementation of the $L^\#$ algorithm was contributed by Ferreira et al. as part of their work in [27].

The amount of system inputs can easily cause performance problems, too. To address this issue, we implemented the concept of *automated alphabet abstraction refinement* (AAAR) [42]. AAAR introduces an orthogonal learning process on the behavioral equivalence classes of the input symbols (as long as such a finite partition exists), incorporating input symbols in the learning process only when really needed. It is worth noting that AAAR is not a single algorithm but a generic concept which can be combined with various of the existing (regular) learning algorithms.

Finally, Bayram [14] extended some of the existing learning algorithms to natively support inferring Moore machines [58]. Being able to record intermediate state outputs can increase the expressiveness of membership queries, boosting the performance of learning processes in case the SUL supports these semantics, too.

Another challenge for practical automata learning is the question whether the chosen formalism is expressive enough to capture the system properties of interest. We extended the scope of LearnLib to support the active inference of context-free (or procedural) systems. The notion of *systems of procedural automata* (SPAs) [35], *systems of behavioral automata* (SBAs) [36], and *systems of procedural Mealy machines* (SPMMs) [34] describe systems that are composed of multiple regular procedures that can mutually call each other. Similar to AAAR, this allows for a generic *meta-learner* that can be parameterized in the concrete learner(s) used for the internal procedures. Furthermore, the existing OP algorithm [40] and TTT algorithm [46] have been extended [44] to support the inference of *visibly push-down automata* (VPAs) [8].

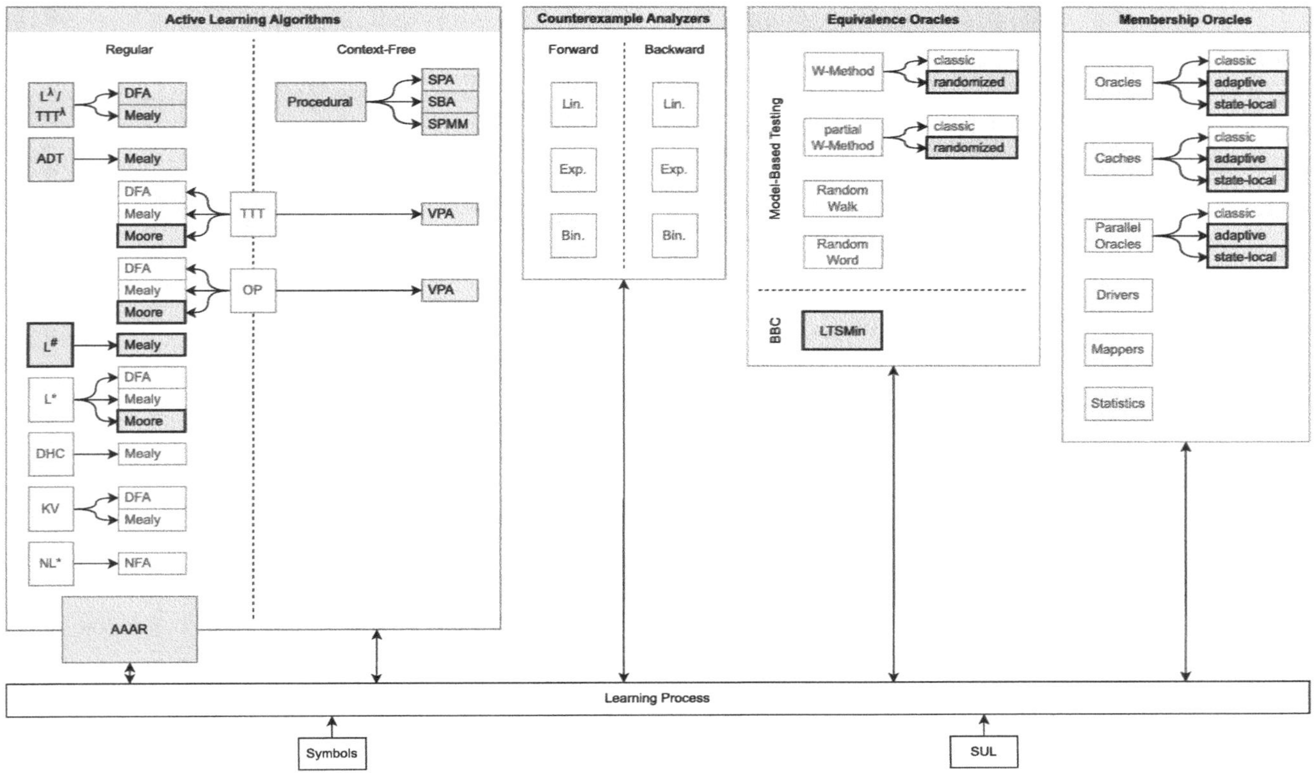

Fig. 1. An overview of the current active automata learning features of LearnLib. Gray nodes represent features from [45] and colored nodes represent new features. Blue marks learning-related concepts, green marks equivalence testing-related concepts, and orange marks membership query-related concepts. Components with bold outlines have been contributed by external community members.

Equivalence Oracles Meijer and Pol [57] integrated the model checker LTSmin [48] into LearnLib and therefore provided a means for *black-box checking* (BBC) [63]. Due to the clever use of LearnLib's modular structure, the authors implement the model checker as a special form of equivalence oracle which seamlessly integrates into the existing hierarchy.

Smetsers et al. [73] discovered that adding fuzzying to methods from model-based testing such as the (partial) W-method [21, 37] is able to boost the performance of counterexample search. The implementations of the authors can be used as drop-in replacements for the classic procedures.

Membership Oracles As an alternative to algorithmic properties for the reduction of membership queries during learning, Geske [38] investigated the concept of state-local alphabets which allow queries to be answered early if non-available input symbols are encountered. This concept is implemented as an independent query filter, making the approach compatible with various existing types of membership oracles.

Another practical means to boost performance concerns the caching and parallelization of queries. Vitorovic [80] introduced a new type of *adaptive membership queries* which model a symbol-by-symbol style communication, contrasting the typical preset queries. His work includes the respective caches and parallel oracles which are implemented in a generic fashion so that they can be shared by adaptive algorithms such as ADT and $L^{\#}$.

Performance Besides algorithmic properties, implementation details such as architectural design decisions or the chosen programming language may also impact (learning) performance. Typically, comparisons of tools (e.g., in [59]) are not conclusive and often depend on the considered use-cases. As a result, we focused more on advancing conceptual features. For example, we improved existing learner implementations by optimizing their batching of queries in order to support a higher degree of parallelization if applicable and we added support for suspending and resuming learning processes to allow for re-using intermediate results in more sophisticated learning setups.

3   Construction of Custom Learning Processes

In this section we illustrate how LearnLib supports the construction of learning processes tailored to specific requirements profiles. The example is included in the artifact and can be used as the basis for experimentation. Additionally, the entire learning process can also be easily implemented with the latest public release of LearnLib (version 0.18.0).

3.1   Requirements

Let us assume that we are interested in controlling a procedural system (systems that may comprise recursion) in a monitoring-based fashion to implement the concept of *life-long learning* [15]. This implies that

- we need a procedural learner and
- monitoring requires us to support
  - prefix-closed semantics as the monitor, ideally, records the subsequent reactions to individual inputs, and
  - extremely long counterexamples since the monitor may detect issues only after days worth of operation.

Immediately, this makes certain options preferable over others.

❶ For modelling prefix-closed procedural systems either SBAs or SPMMs can be used. Since our monitor records individual outputs, we choose SPMMs.
❷ Specific to procedural learners is the choice of a local learner for inferring the involved procedures. We choose the TTT algorithm for this task as it is specifically designed to handle the long counterexamples provided by monitoring.

Another important characteristics of the chosen example is that it comprises two phases:

- a phase for inferring a model for constructing the initial monitor, and
- the monitoring-based life-long learning phase.

In this paper, we focus on the first phase which is interesting because it comes with quite some potential for optimization: we want to speed up the learning process.

❸ Since we can easily spawn multiple local instances of our application, we want to answer queries in parallel.
❹ To reduce the load on our application, we also want to remove duplicate queries via the use of caching.
❺ Furthermore, we have specified a set of critical runs of our system that we want to check during learning to not deploy a knowingly faulty application.

In contrast, the monitoring phase is a purely technical issue. One only has to specify how the monitor can access the current hypothesis model and how monitored traces can be used to refine the hypothesis model.

3.2   Implementation

Listing 1.1 sketches how these requirements can be implemented with LearnLib.

```
 1  // setup
 2  var alphabet = ...
 3  var instance1 = ...
 4  var instance2 = ...
 5
 6  // membership oracles
 7  var parallel =
        ParallelOracleBuilders.newStaticParallelOracle(instance1,
        instance2).create(); ❸
 8  var mqo = MealyCaches.createCache(alphabet, parallel); ❹
 9
10  // equivalence oracles
11  var sample = new SampleSetEQOracle<Input,
        Word<Output>>().addAll(requirements); ❺
12  var wMethod = new WMethodEQOracle<>(mqo);
13  var eqo = new EQOracleChain<>(sample, wMethod);
14
15  // learner
16  var learner = new SPMMLearner<>(alphabet, Output.ERROR, mqo,
        TTTAdapterMealy::new ❷ ); ❶
17
18  // learning loop
19  learner.startLearning();
20  var hyp = learner.getHypothesisModel();
21  DefaultQuery<Input, Word<Output>> cex;
22  while ((cex = eqo.findCounterExample(hyp, alphabet)) != null) {
23      learner.refineHypothesis(cex);
24      hyp = learner.getHypothesisModel();
25  }
26
27  // continue to work with the model
28  startMonitor(learner);
```

Listing 1.1. Construction of the discussed learning process. Encircled numbers reference the respective requirements of the example.

Membership Oracle After the initial setup of symbolic interactions and instantiating our local testing instances, we begin with constructing the main membership oracle that is going to be used by the learner (for exploration) and the equivalence oracle (for verification). LearnLib's design of membership oracles innately supports the processing of query *batches*. Via convenient factory methods, LearnLib provides special *parallel oracles* that split these batches according to a selectable strategy and distribute the (sub-) batches to the provided oracle instances. Yet, due to clever use of abstraction, these oracles appear as regular membership oracles to the outside. As a result, we can use the same instance as a delegate for our query cache. Note that we simply re-use a Mealy cache for this purpose because both formalisms are transition output systems. Using a simple decorator pattern, users are able to construct powerful query chains which can easily integrate custom extensions such as query filters (e.g., to only focus on a specific part of the system) or counters (e.g., to measure the workload on the SUL).

Equivalence Oracle In a similar fashion, equivalence oracles can be composed. LearnLib provides out-of-the-box implementations for many of the conventional equivalence tests. The power comes from being able to combine them. In our example, we build an equivalence oracle chain which sequentially asks each of its inner oracles for counterexamples. First, we use a sampling oracle that simply checks the traces from our previously prepared requirements. Once these traces no longer expose any in-equivalences, we use the W-method for a more methodical test-case generation. Due to the oracle chain, we can abstract all these steps (and potentially more) behind a simple object.

Learner Finally, the learner is set up. As discussed in our requirements, specific to procedural systems is the concept of a *meta-learner* which can be parameterized in its sub-learner(s). Here, we instantiate the SPMM learner and select the TTT algorithm as its procedural learner. The SPMM learner only requires a learner for (regular) Mealy machines, so many other algorithms in LearnLib (or custom ones) can be used, too.

It should be noted that learners can typically be configured with specific counterexample analysis strategies. In our case, however, we can omit this step for two reasons.

- Because SPMMs are context-free, the prefix-closed semantics guarantees that no analysis is required to identify the procedure call responsible for an error, because it is always the same as the procedure call where the error is observed.
- LearnLib uses convention over configuration when reasonable. For the procedural learner, we consider the default binary search-based analysis as adequate.

For other settings, like SPAs or SBAs, LearnLib provides 36 options alone for the (combined) choices of global and procedural counterexample analysis algorithms.

Learning Loop The actual learning process is a simple `while`-loop that alternates between the exploration and verification phase (cf. Section 2). The loop terminates once the equivalence oracle is no longer able to find counterexamples.

Monitoring The learner and the equivalence oracle only communicate via counterexamples. As a result, the very same learner can simply receive counterexamples from the monitor and continue its original learning process. In particular, we do not need to reset any progress but can seamlessly integrate the existing components in the new context. Due to space reasons, we skip the details of the monitor execution. However, from the learning loop, it should be clear how the monitor can access the current hypothesis model and how monitored traces can be used to refine the hypothesis model. The involved workflow is identical to the presented one.

3.3   Takeaways

With LearnLib it is possible to construct complex and intricate learning setups by composing them from simple and easy-to-understand components. The driving forces behind this ability are the rigorous notion of abstraction and composition. For users, this manifests in two ways.

First, LearnLib provides the building blocks for highly specialized learning setups, all while maintaining compatibility between the involved structures. For example, had we chosen the acceptor-based SBA formalism instead of the transducer-based SPMM formalism, only the output type would have changed from Word<Output> to Boolean. For the rest, the same notion of composition for membership oracles, equivalence oracles, and (procedural) learners would have been available.

Second, LearnLib establishes functional contracts which allow for highly extensible implementations. In Listing 1.1, each concept ((procedural) learning algorithm, membership oracle, equivalence oracle, etc.) could have been replaced with a custom implementation without impeding the overall workflow.

From a practitioner's perspective this allows for easy building of use-case specific adaptations and optimizations to improve the overall experience when applying automata learning in practice. From a researcher's perspective, LearnLib provides a rich framework in which novel concepts can be implemented and directly evaluated in a multitude of different contexts.

4   Impact on the Community

Over the years, we continuously improved the experience for potential users. On the technical side, we enhanced the build process of LearnLib to include several industry standards (such as static code analysis and test coverage analysis) and transparently offer them in continuous integration and deployment pipelines to enable high-quality community contributions (cf. Section 2). By supporting modern technologies (such as the *Java Platform Module System* (JPMS) for building custom application installers) and improving integrability (e.g., by switching to the logging facade SLF4J and dropping dependencies with proprietary licenses), LearnLib should become much more attractive for professional environments as well.

On the social side, we further integrated with LearnLib's hosting platform GitHub. We replaced previous mailing lists with GitHub's discussion feature[5] which allows for a much more integrated communication about ideas, issues, and pull requests. Judging from the activity, this change seems to have been positively received by the community as well. Furthermore, we open-sourced the

---

[5] https://github.com/LearnLib/learnlib/discussions

LearnLib website[6] to enable external contributors to improve and extend existing documentation, e.g., by referencing their own related projects to help connecting different research groups. Our efforts enable users to profit from LearnLib at different levels:

Tool-Level There are numerous cases where LearnLib is simply used as a tool [72, 68, 29, 31, 76, 10, 6, 5, 7, 12, 65, 22, 82, 39, 52, 66, 24, 18, 56, 55]. Here, LearnLib provides a service that is either used qualitatively (simply to infer a model) or quantitatively (to compare the performance of different learning algorithms). In these situations, the researchers typically only need to provide an interface to their systems under learning[7] in order to execute their experiments.

Library-Level Other work presents tools that have been built using LearnLib essentially as a library [13, 75, 79, 51, 81, 71, 54, 28, 30, 27, 77, 60, 69]. In this case, LearnLib is used as a library on which the respective tools depend. These situations show how the modularization, the APIs, and the deployment of LearnLib aligns with modern software development.

Framework-Level Cooperation at this level profits most from LearnLib's flexible architecture. Typical here is the extension of LearnLib with custom functionality [57, 23, 50, 17, 26] such as symbol filters or supporting conflicting queries. A particularly fruitful example of this is RALib [19] which is a standalone tool for active learning of register automata. RALib is based on LearnLib and heavily extends its different components with custom learning algorithms and equivalence algorithms (cf. Figure 1). Such extensions, in particular when they are re-integrated again into LearnLib (e.g., [57]), motivate our efforts to increase the flexibility of LearnLib's architecture.

5   Conclusion & Future Work

We have highlighted the advancements of LearnLib over the past decade, aiming to establish it as the central resource for (active) automata learning. Compositionality and extensibility have been the driving forces behind its development, as there cannot be a one-size-fits-all solution in automata learning. Instead, the ability to easily create custom learning processes tailored to specific application profiles is crucial for practical success. It allows researchers to easily benchmark their new learning algorithms against the state of the art by simply replacing components in established learning processes, while application developers can seamlessly compose tailored learning processes to evaluate their suitability for specific requirements. We have illustrated this flexibility by developing a learning process for the life-long learning of procedural systems.

We are continuously working on integrating new technologies. For example, LearnLib has already received initial support for *passive* automata learning via algorithms such as RPNI [61] or OSTIA [62] (contributed by Aleksander Mendoza-Drosik[8]). One of our next goals is to look at the insights gained by RALib [19] to enhance LearnLib's capability to handle data. In the long term, we aim to establish a LearnLib-based benchmark suite as an industry standard for evaluating and comparing active automata learning algorithms.

---

[6] https://github.com/LearnLib/learnlib.github.io
[7] Sometimes, the definition of this interface is the actual research being conducted.
[8] https://github.com/aleksander-mendoza

LearnLib is open-source. We encourage users to replicate and experiment with the concepts presented in this paper and are looking forward to future collaborations which we see as key to the long-term success of LearnLib.

Disclosure of Interests Markus Frohme is funded by Deutsche Forschungsgemeinschaft (DFG), Grant 528775176. The authors are directly involved with development and maintenance of the presented tool. The authors declare they have no financial interests.

References

[1] Fides Aarts. "Tomte : bridging the gap between active learning and real-world systems". PhD thesis. Radboud Universiteit Nijmegen, Netherlands, Oct. 2014. DOI: 2066/130428.

[2] Fides Aarts, Joeri de Ruiter, and Erik Poll. "Formal Models of Bank Cards for Free". In: *Sixth IEEE International Conference on Software Testing, Verification and Validation, ICST 2013 Workshops Proceedings, Luxembourg, Luxembourg, March 18-22, 2013*. IEEE Computer Society, 2013, pp. 461–468. DOI: 10.1109/ICSTW.2013.60.

[3] Fides Aarts, Julien Schmaltz, and Frits W. Vaandrager. "Inference and Abstraction of the Biometric Passport". In: *Leveraging Applications of Formal Methods, Verification, and Validation - 4th International Symposium on Leveraging Applications, ISoLA 2010, Heraklion, Crete, Greece, October 18-21, 2010, Proceedings, Part I*. Ed. by Tiziana Margaria and Bernhard Steffen. Vol. 6415. Lecture Notes in Computer Science. Springer, 2010, pp. 673–686. DOI: 10.1007/978-3-642-16558-0_54.

[4] Fides Aarts et al. "Generating models of infinite-state communication protocols using regular inference with abstraction". In: *Formal Methods Syst. Des.* 46.1 (2015), pp. 1–41. DOI: 10.1007/s10703-014-0216-x.

[5] Bernhard K. Aichernig, Christian Burghard, and Robert Korosec. "Learning-Based Testing of an Industrial Measurement Device". In: *NASA Formal Methods - 11th International Symposium, NFM 2019, Houston, TX, USA, May 7-9, 2019, Proceedings*. Ed. by Julia M. Badger and Kristin Yvonne Rozier. Vol. 11460. Lecture Notes in Computer Science. Springer, 2019, pp. 1–18. DOI: 10.1007/978-3-030-20652-9_1.

[6] Bernhard K. Aichernig and Martin Tappler. "Efficient Active Automata Learning via Mutation Testing". In: *J. Autom. Reason.* 63.4 (2019), pp. 1103–1134. DOI: 10.1007/S10817-018-9486-0.

[7] Bernhard K. Aichernig et al. "Learning a Behavior Model of Hybrid Systems Through Combining Model-Based Testing and Machine Learning". In: *Testing Software and Systems - 31st IFIP WG 6.1 International Conference, ICTSS 2019, Paris, France, October 15-17, 2019, Proceedings*. Ed. by Christophe Gaston, Nikolai Kosmatov, and Pascale Le Gall. Vol. 11812. Lecture Notes in Computer Science. Springer, 2019, pp. 3–21. DOI: 10.1007/978-3-030-31280-0_1

[8] Rajeev Alur and P. Madhusudan. "Visibly pushdown languages". In: *Proceedings of the 36th Annual ACM Symposium on Theory of Computing, Chicago, IL, USA, June 13-16, 2004*. Ed. by László Babai. ACM, 2004, pp. 202–211. DOI: 10.1145/1007352.1007390.

[9]   Dana Angluin. "Learning Regular Sets from Queries and Counterexamples". In: *Information and Computation* 75.2 (1987), pp. 87–106. DOI: 10.1016/0890-5401(87)90052-6.

[10]   Paolo Arcaini, Angelo Gargantini, and Elvinia Riccobene. "Regular Expression Learning with Evolutionary Testing and Repair". In: *Testing Software and Systems - 31st IFIP WG 6.1 International Conference, ICTSS 2019, Paris, France, October 15-17, 2019, Proceedings*. Ed. by Christophe Gaston, Nikolai Kosmatov, and Pascale Le Gall. Vol. 11812. Lecture Notes in Computer Science. Springer, 2019, pp. 22–40. DOI: 10.1007/978-3-030-31280-0_2.

[11]   Denis Arrivault et al. "Sp2Learn: A Toolbox for the Spectral Learning of Weighted Automata". In: *Proceedings of the 13th International Conference on Grammatical Inference, ICGI 2016, Delft, The Netherlands, October 5-7, 2016*. Ed. by Sicco Verwer, Menno van Zaanen, and Rick Smetsers. Vol. 57. JMLR Workshop and Conference Proceedings. JMLR.org, 2016, pp. 105–119. URL: http://proceedings.mlr.press/v57/arrivault16.html.

[12]   Kousar Aslam et al. "Interface protocol inference to aid understanding legacy software components". In: *Softw. Syst. Model.* 19.6 (2020), pp. 1519–1540. DOI: 10.1007/S10270-020-00809-2.

[13]   Alexander Bainczyk et al. "ALEX: Mixed-Mode Learning of Web Applications at Ease". In: *Leveraging Applications of Formal Methods, Verification and Validation: Discussion, Dissemination, Applications - 7th International Symposium, ISoLA 2016, Imperial, Corfu, Greece, October 10-14, 2016, Proceedings, Part II*. Ed. by Tiziana Margaria and Bernhard Steffen. Vol. 9953. Lecture Notes in Computer Science. 2016, pp. 655–671. DOI: 10.1007/978-3-319-47169-3_51.

[14]   Mohamad Bayram. "Moore-basierte Anfragen zur Query-Optimierung beim aktiven Automatenlernen". In german. Bachelor's thesis. TU Dortmund University, 2022.

[15]   Antonia Bertolino et al. "Never-stop Learning: Continuous Validation of Learned Models for Evolving Systems through Monitoring". In: *ERCIM News* 2012.88 (2012). URL: http://ercim-news.ercim.eu/en88/special/never-stop-learning-continuous-validation-of-learned-models-for-evolving-systems-through-monitoring.

[16]   Benedikt Bollig et al. "libalf: The Automata Learning Framework". In: *Computer Aided Verification, 22nd International Conference, CAV 2010, Edinburgh, UK, July 15-19, 2010. Proceedings*. Ed. by Tayssir Touili, Byron Cook, and Paul B. Jackson. Vol. 6174. Lecture Notes in Computer Science. Springer, 2010, pp. 360–364. DOI: 10.1007/978-3-642-14295-6_32.

[17]   Véronique Bruyère, Guillermo A. Pérez, and Gaëtan Staquet. "Learning Realtime One-Counter Automata". In: *Tools and Algorithms for the Construction and Analysis of Systems - 28th International Conference, TACAS 2022, Held as Part of the European Joint Conferences on Theory and Practice of Software, ETAPS 2022, Munich, Germany, April 2-7, 2022, Proceedings, Part I*. Ed. by Dana Fisman and Grigore Rosu. Vol. 13243. Lecture Notes in Computer Science. Springer, 2022, pp. 244–262. DOI: 10.1007/978-3-030-99524-9_13

[18] Véronique Bruyère, Guillermo A. Pérez, and Gaëtan Staquet. "Validating Streaming JSON Documents with Learned VPAs". In: *Tools and Algorithms for the Construction and Analysis of Systems - 29th International Conference, TACAS 2023, Held as Part of the European Joint Conferences on Theory and Practice of Software, ETAPS 2022, Paris, France, April 22-27, 2023, Proceedings, Part I*. Ed. by Sriram Sankaranarayanan and Natasha Sharygina. Vol. 13993. Lecture Notes in Computer Science. Springer, 2023, pp. 271–289. DOI: 10.1007/978-3-031-30823-9_14.

[19] Sofia Cassel, Falk Howar, and Bengt Jonsson. "RALib: A LearnLib extension for inferring EFSMs". In: *DIFTS* 5 (2015).

[20] Chia Yuan Cho et al. "Inference and analysis of formal models of botnet command and control protocols". In: *Proceedings of the 17th ACM Conference on Computer and Communications Security, CCS 2010, Chicago, Illinois, USA, October 4-8, 2010*. Ed. by Ehab Al-Shaer, Angelos D. Keromytis, and Vitaly Shmatikov. ACM, 2010, pp. 426–439. DOI: 10.1145/1866307.1866355.

[21] Tsun S. Chow. "Testing Software Design Modeled by Finite-State Machines". In: *IEEE Transactions on Software Engineering* 4.3 (1978), pp. 178–187. DOI: 10.1109/TSE.1978.231496.

[22] Carlos Diego Nascimento Damasceno, Mohammad Reza Mousavi, and Adenilso da Silva Simão. "Learning by sampling: learning behavioral family models from software product lines". In: *Empir. Softw. Eng.* 26.1 (2021), p. 4. DOI: 10.1007/S10664-020-09912-W.

[23] Carlos Diego Nascimento Damasceno, Mohammad Reza Mousavi, and Adenilso da Silva Simão. "Learning to Reuse: Adaptive Model Learning for Evolving Systems". In: *Integrated Formal Methods - 15th International Conference, IFM 2019, Bergen, Norway, December 2-6, 2019, Proceedings*. Ed. by Wolfgang Ahrendt and Silvia Lizeth Tapia Tarifa. Vol. 11918. Lecture Notes in Computer Science. Springer, 2019, pp. 138–156. DOI: 10.1007/978-3-030-34968-4_8.

[24] Simon Dierl et al. "Learning Symbolic Timed Models from Concrete Timed Data". In: *NASA Formal Methods - 15th International Symposium, NFM 2023, Houston, TX, USA, May 16-18, 2023, Proceedings*. Ed. by Kristin Yvonne Rozier and Swarat Chaudhuri. Vol. 13903. Lecture Notes in Computer Science. Springer, 2023, pp. 104–121. DOI: 10.1007/978-3-031-33170-1_7.

[25] Samuel Drews and Loris D'Antoni. "Learning Symbolic Automata". In: *Tools and Algorithms for the Construction and Analysis of Systems - 23rd International Conference, TACAS 2017, Held as Part of the European Joint Conferences on Theory and Practice of Software, ETAPS 2017, Uppsala, Sweden, April 22-29, 2017, Proceedings, Part I*. Ed. by Axel Legay and Tiziana Margaria. Vol. 10205. Lecture Notes in Computer Science. 2017, pp. 173–189. DOI: 10.1007/978-3-662-54577-5_10.

[26] Tiago Ferreira, Gerco van Heerdt, and Alexandra Silva. "Tree-Based Adaptive Model Learning". In: *A Journey from Process Algebra via Timed Automata to Model Learning - Essays Dedicated to Frits Vaandrager on the Occasion of His 60th Birthday*. Ed. by Nils Jansen, Mariëlle Stoelinga, and Petra van den Bos. Vol. 13560. Lecture Notes in Computer Science. Springer, 2022, pp. 164–179. DOI: 10.1007/978-3-031-15629-8_10.

[27]   Tiago Ferreira et al. "Conflict-Aware Active Automata Learning". In: *Proceedings of the Fourteenth International Symposium on Games, Automata, Logics, and Formal Verification, GandALF 2023, Udine, Italy, 18-20th*

[28]   Tiago Ferreira et al. "Prognosis: closed-box analysis of network protocol implementations". In: *ACM SIGCOMM 2021 Conference, Virtual Event, USA, August 23-27, 2021*. Ed. by Fernando A. Kuipers and Matthew C. Caesar. ACM, 2021, pp. 762–774. DOI: 10.1145/3452296.3472938.

[29]   Paul Fiterau-Brostean, Ramon Janssen, and Frits W. Vaandrager. "Combining Model Learning and Model Checking to Analyze TCP Implementations". In: *Computer Aided Verification - 28th International Conference, CAV 2016, Toronto, ON, Canada, July 17-23, 2016, Proceedings, Part II*. Ed. by Swarat Chaudhuri and Azadeh Farzan. Vol. 9780. Lecture Notes in Computer Science. Springer, 2016, pp. 454–471. DOI: 10.1007/978-3-319-41540-6_25.

[30]   Paul Fiterau-Brostean et al. "DTLS-Fuzzer: A DTLS Protocol State Fuzzer". In: *15th IEEE Conference on Software Testing, Verification and Validation, ICST 2022, Valencia, Spain, April 4-14, 2022*. IEEE, 2022, pp. 456–458. DOI: 10.1109/ICST53961.2022.00051.

[31]   Paul Fiterau-Brostean et al. "Model learning and model checking of SSH implementations". In: *Proceedings of the 24th ACM SIGSOFT International SPIN Symposium on Model Checking of Software, Santa Barbara, CA, USA, July 10-14, 2017*. Ed. by Hakan Erdogmus and Klaus Havelund. ACM, 2017, pp. 142–151. DOI: 10.1145/3092282.3092289.

[32]   Paul Fiterău-Broştean and Falk Howar. "Learning-Based Testing the Sliding Window Behavior of TCP Implementations". In: *Critical Systems: Formal Methods and Automated Verification - Joint 22nd International Workshop on Formal Methods for Industrial Critical Systems - and - 17th International Workshop on Automated Verification of Critical Systems, FMICS-AVoCS 2017, Turin, Italy, September 18-20, 2017, Proceedings*. Ed. by Laure Petrucci, Cristina Seceleanu, and Ana Cavalcanti. Vol. 10471. Lecture Notes in Computer Science. Springer, 2017, pp. 185–200. DOI: 10.1007/978-3-319-67113-0_12.

[33]   Markus Frohme. "Active Automata Learning with Adaptive Distinguishing Sequences". In: *CoRR* abs/1902.01139 (2019). arXiv: 1902.01139.

[34]   Markus Frohme. "Model-based quality assurance of intrumented context-free systems". PhD thesis. Technical University of Dortmund, Germany, 2023. DOI: 10.17877/DE290R-24032.

[35]   Markus Frohme and Bernhard Steffen. "Compositional learning of mutually recursive procedural systems". In: *Int. J. Softw. Tools Technol. Transf.* 23.4 (2021), pp. 521–543. DOI: 10.1007/S10009-021-00634-Y.

[36]   Markus Frohme and Bernhard Steffen. "From Languages to Behaviors and Back". In: *A Journey from Process Algebra via Timed Automata to Model Learning - Essays Dedicated to Frits Vaandrager on the Occasion of His 60th Birthday*. Ed. by Nils Jansen, Mariëlle Stoelinga, and Petra van den Bos. Vol. 13560. Lecture Notes in Computer Science. Springer, 2022, pp. 180–200. DOI: 10.1007/978-3-031-15629-8_11.

[37] Susumu Fujiwara et al. "Test Selection Based on Finite State Models". In: *IEEE Transactions on Software Engineering* 17.6 (1991), pp. 591–603. DOI: 10.1109/32.87284.

[38] Maren Geske. "Implementation and performance evaluation of an active learning algorithm for visible state-local alphabets". Master's thesis. TU Dortmund University, 2018.

[39] Dennis Hendriks and Kousar Aslam. "A Systematic Approach for Interfacing Component-Based Software with an Active Automata Learning Tool". In: *Leveraging Applications of Formal Methods, Verification and Validation. Software Engineering - 11th International Symposium, ISoLA 2022, Rhodes, Greece, October 22-30, 2022, Proceedings, Part II*. Ed. by Tiziana Margaria and Bernhard Steffen. Vol. 13702. Lecture Notes in Computer Science. Springer, 2022, pp. 216–236. DOI: 10.1007/978-3-031-19756-7_13.

[40] Falk Howar. "Active Learning of Interface Programs". PhD thesis. TU Dortmund University, 2012. DOI: 10.17877/DE290R-4817.

[41] Falk Howar and Bernhard Steffen. "Active Automata Learning as Black-Box Search and Lazy Partition Refinement". In: *A Journey from Process Algebra via Timed Automata to Model Learning - Essays Dedicated to Frits Vaandrager on the Occasion of His 60th Birthday*. Ed. by Nils Jansen, Mariëlle Stoelinga, and Petra van den Bos. Vol. 13560. Lecture Notes in Computer Science. Springer, 2022, pp. 321–338. DOI: 10.1007/978-3-031-15629-8_17.

[42] Falk Howar, Bernhard Steffen, and Maik Merten. "Automata Learning with Automated Alphabet Abstraction Refinement". In: *Verification, Model Checking, and Abstract Interpretation - 12th International Conference, VM-CAI 2011, Austin, TX, USA, January 23-25, 2011. Proceedings*. Ed. by Ranjit Jhala and David A. Schmidt. Vol. 6538. Lecture Notes in Computer Science. Springer, 2011, pp. 263–277. DOI: 10.1007/978-3-642-18275-4_19.

[43] Falk Howar et al. "The Teachers' Crowd: The Impact of Distributed Oracles on Active Automata Learning". In: *Leveraging Applications of Formal Methods, Verification, and Validation - International Workshops, SARS 2011 and MLSC 2011, Held Under the Auspices of ISoLA 2011 in Vienna, Austria, October 17-18, 2011. Revised Selected Papers*. Ed. by Reiner Hähnle et al. Vol. 336. Communications in Computer and Information Science. Springer, 2011, pp. 232–247. DOI: 10.1007/978-3-642-34781-8_18.

[44] Malte Isberner. "Foundations of active automata learning: an algorithmic perspective". PhD thesis. Technical University Dortmund, Germany, 2015. URL: https://hdl.handle.net/2003/34282.

[45] Malte Isberner, Falk Howar, and Bernhard Steffen. "The Open-Source LearnLib - A Framework for Active Automata Learning". In: *Computer Aided Verification - 27th International Conference, CAV 2015, San Francisco, CA, USA, July 18-24, 2015, Proceedings, Part I*. Ed. by Daniel Kroening and Corina S. Pasareanu. Vol. 9206. Lecture Notes in Computer Science. Springer, 2015, pp. 487–495. DOI: 10.1007/978-3-319-21690-4_32

[46] Malte Isberner, Falk Howar, and Bernhard Steffen. "The TTT Algorithm: A Redundancy-Free Approach to Active Automata Learning". In: *Runtime Verification - 5th International Conference, RV 2014, Toronto, ON, Canada, September 22-25, 2014. Proceedings*. Ed. by Borzoo Bonakdarpour and Scott A. Smolka. Vol. 8734. Lecture Notes in Computer Science. Springer, 2014, pp. 307–322. DOI: 10.1007/978-3-319-11164-3_26.

[47] Valérie Issarny et al. "CONNECT Challenges: Towards Emergent Connectors for Eternal Networked Systems". In: *14th IEEE International Conference on Engineering of Complex Computer Systems, ICECCS 2009, Potsdam, Germany, 2-4 June 2009*. IEEE Computer Society, 2009, pp. 154–161. DOI: 10.1109/ICECCS.2009.44.

[48] Gijs Kant et al. "LTSmin: High-Performance Language-Independent Model Checking". In: *Tools and Algorithms for the Construction and Analysis of Systems - 21st International Conference, TACAS 2015, Held as Part of the European Joint Conferences on Theory and Practice of Software, ETAPS 2015, London, UK, April 11-18, 2015. Proceedings*. Ed. by Christel Baier and Cesare Tinelli. Vol. 9035. Lecture Notes in Computer Science. Springer, 2015, pp. 692–707. DOI: 10.1007/978-3-662-46681-0_61.

[49] Ali Khalili and Armando Tacchella. "Learning Nondeterministic Mealy Machines". In: *Proceedings of the 12th International Conference on Grammatical Inference, ICGI 2014, Kyoto, Japan, September 17-19, 2014*. Ed. by Alexander Clark, Makoto Kanazawa, and Ryo Yoshinaka. Vol. 34. JMLR Workshop and Conference Proceedings. JMLR.org, 2014, pp. 109–123. URL: http://proceedings.mlr.press/v34/khalili14a.html

[50] Paul Kogel, Verena Klös, and Sabine Glesner. "TTT/ik: Learning Accurate Mealy Automata Efficiently with an Imprecise Symbol Filter". In: *Formal Methods and Software Engineering - 23rd International Conference on Formal Engineering Methods, ICFEM 2022, Madrid, Spain, October 24-27, 2022, Proceedings*. Ed. by Adrián Riesco and Min Zhang. Vol. 13478. Lecture Notes in Computer Science. Springer, 2022, pp. 227–243. DOI: 10.1007/978-3-031-17244-1_14.

[51] Martin Kölbl, Stefan Leue, and Thomas Wies. "TarTar: A Timed Automata Repair Tool". In: *Computer Aided Verification - 32nd International Conference, CAV 2020, Los Angeles, CA, USA, July 21-24, 2020, Proceedings, Part I*. Ed. by Shuvendu K. Lahiri and Chao Wang. Vol. 12224. Lecture Notes in Computer Science. Springer, 2020, pp. 529–540. DOI: 10.1007/978-3-030-53288-8_25.

[52] Eric Lesiuta, Victor Bandur, and Mark Lawford. "SLIME: State Learning in the Middle of Everything for Tool-Assisted Vulnerability Detection". In: *Computer Security. ESORICS 2022 International Workshops - CyberICPS 2022, SECPRE 2022, SPOSE 2022, CPS4CIP 2022, CDT&SECOMANE 2022, EIS 2022, and SecAssure 2022, Copenhagen, Denmark, September 26-30, 2022, Revised Selected Papers*. Ed. by Sokratis K. Katsikas et al. Vol. 13785. Lecture Notes in Computer Science. Springer, 2022, pp. 686–704. DOI: 10.1007/978-3-031-25460-4_39.

[53]   Yong Li et al. "A Novel Learning Algorithm for Büchi Automata Based on Family of DFAs and Classification Trees". In: *Tools and Algorithms for the Construction and Analysis of Systems - 23rd International Conference, TACAS 2017, Held as Part of the European Joint Conferences on Theory and Practice of Software, ETAPS 2017, Uppsala, Sweden, April 22-29, 2017, Proceedings, Part I*. Ed. by Axel Legay and Tiziana Margaria. Vol. 10205. Lecture Notes in Computer Science. 2017, pp. 208–226. DOI: 10.1007/978-3-662-54577-5_12.

[54]   Tiziana Margaria and Alexander Schieweck. "Towards Engineering Digital Twins by Active Behaviour Mining". In: *Model Checking, Synthesis, and Learning - Essays Dedicated to Bengt Jonsson on The Occasion of His 60th Birthday*. Ed. by Ernst-Rüdiger Olderog, Bernhard Steffen, and Wang Yi. Vol. 13030. Lecture Notes in Computer Science. Springer, 2021, pp. 138–163. DOI: 10.1007/978-3-030-91384-7_8.

[55]   Stefan Marksteiner, Peter Priller, and Markus Wolf. "Approaches for Automating Cybersecurity Testing of Connected Vehicles". In: *Intelligent Secure Trustable Things*. Ed. by Michael Karner et al. Cham: Springer Nature Switzerland, 2024, pp. 219–234. DOI: 10.1007/978-3-031-54049-3_13.

[56]   Stefan Marksteiner, Marjan Sirjani, and Mikael Sjödin. "Using Automata Learning for Compliance Evaluation of Communication Protocols on an NFC Handshake Example". In: *Engineering of Computer-Based Systems - 8th International Conference,ECBS 2023, Västerås, Sweden, October 16-18, 2023, Proceedings*. Ed. by Jan Kofron, Tiziana Margaria, and Cristina Seceleanu. Vol. 14390. Lecture Notes in Computer Science. Springer, 2023, pp. 170–190. DOI: 10.1007/978-3-031-49252-5_13.

[57]   Jeroen Meijer and Jaco van de Pol. "Sound Black-Box Checking in the LearnLib". In: *NASA Formal Methods - 10th International Symposium, NFM 2018, Newport News, VA, USA, April 17-19, 2018, Proceedings*. Ed. by Aaron Dutle, César A. Muñoz, and Anthony Narkawicz. Vol. 10811. Lecture Notes in Computer Science. Springer, 2018, pp. 349–366. DOI: 10.1007/978-3-319-77935-5_24.

[58]   Edward F. Moore. "Gedanken-Experiments on Sequential Machines". In: *Automata Studies*. Ed. by C. E. Shannon and J. McCarthy. Princeton: Princeton University Press, 1956, pp. 129–154. DOI: doi:10.1515/9781400882618-006.

[59]   Edi Muskardin et al. "AALpy: An Active Automata Learning Library". In: *Automated Technology for Verification and Analysis - 19th International Symposium, ATVA 2021, Gold Coast, QLD, Australia, October 18-22, 2021, Proceedings*. Ed. by Zhe Hou and Vijay Ganesh. Vol. 12971. Lecture Notes in Computer Science. Springer, 2021, pp. 67–73. DOI: 10.1007/978-3-030-88885-5_5.

[60]   Thomas Neele and Matteo Sammartino. "Compositional Automata Learning of Synchronous Systems". In: *Fundamental Approaches to Software Engineering - 26th International Conference, FASE 2023, Held as Part of the European Joint Conferences on Theory and Practice of Software, ETAPS 2023, Paris, France, April 22-27, 2023, Proceedings*. Ed. by Leen Lambers and Sebastián Uchitel. Vol. 13991. Lecture Notes in Computer Science. Springer, 2023, pp. 47–66. DOI: 10.1007/978-3-031-30826-0_3.

[61] José Oncina and Pedro García. "Inferring regular languages in polynomial update time". In: *World Scientific* (Jan. 1992), pp. 49–61. DOI: 10.1142/9789812797902_0004.

[62] José Oncina, Pedro García, and Enrique Vidal. "Learning Subsequential Transducers for Pattern Recognition Interpretation Tasks". In: *IEEE Trans. Pattern Anal. Mach. Intell.* 15.5 (1993), pp. 448–458. DOI: 10.1109/34.211465.

[63] Doron Peled, Moshe Y. Vardi, and Mihalis Yannakakis. "Black Box Checking". In: *Formal Methods for Protocol Engineering and Distributed Systems: FORTE XII / PSTV XIX. IFIP Advances in Information and Communication Technology.* Ed. by Jianping Wu, Samuel T. Chanson, and Qiang Gao. Boston, MA: Springer US, 1999, pp. 225–240. DOI: 10.1007/978-0-387-35578-8_13.

[64] Andrea Pferscher and Bernhard K. Aichernig. "Fingerprinting Bluetooth Low Energy Devices via Active Automata Learning". In: *Formal Methods - 24th International Symposium, FM 2021, Virtual Event, November 20-26, 2021, Proceedings.* Ed. by Marieke Huisman, Corina S. Pasareanu, and Naijun Zhan. Vol. 13047. Lecture Notes in Computer Science. Springer, 2021, pp. 524–542. DOI: 10.1007/978-3-030-90870-6_28.

[65] Andrea Pferscher and Bernhard K. Aichernig. "Learning Abstracted Non-deterministic Finite State Machines". In: *Testing Software and Systems - 32nd IFIP WG 6.1 International Conference, ICTSS 2020, Naples, Italy, December 9-11, 2020, Proceedings.* Ed. by Valentina Casola, Alessandra De Benedictis, and Massimiliano Rak. Vol. 12543. Lecture Notes in Computer Science. Springer, 2020, pp. 52–69. DOI: 10.1007/978-3-030-64881-7_4.

[66] Swantje Plambeck, Lutz Schammer, and Görschwin Fey. "On the Viability of Decision Trees for Learning Models of Systems". In: *27th Asia and South Pacific Design Automation Conference, ASP-DAC 2022, Taipei, Taiwan, January 17-20, 2022.* IEEE, 2022, pp. 696–701. DOI: 10.1109/ASP-DAC52403.2022.9712579.

[67] Harald Raffelt, Bernhard Steffen, and Tiziana Margaria. "Dynamic Testing Via Automata Learning". In: *Hardware and Software: Verification and Testing, Third International Haifa Verification Conference, HVC 2007, Haifa, Israel, October 23-25, 2007, Proceedings.* Ed. by Karen Yorav. Vol. 4899. Lecture Notes in Computer Science. Springer, 2007, pp. 136–152. DOI: 10.1007/978-3-540-77966-7_13.

[68] Joeri de Ruiter and Erik Poll. "Protocol State Fuzzing of TLS Implementations". In: *24th USENIX Security Symposium, USENIX Security 15, Washington, D.C., USA, August 12-14, 2015.* Ed. by Jaeyeon Jung and Thorsten Holz. USENIX Association, 2015, pp. 193–206. URL: https://www.usenix.org/conference/usenixsecurity15/technical-sessions/presentation/de-ruiter.

[69] Ocan Sankur. "Timed Automata Verification and Synthesis via Finite Automata Learning". In: *Tools and Algorithms for the Construction and Analysis of Systems - 29th International Conference, TACAS 2023, Held as Part of the European Joint Conferences on Theory and Practice of Software, ETAPS 2022, Paris, France, April 22-27, 2023, Proceedings, Part II*. Ed. by Sriram Sankaranarayanan and Natasha Sharygina. Vol. 13994. Lecture Notes in Computer Science. Springer, 2023, pp. 329–349. DOI: 10.1007/978-3-031-30820-8_21.

[70] Muhammad Muzammil Shahbaz. "Reverse Engineering Enhanced State Models of Black Box Software Components to support Integration Testing". PhD thesis. Institut Polytechnique de Grenoble, France, Dec. 2008.

[71] Junya Shijubo, Masaki Waga, and Kohei Suenaga. "Efficient Black-Box Checking via Model Checking with Strengthened Specifications". In: *Runtime Verification - 21st International Conference, RV 2021, Virtual Event, October 11-14, 2021, Proceedings*. Ed. by Lu Feng and Dana Fisman. Vol. 12974. Lecture Notes in Computer Science. Springer, 2021, pp. 100–120. DOI: 10.1007/978-3-030-88494-9_6.

[72] Wouter Smeenk et al. "Applying Automata Learning to Embedded Control Software". In: *Formal Methods and Software Engineering - 17th International Conference on Formal Engineering Methods, ICFEM 2015, Paris, France, November 3-5, 2015, Proceedings*. Ed. by Michael J. Butler, Sylvain Conchon, and Fatiha Zaïdi. Vol. 9407. Lecture Notes in Computer Science. Springer, 2015, pp. 67–83. DOI: 10.1007/978-3-319-25423-4_5.

[73] Rick Smetsers et al. "Complementing Model Learning with Mutation-Based Fuzzing". In: *CoRR* abs/1611.02429 (2016). arXiv: 1611.02429.

[74] Bernhard Steffen, Falk Howar, and Maik Merten. "Introduction to Active Automata Learning from a Practical Perspective". In: *Formal Methods for Eternal Networked Software Systems - 11th International School on Formal Methods for the Design of Computer, Communication and Software Systems, SFM 2011, Bertinoro, Italy, June 13-18, 2011. Advanced Lectures*. Ed. by Marco Bernardo and Valérie Issarny. Vol. 6659. Lecture Notes in Computer Science. Springer, 2011, pp. 256–296. DOI: 10.1007/978-3-642-21455-4_8.

[75] Chris McMahon Stone, Tom Chothia, and Joeri de Ruiter. "Extending Automated Protocol State Learning for the 802.11 4-Way Handshake". In: *Computer Security - 23rd European Symposium on Research in Computer Security, ESORICS 2018, Barcelona, Spain, September 3-7, 2018, Proceedings, Part I*. Ed. by Javier López, Jianying Zhou, and Miguel Soriano. Vol. 11098. Lecture Notes in Computer Science. Springer, 2018, pp. 325–345. DOI: 10.1007/978-3-319-99073-6_16.

[76] Martin Tappler, Bernhard K. Aichernig, and Roderick Bloem. "Model-Based Testing IoT Communication via Active Automata Learning". In: *2017 IEEE International Conference on Software Testing, Verification and Validation, ICST 2017, Tokyo, Japan, March 13-17, 2017*. IEEE Computer Society, 2017, pp. 276–287. DOI: 10.1109/ICST.2017.32.

[77] Frits W. Vaandrager, Masoud Ebrahimi, and Roderick Bloem. "Learning Mealy machines with one timer". In: *Inf. Comput.* 295.Part B (2023), p. 105013. DOI: 10.1016/J.IC.2023.105013

[78] Frits W. Vaandrager et al. "A New Approach for Active Automata Learning Based on Apartness". In: *Tools and Algorithms for the Construction and Analysis of Systems - 28th International Conference, TACAS 2022, Held as Part of the European Joint Conferences on Theory and Practice of Software, ETAPS 2022, Munich, Germany, April 2-7, 2022, Proceedings, Part I*. Ed. by Dana Fisman and Grigore Rosu. Vol. 13243. Lecture Notes in Computer Science. Springer, 2022, pp. 223–243. DOI: 10.1007/978-3-030-99524-9_12.

[79] Pepe Vila et al. "CacheQuery: learning replacement policies from hardware caches". In: *Proceedings of the 41st ACM SIGPLAN International Conference on Programming Language Design and Implementation, PLDI 2020, London, UK, June 15-20, 2020*. Ed. by Alastair F. Donaldson and Emina Torlak. ACM, 2020, pp. 519–532. DOI: 10.1145/3385412.3386008.

[80] Leon Vitorovic. "Query-Parallelisierung des ADT Learners in der LearnLib". In german. Bachelor's thesis. TU Dortmund University, 2024.

[81] Masaki Waga. "Falsification of cyber-physical systems with robustness-guided black-box checking". In: *HSCC '20: 23rd ACM International Conference on Hybrid Systems: Computation and Control, Sydney, New South Wales, Australia, April 21-24, 2020*. Ed. by Aaron D. Ames, Sanjit A. Seshia, and Jyotirmoy Deshmukh. ACM, 2020, 11:1–11:13. DOI: 10.1145/3365365.3382193.

[82] Masaki Waga et al. "Dynamic Shielding for Reinforcement Learning in Black-Box Environments". In: *Automated Technology for Verification and Analysis - 20th International Symposium, ATVA 2022, Virtual Event, October 25-28, 2022, Proceedings*. Ed. by Ahmed Bouajjani, Lukás Holık, and Zhilin Wu. Vol. 13505. Lecture Notes in Computer Science. Springer, 2022, pp. 25–41. DOI: 10.1007/978-3-031-19992-9_2.

Branching Bisimulation Learning

Alessandro Abate[1], Mirco Giacobbe[2], Christian Micheletti[3],
and Yannik Schnitzer[1($\boxtimes$)]

[1] University of Oxford, Oxford, UK
{alessandro.abate,yannik.schnitzer}@cs.ox.ac.uk
[2] University of Birmingham, Birmingham, UK
m.giacobbe@bham.ac.uk
[3] University of Padua, Padua, Italy
christian.micheletti@studenti.unipd.it

Abstract. We introduce a bisimulation learning algorithm for non-deterministic transition systems. We generalise bisimulation learning to systems with bounded branching and extend its applicability to model checking branching-time temporal logic, while previously it was limited to deterministic systems and model checking linear-time properties. Our method computes a finite stutter-insensitive bisimulation quotient of the system under analysis, represented as a decision tree. We adapt the proof rule for well-founded bisimulations to an iterative procedure that trains candidate decision trees from sample transitions of the system, and checks their validity over the entire transition relation using SMT solving. This results in a new technology for model checking CTL* without the next-time operator. Our technique is sound, entirely automated, and yields abstractions that are succinct and effective for formal verification and system diagnostics. We demonstrate the efficacy of our method on diverse benchmarks comprising concurrent software, communication protocols and robotic scenarios. Our method performs comparably to mature tools in the special case of LTL model checking, and outperforms the state of the art in CTL and CTL* model checking for systems with very large and countably infinite state space.

Keywords: Data-driven Verification · Abstraction · Non-deterministic Systems · Stutter-insensitive Bisimulations · CTL* Model Checking

1 Introduction

Bisimulation establishes equivalence between transition systems, ensuring they exhibit identical observable behaviour across all possible computation trees. It captures not only the linear traces of system interactions but also the branching structure of their potential evolutions, making it a powerful characterisation for the abstraction of systems. This enables the efficient analysis of complex concrete systems by reducing them to simpler abstract systems that capture the behaviour that is essential for model checking a formal specification. When the concrete system and its abstract counterpart are in a bisimulation relation, their

© The Author(s) 2025
R. Piskac and Z. Rakamarić (Eds.): CAV 2025, LNCS 15934, pp. 161–184, 2025.
https://doi.org/10.1007/978-3-031-98685-7_8

observable branching behaviour is indistinguishable. As a result, model checking linear- and branching-time temporal logic yield the same result on the abstract and the concrete system, even in the presence of non-determinism.

Algorithms for computing bisimulations have been developed extensively for systems with finite state spaces. The Paige-Tarjan algorithm for partition refinement laid the foundations for the automated constructions of bisimulation relations and their respective quotients [67]. Partition refinement is the state of the art for this purpose, and has lent itself to extension towards on-the-fly quotient construction and symbolic as well as parallel implementations [20,34,57,58,60]. These produce the coarsest bisimulation quotient, namely the most succinct representation possible of a bisimulation. Yet, this can be prohibitively expensive to compute for systems with large state spaces and complex arithmetic pathways, both when using explicit-state and symbolic algorithms. Consequently, model-checking techniques based on the partition refinement algorithm are typically restricted to systems with smaller state spaces and simpler transition logic.

Counterexample-guided abstraction refinement (CEGAR) has enabled the incremental construction of abstract systems using satisfiability modulo theory (SMT) solvers, benefitting from their ability to reason effectively over arithmetic constraints [10,28]. Modern software, hardware and cyber-physical systems are rich in arithmetic operations and have often very large state spaces. As a result, significant progress in software model checking and the verification of cyber-physical systems has been driven by advancements in CEGAR [13,14,36,47, 50,72], specifically designed to compute simulation quotients to prove safety properties [40]. However, for model checking liveness properties and linear-time logic, CEGAR requires non-trivial adaptation [29,31,69], and branching-time logic is entirely out of scope for simulation quotients.

Bisimulation learning has introduced an incremental approach to computing bisimulation quotients [4], where information about the system is learned from counterexample models—as happens in counterexample-guided inductive synthesis (CEGIS) [71]—as opposed to counterexample proofs—as happens in CEGAR [46,61]. Bisimulation learning relies on a parameterised representation of a quotient, such as a decision tree, and trains its parameters to *fit* a bisimulation quotient over sampled transitions of the system. Then, an adversarial component, such as an SMT solver, is used to check whether the quotient satisfies the bisimulation property across the entire state space and, upon a negative answer, propose counterexample transitions for further re-training of the quotient parameters. While in principle bisimulation relations preserve branching-time logic and support non-determinism, bisimulation learning was limited to deterministic systems and linear-time logic specifications [3,4].

We introduce a new, generalised bisimulation learning algorithm. Our result builds upon the proof rule for well-founded bisimulation [65], which we specialise to systems with bounded branching and integrate it within a bisimulation learning algorithm for non-deterministic systems. While well-founded bisimulations were originally developed for interactive theorem proving, our result enables their fully automated construction. We represent finite stutter-insensitive bisimulation quotients of non-deterministic systems, and enable the effective abstraction of systems with very large or countably infinite state space.

Stutter-insensitive bisimulations are indistinguishable to an external observer that cannot track intermediate transitions lacking an observable state change in a system. It is a standard result that stutter-insensitive bisimulation is an abstract semantics for $CTL^*_{\setminus\bigcirc}$—the branching-time logic CTL^* without the next-time operator [33]. In other words, when the abstract system corresponds to a stutter-insensitive bisimulation quotient and distinguishes at least the atomic propositions of the $CTL^*_{\setminus\bigcirc}$ formula ϕ, then the answers to model checking ϕ on the abstract system and the concrete system agree.

We demonstrate the efficacy of our method on a standard set of benchmarks for the formal verification of finite and infinite state systems against linear-time and branching-time temporal logic. We compare the runtime performance of our prototype with mature tools for the termination analysis of software (CPAChecker and Ultimate), LTL and CTL model checking finite-state systems (nuXmv), LTL model checking infinite-state systems (nuXmv and UltimateLTL), and CTL^* model checking infinite-state systems (T2). Our method performs comparably to mature tools for termination analysis, finite-state model checking, and LTL model checking infinite-state systems, while yielding superior results in branching-time model checking infinite-state systems. Overall, our technology addresses the general CTL^* model checking problem for infinite-state systems, performs comparably to specialised tools for linear-time properties, and establishes a new state of the art in branching-time model checking.

Our contribution is threefold. First, we generalise bisimulation learning to non-deterministic transition systems, leveraging the proof rule for well-founded bisimulations which we fully automate. Second, we introduce a new model checking algorithm for infinite-state systems against CTL^* without the next-time operator. Third, we demonstrate the efficacy of our general approach on standard benchmarks which not only compares favourably with the state of the art but also provides more informative results. Our method produces succinct stutter-insensitive bisimulation quotients of the system under analysis. In conjunction with a fix-point based model checking algorithm, this yields the exact initial conditions for which the concrete system satisfies a given specification.

2   Model Checking

We consider the problem of determining whether state transition systems with countable (possibly infinite) state space satisfy linear-time and branching-time temporal logic specifications. More precisely, we consider the model checking problem of non-deterministic transition systems with bounded branching with respect to linear-time and branching-time specifications expressed in CTL^* without the next-time operator. This encompasses a broad variety of formal verification questions for software systems with concurrency, reactive systems including synchronisation and communication protocols, as well as cyber-physical systems over finite or infinite discrete grid worlds.

Definition 1 (Transition Systems). *A transition system $\mathcal{M}$ consists of*

- *a state space S,*
- *an initial region $I \subseteq S$, and*
- *a transition relation $\rightarrow \subseteq S \times S$.*

We consider transition systems that are non-blocking and have bounded branching. In other words, every state $s \in S$ has at least one and at most $k \in \mathbb{N}$ successors, i.e., $0 < |\{t \in S : s \rightarrow t\}| \leq k$, where we say that $\mathcal{M}$ has k-bounded branching. We say that $\mathcal{M}$ is labelled when it additionally comprises

- *a set of atomic propositions Π (the observables), and*
- *a labelling (or observation) function $\langle\!\langle \cdot \rangle\!\rangle : S \rightarrow \mathcal{P}(\Pi)$.*

A path $\pi = s_0 s_1 \ldots$ of $\mathcal{M}$ is a sequence of states such that $s_i \rightarrow s_{i+1}$, for all $i \geq 0$. Since transition systems are non-blocking, every path extends to infinite length. We denote the set of all infinite paths starting in state s as $\text{Paths}(s)$.

Remark 1 (Bounded vs. Finite Branching). Bounded branching requires a constant k that bounds the number of successors across the entire state space, whereas *finite branching* is weaker, requiring every state to have finitely many successors, not imposing a constant upper bound. We note that bounded branching is a mild modelling restriction, which encompasses concurrency with finitely many processes, non-deterministic guarded commands and conditional choices, and non-deterministic variables or inputs with finite static domain. It excludes non-deterministic variables with infinite or state-dependent domain size.   □

We consider the branching-time temporal logic CTL* without the next-time operator (CTL*$_{\backslash\bigcirc}$) as our formal specification language for the temporal behaviour of systems [8,35]. This subsumes and generalises Linear Temporal Logic (LTL) [68] and Computation Tree Logic (CTL) [27] (excluding the next-time operator), expressing both linear-time and branching-time properties. The CTL*$_{\backslash\bigcirc}$ formulae are constructed according to the following grammar:

$$\phi ::= \text{true} \mid p \in \Pi \mid \phi \wedge \phi \mid \neg\phi \mid \exists\psi$$
$$\psi ::= \phi \mid \psi \wedge \psi \mid \neg\psi \mid \psi \, U \, \psi.$$

The model checking problem for CTL*$_{\backslash\bigcirc}$ is to decide whether transition system $\mathcal{M}$ satisfies a given CTL*$_{\backslash\bigcirc}$ formula ϕ. The satisfaction relation $\models$ for state formulae ϕ is defined over states $s \in S$ by:

$$
\begin{aligned}
&s \models \text{true} \\
&s \models p && \text{iff } p \in \langle\!\langle s \rangle\!\rangle \\
&s \models \phi_1 \wedge \phi_2 && \text{iff } s \models \phi_1 \text{ and } s \models \phi_2 \\
&s \models \neg\phi && \text{iff } s \not\models \phi \\
&s \models \exists\psi && \text{iff } \exists\pi \in \text{Paths}(s) : \pi \models \psi.
\end{aligned}
$$

For a path π, the satisfaction relation $\models$ for path formulae ψ is given by:

$$
\begin{aligned}
\pi \models \phi \quad & \text{iff } s_0 \models \phi \\
\pi \models \psi_1 \wedge \psi_2 \quad & \text{iff } \pi \models \psi_1 \text{ and } \pi \models \psi_2 \\
\pi \models \neg\psi \quad & \text{iff } \pi \not\models \psi \\
\pi \models \psi_1 \, U \, \psi_2 \quad & \text{iff } \exists k \in \mathbb{N} \colon \pi[k..] \models \psi_2 \text{ and} \\
& \qquad \forall 0 \leq l < k \colon \pi[l..] \models \psi_1,
\end{aligned}
$$

where for path $\pi = s_0 s_1 \ldots$ and $i \in \mathbb{N}$, $\pi[i..] = s_i s_{i+1} \ldots$ denotes the suffix starting from index i. The satisfaction relation of a state formula ϕ is lifted to the entire transition system by requiring that every initial state must satisfy ϕ:

$$
\mathcal{M} \models \phi \text{ iff } \forall s \in I \colon s \models \phi.
$$

We also introduce the derived path operators *"eventually"* $\Diamond$ and *"globally"* $\Box$. The formula $\Diamond\psi := \text{true} \, U \, \psi$ states that ψ must be true in some state on the path. The formula $\Box\psi := \neg(\Diamond\neg\psi)$ requires that ψ holds true in all states of the path. The universal quantification over paths $\forall\psi$ can be expressed as $\neg\exists\neg\psi$. We do not include the *"next-time"* operator $\bigcirc$ from full CTL*, since we are interested in stutter-insensitive bisimulations, which do not preserve a system's stepwise behaviour, as expressed by $\bigcirc$.

3 Stutter-Insensitive Bisimulations

This section introduces the concept of abstraction, specifically that of stutter-insensitive bisimulation, which preserves all linear- and branching-time behaviour up to externally unobservable stutter steps, as captured by CTL$^*_{\setminus\bigcirc}$.

Definition 2 (Partitions). *A partition on $\mathcal{M}$ is an equivalence relation $\simeq \subseteq S \times S$ on S, which defines the quotient space $S/_\simeq$ of pairwise-disjoint regions of S whose union is S, i.e., $S/_\simeq$ is the set of equivalence classes of $\simeq$. A partition is called label-preserving (or observation-preserving) iff $s \simeq t \implies \langle\!\langle s \rangle\!\rangle = \langle\!\langle t \rangle\!\rangle$.*

A partition induces an abstract transition system – the *quotient*, which aggregates equivalent states and their behaviours into representative states.

Definition 3 (Quotient). *The quotient of $\mathcal{M}$ under the partition $\simeq$ is the transition system $\mathcal{M}/_\simeq$ with*

- *state space $S/_\simeq$,*
- *initial region $I/_\simeq$ where $R \in I/_\simeq$ iff $R \cap I \neq \emptyset$, and*
- *transition relation $\rightarrow/_\simeq$, with $R \rightarrow/_\simeq Q$ iff either:*
  1. *$R \neq Q$ and $\exists s \in R, t \in Q \colon s \rightarrow t$,*
  2. *$R = Q$ and $\forall s \in R \, \exists t \in R \colon s \rightarrow t$.*

If the partition $\simeq$ is label-preserving, the quotient further comprises a well-defined labelling function given by $\langle\!\langle R \rangle\!\rangle/_\simeq = \langle\!\langle s \rangle\!\rangle$, for any $s \in R$.

An *abstract* state in the quotient represents an equivalence class of the underlying partition, inheriting the behaviours of included states. Depending on the partition, the quotient preserves temporal properties of the concrete system, such that model checking results carry over from the quotient [67].

A prominent notion of equivalence on states is *strong bisimilarity* [23,45]. Strong bisimilarity demands that related states can replicate each other's transitions, with transitions leading to states that are themselves related. This ensures temporal equivalence in both linear- and branching-time, making it a suitable abstract semantics for full CTL*, including the *next*-operator [62]. However, preserving exact stepwise behavior limits the potential for state-space reduction when constructing the corresponding quotient. Alternatively, we consider the weaker notion of *stutter-insensitivity*, which abstracts from exact steps in the concrete system that are externally unobservable. This results in potentially smaller quotients while preserving specifications expressible in $CTL^*_{\backslash \bigcirc}$.

Definition 4 (Stutter-insensitive Bisimulation). *A label-preserving partition $\simeq$ is a stutter-insensitive bisimulation if, for all states $s, s' \in S$ with $s \simeq s'$ and paths $\pi \in Paths(s)$, there exists a path $\pi' \in Paths(s')$, such that π and π' can be split into an equal number of non-empty finite subsequences $\pi = B_1 B_2 \ldots$ and $\pi' = B'_1 B'_2 \ldots$, for which it holds that $\forall i \geq 0 \, \forall t \in B_i, t' \in B'_i : t \simeq t'$.*

Stutter-insensitive bisimulation requires that related states have outgoing paths composed of identical subsequences of equivalence classes, regardless of the lengths of these subsequences. This guarantees that related states are roots to computation trees that are externally indistinguishable up to exact step counts. Figure 1 illustrates this condition.

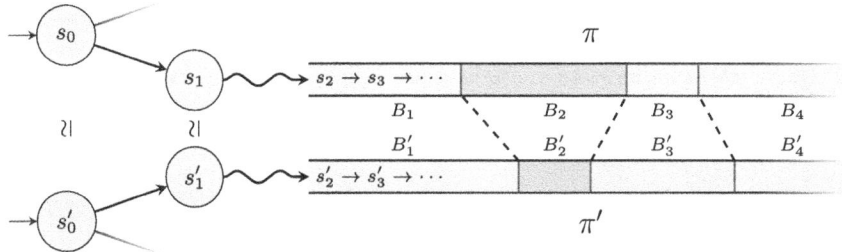

Fig. 1. States related under stutter-insensitive bisimulation, with examples of matching paths, consisting of identical subsequences of equivalence classes.

Remark 2. The case distinction for the quotient transition relation in Definition 3 is needed to prevent spurious self-loops in the quotient system, which may arise from unobservable stuttering steps in the original system [65]. We have to exclude unobservable intra-class transitions from the quotient, except when they reflect diverging behaviour, i.e., when all states within a class can remain in the class indefinitely (Case 2). Figure 2 shows an example system and its stutter-insensitive bisimulation quotient.   □

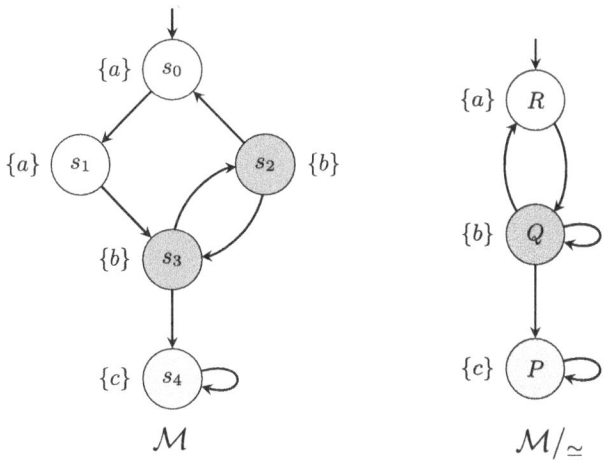

Fig. 2. A system $\mathcal{M}$ and a possible stutter-insensitive bisimulation quotient $\mathcal{M}/_\simeq$. The abstract state R lacks a self-loop despite an intra-class transition, as all represented concrete states eventually transition to Q. Conversely, Q has a self-loop since its concrete states can remain within the class indefinitely.

Since states related by a stutter-insensitive bisimulation are indistinguishable in linear- and branching-time up to exact stepwise behaviour, the model checking question for $\text{CTL}^*_{\backslash\bigcirc}$, as introduced in Sect. 2, yields the same result for a system and its potentially much smaller stutter-insensitive bisimulation quotient.

Theorem 1 ([23, Theorem 4.2]). *Let $\mathcal{M}$ be a labelled transition system and let $\simeq$ be a label-preserving stutter-insensitive bisimulation on $\mathcal{M}$. For every $CTL^*_{\backslash\bigcirc}$ formula ϕ, it holds that $\mathcal{M} \models \phi$ if and only if $\mathcal{M}/_\simeq \models \phi$.*   □

4   Well-Founded Bisimulations with Bounded Branching

We revisit *well-founded* bisimulation [59,65] as an alternative formulation of stutter-insensitive bisimulation. This notion builds on entirely local conditions for states and their transitions that ensure the existence of matching infinite paths. We show how this definition generalises the deterministic version used in bisimulation learning [4] and characterises stutter-insensitive bisimulations for non-deterministic systems. By specialising this notion to systems with bounded branching, we are able to effectively encode the local conditions into quantifier-free first order logic formulas over states and their successors, which we leverage in the design of a counterexample-guided bisimulation learning approach. To the best of our knowledge, this is the first approach for the fully automatic computation of well-founded bisimulations on potentially infinite-state non-deterministic systems, which was originally designed as a proof rule for theorem proving and relied on manually crafted relations. If terminated successfully, the novel bisimulation learning procedure generates a finite quotient system, enabling state-of-the-art finite-state model checkers to verify $\text{CTL}^*_{\setminus \bigcirc}$ properties whose results directly carry over to the original, possibly infinite system.

The proof rule for well-founded bisimulations uses *ranking functions* over a well-founded set, which decrease along stuttering steps and eventually lead to a matching transition. Since well-founded sets preclude infinite descending sequences, this guarantees the finiteness of stuttering and ensures the existence of matching infinite paths between related states based solely on local conditions.

Theorem 2 ([65, **Theorem 1**]). *Let $\mathcal{M}$ be a transition system and let $\simeq$ be a label-preserving partition on $\mathcal{M}$. Suppose there exists a function $r\colon S \times S \to \mathbb{N}$ such that, for every $s, s', t \in S$ with $s \simeq t$ and $s \to s'$, the following holds:*

$$\exists t' \in S\colon t \to t' \wedge s' \simeq t' \vee \tag{1}$$

$$s \simeq s' \wedge r(s', s) < r(s, s) \vee \tag{2}$$

$$\exists t' \in S\colon t \to t' \wedge t \simeq t' \wedge r(s', t') < r(s', t). \tag{3}$$

Then $\simeq$ is a stutter-insensitive bisimulation on $\mathcal{M}$.   □

In this work, we focus on ranking functions $r\colon S \times S \to \mathbb{N}$ mapping to the natural numbers, though all results extend to arbitrary well-founded sets.

The intuition behind Theorem 2 is as follows: For any states $s \simeq t$ with $s \to s'$, there are three possibilities. First, there may be an immediate matching transition for t (Case (1)). If the first case does not apply, and $s \simeq s'$, the rank decreases (Case (2)). Since r is defined over a well-founded set bounded from below, this can happen only finitely many times. In the remaining case, where $s \not\simeq s'$, there must exist a transition $t \to t'$ such that $t \simeq t'$ and the rank decreases (Case (3)). Again, by the well-foundedness of $(\mathbb{N}, <)$, this can also happen only finitely many times. Thus, a state related to s' is eventually reached from t after at most finite stuttering in the same equivalence class [65]. This ensures the existence of matching infinite paths, as per Definition 4, based solely on local reasoning over states and their immediate transitions.

The notion of well-founded bisimulations in Theorem 2 generalises the proof rule used in deterministic bisimulation learning [4], which essentially consists of restricted sub-conditions of Cases (1) and (2) and is thus limited to deterministic systems [4, Theorem 2]. Notice that, since states in non-deterministic systems can have multiple outgoing transitions, the proof rule in Theorem 2 incorporates quantification over successors. For the design of an effective and efficient counterexample-guided bisimulation learning approach to the synthesis of well-founded bisimulations and their quotients, it is crucial to express these conditions in a quantifier-free fragment of a decidable first-order theory [1]. In the deterministic case addressed in previous work [4], this is straightforward, since each state has a single outgoing transition, so the conditions do not involve quantification. To address this in the non-deterministic case, instead, we leverage the assumption of bounded branching, which allows the quantification over successors to be reformulated as a finite disjunction.

For a transition system $\mathcal{M}$ that has k-bounded branching, the transition relation $\rightarrow$ can be expressed as the union of k deterministic transition functions $\sigma_i \colon S \rightarrow S$, for $1 \leq i \leq k$:

$$\rightarrow \; = \; \bigcup_{i=1}^{k} \sigma_i. \tag{4}$$

We assume that every state has exactly k successors. This assumption is without loss of generality, as states with fewer than k successors can have their successors duplicated. With that, we can state a version of Theorem 2 for transition systems with bounded branching that eliminates quantification over successors.

Theorem 3. *Let $\mathcal{M}$ be a transition system that has k-bounded branching and let $\simeq$ be a label-preserving partition on $\mathcal{M}$. Suppose there exists a function $r \colon S \times S \rightarrow \mathbb{N}$ such that, for every $s, t \in S$ with $s \simeq t$, the following holds:*

$$\bigwedge_{i=1}^{k} \Big(\bigvee_{j=1}^{k} \sigma_i(s) \simeq \sigma_j(t) \vee \tag{5}$$

$$s \simeq \sigma_i(s) \wedge r\left(\sigma_i(s), \sigma_i(s)\right) < r(s, s) \vee \tag{6}$$

$$\bigvee_{j=1}^{k} t \simeq \sigma_j(t) \wedge r(\sigma_i(s), \sigma_j(t)) < r(\sigma_i(s), t)\Big). \tag{7}$$

Then $\simeq$ is a stutter-insensitive bisimulation on $\mathcal{M}$.

Proof. We show that Eq. (5) implies Eq. (1) of Theorem 2. The remaining disjuncts can be treated analogously. Let $s, t \in S$ such that $s \simeq t$ and

$$\bigwedge_{i=1}^{k} \Big(\bigvee_{j=1}^{k} \sigma_i(s) \simeq \sigma_j(t)\Big).$$

Since $\mathcal{M}$ has k-bounded branching, both s and t have exactly k successors, represented by the k deterministic transition functions $\sigma_i, 1 \leq i \leq k$. A conjunction over all k successors corresponds to a universal quantification over the successors, while a disjunction corresponds to an existential quantification. Consequently, the above expression can be rewritten as:

$$\forall s' \in S \colon \Big(s \rightarrow s' \implies \bigvee_{j=1}^{k} s' \simeq \sigma_j(t)\Big)$$

$$\Leftrightarrow \forall s' \in S \colon \Big(s \rightarrow s' \implies \exists t' \in S \colon (t \rightarrow t' \wedge s' \simeq t')\Big),$$

which is precisely Eq. (1) of Theorem 2. $\qquad\square$

5   Bisimulation Learning for Non-deterministic Systems

We can now leverage the quantifier-free formulation of well-founded bisimulations from Theorem 3 to design a counterexample-guided bisimulation learning procedure for synthesising stutter-insensitive bisimulation quotients. The problem of identifying a suitable partition and ranking function that satisfy the conditions of a well-founded bisimulation is framed as a learning problem. To this end, we introduce the concept of *state classifiers*.

Definition 5 (State Classifier). *A state classifier on a labelled transition system with state space S is any function $f\colon S \to C$ that maps states to a finite set of classes C. It is label-preserving if $f(s) = f(t)$ implies $\langle\!\langle s \rangle\!\rangle = \langle\!\langle t \rangle\!\rangle$. A classifier induces the partition $\simeq_f$ defined as $\simeq_f = \{(s,t) \mid f(s) = f(t)\}$, which is label-preserving iff f is label-preserving.*

We reduce the problem of identifying a suitable state classifier and ranking function to finding appropriate parameters for parametric function templates $f\colon \Theta \times S \to C$ and $r\colon H \times S \times S \to \mathbb{N}$. These templates define mappings that are fully determined by the parameters $\theta \in \Theta$ and $\eta \in H$, where Θ and H are arbitrary parameter spaces. A state classifier template is label-preserving if the induced classifier is label-preserving for any parameterisation $\theta \in \Theta$. The specific parametric function templates used in our procedure are discussed in Sect. 6. We write $f_\theta(s)$ for $f(\theta, s)$ and $r_\eta(s, s')$ for $r(\eta, s, s')$.

Since state classifiers over a finite set of classes correspond to finite partitions, Theorem 3 extends directly to this setting. Additionally, parametric function templates enable us to express the problem in first-order logic by shifting the focus from reasoning about the existence of suitable functions to reasoning about the existence of suitable parameters. We formalise this in the following corollary.

Corollary 1. *Let $\mathcal{M}$ be a labelled transition system with k-bounded branching, $f\colon \Theta \times S \to C$ be a label-preserving state classifier template and $r\colon H \times S \times S \to \mathbb{N}$ be a ranking function template. Let*

$$\Psi(\theta, \eta, s, t) = \bigwedge_{i=1}^{k} \Big(\bigvee_{j=1}^{k} f_\theta(\sigma_i(s)) = f_\theta(\sigma_j(t)) \ \vee \tag{8}$$

$$f_\theta(s) = f_\theta(\sigma_i(s)) \wedge r_\eta\left(\sigma_i(s), \sigma_i(s)\right) < r_\eta(s, s) \ \vee \tag{9}$$

$$\bigvee_{j=1}^{k} f_\theta(t) = f_\theta(\sigma_j(t)) \wedge r_\eta\left(\sigma_i(s), \sigma_j(t)\right) < r_\eta(\sigma_i(s), t)\Big). \tag{10}$$

Suppose that

$$\exists \theta \in \Theta, \eta \in H \ \forall s, t \in S\colon f_\theta(s) = f_\theta(t) \implies \Psi(\theta, \eta, s, t). \tag{11}$$

Then, $\simeq_f$ is a stutter-insensitive bisimulation on $\mathcal{M}$.   □

Corollary 1 reformulates the conditions of Theorem 3 in terms of parametric function templates. Branching bisimulation learning seeks to identify suitable parameters θ and η that induce a valid well-founded bisimulation.

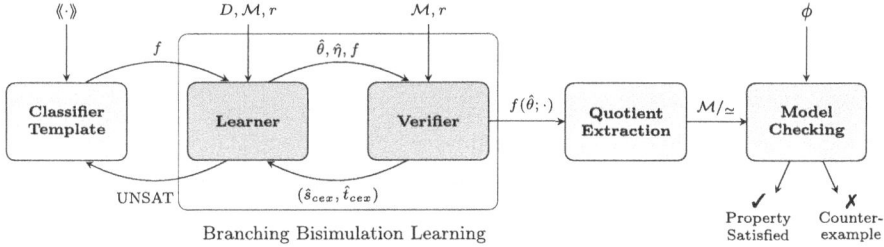

Fig. 3. Architecture of branching bisimulation learning.

5.1 Procedure

Our procedure involves two interacting components, the *learner* and the *verifier* that implement a CEGIS loop [1,7]. The learner proposes candidate parameters that define a classifier and a ranking function, satisfying the conditions of Corollary 1 over a finite set of sample states. The verifier then checks whether these induced mappings satisfy the conditions across the entire state space. If the verifier confirms that the conditions hold globally, the procedure has successfully synthesised a valid stutter-insensitive bisimulation, as induced by the classifier. From this, the corresponding finite quotient system is extracted, which can be verified using off-the-shelf finite-state model checkers, with results directly applicable to the original, potentially infinite system. If the induced mappings fail to generalise to the entire state space, the verifier generates a counterexample pair of states that violates the conditions. This counterexample is returned to the learner, which refines the parameters to eliminate the violation. An overview of the procedure is depicted in Fig. 3, and we elaborate on its individual components in the following sections.

Learner. The learner aims to find suitable parameters for a label-preserving state classifier template $f: \Theta \times S \to C$ and a ranking function template $r: H \times S \times S \to \mathbb{N}$ that satisfy the conditions of Corollary 1 over a finite set of state pairs $D \subseteq S \times S$. Specifically, it attempts to solve:

$$\exists \theta \in \Theta, \eta \in H: \bigwedge_{(\hat{s}, \hat{t}) \in D} f_\theta(\hat{s}) = f_\theta(\hat{t}) \implies \Psi(\theta, \eta, \hat{s}, \hat{t}). \tag{12}$$

In our instantiation of the procedure, the learner is an SMT solver that seeks a satisfying assignment for the parameters θ and η within the quantifier-free inner formula of (12). If the learner successfully identifies parameters that satisfy the conditions over the sample states, the resulting classifier and ranking function are passed to the verifier. However, if the learner fails to find suitable parameters, this indicates that the current function templates cannot be instantiated to comply with Corollary 1 for the finite set of state pairs D. This failure may arise for two reasons: First, since the model checking problem for infinite state systems is generally undecidable, the concrete system might not admit a finite stutter-insensitive bisimulation quotient, meaning no classifier or ranking function can satisfy the conditions of Corollary 1. Second, if a finite quotient does exist, the employed templates lack the expressiveness required to represent it. In this case, we must choose more expressive templates and continue the synthesis loop. In Sect. 6, we detail how our instantiation of the procedure automatically increases the expressiveness of the templates as needed.

Equation (12) employs a single ranking function parameter $\eta \in H$ for the entire state space. To enhance flexibility, the ranking function can instead be defined piecewise with multiple parameters $\boldsymbol{\eta} = (\eta_c)_{c \in C}$, effectively assigning a separate ranking function to each class $c \in C$. While logically equivalent, this approach may enable the use of simpler templates by exploiting similarities in the temporal behavior of equivalent states. The learner then seeks to solve:

$$\exists \theta \in \Theta, \boldsymbol{\eta} \in H^{|C|}: \bigwedge_{c \in C} \bigwedge_{(\hat{s}, \hat{t}) \in D} f_\theta(\hat{s}) = f_\theta(\hat{t}) = c \implies \Psi(\theta, \eta_c, \hat{s}, \hat{t}). \tag{13}$$

Verifier. The verifier checks whether the functions induced by the candidate parameters $\hat{\theta}$ and $\hat{\eta}$, proposed by the learner, generalise to the entire state space. For this, it attempts to solve the negation of the learner formula (12) for a counterexample pair of states:

$$\exists s, t \in S: f_{\hat{\theta}}(s) = f_{\hat{\theta}}(t) \wedge \neg \Psi(\hat{\theta}, \hat{\eta}, s, t). \tag{14}$$

Similar to the learner, the verifier utilises an SMT solver, to which we provide the quantifier-free inner formula of (14). If a satisfying assignment for a counterexample pair $(\hat{s}, \hat{t})$ is found, it is added to D and returned to the learner, which refines the induced mappings to eliminate the counterexample. If the formula is unsatisfiable, this proves that Corollary 1 holds for the entire state space, and the synthesis loop terminates with a valid stutter-insensitive bisimulation $\simeq_f$.

If the learner employs a piecewise-defined ranking function as per Eq. (13), the verifier instead checks the satisfiability of:

$$\exists s, t \in S: \bigvee_{c \in C} f_{\hat{\theta}}(s) = f_{\hat{\theta}}(t) = c \wedge \neg \Psi(\hat{\theta}, \hat{\eta}_c, s, t), \tag{15}$$

for the candidate parameters $\hat{\theta}$ and $\hat{\boldsymbol{\eta}} = (\hat{\eta}_c)_{c \in C}$. The disjunction over the finite set of classes C can be treated as independent and parallelisable SMT queries.

Quotient Extraction. The learner-verifier framework yields a state classifier $f_{\hat{\theta}}(\cdot)$ that induces a valid stutter-insensitive bisimulation $\simeq_f$, provided it terminates successfully. From this, the corresponding finite quotient $\mathcal{M}/_\simeq$ is derived by constructing the abstract transition relation $\rightarrow/_\simeq$ and the initial states $I/_\simeq$. The abstract state space $S/_\simeq$ corresponds to the finite set of classes C.

To construct the abstract transition relation, we express the conditions from Definition 3 as quantifier-free first-order logic formulas, enabling efficient evaluation by an SMT solver. We then perform a series of independent, parallelisable queries for each pair of abstract states $c, d \in C$.

– An abstract transition $c \rightarrow/_{\simeq} d$ where $c \neq d$ is established if:

$$\exists s \in S \colon f_{\hat{\theta}}(s) = c \wedge \bigvee_{i=1}^{k} f_{\hat{\theta}}(\sigma_i(s)) = d. \tag{16}$$

– An abstract transition $c \rightarrow/_{\simeq} c$ is established if:

$$\nexists s \in S \colon f_{\hat{\theta}}(s) = c \wedge \bigwedge_{i=1}^{k} f_{\hat{\theta}}(\sigma_i(s)) \neq c. \tag{17}$$

Both types of queries in Eqs. (16) and (17) are evaluated by passing the quantifier-free inner formula with the free variable $s \in S$ to an SMT solver. Note that a self-loop $c \rightarrow/_{\simeq} c$ is established if the solver *cannot* find a state s classified to c where all successors leave the class. This implies that every state in c has at least one successor within the same class.

To extract the abstract initial region $I/_{\simeq}$, a single SMT query is sufficient for each abstract state. An abstract state is initial $c \in I/_{\simeq}$ if and only if:

$$\exists s \in S \colon f_{\hat{\theta}}(s) = c \wedge s \in I. \tag{18}$$

Note that the synthesised ranking functions are not required for extracting the quotient. They are auxiliary in the synthesis of a valid stutter-insensitive bisimulation, while the resulting quotient depends solely on the final partition.

6   Bisimulation Learning with Binary Decision Trees

In this section, we detail our instantiation of the bisimulation learning procedure for non-deterministic systems. We define parametric function templates for state classifiers and ranking functions employed in branching bisimulation learning, focusing on systems with discrete integer state spaces $S \subseteq \mathbb{Z}^n$.

For state classifiers, we use binary decision tree templates with parametric decision nodes and leaves corresponding to a finite set of classes [4].

Definition 6 (Binary Decision Tree Templates). *The set of binary decision tree (BDT) templates* $\mathbb{T}$ *over a finite set of classes* C *and parameters* Θ *consists of trees* T, *which are defined as either:*

– *a leaf node* LEAF(c), *where* $c \in C$, *or*
– *a decision node* NODE(μ, T_l, T_r), *where* $T_l, T_r \in \mathbb{T}$ *are the left and right subtrees, and* $\mu \colon \Theta \times S \to \mathbb{B}$ *is a parameterised predicate on the states.*

A parametric tree template $T \in \mathbb{T}$ *over classes* C *and parameters* Θ *defines the state classifier template* $f^T \colon \Theta \times S \to C$ *as:*

$$f_{\theta}^{T}(s) = \begin{cases} c & \text{if } T = \text{LEAF}(c), \\ f_{\theta}^{T_l}(s) & \text{if } T = \text{NODE}(\mu, T_l, T_r) \text{ and } \mu_{\theta}(s), \\ f_{\theta}^{T_r}(s) & \text{if } T = \text{NODE}(\mu, T_l, T_r) \text{ and } \neg\mu_{\theta}(s). \end{cases}$$

Binary decision trees are well-suited as state classifier templates due to their expressivity, interpretability, and straightforward translation into quantifier-free expressions over states and parameters.

To ensure that BDT templates are label-preserving, i.e., the induced classifiers respect the labelling of the original system for any parameterisation $\theta \in \Theta$, we associate atomic propositions $p \in \Pi$ with predicates $\mu_p \colon S \to \mathbb{B}$, such that:

$$\langle\!\langle s \rangle\!\rangle = \{p \in \Pi \mid \mu_p(s)\}. \tag{19}$$

Label preservation is enforced by fixing parameter-free predicates for observations at the top nodes of the tree, with parametric decision nodes placed below them to refine the observation partition. This follows a similar principle as partition refinement [67], which starts from the observation partition and iteratively refines it. In our instantiation, we use BDTs with affine predicates of the form $\mu_\theta(s) := \theta_1 \cdot s + \theta_2 \leq 0$ at each parametric decision node, where θ is drawn from the reals with appropriate dimension.

BDTs facilitate an automatic increase of expressivity when the learner cannot find parameters that satisfy the well-founded bisimulation conditions over the finite set of sample states (cf. Sect. 5.1). The initial BDT templates are built automatically from the provided observation partition and include parameter-free top nodes that fix the labelling and a single layer of parametric decision nodes below. If suitable parameters cannot be found, we add another layer of parametric decision nodes, allowing further refinement of each class.

For parametric ranking function templates, we use affine functions of the form $r_\eta(s,t) = \eta_1 \cdot s + \eta_2 \cdot t + \eta_3$, where η is an integer vector of appropriate dimension. These parameters must define a function that is bounded from below on its domain. For this, some systems may require a piecewise-defined ranking function. Using affine predicates ensures that all conditions remain within a decidable fragment of first-order logic with linear arithmetic and efficient solution methods. While more expressive templates, such as non-linear ones, can be used, they require solving more complex SMT problems involving non-linear arithmetic, which are computationally expensive and, in some cases, undecidable [54].

6.1   An Illustrative Example

We illustrate our instantiation of branching bisimulation learning for the non-deterministic example program in Fig. 4a. The program takes two arbitrary integers x and y as inputs and iterates while $x > 0$. Based on variable values and a non-deterministic choice, it subtracts either x from y or vice versa, inducing an infinite non-deterministic transition system over $S = \mathbb{Z}^2$. States are labelled by $x \leq 0$ and $x > 0$, indicating whether computation has terminated or is still running. Despite having infinitely many states, the program has bounded branching, as the single non-deterministic choice yields at most two successors.

Determining which states have terminating or diverging branches is non-trivial. We use branching bisimulation learning to identify conditions under which states share identical computation trees up to exact step counts and

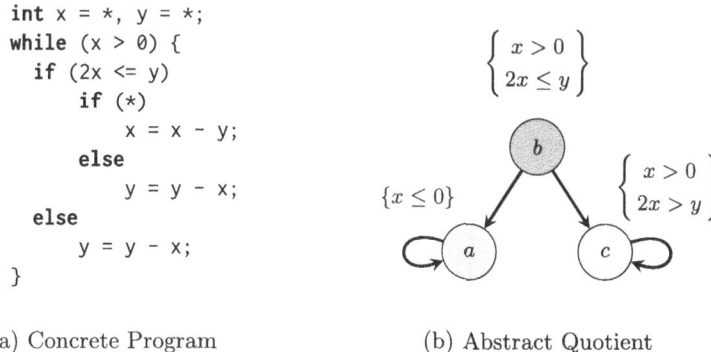

(a) Concrete Program   (b) Abstract Quotient

Fig. 4. A non-deterministic program and the corresponding stutter-insensitive bisimulation quotient synthesised with branching bisimulation learning.

extract the stutter-insensitive bisimulation quotient. Our initial BDT template fixes the labelling at a single non-parametric top node with predicate $x \leq 0$ and includes a parametric decision node to refine the partition labelled $x > 0$.

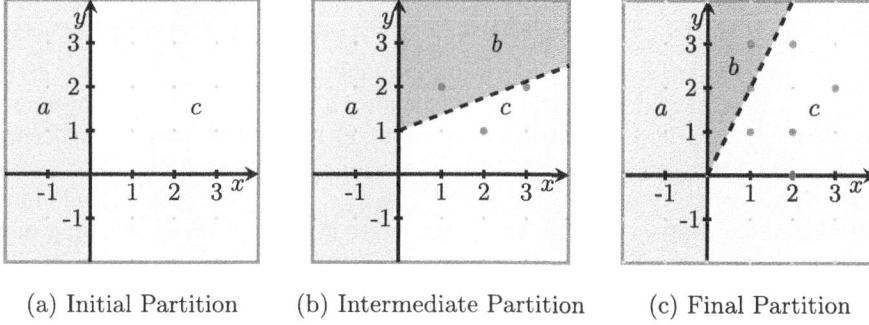

(a) Initial Partition   (b) Intermediate Partition   (c) Final Partition

Fig. 5. Iterative process of branching bisimulation learning, illustrating three stages with generated counterexample states (purple dots). (Color figure online)

The process of branching bisimulation learning is illustrated in Fig. 5. Starting from an arbitrary initial partition (Fig. 5a), the procedure iteratively generates counterexample states and refines the partition to meet the conditions of a well-founded bisimulation over the finite sample set (Fig. 5b). The process terminates when no counterexample states remain (Fig. 5c).

The resulting partition certifies that refining the non-terminated class labeled $x > 0$ along the predicate $2x - y \leq 0$ induces a valid stutter-insensitive bisimulation. From this partition, we extract the stutter-insensitive bisimulation quotient, shown in Fig. 4b. Initial states are omitted, as branching bisimulation learning is independent of initial states. It is stronger in that it determines the conditions defining a state's characteristics, as reflected by its outgoing computation tree, for all states simultaneously. In the quotient, the class b precisely represents states with both terminating and diverging outgoing paths, as expressed by the $\mathrm{CTL}^*_{\backslash\bigcirc}$ formula $\phi = \exists\lozenge\square(x \leq 0) \wedge \exists\square(x > 0)$.

In this example, the initial BDT template was sufficiently expressive to capture a valid stutter-insensitive bisimulation on the state space. If the learner fails to find a partition that satisfies the conditions in Sect. 5.1 over the finite set of sample states, BDTs enable an automatic increase in expressivity by adding an extra layer of decision nodes which further refine the partition.

7   Experimental Evaluation

We implemented our instantiation of branching bisimulation learning with BDT classifier templates in a software prototype and evaluated it across a diverse range of case studies, including deterministic and concurrent software, communication protocols, and reactive systems. Our procedure is benchmarked against state-of-the-art tools, including the nuXmv model checker [21,24,26], the Ultimate [44] and CPAChecker [14] software verifiers, and the T2 [22] infinite-state branching-time model checker. We employ the Z3 SMT solver [63] in both the learner and verifier components of the learning loop and use the nuXmv model checker to verify the obtained finite stutter-insensitive bisimulation quotients.

Setup. Branching bisimulation learning provides a unified approach for verifying infinite-state non-deterministic systems with respect to $\mathrm{CTL}^*_{\backslash\bigcirc}$ specifications. Since our procedure encompasses a broad range of system and specification classes, we compare its performance against specialised state-of-the-art tools. Specifically, we evaluate its effectiveness on key special cases, including deterministic infinite-state and large finite-state systems, before extending our analysis to the full generality of infinite-state and non-deterministic systems. Concretely, we consider:

1. Deterministic finite-state clock synchronisation protocols [4,55], including TTEthernet [18,19] and an interactive convergence algorithm [56], ensuring agents synchronise despite clock drift. We verify safety (clocks stay within a safe distance) and liveness (agents repeatedly synchronise). We compare against nuXmv using IC3 and BDD-based symbolic model checking, and deterministic bisimulation learning [4], which is tailored to this type of system. We evaluate multiple instances with varying time discretisations, where smaller time steps lead to larger state spaces.
2. Conditional termination of infinite-state deterministic software from the SV-COMP termination category [14]. We compare against nuXmv using IC3, Ultimate, CPAChecker, and deterministic bisimulation learning. Here, non-bisimulation-based approaches require separate benchmark instances, as they can only verify termination or non-termination of all initial states. In contrast, bisimulation learning synthesises a quotient, precisely identifying conditions for termination and divergence (see Fig. 4).

3. Infinite-state concurrent software and reactive systems with non-deterministic inputs. We consider non-deterministic conditional termination benchmarks, concurrent software from the T2 verifier benchmark set [11, 22], and reactive robotics where agents navigate while avoiding collisions. For LTL$_{\setminus\bigcirc}$ specifications, we compare against nuXmv (IC3) and Ultimate. For CTL$_{\setminus\bigcirc}$ and CTL$^{*}_{\setminus\bigcirc}$, we compare against T2, the only tool for branching-time verification of infinite-state non-deterministic systems. We also consider finite-state versions verified for CTL$_{\setminus\bigcirc}$ using nuXmv with BDDs.

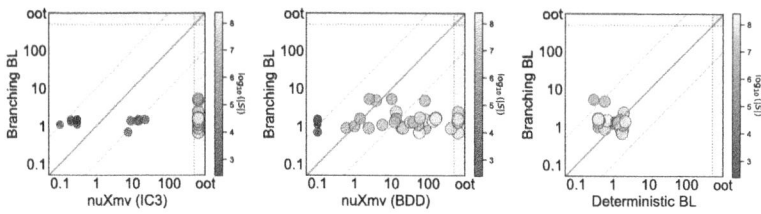

Fig. 6. Deterministic finite-state clock synchronisation benchmarks, verified against LTL$_{\setminus\bigcirc}$ specifications. Data-point colours indicate state-space size.

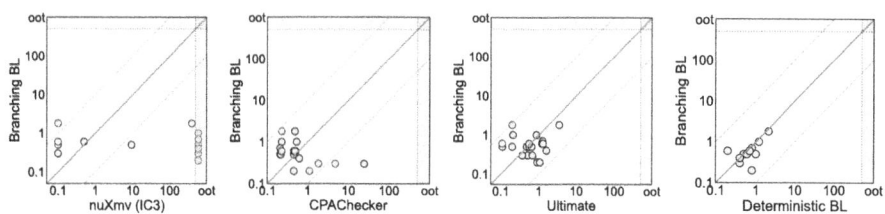

Fig. 7. Deterministic infinite-state termination analysis benchmarks.

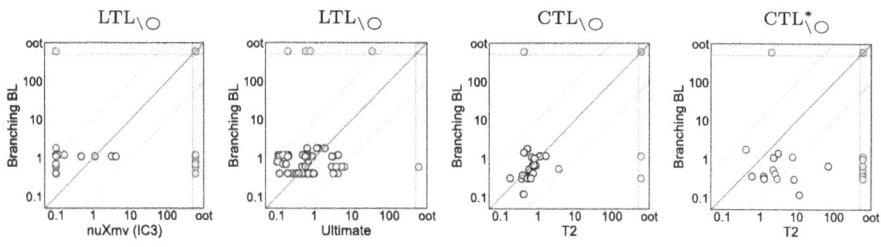

Fig. 8. Non-deterministic infinite-state benchmarks.

Results. We present the resulting verification runtimes in Figs. 6, 7 and 8. Detailed results can be found in the technical report [2]. Each figure compares branching bisimulation learning with BDT templates against applicable baseline tools. Runtimes are shown in seconds, with dashed diagonals indicating 10-fold differences. Each data point represents a case-study and formula combination.

Timeouts in the red areas correspond to runtimes exceeding 500 s. For baselines, we report only analysis time, excluding any preprocessing of programs. Since bisimulation learning depends on the sequence of produced counterexamples, which is generally non-deterministic, we run each benchmark 10 times. The plots report average runtimes, with variances detailed in the technical report [2].

Discussion. The results demonstrate that branching bisimulation learning is an effective and general verification approach across key system and specifications classes, extending to the full generality of non-deterministic infinite-state systems with $CTL^*_{\setminus \bigcirc}$ specifications, where T2 is the only competitor.

For deterministic clock synchronisation and termination benchmarks, branching bisimulation learning remains competitive with baseline tools and even deterministic bisimulation learning [4], despite using a more expressive proof rule. This is presumably due to the separation of partition learning and quotient extraction, reducing the complexity of used SMT queries. As a result, it retains the advantages of deterministic bisimulation learning. For termination benchmarks, our approach achieves runtimes comparable to state-of-the-art tools while also producing interpretable binary decision trees that characterise the conditions under which states terminate, aiding system diagnostics and fault analysis.

For non-deterministic infinite-state benchmarks, the results confirm that branching bisimulation learning is effective in synthesising succinct stutter-insensitive bisimulation quotients, enabling efficient $CTL^*_{\setminus \bigcirc}$ verification by an off-the-shelf finite-state model checker. Notably, for pure $CTL^*_{\setminus \bigcirc}$ properties beyond $LTL_{\setminus \bigcirc}$ or $CTL_{\setminus \bigcirc}$, our approach outperforms T2, the only available alternative, on its benchmark set. This shows the advantage of branching bisimulation learning in making the verification of complex branching-time properties scalable and practical for non-deterministic infinite-state systems.

We note that bisimulation learning is not a stand-alone procedure but a lightweight preprocessing technique that synthesises succinct finite quotients for infinite-state systems, enabling their verification with standard finite-state model checkers. Since model checking for this general class of systems is undecidable, our approach is necessarily incomplete, as not all systems admit a finite stutter-insensitive bisimulation quotient. However, our experiments demonstrate that many standard benchmarks do yield finite quotients, and branching bisimulation learning is able to efficiently derive them from sampled system behaviours.

8   Related Work

Notions of abstractions, particularly bisimulation relations and their efficient computation, have been widely studied in the literature [5,9,51,62]. The primary notion is *strong* bisimulation, which requires related states to match each other's transitions exactly at every step, thereby preserving all linear- and branching-time properties expressible in common specification logics such as LTL, CTL*, and even the μ-calculus [53]. This notion has been relaxed into weaker variants that preserve only the externally observable behaviour, abstracting from exact stepwise equivalence, such as *stutter-insensitive* bisimulation [23,33]. These variants allow for much more succinct quotients while still preserving properties that do not include the exact stepwise *next*-operator, such as formulas in CTL$^*_{\setminus \bigcirc}$.

Stutter-insensitive bisimulations are closely related to *branching* bisimulations [39], which serve as the natural analogue when actions rather than states are labelled [42]. Any stutter-insensitive bisimulation on a state-labelled transition system forms a branching bisimulation on the corresponding action-labelled transition system, with both representations interconvertible via a standard construction [41,42]. This observation motivates the name of our procedure, which extends the applicability of bisimulation learning to nondeterministic systems and branching-time specifications, while also enabling the computation of branching bisimulations for action-labelled transition systems, even though our focus remains on state-labelled systems [4].

The standard approach to computing bisimulation relations are partition refinement algorithms, such as the Paige-Tarjan algorithm [37,48,67]. These algorithms iteratively refine an equivalence relation with respect to the bisimulation conditions until the partition stabilises into a valid bisimulation. This generalises to stutter-insensitive and branching bisimulations, although it requires computing unbounded pre or post images of the transition relation to determine the refinement [41,42,49]. Since partition refinement must process the entire state space, it can fall short on large systems. Moreover, for infinite state systems, symbolic procedures are required, incurring costly quantifier elimination [6,20,64]. Bisimulation learning introduces an incremental approach based on inductive synthesis that computes stutter-insensitive bisimulations by generalising from sample transitions, thereby circumventing the need to process the entire state space and enabling efficient computation for infinite state systems [1,3,4].

Model checking of infinite-state systems with respect to branching-time properties has been explored through techniques based on the satisfiability of Horn clauses [15–17,43], a class of universally quantified first-order logic formulas. These clauses are particularly effective for encoding safety properties of nondeterministic infinite-state systems. When extended with existential quantification, they facilitate the verification of full CTL* properties [11,12,25,52]. This approach is implemented in the T2 verification framework [22,30]. However, existential Horn clauses introduce quantifier alternation, which is computationally expensive even for mature symbolic first-order logic solvers [38,70]. An alternative approach reduces CTL* formulas to the modal μ-calculus and verifies the resulting expression by solving a parity game [32,66]. However, the translation from CTL* to the μ-calculus incurs a doubly-exponential blowup in the size of the formula, rendering the approach infeasible for many practical examples.

9   Conclusion

We have presented a generalised branching bisimulation learning algorithm for non-deterministic systems with bounded branching, and enabled effective model checking of finite- and infinite-state systems against $\text{CTL}^*_{\setminus\bigcirc}$ specifications. Our lightweight approach implements the proof rule for well-founded bisimulations within a counterexample-guided inductive synthesis loop, which performs comparably to mature tools for the special case of linear-time properties and establishes a new state of the art for branching-time properties. Our method produces stutter-insensitive bisimulations of the system under analysis for proving branching- and linear-time temporal properties as well as providing genuine abstract counterexamples or the exact initial conditions for which the property is satisfied. Our contribution provides the groundwork for the development of efficient model checkers that integrate bisimulation learning as a technique to reduce non-deterministic systems with very large or infinite state spaces to equivalent systems with finite and succinct state space.

Acknowledgments. This work was funded in part by the Advanced Research + Invention Agency (ARIA) under the Safeguarded AI programme.

Disclosure of Interests. The authors have no competing interests to declare that are relevant to the content of this article.

References

1. Abate, A., David, C., Kesseli, P., Kroening, D., Polgreen, E.: Counterexample guided inductive synthesis modulo theories. In: CAV (1). Lecture Notes in Computer Science, vol. 10981, pp. 270–288. Springer (2018)
2. Abate, A., Giacobbe, M., Micheletti, C., Schnitzer, Y.: Branching bisimulation learning (technical report). CoRR abs/2504.12246 (2025)
3. Abate, A., Giacobbe, M., Roy, D., Schnitzer, Y.: Model checking and strategy synthesis with abstractions and certificates. In: Principles of Verification (2). Lecture Notes in Computer Science, vol. 15261, pp. 360–391. Springer (2024)
4. Abate, A., Giacobbe, M., Schnitzer, Y.: Bisimulation learning. In: CAV (3). Lecture Notes in Computer Science, vol. 14683, pp. 161–183. Springer (2024)
5. Aceto, L., Ingólfsdóttir, A., Srba, J.: The algorithmics of bisimilarity. In: Advanced Topics in Bisimulation and Coinduction, Cambridge Tracts in Theoretical Computer Science, vol. 52, pp. 100–172. Cambridge University Press (2012)
6. de Alfaro, L., Henzinger, T.A., Majumdar, R.: Symbolic algorithms for infinite-state games. In: Larsen, K.G., Nielsen, M. (eds.) CONCUR 2001. LNCS, vol. 2154, pp. 536–550. Springer, Heidelberg (2001). https://doi.org/10.1007/3-540-44685-0_36
7. Alur, R., et al.: Syntax-guided synthesis. In: FMCAD, pp. 1–8. IEEE (2013)
8. Baier, C., Katoen, J.: Principles of Model Checking. MIT Press (2008)
9. Balcázar, J.L., Gabarró, J., Santha, M.: Deciding bisimilarity is P-complete. Formal Aspects Comput. 4(6A), 638–648 (1992)

10. Barrett, C.W., Sebastiani, R., Seshia, S.A., Tinelli, C.: Satisfiability modulo theories. In: Handbook of Satisfiability, Frontiers in Artificial Intelligence and Applications, vol. 336, pp. 1267–1329. IOS Press (2021)

11. Beyene, T.A., Popeea, C., Rybalchenko, A.: Solving existentially quantified horn clauses. In: Sharygina, N., Veith, H. (eds.) CAV 2013. LNCS, vol. 8044, pp. 869–882. Springer, Heidelberg (2013). https://doi.org/10.1007/978-3-642-39799-8_61

12. Beyene, T.A., Popeea, C., Rybalchenko, A.: Efficient CTL verification via horn constraints solving. In: HCVS@ETAPS. EPTCS, vol. 219, pp. 1–14 (2016)

13. Beyer, D., Henzinger, T.A., Jhala, R., Majumdar, R.: The software model checker blast. Int. J. Softw. Tools Technol. Transf. **9**(5–6), 505–525 (2007)

14. Beyer, D., Keremoglu, M.E.: CPACHECKER: a tool for configurable software verification. In: Gopalakrishnan, G., Qadeer, S. (eds.) CAV 2011. LNCS, vol. 6806, pp. 184–190. Springer, Heidelberg (2011). https://doi.org/10.1007/978-3-642-22110-1_16

15. Bjørner, N., Gurfinkel, A., McMillan, K., Rybalchenko, A.: Horn clause solvers for program verification. In: Beklemishev, L.D., Blass, A., Dershowitz, N., Finkbeiner, B., Schulte, W. (eds.) Fields of Logic and Computation II. LNCS, vol. 9300, pp. 24–51. Springer, Cham (2015). https://doi.org/10.1007/978-3-319-23534-9_2

16. Bjørner, N.S., McMillan, K.L., Rybalchenko, A.: Program verification as satisfiability modulo theories. In: SMT@IJCAR. EPiC Series in Computing, vol. 20, pp. 3–11. EasyChair (2012)

17. Bjørner, N., McMillan, K., Rybalchenko, A.: On solving universally quantified horn clauses. In: Logozzo, F., Fähndrich, M. (eds.) SAS 2013. LNCS, vol. 7935, pp. 105–125. Springer, Heidelberg (2013). https://doi.org/10.1007/978-3-642-38856-9_8

18. Bogomolov, S., Frehse, G., Giacobbe, M., Henzinger, T.A.: Counterexample-guided refinement of template polyhedra. In: Legay, A., Margaria, T. (eds.) TACAS 2017. LNCS, vol. 10205, pp. 589–606. Springer, Heidelberg (2017). https://doi.org/10.1007/978-3-662-54577-5_34

19. Bogomolov, S., Herrera, C., Steiner, W.: Verification of fault-tolerant clock synchronization algorithms. In: ARCH@CPSWeek. EPiC Series in Computing, vol. 43, pp. 36–41. EasyChair (2016)

20. Bouajjani, A., Fernandez, J., Halbwachs, N.: Minimal model generation. In: CAV. Lecture Notes in Computer Science, vol. 531, pp. 197–203. Springer (1990)

21. Bradley, A.R.: SAT-based model checking without unrolling. In: Jhala, R., Schmidt, D. (eds.) VMCAI 2011. LNCS, vol. 6538, pp. 70–87. Springer, Heidelberg (2011). https://doi.org/10.1007/978-3-642-18275-4_7

22. Brockschmidt, M., Cook, B., Ishtiaq, S., Khlaaf, H., Piterman, N.: T2: temporal property verification. In: Chechik, M., Raskin, J.-F. (eds.) TACAS 2016. LNCS, vol. 9636, pp. 387–393. Springer, Heidelberg (2016). https://doi.org/10.1007/978-3-662-49674-9_22

23. Browne, M.C., Clarke, E.M., Grumberg, O.: Characterizing finite Kripke structures in propositional temporal logic. Theor. Comput. Sci. **59**, 115–131 (1988)

24. Burch, J.R., Clarke, E.M., McMillan, K.L., Dill, D.L., Hwang, L.J.: Symbolic model checking: 10^{20} states and beyond. Inf. Comput. **98**(2), 142–170 (1992)

25. Carelli, M., Grumberg, O.: CTL* verification and synthesis using existential horn clauses. In: ATVA (2). Lecture Notes in Computer Science, vol. 15055, pp. 177–197. Springer (2024)

26. Cavada, R., et al.: The NUXMV Symbolic Model Checker. In: Biere, A., Bloem, R. (eds.) CAV 2014. LNCS, vol. 8559, pp. 334–342. Springer, Cham (2014). https://doi.org/10.1007/978-3-319-08867-9_22

27. Clarke, E.M., Emerson, E.A.: Design and synthesis of synchronization skeletons using branching-time temporal logic. In: Logic of Programs. Lecture Notes in Computer Science, vol. 131, pp. 52–71. Springer (1981)
28. Clarke, E.M., Grumberg, O., Jha, S., Lu, Y., Veith, H.: Counterexample-guided abstraction refinement. In: CAV. Lecture Notes in Computer Science, vol. 1855, pp. 154–169. Springer (2000)
29. Cook, B., Gotsman, A., Podelski, A., Rybalchenko, A., Vardi, M.Y.: Proving that programs eventually do something good. In: POPL, pp. 265–276. ACM (2007)
30. Cook, B., Khlaaf, H., Piterman, N.: On Automation of CTL* verification for infinite-state systems. In: Kroening, D., Păsăreanu, C.S. (eds.) CAV 2015. LNCS, vol. 9206, pp. 13–29. Springer, Cham (2015). https://doi.org/10.1007/978-3-319-21690-4_2
31. Cook, B., Podelski, A., Rybalchenko, A.: Abstraction refinement for termination. In: Hankin, C., Siveroni, I. (eds.) SAS 2005. LNCS, vol. 3672, pp. 87–101. Springer, Heidelberg (2005). https://doi.org/10.1007/11547662_8
32. Dam, M.: CTL* and ECTL* as fragments of the modal mu-calculus. Theor. Comput. Sci. **126**(1), 77–96 (1994)
33. De Nicola, R., Vaandrager, F.W.: Three logics for branching bisimulation. J. ACM **42**(2), 458–487 (1995)
34. van Dijk, T., van de Pol, J.: Multi-core symbolic bisimulation minimisation. Int. J. Softw. Tools Technol. Transf. **20**(2), 157–177 (2018)
35. Emerson, E.A., Halpern, J.Y.: "Sometimes" and "Not Never" revisited: on branching versus linear time. In: POPL, pp. 127–140. ACM Press (1983)
36. Ermis, E., Nutz, A., Dietsch, D., Hoenicke, J., Podelski, A.: Ultimate Kojak. In: Ábrahám, E., Havelund, K. (eds.) TACAS 2014. LNCS, vol. 8413, pp. 421–423. Springer, Heidelberg (2014). https://doi.org/10.1007/978-3-642-54862-8_36
37. Fernandez, J.-C., Mounier, L.: A tool set for deciding behavioral equivalences. In: Baeten, J., Groote, J.F. (eds.) CONCUR 1991. LNCS, vol. 527, pp. 23–42. Springer, Heidelberg (1991). https://doi.org/10.1007/3-540-54430-5_78
38. Garcia-Contreras, I., K., H.G.V., Shoham, S., Gurfinkel, A.: Fast approximations of quantifier elimination. In: CAV (2). Lecture Notes in Computer Science, vol. 13965, pp. 64–86. Springer (2023)
39. van Glabbeek, R.J., Weijland, W.P.: Branching time and abstraction in bisimulation semantics. J. ACM **43**(3), 555–600 (1996)
40. Graf, S., Saïdi, H.: Construction of abstract state graphs with PVS. In: CAV. Lecture Notes in Computer Science, vol. 1254, pp. 72–83. Springer (1997)
41. Groote, J.F., Jansen, D.N., Keiren, J.J.A., Wijs, A.: An $O(m \log n)$ algorithm for computing stuttering equivalence and branching bisimulation. ACM Trans. Comput. Log. **18**(2), 13:1–13:34 (2017)
42. Groote, J.F., Vaandrager, F.: An efficient algorithm for branching bisimulation and stuttering equivalence. In: Paterson, M.S. (ed.) ICALP 1990. LNCS, vol. 443, pp. 626–638. Springer, Heidelberg (1990). https://doi.org/10.1007/BFb0032063
43. Gurfinkel, A.: Program verification with constrained horn clauses (invited paper). In: CAV (1). Lecture Notes in Computer Science, vol. 13371, pp. 19–29. Springer (2022)
44. Heizmann, M., et al.: Ultimate automizer and the commuhash normal form - (competition contribution). In: TACAS (2). Lecture Notes in Computer Science, vol. 13994, pp. 577–581. Springer (2023)
45. Hennessy, M., Milner, R.: Algebraic laws for nondeterminism and concurrency. J. ACM **32**(1), 137–161 (1985)

46. Henzinger, T.A., Jhala, R., Majumdar, R., McMillan, K.L.: Abstractions from proofs. In: POPL, pp. 232–244. ACM (2004)
47. Henzinger, T.A., Jhala, R., Majumdar, R., Sutre, G.: Lazy abstraction. In: POPL, pp. 58–70. ACM (2002)
48. Hopcroft, J.: An $n \log n$ algorithm for minimizing states in a finite automaton. In: Kohavi, Z., Paz, A. (eds.) Theory of Machines and Computations, pp. 189–196. Academic Press (1971)
49. Jansen, D.N., Groote, J.F., Keiren, J.J.A., Wijs, A.: A simpler $O(m \log n)$ algorithm for branching bisimilarity on labelled transition systems. CoRR abs/1909.10824 (2019)
50. Kahsai, T., Rümmer, P., Sanchez, H., Schäf, M.: JayHorn: a framework for verifying Java programs. In: Chaudhuri, S., Farzan, A. (eds.) CAV 2016. LNCS, vol. 9779, pp. 352–358. Springer, Cham (2016). https://doi.org/10.1007/978-3-319-41528-4_19
51. Kanellakis, P.C., Smolka, S.A.: CCS expressions, finite state processes, and three problems of equivalence. Inf. Comput. **86**(1), 43–68 (1990)
52. Kesten, Y., Pnueli, A.: A compositional approach to CTL* verification. Theor. Comput. Sci. **331**(2–3), 397–428 (2005)
53. Kozen, D.: Results on the propositional μ-calculus. In: ICALP. Lecture Notes in Computer Science, vol. 140, pp. 348–359. Springer (1982)
54. Kroening, D., Strichman, O.: Decision Procedures - An Algorithmic Point of View, Second Edition. Texts in Theoretical Computer Science. An EATCS Series, Springer (2016)
55. Lamport, L.: What good is temporal logic? In: IFIP Congress. pp. 657–668. North-Holland/IFIP (1983)
56. Lamport, L., Melliar-Smith, P.M.: Byzantine clock synchronization. In: PODC, pp. 68–74. ACM (1984)
57. Lee, D., Yannakakis, M.: Online minimization of transition systems (extended abstract). In: STOC, pp. 264–274. ACM (1992)
58. Lee, I., Rajasekaran, S.: A parallel algorithm for relational coarsest partition problems and its implementation. In: Dill, D.L. (ed.) CAV 1994. LNCS, vol. 818, pp. 404–414. Springer, Heidelberg (1994). https://doi.org/10.1007/3-540-58179-0_71
59. Manolios, P., Namjoshi, K.S., Summers, R.: Linking theorem proving and model-checking with well-founded bisimulation. In: CAV. Lecture Notes in Computer Science, vol. 1633, pp. 369–379. Springer (1999)
60. Martens, J., Groote, J.F., van den Haak, L., Hijma, P., Wijs, A.: A linear parallel algorithm to compute bisimulation and relational coarsest partitions. In: Salaün, G., Wijs, A. (eds.) FACS 2021. LNCS, vol. 13077, pp. 115–133. Springer, Cham (2021). https://doi.org/10.1007/978-3-030-90636-8_7
61. McMillan, K.L.: Lazy abstraction with interpolants. In: Ball, T., Jones, R.B. (eds.) CAV 2006. LNCS, vol. 4144, pp. 123–136. Springer, Heidelberg (2006). https://doi.org/10.1007/11817963_14
62. Milner, R. (ed.): A Calculus of Communicating Systems. LNCS, vol. 92. Springer, Heidelberg (1980). https://doi.org/10.1007/3-540-10235-3
63. de Moura, L., Bjørner, N.: Z3: An efficient SMT solver. In: Ramakrishnan, C.R., Rehof, J. (eds.) TACAS 2008. LNCS, vol. 4963, pp. 337–340. Springer, Heidelberg (2008). https://doi.org/10.1007/978-3-540-78800-3_24
64. Mumme, M., Ciardo, G.: A fully symbolic bisimulation algorithm. In: Delzanno, G., Potapov, I. (eds.) RP 2011. LNCS, vol. 6945, pp. 218–230. Springer, Heidelberg (2011). https://doi.org/10.1007/978-3-642-24288-5_19
65. Namjoshi, K.S.: A simple characterization of stuttering bisimulation. In: FSTTCS. Lecture Notes in Computer Science, vol. 1346, pp. 284–296. Springer (1997)

66. Niwinski, D., Walukiewicz, I.: Games for the mu-calculus. Theor. Comput. Sci. **163**(1&2), 99–116 (1996)
67. Paige, R., Tarjan, R.E.: Three partition refinement algorithms. SIAM J. Comput. **16**(6), 973–989 (1987)
68. Pnueli, A.: The temporal logic of programs. In: FOCS. pp. 46–57. IEEE Computer Society (1977)
69. Prabhakar, P., Soto, M.G.: Counterexample guided abstraction refinement for stability analysis. In: Chaudhuri, S., Farzan, A. (eds.) CAV 2016. LNCS, vol. 9779, pp. 495–512. Springer, Cham (2016). https://doi.org/10.1007/978-3-319-41528-4_27
70. S, S.P., Fedyukovich, G., Madhukar, K., D'Souza, D.: Specification synthesis with constrained horn clauses. In: PLDI. pp. 1203–1217. ACM (2021)
71. Solar-Lezama, A., Tancau, L., Bodík, R., Seshia, S.A., Saraswat, V.A.: Combinatorial sketching for finite programs. In: ASPLOS, pp. 404–415. ACM (2006)
72. Tóth, T., Hajdu, A., Vörös, A., Micskei, Z., Majzik, I.: Theta: a framework for abstraction refinement-based model checking. In: FMCAD, pp. 176–179 (2017)

A Misconception-Driven Adaptive Tutor
for Linear Temporal Logic

Siddhartha Prasad[1](✉) [iD], Ben Greenman[2] [iD], Tim Nelson[1] [iD],
and Shriram Krishnamurthi[1] [iD]

[1] Brown University, Providence, USA
siddhartha.a.prasad@gmail.com,
{timothy_nelson,shriram}@brown.edu
[2] University of Utah, Salt Lake, USA
benjamin.l.greenman@gmail.com

Abstract. Linear Temporal Logic (LTL) is used widely in verification,
planning, and more. Unfortunately, users often struggle to learn it. To
improve their learning, they need drill, instruction, and adaptation to
their strengths and weaknesses. Furthermore, this should fit into whatever learning process they are already part of (such as a course).

In response, we have built a *misconception-based* automated tutoring system. It assumes learners have a basic understanding of logic,
and focuses on their understanding of LTL operators. Crucially, it takes
advantage of multiple years of research (by our team, with collaborators)
into misconceptions about LTL amongst both novices and experts.

The tutor generates questions using these known learner misconceptions; this enables the tutor to determine which concepts learners are
strong and weak on. When learners get a question wrong, they are offered
immediate feedback in terms of the concrete error they made. If they
consistently demonstrate similar errors, the tool offers them feedback in
terms of more general misconceptions, and tailors subsequent question
sets to exercise those misconceptions.

The tool is hosted for free on-line, is available open source for self-
hosting, and offers instructor-friendly features.

Keywords: LTL · misconceptions · adaptive tutor

1 Introduction

Linear Temporal Logic is a cornerstone of verification [62], and is also used for
synthesis [3,4,9,12,16,44,48,58,66], robotics [6,7,11,24,32,34,35,40,55,63,65],
embedded systems [10,59], business processes [1,14,17,18,43], and more [46,60].

Since an incorrect specification can cause bugs to go undetected or derail
a system's functionality, it is critical that users (from students to profession-
als) can write and understand LTL specifications correctly. This has spurred a
growing body of research focused on improving the process of authoring and
interpreting LTL specifications. These efforts include tools designed to represent
specifications in terms of alternate formalisms (e.g., Büchi automata [8,20]),

© The Author(s) 2025
R. Piskac and Z. Rakamarić (Eds.): CAV 2025, LNCS 15934, pp. 185–200, 2025.
https://doi.org/10.1007/978-3-031-98685-7_9

scaffold common specification patterns [23,57], explain formulae via visualization [36,64], and generate specifications from natural language [15,25].

Another way to tackle the problem is to better understand *what* aspects of
LTL are difficult. For several years [28,31], with collaborators, we have focused on
this question. Our findings have resulted in a catalog of common misconceptions,
and these have been distilled into multiple-choice question/answer sets.

However, simply deploying a question/answer sheet as, say, an electronic survey is not enough. To learn well, learners need lots of examples and periodic drill
(even refreshers). When they make mistakes, they need feedback to understand
what they got wrong. This feedback should occur at two levels. On individual
questions, learners may have made a mis*take*. Though they need concrete feedback (e.g., showing traces), the error could also be due to a lack of attention
or even a slip of the finger. If, however, they make the same kind of error consistently, they may have a mis*conception*; addressing that requires correcting
conceptual knowledge. In turn, they need additional questions that target their
errors to confirm that they have internalized the feedback.

We have operationalized all of the above into an on-line, adaptive *tutor*, the
LTL Tutor. It is hosted for free online:

https://ltl-tutor.xyz

To be privacy-protecting, the tutor does not gather any identifying information.
Educators can create a "course" and get aggregated data of how students in it are
performing. For those who have additional data privacy concerns, the software is
also available open source and designed for self-hosting. The tutor also supports
both the classical LTL syntax (used in this paper) as well as variants used by
recent tools [13,45] that use keywords (e.g., `always`, `after`).

Some tutoring systems are designed to teach a topic from scratch. As educators, we recognize this can be very disruptive because it assumes a specific context, preparation, amount of available time, and so on. Instead, the LTL Tutor
is designed to be a *companion* that complements whatever pedagogy is already
in use, rather than a substitute. We assume students have a basic grounding in
formal logic, and may have heard a lecture or two about LTL in the instructor's
preferred style. What the LTL Tutor does is save the instructor from having to
provide *drill*, feedback, and corrections; and it leverages our extensive catalog
of LTL difficulty without the instructor needing to learn it in depth themselves.
Effectively, the LTL Tutor tries to learn, and then correct, the *latent* conceptual
model of LTL that the student has in their mind—however it is obtained.

Finally, we note the increased interest in LTL in industrial settings. It can be
especially difficult for industrial practitioners to get assistance the way a student
in a course can from instructors and teaching assistants. Thus, the LTL Tutor
should be of particular value to practitioners.

This paper describes the design and implementation of the LTL Tutor. After
providing a high-level overview (Sect. 3), it especially focuses on two aspects:

- A misconception driven process for generating novel question sets tailored to
  individual learners (Sect. 4).

– Mechanisms designed to provide learners with insight both into the questions they get wrong and the underlying misconceptions that may be driving these errors (Sect. 5).

2 Related Work

Our work is inspired by the seminal work on *concept inventories* [33] from physics education. A concept inventory is a collection of multiple-choice questions where each wrong answer (often called a *distractor*) is not merely wrong, but corresponds to a *specific misconception*. Thus, if students choose a certain distractor, the instructor can be confident about what the student's confusion is. Our prior work [28–31] takes steps toward such an instrument for LTL (and introduces a catalog of misconceptions), which this work leverages to make generative.

To make it generative, we need a way to not only create new problems but also create misconception-based distractors. While mutation testing [2] is appealing here, the mutants created may be trivial, redundant [53], or even functionally identical to the original [42]. We thus draw inspiration from Prasad et al. [50]'s work on "conceptual" mutation to address these problems. Their work (not for LTL!), however, is only partially automated and requires significant expert intervention. A key technical contribution of this work (Sect. 4) is to perform conceptual mutation in a completely automated way.

When learners make conceptual errors, we have to provide high-level feedback (Sect. 5.2). We draw on the literature of conceptual change [49], specifically using *refutation texts*, which has been found effective in many settings [54]. (The SMoL Tutor for programming language semantics [41] also uses these, and is also driven by misconceptions.)

Our tutor is inspired by vanLehn's two-loop model for tutoring systems [61], in which an inner loop provides immediate feedback and an outer loop selects the next task. The LTL Tutor builds on this framework, extending the outer loop to also target misconceptions (Fig. 5).

We are also inspired by works on cognitive tutoring [5,47,56], which capture how an expert would solve a problem and try to get learners to mimic that approach. This approach is too resource-intensive for our lightweight setting, as it requires extensive effort to model and encode expert problem-solving methods.

Finally, we describe existing tutors for formal logic. These systems rely on hand-crafted questions or generate questions without a guiding principle (akin to conventional mutation testing). In contrast, the LTL Tutor stands out by generating novel questions based on an inventory of conceptual errors.

Iltis is a web-based tutor designed to teach learners about the logical foundations of computer science [26,27]. The system has two primary focuses: allowing instructors to easily construct, compose, and pipeline questions and question sets, and the ability to provide students with instant meaningful feedback and explanations for errors. Unlike the LTL Tutor, this means that Iltis modules are designed to be closely tied to specific courses of study (e.g., a modal logic module [19]).

Lodder et al. have developed logic tutors [37–39]. Rather than requiring experts to specify the steps of a solution, the tutors automatically generate authoritative step-by-step proofs for instructor-specified problems. Students are given feedback when their proof steps diverge from the generated authoritative proof. However, this work is (a) proof-, not model-theoretic and (b) not for LTL.

3   The LTL Tutor

A user of the LTL Tutor sees a series of multiple-choice questions. There are two kinds of problems:

English-to-LTL questions ask learners to identify which LTL formula best captures a given English description. Figure 1 shows an example of a question and the feedback for a wrong answer.

Trace Satisfaction questions ask learners to decide whether a temporal trace satisfies a given LTL formula. These questions come in two forms: yes/no questions (Fig. 3) in the style of the quizzes we used to build the misconception catalog [29,30], or a multiple-choice variant that asks learners to choose the one satisfying trace from among several possibilities (Fig. 2). The LTL Tutor also provides an LTL Stepper (Fig. 4), where learners can step through a formula and trace simultaneously to develop a better operational understanding of the language.

The LTL Tutor had about 254 unique users by April 2025, who answered a total of 2261 questions. Of these, 530 (23.44%) answers were incorrect. The wrong answers most commonly corresponded to the following misconceptions:

1. Implicit G (28.68%): Expecting a G operator to apply, even when it was not explicitly present. For example, expecting $G(x \implies y)$ to behave like $G(x \implies (Gy))$.
2. Other Implicit (23.58%): Expecting formulae to be stronger than their actual meaning. For example, expecting Fx to capture the behavior of $(\neg x)Ux$.
3. Bad State Quantification (19.25%): Confusing how "fan out" operators (F, G, U) apply to different states in a trace. For example, expecting $(Gx)Uy$ to behave like $x\,Uy$.

Detailed explanations of these misconceptions are available in [31, Figure 4].

Because of the nature of generated formulas (Sect. 4), when learners make mistakes, we can associate these with known misconceptions. Therefore, over time, the LTL Tutor builds a model of the learner's overall understanding of LTL. Each learner mistake is given a score, with recent mistakes weighted more heavily using a decay function inversely proportional to the time elapsed since the mistake. Starting from a uniform prior, each misconception's relative likelihood is then calculated from the sum of the associated mistake scores. The effect of this is that the predicted likelihood of a learner having a misconception is higher if they have made recent mistakes associated with that misconception.

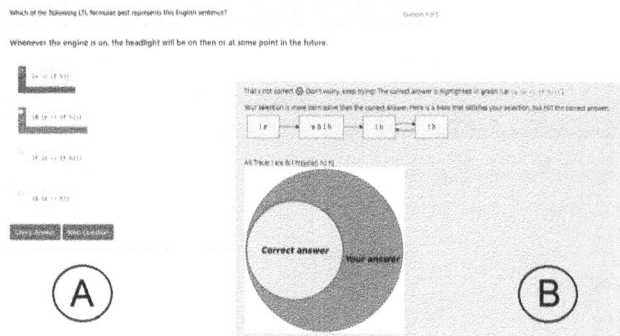

Fig. 1. An English-to-LTL question, with feedback about a learner's mistake. Here (A) the learner selects an incorrect answer, associated with the Implicit G misconception, and is shown (B) a concrete example of why their answer is incorrect, and the relationship between their answer and the correct solution.

Each time the tutor generates a question set, it uses these predictions to inform the kinds of questions it generates. If learners consistently demonstrate a misconception, then the tutor provides *concept-level* feedback, which we discuss in Sect. 5.2. The overall flow is shown in Fig. 5.

4   Generating Problems

From the above, we can see that the heart of the tutor lies in generating good sets of related formulas. Both kinds of questions are generated from a *seed formula*. This formula is randomly generated by the SPOT randltl tool [20], with the likelihood of each operator's occurence determined by the learner's predicted likelihood of having a related misconception. For example, if the learner has a high likelihood of the Implicit G misconception, the formula generation process will bias the seed formula towards the G operator. All seed formulae are generated to have at most 4 unique propositions, enough to allow for reasonably complex formulas, but low enough to limit extraneous cognitive load.

For English-to-LTL, the LTL Tutor generates a simple English description of the seed formula, which is used as the question prompt. We describe this translation process in Sect. 7. The seed formula represents the correct answer to the question. It is mutated to create distractors, as we describe below.

For trace satisfaction, the seed formula serves as the question prompt. Traces accepted by the seed formula and its mutants (also created as below) are then used as candidate answers and distractors, respectively. These traces are generated by translating the LTL formulas into Büchi automata using the SPOT tool for ω-automata manipulation [20,21] and then extracting accepting runs. If an accepting run includes a state with multiple possible transitions, we randomly choose one of the branches to resolve the ambiguity. No specific preference is given to one trace over another beyond this random selection.

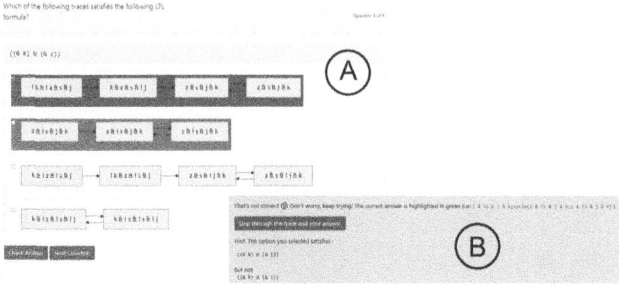

Fig. 2. A Trace Satisfaction (Multiple Choice) (A) question, with (B) feedback about a learner's mistake.

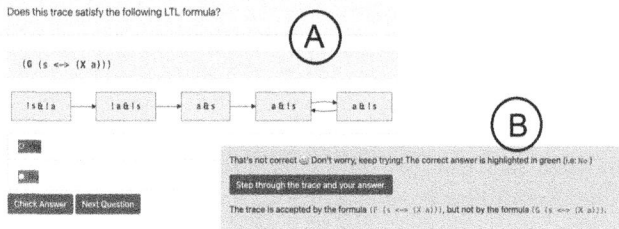

Fig. 3. A Trace Satisfaction (Y/N) (A) question, with (B) feedback about a learner's mistake. Figure 4 shows how the stepper can help shed further light on the mistake.

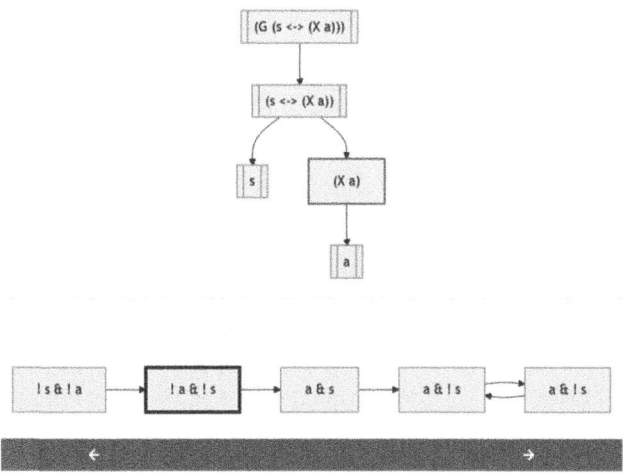

Fig. 4. LTL Stepper: The syntax tree (top) shows how each sub-formula of $G(s \iff (Xa))$ is satisfied (green border) or not satisfied (orange double border) at a given trace step. The trace (bottom) highlights the trace step under study and shows the assignment of truth values to literals at each step. (Color figure online)

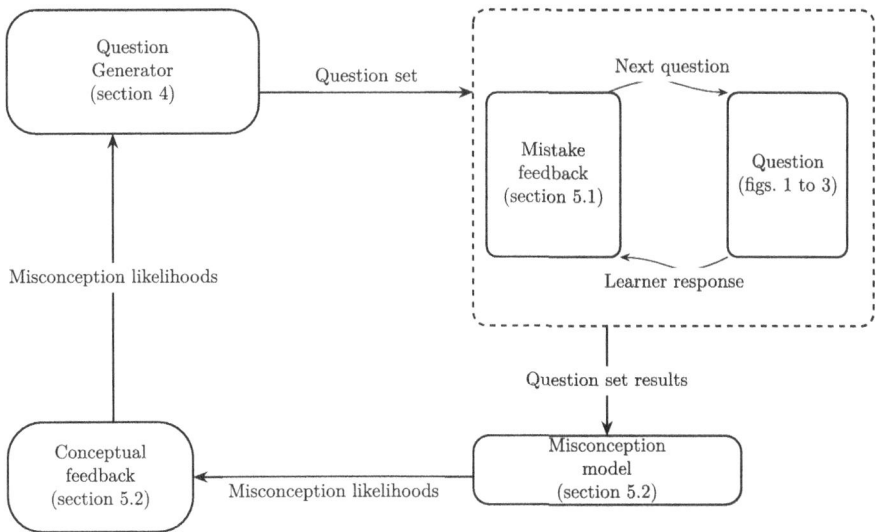

Fig. 5. The overall flow of the LTL Tutor.

Generating Good Mutants. The key to generating useful problems comes down to creating good mutants. Doing so well is a central contribution of the LTL Tutor.

An English-to-LTL question, for example, might be founded in the following seed formula and English sentence pair:

$$G(e \implies (Fh))$$

Whenever the engine is on, the headlight will be on then or at some point in the future.

As we have noted, it is natural to mutate this seed formula to create mutants. Because LTL equality is decidable [62], we can easily rule out syntactic variants that are not semantically different. Thus, we could adapt typical syntactic mutation techniques from programming to LTL formulae: for instance, we might randomly change logical operators (Eq. (1)), change operands (Eq. (2)), or swap operand order (Eq. (3)):

$$G(e \implies (Fh)) \xrightarrow{\text{mutate}} G(e \wedge (Fh)) \tag{1}$$

$$G(e \implies (Fh)) \xrightarrow{\text{mutate}} ((Ge) \implies (Fh)) \tag{2}$$

$$G(e \implies (Fh)) \xrightarrow{\text{mutate}} G((Fh) \implies e) \tag{3}$$

While these syntactic mutants of the original formula could be used as distractors in a multiple choice question, they are very unlikely to capture the actual difficulties that learners have. For example, since the *and* operator is nowhere in the English sentence to be translated, it is highly unlikely that a learner would pick $G(e \wedge (Fh))$ (the mutant in Eq. (1)) as an answer. Furthermore, if a learner were to select this option, it is unclear *why* they did so. This limits the kinds of feedback that can be provided to the learner.

Table 1. Conceptual mutation rules used by the LTL Tutor, alongside their associated misconceptions. Arbitrary LTL formulae are represented by α, β, and δ. Arbitrary binary operators are represented by $\bowtie$.

Misconception	Mutation Rules
Implicit $\boldsymbol{G}$	$\boldsymbol{G}\alpha \xrightarrow{\text{mutate}} \alpha$
Implicit $\boldsymbol{F}$	$\boldsymbol{F}\alpha \xrightarrow{\text{mutate}} \alpha$
Bad State	$\boldsymbol{G}\alpha \xrightarrow{\text{mutate}} \boldsymbol{F}\alpha$
Quantification	$\boldsymbol{F}\alpha \xrightarrow{\text{mutate}} \boldsymbol{G}\alpha$
	$\alpha\boldsymbol{U}\beta \xrightarrow{\text{mutate}} (\boldsymbol{F}\alpha)\boldsymbol{U}\beta$
	$\alpha\boldsymbol{U}\beta \xrightarrow{\text{mutate}} \alpha\boldsymbol{U}(\boldsymbol{F}\beta)$
	$\alpha\boldsymbol{U}\beta \xrightarrow{\text{mutate}} (\boldsymbol{G}\alpha)\boldsymbol{U}\beta$
	$\alpha\boldsymbol{U}\beta \xrightarrow{\text{mutate}} \alpha\boldsymbol{U}(\boldsymbol{G}\beta)$
	$\alpha\boldsymbol{U}\beta \xrightarrow{\text{mutate}} (\beta\boldsymbol{U}\alpha)$
Precedence	$\alpha\bowtie(\beta\bowtie\delta) \xrightarrow{\text{mutate}} (\alpha\bowtie\beta)\bowtie\delta$
Exclusive $\boldsymbol{U}$	$\alpha\boldsymbol{U}(\neg\alpha\wedge\beta) \xrightarrow{\text{mutate}} \alpha\boldsymbol{U}\beta$
Weak $\boldsymbol{U}$	$\alpha\boldsymbol{U}\beta \xrightarrow{\text{mutate}} (\alpha\boldsymbol{U}\beta)\wedge\boldsymbol{F}\beta$
Bad State	$\delta\boldsymbol{U}(\alpha\wedge(\boldsymbol{F}\beta)) \xrightarrow{\text{mutate}} (\delta\boldsymbol{U}\alpha)\wedge(\boldsymbol{F}\beta)$
Index	$\delta\boldsymbol{U}(\alpha\wedge(\boldsymbol{G}\beta)) \xrightarrow{\text{mutate}} (\delta\boldsymbol{U}\alpha)\wedge(\boldsymbol{G}\beta)$
	$\delta\boldsymbol{U}(\alpha\wedge(\boldsymbol{F}\beta)) \xrightarrow{\text{mutate}} (\delta\boldsymbol{U}\alpha)\wedge(\boldsymbol{F}\beta)$
	$\delta\boldsymbol{U}(\alpha\vee(\boldsymbol{G}\beta)) \xrightarrow{\text{mutate}} (\delta\boldsymbol{U}\alpha)\vee(\boldsymbol{G}\beta)$
	$\delta\boldsymbol{U}(\alpha\implies(\boldsymbol{F}\beta)) \xrightarrow{\text{mutate}} (\delta\boldsymbol{U}\alpha)\implies(\boldsymbol{F}\beta)$
	$\delta\boldsymbol{U}(\alpha\implies(\boldsymbol{G}\beta)) \xrightarrow{\text{mutate}} (\delta\boldsymbol{U}\alpha)\implies(\boldsymbol{G}\beta)$
	$\boldsymbol{X}(\alpha\wedge\beta) \xrightarrow{\text{mutate}} (\boldsymbol{X}\alpha)\wedge\beta$
	$\boldsymbol{X}(\boldsymbol{X}(\boldsymbol{X}\ldots\boldsymbol{X}\alpha)) \xrightarrow{\text{mutate}} \boldsymbol{X}\alpha$
Other Implicit	$(\neg\alpha\boldsymbol{U}\alpha) \xrightarrow{\text{mutate}} \boldsymbol{F}\alpha$
	$(\alpha\boldsymbol{U}(\boldsymbol{G}\alpha)) \xrightarrow{\text{mutate}} \alpha\wedge(\boldsymbol{F}(\boldsymbol{G}\alpha))$
	$(\boldsymbol{F}\alpha)\wedge(\boldsymbol{G}(\beta\implies(\boldsymbol{X}(\boldsymbol{G}\beta)))) \xrightarrow{\text{mutate}} \alpha\wedge(\boldsymbol{X}(\boldsymbol{G}\beta))$
	$\boldsymbol{X}\alpha \xrightarrow{\text{mutate}} \boldsymbol{F}\alpha$
	$\alpha\bowtie\beta \xrightarrow{\text{mutate}} \alpha$
	$\alpha\bowtie\beta \xrightarrow{\text{mutate}} \beta$
	$\neg\alpha \xrightarrow{\text{mutate}} \alpha$

Instead, the LTL Tutor uses our well-substantiated catalogs of LTL misconceptions [28,31] to guide the mutation process. This process of *conceptual* mutation is achieved by associating each misconception with mutation rules (Table 1). Applying any of these mutation rules to a given LTL formula (or sub-formula) generates a mutant that embodies the corresponding misconception. The seed formula above, for example, could be mutated to explicitly embody multiple misconceptions, with the misconception given as a label:

$$G(e \implies (Fh)) \xrightarrow{\text{mutate}} e \implies (Fh) \qquad \text{(Implicit } G)$$

$$G(e \implies (Fh)) \xrightarrow{\text{mutate}} G(e \implies h) \qquad \text{(Implicit } F)$$

$$G(e \implies (Fh)) \xrightarrow{\text{mutate}} F(e \implies h) \qquad \text{(Bad State Quantification)}$$

Crucially, each distractor is now associated with a known misconception.[1] Not only do these distractors reflect the actual difficulties that learners are known to have, when chosen, they also provide insight into the underlying misconceptions. Thus, for instance, if a learner selects the first conceptual mutant above (as shown in Fig. 1), it is likely that they have the Implicit G misconception. We next discuss how we operationalize this insight.

5   Helping Learners Learn

As mentioned in Sect. 1, we draw a meaningful distinction between learner mis*takes* and mis*conceptions*. While mistakes can be addressed via feedback in terms of the problem at hand (Sect. 5.1), misconception feedback must be provided in terms of the misunderstood concept (Sect. 5.2).

5.1   Addressing Learner Mistakes

The first thing the LTL tutor does is give feedback at the question level. When a learner selects a distractor to an English-to-LTL question (e.g., Fig. 1), they are shown a concrete example of why their answer is incorrect and the relationship between their answer and the correct solution. Feedback for trace satisfaction questions involves the formula used to generate the (incorrect) trace alongside the correct formula (Fig. 2, Fig. 3). If the learner wants further insight, they can walk through the evaluation of the trace they selected over the correct formula trace using an interactive trace stepper. Figure 4 shows how the stepper can help shed light on the learner's mistake in Fig. 3.

5.2   Addressing Learner Misconceptions

A single mistake, however, is not enough to identify a pervasive misconception. A learner could have misread the question, mis-clicked, or just had a minor misunderstanding. However, if a learner consistently makes the same mistake, it is likely that they have a misconception.

As described in Sect. 3, the LTL Tutor models the likelihood of a learner having a misconception based on their previous mistakes. This model informs

---

[1] When multiple mutants are *syntactically* equal, we present only one to the learner, but associate all relevant misconceptions with that distractor.

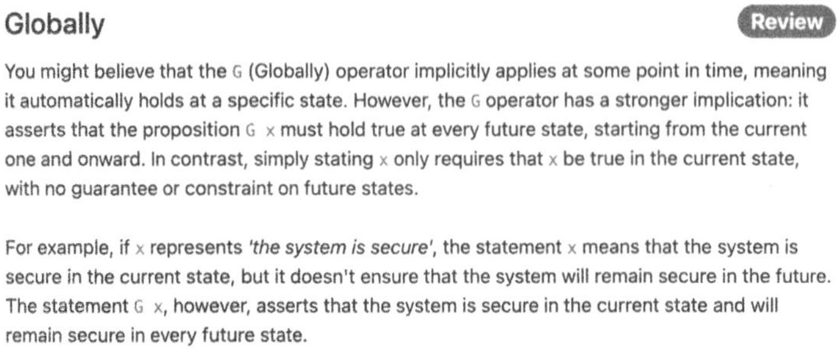

Globally   `Review`

You might believe that the G (Globally) operator implicitly applies at some point in time, meaning it automatically holds at a specific state. However, the G operator has a stronger implication: it asserts that the proposition G x must hold true at every future state, starting from the current one and onward. In contrast, simply stating x only requires that x be true in the current state, with no guarantee or constraint on future states.

For example, if x represents 'the system is secure', the statement x means that the system is secure in the current state, but it doesn't ensure that the system will remain secure in the future. The statement G x, however, asserts that the system is secure in the current state and will remain secure in every future state.

Fig. 6. Feedback for the Implicit G misconception.

seed formula generation, and thus the likelihood of a learner encountering a question that exercises a particular misconception.

Once the learner has got at least 5 questions incorrect, the tutor provides textual feedback about their most probable misconception.[2] Crucially, this feedback does not refer to a specific question encountered by the learner, but rather the general misconception itself. Using the refutation text format (Sect. 2), this feedback confronts the learner with their misconception and provides a rebuttal to it. For example, the feedback for the Implicit G misconception (Fig. 6) presents a hypothesis of the learner's idea of how the G operator behaves, explains the correct semantics of the operator, and provides an example to illustrate the difference.

6   Instructor Support

Many of our existing users are instructors who employ the LTL Tutor in the context of a course. They would benefit from having feedback on how their students are doing, not only to track progress but also to detect class-wide persistent misconceptions (which may suggest weaknesses in their materials).

Therefore, the LTL Tutor provides instructors the option of creating a notion of a "course". This generates a code that students use when submitting work. Instructors can then use the course instance to track student progress by identifier or class progress via aggregate statistics.

Because we host the LTL Tutor, this can create discomfort or problems for some instructors regarding student privacy. For that reason, the tutor is available as an open-source system [52] with instructions for running local copies [51]. While we appreciate instructors providing us with summary statistics (which

---

[2] This threshold is arbitrary but chosen with some thought. We wanted it to be high enough that users gain familiarity with the tutor, to avoid misidentifying early mistakes as misconceptions. At the same time, it is low enough to ensure that users don't go too long without receiving conceptual feedback.

Table 2. Example patterns used to translate LTL to English.

LTL Pattern	English Translation
$G(\alpha \implies (F\beta))$	Whenever α (holds), eventually β will (hold)
$G(F\alpha)$	There will always be a point in the future where α (holds)
$F(G\neg\alpha)$	Eventually, it will never be the case that α (holds)
$XX...X\alpha$	In n states, α (will hold)
$G(\alpha \implies (X(\beta U\delta)))$	Whenever α (happens), β (will hold) until δ (holds)

help us keep track of both global student understanding of LTL[3] and the tutor's performance), we do not require this.

7   LTL to English

The creation of English-to-LTL questions requires the translation of a seed formula into English. To do this, the LTL Tutor first attempts to match the LTL formula to a set of common patterns (inspired by Dwyer et al.'s work on patterns in property specifications [22,23]), some of which are described in Table 2.

Formulae that do not match any of these patterns are recursively translated into English via mechanical description of their logical operators. For instance, a formula like $G(p \wedge Xq)$ might be broken into "Globally, p and Xq," where Xq is further translated as "in the next state, q." This ensures even complex or unconventional formulae receive a systematic, if literal, English description. However, these translations may be stilted or ambiguous, as the translation method ignores systematic dependencies between subformulae. For instance, the formula $F(n \rightarrow Gz)$, translates to "Eventually, globally, z holds is necessary for n holds". We readily acknowledge that this recursively-generated phrasing is both confusing and unnatural; future work should look to improve this output.

While translations could be improved with language models, we are wary of potential "hallucinations" that could lead to incorrect translations. The demands of the educational context require that English translations never be *incorrect*.

8   Limitations

Given the tutor's support for English-to-LTL, it is natural to wonder why it does not also support LTL-to-English. This is particularly relevant since the work we build upon [29,30] identified misconceptions in both directions. However, LTL-to-English requires the ability to check English output. Naturally, it may be possible to employ language models for this. However, we have not done this because of our desire for reliability in evaluating output, which seems hard to

---

[3] Because LTL operators are tied to natural language, it is conceivable that different linguistic backgrounds would have different performance and misconceptions.

achieve. Furthermore, in prior work, people demonstrated strong performance in this direction [31], reducing its priority. In addition, language models can significantly drive up computational costs (complicating our hosting) or require use of external paid services (which is difficult at scale).

A natural weakness of the current tutor is that it centers around our existing catalog of misconceptions. Though this has been built up over many years, there may yet be other misconceptions in the wild. One of our goals is to adapt the tutor to be more open to these: e.g., using some of the purely syntactic mutants that we rejected earlier (Sect. 4) to see whether they yield unexpected answers. The reason we have not done this already is that turning these mistakes into misconceptions ideally requires learners to provide textual explanations of their choices, and making the interface for this useful to us while not irritating to them is a challenge.

Acknowledgments. This work was partially supported by US NSF grant DGE-2208731. We thank Sriram Sankaranarayanan for his advice. We are also grateful to Skyler Austen, Elijah Rivera, Gavin Gray, and Kuang-Chen Lu for alpha testing the LTL Tutor and providing valuable feedback. Finally, we thank the instructors and learners who have used the LTL Tutor, both in classrooms and in the wild.

Disclosure of Interests. All authors declare that they have no competing interests.

References

1. Van der Aalst, W.M., de Beer, H.T., van Dongen, B.F.: Process mining and verification of properties: an approach based on temporal logic. In: On the Move to Meaningful Internet Systems 2005: CoopIS, DOA, and ODBASE: OTM Confederated International Conferences, CoopIS, DOA, and ODBASE 2005, Agia Napa, Cyprus, October 31-November 4, 2005, Proceedings, Part I, pp. 130–147. Springer (2005)
2. Acree, A., Budd, T., Demillo, R., Lipton, R., Sayward, F.: Mutation analysis. Technical report. ADA076575, Georgia Inst. of Tech. Atlanta School of Information and Computer Science (1979). https://apps.dtic.mil/sti/citations/ADA076575
3. Alur, R., Bansal, S., Bastani, O., Jothimurugan, K.: A framework for transforming specifications in reinforcement learning. In: Principles of Systems Design - Essays Dedicated to Thomas A. Henzinger on the Occasion of His 60th Birthday, pp. 604–624. Springer (2022). https://doi.org/10.1007/978-3-031-22337-2_29
4. Amram, G., Bansal, S., Fried, D., Tabajara, L.M., Vardi, M.Y., Weiss, G.: Adapting behaviors via reactive synthesis. In: CAV, pp. 870–893. Springer (2021). https://doi.org/10.1007/978-3-030-81685-8_41
5. Anderson, J.R., Corbett, A.T., Koedinger, K.R., Pelletier, R.: Cognitive tutors: lessons learned. J. Learn. Sci. **4**(2), 167–207 (1995)
6. Antoniotti, M., Mishra, B.: Discrete events models + temporal logic = supervisory controller: automatic synthesis of locomotion controllers. In: ICRA, pp. 1441–1446. IEEE (1995). https://doi.org/10.1109/ROBOT.1995.525480
7. Araki, B., Li, X., Vodrahalli, K., DeCastro, J.A., Fry, M.J., Rus, D.: The logical options framework. In: ICML, vol. 139, pp. 307–317. PMLR (2021). http://proceedings.mlr.press/v139/araki21a.html

8. Babiak, T., Křetínský, M., Řehák, V., Strejček, J.: LTL to Büchi automata translation: Fast and more deterministic. In: International Conference on Tools and Algorithms for the Construction and Analysis of Systems, pp. 95–109. Springer (2012)

9. Bansal, S., Li, Y., Tabajara, L.M., Vardi, M.Y., Wells, A.: Model checking strategies from synthesis over finite traces. In: ATVA, pp. 227–247. Springer (2023). https://doi.org/10.1007/978-3-031-45329-8_11

10. Benny, A., Chandran, S., Kalayappan, R., Phawade, R., Kurur, P.P.: faRM-LTL: a domain-specific architecture for flexible and accelerated runtime monitoring of LTL properties. In: International Conference on Runtime Verification, pp. 109–127. Springer (2024)

11. Bhatia, A., Kavraki, L.E., Vardi, M.Y.: Sampling-based motion planning with temporal goals. In: ICRA, pp. 2689–2696. IEEE (2010). https://doi.org/10.1109/ROBOT.2010.5509503

12. Bloem, R., Jobstmann, B., Piterman, N., Pnueli, A., Sa'ar, Y.: Synthesis of reactive(1) designs. J. Comput. Syst. Sci. **78**(3), 911–938 (2012). https://doi.org/10.1016/j.jcss.2011.08.007

13. Brunel, J., Chemouil, D., Cunha, A., Macedo, N.: The Electrum analyzer: model checking relational first-order temporal specifications. In: ASE, pp. 884–887. ACM (2018)

14. Ciccio, C.D., Montali, M.: Declarative process specifications: Reasoning, discovery, monitoring. In: Process Mining Handbook, Lecture Notes in Business Information Processing, vol. 448, pp. 108–152. Springer (2022). https://doi.org/10.1007/978-3-031-08848-3_4

15. Cosler, M., Hahn, C., Mendoza, D., Schmitt, F., Trippel, C.: nl2spec: interactively translating unstructured natural language to temporal logics with large language models. In: CAV, pp. 383–396. Springer (2023). https://doi.org/10.1007/978-3-031-37703-7_18

16. Cui, L., Rothkopf, R., Santolucito, M.: Towards reactive synthesis as a programming paradigm (2024). https://doi.org/10.1184/R1/25587741.v1, https://kilthub.cmu.edu/articles/conference_contribution/Towards_Reactive_Synthesis_as_a_Programming_Paradigm/25587741

17. De Giacomo, G., De Masellis, R., Grasso, M., Maggi, F.M., Montali, M.: Monitoring business metaconstraints based on LTL and LDL for finite traces. In: BPM, pp. 1–17. Springer (2014). https://doi.org/10.1007/978-3-319-10172-9_1

18. De Giacomo, G., Maggi, F.M., Marrella, A., Patrizi, F.: On the disruptive effectiveness of automated planning for LTLf-based trace alignment. In: Artificial Intelligence, pp. 1–7. AAAI (2017). https://doi.org/10.1609/aaai.v31i1.11020

19. Dortmund, T.U.: Logic WiSe 2022 (2022). https://iltis.cs.tu-dortmund.de/Logic-WiSe2022-external/en/#chapterB1

20. Duret-Lutz, A.: Manipulating LTL formulas using Spot 1.0. In: Proceedings of the 11th International Symposium on Automated Technology for Verification and Analysis (ATVA'13), pp. 442–445. Springer (2013). https://doi.org/10.1007/978-3-319-02444-8_31

21. Duret-Lutz, A., et al.: From Spot 2.0 to Spot 2.10: what's new? In: Proceedings of the 34th International Conference on Computer Aided Verification (CAV'22), Lecture Notes in Computer Science, vol. 13372, pp. 174–187. Springer (2022). https://doi.org/10.1007/978-3-031-13188-2_9

22. Dwyer, M.B.: Patterns for LTL translation (2025). https://matthewbdwyer.github.io/psp/patterns/ltl.html. Accessed 08 Jan 2025

23. Dwyer, M., Avrunin, G., Corbett, J.: Patterns in property specifications for finite-state verification. In: Proceedings of the 1999 International Conference on Software Engineering (IEEE Cat. No.99CB37002), pp. 411–420 (1999). https://doi.org/10.1145/302405.302672
24. Fainekos, G.E., Kress-Gazit, H., Pappas, G.J.: Temporal logic motion planning for mobile robots. In: ICRA, pp. 2020–2025. IEEE (2005). https://doi.org/10.1109/ROBOT.2005.1570410
25. Fuggitti, F., Chakraborti, T.: NL2LTL – a Python package for converting natural language (NL) instructions to linear temporal logic (LTL) formulas. AAAI Conf. Artif. Intell. **37**(13), 16428–16430 (2023). https://doi.org/10.1609/aaai.v37i13.27068
26. Geck, G., Ljulin, A., Peter, S., Schmidt, J., Vehlken, F., Zeume, T.: Introduction to ILTIS: an interactive, web-based system for teaching logic. In: ITiCSE, pp. 141–146. ACM (2018). https://doi.org/10.1145/3197091.3197095
27. Geck, G., et al.: ILTIS: teaching logic in the Web. CoRR abs/2105.05763 (2021)
28. Greenman, B., et al.: Misconceptions in finite-trace and infinite-trace linear temporal logic. In: International Symposium on Formal Methods. pp. 579–599. Springer (2024)
29. Greenman, B., et al.: Artifact for misconceptions in finite-trace and infinite-trace linear temporal logic (2024). https://doi.org/10.5281/zenodo.12770102
30. Greenman, B., Saarinen, S., Nelson, T., Krishnamurthi, S.: Accepted artifact for little tricky logic: misconceptions in the understanding of LTL (2022). https://doi.org/10.5281/zenodo.6988909
31. Greenman, B., Saarinen, S., Nelson, T., Krishnamurthi, S.: Little tricky logic: misconceptions in the understanding of LTL. Programming **7**(2), 7:1–7:37 (2023). https://doi.org/10.22152/programming-journal.org/2023/7/7
32. Gundana, D., Kress-Gazit, H.: Event-based signal temporal logic synthesis for single and multi-robot tasks. IEEE Robot. Autom. Lett. **6**(2), 3687–3694 (2021). https://doi.org/10.1109/LRA.2021.3064220
33. Hestenes, D., Wells, M., Swackhamer, G.: Force concept inventory. Phys. Teach. **30**(3), 141–158 (1992). https://doi.org/10.1119/1.2343497
34. Kantaros, Y., Zavlanos, M.M.: STyLuS*: a temporal logic optimal control synthesis algorithm for large-scale multi-robot systems. Int. J. Robot. Res. **39**(7), 812–836 (2020). https://doi.org/10.1177/0278364920913922
35. Lahijanian, M., Almagor, S., Fried, D., Kavraki, L., Vardi, M.: This time the robot settles for a cost: a quantitative approach to temporal logic planning with partial satisfaction. In: AAAI, pp. 3664–3671. AAAI Press (2015). https://shaull.github.io/pub/LAFKV15.pdf
36. Li, R., Gurushankar, K., Heule, M.J., Rozier, K.Y.: What's in a name? linear temporal logic literally represents time lines. In: 2023 IEEE Working Conference on Software Visualization (VISSOFT), pp. 73–83. IEEE (2023)
37. Lodder, J., Heeren, B., Jeuring, J.: A comparison of elaborated and restricted feedback in LogEx, a tool for teaching rewriting logical formulae. J. Comput. Assist. Learn. **35**(5), 620–632 (2019)
38. Lodder, J., Heeren, B., Jeuring, J.: Providing hints, next steps and feedback in a tutoring system for structural induction. arXiv preprint arXiv:2002.12552 (2020)
39. Lodder, J., Heeren, B., Jeuring, J., Neijenhuis, W.: Generation and use of hints and feedback in a Hilbert-style axiomatic proof tutor. Int. J. Artif. Intell. Educ. **31**, 99–133 (2021)

40. Loizou, S.G., Kyriakopoulos, K.J.: Automatic synthesis of multi-agent motion tasks based on LTL specifications. In: CDC, pp. 153–158. IEEE (2004). https://doi.org/10.1109/CDC.2004.1428622

41. Lu, K.C., Krishnamurthi, S.: Identifying and correcting programming language behavior misconceptions. Proc. ACM Program. Lang. **8**(OOPSLA1), 334–361 (2024)

42. Madeyski, L., Orzeszyna, W., Torkar, R., Jozala, M.: Overcoming the equivalent mutant problem: a systematic literature review and a comparative experiment of second order mutation. IEEE Trans. Software Eng. **40**(1), 23–42 (2013)

43. Maggi, F.M., Montali, M., Westergaard, M., Van Der Aalst, W.M.: Monitoring business constraints with linear temporal logic: an approach based on colored automata. In: Business Process Management: 9th International Conference, BPM 2011, Clermont-Ferrand, France, August 30-September 2, 2011. Proceedings 9. pp. 132–147. Springer (2011)

44. Manna, Z., Wolper, P.: Synthesis of communicating processes from temporal logic specifications. TOPLAS **6**(1), 68–93 (1984). https://doi.org/10.1145/357233.357237

45. Nelson, T., et al.: Forge: a tool and language for teaching formal methods. Proc. ACM Program. Lang. **8**(OOPSLA1), 613–641 (2024)

46. O'Connor, L., Wickström, O.: Quickstrom: property-based acceptance testing with LTL specifications. In: PLDI, pp. 1025–1038. ACM (2022). https://doi.org/10.1145/3519939.3523728

47. Pane, J.F., Griffin, B.A., McCaffrey, D.F., Karam, R.: Effectiveness of cognitive tutor algebra I at scale. Educ. Eval. Policy Anal. **36**(2), 127–144 (2014)

48. Pnueli, A., Rosner, R.: On the synthesis of a reactive module. In: POPL, pp. 179–190. ACM (1989). https://doi.org/10.1145/75277.75293

49. Posner, G.J., Strike, K.A., Hewson, P.W., Gertzog, W.A.: Accommodation of a scientific conception: toward a theory of conceptual change. Sci. Educ. **66**(2), 211–227 (1982)

50. Prasad, S., Greenman, B., Nelson, T., Krishnamurthi, S.: Conceptual mutation testing for student programming misconceptions. Art Sci. Eng. Program. **8**(2) (2023). https://doi.org/10.22152/programming-journal.org/2024/8/7

51. Prasad, S., Greenman, B., Nelson, T., Krishnamurthi, S.: Hosting the LTL Tutor (2024). https://github.com/brownplt/LTLTutor/wiki/Hosting-the-LTL-Tutor

52. Prasad, S., Greenman, B., Nelson, T., Krishnamurthi, S.: LTL tutor (2024). https://github.com/brownplt/ltltutor

53. Rojas, J.M., White, T.D., Clegg, B.S., Fraser, G.: Code defenders: crowdsourcing effective tests and subtle mutants with a mutation testing game. In: 2017 IEEE/ACM 39th International Conference on Software Engineering (ICSE), pp. 677–688. IEEE (2017)

54. Schroeder, N.L., Kucera, A.C.: Refutation text facilitates learning: a meta-analysis of between-subjects experiments. Educ. Psychol. Rev. **34**(2), 957–987 (2022)

55. Shah, A., Kamath, P., Shah, J.A., Li, S.: Bayesian inference of temporal task specifications from demonstrations. In: NeurIPS, pp. 3808–3817 (2018)

56. Sieg, W.: The AProS project: strategic thinking & computational logic. Logic J. IGPL **15**(4), 359–368 (2007)

57. Smith, R., Avrunin, G., Clarke, L., Osterweil, L.: PROPEL: an approach supporting property elucidation. In: Proceedings of the 24th International Conference on Software Engineering. ICSE 2002, pp. 11–21 (2002). https://doi.org/10.1109/ICSE.2002.1007952

58. Tabajara, L.M., Vardi, M.Y.: LTLf synthesis under partial observability: from theory to practice. In: GandALF, pp. 1–17. Open Publishing Association (2020). https://doi.org/10.4204/eptcs.326.1
59. Tracy II, T., Tabajara, L.M., Vardi, M., Skadron, K.: Runtime verification on FPGAs with LTLf specifications. In: FMCAD, pp. 36–46. IEEE Computer Society (2020). https://doi.org/10.34727/2020/isbn.978-3-85448-042-6_10
60. Umili, E., Capobianco, R., De Giacomo, G.: Grounding LTLf specifications in images. In: KR, pp. 45–63. ACM (2023). https://doi.org/10.24963/kr.2023/65
61. VanLehn, K.: The behavior of tutoring systems. Int. J. Artif. Intell. Educ. **16**(3), 227–265 (2006)
62. Vardi, M.Y., Wolper, P.: An automata-theoretic approach to automatic program verification. In: 1st Symposium in Logic in Computer Science (LICS). IEEE Computer Society (1986)
63. Wang, Y., Figueroa, N., Li, S., Shah, A., Shah, J.: Temporal logic imitation: learning plan-satisficing motion policies from demonstrations. In: Conference on Robot Learning, CoRL, pp. 94–105. PMLR (2022). https://proceedings.mlr.press/v205/wang23a.html
64. Wickström, O.: LTL visualizer (2023). https://github.com/quickstrom/ltl-visualizer
65. Wongpiromsarn, T., Ulusoy, A., Belta, C., Frazzoli, E., Rus, D.: Incremental temporal logic synthesis of control policies for robots interacting with dynamic agents. In: IROS, pp. 229–236. IEEE (2012). https://doi.org/10.1109/IROS.2012.6385575
66. Zhu, S., Tabajara, L.M., Li, J., Pu, G., Vardi, M.Y.: Symbolic LTLf synthesis. In: IJCAI, pp. 1362–1369 (2017). https://doi.org/10.24963/ijcai.2017/189

Scaling GR(1) Synthesis via a Compositional Framework for LTL Discrete Event Control

Hernan Gagliardi[1(✉)], Victor Braberman[1,2], and Sebastian Uchitel[1,2,3]

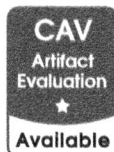

[1] Universidad de Buenos Aires, Buenos Aires, Argentina
hgagliardi@dc.uba.ar
[2] CONICET, Buenos Aires, Argentina
[3] Imperial College London, London, UK

Abstract. We present a compositional approach to controller synthesis of discrete event system controllers with linear temporal logic (LTL) goals. We exploit the modular structure of the plant to be controlled, given as a set of labelled transition systems (LTS), to mitigate state explosion that monolithic approaches to synthesis are prone to. Maximally permissive safe controllers are iteratively built for subsets of the plant LTSs by solving weaker control problems. Observational synthesis equivalence is used to reduce the size of the controlled subset of the plant by abstracting away local events. The result of synthesis is also compositional, a set of controllers that when run in parallel ensure the LTL goal. We implement synthesis in the MTSA tool for an expressive subset of LTL, GR(1), and show it computes solutions to that can be up to 1000 times larger than those that the monolithic approach can solve.

Keywords: Modular Discrete Event System Control · Compositional Controller Synthesis · LTL · GR(1)

1 Introduction

The problem of automatically constructing control rules from a specification (i.e., synthesis) has been addressed by different areas in Computer Science including Control of Discrete Event Systems (DES) [28], Reactive Synthesis [27] and Automated Planning [13]. Each has distinct perspectives on representational and computational aspects. All three use different input languages to provide compact problem descriptions for an underlying semantics that can grow exponentially. These different input languages have led to different algorithmic approaches to achieve more efficient ways to solve synthesis problems.

In this paper, we study control of DES described modularly as the parallel composition of interacting transition systems. The semantics is a monolithic automaton whose state space can grow exponentially with respect to the number of intervening components. This state explosion makes tractability of DES control problems a challenge. Modularity has enabled compositional reasoning in

© The Author(s) 2025
R. Piskac and Z. Rakamarić (Eds.): CAV 2025, LNCS 15934, pp. 201–223, 2025.
https://doi.org/10.1007/978-3-031-98685-7_10

supervisory control. Notably, in [25] a compositional framework is described for synthesis of non-blocking supervisory controllers for safety goals. Compositional DES control for liveness goals (e.g., [6,26,30]) has not been studied.

We present a compositional synthesis framework for modular DES control problems with LTL goals. Our compositional approach does not compose the transition systems describing the plant and then compute a discrete event controller as does [6]. Instead, roughly, we iteratively pick a subset of plant transition systems, we compute a safe controller for the subset, and replace the subset with a minimized controlled version of the subset that abstracts events not shared with the rest of the plant. Each iteration does a *partial synthesis* of the original control problem.

The *final result is a controller expressed as a set of controllers* that can be run in parallel to control the original plant, reducing memory footprint and mitigating state explosion of the composed controller.

Our approach is inspired by [25] for building modular non-blocking supervisors for finite regular languages.

Moving to ω-regular languages such as those expressed using LTL introduces various challenges. First, in contrast to supervisory control for non-blocking supervisors, maximally permissive controllers for LTL control problems are not guaranteed to exist. We compute *safe controllers* for a weaker goal, that allows maximally permissive controllers and supports deferring the construction of a *live controller* that ensures LTL in the final step. Second, although we use the synthesis observational equivalence [25] for minimization, the equivalence does not actually preserve LTL equirealizability as it introduces uncontrollable loops which require special considerations. Last, in [25] non-blocking conditions are represented modularly with marked states in each plant automaton. Thus, non-blocking can be analysed straightforwardly for subplants. In contrast, LTL is a condition that refers to the behaviour of the composed plant and must be decomposed when analysing subplants.

We assess if the compositional synthesis can perform better than a monolithic approach in which the plant composition is constructed in full. For this we implemented the approach in the MTSA tool [5] which is the only tool we are aware of that is available and *natively* supports controller synthesis for modular DES plants. MTSA supports a specific class of LTL formulae referred to as GR(1) [26]. *We show that using the same GR(1) explicit state synthesis engine, implemented in MTSA, the compositional approach solves control problems up to* $1000\times$ *larger than what a monolithic approach can.* In addition, we show that the compositional framework can sometimes yield more effective results when symbolic synthesis engines such as Strix [23] and Spectra [20] are used for DES controller synthesis via a translation [16].

The remainder of this paper presents background in Sect. 2, an overview in Sect. 3, novel definitions and results for compositional synthesis in Sect. 4, the compositional algorithm in Sect. 5, and an evaluation in Sect. 6. We conclude in Sects. 7 and 8 with related work and conclusions.

2   Preliminaries

We model discrete event systems by composing Labelled Transition Systems.

Definition 1 (Labelled Transition System). *A Labelled Transition System (LTS) is a tuple* $(S, \Sigma, \rightarrow, \hat{s})$ *where* S *is a finite set of states;* Σ *is a finite set of event labels;* $\rightarrow \subseteq S \times \Sigma \times S$ *are transitions; and* $\hat{s} \in S$ *is the initial state.*

Definition 2 (Parallel composition). *Let* $M_i = (S_i, \Sigma_i, \rightarrow_{M_i}, \hat{s}_i)$ *with* $i \in \{1, 2\}$ *be two LTSs, their parallel composition is an LTS* $M_1 \| M_2 = (S_1 \times S_2, \Sigma_1 \cup \Sigma_2, \rightarrow_{M_1 \| M_2}, (\hat{s}_1, \hat{s}_2))$, *where* $\rightarrow_{M_1 \| M_2}$ *is the smallest relation that satisfies:*

- *if* $s_1 \xrightarrow{l}_{M_1} s_1'$ *and* $l \in \Sigma_1 \setminus \Sigma_2$, *then* $(s_1, s_2) \xrightarrow{l}_{M_1 \| M_2} (s_1', s_2)$
- *if* $s_2 \xrightarrow{l}_{M_2} s_2'$ *and* $l \in \Sigma_2 \setminus \Sigma_1$, *then* $(s_1, s_2) \xrightarrow{l}_{M_1 \| M_2} (s_1, s_2')$
- *if* $s_1 \xrightarrow{l}_{M_1} s_1', s_2 \xrightarrow{l}_{M_2} s_2'$ *and* $l \in \Sigma_1 \cap \Sigma_2$, *then* $(s_1, s_2) \xrightarrow{l}_{M_1 \| M_2} (s_1', s_2')$

Parallel composition is associative and commutative. If $\mathcal{M} = \{M_1, M_2, .., M_n\}$ is a set of LTS, we may refer to $M_1 \| M_2 \| .. \| M_n$ as $\mathcal{M}$ too.

We use Σ^* for the set of all finite sequences of labels of Σ, i.e., traces. We say $l \in \Sigma$ is enabled in s if there is s' such that $(s, l, s') \in \rightarrow$. We denote $\rightarrow(s)$ as the set of enabled events in s. An LTS is deadlock-free if all states have outgoing transitions. An LTS is deterministic if there is no state that has two outgoing transitions on the same event. We use $\rightarrow$ to denote the transitive closure of transitions and assume it holds for the empty trace: $x \xrightarrow{\epsilon} x$. We say a (finite or infinite) sequence w of labels in Σ is a trace of M if there is an s' such that $s_M \xrightarrow{w} s'$. The concatenation of two traces s and t is written as st. For $\Omega \subseteq \Sigma$, we define the natural projection $P_\Omega : \Sigma^* \rightarrow \Omega^*$ as the operation that removes from a trace $\pi \in \Sigma^*$ all events not in Ω.

We model controllers with legal LTS that must not block the DES.

Definition 3 (Legal LTS). *Given LTS* $M = (S_M, \Sigma, \rightarrow_M, \hat{s_M})$ *and* $C = (S_C, \Sigma_C, \rightarrow_C, \hat{s_C})$ *with* $\Sigma_u \in \Sigma$. *We say that* C *is a legal LTS for* M *with respect to* Σ_u, *if for all* (s_M, s_C) *such that* $(\hat{s_M}, \hat{s_C}) \rightarrow_{M \| C} (s_M, s_C)$ *the following holds:* $\rightarrow_{M \| C} ((s_M, s_C)) \cap \Sigma_u = \rightarrow_M (s_M) \cap \Sigma_u$

We use Linear Temporal Logic to declaratively specify control requirements.

Definition 4 (Linear Temporal Logic (LTL) formula). *An LTL formula is defined inductively using the standard Boolean connectives and temporal operators* X *(next),* U *(strong until) as follows:* $\phi := e \mid \neg\phi \mid \phi \vee \psi \mid X\phi \mid \phi U\psi$, *where* e *is an atomic event. As usual we introduce* $\Diamond$ *(eventually), and* $\square$ *(always) as syntactic sugar. The semantics of an LTL formula is defined via a relation* $\models$ *between infinite traces and LTL formulae, noted* $\pi \models \phi$.

We now define discrete event control problems.

Definition 5 (Control Problem). *Given a set of deterministic LTS $\mathcal{M}$ modelling the plant to be controlled, Σ the union of the alphabets of the LTS in $\mathcal{M}$, a set of controllable events $\Sigma_c \subseteq \Sigma$ and an LTL formula φ over Σ modelling the controller goal, we define $\mathcal{E} = \langle \mathcal{M}, \Sigma_c, \varphi \rangle$ to be an Control Problem. A deterministic LTS C is a solution for $\mathcal{E}$ (i.e., a controller) if C is legal for $\mathcal{M}$ with respect to the set of uncontrolled events $\Sigma_u = \Sigma \setminus \Sigma_c$, $\mathcal{M} \| C$ is deadlock-free and for every infinite trace π in $\mathcal{M} \| C$ we have $\pi \vDash \varphi$.*

$\mathcal{E}$ is realizable if a solution for $\mathcal{E}$ exists. A solution C is *maximally permissive* [15] if for any solution C', if π is a trace of C' then it is a trace of C.

Definition 6 (Winning States). *Let $\mathcal{E} = \langle \mathcal{M}, \Sigma_c, \varphi \rangle$ a control problem with $\hat{s}$ the initial state of $\mathcal{M}$. We say $s \in S_\mathcal{M}$ is a winning state if there is a solution C for $\mathcal{E}$ with initial state $\hat{c}$, a state $c \in S_c$ and a trace π such that $(\hat{c}, \hat{s}) \xrightarrow{\pi}_{C\|M} (c, s)$.*

We focus on a particular form of controller goals referred to as GR(1).

Definition 7 (Generalised Reactivity(1) [26]). *A GR(1) formula φ is an LTL formula restricted with this structure $\varphi = \wedge_{i \in n} \Box \Diamond \phi_i \implies \wedge_{j \in m} \Box \Diamond \gamma_j$ where ϕ_i and γ_j are boolean combination of events.*

Note that realizable GR(1) control problems may not have a maximally permissive controller. An intuition is that a controller may delay achieving its goal an unbounded but finite number of times. This cannot be captured as an LTS.

Also note that for a realizable GR(1) control problem, if a plant state is losing (i.e., not winning) it will never be traversed when the plant is being controlled. Also note that stripping a plant of its losing states not only preserves realizability but also results in the smallest sub-plant that preserves realizability.

We use an observational equivalence taken from [25]. In [25] the relation to reduce the size of the plant, hiding local events Υ while preserving solutions to supervisory control problems with non-blocking goals. The equivalence does not preserve realizability of GR(1) control problems; an adaptation is required.

Definition 8 (Synthesis observation equivalence [25]). *Let $M = (S, \Sigma, \rightarrow, \hat{s})$ be a LTS with $\Sigma = \Omega \mathbin{\dot{\cup}} \Upsilon$, Σ_c is the set of controllable events and Σ_u is the set of uncontrollable events. An equivalence relation $\sim_\Upsilon \subseteq S \times S$ is a synthesis observational equivalence on M with respect to Υ if the following conditions hold for all $x_1, x_2 \in S$ such that $x_1 \sim_\Upsilon x_2$:*

1. *if $x_1 \xrightarrow{u} y_1$ for $u \in \Sigma_u$, then there exist $\pi_1, \pi_2 \in (\Upsilon \cap \Sigma_u)^*$ such that $x_2 \xrightarrow{\pi_1 P_\Omega(u) \pi_2} y_2$ and $y_1 \sim_\Upsilon y_2$*

2. *if $x_1 \xrightarrow{c} y_1$ for $c \in \Sigma_c$, then there exists a path $x_2 = x_2^0 \xrightarrow{\tau_1} \ldots \xrightarrow{\tau_n} x_2^n \xrightarrow{P_\Omega(c)} y_2$ such that $y_1 \sim_\Upsilon y_2$ and $\tau_1, .., \tau_n \in \Upsilon$, and if $\tau_{i \in \{1..n\}} \in \Sigma_c$ then $x_1 \sim_\Upsilon x_2^i$*

Definition 9 (Quotient LTS). *Let $M = (S, \Sigma, \rightarrow, \hat{s})$ be an LTS, and $\sim \subseteq S \times S$ be an equivalence relation. The quotient LTS of M modulo $\sim$ is $M/\sim = (S/\sim, \Sigma, \rightarrow/\sim, [\hat{s}])$ where $S/\sim$ is the set of equivalences classes of $\sim$ and $\rightarrow/\sim = \{([s], \sigma, [s']) \cdot s \xrightarrow{\sigma} s'\}$*

3   Overview

In this section we first provide an overview of our approach that does not include an equivalence minimization step. We then revisit the overview explaining where some aspects of minimization require special treatment.

Overview Without Minimization. Consider a control problem $\mathcal{E} = \langle \mathcal{M}, \Sigma_c, \varphi \rangle$ where $\mathcal{M}$ is a set of LTS. A monolithic approach to solving the problem (e.g., [6]) composes all the LTSs in $\mathcal{M}$ and then computes a controller. Our approach starts with $\mathcal{M}$ and an empty set $\mathcal{C}$ which will store *safe controllers* (we discuss them below). We iteratively extract a subset $\mathcal{M}'$ of $\mathcal{M}$ of size greater than 1, compose the LTSs in $\mathcal{M}'$, compute a safe controller for the composition (with a weaker property φ' and a larger controllable alphabet – we explain why below) and store it in $\mathcal{C}$. In addition, we reintroduce a controlled version of $\mathcal{M}'$ to $\mathcal{M}$, we refer to this LTS as an *controlled subplant* (we explain these below).

In each iteration, $\mathcal{C}$ increases by one and $\mathcal{M}$ decreases by at least one. The iteration ends if the subset $\mathcal{M}'$ (which is picked by a heuristic) is equal to $\mathcal{M}$, typically when $\mathcal{M}$'s size is 1 or 2. At this point we apply the standard monolithic approach for φ to $\mathcal{M}'$. The controller built in this last step of the algorithm can be thought of as a *live controller* in contrast to the safe controllers built before.

The *solution* to the original control problem $\mathcal{E}$ is the composition of the safe controllers in $\mathcal{C}$ with the live controller computed after the iterations.

Safe Controllers. We provide an intuition of what is referred to as safe controllers and why they are computed for a property φ' that is weaker than φ and an expanded controllable alphabet. We do so by working through an example.

Consider the control problem $\langle \mathcal{M}, \Sigma_c, \varphi \rangle$ depicted in Fig. 1. A monolithic synthesis approach would first compose the three LTSs in $\mathcal{M}$ and then compute a controller. The composition (see Fig. 10 of the Appendix in the technical report submitted in Arxiv) has 23 states.

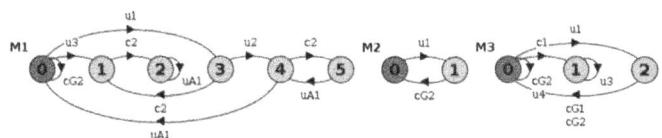

Fig. 1. Modular plant for a control problem $\mathcal{E}$ with $\mathcal{M} = \{M_1, M_2, M_3\}$, GR(1) goal $\varphi = \Box \Diamond uA1 \implies \Box \Diamond cG1 \wedge \Box \Diamond cG2$ and controllable alphabet $\Sigma_c = \{cG1, cG2, c1, c2\}$.

Consider a first iteration of our algorithm in which a heuristic selects the subset $\mathcal{M}' = \{M_1, M_2\}$ and computes it composition (see Fig. 2).

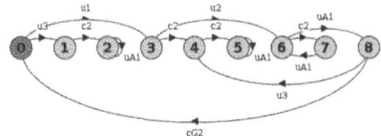

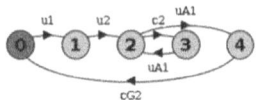

Fig. 2. Parallel composition of subplant $\mathcal{M}' = \{M_1, M_2\} \subset \mathcal{M}$, i.e., $M_1 \| M_2$.

Fig. 3. Safe Controller $(\mathcal{M}_1 \| \mathcal{M}_2)_{safe}$ for subplant $M_1 \| M_2$, $\varphi' = \Box \Diamond uA1 \implies \top \wedge \Box \Diamond cG2$, controllable events $\Sigma_c \cup \{u3\}$, and $\mu = \emptyset$.

We would like to control $\mathcal{M}'$ to achieve φ. However, this is not possible as φ refers to $cG1$ that is not in the alphabet of the LTS in $\mathcal{M}'$. Thus, we weaken φ by *projecting* it to the alphabet of $\mathcal{M}'$: $\varphi' = \Box \Diamond uA1 \implies \top \wedge \Box \Diamond cG2$.

Now we would like to control $\mathcal{M}'$ to achieve the weaker φ'. Yet this is not possible because a controller cannot prevent the occurrence of $u3$ in the initial state of $\mathcal{M}'$. But event $u3$ would never occur in the initial state of the plant $\mathcal{M}$ because $M_3 \notin \mathcal{M}'$ disallows it in its initial state! Indeed, when computing a controller for $\mathcal{M}'$ we must account for the fact that certain aspects of the problem may be solvable when considering the rest of the plant. For this we *expand the controllable alphabet* to include all uncontrollable events shared with LTS in $\mathcal{M} \setminus \mathcal{M}'$ (i.e., $u3$).

We now explain why we compute a *safe* controller for the weaker formula φ' and the extended set of controllable events: There may be controllers that can realize φ' in different ways (often called strategies). Some of these strategies may be conflicting with restrictions imposed by LTS in $\mathcal{M} \setminus \mathcal{M}'$ or parts of the goal lost in the projection of φ. Ideally, we would compute a controller that includes all such strategies, but this is impossible. Liveness goals such as GR(1) do not allow maximally permissive controllers. Instead of constructing a controller that achieves φ' we build one that avoids states in $\mathcal{M}'$ that a controller that guarantees φ' may traverse. In other words, we build a controller that stays in winning states of φ'. This is a safety property, and if there is a controller, there is a maximally permissive one.

The safe (maximally permissive) controller for $\mathcal{M}'$, φ, and $\Sigma_c \cup \{u3\}$, referred to as $(M_1 \| M_2)_{safe}$ is shown in Fig. 3 and is added to $\mathcal{C}$.

Controlled Subplant. We now provide an intuition of what controlled subplants are. Having computed a safe controller for $M_1 \| M_2$ for a weaker goal than φ we must describe what remains to be controlled.

A naive approach would be to add to $\mathcal{M}$ the controlled version of $M_1 \| M_2$, in other words $(M_1 \| M_2)_{safe} \| (M_1 \| M_2)$. However, the $(M_1 \| M_2)_{safe}$ was built assuming it controlled $u3$ when in fact it does not. Indeed, the composition would not let the subplant $M_1 \| M_2$ take a $u3$ transitions from states 0 and 8.

To adequately model the behavior of the controlled subplant (see Fig. 4) we must re-introduce $u3$ transitions to the safe controller. Specifically, we must add them to states 0 and 4 of the controller, these are the states the controller would be in if it were composed with the subplant and the subplant were in states 0 or 8. Added transitions are sent to a deadlock state because we know that from this point on, it is impossible to achieve φ' and thus impossible to achieve φ.

Indeed, the safe controller with the added transitions and deadlock state represent the safe controller with the assumptions it makes on when uncontrolled shared events should not happen. The deadlock state is in a sense abstracting states 1, 2, 4 and 5 of the subplant $M_1\|M_2$ of Fig. 2 as bad states.

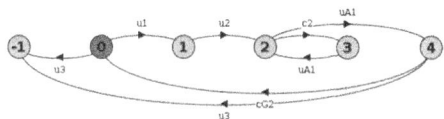

Fig. 4. Controlled Subplant $(M_1\|M_2)_{cont}$ built from the safe controller $(M_1\|M_2)_{safe}$ in Fig. 3 by adding $u3$ transitions from state 0 and state 4 to a deadlock state

After the First Iteration. At the end of the first iteration of our simplified algorithm we have: $\mathcal{M} = \{M_3, (M_1\|M_2)_{cont}\}$ and $\mathcal{C} = \{(M_1\|M_2)_{safe}\}$. As the subplants are required to be of size larger than 1, the only possible $\mathcal{M}' \subseteq \mathcal{M}$ is actually $\mathcal{M}$. Here termination of the iterations kicks in and the algorithm proceeds to build a live controller using a monolithic approach for: $\langle\{M_3, (M_1\|M_2)_{cont}\}, \Sigma_c, \varphi\rangle$. In other words, it builds the plant $M_3\|(M_1\|M_2)_{cont}$ (see Fig. 11 in Appendix of the technical report submitted in Arxiv), computes a controller $(M_3\|(M_1\|M_2)_{cont})_{live}$ (see Fig. 5) and returns the solution $\mathcal{C} = \{(M_3\|(M_1\|M_2)_{cont})_{live}, (M_1\|M_2)_{safe}\}$.

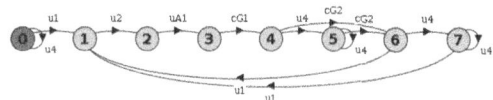

Fig. 5. Controller $(M_3\|(M_1\|M_2)_{cont})_{live}$ for Fig. 11.

Note that the largest LTS for which the compositional algorithm built a controller was of size 14, whilst a monolithic approach applied to $M_1\|M_2\|M_3$ would have had to analyse an LTS of size 22.

Introducing Minimization. The approach to synthesis presented formally in the next sections relies heavily on minimization to perform well: It minimizes the controlled subplants before adding them to $\mathcal{M}$. The minimization procedure preserves the synthesis observational equivalence defined in [24]. We apply minimization, as does [24], hiding events that are local to the controlled subplant (i.e., events that are not part of the alphabet of the remaining LTSs in $\mathcal{M}$). In Fig. 6 we depict the minimized version of $(M_1\|M_2)_{cont}$ using local events

$\Upsilon = \{u2, uA1, c2\}$. Note that minimization may introduce non-determinism that can be solved, as in [24] using relabeling.

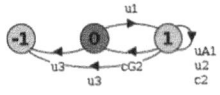

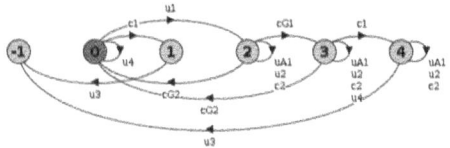

Fig. 6. $(M_1 \| M_2)_{cont}/ \sim_\Upsilon$, a minimized version of $(M_1 \| M_2)_{cont}$ with local events $\Upsilon = \{u2, uA1, c2\}$.

Fig. 7. Plant $(M_1 \| M_2)^c/ \sim_\Upsilon \| M_3$ to be controlled assuming $\Box \Diamond (\neg u2 \wedge \neg uA1 \wedge \neg c2)$

The approach proceeds by composing $(M_1 \| M_2)_{cont}/\sim_\Upsilon$ and M_3 (see Fig. 7) and attempts to build a controller for φ. However, such a controller does not exists as the trace $u1.uA1^\omega$ cannot be avoided. Yet such a trace is not possible in $(M_1 \| M_2 \| M_3)$ (see Fig. 10 in Appendix of the technical report submitted in Arxiv). This mismatch can be traced back to the minimization procedure that introduces a looping transition labelled $uA1$ in state 1 in $(M_1 \| M_2)_{cont}/\sim_\Upsilon$ which $(M_1 \| M_2)_{cont}$ does not have. Note that these loops are not a problem for compositional control for finite traces such as in [24].

Having introduced uncontrollable looping transitions, they must be kept track of (we add them to a set μ) and solve control problems in future iterations that assume events in μ do not occur infinitely (i.e., $\Box \Diamond \bigwedge_{l \in \mu} \neg l \implies \varphi$). Although not a GR(1) formula, it can be solved using GR(1) synthesis.

The live controller for $(M_1 \| M_2)_{cont}/ \sim_\Upsilon \| M_3$ and property $\Box \Diamond \bigwedge_{l \in \mu} \neg l \implies \varphi$ is depicted on the left of Fig. 8. This live controller plus the safe controller in Fig. 3 are a modular solution to $\mathcal{E}$.

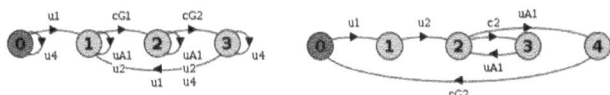

Fig. 8. Modular representation of a controller for the discrete event problem $\mathcal{M} = \{M_1, M_2, M_3\}$ to be controlled to satisfy $\varphi = \Box \Diamond uA1 \implies \Box \Diamond cG1 \wedge \Box \Diamond cG2$ with controllable alphabet $\Sigma_c = \{cG1, cG2, c1, c2, c3\}$. Controller on the left is a solution to Fig. 7, controller on the right is the safe controller from Fig. 3.

Note that using minimization, the largest LTS for which synthesis was computed for has 5 states, while a monolithic approach would have computed a controller for a plant of 22 states. This exemplifies how state explosion of the composed plant might be avoided using our compositional approach.

Subplant minimization can result in a non-deterministic monitor. To remove non-determinism we use a the same procedure as in [24]. Due to space restrictions we do not discuss renaming in this paper, but our implementation and experimentation includes it. We refer the reader to [24] for more information.

4   Compositional Synthesis

This section defines a data structure used by the compositional synthesis algorithm, two operations over the data structure, and theorems that enunciate when these operations preserve the semantics of the data structure.

During algorithm execution three variables are maintained, ($\mathcal{M}$, $\mathcal{C}$ and μ) that form what we refer to as a synthesis tuple. They were discussed in Sect. 3.

Definition 10 (Synthesis tuple). *A synthesis tuple is tuple* $(\mathcal{M}, \mathcal{C}, \mu)$, *where* $\mathcal{M}$ *is a set of deterministic LTSs modelling a modular plant,* $\mathcal{C}$ *is a set of LTSs modelling safe controllers, and* μ *is a set of events in the alphabet of* $\mathcal{M}$.

When solving a control problem $\mathcal{E} = \langle \mathcal{M}, \Sigma_c, \varphi \rangle$, the algorithm starts with a synthesis tuple of the following form: $(\mathcal{M}, \emptyset, \emptyset)$. The algorithm will iteratively reduce the size of $\mathcal{M}$ while populating $\mathcal{C}$ and μ. Each intermediate step will yield a synthesis tuple that preserves the control problem to be solved. To formalize this notion of preservation we define the set of controllers that are a solution to a synthesis tuple. This set of controllers will serve as an invariant.

Definition 11 (Controllers of a Synthesis Tuple). *Let* $T = (\mathcal{M}, \mathcal{C}, \mu)$ *be a synthesis tuple with* $\mathcal{C} = \{C_1, \ldots, C_n\}$, $\Sigma_c \subseteq \Sigma$ *a controllable alphabet, and* φ *an LTL formula. We define the controllers of a synthesis tuple as* $Cont_{\Sigma_c, \varphi}(T) = \{\mathcal{C}_M || C_1 || \ldots || C_n \cdot \mathcal{C}_M$ *is a solution to* $\mathcal{E}\}$ *where* $\mathcal{E} = \langle \mathcal{M}, \Sigma_c, \Box \Diamond \bigwedge_{l \in \mu} \neg l \Longrightarrow \varphi \rangle$.

Remark 1. Given the synthesis tuple $T = (\mathcal{M}, \emptyset, \emptyset)$ then the controllers in $Cont_{\Sigma_c, \varphi}(T)$ are the same as those for the control problem $\mathcal{E} = \langle \mathcal{M}, \Sigma_c, \varphi \rangle$.

We say that two *synthesis tuples* T and T' *are equivalent* with respect to a controllable alphabet Σ_c and an LTL formula φ if they have the same set of controllers: $T \cong_{\Sigma_c, \varphi} T'$ iff $Cont_{\Sigma_c, \varphi}(T) = Cont_{\Sigma_c, \varphi}(T')$

In the following we introduce two equivalence preserving transformation operations over synthesis tuples. The compositional synthesis algorithm in Sect. 5 iteratively applies these equivalence preserving transformations.

4.1   Composition

This synthesis tuple transformation method reduces the size of $\mathcal{M}$ in a synthesis tuple by composing in parallel a subset of the LTS in $\mathcal{M}$. It is straightforward to see that parallel composition preserves equivalence of synthesis tuples.

Theorem 1 (Composition preserves controllers). *Let* φ *be an LTL formula,* Σ_c *a set of controllable events, and* T, T' *synthesis tuples* $(\mathcal{M}, \mathcal{C}, \mu)$ *and* $(\mathcal{M}', \mathcal{C}, \mu)$ *respectively. If* $\mathcal{M}_1$ *and* $\mathcal{M}_2$ *are a partition of* $\mathcal{M}$ *such as* $\mathcal{M}' = M \cup \mathcal{M}_2$ *where* M *is the parallel composition of the LTS in* $\mathcal{M}_1$, *then* $T \cong_{\Sigma_c, \varphi} T'$

The theorem follows from the fact that parallel composition is associative.

4.2   Partial Synthesis

Partial Synthesis is the key transformation operation over synthesis tuples. Given a tuple $(\mathcal{M}, \mathcal{C}, \mu)$ it removes one LTS M from $\mathcal{M}$, computes a safe controller C for a weaker property φ' and adds the safe controller to $\mathcal{C}$. It also adds a minimized LTS modelling the controlled subplant, i,e. the result of C controlling M_i but hiding local events Υ. In addition it updates μ.

We define the projection of a formula the alphabet of a subsystem.

Definition 12 (Formula projection). *A formula projection is a function* $\alpha : LTL \times 2^{\Sigma} \rightarrow LTL$ *such that for any formula* φ *and set* $\Sigma' \subseteq \Sigma$ *we have* $\varphi \implies \alpha(\varphi, \Sigma')$ *and* $\alpha(\varphi, \Sigma')$ *is a formula that only refers to events in* Σ'.

To achieve completeness, it is essential partial controllers built are maximally permissive. That is, there is a controller that is maximal in terms of traces it allows. Maximally permissive controllers in general do not exist. Therefore, we construct *safe controllers* that avoid reaching a state in the plant from which achieving a the goal is certainly impossible. That is, a controller that keeps the plant in potentially winning states but does not guarantee traces that satisfy the liveness property. Liveness is achieved in the algorithm's last step.

Definition 13 (Safe Controller). *Let* $\mathcal{E} = \langle \mathcal{M}, \Sigma_c, \varphi \rangle$ *be a control problem with* $\mathcal{M} = (S, \Sigma, \rightarrow, \hat{s})$. *If* $\mathcal{E}$ *is realizable, we say* $(\hat{S}, \Sigma, \rightarrow_S, \hat{s})$ *is the safe controller for* $\mathcal{E}$ *where* $\hat{S}$ *is a superset of the set of winning states in* S *for* $\mathcal{E}$ *and* $\rightarrow_S$ *contains all the transitions in* $\mathcal{M}$ *between states* $s \in \hat{S}$.

As explained in the overview, a model of the subplant controlled by the safe controller must be reintroduced into $\mathcal{M}$, however this cannot be done by simply introducing their parallel composition as the safe controller will have been built with an extended controllable alphabet. We build a *controlled subplant* LTS that models M being controlled by the safe controller C with shared uncontrollable events Ω. Recall from the overview (see Fig. 4) that we must add to the safe controller transitions to a deadlock state representing the safe controller's assumptions on when uncontrolled shared events should not happen.

Definition 14 (Controlled Subplant). *Let* $C = (S_C, \Sigma_C, \rightarrow_C, \hat{s_C})$ *be a safe controller for* $\mathcal{E} = \langle M, \Sigma_c \cup \Omega, \varphi \rangle$ *with* $M = \langle S_M, \Sigma_M, \rightarrow_M, \hat{s_M} \rangle$, φ *an LTL formula, and* $\Omega \subseteq \Sigma_u$ *the set of uncontrolled shared events. The controlled subplant* M *by* C *with respect to* Ω *is* $\langle S_C \cup \{\bot\}, \Sigma_C, \rightarrow, \hat{s_C} \rangle$ *where* $\rightarrow = \rightarrow_C \cup \{(s, l, \bot) \mid l \in \Omega \wedge s \in S_C \wedge \exists s' \in S_M \cdot s \xrightarrow{l}_M s' \wedge \forall s' \in S_M \cdot (s, l, s') \notin \rightarrow_C\}$.

We now enunciate how the definitions above can be used to evolve a synthesis tuple by computing a safe controller and adding a minimized controlled subplant.

Roughly, the theorem states that the solution to a synthesis tuple remains the same if given a tuple $(\mathcal{M}, \mathcal{C}, \mu)$, (i) we take one of the LTS in the plant to be controlled ($M_1 \in \mathcal{M}$), (ii) compute a safe controller for M_1, the projection of φ to the alphabet of M_1, and an controllable alphabet extended with the uncontrollable events shared by M_1 and $\mathcal{M} \setminus \{M_1\}$, (iii) add the safe controller to $\mathcal{C}$, (iv) add a minimized version of the subplant M_1 controlled by the safe controller to $\mathcal{M}$ by quotienting it to remove transitions on local events, and (v) add any uncontrollable events on self loops induced by the quotient into μ. The proof of this theorem is included in the technical report submitted in Arxiv.

Theorem 2 (Partial synthesis preserves controllers). *Given a synthesis tuple* $(\mathcal{M},\mathcal{C},\mu)$, *an LTL formula* φ, *and a set* Σ_c *of controllable events. Let* $M \subseteq \mathcal{M}$ *with alphabet* $\Sigma_M = \Upsilon \dot\cup \Omega$ *where* Υ *has the events not shared with any other LTS in* $\mathcal{M} \setminus M$ *nor in* φ. *Let* φ' *be a projection of* φ *to* Σ_M. *Let* M_{safe} *be a safe controller for* $\langle M, \Sigma_c, \square \lozenge \bigwedge_{l \in \mu} \neg l \implies \varphi \rangle$. *Let* M_{cont} *be the subplant* M *controlled by* M_{safe} *with shared events* Ω.

If $M_{cont}/\!\sim_\Upsilon$ *is deterministic and* μ' *is the set of self-loop events added by* $\sim_\Upsilon$ *reduction, then* $(\mathcal{M},\mathcal{C},\mu) \cong_{\Sigma_c,\varphi} (\mathcal{M} \setminus \{M\} \cup \{M_{cont}/\!\sim_\Upsilon\}, \mathcal{C} \cup \{M_{safe}\}, \mu \cup \mu')$.

Note that the theorem requires $M_{cont}/\!\sim_\Upsilon$ to be deterministic, which is not always the case. Non-determinism can be avoided by renaming labels in M and using distinguishers [24]. We avoid presenting these due to space restrictions.

5 Compositional Synthesis Algorithm

The algorithm has as inputs a control problem $\mathcal{E} = \langle \mathcal{M}, \varphi, \Sigma_c \rangle$ and a heuristic that returns a subset of the plant of size greater than 1.

CompSynthesis$(\langle \mathcal{M}, \varphi, \Sigma_c \rangle$, heuristic)	**PartialSynthesis**$(\mathcal{M}, \mathcal{C}, \text{sp}, \Sigma_c, \varphi)$
1: $\mathcal{C} \leftarrow \{\}$, $\mu \leftarrow \{\}$	1: $\varphi' \leftarrow \text{getProjection}(\varphi, \Sigma_{\text{sp}})$
2: **while** *true* **do**	2: $\Sigma_{\varphi'} \leftarrow \text{getAlphabet}(\varphi')$
3: sp $\leftarrow$ getSubplant($\mathcal{M}$, heuristic)	3: $\Upsilon \leftarrow \Sigma_{\text{sp}} \setminus (\Sigma_{\mathcal{M}} \cup \Sigma_{\varphi'})$
4: $\mathcal{M} \leftarrow \mathcal{M} \setminus \text{sp}$	4: $M_{safe} \leftarrow \text{getSafeController}_\Upsilon(\langle \text{sp}, \Sigma_c, \varphi' \rangle, \mu)$
5: **if** $|\mathcal{M}| == 0$ **then**	5: **if** $\neg\text{isRealizable}(M_{safe})$ **then**
6: lc $\leftarrow$ getLiveController($\langle \text{sp}, \Sigma_c, \varphi \rangle, \mu$)	6: **return** UNREALIZABLE
7: **if** $\neg\text{isRealizable(lc)}$ **then**	7: **end if**
8: **return** UNREALIZABLE	8: $M_{cont} \leftarrow \text{getControlledSubplant}_\Upsilon(M_{safe}, \text{sp})$
9: **end if**	9: $\mathcal{C} \leftarrow \mathcal{C} \cup M_{safe}$
10: **return** $\mathcal{C} \cup \{\text{ lc }\}$	10: $\langle M_{cont}^\sim, \mu' \rangle \leftarrow \text{minimize}(M_{cont}, \Upsilon)$
11: **end if**	11: $\mu \leftarrow \mu \cup \mu'$, $\mathcal{M} \leftarrow \mathcal{M} \cup \{M_{cont}^\sim\}$
12: PartialSynthesis($\mathcal{M}, \mathcal{C}, \text{sp}, \Sigma_c, \varphi$)	
13: **end while**	

The synthesis tuple is initialized and a loop that strictly monotonically reduces the size of $\mathcal{M}$ starts. In the loop, the heuristic first selects and removes a subset of $\mathcal{M}$. If $\mathcal{M}$ is not empty, we project φ to the alphabet of the subplant, compute the local alphabet (Υ) used to perform minimization, compute the safe controller and the controlled subplant. If there is no solution when computing the safe controller, then the algorithm returns UNREALIZABLE. Otherwise, it adds the safe controller to $\mathcal{C}$ and computes both the quotient of the controlled subplant and the events that the quotient introduces loops for.

The loop terminates when the subplant selected has all LTS in $\mathcal{M}$. At this point we compute a live solution for the remaining control problem and return it with all previously computed partial controllers.

Procedure *getSubplant* returns a subplant of $\mathcal{M}$ using the *heuristic*. Procedures *getLiveController* and *getSafeController* solve control problems of the form $\langle sp, \Sigma_c, \Box\Diamond \bigwedge_{l \in \mu} \neg l \implies \varphi \rangle$ according to Definitions 5 and 13. Procedure *getControlledSubplant* returns a controlled subplant according to Definition 14, and *minimize* applies minimization based for the equivalence defined in Definition 8 and also returns the events for which self-loops have been introduced.

The correctness and completeness argument for the algorithm is as follows. The algorithm encodes the original problem $\mathcal{E} = \langle \mathcal{M}, \Sigma_c, \varphi \rangle$ as a synthesis tuple $T = (\mathcal{M}, \emptyset, \emptyset)$. The solutions of T by definition are $Cont_{\Sigma_c, \varphi}(T)$ are exactly those of $\mathcal{E}' = \langle \mathcal{M}, \Sigma_c, \varphi \rangle$ (see Remark 1 after Definition 11). It is straightforward to see that after each iteration of the while loop, the tuple is updated via two solution preserving operations (parallel composition and partial synthesis). The loop terminates because we assume that the heuristic will never infinitely often return subsets of size 1 when $|\mathcal{M}| > 1$ size greater than one is replaced in $\mathcal{M}$ with its composition. Thus, the set of partial controllers by the algorithm, when composed in parallel is a solution to the original problem.

6   Evaluation

The purpose of the evaluation is to assess if a compositional synthesis of controllers for modular DES plants and LTL goals can perform better than a monolithic approach in which the plant composition is constructed in full.

For this we implemented compositional synthesis within MTSA [6]. The only tool we are aware of that is available and *natively* supports controller synthesis for modular DES plants and infinite-trace goals. By this we mean means that other tools do not support describing the system to be controlled as a parallel composition of a set of DES along with some form of specifying liveness guarantees that are to be achieved. Notably, [19] and [12] do modular DES plants, but only allow specifying safety goals. MTSA tool supports GR(1) formulae. We compare MTSA with and without compositional synthesis.

We also study how reactive synthesis tools perform on translated versions of GR(1) DES control problems, both monolithically and compositionally. Specifically, we study *Spectra* [20] (a synthesis tool specialized in GR(1)) and Strix [23] (a compositional LTL synthesis tool, winner at SyntComp 2023). Note that we did not implement the compositional approach within *Spectra* and *Strix*, rather we had MTSA call them to measure how much time they take to solve the intermediate control problems compositional synthesis necessitates.

A replication package including tool and control problems is available in [1].

6.1   Compositional Synthesis of DES for GR(1) Goals

Applying the composition synthesis algorithm to control problems where φ is a GR(1) formula involves three challenges. First and foremost, procedures *getLiveController* and *getSafeController* must solve control problems that in principle are not GR(1) (i.e., $\Box\Diamond \bigwedge_{l \in \mu} \neg l \implies \varphi$). However, these problems can actually be solved using a GR(1) synthesis algorithm due to the shape of the subplant under analysis (the only loops consisting of uncontrollable events that can be found in the subplant are in μ and are self-loops) and the fact that GR(1) formulae are closed under stuttering. The procedure is to remove in the plant all self-loop transitions labeled with some $l \in \mu \subseteq \Sigma_u$, compute a controller for φ, and add to the controller the self-loop transitions previously removed to make it legal. This procedure is correct and complete (see proof in Appendix of the technical report submitted in Arxiv).

Theorem 3. *Given control problems* $\mathcal{E} = \langle \mathcal{M}' \setminus \{(s,l,s) \mid l \in \mu \cup \mu'\}, \Sigma_c, \varphi \rangle$ *and* $\mathcal{E}' = \langle \mathcal{M}', \Sigma_c, \Box \Diamond (\bigwedge_{l \in (\mu \cup \mu')} \neg l) \implies \varphi \rangle$ *where* $\mathcal{M}' = \mathcal{M} \setminus \{M_{sub}\} \cup \{M_{cont}/ \sim_\Upsilon\}$, $\Sigma_c \subseteq \Sigma$ *is a set of controllable events,* μ *and* μ' *are sets of events and* M_{cont} *is a controlled subplant for* $\langle M_{sub}, \Sigma_c, \Box \Diamond (\bigwedge_{l \in \mu} \neg l) \implies \varphi \rangle$ *where* $M_{sub} \subseteq \mathcal{M}$. *If there is a solution* $C = (S_c, \Sigma, \to_c, \hat{s}_c)$ *for control problem* $\mathcal{E}$, *then* C' *is a solution for* $\mathcal{E}'$ *where* $C' = (S_{c'}, \Sigma, \to_{c'}, \hat{s}_c)$ *is defined as follows:*

- $S_{C'} = S_C$
- $\to_{C'} = \to_C \ \cup \ \{(s,l,s) \mid s \in S_c \ \wedge \ l \in \Sigma_u \cap (\mu \cup \mu') \ \wedge \ \exists (s_{\mathcal{M}'}, s_c) \in S_{\mathcal{M}' \| C} \cdot (s_{\hat{\mathcal{M}}'}, \hat{s_C}) \to_{\mathcal{M}' \| C} (s_{\mathcal{M}'}, s_C) \ \wedge \ (s_{\mathcal{M}'}, l, s_{\mathcal{M}'}) \in \to_{\mathcal{M}'}\}.$

Also, if there is no solution for $\mathcal{E}$ *then there is no solution for* $\mathcal{E}'$.

A second challenge is an efficient way to compute a safe controller, that is a controller that keeps a plant in states that are non-losing. Furthermore, that the over-approximation of winning states is sufficiently small to achieve state space reductions that make the compositional approach efficient. This can be achieved for GR(1) formulae straightforwardly as the arena for which the underlying game is solved maps back one-to-one to states of the plant. In addition, the GR(1) synthesis procedure [26] establishes precisely all winning states of the arena.

Finally, projecting a GR(1) formula to a weaker formula can be done straightforwardly. In our implementation we use the following procedure: For formulae of the form $\varphi = \bigwedge_{i \in n} \Box \Diamond \phi_i \implies \bigwedge_{j \in m} \Box \Diamond \gamma_j$ where ϕ_i and γ_j are boolean combination of events in conjunctive normal form and $\Sigma' \in \Sigma$ do the following. For every $l \in \Sigma'$, replace every occurrence of l and $\neg l$ with F in every ϕ_i and replace every occurrence of l and $\neg l$ with $\top$ in every γ_j. It is straightforward to see that this projection yields weaker formulae: $\varphi \implies \alpha(\varphi, \Sigma')$.

6.2 GR(1) DES Synthesis via Reactive Synthesis

To study the performance of GR(1) compositional synthesis for DES via reactive synthesis we implemented a translation of MTSA inputs using an approach based on [17]. Nonetheless, we developed two different translations. The first translates each LTS of the plant and also encodes parallel composition rules. We refer to this translation as *modular*. The second translates the composed plant, a single LTS. We refer to this translation as *non-modular*. Note that the translation is orthogonal to whether monolithic or compositional synthesis will be applied.

For *Strix* we use a binary-encoding for events and local states to reduce the number of atomic propositions needed. Such an encoding is unnecessary for *Spectra* as it supports variables (and performs binary-encoding internally).

For both *Strix* and *Spectra* we first evaluate how they perform using the modular and non-modular translations for various instances of the benchmark. We then take the best performing translation for each tool to evaluate how a monolithic synthesis approach compares with a compositional one.

Monolithic synthesis with *Strix* and *Spectra* is achieved by simply translating the plant of the control problem and executing the reactive synthesis tool.

To avoid modifying *Strix* and *Spectra* to do compositional synthesis, performance is approximated by running a modified version of the compositional MTSA implementation. Every time MTSA calls its internal GR(1) synthesis procedure with a subplant, we mimick the call by calling the synthesis procedure of *Strix* or *Spectra* with a translation of the subplant. The output of reactive synthesis procedure is discarded, and the result of the native GR(1) synthesis procedure is used. We compute the overall time by subtracting the time spent by internal MTSA synthesis procedure. We refer to these approximations of native compositional implementations as *DES Strix* and *DES Spectra*.

6.3   Benchmark

We use modular DES GR(1) control problems taken from multiple sources. Control problems are parameterizable some scale in two dimensions (number of intervening components, n, and number of states per component, k) and some scale only in the number of intervening components.

For the case studies scalable in two dimensions, we use all problem families introduced in [2], modified from supervisory control problems to GR(1) control problems: Air Traffic (AT), Bidding Workflow (BW) and Travel Agency (TA), Transfer Line (TL), and Cat and Mouse (CM). We also used a Robot Search Mission (RS) taken from robotic literature [31]. All the n-k instances for these problems are known to be realizable, except for those in AT where $n \leq k$ must hold. Thus, we report separately on instances that are realizable (AT_R) and those that are not ($AT_{!R}$). We studied for instances with $n, k \leq 9$.

The one-dimension control problems we use are the classic concurrency Dinning Philosophers (DP) problem and the AI planning problem Gripper (GR) [29]. Finally, we also use a SYNTECH [20] case study named Moving Obstacle (MO) originally specified as a reactive synthesis problem (i.e., a turn-based game in which each player can update all its variables in each turn). We translated MO manually into a modular discrete event problem by developing one LTS for each safety property of the specification plus some additional LTS to replicate the turn-based logic of reactive synthesis control. The maximum value for n varies depending on how large the plant for the control problems grows.

Experiments were run on a computer with an Intel i7-7700 CPU @ 3.60GHz, with 8GB of RAM, and a timeout of 30 min. In addition, we use a simple deterministic heuristic for selecting subplants that always chooses the first two LTS from the vector representation of the set $\mathcal{M}$.

Table 1. Experimental Results for Native DES GR(1) Controller Synthesis.

Inst.	Solved Instances		Largest instance solved by both Mono and Comp										State space
					State space	Comp Perf.		Reduction		Controller			space
	Mono	Comp	n	k	space	States	Time	States	Time	LTSs	States	Red.	lgst. inst.
AT_R	45	**35**	20	4	4	2^{38}	6244	110 s	−91%	−99.63%	9	6545	−95.6%	2^{41}
$AT_{!R}$	36	**21**	15	9	1	2^{42}	17920	24 s	33%	93%	−	−	−	2^{46}
BW	81	45	**50**	9	1	2^{22}	1604	3 s	99.6%	96.2%	9	2499	95.6%	2^{28}
CM	81	20	**21**	4	2	2^{32}	229993	1251 s	−51%	−81.1%	7	242865	−91%	2^{32}
RS	81	17	**29**	3	3	2^{24}	24285	230 s	90%	84%	6	212664	94.3%	2^{30}
TA	81	50	**71**	6	4	2^{50}	6560	98 s	97.2%	93.4%	13	7951	83.3%	2^{67}
TL	81	**30**	29	3	6	2^{20}	374993	231 s	−6%	−49%	6	377790	−99.8%	2^{20}
DP	10	4	**9**	5	-	2^{20}	185	1 s	88%	96.8%	9	391	97.3%	2^{36}
GR	20	8	**11**	8	-	2^{29}	378	1 s	99.22%	96%	17	853	78%	2^{38}
MO	4	3	**4**	6	-	2^{100}	5180	380 s	59%	34%	38	14011	44%	2^{127}
PC	10	4	**10**	5	-	2^{28}	6561	220 s	94.8%	−87%	11	7152	94.3%	2^{50}

6.4   Results

Monolithic vs. Compositional GR(1) DES Controller Synthesis.
Table 1 shows results for all case studies. The first column has problem family names. The next three aggregate information of entire problem families: we
show the total number of instances per problem family (Column Inst) and the
number of solved instances by the monolithic (Mono) and compositional (Comp)
methods.

These first three columns show that *for 8 out of 10 control problem families,
the compositional method improves over the monolithic one* (we count AT_R and
$AT_{!R}$ as the same family). In all cases the solved instances one of the methods
is a superset of the instances solved by the other.

All problems that the monolithic approach could not solve were due to running out of memory. Also note that providing more RAM to the monolithic
method makes little difference in dealing with the combinatorial growth of the
state space resulting from increasing the size of problems using k and n. Indeed,
doubling memory from 8Gb to 16Gb allows the monolithic approach to add less
than 5% more instances. The two problem families in which monolithic performs
better than compositional can be explained by looking at the remaining columns.

From the 5th column onwards we focus on the instance with the largest
composed plant that was solved by both monolithic and compositional methods.
We first report on the values n and k for the instance and its potential state
space (i.e., the product of the sizes of all LTS of the plant). We then report the
performance of the compositional method by showing the number of states of
the largest plant which the compositional approach solves a control problem for,
and the end-to-end time to compute the final controller. The next two columns
report the reduction in the largest control problem to be solved with respect to
the monolithic method, and the reduction in time to build the final controller

compared to the monolothic approach. Negative values in this column indicate that the monolithic approach did better than the compositional.

For all but three problem families, when considering the largest instance solved by both methods, the compositional approach was able to significantly reduce the plant on which it computes a live controller. This is an indication of why for these problem families the compositional method has better performance. The exception being $AT_!R$ for which, despite achieving reductions, the total number of instances solved by the compositional approach was not greater. This may indicate some bias of our approach towards realizable problems.

The three instances for which we report a negative reduction ($AT_R(n = 4, k = 4)$, $CM(n = 4, k = 2)$, and $TL(n = 3, k = 6)$) show that state explosion of subplants can occur and is a likely cause for poor (or in the case of CM, not significantly better) performance of compositional synthesis.

Notice that treating smaller (sub)plants does not necessarily mean a reduction in time. Instance $PC(n = 5)$ shows that the compositional method is good at reducing size, but a price is paid in time (mostly spent minimizing subplants).

The next three columns, show the size of the controller computed by the compositional method. We report in column LTSs how many LTSs is the controller composed of. The States column reports the sum of the states of each of these LTS, other words, a measure of the memory required to store the controller on the computer that will enact the controller. We also show the reduction in memory, measured in states, with respect to the (monolithic) controller computed by the monolithic method. *Note that there are significant reductions in the size of the compositional controller for all case studies except for the three in which there are intermediate state explosions of subplants.*

The final column shows the theoretical size of the biggest instance solved by either of the methods. Subtracting column 7 ("state space") we obtain how much bigger was the biggest problem solved by one approach than the biggest of the other: For 4 out of 10 problem families, the compositional approach was able to solve instances at least 3 orders of magnitude ($\times 2^{10}$) bigger than the monolithic approach. For 3 out 10, the increase in size that the compositional algorithm was able to manage was of at least 2^6 larger. On the other hand for the 3 case studies where monolithic fared better, the largest instances it was able to solve were only 2^6 times bigger.

The final column reports on the state space of the largest instance solved, be it the compositional or the monolithic method. For 4 out of 10 case studies, the compositional approach was able to solve instances at least 3 orders of magnitude ($\times 2^{10}$) bigger than the monolithic approach. For 3 out 10, the increase in size that the compositional algorithm was able to manage was of at least 2^6 larger. On the other hand for the 3 case studies where monolithic fared better, the largest instances it was able to solve were only 2^6 times bigger.

The survival plot on the top left of Fig. 9 provides a graphical summary of the comparative performance of monolithic vs. compositional GR(1) DES controller synthesis implemented in MTSA. Overall compositional can solve more (and significantly larger) subjects but takes more time than monolithic.

We now discuss possible causes for variable performance of compositional synthesis across different problem families. We hypothesise that compositional synthesis has opportunities for increased performance when intermediate subsystems can be reduced due to minimization with respect to local events, and when reduction is achieved by reducing reachable states when the subsystem is controlled via partial synthesis. The main threat to performance is, we believe, having intermediate subsystem state explosion as a result of composing LTS that are very loosely synchronized (worst case being that the composition yields the cartesian product of states). Below we analyze two problem families where compositional synthesis performance was worse than monolithic (AT TL) and one in which it was better (DP).

For AT, there are two classes of LTS affected by parameters n and k: The number of airplane LTS is determined by n and the number of height monitors (that check that at a particular height, there is never more than one airplane) is determined by k. The height monitors interact very little with each other, while each one interacts frequently with all airplanes. Additionally, there is always just one ramp and one response monitor. The response monitor interacts with each airplane on a specific label that is local to that airplane.

The simple heuristic used composes incrementally height monitors inducing, early on, an intermediate state explosion as their composition yields a state space that is almost the size of the cartesian product of height monitors' states. In addition, there are no local shared events that can lead to intermediate reductions. We speculate that a heuristic that starts with the response monitor and adds one airplane at a time will perform better because local shared variables provide opportunities for reduction. Indeed, initial explorations seem to indicate this.

In instances of TL, there are LTSs representing the machines connected by buffers on a transfer line and an LTS at the end, the Testing Unit (TU), that takes a work piece from the last buffer and accepts it or rejects and returns it to the first buffer for reprocessing.

The naive heuristic we used selects Machines and Buffers in order from the beginning, thus the TU machine is included in the composition towards the end. These intermediate subsystems have permissive controllers because the projected formula (that only talks about events in the TU) is trivial, so they cannot be reduced by partial synthesis. We speculate that a heuristic that starts with TU and adds consecutive machines and buffers from the end towards the beginning of the line will perform better. Initial exploration indicate this is the case.

In contrast, consider instances of DP, where the compositional approach performs better. The heuristic chooses to add LTSs following the ring architecture defined by the philosophers sitting round the table. Thus, as one more adjacent LTS is added to the subsystem, some new local shared events (between a particular philosopher and a particular fork) can be minimized. Also, since this problem has a formula that refers to events in all philosophers, there are opportunities of minimize by partial synthesis solving control problem for each subsystem.

Monolithic vs Composition GR(1) Synthesis via Reactive Synthesis.
Strix performed consistently better when using the non-modular translation than
when using the modular one. This provides some evidence that *the compositional
approach Strix has built in (where smaller problems are solved by selecting subsets
of formulae) is not able to exploit the modular nature of the DES control problem.*
Results for *Spectra* were opposite. The tool performed consistently better when
applied to modular translations of the control problems instead of non-modular
ones. Thus, for the remaining experiments we used modular translations for
Spectra and non-modular ones for *Strix*.

Top right and bottom left survival plots of Fig. 9 show comparative performance of compositional vs monolithic *DES Strix* and *DES Spectra*. *DES
Strix* solved the same number of cases with both approaches, but the monolithic method took over 50% more time. Conversely, bottom left survival plot
shows that in *DES Spectra* compositional and monolithic solve the same number
of cases, but the monolithic approach is slightly over 20% faster.

A closer look at *DES Spectra* results reveal that the monolithic tends to
perform better on problems with shorter and more centralized formulas (i.e.,
share alphabet with less LTS). By splitting problem families based on whether
monolithic or compositional *DES Spectra* does better we can see (bottom right of
Fig. 9) that for one set of problem families compositional cumulative time grows
much less than that of monolithic, while for the other, compositional cumulative
time is higher but grows at a closer rate to that of monolithic.

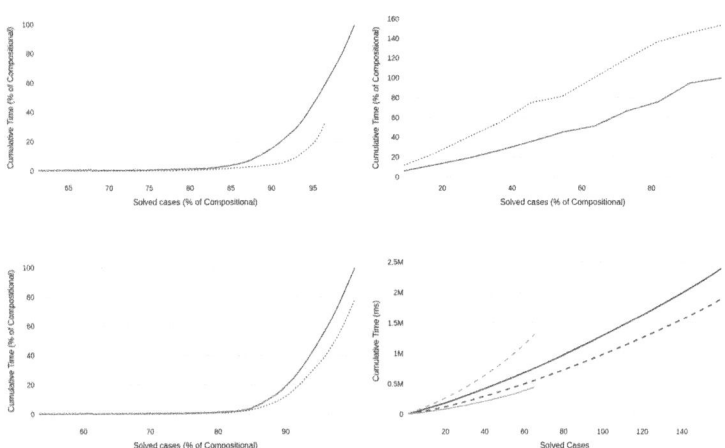

Fig. 9. Survival plots for Compositional (solid) and Monolithic (dashed) for *DES
MTSA* -top left-, *DES Strix* -top right-, and *DES Spectra* -bottom left-) relative to compositional performance. Bottom right is for *DES Spectra* divided into problem families
for which compositional performs better (purple) and worse (cyan) than monolithic.
(Color figure online)

Summary. The evaluation presented above contributes evidence that compositional synthesis can achieve improvements in scale compared to monolithic DES control, both for native GR(1) DES (explicit state) synthesis, and can achieve improvements in time for DES control via reactive (symbolic state) synthesis.

For the case of native GR(1) DES synthesis, we observe that performance can degrade if there is intermediate state explosion. Exploring heuristics for choosing subplants that may mitigate this problem. In [25] various heuristics are reported to make significant improvements for supervisory control for finite traces. These may also achieve better performance for GR(1) goals.

7   Related Work

Out of the three classic areas that focus on automatically constructing control rules from a specification, Discrete Event Control [28], Reactive Synthesis [27] and Automated Planning [13], this paper is more related to the first two.

Discrete Event Control was first formulated for *-regular languages [28] and then extended to ω-regular languages. In [30], Thistle addresses control problems described using a deterministic finite automaton (DFA) equipped with two acceptance conditions for ω-languages, one representing a specification and the other representing an assumption. Supervisors are required to generate infinite words that belong to the specification ω-language under the supposition that the environment generates finite traces of the DFA and infinite traces of the assumption ω-language. The supervisor is also required to not block the environment from generating some trace in the assumption ω-language. In [17], this is referred to as a *non-conflicting* requirement. In [30], Thistle presents a supervisor synthesis algorithm that is polynomial in the number of states of the automaton and exponential in the acceptance condition size.

The control problem we study in this paper can be presented as an instance of the general supervisory control problem for ω-regular languages where the ω-regular language for the specification is given as an LTL formula. Whereas the *-regular language for assumptions is given by a composition of LTS (i.e., the plant) and the ω-regular language for assumptions is the entire set of infinite traces of the plant.

Our work is related to reactive synthesis where the control problem is solely expressed by means of a logical formulae, LTL is commonly used. The system-to-be is a reactive module that shares state variables with the environment. Assumed environment behaviour is also described by means of logical formulae. The underlying interaction model between the controller and the environment differs from that of supervisory control. Reactive synthesis assumes a turn based interaction where each part can change in their turn all the variables it controls. In supervisory control, there are no turns and the environment may win all races.

The relation between supervisory control and reactive synthesis has received much attention in the last years [7]. Notably, [17] shows that the non-conflicting/non-blocking requirement of supervisory control requires solving games, obliging games, of higher complexity than those classically used for reactive synthesis.

The control problem we study does not suffer from this as the non-conflicting requirement is trivially satisfied.

The class of GR(1) LTL formulae have been studied extensively as controllers for them can be computed polynomially [26] as opposed to the double exponential complexity of general LTL [27]. GR(1) has been studied extensively as a specification language for reactive systems (e.g. [21,22]) and various variants have been proposed (e.g., [16]).

GR(1) control of DES as defined in this paper was originally proposed in [6], a monolithic synthesis algorithm is defined. Later, on-the-fly composition construction has been proposed [2,4].

The reactive synthesis community has explored compositionality as a way to scale synthesis by identifying and performing independent synthesis tasks [8–10]. For instance, in [8] LTL synthesis is solved compositionally by first computing winning strategies for each conjunct that appears in the large formula using an incomplete heuristic. The decomposition algorithm of [9] works for LTL and decomposes the formulae into subspecifications that do not share output variables. A dependency graph used for finding the decomposition-critical propositions that, in turn, are key to soundness and completeness of the approach. In [10] decomposition means partitioning system's input and output variables and then applying incremental synthesis of dominant strategies. Dependency graphs must be constructed to identify components and synthesis order that would ensure completeness. On the other hand, our technique works compositionally in terms of environment's safety assumptions (involving input, output and synchronization events) which are described as synchronizing LTS. Goal formula decomposition is a consequence of projection of the formula onto intermediate subsystems. Grouping and ordering of compositions does not affect neither soundness nor completeness (although it may affect performance).

Traditional compositional verification [3,14] mitigates the state-space explosion by leveraging modular structure of system-under-verification. In that vein, compositional synthesis for plants expressed as finite-state systems has been studied by the community of supervisory control for non-blocking goals [11,18]. There, synthesis is addressed by incrementally composing (and reducing) plant's component. Also, resulting controllers are modular: they are made up by automata that interact by mean of shared labels. Our solution is inspired in such works but it addresses intfinite trace goals for which there is no guarantee for the existence of maximal solutions.

8   Conclusions and Future Work

The modular representation of discrete event systems can be exploited by composition synthesis to mitigate the state explosion problem that monolithic synthesis suffers. In this paper we present how compositional synthesis can be applied to LTL. We implement compositional synthesis for GR(1) goals and show that with a very basic heuristic for selecting subplants the compositional synthesis already achieves significant gains with respect to a monolithic method, both in a native DES synthesis tool and using reactive synthesis tools via translations.

Future work must look into avoiding intermediate state explosion by means of smarter heuristics that impact the order in which a plant LTS are composed. An implementation of the compositional framework for LTL requires defining a projection function (which can simply be an existential elimination of literals) and a method for computing safe controllers. The latter can be trivialized by the conservative decision of not removing any states at all, to ensure that no winning states are lost. However, this is unlikely to provide good performance results. Thus, the challenge with full LTL is to find an effective way of removing a significant portion of subplant losing states.

Acknowledgements. This work was partially supported by proyects ANPCYT PICT 2019-1442, 2021-4862, UBACYT 2023-0134, and CONICET PIP 1220220100470CO.

References

1. Replication package: tool and control problems (2025). https://zenodo.org/records/13913744
2. Ciolek, D.A., Braberman, V.A., D'Ippolito, N.R., Uchitel, S., Sardiña, S.: Compositional supervisory control via reactive synthesis and automated planning. IEEE Trans. Autom. Control **65**(8), 3502–3516 (2020). https://doi.org/10.1109/TAC.2019.2948270
3. Clarke, E.M., Grumberg, O., Long, D.E.: Model checking and abstraction. In: Sethi, R. (ed.) Conference Record of the Nineteenth Annual ACM SIGPLAN-SIGACT Symposium on Principles of Programming Languages, Albuquerque, New Mexico, USA, 19–22 January 1992, pp. 342–354. ACM Press (1992). https://doi.org/10.1145/143165.143235
4. Delgado, T., Sorondo, M.S., Braberman, V.A., Uchitel, S.: Exploration policies for on-the-fly controller synthesis: a reinforcement learning approach. In: Koenig, S., Stern, R., Vallati, M. (eds.) Proceedings of the Thirty-Third International Conference on Automated Planning and Scheduling, Prague, Czech Republic, 8–13 July 2023, pp. 569–577. AAAI Press (2023). https://doi.org/10.1609/ICAPS.V33I1.27238
5. D'Ippolito, N., Fischbein, D., Chechik, M., Uchitel, S.: MTSA: the modal transition system analyser. In: 2008 23rd IEEE/ACM International Conference on Automated Software Engineering, pp. 475–476 (2008). https://doi.org/10.1109/ASE.2008.78
6. D'Ippolito, N., Fischbein, D., Chechik, M., Uchitel, S.: MTSA: the modal transition system analyser. In: Proceedings of the International Conference on Automated Software Engineering (ASE) (2008)
7. Ehlers, Tripakis: Supervisory Control and Reactive Synthesis: A Comparative Introduction (2017)
8. Filiot, E., Jin, N., Raskin, J.-F.: Compositional algorithms for LTL synthesis. In: Bouajjani, A., Chin, W.-N. (eds.) ATVA 2010. LNCS, vol. 6252, pp. 112–127. Springer, Heidelberg (2010). https://doi.org/10.1007/978-3-642-15643-4_10
9. Finkbeiner, B., Geier, G., Passing, N.: Specification decomposition for reactive synthesis. Innov. Syst. Softw. Eng. **19**(4), 339–357 (2023). https://doi.org/10.1007/S11334-022-00462-6

10. Finkbeiner, B., Passing, N.: Dependency-based compositional synthesis. In: Hung, D.V., Sokolsky, O. (eds.) ATVA 2020. LNCS, vol. 12302, pp. 447–463. Springer, Cham (2020). https://doi.org/10.1007/978-3-030-59152-6_25

11. Flordal, H., Malik, R., Fabian, M., Åkesson, K.: Compositional synthesis of maximally permissive supervisors using supervision equivalence. Discret. Event Dyn. Syst. **17**(4), 475–504 (2007). https://doi.org/10.1007/S10626-007-0018-Z

12. Fokkink, W.J., et al.: Eclipse ESCET^{TM}: the eclipse supervisory control engineering toolkit. In: Sankaranarayanan, S., Sharygina, N. (eds.) Tools and Algorithms for the Construction and Analysis of Systems, pp. 44–52. Springer, Cham (2023)

13. Ghallab, M., Nau, D., Traverso, P.: Automated Planning: Theory and Practice. Elsevier, San Francisco (2004)

14. Graf, S., Steffen, B.: Compositional minimization of finite state systems. In: Clarke, E.M., Kurshan, R.P. (eds.) Computer Aided Verification, 2nd International Workshop, CAV 1990, New Brunswick, NJ, USA, 18–21 June 1990, Proceedings. Lecture Notes in Computer Science, vol. 531, pp. 186–196. Springer (1990). https://doi.org/10.1007/BFB0023732

15. Huang, J., Kumar, R.: Directed control of discrete event systems for safety and nonblocking. IEEE Trans. Autom. Sci. Eng. **5**(4), 620–629 (2008). https://doi.org/10.1109/TASE.2008.923820

16. Majumdar, R., Piterman, N., Schmuck, A.K.: Environmentally-friendly GR(1) Synthesis (2019). https://doi.org/10.48550/arXiv.1902.05629. http://arxiv.org/abs/1902.05629. arXiv:1902.05629

17. Majumdar, R., Schmuck, A.K.: Supervisory Controller Synthesis for Nonterminating Processes is an Obliging Game (2021). https://doi.org/10.48550/arXiv.2007.01773. http://arxiv.org/abs/2007.01773. arXiv:2007.01773

18. Malik, R., Mohajerani, S., Fabian, M.: A survey on compositional algorithms for verification and synthesis in supervisory control. Discret. Event Dyn. Syst. **33**(3), 279–340 (2023). https://doi.org/10.1007/S10626-023-00378-8

19. Malik, R., Åkesson, K., Flordal, H., Fabian, M.: Supremica–an efficient tool for large-scale discrete event systems. IFAC-PapersOnLine **50**(1), 5794–5799 (2017). https://doi.org/10.1016/j.ifacol.2017.08.427. https://www.sciencedirect.com/science/article/pii/S2405896317307772. 20th IFAC World Congress 20th IFAC World Congress 20th IFAC World Congress

20. Maoz, S., Ringert, J.O.: Spectra: a specification language for reactive systems. Softw. Syst. Model. **20**(5), 1553–1586 (2021). https://doi.org/10.1007/s10270-021-00868-z

21. Menghi, C., et al.: Mission specification patterns for mobile robots: providing support for quantitative properties. IEEE Trans. Software Eng. **49**(4), 2741–2760 (2023). https://doi.org/10.1109/TSE.2022.3230059

22. Menghi, C., Tsigkanos, C., Pelliccione, P., Ghezzi, C., Berger, T.: Specification Patterns for Robotic Missions (2019). https://doi.org/10.48550/arXiv.1901.02077. http://arxiv.org/abs/1901.02077. arXiv:1901.02077

23. Meyer, P.J., Sickert, S., Luttenberger, M.: Strix: explicit reactive synthesis strikes back! In: Chockler, H., Weissenbacher, G. (eds.) CAV 2018. LNCS, vol. 10981, pp. 578–586. Springer, Cham (2018). https://doi.org/10.1007/978-3-319-96145-3_31

24. Mohajerani, S., Malik, R., Fabian, M.: An algorithm for weak synthesis observation equivalence for compositional supervisor synthesis. IFAC Proc. Vol. **45**(29), 239–244 (2012). https://doi.org/10.3182/20121003-3-MX-4033.00040. https://www.sciencedirect.com/science/article/pii/S1474667015401776

25. Mohajerani, S., Malik, R., Fabian, M.: A framework for compositional synthesis of modular nonblocking supervisors. IEEE Trans. Autom. Control **59**(1), 150–162 (2014). https://doi.org/10.1109/TAC.2013.2283109. http://ieeexplore.ieee.org/document/6606831/

26. Piterman, N., Pnueli, A., Sa'ar, Y.: Synthesis of reactive(1) designs. In: Emerson, E.A., Namjoshi, K.S. (eds.) VMCAI 2006. LNCS, vol. 3855, pp. 364–380. Springer, Heidelberg (2005). https://doi.org/10.1007/11609773_24

27. Pnueli, A., Rosner, R.: A framework for the synthesis of reactive modules. In: Vogt, F.H. (ed.) CONCURRENCY 1988. LNCS, vol. 335, pp. 4–17. Springer, Heidelberg (1988). https://doi.org/10.1007/3-540-50403-6_28

28. Ramadge, P., Wonham, W.: Supervisory control of a class of discrete event systems **25**, 206–230 (1987). https://doi.org/10.1137/0325013

29. Silver, T., Dan, S., Srinivas, K., Tenenbaum, J.B., Kaelbling, L.P., Katz, M.: Generalized planning in PDDL domains with pretrained large language models. CoRR abs/2305.11014 (2023). https://doi.org/10.48550/ARXIV.2305.11014

30. Thistle, J.G.: On control of systems modelled as deterministic Rabin automata. Discrete Event Dyn. Syst. Theory Appl. **5**(4), 357–381 (1995). https://doi.org/10.1007/BF01439153

31. Zudaire, S., Nahabedian, L., Uchitel, S.: Assured mission adaptation of UAVs **16**(3), 1–27 (2021). https://doi.org/10.1145/3513091. http://arxiv.org/abs/2107.10173

Counter Example Guided Reactive Synthesis for LTL Modulo Theories*

Andoni Rodríguez[1,2] , Felipe Gorostiaga[1(✉)] , and Cesar Sánchez[1]

[1] IMDEA Software Institute, Madrid, Spain
felipe.gorostiaga@imdea.org
[2] Universidad Politécnica de Madrid, Madrid, Spain

Abstract. Reactive synthesis is the process of automatically generating a correct system from a given temporal specification. In this paper, we address the problem of reactive synthesis for LTL modulo theories (LTL$^\mathcal{T}$), which extends LTL with literals from a first-order theory *and allows relating the values of data across time*. This logic allows describing complex dynamics both for the system and for the environment—such as a numeric variable increasing monotonically over time. The logic also allows defining relations (and not only assignment) between variables, enabling permissive shielding.

We propose a sound algorithm called Counter-Example Guided Reactive Synthesis modulo theories (CEGRES), whose core is the novel concept of *reactive tautology*, which are valid temporal formulas that preserve the semantics of the specification but make the algorithm conclusive. Although realizability for full LTL$^\mathcal{T}$ is undecidable in general, we prove that CEGRES is terminating for some important theories and for arbitrary theories when specifications do not fetch data across time. We include an empirical evaluation that shows that CEGRES can solve many reactive synthesis problems of practical interest.

1 Introduction

Reactive synthesis [33,34] is the problem of automatically producing a correct controller given a temporal specification, whose Boolean variables (i.e., atomic propositions) are split into those controlled by the environment and those controlled by the system. Realizability is the decision problem of deciding whether such a system exists. Reactive synthesis corresponds to a two-player game between a system and an environment. A specification is realizable if the system player has a winning strategy. Realizability has been widely studied for LTL [32].

At the same time, there is a growing interest in LTL modulo theories (LTL$^\mathcal{T}$), which allows reasoning about values in the domains of first-order theories. For example, [10,16,43] study satisfiability for variants of LTL with data. Also, [15]

This work was funded in part by the DECO Project (PID2022-138072OB-I00) funded by MCIN/AEI/10.13039/501100011033 and by the ESF+.

R. Piskac and Z. Rakamarić (Eds.): CAV 2025, LNCS 15934, pp. 224–248, 2025.
https://doi.org/10.1007/978-3-031-98685-7_11

considers a variant of LTL^T for finite traces which allows retrieving values of variables at the previous or following instants. However, reactive synthesis is not studied in [15,17]. Later, [37] showed the decidability of realizability for a fragment of LTL^T (which we call $LTL_{\mathcal{A}}^T$ here) without lookup, later extended in [36,38] into a full synthesis procedure. The method in [37] takes an $LTL_{\mathcal{A}}^T$ φ, and generates an equi-realizable Boolean LTL abstraction $\varphi^{\mathbb{B}}$. The practical application is however limited because (1) the method exhaustively explores all possible system reactions, which compromises scalability; and (2) the logic restricts the transfer of data values across time. In [37] the controller can remember the valuation of a literal, (e.g. whether x was odd in the previous timestep), but cannot remember the concrete value of x. Other works consider temporal logics that allow numeric information to flow across time, but with different expressive limitations like the temporal fragment [14,21,26] or the lack of operators to compare values at different time instants [7,18,20,25,26,40–42].

In this paper we study reactive synthesis for full LTL^T, which essentially consists of LTL temporal operators, literals from the theory $\mathcal{T}$ and the lookup operator $\lhd$ (also called *fetch*). This additional expressivity enables more realistic scenarios, including for example complex dynamics like $G(|\lhd v - v| \leq 30)$, which means that a current velocity v cannot change in more than 30 units from timestep to timestep. We introduce a novel method called Counter-Example Guided Reactive Synthesis (CEGRES) for temporal logics modulo theory, which is a general algorithm based on refinements (in a CEGAR [8] fashion). CEGRES attempts an abstraction to a simpler reactive synthesis problem, studies the strategy proposed as solution and refines the abstraction by learning from illegal actions of the strategy (whose legality was not preserved in the abstraction). In summary, the contributions of this paper are the following:

(1) A general CEGRES method for reactive synthesis of temporal logics with data.
(2) An instance of the general method for $LTL_{\mathcal{A}}^T$ which significantly improves scalability for this decidable fragment. This is used as a building block in the following steps.
(3) An instance of CEGRES for full LTL^T, which is a sound synthesis procedure (yet possibly not terminating because LTL^T realizability is in general undecidable). This method introduces the novel concept of *reactive tautologies*, which are valid temporal formulas that improve the equi-realizability between the original LTL^T specification and its abstraction. These tautologies are to realizability modulo theories what inductive invariants are to invariant proving. The refinement phase of CEGRES for general LTL^T is guaranteed to progress by generating these tautologies.
(4) We show that our method always terminates for theories with bounded domains (very common in embedded systems) and avoids blasting the variables into a Boolean specification.
(5) We showcase the applicability of CEGRES with a large set of benchmarks.

We emphasize our synthesis problem is different, because (in contrast with TSL-MT) it allows choosing different values at different time-steps. To the best of our knowledge, this is the first method to solve this problem.

Related Work. Reactive synthesis has been shown to be decidable for $\mathrm{LTL}^{\mathcal{T}}_{\mathcal{A}}$ (see [36–39]), but our CEGRES method for $\mathrm{LTL}^{\mathcal{T}}_{\mathcal{A}}$ is faster because it avoids an upfront exhaustive exploration of the set of reactions. However, $\mathrm{LTL}^{\mathcal{T}}_{\mathcal{A}}$ does not allow data temporal relations which limits its application in some realistic domains. A more expressive variant of $\mathrm{LTL}^{\mathcal{T}}$ was presented in [15,17] for finite traces, but they address the satisfiability problem and not reactive synthesis.

A close specification language to $\mathrm{LTL}^{\mathcal{T}}$ is Temporal Stream Logic Modulo Theories (TSL-MT), which was first introduced for satisfiability [12,13]. Reactive synthesis for TSL-MT specifications is addressed in [25] using abstraction-refinement, which is often not tractable for the presented benchmarks. The work in [7] presents an abstraction-refinement method introducing *data transformation obligations* (similar in spirit to our reactive tautologies), but obligations are in a `Precondition|State|Postcondition` style that is less general than our reactive tautologies. For instance, their obligation $G[(a = 0 \wedge X(a = \triangleleft a + 1) \wedge X^2(a = \triangleleft a + 1) \rightarrow X^2(a = 2)]$ does not capture enough information about what happens when a increases over three timesteps, or what if addition does not happen two timesteps in a row. In contrast, our tautologies capture a more general relation across time.

The work in [20] provides rules and an invariant notion similar to our tautologies (and to [7,25]), for RP-LTL. RP-LTL is similar to $\mathrm{LTL}^{\mathcal{T}}$ but does not allow to directly refer to previous environment variables and the environment controls all variables in the first instant, making the move of the system in the first timestep irrelevant. Also, [20] is based on symbolic game solving and the implementation and empirical evaluation in [20] is still restricted to TSL-MT. TSL-MT synthesis is different from $\mathrm{LTL}^{\mathcal{T}}$ synthesis because the semantics of TSL-MT only allow to fetch past information via an *update* operation; e.g., $(x = \triangleleft x)$ is legal in TSL-MT, but $(x < \triangleleft x)$ or $(x < \triangleleft x + z)$ are not. This limits the ability to express arbitrary relations in terms of data across time, and precludes the application to the field of shielding modulo theories [35] as post-shields, because a shield that uses equality would force a single fixed move. The reason is that TSL-MT follows a clear design goal: the restriction to updates with equality and restricting the specification to a finite number of possible assignments facilitates extracting controllers as programs. In contrast, $\mathrm{LTL}^{\mathcal{T}}$ is a specification language with more non-determinism.

Another important recent approach is [18,42], which use acceleration-based game solving for expressive reactive synthesis problems. However, the specification allows infinite data domains only in the environment inputs, and not in the system outputs. Also, [18,42] does not reduce to simpler synthesis problems. Instead, they create directly 2-player games and then search strategies in the corresponding arenas. Similarly, [40,41] proposes a fixpoint-based solver for infinite-state safety game-arenas. In addition, [14,21,26] also perform synthesis of modulo theories specifications, but their techniques only apply to safety, assume-guarantee and GR(1) fragments, respectively. In contrast, our method works for any temporal fragment (as long as the underlying solver can handle the fragment).

2   Preliminaries

Let AP be a set of *atomic propositions* and $\Sigma = 2^{AP}$ be the propositional *alphabet*, where we call each element of Σ a *letter*. A *trace* is an infinite sequence $\sigma = a_0 a_1 \cdots$ of letters from Σ, where we use $\sigma(i)$ for a_i. We denote the set of all infinite traces by Σ^ω. A *pointed trace* is a pair (σ, p), where $p \in \mathbb{N}$ is a natural number (called the *pointer*).

LTL and Reactive Synthesis. Linear Temporal Logic (LTL) [28,32] extends propositional logic with time modalities. LTL has the following syntax:

$$\varphi ::= \top \mid a \mid \varphi \vee \varphi \mid \neg \varphi \mid \mathsf{X}\,\varphi \mid \varphi \mathcal{U} \varphi,$$

where a ranges from an atomic set of propositions AP, $\top$ is the true value, $\vee$, $\wedge$ and $\neg$ are the usual Boolean operators, and X and $\mathcal{U}$ are the *next* and *until* temporal operators. The semantics of LTL associates traces $\sigma \in \Sigma^\omega$ (where $\Sigma = 2^{AP}$) with formulas as follows (we omit Boolean operators which are standard):

$(\sigma, i) \models a$ iff $a \in \sigma(i)$
$(\sigma, i) \models \mathsf{X}\varphi$ iff $(\sigma, i+1) \models \varphi$
$(\sigma, i) \models \varphi \mathcal{U} \psi$ iff   for some $j \geq i$, $(\sigma, j) \models \psi$ and for all $i \leq k < j, (\sigma, k) \models \varphi$

We use $\sigma \models \varphi$ for $(\sigma, 0) \models \varphi$.

Reactive synthesis [11,33,34] is the problem of automatically constructing a reactive system from an LTL specification φ. The atomic propositions AP of φ are partitioned into propositions $\overline{e} = Vars_E(\varphi)$ controlled by the environment and $\overline{s} = Vars_S(\varphi)$ controlled by the system (with $\overline{e} \cup \overline{s} = AP$ and $\overline{e} \cap \overline{s} = \emptyset$). Reactive Synthesis corresponds to a turn-based game in an arena where the environment and system players alternate. In each turn, the environment produces values for $\overline{e}$, and the system responds with values for $\overline{s}$. We use $val(\overline{e})$ and $val(\overline{s})$ for valuations. A play is an infinite sequence of turns, which induces a trace σ by joining at each position the valuations that the environment and system players choose. The system player wins a play σ whenever $\sigma \models \varphi$.

We introduce now a slightly non-standard notion of strategy as a Mealy machine, which is a common output from synthesis tools like Strix [30]. This definition is convenient in this paper because it is common for both players—environment and system—and eases the description of the algorithms in Sects. 4 and 5. A strategy is a tuple $M : \langle Q, q_0, T \rangle$ where Q is a finite set of states, $q_0 \in Q$ is the initial state and $T \subseteq Q \times Q \times val(\overline{e}) \times val(\overline{s})$. Given $t = (q, q', e, s)$ we use $t.from$ for the pre-state q, $t.to$ for the post-state q', $t.env$ for the valuation e of environment variables and $t.sys$ for the valuation s of system variables. We use T_q for $\{t \mid t.from = q\}$. We say that a strategy M is *legal for the system* if, for all states q, all environment valuations are considered in some transition, that is for every q and every $\bar{a} \in val(\bar{e})$ there is a $t \in T_q$ with $t.env = \bar{a}$. Similarly, a strategy M is *legal for the environment* if for all states q, all sets of outgoing transitions that agree on the environment move, cover all possible moves of the system. Formally, for every state q (1) there is a $\bar{a} \in val(\bar{e})$ and a transition $t \in T_q$ with $t.env = \bar{a}$; and (2) for every $\bar{a} \in val(\bar{e})$ such that there is a $t \in T_q$ with $t.env = \bar{a}$, then for every $\bar{c}$ in $val(\bar{s})$ there is a $t' \in T_q$ with $t'.env = \bar{a}$ and $t'.sys = \bar{c}$. Of course, in practice T can be represented explicitly, or symbolically as formulas covering many valuations.

A trace $((\bar{a}_0, \bar{c}_0), (\bar{a}_1, \bar{c}_1), \dots)$ is played according to a strategy M if there is a sequence $(q_0, q_1, \dots)$ such that $(q_i, q_{i+1}, \bar{a}_i, \bar{c}_i) \in T$ for all $i \geq 0$. We use *Traces(M)* for the set of traces played according to M. A strategy M is winning for the system if M is legal for the system and $Traces(M) \models \varphi$. A strategy M is winning for the environment if M is legal for the environment and $Traces(M) \models \neg\varphi$. If there is a winning strategy for the system, then φ is *realizable*.

Theories. A first-order theory $\mathcal{T}$ (see e.g. [4]) is described by a signature that consists of a finite set of functions and predicates, a set of variables, and a domain, which is the sort of its variables. For simplicity in the presentation we assume single-sorted theories but all our results can be extended to multi-sorted theories. For example, the domain of linear integer arithmetic $\mathcal{T}_{\mathbb{Z}}$ is $\mathbb{Z}$ and we denote this by $\mathbb{D}(\mathcal{T}_{\mathbb{Z}}) = \mathbb{Z}$. A predicate α in a theory $\mathcal{T}$ is valid iff $I \models \alpha$ for every interpretation I of $\mathcal{T}$. A literal is a predicate or its negation. We use $Terms_{\mathcal{T}}(V)$ for the terms that can be built from variables in V using the constructors of $\mathcal{T}$. Similarly, $Lits_{\mathcal{T}}(V)$ is the set of literals. We drop $\mathcal{T}$ from $Lits_{\mathcal{T}}$ and $Terms_{\mathcal{T}}$ when clear from the context. We use $Vars(l)$ for the set of variables in the literal l and $Vars(\varphi)$ for the union of the variables that occur in the literals of the formula φ. A valuation for a set of variables $\bar{z}$ is a map from $\bar{z}$ into $\mathbb{D}(\mathcal{T})$. We assume that every theory assigns a meaning to each function f and predicate symbol l such that $[\![f]\!]$ gives a value of the domain and $[\![l]\!]$ gives a truth value given values of the arguments. We also assume a default value d in $\mathbb{D}(\mathcal{T})$.

3   LTL Modulo Theories

Syntax and Semantics. LTL modulo theories extends LTL using first-order theories. Given a set of $\mathcal{T}$ variables, V the *alphabet* is a map $\Sigma_{\mathcal{T}} : V \to \mathbb{D}(\mathcal{T})$. Given an alphabet a over a set of variables V and a term t with $Vars(t) \subseteq V$, we use $t(a)$ as the value obtained by substituting every variable in t according to a and evaluating $[\![t]\!]$. Similarly we use $l(a)$ for a predicate l.

LTL modulo Theories (LTL$^{\mathcal{T}}$) extends LTL in the following way. First, the atomic predicates AP are substituted with literals from the theory. Second, LTL$^{\mathcal{T}}$ introduces two new term constructors $\triangleleft x$ and $\triangleright x$ (that apply to variables) with the intended meaning of retrieving the value of variable x. We use *fetch* (or look back) to refer to the $\triangleleft$ operator and *look ahead* for $\triangleright$. Then, for a set of variables V, we use $F(V)$ for the set of terms $V \cup \{\triangleleft x | x \in V\} \cup \{\triangleright x | x \in V\}$ and we extend the set of terms to $Terms(F(V))$ and the set of literals to $Lits(F(V))$. Then, the syntax of an LTL^T formula over variables V is

$$\varphi ::= T \mid l \mid \varphi \vee \varphi \mid \neg \varphi \mid \mathsf{X}\,\varphi \mid \varphi \mathcal{U} \varphi,$$

where $l \in Lits(F(V))$. Given a trace $\sigma \in \Sigma_T(V)^\omega$ we define the valuation of a variable as $[\![x]\!]_{(\sigma,i)} \overset{\text{def}}{=} \sigma(i)(x)$, and the valuation $[\![t]\!]_{(\sigma,i)}$ of a term $t \in Terms(F(V))$ (and of a literals $l \in Lits_T(F(V))$) at position i as recursively:

$$[\![\triangleleft x]\!]_{(\sigma,i)} \overset{\text{def}}{=} \sigma(i-1)(x) \text{ (or } d \text{ if } i = 0)$$
$$[\![\triangleright x]\!]_{(\sigma,i)} \overset{\text{def}}{=} \sigma(i+1)(x)$$
$$[\![t(s_1,\ldots,s_n)]\!]_{(\sigma,i)} \overset{\text{def}}{=} [\![t]\!]([\![s_1]\!]_{(\sigma,i)},\ldots,[\![s_1]\!]_{(\sigma,i)})$$
$$[\![l(s_1,\ldots,s_n)]\!]_{(\sigma,i)} \overset{\text{def}}{=} [\![l]\!]([\![s_1]\!]_{(\sigma,i)},\ldots,[\![s_1]\!]_{(\sigma,i)})$$

Then, the semantics of LTL^T associates traces $\sigma \in \Sigma_T(Vars(\varphi))^\omega$ with formulas φ as in LTL but considering the base case: $(\sigma,i) \models l$ whenever $[\![l]\!]_{(\sigma,i)}$ holds. The logic defined here is essentially equivalent (but for infinite traces) to LTL modulo theories in [15]. The previous syntax can be extended to allow nested $\triangleleft$ and $\triangleright$ operators, which can be eliminated linearly into equivalent formulas.

Eliminating $\triangleleft\triangleleft x$. Consider an arbitrary formula φ and a term $\triangleleft \triangleleft x$ in φ. Assume that y is assigned to the system. Let φ' be the formula $(\mathsf{X}\,\mathsf{G}\,(y_{new} = \triangleleft y) \wedge \varphi[\triangleleft y \leftarrow y_{new}])$. Let σ be a trace for φ and let us extend σ into σ' by adding the assignment to the new variable y_{new}, $\sigma'(i+1)(y_{new}) = \sigma(i)(y)$ and $\sigma'(0)(y_{new}) = d$. It is easy to see that $\sigma' \models \mathsf{X}\,\mathsf{G}\,(y_{new} = \triangleleft y)$, that $\sigma' \models \varphi$ if and only if $\sigma \models \varphi$, and that $\sigma' \models \varphi$ if and only if $\sigma' \models \varphi'$. The same argument can be followed for a variable x assigned to the environment creating φ' as $(\mathsf{X}\,\mathsf{G}\,(x_{new} = \triangleleft x) \rightarrow \varphi[\triangleleft x \leftarrow x_{new}])$.

Similarly, $\triangleright$ can also be eliminated by adding a X operator and shifting the variables in the formula introducing $\triangleleft$ if necessary.

Eliminating $\triangleright$. Consider a formula φ that contains a literal l with a term t that has $\triangleright x$ as a sub-term. We create a literal l' from l by replacing every term $\triangleright y$ with x, every term $\triangleleft y$ with $\triangleleft\triangleleft y$, and every variable z not preceded with $\triangleright$ or $\triangleleft$ with $\triangleleft z$. It is easy to see following the definitions of semantics and valuations that for every (σ,i) a $[\![l]\!]_{(\sigma,i)} = [\![l']\!]_{(\sigma,i+1)}$. Then, we replace l with $\mathsf{X}l'$ in φ and obtain a new equivalent formula φ'.

Based on the previous elimination methods, in the rest of the paper we consider LTL^T with only $\triangleleft$ in front of variables. The fragment of LTL^T that does not use the $\triangleleft$ operator is denoted by $\text{LTL}^T_{\not\triangleleft}$, which is the fragment used in [37]. We sometimes refer to this fragment as fetch-less LTL^T, which is exactly the logic obtained by replacing in LTL atomic propositions with literals from T.

Fetch within Bounds. Given an LTL^T formula, we say that the formula φ *fetches within bounds* whenever every evaluation of a term required to evaluate $(\sigma,i) \models \varphi$ for every σ and i does not require the default value d in the rule for evaluating $[\![\triangleleft x]\!]_{(\sigma,i)}$. If every term that contains a fetch variable $\triangleleft x$ occurs in a literal l that is within the scope of a X operator in φ, then φ fetches within bounds. All the formulas in the paper fetch within bounds.

Applying ◁ to Terms. Extending $\text{LTL}^{\mathcal{T}}$ and allowing ◁ to be applied to arbitrary term t does not add expressiveness, because we can apply recursively the rewriting $◁f(s_1, \ldots, s_n) \mapsto f(◁s_1, \ldots, ◁s_n)$ until ◁ is applied only to variables. It is easy to see that this rewriting preserves semantics, since $[\![◁f(s_1, \ldots, s_n)]\!]_{(\sigma,i)} = [\![f(◁s_1, \ldots, ◁s_n)]\!]_{(\sigma,i)}$ for every σ and i.

Reactive Synthesis for $\text{LTL}^{\mathcal{T}}$. Given an $\text{LTL}^{\mathcal{T}}$ formula φ the reactive synthesis problem for $\text{LTL}^{\mathcal{T}}$ splits the set of (theory) variables in $Vars(\varphi)$ between environment variables V_E and system variables V_S. In the corresponding game the environment and system players alternate choosing valuations of the variables they control, whose valuations are now theory values. An infinite sequence of moves forms now a trace σ in $\Sigma_{\mathcal{T}}(V_E \cup V_S)^{\omega}$, which is winning for the system if $\sigma \models \varphi$.

We classify the literals in φ as $L_E = \{l \mid Vars(l) \subseteq V_E\}$ and $L_S = Lits(\varphi) \setminus L_E$. A strategy is again a tuple $M : \langle Q, q_0, T \rangle$ where Q is a finite set of states, $q_0 \in Q$ is the initial state and $T \subseteq Q \times Q \times (2^{L_E}) \times (2^{L_S})$. In this case $t.env$ is a valuation of the environment literals and $t.sys$ is a valuations of the system literals. Given a transition t the $\mathcal{T}$ formulas E_t and S_t characterize the valuations of theory variables that satisfy the valuations of the literals in t:

$$E_t(\overline{x}) : \bigwedge_{l_e \in t.env} l_e(\overline{x}) \wedge \bigwedge_{l_e \notin t.env} \neg l_e(\overline{x})$$

$$S_t(\overline{x}, \overline{y}) : \bigwedge_{l_s \in t.sys} l_s(\overline{x}, \overline{y}) \wedge \bigwedge_{l_s \notin t.sys} \neg l_s(\overline{x}, \overline{y}) \qquad t(\overline{x}, \overline{y}) : E_t(\overline{x}) \wedge S_t(\overline{x}, \overline{y})$$

We call E_t and S_t the *characteristic formulas* of a transition. The notion of legal strategy for the environment and the system are analogous to the Boolean cases (for the environment legality all valuations of the variables of the system are considered for each environment move, and for the system legality all environment moves have a response). The following holds:

Theorem 1. *Let φ be an $\text{LTL}^{\mathcal{T}}$ specification.*

- *If there is winning strategy for the system player then φ is realizable.*
- *If there is winning strategy for the environment player then φ is unrealizable.*

Proof. (Sketch). Let φ be an $\text{LTL}^{\mathcal{T}}$ specification. Assume there is a winning strategy M for the system player. Hence, $Traces(M) \models \varphi$. We show that at each step the environment can play every possible move, i.e., for every suffix $(\overline{x}_0, \overline{y}_0) \ldots (\overline{x}_k, \overline{y}_k))$ of a trace $\sigma \in Traces(M)$ and every valuation $\overline{x}_{k+1}$ there is a $\overline{y}_{k+1}$ and trace σ' in $Traces(M)$ whose prefix is $(\overline{x}_0, \overline{y}_0) \ldots (\overline{x}_k, \overline{y}_k)(\overline{x}_{k+1}, \overline{y}_{k+1})$. Since M is legal for the system, for every q and $\overline{x}$ there is a transition t such that (1) $E_t(\overline{x})$ and (2) there is $\overline{y}$ with $S_t(\overline{x}, \overline{y})$. For $i = 0$ to k let us pick one such transition such that (1) and (2) hold for $\overline{x}_i$ and $\overline{y}_i$. Let q be the state reached.

For $k + 1$ let us pick a transition t out of q such that $E_t(\overline{x}_{k+1})$ holds and let $\overline{y}_{k+1}$ be such that $S_t(\overline{x}_{k+1}, \overline{y}_{k+1})$ holds. Let q' be the state reached. Since k is arbitrary the result holds. The result for the environment is analogous.   □

Note that, unfortunately, the opposite implications do not hold in general. If they did, one could enumerate the strategies of the system and the environment and traverse these sets in parallel, checking whether the strategies are legal and winning for the corresponding player. One of the two searches is guaranteed to terminate revealing the correct answer to realizability for $\mathrm{LTL}^{\mathcal{T}}$, which is undecidable, contradicting Theorem 3. It is also easy to show that the reverse implications cannot hold for every specification for the system (or for every specification for the environment). Given an $\mathrm{LTL}^{\mathcal{T}}$ specification φ we can construct another $\mathrm{LTL}^{\mathcal{T}}$ specification φ' over the same theory such that φ is realizable if and only if φ' is unrealizable.

The following is shown in [37], which is extended in [36,38] to full synthesis procedures using Skolem function generation or SMT queries to generate concrete theory outputs.

Theorem 2. *Realizability of* $\mathrm{LTL}^{\mathcal{T}}_{\mathcal{A}}$ *specifications is decidable.*

Example 1. Consider $\mathcal{T} = \mathcal{T}_{\mathbb{Z}}$ and the following specification φ_1 (left):

$$\varphi_1 : \mathsf{G} \left(\begin{array}{cc} (x < 0) \rightarrow \mathsf{X}(y \geq x) & \wedge \\ (x \geq 0) \rightarrow (y < x) & \end{array} \right) \qquad \varphi_1^{\mathbb{B}} : \mathsf{G} \left(\begin{array}{cc} l_0 \rightarrow \mathsf{X}l_2 & \wedge \\ l_1 \rightarrow l_3 & \end{array} \right)$$

where the variable x belongs to the uncontrollable environment and the variable y to the system. The environment strategy that assigns $x : -1$ at timestep 0 and $x : 1$ at timestep 1 is winning, so φ_1 is unrealizable. Note that the arena of the corresponding game is infinite so a naive explicit representation is not feasible. One approach to realizability [37] is to abstract φ_1 into an equi-realizable LTL specification. A naive abstraction of φ_1 is to replace each literal by a fresh Boolean variable like $\varphi_1^{\mathbb{B}}$ (right), where l_0 and l_1 belong to the environment and l_2 and l_3 belong to the system. Unfortunately, realizability between φ_1 and $\varphi_1^{\mathbb{B}}$ is not preserved because, in φ_1, literals $(y \geq x)$ and $(y < x)$ cannot happen at the same time, whereas l_2 and l_3 forget this constraint in $\varphi_1^{\mathbb{B}}$. Thus, a sound abstraction method would require to add additional constraints to $\varphi_1^{\mathbb{B}}$ that capture the dependencies between the literals.

If the system controls all variables, reactive synthesis becomes satisfiability, which is undecidable for $\mathrm{LTL}^{\mathcal{T}}_{\mathcal{A}}$ [15] (and can be trivially extended for $\mathrm{LTL}^{\mathcal{T}}$).

Theorem 3. *Realizability of arbitrary* $\mathrm{LTL}^{\mathcal{T}}$ *specifications is undecidable.*

Example 2. Recall φ_1 from Example 1 and consider $\varphi_2 : \left(\mathsf{X}\,\mathsf{G}\,[x < \triangleleft x] \rightarrow \mathsf{X}\varphi_1 \right)$, which encodes that x must be monotonically decreasing. Note that the strategy for the environment mentioned in Example 1 does not violate φ_2 because once the environment plays a value of x below 0, the upcoming valuations of x will need to also be below 0 (because of $\mathsf{G}[x < \triangleleft x]$), so the strategy of playing some

x below 0 at timestep k and some x above 0 in timestep $k + 1$ is no longer legal. In fact, φ_2 is realizable. Note that if $\triangleleft x$ is substituted by a fresh variable z controlled by the environment, that is $\varphi_2' : \left(\mathsf{X} \, \mathsf{G} \, [x < z] \rightarrow \mathsf{X}\varphi_1 \right)$ then φ_2' is again unrealizable. This naive abstraction over-approximates the power of the environment removing the monotonicity constraint. In other words, φ_2 and φ_2' are not equi-realizable.

4   Counter Example Guided Reactive Synthesis

We present now a novel method called *Counter-Example Guided Reactive Synthesis* (CEGRES) modulo theories, shown schematically in Fig. 1. Given a specification φ in a logic L, the CEGRES method first computes an abstraction φ' in a less expressive variant L'. The formulas φ and φ' are not necessarily equi-realizable. Then, a synthesis tool for L' is used to get the verdict v' (whether φ' is `real` or `unreal`), and a strategy M' for the winning player. Then, the method examines M' to check whether it corresponds to a consistent strategy for the higher logic L. If M' is consistent in L, then the verdict is conclusive, and we derive a machine M in L based on the machine M' in L', returning v' as verdict and M as answer. If, on the other hand, M' is inconsistent in L then the outcome is not conclusive. The method then finds a counterexample based on the inconsistencies in M and computes additional constraints which are incorporated to φ, reiterating the process with the strengthened formula. Note how in CEGRES we use an existing synthesis tool for a simpler logic to build a synthesis method for a richer logic. Both methods receive a temporal logic formula, with a split of the set of variables between environment and system, and both return a realizability outcome with a finite machine as witness.

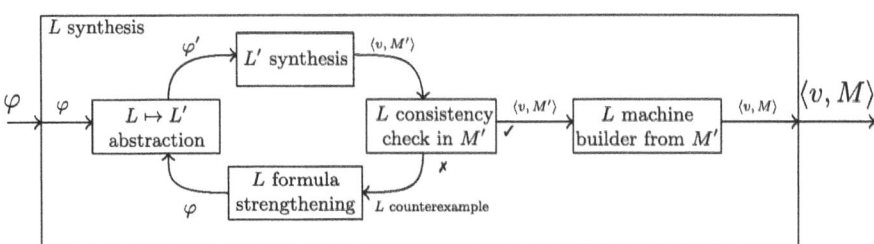

Fig. 1. CEGRES to generate a verdict v (real/unreal) and strategy M from φ.

CEGRES for LTL$_{\nexists}^{\mathcal{T}}$. We first illustrate the CEGRES method for LTL$_{\nexists}^{\mathcal{T}}$ specifications, using classical LTL as the internal synthesis tool box. The reactive synthesis problem for LTL$_{\nexists}^{\mathcal{T}}$ was solved in [37] using an explicit exhaustive exploration method. In contrast, CEGRES is much more lightweight because it captures only the necessary $\mathcal{T}$ information and avoids exploring all the potential reactions. As we will see in Sect. 6 this is the fastest algorithm up to date for realizability and synthesis for $\text{LTL}_{\cancel{A}}^{\mathcal{T}}$. The abstraction in CEGRES for $\text{LTL}_{\cancel{A}}^{\mathcal{T}}$ combines a naive abstraction $\varphi_{-}^{\mathbb{B}}$ of φ—that simply translates literals to Boolean variables—with a set of assumptions A that constrain the plays of the environment and a set of guarantees G that constrain the legal responses of the system. The resulting formula is $\varphi^{\mathbb{B}}$: $GA \to (GG \wedge \varphi_{-}^{\mathbb{B}})$, where A and G are non-temporal Boolean formulas that constrain the combinations of literal valuations preventing $\mathcal{T}$ inconsistencies.

We instantiate the CEGRES components for $\text{LTL}_{\cancel{A}}^{\mathcal{T}}$ as follows:

- L is $\text{LTL}_{\cancel{A}}^{\mathcal{T}}$ (φ is an $\text{LTL}_{\cancel{A}}^{\mathcal{T}}$ formula) and L' is LTL;
- φ' is the (propositional) LTL formula obtained by replacing literals by fresh Boolean variables (the Boolean variables that abstract L_E are assigned to the environment, and the variables that abstract L_S, to the system);
- the internal solver is an off-the-shelf LTL synthesis tool (e.g., Strix [30]) and M' is a Mealy machine encoding a strategy of the winning player.
- the derivation of M from M' uses either Skolem function generation [36] or SMT queries [38] on $\forall\exists$ queries that are guaranteed to be satisfiable.
- the CEGRES refinement is based on the following lemma, where a counterexample is a tautology in $\mathcal{T}$ that is falsified in a transition of M'.

Lemma 1. *Given a strategy M' for a φ' that is realizable (resp. unrealizable), if for every transition $t \in M'$, the formula: $\exists\overline{x}.E_t(\overline{x}) \wedge \forall\overline{x}.(E_t(\overline{x}) \to \exists\overline{y}.S_t(\overline{x},\overline{y}))$ is valid, then φ is realizable (resp. unrealizable).*

The proof proceeds by contradiction, assuming that φ is not equi-realizable with respect to φ', taking a loosing play according to M and generating a loosing play played according to M', which is a contradiction.

The CEGRES method for $\text{LTL}_{\cancel{A}}^{\mathcal{T}}$ is shown in Algorithm 1 and it works as follows.

Algorithm 1: CEGRES for $\text{LTL}_{\cancel{A}}^{\mathcal{T}}$.

---

1 **Require:** φ
2 $A, G \leftarrow true$
3 $done \leftarrow false$
4 **while** $\neg done$ **do**
5     $\varphi^{\mathbb{B}} \leftarrow abstract(A \to (G \wedge \varphi))$
6     $is\_real, \mathcal{M} \leftarrow synth(\varphi^{\mathbb{B}})$
7     $T \leftarrow get\_trans(\mathcal{M})$
8     $done \leftarrow true$
9   **if** $\neg is\_real$ **then**
10   **foreach** $t{:}T$ **do** $check\_env(t)$;
11   **else**
12   **foreach** $t{:}T$ **do** $check\_sys(t)$;
13 **return** $is\_real, \mathcal{M}$

14 $check\_env(t)$
15     $E(\overline{x}) \leftarrow t.env$
16   **if** $\exists\overline{x}.E(\overline{x})$ *invalid* **then**
17         $A \leftarrow A \wedge \neg E(\overline{x})$
18         $done \leftarrow false$

19 $check\_sys(t)$
20     $E(\overline{x}) \leftarrow t.env$
21     $S(\overline{x},\overline{y}) \leftarrow t.sys$
22   **if** $\left(\begin{array}{c}\forall\overline{x}.E(\overline{x}) \to \\ \exists\overline{y}.S(\overline{x},\overline{y})\end{array}\right)$ *invalid* **then**
23         $G \leftarrow G \wedge (S(\overline{x},\overline{y}) \to \exists\overline{y}.S(\overline{x},\overline{y}))$
24         $done \leftarrow false$

- The abstraction method (line 5) assigns a fresh Boolean variable for each literal, and tags it as controlled by the environment if it only contains variables from the environment, and controlled by the system otherwise. Then, $\varphi^{\mathbb{B}}$ is obtained from φ by replacing each literal by its associated Boolean variable.
- Then, an off-the-shelf synthesis tool receives $\varphi^{\mathbb{B}}$ as input and produces a Mealy machine M as a winning strategy for the system if $\varphi^{\mathbb{B}}$ is realizable, or for the environment if $\varphi^{\mathbb{B}}$ is unrealizable.
- If $\varphi^{\mathbb{B}}$ is unrealizable, the method *check_env* is invoked for each transition t, and line 16 checks whether $\exists \overline{x}.E_t(\overline{x})$ is valid. If the check fails for some transition, the result is inconclusive because the environment may be winning by using illegal moves. In this case line 17 incorporates to A the fact that $E_t(\overline{x})$ is unsatisfiable and restarts the process with the refined formula. This is performed for all illegal environment moves detected.
- If $\varphi^{\mathbb{B}}$ is realizable, *check_sys* is invoked for every transition t, which checks for every $\overline{x}$ that makes $E_t(\overline{x})$ hold, there is a $\overline{y}$ that makes $S_t(\overline{x},\overline{y})$ hold as well (in line 22). If the formula is not valid, then the transition t is illegal: there is an $\overline{x}$ that satisfies $E_t(\overline{x})$ for which there is no $\overline{y}$ that satisfies $S_t(\overline{x},\overline{y})$. That is, $(\exists \overline{x}.E_t(\overline{x}) \wedge \neg(\exists \overline{y}.S_t(\overline{x},\overline{y})))$ is valid. In particular, $(\exists \overline{x}.\neg(\exists \overline{y}.S_t(\overline{x},\overline{y})))$ holds. That is, we found that the system can make the formula $S_t(\overline{x},\overline{y})$ hold only if the environment makes the formula $\exists \overline{y}.S_t(\overline{x},\overline{y})$ hold. We incorporate this information as a strengthening predicate into the specification $S_t(\overline{x},\overline{y}) \rightarrow \exists \overline{y}.S_t(\overline{x},\overline{y})$ to G, and we reiterate the process with the updated formula.

Algorithm 1 finishes when there are no inconsistencies in M according to Theorem 1, generating a correct verdict and strategy. Algorithm 1 is guaranteed to terminate, generating no more strengthening predicates than "reactions" allowed by the set of literals in the formula (see [37]). In practice this method generates considerably fewer strengthenings (which is the why it dramatically improves scalability). The following theorem establishes the correctness of CEGRES for $LTL^{\mathcal{T}}$.

Theorem 4 (Correctness of Algorithm *1*). *Algorithm 1 terminates and produces an equi-realizable LTL formula $\varphi^{\mathbb{B}}$ along with a strategy for the winning player in φ.*

Proof. (Sketch). Consider an execution of Algorithm 1. If the algorithm terminates, the strategy found is legal and winning for the corresponding player, so according to Theorem 1 the result is correct. Therefore we only need to prove termination. The formulas in line 21 are bounded by combinations of L_S so the set is bounded by $2^{|L_S|}$. In turn, the set of predicates $E(\overline{x})$ is bounded by $|L_E|$ plus the new literals that can be generated in the quantifier elimination of line 23 (the elimination of $\overline{y}$ in $\exists \overline{y}.S(\overline{x},\overline{y})$ can generate a new environment literal). Therefore the size of the set of environment literals in combinations from E is also bounded by $|L_E| + 2^{|L_S|}$. This also limits the number of $E(\overline{x})$ formulas in line 16. In every iteration either the main loop terminates or at least a new formula from a finite set is added to A or to G. Hence, Algorithm 1 terminates with the correct answer. □

5   Reactive Synthesis for LTL$^{\mathcal{T}}$

We now study CEGRES for LTL$^{\mathcal{T}}$. The main idea is to (1) abstract all fetch terms by fresh variables controlled by the environment (thus over-approximating the power of the environment). Then (2) solve the resulting LTL$^{\mathcal{T}}_{\mathcal{A}}$ specification and analyze the winning strategy, which is either conclusive, or we learn how to limit the over-approximation power of the environment to avoid similar illegal moves.

Example 3. Consider the LTL$^{\mathcal{T}}$ specification over $V_E : \{x\}$ and $V_S : \{y\}$:

$$\mathsf{G}\,(x < 10) \to \mathsf{X}\,\mathsf{G}\,(x < \lhd y).$$

This specification states that, assuming that the environment variable x is always less than 10, then the system can provide a value y that is always greater than the next value of x. This specification is realizable (for example, by simply producing $y : 11$ at all instants). If we replace the expression $\lhd y$ by a fresh variable y' that represents the previous value of y and assign it *to the environment*, we obtain a property in LTL$^{\mathcal{T}}_{\mathcal{A}}$ over $V_E : \{x, y'\}$ and $V_S : \{y\}$:

$$\mathsf{G}\,(x < 10) \to \mathsf{X}\,\mathsf{G}\,(x < y')$$

which is trivially unrealizable because the environment can play $x : 9, y' : 9$ at all instants. However, if we strengthen the assumption with $\mathsf{X}(y' < 10) \to (y < 10)$ (which is trivially an LTL$^{\mathcal{T}}$ temporal validity, that is, it holds at all instants of all traces), which is equivalent to $\neg(y < 10) \to \mathsf{X}\neg(y' < 10)$):

$$\mathsf{G}\,[(x < 10) \wedge \big(\mathsf{X}\,(y' < 10) \to (y < 10)\big)] \to \mathsf{X}\,\mathsf{G}\,(x > y')$$

The resulting LTL$^{\mathcal{T}}$ formula is realizable.

5.1   A General CEGRES Method for LTL$^{\mathcal{T}}$

We instantiate the CEGRES components in Fig. 1 as follows:

- the input logic L is LTL$^{\mathcal{T}}$, so φ is an LTL$^{\mathcal{T}}$ formula.
- the logic L' after the abstraction is LTL$^{\mathcal{T}}_{\mathcal{A}}$ and φ' is the formula obtained by replacing every expression $\lhd v$ by a fresh *environment variable* v'.
- the inner solver is Algorithm 1 from Sect. 4.

Before we describe the method in detail we need some auxiliary definitions. We use $\bar{v}s' : V_F$ to describe the set of primed variables that have replaced the fetch terms. For example, in the example above, we have $V_E : \{x\}$, $V_S : \{y\}$, and $V_F : \{y'\}$. The variables in V_F belong to the environment.

The next definition captures a constraint that every pair of consecutive steps in a strategy M must satisfy for M to be legal according to the semantics of $\lhd$.

Definition 1. *Given a candidate strategy M and given two consecutive transitions t_{pre} and t (i.e., $t_{pre}.to = t.from$), the following formula $C_{t_{pre},t}$ is the consistency condition for (t_{pre}, t).*

$$\forall(\overline{x}_0 : V_E), (\overline{v}'_0 : V_F), (\overline{y}_0 : V_S).t_{pre}(\overline{x}_0 \cup \overline{v}'_0, \overline{y}_0) \rightarrow$$
$$\begin{pmatrix} \exists(\overline{x}_1 : V_E), (\overline{v}'_1 : V_F).(\varphi_{pr} \wedge E_t(\overline{x}_1 \cup \overline{v}'_1)) \wedge \\ \forall(\overline{x}_1 : V_E), (\overline{v}'_1 : V_F).(\varphi_{pr} \wedge E_t(\overline{x}_1 \cup \overline{v}'_1) \rightarrow (\exists \overline{y}_1 : V_S).t(\overline{x}_1 \cup \overline{v}'_1, \overline{y}_1)) \end{pmatrix}$$

where

$$\varphi_{pr} \stackrel{def}{=} \bigwedge_{v'_1 \in \overline{v}'_1} (v'_1 = v_0).$$

This formula essentially captures that the values of the variables in a transition coincide with the values of their corresponding fetched variables in the successive transition.

The following theorem guarantees that if a strategy for an abstracted formula satisfies the constraint for all two consecutive transitions, then the strategy is valid for the original $LTL^{\mathcal{T}}$ formula.

Theorem 5. *Let φ be an $LTL^{\mathcal{T}}$ formula and φ' the $LTL^{\mathcal{T}}_{\mathcal{A}}$ formula obtained by replacing all fetch terms by primed variables. Given a winning strategy M' for φ', if every two consecutive transitions t_{pre} and t satisfy $C_{t_{pre},t}$, then we can obtain a winning strategy M for the same player for φ.*

Proof. (Sketch). It is enough to build a winning strategy M for φ from M'. M contains the same states and transitions as M', but at every step the environment player is additionally given the values of the fetched variables at the previous instant, and its characteristic formula constrained to choose these values at every point (except at the first instant). It holds that the environment characteristic formula with these additional constraints is always satisfiable (due to the check performed before terminating). This strategy M preserves the semantics of the operators, it is a legal strategy and it is a winning strategy for the same player as the winner of M'. $\square$

If $C_{t_{pre},t}$ fails for some consecutive t_{pre} and t, the CEGRES method will strengthen the environment assumptions of φ by learning tautologies using the following concepts.

Definition 2 (Environment Ability). *Given a strategy M and transition t with environment and characteristic formulas E_t and S_t, the following formula*

$$A_t(\overline{v}) \stackrel{def}{=} \exists(\overline{x} : V_E).E_t(\overline{x} \cup \overline{v})$$

captures the ability of the environment of choosing environment variables $\overline{x}$ and satisfy the environment play of t, given the variables $\overline{v}$.

Given an ability formula A_t extracted from transition t we assign $R_t(\overline{v})$ to be the formula $X A_t(\overline{v}') \rightarrow A_t(\overline{v})$. The following lemma justifies that formulas of the form of R_t are tautologies, called *reactive tautologies*.

Lemma 2. *Given a trace σ, an instant i such that, for every $v' : V_F$, $\sigma(i)(v) = \sigma(i+1)(v')$. Let $Q(\overline{v}')$ be a predicate over V_F. Then, $(\sigma, i) \models XQ(\overline{v}') \rightarrow Q(\overline{v})$.*

The lemma follows immediately because the value of $Q(v')$ at time $i + 1$ is exactly the value of $Q(v)$ at time i.

An example of reactive tautology, shown in Example 3 above is $(\ X\ (y' < 10) \rightarrow (y < 10))$, obtained from $y' < 10$. Given a formula $C_{t_{pre},t}$ for a pair of consecutive transitions, adding R_t (the reactive tautology of the second transition) to the environment assumptions of φ prevents the inner synthesis step from searching similarly illegal transitions in the next iteration of the CEGRES method. Unfortunately, this does not guarantee termination because the machine in the new iteration can contain other transitions with new literals and formulas.

Algorithm 2: CEGRES for Full LTL^T.

---

1 **Require:** φ
2 **while** *true* **do**
3     $\varphi^e \leftarrow overApprEnv(\varphi)$
4     $M \leftarrow synth(\varphi^e)$
5   **if** φ^e *is* **real then**
6 | **return real**
7   **else if** $consTmp(M)$ **then**
8 | **return unreal**
9   **else**
10       $\lfloor\ \varphi \leftarrow addTempTaut(M, \varphi)$

Based on Theorem 5 we present a CEGRES algorithm that uses the concept of reactive tautology in the learning phase, in Algorithm 2 (left). Since our method over-approximates the power of the environment, a **real** verdict immediately implies that the original specification φ is realizable with the strategy found. Otherwise, the checker component checks (line 7) whether for every pair of successive transitions t_{pre} and t, the formula $C_{t_{pre};t}$ in Theorem 5 holds. If every pair is fine, Theorem 5 implies that the machine obtained is winning for the environment. Otherwise, the reactive tautologies R_t learned are added (line 10) to the environment assumptions of φ for every outgoing transition t of a failing pair.

The check for $C_{t_{pre};t}$ above can be accelerated using the following result.

Lemma 3. *If R_t is in the environment assumption of φ, then every pair of consecutive transitions t_{pre} and t satisfies $C_{t_{pre};t}$ in Theorem 5.*

Proof. (Sketch). Follows from simple algebraic transformations   □

Example 4. Consider again $\varphi : G(x > 10) \rightarrow X\ G\ (x > \triangleleft y)$ from Example 3. Algorithm 2 proceeds as follows:

1. Abstract φ into φ'.
2. The inner LTL^T computes internally the abstraction $\varphi^{\mathbb{B}} : Gl_0 \rightarrow X\ G\ (l_1)$, where both l_0 and l_1 belong to the environment.
3. Next, an LTL synthesis tool discovers that $\varphi^{\mathbb{B}}$ is unrealizable and provides a Mealy machine $M_{\mathbb{B}}$ that witnesses the strategy of the environment. $M_{\mathbb{B}}$ has a single transition t, whose corresponding environment play is $E_t = (x \leq y') \wedge (x > 10)$ and the system play is $S_t = true$, which means that the system's choice is irrelevant.

4. CEGRES for LTL$_\lhd^\mathcal{T}$ (Algorithm 1) checks that $M_\mathbb{B}$ has no inconsistencies in $\mathcal{T}$.

5. Then, the temporal analysis reveals that $M_\mathbb{B}$ might not be valid because the check of traversing t twice:

$$\forall x_0, y_0', y_0.((x_0 \leq y_0') \wedge (x_0 > 10)) \rightarrow$$
$$\left(\begin{array}{l} \exists x_1, y_1'.((y_0 = y_1') \wedge ((x_1 \leq y_1') \wedge (x_1 > 10))) \wedge \\ \forall x_1, y_1'.((y_0 = y_1') \wedge (x_1 \leq y_1') \wedge (x_1 > 10)) \rightarrow (\exists y_1).((x_1 \leq y_1') \wedge (x_1 > 10)) \end{array} \right)$$

is not valid. In particular, it is not true that for every y_0 there are x_1 and y_1' such that $(y_0 = y_1') \wedge ((x_1 \leq y_1') \wedge (x_1 > 10))$—it suffices to take any y_0 lower than 11. From the transition t, the algorithm explores the conditions that system-controlled variables must meet to make E_t satisfiable, in particular, it explores the ability $A_t(y') = \exists x.(x \leq y') \wedge (x > 10)$ or, equivalently via quantifier elimination, $A_t(y') = (y' < 11)$.

6. Then, $R_t : \mathsf{X}(y' < 11) \rightarrow (y < 11)$ is added to φ, obtaining $\varphi' : R_t \rightarrow \varphi$, invoking again the abstraction and LTL synthesis and obtaining a new M', that this time is consistent in LTL$^\mathcal{T}$.

7. Finally, the algorithm constructs a machine M in LTL$^\mathcal{T}$ from M' and returns the realizability verdict along with the witness M^1.

5.2   CEGRES for Bounded Domains

We now study CEGRES for LTL$^\mathcal{T}$ for a very important practical domain: bounded theories and in particular bounded arithmetic. This theory is very important in the specification of embedded critical systems. A typical scenario in embedded systems uses numeric domains (like 32 bit integers) where bit operations are used instead of ideal integers.

In theory, one can blast all variables in the specification, for example for an 8 bit signed variable d, one would introduce 256 Boolean variables $d_{-127} \ldots d_{128}$, and include all corresponding precise rules of arithmetic, like $d_0 < d_1$, $d_1 < d_2$, $\ldots$, and temporal rules $d_0 \rightarrow \mathsf{X}{\lhd}d_0$ and $d_1 = d_0 + 1$, etc. This blasting method generates 256 atomic propositions for each 8-bit numeric variable which does not scale for the example above. Even though one can use a logarithmic encoding and capture arithmetic operations and relations, LTL synthesis does not scale either. Instead, we propose using Algorithm 2 directly—which results in a much faster procedure, and it is guaranteed to terminate for bounded domains. Specifications in LTL$^\mathcal{T}$ are much more succinct and close to the human intention than their blasted versions.

We envision the impact of our solution to be analogous to bit-vectors solvers in SMT, in the sense that practitioners can trust precise solutions which can also be much faster (and in our case produce much simpler strategies). For the sake of simplicity we consider LTL$^\mathcal{T}$ for the theory $\mathcal{T} = \mathbb{Z}^k$ of bounded integer arithmetic (for example $\mathbb{Z}^{32}$ for 32 bit signed integer arithmetic).

---

[1] The construction of the full machine for φ from the inner M' can be done analogously to [36,38] but the details are not included here due to space limitations.

Example 5. Consider the following scenario of a water tank evolution. At each timestep, the environment provides a *stamina* value d (between 0 and 40) that models the effect on the water tank of inflow and outflow of water, where two valves (input and output) control the income and output of water into the tank. Additionally, there is a non-observable *rain* of extra water that can be added to the tank when the input valve is opened, and also some non-observable *leak* of water that controls the amount of outgoing water when the output valve is opened. We model the effect of the valves as inequalities rather than exact equalities. The safety goal of the controller is to make the water level wl, which the system controls, between 0 and 1000. We express this as the following $\text{LTL}^{\mathcal{T}}$ specification with, for example, domain $\mathbb{Z}^{16}$ (that is, 16-bit integers).

$$\varphi : \mathsf{G}(0 < d < 40) \to \mathsf{G}\left(\begin{array}{ccc} \mathsf{X}(wl > \lhd wl + d) & \vee & \mathsf{X}(wl < \lhd wl - d) \\ & \wedge & \\ & (0 < wl < 1000) & \end{array}\right)$$

One simple strategy that our method finds is to let the tank fill until it is close to being full or let it drain until it is nearly empty.

One important question is whether CEGRES for $\text{LTL}^{\mathcal{T}}$ and bounded domains like $\mathbb{Z}^{32}$ terminates. The following theorem provides a positive answer.

Theorem 6. *Algorithm 2 terminates for every* $\text{LTL}^{\mathcal{T}}$ *formula with a bounded domain.*

Proof. (Sketch). The idea of the proof is to first observe that all reactive tautologies that can be found are equivalent to a finite collection of ground axioms of arithmetic for bounded domains, and that this collection is finite. Then, at each iteration of the algorithm, either the correct solution is found or a new reactive tautology is found that corresponds to a new set of axiom that the previous tautologies did not cover. In other words, every new tautologies strictly expands the set of axioms covered. Since the largest set of axioms is finite, after a finite number of iterations, either the algorithm has already converged providing the right answer or all axioms are captured. At this point, the algorithm is guaranteed to terminate in the next iteration. □

Even though the bound provided by Theorem 6 can be large, in practice the algorithm runs much faster and produces a much smaller and understandable controller than a blasting strategy. This is because the algorithm can reuse moves in the strategy for many different states, particularly when the situation is far from the boundaries established in the specification. Many times the algorithm takes comparable time and yields equivalent systems when using 8 bit, 16 bit or 32 bit arithmetic (or changing boundaries like 40 and 1000 to 4000 and 60000 above), where a blasting strategy would not scale for large bound, and generate a convoluted solution when it terminates for small domains.

6   Empirical Evaluation

In order to evaluate the applicability of our approach, we carried out an empirical evaluation that intends to address the following research questions:

- **RQ1**: Is CEGRES faster for $\text{LTL}^{\mathcal{T}}_{\mathcal{A}}$ than previous methods?
- **RQ2**: How well does CEGRES for full $\text{LTL}^{\mathcal{T}}$ perform when solving TSL-MT style specifications?
- **RQ3**: Is CEGRES for full $\text{LTL}^{\mathcal{T}}$ capable of solving arbitrary $\text{LTL}^{\mathcal{T}}$ specifications?

To address these questions, we implemented a prototype tool for synthesizing $\text{LTL}^{\mathcal{T}}$ specifications called `syntheos`[2]. The tool is written in Python and uses Z3 [31] for the SMT queries necessary in the Boolean abstraction, and Strix [30] to check the realizability of the abstraction. Strategies are Mealy machines in the standard `HOA` format. All our tests were run using a MacBook Air (M1, 2020) machine, with processes limited to 16GB.

RQ1: CEGRES for $\text{LTL}^{\mathcal{T}}_{\mathcal{A}}$. In order to address **RQ1**, we consider the industry-inspired benchmarks from [37] and compare with their results. Table 1 shows the name of each benchmark, the number of variables ($|V|$) and literals ($|L|$), the number of strengthenings in eager methods (Prv.), the running time of the different versions of the eager algorithms from [37] with accelerating heuristics (T_{prv}), the time for Algorithm 1 (T_{CG}) TO means time-out after 12 h of execution. As expected, CEGRES outperforms [37] in running time, especially for large instances (which cannot be solved with eager methods). Indeed, these experiments show that eager methods are not tractable for realistic-size instances. We hypothesize that CEGRES performs better because it produces a smaller amount of refinements, that is., the number of literals in the final specification is smaller. This means that the original specification suffers less modifications. Comparing specification interpretability before and after the abstraction processes among different methods is a possible research direction (where the preferred method is the one that modifies the original specification the least).

RQ2: CEGRES for the TSL-MT fragment. In order to answer **RQ2**, we first observe that the syntax of $\text{LTL}^{\mathcal{T}}$ is strictly subsumes that of TSL-MT. We use a complete recent set of benchmarks from [20], which consists of TSL-MT specifications in integer arithmetic. The columns I and O in Table 2 indicate the number of input and output variables in the specification, respectively. The column R? in that table indicates whether the specification is realizable or not. The column CG indicates the time it takes for the CEGRES algorithm to finish. The columns that are not CG correspond to specialized TSL-MT solvers: MO, WI are monitored and non-monitored versions for `tslmt2rpg` [20], RA corresponds to `raboniel` [25] and TE corresponds to `temos` [7]. We ran all the experiments in the same machine. As we can see, in most cases, CG either timeouts (TO)

---

[2] Syntheos is available at https://github.com/imdea-software/syntheos.

Table 1. Comparison of [37] with our CEGRES method (time is in seconds).

#	Name	$|V|$	$|L|$	Prv.	T_{prv}	T_{CG}
1	Lift 1	1	7	2^{2^7}	31.77	1
2	Lift 2	2	4	2^{2^4}	0.7	1
3	Lift 1-2	3	11	$2^{2^{11}}$	TO	1
4	Lift 3	1	3	2^{2^3}	0.52	1
5	Lift 1-3	4	14	2^{2^3}	TO	1
6	Lift 4	1	2	2^{2^2}	0.09	1
7	Lift All	5	16	$2^{2^{16}}$	TO	1
8	Train 1	1	3	2^{2^3}	0.04	1
9	Train 2	2	1	2^{2^1}	0.04	1
10	Train 3	1	3	2^{2^3}	0.21	1
11	Train 4	1	1	2^{2^1}	0.05	1
12	Train 1-4	4	9	2^{2^1}	TO	1
13	Train 5	4	5	2^{2^5}	112.5	1
14	Train 6	3	5	2^{2^5}	359.3	1
15	Train 7	4	12	$2^{2^{12}}$	6571	1
16	Train 5-7	11	22	$2^{2^{12}}$	TO	1
17	Train All	19	26	$2^{2^{26}}$	TO	2
18	Connect	2	2	2^{2^2}	0.09	1
19	Cooker	3	5	2^{2^5}	2.81	1
20	Usb 1	2	3	2^{2^3}	0.17	1
21	Usb 2	3	5	2^{2^5}	231.9	1
22	Usb All	5	8	2^{2^8}	TO	1
23	Stages 1	8	8	2^{2^8}	18.19	1
24	Stages 2	3	6	2^{2^6}	194.8	1
25	Stages All	11	14	$2^{2^{14}}$	TO	1

after 20 min or solves the benchmark, but in a worse time than some TSL-MT competitors. This is expected because we are comparing CEGRES—which is a general LTL$^{\mathcal{T}}$ solver—against tools that are specific for TSL-MT. However, we find some instances in which CG finishes but no TSL-MT solver can.

It is very important to note that the most difficult task for CG is to find the appropriate reactive tautologies for each benchmark. Once the tautologies have been found, the proof finishes in one iteration (see **RQ3**), so checking proofs once the appropriate tautologies are provided is fast. Proofs are sometimes simplified by adding facts of the specification like $\mathsf{G}(x > \lhd x)$ or validities like $(\mathsf{G}(x > \lhd x)) \to \mathsf{F}(x > 1000)$. Therefore, a line of future work is to explore the addition of simple arithmetic and temporal facts to specifications; for instance, generation of tautologies via the invariant generation of [20].

RQ3: CEGRES for General LTL$^{\mathcal{T}}$. Since the syntax of TSL-MT is oriented to extracting programs more easily (as the system is restricted to a finite number of known assignments), the previous benchmarks are not able to use all the expressive power of LTL$^{\mathcal{T}}$. An example is `fut-work` from Table 2, which is a benchmark from [20] that cannot be solved (and is not clear how to express) in previous tools because it includes a relation across time: $x = 0 \land \mathsf{X}\,\mathsf{G}\,(x > \lhd x) \land \mathsf{F}(x < 0)$. In practice, these relations are useful because they allow us to express rich dynamics of both players (as in Example 2).

Therefore, we evaluate now the merits of our tool with specifications in general LTL$^{\mathcal{T}}$, with no restriction in $\mathcal{T}$, temporal fragment or operators across time. Since there are no benchmarks to compare with, we randomly took some examples of Table 2, but modified them in order to include relations and randomly

Table 2. Comparison between TSL-MT methods and our approach for all the benchmarks by [20] (measured in s).

Name	I	O	R?	CG	MO	WI	RA	TE	Name	I	O	R?	CG	MO	WI	RA	TE
Box Lim.	2	2	R	TO	7	1	1	MO	thrmF	2	1	R	MO	77	TO	TO	MO
Box	2	2	R	394	33	3	1	TO	thrmFur	2	1	U	MO	142	TO	TO	–
Diagonal	2	1	R	MO	43	1	5	MO	thrmGF	2	1	R	MO	TO	TO	TO	MO
Evasion	4	2	R	MO	82	4	2	TO	thrmGFur	2	1	U	MO	136	TO	TO	–
Follow	4	2	R	TO	TO	18	TO	TO	ordvisit	2	1	R	MO	488	TO	TO	TO
Solitary	2	0	R	278	8	1	1	ER	ptrl-alr	2	2	R	TO	TO	TO	TO	MO
Sqr-5x5	2	2	R	MO	203	10	43	TO	ptrl	2	0	R	MO	277	TO	ER	TO
E.Smp 3	1	0	R	111	27	2	1	MO	charging	3	1	R	6	287	TO	TO	TO
E.Smp 4	1	0	R	333	47	2	1	MO	charge-ur	3	1	U	MO	39	TO	TO	–
E.Smp 5	1	0	R	1124	74	4	4	TO	rtarget	3	1	R	MO	398	TO	TO	MO
E.Smp 8	1	0	R	TO	211	8	23	TO	rtrgt-ur	3	1	U	MO	314	TO	TO	–
E.Smp10	1	0	R	TO	356	11	98	TO	unordvisit	2	0	R	TO	253	TO	ER	TO
E.Sgnl 3	2	1	R	MO	MO	MO	17	MO	helipad	3	6	R	MO	102	MO	TO	MO
E.Sgnl 4	2	1	R	MO	MO	MO	111	MO	delivery	5	2	R	38	88	MO	TO	MO
E.Sgnl 5	2	1	R	TO	MO	MO	735	MO	tasks	3	0	R	191	TO	TO	ER	MO
G-real	3	1	R	MO	330	MO	3	TO	tasks-ur	3	0	U	186	334	TO	ER	–
G-ur-1	2	1	U	MO	27	TO	TO	–	buffer-st	3	1	R	47	TO	TO	45	MO
G-ur-2	2	1	U	1	28	TO	ER	–	heli-cont	2	0	U	1	182	15	TO	–
G-ur-3	1	0	U	1	46	TO	ER	–	ord-ch.	2	0	R	TO	TO	TO	ER	TO
F-real	3	1	R	4	66	TO	ER	ER	precise	2	0	R	12	TO	ER	ER	–
F-unreal	2	1	U	MO	104	TO	TO	–	st.-GF-64	2	0	R	1	TO	TO	ER	MO
FGcntr1	1	0	U	1	34	TO	ER	–	unord-ch	3	0	R	TO	TO	TO	TO	TO
FGcntr2	2	1	U	5	137	TO	1	–	unsat	2	1	U	MO	133	TO	ER	–
GF-real	1	1	R	MO	7	TO	ER	ER	vacuous	2	1	R	MO	24	TO	ER	ER
GF-ur	1	0	U	28	18	TO	TO	–	dschrg-GF	2	1	R	MO	19	TO	TO	ER
GF-contr	1	1	U	TO	8	TO	ER	–	fut-work	2	1	R	1	–	–	–	–

removed some subformulae. We also designed 5 additional benchmarks that illustrate the importance of expressing environment dynamics. In all of them, like in Example 2, an LTL$_{\lhd}^{\mathcal{T}}$ version that does not consider the environment dynamics properly using $\lhd$ results in an unrealizable verdict, whereas the full LTL$^{\mathcal{T}}$ version considers such dynamics and is realizable. Most importantly, the *oracle* version shows that CEGRES terminates in a single iteration of the outer loop (the one solving full LTL$^{\mathcal{T}}$) when key reactive tautologies are added manually in advance (as anticipated in **RQ2**). Table 3 shows the results, where we can see that TSL-MT tools do not express any of these benchmarks, while the reported times in CEGRES were very similar to Table 2. Also, note that all of these bench-

Table 3. Showcasing performance of CEGRES with full LTL$^{\mathcal{T}}$ specifications and limitation of TSL-MT expressivity (measured in s).

Name	I	O	R?	CG	TSL	Name	Auto	Oracle	TSL
Future-Work	1	0	U	1	–	AD-Real	1	1	–
E. Signal-3	2	1	R	6	–	AD-Unreal	1	–	–
E. Signal-4	2	1	R	7	–	TC-Real	3	1	–
E. Signal-5	2	1	R	9	–	TC-Unreal	1	–	–
Ordered-vis.	2	1	R	22	–	SL-Real	84	2	–
Buff-storage	3	1	R	63	–	SL-Unreal	1	–	–
Ordered-vis-ch.	2	0	R	7	–	MS-Real	3	1	–
Prec.-reachab.	2	0	R	6	–	MS-Unreal	1	–	–
Stor.-GF	2	0	R	2	–	PM-Real	16	1	–
Unordered-vs	3	0	R	26	–	PM-Unreal	1	–	–

marks are solved by Algorithm 2 iteration due to the use of CEGRES for LTL$^{\mathcal{T}}_{\mathcal{A}}$ (Algorithm 1).

RQ4: CEGRES for Bounded Domains. Additionally, we ask ourselves the following question: can, in some case, LTL$^{\mathcal{T}}$ be a better specification language than LTL bit-blasting and does CEGRES scales better? Example 5 shows that LTL$^{\mathcal{T}}$ can be more succinct than LTL, because it can symbolically represents numerous states. Now, we consider again Example 5 (WT-Signal) and a version with no environment (WT-Simple) both with different scalability parameters: see Table 4 and the figure at its side (where brown and blue correspond to LTL and black and red to LTL$^{\mathcal{T}}$). The results show that performance is not compromised when the parameters take larger values. Moreover, for Example 5 the blasting approach does not scale to bounds higher than 20, whereas in LTL$^{\mathcal{T}}$ this bound is not relevant for the example, because the technique directly explores fine-grain solutions close to the boundaries and abstracts the rest. Surprisingly, in Example 5, the larger the bounds, the sooner our method is able to check

Table 4. Scalability comparison of LTL$^{\mathcal{T}}$ vs blasting for Example 5.

#	WL-Simple		WL-Signal	
	LTL	LTL$^{\mathcal{T}}$	LTL	LTL$^{\mathcal{T}}$
1	3	5	12	18
10	2738	1222	TO	1926
100	TO	32	TO	44
1000	TO	16	TO	17
10000	TO	13	TO	15
100000	TO	13	TO	13

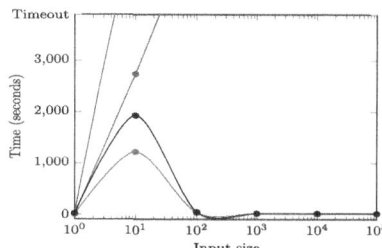

realizability, but this should not be treated as a general result (in this example, this is because large bounds allow a safety boundary to be wider, whereas narrower bounds force the unrealizability search to be more nuances). This is a preliminary set of experiments, not part of the prototype and future work is needed to further assess applicability of $LTL^{\mathcal{T}}$ to more complex embedded system specifications.

7 Conclusions

In this paper we studied reactive synthesis and realizability for full $LTL^{\mathcal{T}}$ which includes a fetching operator that allows specifying expressive data temporal relations. We introduced CEGRES, a counter-example guided reactive synthesis method that uses a novel concept of reactive tautologies. CEGRES is guaranteed to terminate for $LTL^{\mathcal{T}}_{\mathcal{A}}$ and to always progress for general $LTL^{\mathcal{T}}$. We showed that this algorithm is useful for specifications that require rich dynamics and we also showed that it is competitive against less expressive competing tools.

This paper opens the door for exciting future work, as tautologies are to realizability modulo theory what inductive invariants are for invariant proving. We will investigate how to discover and reuse reactive tautologies, for which we envision that TSL-MT invariant generation methods like [7,20,25] and CEGRES will mutually benefit. As for scalability, we will explore how to improve our CEGAR approach via reductions to simpler arena solving based methods internally [20], LTL methods like mode decomposition [5] or with neurosymbolic techniques like [23,24]. As for theory, finding decidable fragments [17] of realizability for $LTL^{\mathcal{T}}$ (other than $LTL^{\mathcal{T}}_{\mathcal{A}}$ or bounded domains) is ongoing work, as well as unifying the contributions with classic reactivity approaches [27] and symbolic model checking [6,29]. Also, we will investigate how to include very recent performant tools for infinite-state reactive synthesis [2,19] under the umbrella of $LTL^{\mathcal{T}}$ specifications. Finally, we are studying applications to safety shield [1,3] synthesis beyond Booleans [9,22,35,44], where rich dynamics of the environment play an important role.

References

1. Alshiekh, M., Bloem, R., Ehlers, R., Könighofer, B., Niekum, S., Topcu, U.: Safe reinforcement learning via shielding. arXiv abs/1708.08611 (2017). https://doi.org/10.48550/ARXIV.1708.08611
2. Azzopardi, S., Piterman, N., Stefano, L.D., Schneider, G.: Symbolic infinite-state LTL synthesis (2024). https://doi.org/10.48550/arXiv.2307.09776
3. Bloem, R., Könighofer, B., Könighofer, R., Wang, C.: Shield synthesis: runtime enforcement for reactive systems. In: Proceedings of the 21st International Conference in Tools and Algorithms for the Construction and Analysis of Systems (TACAS 2015). LNCS, vol. 9035, pp. 533–548. Springer (2015). https://doi.org/10.1007/978-3-662-46681-0_51
4. Bradley, A.R., Manna, Z.: The Calculus of Computation. Springer-Verlag (2007). https://doi.org/10.1007/978-3-540-74113-8

5. Brizzio, M., Gorostiaga, F., Sanchez, C., Degiovanni, R.: Mode-based reactive synthesis. In: Proceedings of the 17th NASA Formal Methods International Symposium (NFM 2025). LNCS (2025). https://doi.org/10.1007/978-3-031-60698-4_1
6. Burch, J.R., Clarke, E.M., McMillan, K.L., Dill, D.L., Hwang, L.J.: Symbolic model checking: 10^{20} states and beyond. In: Proceedings of the 5th Annual Symposium on Logic in Computer Science (LICS 1990), pp. 428–439. IEEE Computer Society (1990). https://doi.org/10.1109/LICS.1990.113767
7. Choi, W., Finkbeiner, B., Piskac, R., Santolucito, M.: Can reactive synthesis and syntax-guided synthesis be friends? In: Proceedings of the 43rd ACM SIGPLAN International Conference on Programming Language Design and Implementation (PLDI 2022), pp. 229–243. ACM (2022). https://doi.org/10.1145/3519939.3523429
8. Clarke, E., Grumberg, O., Jha, S., Lu, Y., Veith, H.: Counterexample-guided abstraction refinement. In: Emerson, E.A., Sistla, A.P. (eds.) CAV 2000. LNCS, vol. 1855, pp. 154–169. Springer, Heidelberg (2000). https://doi.org/10.1007/10722167_15
9. Corsi, D., Amir, G., Rodríguez, A., Katz, G., Sánchez, C., Fox, R.: Verification-guided shielding for deep reinforcement learning. RLJ **4**, 1759–1780 (2024)
10. D'Antoni, L., Veanes, M.: The power of symbolic automata and transducers. In: Proceedings of the 29th International Conference in Computer Aided Verification (CAV 2017), Part I. LNCS, vol. 10426, pp. 47–67. Springer (2017). **https://doi.org/10.1007/978-3-319-63387-9_3**
11. Finkbeiner, B.: Synthesis of reactive systems. In: Dependable Software Systems Engineering, NATO Science for Peace and Security Series - D: Information and Communication Security, vol. 45, pp. 72–98. IOS Press (2016). https://doi.org/10.3233/978-1-61499-627-9-72
12. Finkbeiner, B., Heim, P., Passing, N.: Temporal stream logic modulo theories. In: Proceedings of the 25th International Conference on Foundations of Software Science and Computation Structures (FOSSACS 2022). LNCS, vol. 13242, pp. 325–346. Springer (2022). https://doi.org/10.1007/978-3-030-99253-8_17
13. Finkbeiner, B., Klein, F., Piskac, R., Santolucito, M.: Temporal stream logic: synthesis beyond the Bools. In: Proceedings of the 31st International Conference on Computer Aided Verification (CAV 2019), Part I. LNCS, vol. 11561, pp. 609–629. Springer (2019). https://doi.org/10.1007/978-3-030-25540-4_35
14. Gacek, A., Katis, A., Whalen, M.W., Backes, J., Cofer, D.D.: Towards realizability checking of contracts using theories. In: Proceedings of the 7th International Symposium NASA Formal Methods (NFM 2015). LNCS, vol. 9058, pp. 173–187. Springer (2015). https://doi.org/10.1007/978-3-319-17524-9_13
15. Geatti, L., Gianola, A., Gigante, N.: Linear temporal logic modulo theories over finite traces. In: Proceedings of the 31st International Joint Conference on Artificial Intelligence, (IJCAI 2022), pp. 2641–2647. ijcai.org (2022). https://doi.org/10.24963/ijcai.2022/366
16. Geatti, L., Gianola, A., Gigante, N.: A general automata model for first-order temporal logics. arXive abs/2405.20057 (2024).
17. Geatti, L., Gianola, A., Gigante, N., Winkler, S.: Decidable fragments of LTL_f modulo theories. In: Proceedings of the 26th European Conference on Artificial Intelligence (ECAI 2023). Frontiers in Artificial Intelligence and Applications, vol. 372, pp. 811–818. IOS Press (2023). https://doi.org/10.3233/FAIA230348
18. Heim, P., Dimitrova, R.: Solving infinite-state games via acceleration. Proc. ACM Program. Lang. **8**(POPL), 1696–1726 (2024). https://doi.org/10.1145/3632899

19. Heim, P., Dimitrova, R.: Issy: A comprehensive tool for specification and synthesis of infinite-state reactive systems (2025). https://doi.org/10.48550/arXiv.2502.03013

20. Heim, P., Dimitrova, R.: Translation of temporal logic for efficient infinite-state reactive synthesis. Proc. ACM Program. Lang. **9**(POPL) (2025). https://doi.org/10.1145/3704888

21. Katis, A., Fedyukovich, G., Guo, H., Gacek, A., Backes, J., Gurfinkel, A., Whalen, M.W.: Validity-guided synthesis of reactive systems from assume-guarantee contracts. In: Proceedings of the 24th Int'l Conference on Tools and Algorithms for the Construction and Analysis of Systems, (TACAS 2018), Part II. LNCS, vol. 10806, pp. 176–193. Springer (2018). https://doi.org/10.1007/978-3-319-89963-3_10

22. Kim, K., et al.: Realizable continuous-space shields for safe reinforcement learning. In: Proceedings of the 7th Annual Learning for Dynamics & Control Conference (L4DC 2025). PMLR (2025). https://proceedings.mlr.press/v242/zhou24a.html

23. Kretínský, J., Meggendorfer, T., Prokop, M., Rieder, S.: Guessing winning policies in LTL synthesis by semantic learning. In: Proceedings of the 35th International Conference on Computer Aided Verification (CAV 2023). LNCS, vol. 13964, pp. 390–414. Springer (2023). https://doi.org/10.1007/978-3-031-37706-8_20

24. Křetínský, J., Meggendorfer, T., Prokop, M., Zarkhah, A.: SemML: enhancing automata-theoretic LTL synthesis with machine learning. In: Gurfinkel, A., Heule, M. (eds.) Tools and Algorithms for the Construction and Analysis of Systems, pp. 233–253. Springer Nature Switzerland, Cham (2025)

25. Maderbacher, B., Bloem, R.: Reactive synthesis modulo theories using abstraction refinement. In: Proceedings of the 22nd International Conference on Formal Methods in Computer-Aided Design, (FMCAD 2022), pp. 315–324. IEEE (2022). https://doi.org/10.34727/2022/isbn.978-3-85448-053-2_38

26. Maderbacher, B., Windisch, F., Bloem, R.: Synthesis from infinite-state generalized reactivity(1) specifications. In: Proceedings of the 12th International Symposium On Leveraging Applications of Formal Methods, Verification and Validation on Software Engineering Methodologies, (ISoLA 2024), Part IV. LNCS, vol. 15222, pp. 281–301. Springer (2024). https://doi.org/10.1007/978-3-031-75387-9_17

27. Manna, Z., Pnueli, A.: A hierarchy of temporal properties. In: Proceedings of the 9th Annual ACM Symposium on Principles of Distributed Computing (PODC 1990), pp. 377–410. ACM (1990). https://doi.org/10.1145/93385.93442

28. Manna, Z., Pnueli, A.: Temporal Verification of Reactive Systems - Safety. Springer (1995). https://doi.org/10.1007/978-1-4612-4222-2

29. McMillan, K.L.: Eager abstraction for symbolic model checking. In: Proceedings of the 30th International Conference in Computer Aided Verification (CAV 2018), Part I. LNCS, vol. 10981, pp. 191–208. Springer (2018). https://doi.org/10.1007/978-3-319-96145-3_11

30. Meyer, P.J., Sickert, S., Luttenberger, M.: Strix: explicit reactive synthesis strikes back! In: Chockler, H., Weissenbacher, G. (eds.) CAV 2018. LNCS, vol. 10981, pp. 578–586. Springer, Cham (2018). https://doi.org/10.1007/978-3-319-96145-3_31

31. de Moura, L., Bjørner, N.: Z3: An efficient SMT solver. In: Ramakrishnan, C.R., Rehof, J. (eds.) TACAS 2008. LNCS, vol. 4963, pp. 337–340. Springer, Heidelberg (2008). https://doi.org/10.1007/978-3-540-78800-3_24

32. Pnueli, A.: The temporal logic of programs. In: Proceedings of the 18th IEEE Symposium on Foundations of Computer Science (FOCS 1977), pp. 46–67. IEEE CS Press (1977)

33. Pnueli, A., Rosner, R.: On the synthesis of a reactive module. In: Proceedings of the 16th Annual ACM Sympoisum on Principles of Programming Languages (POPL 1989), pp. 179–190. ACM Press (1989)

34. Pnueli, A., Rosner, R.: On the synthesis of an asynchronous reactive module. In: Ausiello, G., Dezani-Ciancaglini, M., Della Rocca, S.R. (eds.) ICALP 1989. LNCS, vol. 372, pp. 652–671. Springer, Heidelberg (1989). https://doi.org/10.1007/BFb0035790

35. Rodríguez, A., Amir, G., Corsi, D., Sánchez, C., Katz, G.: Shield synthesis for LTL modulo theories. In: Proceedings of the 39th AAAI Conference on Artificial Intelligence (AAAI 2025), pp. 15134–15142. AAAI Press (2025). https://doi.org/10.1609/AAAI.V39I14.33660

36. Rodríguez, A., Gorostiaga, F., Sánchez, C.: Predictable and performant reactive synthesis modulo theories via functional synthesis. In: Akshay, S., Niemetz, A., Sankaranarayanan, S. (eds.) Proceedings of 22nd the International Symposium on Automated Technology for Verification and Analysis (ATVA 2024). Springer (2024). https://doi.org/10.1007/978-3-031-78750-8_2

37. Rodríguez, A., Sánchez, C.: Boolean abstractions for realizabilty modulo theories. In: Proceedings of the 35th International Conference on Computer Aided Verification (CAV 2023). LNCS, vol. 13966. Springer, Cham (2023). https://doi.org/10.1007/978-3-031-37709-9_15

38. Rodríguez, A., Sánchez, C.: Adaptive reactive synthesis for LTL and LTLf modulo theories. In: Proceedings of the 38th AAAI Conference on Artificial Intelligence (AAAI 2024), pp. 10679–10686. AAAI Press (2024). https://doi.org/10.1609/AAAI.V38I9.28939

39. Rodríguez, A., Sánchez, C.: Realizability modulo theories. J. Logical Algebraic Methods Program. **140**, 100971 (2024). https://doi.org/10.1016/j.jlamp.2024.100971

40. Samuel, S., D'Souza, D., Komondoor, R.: GenSys: a scalable fixed-point engine for maximal controller synthesis over infinite state spaces. In: Proc. of the 29th ACM Joint European Software Engineering Conference and Symposium on the Foundations of Software Engineering (ESEC/FSE 2021), pp. 1585–1589. ACM (2021). https://doi.org/10.1145/3468264.3473126

41. Samuel, S., D'Souza, D., Komondoor, R.: Symbolic fixpoint algorithms for logical LTL games. In: Proceedings of the 38th IEEE/ACM International Conference on Automated Software Engineering (ASE 2023), pp. 698–709. IEEE (2023). https://doi.org/10.1109/ASE56229.2023.00212

42. Schmuck, A., Heim, P., Dimitrova, R., Nayak, S.P.: Localized attractor computations for infinite-state games. In: Proceedings of the 36th Int'l Conf. on Computer Aided Verification (CAV 2024), Part III. LNCS, vol. 14683, pp. 135–158. Springer (2024). https://doi.org/10.1007/978-3-031-65633-0_7

43. Veanes, M., Ball, T., Ebner, G., Zhuchko, E.: Symbolic automata: ω-regularity modulo theories. Proc. ACM Program. Lang. **9**(POPL) (2025). https://doi.org/10.1145/3704838

44. Wu, M., Wang, J., Deshmukh, J., Wang, C.: Shield synthesis for real: enforcing safety in cyber-physical systems. In: Proceedings of 19th Formal Methods in Computer Aided Design, (FMCAD 2019), pp. 129–137. IEEE (2019). https://doi.org/10.23919/FMCAD.2019.8894264

Automatic Synthesis of Smooth Infinite Horizon Paths Satisfying Linear Temporal Logic Specifications

Samuel Williams$^{(\boxtimes)}$ and Jyotirmoy Deshmukh

University of Southern California, Los Angeles, CA 90310, USA
{samwilliams,jyotirmoy.deshmukh}@usc.edu

Abstract. Automatically constructing smooth paths that satisfy a formal specification is a challenging problem. Existing methods struggle to scale to long horizon specifications and challenging environments. We present a method that uses abstraction, model checking, and convex optimization to solve for a smooth Bézier spline that is guaranteed to satisfy a Linear Temporal Logic specification. Our approach uses a coarse abstraction to avoid the state explosion of other abstraction based methods, and successfully avoids the computational challenges of directly optimizing the non-convex temporal logic semantics. We prove our method is sound and complete and demonstrate a significant computational advantage relative to state of the art approaches. Generating such smooth paths has natural applications in path planning for autonomous robots, and we demonstrate the applicability of our method on path planning for a quadrotor.

Keywords: Temporal logic · Path synthesis · Bézier splines

1 Introduction

Path planning for robotic systems is an important and challenging problem [24]. Typically, a planner is provided with the description of the robot's workspace including an initial configuration, a desired goal configuration, obstacles, and a transition relation encoding the effect of robot actions on its configurations. Most autonomous robots perform planning in a layered manner: a high-level planner first identifies a (possibly dense) sequence of way-points for the robot to follow that achieves a collision-free path through the workspace that satisfies the robot's goal. The *path* is then handed off to a lower-level controller that ensures that the robot's actual trajectory follows the path with minimal tracking error. While there are many planning algorithms for robots that help identify paths over finite planning horizons, specification of infinite horizon objectives and path planning for such objectives remains a significant challenge. A popular formalism to describe infinite horizon behavior of the system, such as invariance or persistence, is Linear Temporal Logic [42]. For most autonomous robots, a

© The Author(s) 2025
R. Piskac and Z. Rakamarić (Eds.): CAV 2025, LNCS 15934, pp. 249–273, 2025.
https://doi.org/10.1007/978-3-031-98685-7_12

feasible lower-level control scheme often imposes constraints on the high-level paths to ensure dynamic feasibility. Following paths that require abrupt changes may impose unrealistic demands on the low-level control that violate actuation constraints. Thus, producing paths that are sufficiently smooth usually makes the low-level control problem easier.

In this paper, we tackle two challenges: (1) generating smooth paths through the robot's workspace, (2) ensuring that these paths can satisfy arbitrary *infinite horizon* planning objectives specified in LTL. A key observation that we use in our approach is that for any labeled transition system that satisfies an LTL (or any other ω-regular) specification: if a satisfying path exists, then a *lasso-shaped* satisfying path exists in the system. These lassos describe an infinite sequence of system states as a finite prefix followed by an infinitely repeating finite suffix.

Related Work on Abstraction-Based Control Synthesis. There is significant work on constructing controllers for dynamical systems that guarantee that the resulting closed-loop system satisfies Linear Temporal Logic (LTL) specifications using approaches from reactive synthesis [5,18,21] and abstraction-guided control [46,48,52]. Our approach falls under the broad category of automata based methods that model a finite state abstraction of the control system as a finite transition system [4,7,12,20,32,37,41,53,55,59]. These approaches use model checking [2,8] or other algorithms on automata to produce a satisfying lasso through the abstract transition system. However, it is challenging to map the abstract lasso to a controller of the robotic system. Additionally, it is computationally challenging to use these methods on large abstract systems as algorithms operate on the product of the abstract system with a translated Büchi automaton for the specification, which is exponentially large in the size of the formula [2]. Sampling based planners address this problem by either incrementally building a sparse abstract system through sampling system dynamics [4,19,35,57] or avoiding the construction of an abstract system altogether by simultaneously exploring the state space and translated Büchi automaton [31].

Our Approach: Path Synthesis. Our method addresses the computational challenges of related methods by synthesizing paths instead of a controller. Relative to other abstraction-based methods, we can leverage a more coarse abstraction as interpolating discrete transitions with a Bézier spline reduces the need for a fine-grained abstraction. This can be seen as an alternative to sampling-based abstract planning as both approaches seek to reduce the size of the abstract system, though our method is control-agnostic. Additionally, our method handles infinite horizon paths. We theoretically guarantee the discrete trace of the synthesized path satisfies an LTL specification and that our method will always construct one if such a path exists. However, these guarantees are on the synthesized paths and extending guarantees to a controller is a challenging problem. For the special case of *differentially flat systems*, we demonstrate how existing trajectory tracking controllers can be used to track the planned spline.

Kurtz and Lin [23] present the most similar method. They solve for a Bézier spline that satisfies an LTL specification by formulating the problem as a shortest path problem in a graph of convex sets [33,34], which is NP-hard but has a tight convex relaxation. They give soundness and completeness guarantees for the synthesized trajectory for the co-safe fragment of LTL formulas, but are unable to give a completeness guarantee for full LTL. A Bézier spline that satisfies the formula may exist when their method fails. *We present an alternative method that uses model checking tools to achieve soundness and completeness for full LTL.* Sun et al. [50] present another similar method that solves for piecewise linear paths that satisfy an STL formula by encoding the satisfaction of the formula as an MILP. Although they consider satisfaction of a different temporal logic, the Bézier splines used in our method generalize piecewise linear paths, and under some conditions we can translate the same problem instance into our setting. In contrast to solving an NP-hard MILP, our method splits the problem into a model checking step and a convex optimization step. This shares an exponential worst-case complexity but we demonstrate a computational advantage relative to both of these alternative methods.

Contributions and Organization. Summarizing our main contributions:

1. We present an abstraction-based method that uses model checking and convex optimization to automatically synthesize a Bézier spline that satisfies an LTL specification.
2. We prove our method is sound and complete. Our method will return a spline that satisfies the specification if and only if one exists.
3. We compare our method against recent approaches to path synthesis [23,50] and find a **5x** to **1255x** times computational speedup in simulated experiments of varying size.
4. We demonstrate how synthesized splines can be used in conjunction with trajectory tracking controllers for differentially flat systems to solve the control synthesis problem.

We cover preliminary material on LTL and Bézier splines in Sect. 2. In Sect. 3, we formally define our problem and describe our approach to use model checking and optimization to synthesize a Bézier spline. Section 4 presents a simulated experimental comparison with related work. In Sect. 5, we review abstractions of control systems and demonstrate how our method can be combined with trajectory tracking controllers for differentially flat systems.

2   Preliminaries

2.1   Linear Temporal Logic

For a more complete treatment, see [2]. Linear Temporal Logic (LTL) is a formalism that extends propositional logic with modalities to express requirements on the infinite discrete behavior of a system. Define a set of atomic propositions AP which represent Boolean properties of a system.

Definition 1 (Syntax of LTL). *The syntax of LTL is as follows.*

$$\varphi ::= T \mid a \mid \neg\varphi \mid \varphi_1 \wedge \varphi_2 \mid \mathbf{X}\,\varphi \mid \varphi_1 \, \mathbf{U}\, \varphi_2$$

where T denotes "true", $a \in AP$, $\neg$ is the negation operator, $\wedge$ is the conjunction operator, $\mathbf{X}$ is the "next" temporal operator, and $\mathbf{U}$ is the "until" temporal operator.

Other typical boolean connectors $(\vee, \Rightarrow)$ and temporal operators ($\mathbf{G}$ for "globally" and $\mathbf{F}$ for "eventually") are derived from the above rules. $\varphi_1 \vee \varphi_2 := \neg(\neg\varphi_1 \wedge \neg\varphi_2)$, $\varphi_1 \Rightarrow \varphi_2 := \neg\varphi_1 \vee \varphi_2$, $\mathbf{F}\,\varphi := \mathbf{T}\,\mathbf{U}\,\varphi$, $\mathbf{G}\,\varphi := \neg\mathbf{F}\,\neg\varphi$. The semantics of an LTL formula φ is defined as a language over infinite words with the alphabet 2^{AP}. A *word* $\sigma = A_0 A_1 A_2 \ldots \in (2^{AP})^\omega$ is an infinite sequence of sets of atomic propositions. Denote the j-th letter of σ as $\sigma[j] = A_j$ and denote the suffix of σ starting at index j as $\sigma[j\ldots] = A_j A_{j+1}\ldots$.

Definition 2 (Semantics of LTL). *Define satisfaction relation $\vDash \subseteq (2^{AP})^\omega \times$ LTL to be the smallest relation satisfying:*

$$\sigma \vDash T$$
$$\sigma \vDash a \qquad\qquad \Leftrightarrow \quad a \in A_0$$
$$\sigma \vDash \neg\varphi \qquad\qquad \Leftrightarrow \quad \sigma \nvDash \varphi$$
$$\sigma \vDash \varphi_1 \wedge \varphi_2 \qquad \Leftrightarrow \quad \sigma \vDash \varphi_1 \wedge \sigma \vDash \varphi_2$$
$$\sigma \vDash \mathbf{X}\,\varphi \qquad\qquad \Leftrightarrow \quad \sigma[1\ldots] \vDash \varphi$$
$$\sigma \vDash \varphi_1 \, \mathbf{U}\, \varphi_2 \qquad \Leftrightarrow \quad \text{there exists } j \geq 0 \text{ s.t. } \sigma[j\ldots] \vDash \varphi_2$$
$$\text{and for all } 0 \leq i < j \colon \sigma[i\ldots] \vDash \varphi_1.$$

The semantics of the derived temporal operators $\mathbf{G}$ and $\mathbf{F}$ follow.

$$\sigma \vDash \mathbf{G}\,\varphi \Leftrightarrow \text{ for all } j \geq 0 \colon \sigma[j\ldots] \vDash \varphi, \qquad \sigma \vDash \mathbf{F}\,\varphi \Leftrightarrow \text{ exists } j \geq 0 \colon \sigma[j\ldots] \vDash \varphi$$

The statement $\sigma \vDash \varphi$ is read as σ "satisfies" φ. Denote the set of words that satisfy φ as $\text{Words}(\varphi) = \{\sigma \in (2^{AP})^\omega \mid \sigma \vDash \varphi\}$. Finally, recall any LTL formula can be translated into a non-deterministic Büchi automaton.

Definition 3 (Büchi automaton). *A non-deterministic Büchi automaton (NBA) is a tuple $M = (Q, 2^{AP}, \delta, Q_0, F)$ where Q is a finite state space, 2^{AP} is an alphabet, $Q_0 \subseteq Q$ is a set of initial states, $\delta\colon Q \times 2^{AP} \to 2^Q$ is a transition relation, and $F \subseteq Q$ is the acceptance set. The language $L_\omega(M)$ is the set of infinite words in $(2^{AP})^\omega$ that have at least one infinite run $q_0 q_1 q_2 \ldots$ in M where $q_i \in F$ for infinitely many indices i.*

The construction of an NBA M_φ where $\sigma \in \text{Words}(\varphi)$ iff $\sigma \in L_\omega(M_\varphi)$ takes $2^{\mathcal{O}(|\varphi|)}$ time and space, yet has been successfully applied in model checking tools that are capable of handling modestly sized formulas.

Definition 4 (Kripke Structure). *A Kripke structure over a set of atomic propositions AP is defined as a tuple $K = (S, I, R, h_S)$ where S is a finite set of states, $I \subseteq S$ is a set of initial states, $R \subseteq S \times S$ is a transition relation satisfying $\forall s \in S, \exists s' \in S$ s.t. $(s, s') \in R$. The function $h_S \colon S \to 2^{AP}$ is called the output function and labels a set of atomic propositions that hold in S.*

A *path* through K is an infinite sequence of states $\rho = s_1 s_2 s_3 \dots$ where $s_1 \in I$ and each $s_i \in S$ such that for each $i \geq 1$, $(s_i, s_{i+1}) \in R$. Denote $\mathtt{Trace}(\rho)$ as the word defined by the sequence of labels of each state $\mathtt{Trace}(\rho) = h_S(s_1) h_S(s_2) h_S(s_3) \dots \in (2^{AP})^\omega$. The *model checking* [2,8] problem decides whether all words generated by a Kripke structure K satisfy an LTL formula φ. To do so, the standard algorithm takes the product automaton $A := K \otimes M_{\neg\varphi}$ where $M_{\neg\varphi}$ is the NBA constructed from $\neg\varphi$ and checks whether A accepts any words. Iff the language $L_\omega(A)$ is empty, $K \vDash \varphi$. Model checkers produce a witness (or counterexample) when $K \nvDash \varphi$ which is of the form $\rho = \rho_1(\rho_2)^\omega$ where $\rho_1 = s_1 \dots s_n$ is a finite prefix and $\rho_2 = s_{n+1} \dots s_m$ is an infinitely repeated finite suffix. Each s_i is a state in the product automaton $K \otimes M_{\neg\varphi}$ which can be projected onto S to produce a path of K where the associated word $\mathtt{Trace}(\rho) \nvDash \varphi$.

2.2 Bézier Splines

We use Bézier splines to map discrete witnesses ρ to smooth paths. Bézier splines [40] are a method of interpolation that have been used extensively in the motion planning literature (e.g. [25,43,56,60]). A Bézier spline of degree $k \in \mathbb{N}$ is defined by the concatenation of several curves (or segments) which are each defined using a particular set of polynomial basis functions, the Bernstein basis polynomials. For spline degree k, there are $k + 1$ Bernstein basis polynomials.

Definition 5 (Bernstein Basis Polynomial). *For $i \in \{0, \dots, k\}$, the Bernstein basis polynomial $B_{i,k} \colon [0, \Delta_t] \to \mathbb{R}$ is defined by:*

$$B_{i,k}(t) = \binom{k}{i} \left(1 - \frac{t}{\Delta_t}\right)^{k-i} \left(\frac{t}{\Delta_t}\right)^i \tag{1}$$

Where $\Delta_t \in \mathbb{R}_{++}$ is a strictly positive real number. Typically $\Delta_t = 1$ but we allow the parameter to range to enable greater flexibility on the timing of planned curves. We later refer to the following properties of Bernstein basis polynomials:

$$\sum_{i=0}^{k} B_{i,k}(t) = 1, \quad B_{i,k}(t) \geq 0 \text{ for } t \in [0, \Delta_t], \quad B_{i,k}(t) > 0 \text{ for } t \in (0, \Delta_t) \tag{2}$$

$$B_{i,k}(0) = \delta_{i,0}, \quad B_{i,k}(\Delta_t) = \delta_{i,k} \tag{3}$$

$$\frac{\mathrm{d}B(t)_{i,k}}{\mathrm{d}t} = \frac{k}{\Delta_t}(B_{i-1,k-1}(t) - B_{i,k-i}(t)) \tag{4}$$

Where $\delta_{i,j}$ is the Kronecker delta function i.e. $\delta_{i,j} = 1$ if $i = j$ and 0 otherwise. A Bézier curve is defined using the Bernstein basis polynomials as the coefficients of a convex combination of $k + 1$ chosen control points $(p_0, \dots, p_k)$ where each $p_i \in \mathbb{R}^n$ for $i \in \{0, \dots, k\}$.

Definition 6 (Bézier Curve). *A Bézier curve* $b: [0, \Delta_t] \rightarrow \mathbb{R}^n$ *is defined as*

$$b(t) := \sum_{i=0}^{k} B_{i,k}(t) p_i \tag{5}$$

Bézier curves have a few useful properties that immediately follow from (2–4):

a. The curve interpolates the first and last points $b(0) = p_0$ and $b(\Delta_t) = p_k$.
b. The derivative of a Bézier curve is another Bézier curve of degree $k - 1$.
c. The curve is bounded by the convex hull of the control points.

Applying (4) yields an expression for the derivative of a Bézier curve.

Lemma 1. *The derivative of the Bézier curve with control points* $(p_0, \ldots, p_k)$ *is a Bézier curve of degree* $k - 1$ *with control points* $(\frac{k}{\Delta_t}(p_1 - p_0), \ldots, \frac{k}{\Delta_t}(p_k - p_{k-1}))$

$$\frac{db(t)}{dt} := \sum_{i=0}^{k-1} B_{i,k-1}(t) \frac{k}{\Delta_t}(p_{i+1} - p_i) \tag{6}$$

Applying Lemma 1 recursively yields an expression for the d-th derivative of a Bézier curve.

Lemma 2. *The d-th derivative of a Bézier curve is given by*

$$\frac{d^d b(t)}{dt^d} := \sum_{i=0}^{k-d} B_{i,k-d}(t) \frac{k!}{(\Delta_t)^d (k-d)!} \sum_{\nu=0}^{d} \binom{d}{\nu} (-1)^{\nu+d} p_{i+\nu} \tag{7}$$

Corollary 1. *If* $p_0 = p_1 = \ldots = p_d$, *(3) and the "polarity" property of Pascal's triangle* $\sum_{\nu=0}^{d} \binom{d}{\nu}(-1)^{\nu+d} = 0$ *imply* $\frac{d^d b(0)}{dt^d} = 0$. *Similarly, if* $p_{k-d} = \ldots = p_k$, *(3) and the "polarity" property imply* $\frac{d^d b(\Delta_t)}{dt^d} = 0$.

A Bézier spline $\mathcal{B} = (b^1, \ldots, b^m)$ is constructed by concatenating m Bézier curves in time. The spline is called *uniform* if all curves share the same Δ_t and *non-uniform* otherwise. For non-uniform splines, denote the sequence of time deltas as $\Delta := (\Delta_t^1, \ldots, \Delta_t^m)$. As each Bézier curve is a polynomial function, ensuring the spline is C^d, or d-times continuously differentiable, amounts to checking equivalence of the first d derivatives at the knot points. *Knot points are points where one curve ends and the next begins.* From Lemma 2, the control points of the d-th derivative are a linear function of the control points $(p_0, \ldots, p_k)$, so this amounts to a set of linear constraints. Corollary 1 is useful to prove these constraints are satisfiable. If the spline is non-uniform, these constraints are instead quadratic as the $(\Delta_t)^d$ expression is multiplied by the control points. For example, C^1 continuity requires between the curves j and $j + 1$:

$$\frac{p_k^j - p_{k-1}^j}{\Delta_t^j} = \frac{p_1^{j+1} - p_0^{j+1}}{\Delta_t^{j+1}}. \tag{8}$$

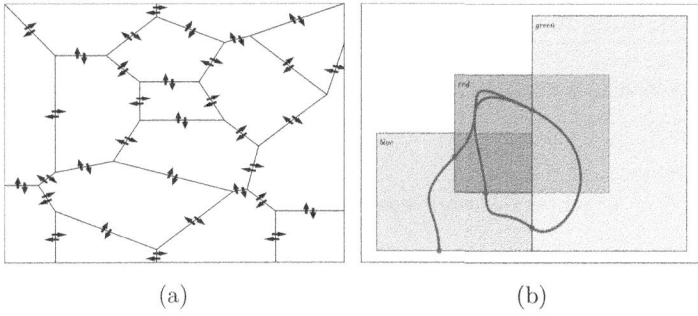

(a)   (b)

Fig. 1. (a) Example partition $\mathcal{P}$. Arrows display the transitions of K_{abs} defined on $\mathcal{P}$. (b) Example C^1 lasso spline $\mathcal{B} = (b^1, b^2, b^3, b^4, b^5)$ composed of 5 segments where (b^1, b^2) is a prefix and (b^3, b^4, b^5) is an infinitely repeating suffix. The red points mark the start of each segment. $\texttt{Trace}(\mathcal{B}) = \{blue\}\{blue, red\}\{red\}(\{red, green\}\{green\}\{blue\}\{blue, red\}\{red\})^\omega$. (Color figure online)

3   Path Synthesis

In this Section, we first present a formal definition of our problem, then present an algorithm that solves our problem along with formal soundness and completeness guarantees. Finally, we analyze the worst-case time complexity of our algorithm.

3.1   Problem Definition

Define the *workspace* $\mathbb{X} \subset \mathbb{R}^n$. We are given a partition $\mathcal{P} = (P_1, \ldots, P_r)$ of $\mathbb{X}$ into r convex regions i.e. $P_i \cap P_j = \emptyset$ for $i \neq j$ and $\bigcup_{i=1,\ldots,r} P_i = \mathbb{X}$. Let $\text{int}(P)$ and $\overline{P}$ denote the interior and closure of the set P respectively. We assume $\text{int}(P) \neq \emptyset$ for each $P \in \mathcal{P}$. Denote the *absorbing region* $P_* = \mathbb{R}^n \setminus \mathbb{X}$. We are given a set of atomic propositions AP and a labeling function $L: \mathcal{P} \cup P_* \to 2^{AP}$. Define $\texttt{Regions}(\mathcal{B}) = P^0 P^1 \ldots$ to be the sequence of regions $\mathcal{B}$ enters where for each $i = 0, 1, \ldots$ each $P^i \in \mathcal{P}$ and there exists a strictly increasing non-Zeno time sequence $(t_0, t_1, \ldots)$ where $\mathcal{B}(t_i) \in P^i$ and there exists $\epsilon_i \in (0, t_{i+1} - t_i)$ where either:

a. For all $t \in [t_i, t_i + \epsilon_i)$: $\mathcal{B}(t) \in P^i$ and $t \in [t_i + \epsilon_i, t_{i+1}]$: $\mathcal{B}(t) \in P^{i+1}$
b. For all $t \in [t_i, t_i + \epsilon_i]$: $\mathcal{B}(t) \in P^i$ and $t \in (t_i + \epsilon_i, t_{i+1}]$: $\mathcal{B}(t) \in P^{i+1}$

We define the trace of $\mathcal{B}$ as the sequence of labels of $\texttt{Regions}(\mathcal{B})$. $\texttt{Trace}(\mathcal{B}) := \sigma \in (2^{AP})^\omega$ where $\sigma = L(P^0)L(P^1)\ldots$, $\texttt{Regions}(\mathcal{B}) = P^0 P^1 \ldots$. Figure 1 displays an example $\mathcal{B}$.

Remark 1. Requiring a convex partition is useful as constraints to require a Bézier curve remains within a convex region are convex. We assume this partition

---

Algorithm 1: Path Synthesis from LTL Objectives

---

input: Partition $\mathcal{P}$, Starting states I, LTL formula φ, Label function L
1 $K_{\mathrm{abs}} \leftarrow$ ConstructKripke$(\mathcal{P}, I, L)$
2 $M_{\varphi} \leftarrow$ LTLtoNBA(φ)
3 $\rho \leftarrow$ EmptinessCheck$(K_{\mathrm{abs}} \otimes M_{\varphi})$
4 $\mathcal{B} \leftarrow$ SynthesizeBézier(ρ)
   /* Check if SynthesizeBézier was feasible   */
5 **if** $\mathcal{B}$ *is not* ϵ **then**
6 | **return** $\mathcal{B}$
7 **return** ϵ

---

is given, though in practice one could be created by first taking convex over-approximations or under-approximations of labeled regions of interest in the workspace (e.g. obstacles, goal regions, etc.) and subsequently partitioning the remaining space into unlabeled convex regions. Of course this approach is not general and precludes some environments from using our method, though we are able to perform this procedure for a number of interesting environments used in our experiments in Sects. 4 and 5.

Problem Definition. Given convex partition $\mathcal{P}$ of the workspace $\mathbb{X} \subset \mathbb{R}^n$, labeling function $L \colon \mathcal{P} \cup P_* \to 2^{AP}$, and an LTL specification φ over AP, we aim to find a C^d lasso Bézier spline $\mathcal{B}$ that minimizes a given convex cost function J such that Trace$(\mathcal{B}) \vDash \varphi$.

3.2 Synthesis Algorithm

Algorithm 1 details the full algorithm. ConstructKripke() constructs the Kripke structure $K_{\mathrm{abs}} = (S, I, R, h_s)$ where $S = \mathcal{P} \cup P_*$, $I \subseteq S$ is given, $(s_i, s_j) \in R$ if either $i = j$ or $\overline{P_i} \cap \overline{P_j} \neq \emptyset$ where P_i and P_j are the associated sets in the partition for s_i and s_j. Finally, $h_S = L$ is the given labeling function. We abuse notation and use $s \in S$ to refer both to a specific Kripke state and the associated region P. The LTLtoNBA() function constructs the NBA M_{φ} where $L_{\omega}(M_{\varphi}) = \mathrm{Words}(\varphi)$. EmptinessCheck() performs emptiness checking, returning a witness ρ that is accepted by $K_{\mathrm{abs}} \otimes M_{\varphi}$. Practically, we constrain ρ to not include P_* so the path avoids the absorbing region.[1] SynthesizeBézier() performs a convex optimization problem described in the following subsection to produce a Bézier spline $\mathcal{B}$ where Trace$(\mathcal{B}) = $ Trace(ρ). We prove SynthesizeBézier() will always be feasible if the spline order k is large enough, though since the problem defines constraints based on a specific witness, the resulting spline may be suboptimal as an alternative witness may produce a lower cost spline.

---

[1] This can be accomplished by introducing a unique label a to AP for P_* and conjuncting φ with $\mathbf{G} \neg a$.

3.3   Convex Optimization to Synthesize a Bézier Spline

To provide intuition, given path ρ of K_{abs} we define constraints on $\mathcal{B}$ such that each Bézier curve b in $\mathcal{B}$ remains entirely within the associated convex region for a single state in ρ. We additionally append constraints so the knot between each segment of the spline is C^d. This includes between the last segment of the suffix and the first segment of the suffix of ρ, ensuring the synthesized spline is a C^d lasso where the looping section is repeated infinitely to realize the desired behavior.

The SynthesizeBézier() function in Algorithm 1 solves one of the following optimization problems. Given path $\rho = \rho_1(\rho_2)^\omega$ of K_{abs} where $\rho_1 = s_1 \dots s_l$ and $\rho_2 = s_{l+1} \dots s_m$ and user-provided cost function $J \colon \mathbb{R}^{k(m+1)} \to \mathbb{R}$, we construct a Bézier spline $\mathcal{B}$ of order k that is d-times continuously differentiable using $m+1$ segments. Let p_i^j refer to the i-th control point of the j-th segment, where $i \in \{0, \dots, k\}$, and $j \in \{1, \dots, m+1\}$. The spline is constructed by minimizing:

$$(P1) : \min_p J(p) \tag{9}$$

$$\text{s.t. } p_0^1 \in \overline{s_1} \tag{10}$$

$$p_0^j \in \overline{s_{j-1}} \cap \overline{s_j} \qquad\qquad j \in \{2, \dots, m\} \tag{11}$$

$$p_0^{m+1} \in \overline{s_m} \cap \overline{s_{l+1}} \tag{12}$$

$$p_i^j \in \mathrm{int}(s_j) \qquad i \in \{1, \dots, k-1\}, j \in \{1, \dots, m\} \tag{13}$$

$$p_i^{m+1} \in \mathrm{int}(s_{l+1}) \qquad\qquad i \in \{1, \dots, k-1\} \tag{14}$$

$$p_k^j \in \overline{s_j} \cap \overline{s_{j+1}} \qquad\qquad j \in \{1, \dots, m-1\} \tag{15}$$

$$p_k^m \in \overline{s_m} \cap \overline{s_l} \tag{16}$$

$$p_k^{m+1} \in \overline{s_{l+1}} \cap \overline{s_{l+2}} \tag{17}$$

$$\mathcal{B} \in C^d \tag{18}$$

The constraints for the $j = 1$, $j = m$, and $j = m + 1$ curves differ slightly from the constraints for all other curves and are separated for clarity. As each $P \in \mathcal{P}$ is convex, the constraints (10–17) are convex. If we require $\mathcal{B}$ to be uniform, constraint (18) is linear. Otherwise, (18) is quadratic. As long as J is a convex function, this problem can be efficiently solved to global optimality. Typical choices of cost functions include minimizing an approximation of the path length, or the magnitude of higher order derivatives of $\mathcal{B}$. Note $\mathcal{B}$ has one more segment than $|\rho_1\rho_2|$.

$$\mathcal{B} = (b^1, \dots, b^l, b^{l+1}, b^{l+2}, \dots, b^{m+1}) \tag{19}$$

This construction sets $(b^1, \dots, b^{l+1})$ to be the prefix and $(b^{l+2}, \dots, b^{m+1})$ to be the infinitely repeating suffix, effectively shifting ρ from $\rho_1(\rho_2)^\omega$ to $\rho' = \rho_1\rho_2[1](\rho_2[2 \dots]\rho_2[1])^\omega$. Clearly Trace$(\rho) = $ Trace(ρ') but the additional state ensures we can always close the loop on the lasso spline. Included in constraint (18) are constraints that the first d derivatives of the knot point between the last state of the prefix and the first state of the suffix equals the first d derivatives of the knot point between the last state of the suffix and the first state of the suffix. $\mathcal{B}$ defines a C^d lasso trajectory. We prove this construction is sound, the constraints ensure $\mathtt{Trace}(\mathcal{B}) = \mathtt{Trace}(\rho)$.

Theorem 1 (Soundness of $(P1)$). *Given path ρ of K_{abs}, all feasible solutions of $(P1)$ produce a C^d spline $\mathcal{B}$ that satisfies $\mathtt{Trace}(\mathcal{B}) = \mathtt{Trace}(\rho)$.*

Proof. Constraints (10–17) ensure for $j \in \{1, \ldots, m\}$ and $i \in \{0, \ldots, k\}$ each $p_i^j \in \overline{s_j}$, or, $p_i^j \in \overline{P}$ where P is the associated convex region to s_j. Constraints (12), (14), (17) analogously ensure $p_i^{m+1} \in \overline{s_{l+1}}$. As the Bézier curve b^j defined by control points $(p_0^j, \ldots, p_k^j)$ is contained within the convex hull of the control points, $\forall t \in [0, \Delta_t]: b^j(t) \in P$. Constraints (13) and (14) ensures for each spline segment j, there exists some i where $p_i^j \in \mathrm{int}(P)$. Due to (2), $b^j(t)$ for $t \in (0, \Delta_t)$ is a convex combination with strictly positive weight assigned to $p_i^j \in \mathrm{int}(P)$, implying $b^j(t) \in \mathrm{int}(P)$ for all $t \in (0, \Delta_t)$. As $\mathcal{P}$ is a partition, $b^j(t) \notin P'$ for all regions $P' \in \mathcal{P}, P' \neq P$ for all $t \in (0, \Delta_t)$. This holds for all $j \in \{1, \ldots, m+1\}$, therefore $\mathtt{Regions}(\mathcal{B}) = \rho$ and $\mathtt{Trace}(\mathcal{B}) = \mathtt{Trace}(\rho)$.

The constraints of $(P1)$ are sufficient but not necessary to provide a C^d spline $\mathcal{B}$ that satisfies $\mathtt{Trace}(\mathcal{B}) = \mathtt{Trace}(\rho)$. For example, problem $(P1)$ may be infeasible when there could exist a spline that either (a) has a different order k, or (b) relaxes constraint (13) that for every $i \in \{1, \ldots, k-1\}$ we have $p_i^j \in \mathrm{int}(s_j)$. For Theorem 1, we only use the fact that one of $i \in \{1, \ldots, k-1\}$ satisfies (13), but encoding that relaxation introduces integer variables which changes $(P1)$ from a convex program to a mixed-integer convex program. Instead, simply increasing the order k allows us to relax a constraint and guarantee feasibility. If $k \geq 2d+1$, we consider a second optimization problem:

$$(P2) : \min_{p} J(p) \tag{20}$$

$$\text{s.t. } p_0^1 \in \overline{s_1} \tag{21}$$

$$p_0^j \in \overline{s_{j-1}} \cap \overline{s_j} \qquad\qquad j \in \{2, \ldots, m\} \tag{22}$$

$$p_0^{m+1} \in \overline{s_m} \cap \overline{s_{l+1}} \tag{23}$$

$$p_i^j \in \overline{s_j} \qquad\qquad i \in \{1, \ldots d-1\} \cup \{k-d+1, \ldots, k\}, \tag{24}$$
$$j \in \{1, \ldots, m\}$$

$$p_i^j \in \mathrm{int}(s_j) \qquad\qquad i \in \{d, \ldots, k-d\}, j \in \{1, \ldots, m\} \tag{25}$$

$$p_i^{m+1} \in \overline{s_{l+1}} \qquad\qquad i \in \{1, \ldots, d-1\} \cup \{k-d+1, \ldots, k\} \tag{26}$$

$$p_i^{m+1} \in \mathrm{int}(s_{l+1}) \qquad\qquad i \in \{d, \ldots, k-d\} \tag{27}$$

$$p_k^j \in \overline{s_j} \cap \overline{s_{j+1}} \qquad\qquad j \in \{1, \ldots, m-1\} \tag{28}$$

$$p_k^m \in \overline{s_m} \cap \overline{s_{l+1}} \tag{29}$$

$$p_k^{m+1} \in \overline{s_{l+1}} \cap \overline{s_{l+2}} \tag{30}$$

$$\mathcal{B} \in C^d \tag{31}$$

The only changes between $(P1)$ and $(P2)$ is constraint (13) is relaxed to (24) and (25), and constraint (14) is relaxed to (26) and (27). This is only sound when $k \geq 2d + 1$ as $\{d, \ldots, k - d\}$ is nonempty.

Theorem 2 (Soundness of $(P2)$). *Given path ρ of K_{abs}, all feasible solutions of $(P2)$ produce a spline $\mathcal{B}$ that satisfies $\mathtt{Trace}(\mathcal{B}) = \mathtt{Trace}(\rho)$.*

Proof. Follows immediately from the same argument as the proof of Theorem 1.

The assumptions made on $\mathcal{P}$ allow us to prove $(P2)$ is feasible.

Theorem 3 (Feasibility of $(P2)$). *Given path ρ of K_{abs}, $(P2)$ is feasible.*

Proof. Given path $\rho = \rho_1(\rho_2)^\omega$ of K_{abs}, we consider three distinct cases in our construction.

- Considering the first segment $j = 1$, for $i \in \{0, \ldots, k - d\}$ pick p_i^1 to be the same arbitrary point $x \in \mathrm{int}(s_1)$. By assumption $\mathrm{int}(P) \neq \emptyset$ for all $P \in \mathcal{P}$, this point exists. For $i \in \{k - d + 1, \ldots, k\}$ pick p_i^1 to be the same arbitrary point $x' \in \overline{s_1} \cap \overline{s_2}$. Since ρ is a path of K_{abs}, the definition of the transition relation R of K_{abs} ensures $\overline{s_1} \cap \overline{s_2} \neq \emptyset$. By Corollary 1, $\frac{\mathrm{d}^{d'} b^1(0)}{\mathrm{d}t^{d'}} = \frac{\mathrm{d}^{d'} b^1(\Delta_t)}{\mathrm{d}t^{d'}} = 0$ for $d' \in \{1, \ldots, d\}$.

- Considering the intermediate segments $j \in \{2, \ldots, m - 1\}$, by induction, assume for some $(j - 1) \geq 1$, $\frac{\mathrm{d}^{d'} b^{j-1}(0)}{\mathrm{d}t^{d'}} = \frac{\mathrm{d}^{d'} b^{j-1}(\Delta_t)}{\mathrm{d}t^{d'}} = 0$ for $d' \in \{1, \ldots, d\}$ and $p_i^{j-1} = x \in \overline{s_{j-1}} \cap \overline{s_j}$ are all the same point for $i \in \{k - d + 1, \ldots, k\}$. The $j = 1$ case above is the base case. Pick $p_i^j = x$ to be the same point x from the last d points of the previous segment for $i \in \{0, \ldots, d - 1\}$, pick $p_i^j \in \mathrm{int}(s_j)$ to be arbitrary interior points for $i \in \{d, \ldots, k - d\}$, and pick $p_i^j = x' \in \overline{s_j} \cap \overline{s_{j+1}}$ to be the same point for $i \in \{k - d + 1, \ldots, k\}$. By the same arguments in the $j = 1$ case, all of these points exist. By Corollary 1, $\frac{\mathrm{d}^{d'} b^j(0)}{\mathrm{d}t^{d'}} = \frac{\mathrm{d}^{d'} b^j(\Delta_t)}{\mathrm{d}t^{d'}} = 0$ for $d' \in \{1, \ldots, d\}$. All conditions for the inductive hypothesis hold.

- Considering the final segments $j = m$ and $j = m + 1$, the inductive proof above shows we can make m arbitrarily large, but we still need to close the loop for the lasso spline. We construct the m-th segment according to the previous case, except for $i \in \{k - d + 1, \ldots, k\}$ we pick $p_i^m = x \in \overline{s_m} \cap \overline{s_{l+1}}$ according to constraint (29) as s_{m+1} does not exist. We pick the first $i \in \{0, \ldots, d - 1\}$ points of the $m + 1$ segment to be the same point $p_i^{m+1} = x$, and for $i \in \{d, \ldots, k - d\}$ we pick $p_i^{m+1} \in \mathrm{int}(s_{l+1})$ to be arbitrary interior points. From the previous case, $p_i^{l+2} = x' \in \overline{s_{l+1}} \cap \overline{s_{l+2}}$ for $i \in \{0, \ldots, d - 1\}$ is some already chosen point. We pick $p_i^{m+1} = x'$ to be the same point for $i \in \{k - d + 1, \ldots, k\}$. This construction means the last d points of the $m + 1$ segment equals the first d points of the $l + 2$ segment, ensuring a C^d knot by Corollary 1.

Each point exists and has been selected according to the constraints (21–30). As we have proven the first d derivatives of each spline segment at $t = 0$ and $t = \Delta_t$ all equal 0, the spline is clearly C^d. Therefore, this spline also satisfies constraint (31) and is a feasible solution of $(P2)$.

In practice, we expect this construction to be high cost as it likely results in large fluctuations in the higher order derivatives, which can be penalized by sensible choices of cost functions. However, this construction guarantees we can always synthesize a C^d spline $\mathcal{B}$ for ρ, so long as we pick large enough k.

Theorem 4 (Completeness of Algorithm 1 with (P2)). *Algorithm 1 using (P2) for* SynthesizeBézier() *returns a Bézier spline $\mathcal{B}$ with* Trace($\mathcal{B}$) = Trace(ρ).

Proof. Follows from Theorem 2 and Theorem 3 by selecting $k \geq 2d + 1$.

While the convex formulation allows us to find the optimal $\mathcal{B}$ subject to the constraints defined from a given witness ρ, there could exist a different witness ρ' or a different construction that produces a lower cost spline. Enumerating all possible witnesses may be impossible as there can be infinite. In practice, we are interested in a small *diverse* set of witnesses to get an empirically good enough solution and simply randomize the order of transitions in K_{abs} to produce different witnesses.[2] This choice prevents us from guaranteeing $\mathcal{B}$ is the optimal spline that satisfies φ, but we demonstrate in the following section it is very computationally efficient and produces splines of similar cost to related methods.

3.4 Complexity

Focusing on the case where (P1) and (P2) admit polynomial time algorithms to minimize J (e.g. $\mathcal{B}$ is uniform, $\mathcal{P}$ is a set of polyhedra, and J is a linear or convex quadratic function), the complexity of Algorithm 1 is dominated by the model checking step, which is PSPACE-complete [2].

Theorem 5. *Algorithm 1 has worst-case time complexity exponential in the size of the formula $\mathcal{O}(\mathrm{poly}(|K_{abs}| \cdot 2^{|\varphi|}))$.*

Proof. An upper bound for the time and space complexity for LTL model checking can be found by translating the LTL formula into a Büchi automaton and searching for an accepting lasso, which is $\mathcal{O}(|K_{abs}| \cdot 2^{|\varphi|})$ [2]. If no accepting lasso is found, Algorithm 1 terminates. If one is found, w.l.o.g. by the small model theorem it can be bound in length by the size of the product automaton $|\rho| \leq |K_{abs} \otimes M_\varphi| = \mathcal{O}(|K_{abs}| \cdot 2^{|\varphi|})$ as repeated states in the lasso imply redundant sections that can be removed to obtain a lasso that satisfies this size bound. As (P1) and (P2) have a linear number of decision variables with $|\rho|$ and are solvable in polynomial time, the overall time complexity is exponential in the size of the formula $\mathcal{O}(\mathrm{poly}(|K_{abs}| \cdot 2^{|\varphi|}))$.

---

[2] The SPOT model checker deterministically produces witnesses based on the order states and transitions are added to a Kripke structure.

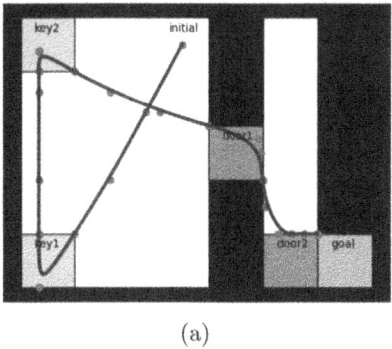
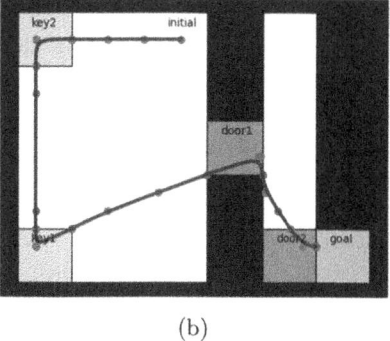

(a)   (b)

Fig. 2. Synthesized C^2 paths with the proposed method for Example 1. Paths satisfy the formula $\varphi = (\neg door_1 \, \mathbf{U} \, key_1) \wedge (\neg door_2 \, \mathbf{U} \, key_2) \wedge (\mathbf{F} \, goal)$. (a) finds a sub-optimal region order and (b) finds the optimal region order returned by different calls to the model checker. Control points are marked with the red circles. Example recreated from [23] (Color figure online).

4   Experimental Results

The following experiments were all performed using a laptop running Ubuntu 20.04 with a 16 core i7-11800H processor at 2.30 GHz, 32 GB ram, and a RTX 2080 GPU. For our method, we use the SPOT model checker [9] to produce witnesses and Gurobi[3] for optimization. We compare our method with [23,50] referred to as GCS for "Graph of Convex Sets" and PWL for "Piecewise Linear" respectively. Implementations of the compared methods on the experiments are provided by the respective authors. All formulas considered in this comparison are syntactically co-safe, and all splines in this section are uniform.

4.1   Numerical Comparison

Example 1 is the simple key-door problem from [23] where a planar robot must pick up both keys before passing through their associated doors in order to reach a goal. Trajectories are synthesized to satisfy the formula:

$$\varphi = (\neg door_1 \, \mathbf{U} \, key_1) \wedge (\neg door_2 \, \mathbf{U} \, key_2) \wedge (\mathbf{F} \, goal). \tag{32}$$

Synthesized trajectories from two different witnesses using our method are shown in Fig. 2. We ran our method and GCS for 50 trials and compared setup times, solve times, and spline costs. As both methods formulate a convex optimization problem to solve for their respective trajectories, we separate the time spent in the optimizer and all other time spent in the program into solve time and setup time. For our method, setup time includes the construction of the Kripke structure, translation of the LTL formula into a Büchi automaton, the model

---

[3] [Online]. Available: https://www.gurobi.com/.

checking step, and setup of the convex optimization problem. For GCS, the setup time includes translation of the LTL formula into a DFA, construction of the graph of convex sets, forming a product automaton between the DFA and the graph, and setup of the convex optimization problem. In order to use the same spline parameters as presented in [23], both methods compute C^2 splines of order $k = 3$ with $\Delta_t = 1$ and minimize the same cost function that computes the L2 norm difference between adjacent control points for the Bézier spline and first and second derivatives. This choice of cost function is convex, so $(P1)$ and $(P2)$ are convex programs for uniform splines. As $k < 2d + 1$ for this experiment, we use $(P1)$ for the SynthesizeBézier() calls and randomize the transition order in the Kripke structure K_{abs} between trials to produce different counterexamples to get a sense of how frequently $(P1)$ is infeasible.

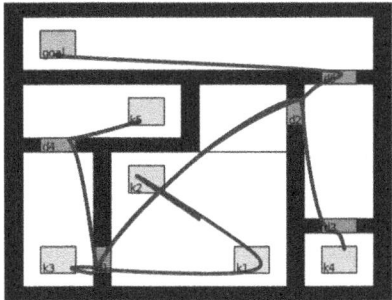

Fig. 3. Synthesized path with the proposed method for Example 2. Path satisfies formula $\varphi = \bigwedge_{i \in \{1,2,3,4,5\}} (\neg door_i \ \mathbf{U} \ key_i) \wedge (\mathbf{F} \ goal)$.

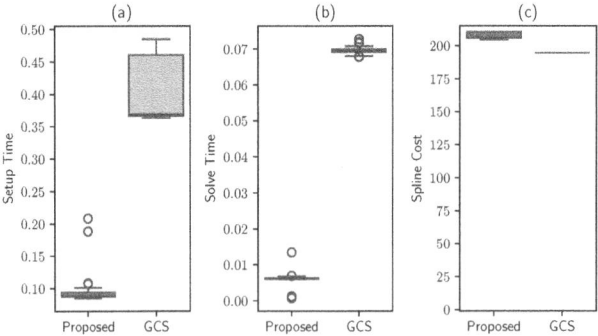

Fig. 4. Comparison with [23] on Example 1. From 50 trials, our method finds a solution on average 5.1x faster and returns splines with 6.7% increased cost. 12 of the 50 trials were infeasible for $(P1)$ to solve.

On average, our proposed method has significantly faster solve times but produces slightly higher cost splines and has variance in the cost of the produced spline. This is partially explained as our method always solves for a lasso spline which adds additional constraints and segments relative to the finite trajectory from the GCS method. Of the sampled 50 trials, 12 were infeasible for $(P1)$ to solve. Figure 4 presents a summary of this comparison.

Table 1. Summary of the comparison on Example 2. Mean values of 50 trials are reported for the proposed method, while a single problem is solved for the compared methods.

	Proposed	GCS [23]	PWL [50]
Setup Time (s)	**0.432**	628.5	1.668
Solve Time (s)	**0.070**	1.919	184.2
Overall Time (s)	**0.502**	630.5	185.9
Mean Spline Cost	849.0	**728.7**	-
Minimum Spline Cost	**667.3**	728.7	-

Example 2 is a significantly more challenging key-door problem originating from [58]. This problem increases the key-door pairs to 5 and features a more complex environment relative to Example 1. In this comparison, we omit the time spent by the GCS method from translating the LTL formula into a DFA from the setup time, but still include the time spent to formulate the graph of convex sets and the product between the DFA and graph. Setup time for the PWL method is only comprised of the time to set up the MILP. A trajectory synthesized with our method is displayed in Fig. 3. For this problem, we again use $(P1)$ to solve for C^2 splines with the same cost function, but increase the order to $k = 4$. The computational benefits from our methods are more obvious on this example and are summarized in Table 1. The GCS method spends significant time in setup by formulating the graph of convex sets and product automaton, which is not an on-the-fly construction like we use. The PWL method encodes the semantics of the specification directly into the optimization problem which is a NP-hard MILP. Our method avoids both these pitfalls. We find the construction of K_{abs}, translation of φ to M_φ, and the model checker runs in less than half a second on average to find a witness ρ, and we only need to provide a simple set of convex constraints to the optimizer that are derived from ρ. This advantage results in a **1255x** speedup compared to GCS and a **370x** speedup compared to PWL on a sample of 50 trials. Of the 50 trials, only 4 were infeasible for $(P1)$ to solve. The cost of the PWL method is incomparable as the splines have different order and PWL uses a different linear cost function. Compared to GCS, we observe our method on average produced splines with 16.5% higher cost but is capable of finding splines with lower cost. Due to the significant computational advantage, it is practical to run our method for several trials to find a lower cost spline in faster time.

4.2   Scalability

To experimentally demonstrate the scalability of our method to splines with high order, we compare the performance of our method using $(P1)$ and $(P2)$ on Example 2. For this comparison, we solve for C^2 splines and range the order from $k = 4$ to $k = 19$, minimizing the same cost function as the previous experiment. We do not run $(P2)$ for $k = 4$ as the order is insufficiently large for the conditions in Theorem 2 to guarantee soundness. We perform 50 random samples for each order and present the mean solve times and spline costs along with confidence intervals in Fig. 5. There is insignificant difference in the mean solve times or spline cost between our two proposed synthesis methods, which is intuitive as $(P2)$ lightly relaxes some constraints of $(P1)$. As the choice of k is independent from the model checking step, the only increase in computational time is due to the convex optimization step. We observe a linear trend in the solve time, shown in (a) of Fig. 5. Intuitively, increasing k reduces the cost of the optimal solution. Only 6 problems were infeasible for $(P1)$ at $k = 4$, all other problems were feasible for both methods, which is guaranteed for $(P2)$ due to Theorem 3.

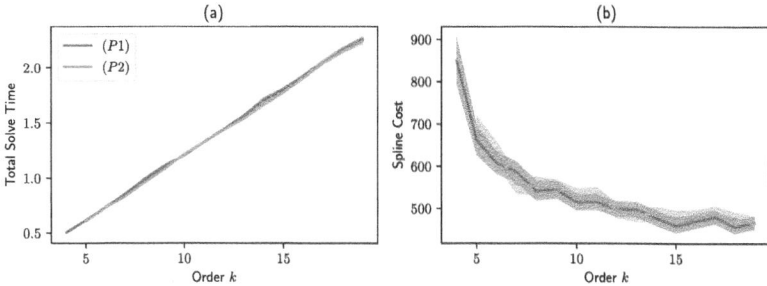

Fig. 5. Comparison between $(P1)$ and $(P2)$ on Example 2 using different spline orders k. Shaded regions present a 95% CI on the mean values for each graph from 50 trials per k.

5   Dynamic Feasibility and Trajectory Tracking

While our method provides a path that achieves a specification, the path may not be dynamically feasible for a specific control system and it is not trivial to design a controller that tracks the path. Moreover, model uncertainty, disturbances, and state estimation errors introduce additional error where the online execution of a synthesized path may now actually violate the specification. This caveat is important to highlight, our soundness and completeness guarantees are with respect to the path and extending those guarantees to a controller is a significantly challenging problem. These issues motivate the usage of sophisticated trajectory tracking controllers to execute planned splines.

5.1 Abstract Control Preliminaries

In this subsection, we review definitions for symbolic abstractions of control systems from [54]. All material in this subsection is preliminary.

Definition 7 (Control System). *A control system is a tuple* $\Sigma = (\mathbb{R}^n, \mathbb{X}_0, \mathbb{U}, f, h_{\mathbb{R}^n})$ *where* $\mathbb{R}^n$ *is the state space,* $\mathbb{X}_0 \subseteq \mathbb{R}^n$ *is the set of initial states,* $\mathbb{U} \subset \mathbb{R}^m$ *is the input space,* $f \colon \mathbb{R}^n \times \mathbb{R}^m \to \mathbb{R}^n$ *is a vector field, and* $h_{\mathbb{R}^n} \colon \mathbb{R}^n \to 2^{AP}$ *is an output function for set of atomic propositions* AP.

We denote the set of input functions U where each $u \in U$ is an essentially bounded piecewise continuous function $u \colon \mathbb{R} \to \mathbb{U}$. A piecewise continuously differentiable function $x \colon (a, b) \to \mathbb{R}^n$ is a trajectory (or solution) of Σ if there exists $u \in U$ satisfying

$$\dot{x}(t) = f(x(t), u(t)), \quad x(0) \in \mathbb{X}_0 \tag{33}$$

where $a < 0 < b$. Denote $[\cdot] \colon \mathbb{R}^n \to \mathcal{P} \cup P_*$ the map from each state to the appropriate set in the partition or absorbing region it belongs to. We assume the output function $h_{\mathbb{R}^n}$ is well-behaved with respect to the given partition and labeling function, i.e. each $x \in \mathbb{R}^n$ satisfies $h_{\mathbb{R}^n}(x) = L([x])$.

Definition 8 (Transition System). *A transition system* $TS = (\mathcal{X}, \mathcal{X}_0, \mathcal{U}, \to, \mathcal{Y}, h_{\mathcal{X}})$. $\mathcal{X}$ *is a set of states,* $\mathcal{X}_0 \subseteq X$ *is a set of initial states,* $\mathcal{U}$ *is a set of inputs,* $\to \subseteq \mathcal{X} \times \mathcal{U} \times \mathcal{X}$ *is a transition relation,* $\mathcal{Y}$ *is an output set,* $h_{\mathcal{X}} \colon \mathcal{X} \to \mathcal{Y}$ *is an output function.*

Define the transition system associated with the control system Σ as $TS_\Sigma = (\mathcal{X}, \mathcal{X}_0, \mathcal{U}, \to, \mathcal{Y})$. The state set $\mathcal{X} = \mathbb{R}^n$, initial states $\mathcal{X}_0 = \mathbb{X}_0$, input set $\mathcal{U} = U$, and output function $h_{\mathcal{X}} = h_{\mathbb{R}^n}$. Transition system TS_Σ records transition $x_i \xrightarrow{u} x_j$ if either:

a. $[x_i] \neq [x_j]$ and there exists $u \in U$ and $\tau \in \mathbb{R}_+$ where $x(t)$ is a trajectory of Σ satisfying $x(0) = x_i, x(\tau) = x_j$. Additionally, there exists $\epsilon \in [0, \tau]$ satisfying either
   1. $[x_i] = [x(t)]$ for $t \in [0, \epsilon)$ and $[x_j] = [x(t)]$ for $t \in [\epsilon, \tau]$.
   2. $[x_i] = [x(t)]$ for $t \in [0, \epsilon]$ and $[x_j] = [x(t)]$ for $t \in (\epsilon, \tau]$.
b. $[x_i] = [x_j]$ and there exists $u \in U$ where $x(t)$ is a trajectory of Σ satisfying $x(0) = x_i, x(\tau) = x_j$ and for all $t \in [0, \tau], [x_i] = [x(t)]$.

Intuitively, TS_Σ is an infinite transition system that records transitions when there exists a control input function that drives the system state to an adjacent set in the partition or to a state within the same set in the partition. We define a finite abstraction of TS_Σ using a Kripke structure $K_\Sigma = (S_\Sigma, I_\Sigma, R_\Sigma, h_{S_\Sigma})$. The state set $S_\Sigma = \mathcal{P} \cup P_*$, initial states $s \in I_\Sigma$ iff there exists $x \in s$ where $x \in \mathbb{X}_0$, and the transition $(s_i, s_j) \in R_\Sigma$ iff there exists $u \in U$ where $x_i \xrightarrow{u} x_j$, $[x_i] = s_i, [x_j] = s_j$. Finally $h_{S_\Sigma} = h_S$ is a given labeling function. Runs of K_Σ describe the possible sequences of labels the control system can achieve using some control input function. There is a simulation relation from TS_Σ to K_Σ, denoted $TS_\Sigma \preceq K_\Sigma$.

Definition 9 (Simulation Relation). *For transition system TS and Kripke structure K, a relation $\mathcal{R} \subseteq \mathcal{X} \times S$ is a simulation relation from TS to K, denoted $TS \preceq K$, if the following conditions are satisfied*

1. *For all $x \in \mathcal{X}_0$, there exists $s \in I$ with $(x, s) \in \mathcal{R}$.*
2. *For all $(x, s) \in \mathcal{R}$, $h_\mathcal{X}(x) = h_S(s)$.*
3. *For all $(x, s) \in \mathcal{R}$, $x \xrightarrow{u} x'$ implies there exists $s' \in S$ where $(s, s') \in R$ and $(x', s') \in \mathcal{R}$.*

Lemma 3. *The Kripke structure K_Σ simulates TS_Σ, $TS_\Sigma \preceq K_\Sigma$*

Proof. The relation $\mathcal{R} = \{(x, P) \mid x \in P, P \in \mathcal{P} \cup P_*\}$ is a simulation relation. The first two conditions immediately follow from the definitions of TS_Σ and K_Σ, the last condition follows from the "only if" of the definition of R_Σ.

5.2   Differential Flatness

Now, we relate our Kripke structure K_{abs} constructed from the given convex partition $\mathcal{P}$ with the abstract control system K_Σ. Specifically, K_{abs} simulates K_Σ, assuming for each $x \in \mathcal{X}_0 \colon [x] \in I$.

Lemma 4. *The Kripke structure K_{abs} simulates K_Σ, $K_\Sigma \preceq K_{\text{abs}}$.*

Proof. Define the relation $\mathcal{R} = \{(s, s) \mid s \in S\}$. As $S = S_\Sigma$, $I_\Sigma \subseteq I$, and $h_S = h_{S_\Sigma}$, the first two conditions of the simulation relation are immediate. For every $(s_i, s_j) \in R_\Sigma$, there exists a piecewise continuous trajectory of Σ from some $x \in P_i$ to some $x' \in P_j$ that does not enter any $P \in \mathcal{P} \cup P_*$ where $P \neq P_i$ and $P \neq P_j$. This implies the intersection of the closures is nonempty, $\overline{P_i} \cap \overline{P_j} \neq \emptyset$, so $(s_i, s_j) \in R$.

As simulation relations are transitive, $TS_\Sigma \preceq K_{\text{abs}}$ follows. This guarantees if there exists a trajectory of Σ that satisfies φ, our algorithm will produce a spline. However, the spline may not be dynamically feasible. One class of systems where Bézier spline paths are well suited for are differentially flat systems [15], control systems where the state and inputs can be written as algebraic functions of selected flat outputs and derivatives. Precisely, Σ is differentially flat if there exists a o-dimensional flat output $z \in \mathbb{R}^o$ that can be computed from an invertible function $\alpha \colon \mathbb{R}^{n \times m^{d+1}} \to \mathbb{R}^o$ that depends on the state x and a finite number d of time derivatives of the input u.

$$z = \alpha(x, u, \dot{u}, \ldots, u^{(d)}). \tag{34}$$

The inverse of α may depend on a different finite number of derivatives ν of z and is split into two functions $\beta \colon \mathbb{R}^{o^{\nu+1}} \to \mathbb{R}^n$ and $\gamma \colon \mathbb{R}^{o^{\nu+1}} \to \mathbb{R}^m$ to recover x and u.

$$x = \beta(z, \dot{z}, \ldots, z^{(\nu)}), \quad u = \gamma(z, \dot{z}, \ldots, z^{(\nu)}) \tag{35}$$

Any C^ν trajectory in the flat output space is dynamically feasible as this inverse transformation directly recovers the state and input trajectory. However, since

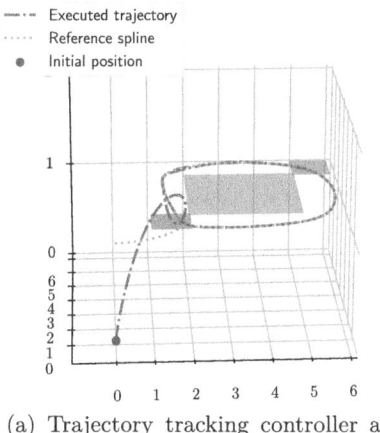

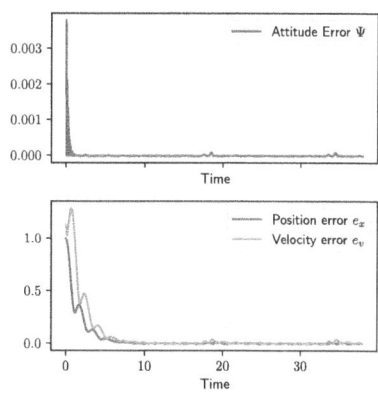

(a) Trajectory tracking controller applied to a planned spline.

(b) Tracking error defined in [27].

Fig. 6. Planned and executed trajectories for a quadrotor satisfying $\varphi = \mathbf{G}\,\mathbf{F}(blue) \wedge \mathbf{G}\,\mathbf{F}(green) \wedge \mathbf{G}(\neg red)$. The quadrotor is initialized with error to the planned trajectory to show the controller can recover. (Color figure online)

convex actuator constraints could map to non-convex regions in the flat output space, including constraints on u typically requires conservatively bounding derivatives [14]. This differential flatness approach is popular to plan trajectories for quadrotors (e.g. [10,36,45,49]). A C^ν curve planned in the flat output space is a dynamically feasible trajectory, but to handle model uncertainty, disturbances, and tracking errors, these methods combine with a trajectory tracking controller where many methods have been studied such as model predictive control (MPC) [1,11,51] and geometric control [26,27]. In this way, our method can plan reference paths in the flat output space while a trajectory tracking controller for the control system of interest can be used to track the planned path.

Quadrotor Trajectory Tracking. We use a simple model of quadrotor dynamics without disturbances or drag, the same presented in [36]. Recall from Sect. 2.2, the constraints to impose velocity and acceleration limits are linear for uniform splines $\mathcal{B}$. We leverage the controller from [27] to track the reference paths. We plan the reference Bézier spline $\mathcal{B}$ in the flat output space $z = (\mathbf{x}, \psi)$ where $\mathbf{x}$ is the 3D position and ψ is the yaw angle of the quadrotor. $\mathcal{B}$ is planned to satisfy $\varphi = \mathbf{G}\,\mathbf{F}(blue) \wedge \mathbf{G}\,\mathbf{F}(green) \wedge \mathbf{G}(\neg red)$. The transformations β and γ from the flat output space to the state and control spaces of the quadrotor requires $\mathbf{x}$ to be C^5 and ψ to be C^3, so we set $d = 5$ and $k = 11$ and use $(P2)$. We constrain the reference spline acceleration to be below $1.5\,\text{m/s}^2$ and velocity to be below $2.5\,\text{m/s}$. These additional constraints means Theorem 3 does not apply, though empirically we did not encounter any infeasible problems when running this experiment. Planned and executed trajectories that drive the quadrotor twice around the looping section in $\mathcal{B}$ are displayed in Fig. 6, along with the trajectory tracking error. Note each region is unbounded in the z axis but presented as a 2D region for clarity. The overall planning time for this problem is 0.75 s.

6   Related Work

A popular method to synthesize controllers for discrete time systems is to formulate satisfaction of the temporal logic objective as a mixed integer linear program (MILP) [3,6,44,47]. This approach has been extended for multi-agent systems [50]. A drawback of this approach is the NP-hardness of the MILP. Additional binary variables are added as the problem horizon increases, making scaling to long horizons and multi-agent systems difficult, and entirely prohibiting infinite horizon trajectories. Additionally, MILP approaches require linear or linearized dynamics and the MILP often does not encode information about the system trajectory between discrete waypoints. Guaranteeing satisfaction of a continuous time system from a discrete time sampled trajectory requires additional reasoning by e.g. strictification [13] or trajectory parameterizations [50].

Optimization and controls methods have been used to directly optimize the robustness of a Signal Temporal Logic (STL) objective by defining smooth approximations of the robustness metric [16,17,38], which can be incorporated into automatic differentiation systems [28]. Methods in this category either directly optimize a parameterized version of the trajectory [39], or formulate an optimal control problem to maximize a smooth robustness by adapting algorithms like SQP [16,38] and DDP [22]. This approach also requires finite time satisfaction of the formula, and the smooth robustness semantics are non-convex so these methods can only guarantee local optimality. Control barrier functions (CBF) for a fragment of STL have been studied in [29,30] which guarantee continuous time satisfaction with control actions that can be solved with convex programming. This method alleviates the computational challenge of the MILP and optimization based approaches, but must rely on expert knowledge to design appropriate CBFs for each formula, and only applies to a restricted fragment of STL.

7   Conclusion

We have presented a sound and complete method that synthesizes a smooth path which automatically satisfies an LTL formula. Additionally, we have demonstrated a significant computational advantage on benchmark problems relative to existing work. In the future, we plan on extending formal guarantees to trajectory tracking controllers, as well as extending our method to multi-agent systems.

Acknowledgments. This work was partially supported by the National Science Foundation through the following grants: CAREER award (SHF-2048094), CNS-1932620, CNS-2039087, FMitF-1837131, CCF-SHF-1932620, IIS-SLES-2417075, funding by Toyota R&D and Siemens Corporate Research through the USC Center for Autonomy and AI, by Northrop Grumman through the IDEAS center at USC, and the Airbus Institute for Engineering Research. This work does not reflect the views or positions of any organization listed.

Disclosure of Interests. The authors have no competing interests to declare.

References

1. Baca, T., Hert, D., Loianno, G., Saska, M., Kumar, V.: Model predictive trajectory tracking and collision avoidance for reliable outdoor deployment of unmanned aerial vehicles. In: 2018 IEEE/RSJ International Conference on Intelligent Robots and Systems (IROS), pp. 6753–6760 (2018). https://doi.org/10.1109/IROS.2018.8594266

2. Baier, C., Katoen, J.P.: Principles of Model Checking. The MIT Press, Cambridge (2008)

3. Belta, C., Sadraddini, S.: Formal methods for control synthesis: an optimization perspective. Annu. Rev. Control Robot. Auton. Syst. **2**, 115–140 (2019). https://doi.org/10.1146/annurev-control-053018-023717

4. Bhatia, A., Kavraki, L.E., Vardi, M.Y.: Sampling-based motion planning with temporal goals. In: 2010 IEEE International Conference on Robotics and Automation, Anchorage, AK, pp. 2689–2696. IEEE (2010). https://doi.org/10.1109/ROBOT.2010.5509503

5. Bloem, R., Jobstmann, B., Piterman, N., Pnueli, A., Sa'ar, Y.: Synthesis of reactive(1) designs. J. Comput. Syst. Sci. **78**(3), 911–938 (2012). https://doi.org/10.1016/j.jcss.2011.08.007

6. Buyukkocak, A.T., Aksaray, D., Yazıcıoğlu, Y.: Planning of heterogeneous multi-agent systems under signal temporal logic specifications with integral predicates. IEEE Robot. Autom. Lett. **6**(2), 1375–1382 (2021). https://doi.org/10.1109/LRA.2021.3057049

7. Camacho, A., Baier, J., Muise, C., McIlraith, S.: Finite LTL synthesis as planning. In: Proceedings of the International Conference on Automated Planning and Scheduling, vol. 28, pp. 29–38 (2018). https://doi.org/10.1609/icaps.v28i1.13908

8. Clarke, E.M., Henzinger, T.A., Veith, H., Bloem, R. (eds.): Handbook of Model Checking. Springer, Cham (2018). https://doi.org/10.1007/978-3-319-10575-8

9. Duret-Lutz, A., et al.: From spot 2.0 to spot 2.10: what's new? In: Shoham, S., Vizel, Y. (eds.) Computer Aided Verification, pp. 174–187. Springer, Cham (2022). https://doi.org/10.1007/978-3-031-13188-2_9

10. Faessler, M., Franchi, A., Scaramuzza, D.: Differential flatness of quadrotor dynamics subject to rotor drag for accurate tracking of high-speed trajectories. IEEE Robot. Autom. Lett. **3**(2), 620–626 (2018). https://doi.org/10.1109/LRA.2017.2776353

11. Faigl, J., Váňa, P.: Surveillance planning with Bézier curves. IEEE Robot. Autom. Lett. **3**(2), 750–757 (2018). https://doi.org/10.1109/LRA.2018.2789844

12. Fainekos, G.E., Loizou, S.G., Pappas, G.J.: Translating temporal logic to controller specifications. In: Proceedings of the 45th IEEE Conference on Decision and Control, pp. 899–904 (2006). https://doi.org/10.1109/CDC.2006.377825

13. Fainekos, G.E., Pappas, G.J.: Robustness of temporal logic specifications for continuous-time signals. Theoret. Comput. Sci. **410**(42), 4262–4291 (2009). https://doi.org/10.1016/j.tcs.2009.06.021

14. Faiz, N., Agrawal, S., Murray, R.: Differentially flat systems with inequality constraints: an approach to real-time feasible trajectory generation. J. Guid. Control. Dyn. **24**(2), 219–227 (2001)

15. Fliess, M., Lévine, J., Martin, P., Rouchon, P.: Flatness and defect of non-linear systems: introductory theory and examples. Int. J. Control **61**(6), 1327–1361 (1995). https://doi.org/10.1080/00207179508921959

16. Gilpin, Y., Kurtz, V., Lin, H.: A smooth robustness measure of signal temporal logic for symbolic control. IEEE Control Syst. Lett. **5**(1), 241–246 (2021). https://doi.org/10.1109/LCSYS.2020.3001875

17. Hashemi, N., Williams, S., Hoxha, B., Prokhorov, D., Fainekos, G., Deshmukh, J.: LB4TL: a smooth semantics for temporal logic to train neural feedback controllers. IFAC-PapersOnLine **58**(11), 183–188 (2024). https://doi.org/10.1016/j.ifacol.2024.07.445

18. Jing, G., Kress-Gazit, H.: Improving the continuous execution of reactive LTL-based controllers. In: 2013 IEEE International Conference on Robotics and Automation, pp. 5439–5445. IEEE (2013)

19. Karaman, S., Frazzoli, E.: Sampling-based motion planning with deterministic μ-calculus specifications. In: Proceedings of the 48h IEEE Conference on Decision and Control (CDC) held jointly with 2009 28th Chinese Control Conference, pp. 2222–2229 (2009). https://doi.org/10.1109/CDC.2009.5400278

20. Kloetzer, M., Belta, C.: Automatic deployment of distributed teams of robots from temporal logic motion specifications. IEEE Trans. Rob. **26**(1), 48–61 (2010). https://doi.org/10.1109/TRO.2009.2035776

21. Kress-Gazit, H., Fainekos, G.E., Pappas, G.J.: Temporal-logic-based reactive mission and motion planning. IEEE Trans. Rob. **25**(6), 1370–1381 (2009). https://doi.org/10.1109/TRO.2009.2030225

22. Kurtz, V., Lin, H.: Trajectory optimization for high-dimensional nonlinear systems under STL specifications. IEEE Control Syst. Lett. **5**(4), 1429–1434 (2021). https://doi.org/10.1109/LCSYS.2020.3038640

23. Kurtz, V., Lin, H.: Temporal logic motion planning with convex optimization via graphs of convex sets. IEEE Trans. Rob. **39**(5), 3791–3804 (2023). https://doi.org/10.1109/TRO.2023.3291463

24. Latombe, J.C.: Robot Motion Planning, vol. 124. Springer (2012)

25. Lau, B., Sprunk, C., Burgard, W.: Kinodynamic motion planning for mobile robots using splines. In: 2009 IEEE/RSJ International Conference on Intelligent Robots and Systems, pp. 2427–2433 (2009). https://doi.org/10.1109/IROS.2009.5354805

26. Lee, T.: Geometric control of quadrotor UAVs transporting a cable-suspended rigid body. IEEE Trans. Control Syst. Technol. **26**(1), 255–264 (2018). https://doi.org/10.1109/TCST.2017.2656060

27. Lee, T., Leok, M., McClamroch, N.H.: Geometric tracking control of a quadrotor UAV on SE(3). In: 49th IEEE Conference on Decision and Control (CDC), pp. 5420–5425 (2010). https://doi.org/10.1109/CDC.2010.5717652

28. Leung, K., Aréchiga, N., Pavone, M.: Backpropagation through signal temporal logic specifications: infusing logical structure into gradient-based methods. Int. J. Robot. Res. **42**(6), 356–370 (2023). https://doi.org/10.1177/02783649221082115

29. Lindemann, L., Dimarogonas, D.V.: Control barrier functions for signal temporal logic tasks. IEEE Control Syst. Lett. **3**(1), 96–101 (2019). https://doi.org/10.1109/LCSYS.2018.2853182

30. Lindemann, L., Dimarogonas, D.V.: Decentralized control barrier functions for coupled multi-agent systems under signal temporal logic tasks. In: 2019 18th European Control Conference (ECC), pp. 89–94 (2019). https://doi.org/10.23919/ECC.2019.8796109

31. Luo, X., Kantaros, Y., Zavlanos, M.M.: An abstraction-free method for multi-robot temporal logic optimal control synthesis. IEEE Trans. Rob. **37**(5), 1487–1507 (2021). https://doi.org/10.1109/TRO.2021.3061983

32. Majumdar, R., Ozay, N., Schmuck, A.K.: On abstraction-based controller design with output feedback. In: Proceedings of the 23rd International Conference on Hybrid Systems: Computation and Control, HSCC 2020, pp. 1–11. Association for Computing Machinery, New York (2020). https://doi.org/10.1145/3365365.3382219

33. Marcucci, T., Petersen, M., von Wrangel, D., Tedrake, R.: Motion planning around obstacles with convex optimization. Sci. Robot. **8**(84), eadf7843 (2023). https://doi.org/10.1126/scirobotics.adf7843

34. Marcucci, T., Umenberger, J., Parrilo, P., Tedrake, R.: Shortest paths in graphs of convex sets. SIAM J. Optim. **34**(1), 507–532 (2024). https://doi.org/10.1137/22M1523790

35. McMahon, J., Plaku, E.: Sampling-based tree search with discrete abstractions for motion planning with dynamics and temporal logic. In: 2014 IEEE/RSJ International Conference on Intelligent Robots and Systems, pp. 3726–3733 (2014). https://doi.org/10.1109/IROS.2014.6943085

36. Mellinger, D., Kumar, V.: Minimum snap trajectory generation and control for quadrotors. In: 2011 IEEE International Conference on Robotics and Automation, pp. 2520–2525 (2011). https://doi.org/10.1109/ICRA.2011.5980409

37. Nilsson, P., Ames, A.D.: Barrier functions: bridging the gap between planning from specifications and safety-critical control. In: 2018 IEEE Conference on Decision and Control (CDC), pp. 765–772 (2018). https://doi.org/10.1109/CDC.2018.8619142

38. Pant, Y.V., Abbas, H., Mangharam, R.: Smooth operator: control using the smooth robustness of temporal logic. In: 2017 IEEE Conference on Control Technology and Applications (CCTA), pp. 1235–1240 (2017). https://doi.org/10.1109/CCTA.2017.8062628

39. Pant, Y.V., Abbas, H., Quaye, R.A., Mangharam, R.: Fly-by-logic: control of multi-drone fleets with temporal logic objectives. In: 2018 ACM/IEEE 9th International Conference on Cyber-Physical Systems (ICCPS), pp. 186–197 (2018). https://doi.org/10.1109/ICCPS.2018.00026

40. Piegl, L., Tiller, W.: The NURBS Book. Monographs in Visual Communication, Springer, Heidelberg (1997). https://doi.org/10.1007/978-3-642-59223-2

41. Plaku, E., Karaman, S.: Motion planning with temporal-logic specifications: progress and challenges. AI Commun. **29**(1), 151–162 (2016). https://doi.org/10.3233/AIC-150682

42. Pnueli, A.: The temporal logic of programs. In: 18th Annual Symposium on Foundations of Computer Science (SFCS 1977), pp. 46–57 (1977). https://doi.org/10.1109/SFCS.1977.32

43. Preiss, J., Hausman, K., Sukhatme, G., Weiss, S.: Trajectory optimization for self-calibration and navigation. In: Robotics: Science and Systems XIII. Robotics: Science and Systems Foundation (2017). https://doi.org/10.15607/RSS.2017.XIII.054

44. Raman, V., Donzé, A., Maasoumy, M., Murray, R.M., Sangiovanni-Vincentelli, A., Seshia, S.A.: Model predictive control with signal temporal logic specifications. In: 53rd IEEE Conference on Decision and Control, pp. 81–87 (2014). https://doi.org/10.1109/CDC.2014.7039363
45. Richter, C., Bry, A., Roy, N.: Polynomial trajectory planning for aggressive quadrotor flight in dense indoor environments. In: Inaba, M., Corke, P. (eds.) Robotics Research. STAR, vol. 114, pp. 649–666. Springer, Cham (2016). https://doi.org/10.1007/978-3-319-28872-7_37
46. Rungger, M., Mazo Jr, M., Tabuada, P.: Specification-guided controller synthesis for linear systems and safe linear-time temporal logic. In: Proceedings of the 16th International Conference on Hybrid Systems: Computation and Control, pp. 333–342 (2013)
47. Saha, S., Julius, A.A.: An MILP approach for real-time optimal controller synthesis with metric temporal logic specifications. In: 2016 American Control Conference (ACC), pp. 1105–1110 (2016). https://doi.org/10.1109/ACC.2016.7525063
48. Schmuck, A.K.: Building Bridges in Abstraction-Based Controller Synthesis: Advancing, Combining, and Comparing Methods From Computer and Control. Technische Universitaet Berlin (Germany) (2015)
49. Sreenath, K., Lee, T., Kumar, V.: Geometric control and differential flatness of a quadrotor UAV with a cable-suspended load. In: 52nd IEEE Conference on Decision and Control, pp. 2269–2274 (2013). https://doi.org/10.1109/CDC.2013.6760219
50. Sun, D., Chen, J., Mitra, S., Fan, C.: Multi-agent motion planning from signal temporal logic specifications. IEEE Robot. Autom. Lett. 7(2), 3451–3458 (2022). https://doi.org/10.1109/LRA.2022.3146951
51. Sun, S., Romero, A., Foehn, P., Kaufmann, E., Scaramuzza, D.: A comparative study of nonlinear MPC and differential-flatness-based control for quadrotor agile flight. IEEE Trans. Rob. 38(6), 3357–3373 (2022). https://doi.org/10.1109/TRO.2022.3177279
52. Tabuada, P.: Symbolic control of linear systems based on symbolic subsystems. IEEE Trans. Autom. Control 51(6), 1003–1013 (2006)
53. Tabuada, P.: An approximate simulation approach to symbolic control. IEEE Trans. Autom. Control 53(6), 1406–1418 (2008). https://doi.org/10.1109/TAC.2008.925824
54. Tabuada, P.: Verification and Control of Hybrid Systems: A Symbolic Approach. Springer, Boston (2009). https://doi.org/10.1007/978-1-4419-0224-5
55. Tabuada, P., Pappas, G.J.: Linear time logic control of discrete-time linear systems. IEEE Trans. Autom. Control 51(12), 1862–1877 (2006). https://doi.org/10.1109/TAC.2006.886494
56. Tordesillas, J., Lopez, B.T., How, J.P.: FASTER: fast and safe trajectory planner for flights in unknown environments. In: 2019 IEEE/RSJ International Conference on Intelligent Robots and Systems (IROS), pp. 1934–1940 (2019). https://doi.org/10.1109/IROS40897.2019.8968021
57. Vasile, C.I., Belta, C.: Sampling-based temporal logic path planning. In: 2013 IEEE/RSJ International Conference on Intelligent Robots and Systems, pp. 4817–4822 (2013). https://doi.org/10.1109/IROS.2013.6697051
58. Vega-Brown, W., Roy, N.: Admissible abstractions for near-optimal task and motion planning. In: Proceedings of the Twenty-Seventh International Joint Conference on Artificial Intelligence, pp. 4852–4859. International Joint Conferences on Artificial Intelligence Organization, Stockholm, Sweden (2018). https://doi.org/10.24963/ijcai.2018/674

59. Wongpiromsarn, T., Topcu, U., Murray, R.M.: Receding horizon control for temporal logic specifications. In: Proceedings of the 13th ACM International Conference on Hybrid Systems: Computation and Control, HSCC 2010, pp. 101–110. Association for Computing Machinery, New York (2010). https://doi.org/10.1145/1755952.1755968

60. Zhou, B., Gao, F., Wang, L., Liu, C., Shen, S.: Robust and efficient quadrotor trajectory generation for fast autonomous flight. IEEE Robot. Autom. Lett. **4**(4), 3529–3536 (2019). https://doi.org/10.1109/LRA.2019.2927938

Full LTL Synthesis over Infinite-State Arenas

Shaun Azzopardi[3(✉)] , Luca Di Stefano[2] , Nir Piterman[1] ,
and Gerardo Schneider[1]

[1] University of Gothenburg and Chalmers University
of Technology, Gothenburg, Sweden
[2] TU Wien, Institute of Computer Engineering,
Treitlstraße 3, 1040 Vienna, Austria
[3] Dedaub, San Gwann, Malta
shaun.a@dedaub.com

Abstract. Recently, interest has increased in applying reactive synthesis to richer-than-Boolean domains. A major (undecidable) challenge in this area is to establish when certain repeating behaviour terminates in a desired state when the number of steps is unbounded. Existing approaches struggle with this problem, or can handle at most deterministic games with Büchi goals. This work goes beyond by contributing the first effectual approach to synthesis with full LTL objectives, based on Boolean abstractions that encode both safety and liveness properties of the underlying infinite arena. We take a CEGAR approach: attempting synthesis on the Boolean abstraction, checking spuriousness of abstract counterstrategies through invariant checking, and refining the abstraction based on counterexamples. We reduce the complexity, when restricted to predicates, of abstracting and synthesising by an exponential through an efficient binary encoding. This also allows us to eagerly identify useful fairness properties. Our discrete synthesis tool outperforms the state-of-the-art on linear integer arithmetic (LIA) benchmarks from literature, solving almost double as many syntesis problems as the current state-of-the-art. It also solves slightly more problems than the second-best realisability checker, in one-third of the time. We also introduce benchmarks with richer objectives that other approaches cannot handle, and evaluate our tool on them.

Keywords: Infinite-state synthesis · Liveness refinement · CEGAR

1 Introduction

Reactive synthesis provides a way to synthesise controllers that ensure satisfaction of high-level *Linear Temporal Logic* (LTL) specifications, against uncontrolled environment behaviour. Classically, synthesis was suggested and applied

This work is funded by the ERC consolidator grant D-SynMA (No. 772459) and the Swedish research council project (No. 2020-04963).

R. Piskac and Z. Rakamarić (Eds.): CAV 2025, LNCS 15934, pp. 274–297, 2025.
https://doi.org/10.1007/978-3-031-98685-7_13

in the Boolean (or finite-range) variable setting [29]. Interest in the infinite-range variable setting was soon to follow. Some of the milestones include the adaptation of the theory of CEGAR to infinite-state games [20] and the early adoption of SMT for symbolic representation of infinite-sized sets of game configurations [5]. However, in recent years, success of synthesis in the finite domain as well as maturity of SMT solvers has led to sharply growing interest in synthesis in the context of infinite-range variables, with several tools becoming available that tackle this problem. We highlight the two different (but related) approaches taken by the community: (a) application of infinite-state reactive synthesis from extensions of LTL where atoms include quantifier-free first-order formulas over infinite-range variables [8,14,22,23] and (b) direct applications to the solution of games with an infinite number of configurations [3,18,19,34]. Two notable examples of the two approaches from the last two years include: (a) the identification of a fragment of LTL with first-order atoms that allows for a decidable synthesis framework [30–32] and (b) the introduction of so-called *acceleration lemmas* [18,19,34] targeting the general undecidable infinite-state synthesis problem. The latter directly attacks a core issue of the problem's undecidability: identify whether certain repeated behaviour can eventually force the interaction to a certain state. Thus, solving the (alternating) termination problem.

Infinite-state reactive synthesis aims at producing a system that manipulates variables with infinite domains and reacts to input variables controlled by an adversarial environment. Given an LTL objective, the *realisability problem* is to determine whether a system may exist that enforces the objective. Then, the *synthesis problem* is to construct such a system, or a *counterstrategy* by which the environment may enforce the negation of the objective. While in the finite-state domain realisability and synthesis are tightly connected, this is not the case in the infinite-state domain and many approaches struggle to (practically) scale from realisability to synthesis. In this paper we focus on the more challenging synthesis problem, rather than mere realisability, to be able to construct implementations. Furthermore, our approach is tailored for the general – undecidable – case.

As mentioned, a major challenge is the identification of repeated behaviour that forces reaching a given state. Most approaches rely on one of two basic techniques: either refine an abstraction based on a mismatch in the application of a transition between concrete and abstract representations, or compute a representation of the set of immediate successors/predecessors of a given set of states. Both have limited effectiveness due to the termination challenge. Indeed, in many interesting cases, such approaches attempt at enumerating paths of unbounded length. For example, this is what happens to approaches relying on refinement [14,22], which is sound but often cannot terminate. It follows that reasoning about the effect of repeated behaviour is crucial.

We know of two attempts at such reasoning. temos [8] identifies single-action loops that terminate in a desired state, but cannot generalise to more challenging cases, e.g., where the environment may momentarily interrupt the loop, and moreover it cannot supply unrealisability verdicts. By contrast, rpgsolve [18] summarises terminating sub-games via acceleration lemmas to construct an argument for realisability, relying on quantifier elimination with uninterpreted functions. However, this approach is limited to at most deterministic Büchi objectives, and is practically more effective for realisability than for synthesis due to the challenges of quantifier elimination. Its extension rpg-STeLA [34] attempts to identify acceleration lemmas that apply to multiple regions and thus solves games compositionally, but only supports realisability.

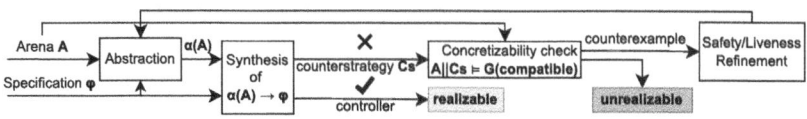

Fig. 1. Workflow of our approach.

In this paper we address the limitations described above, generalising infinite-state reactive synthesis to more expressive objectives. In particular, we consider LTL objectives over infinite-state arenas, without imposing any limit on temporal nesting. Similar to others, our atoms may include quantifier-free first-order formulas. However, we do not restrict the LTL formulas. Furthermore, our approach does not distinguish between realisability and synthesis, and can synthesise both controllers and counterstrategies. As shown in Fig. 1, our approach is based on CEGAR [21], heavily adapted for synthesis. Our main contributions are:

1. An efficient binary encoding of predicates. This reduces complexity, in terms of predicates, of abstraction building/size from exponential to polynomial, and of finite synthesis over abstractions from doubly to singly exponential.
2. A method to check counterstrategy concretisability through invariant checking, that finds minimal counterexamples to concretisability.
3. Two new kinds of liveness refinements: *Structural refinement*, which monitors for terminating concrete loops in the abstract system, and enforces eventual exit; and *Ranking refinement* that relies on the binary encoding, which ensures the well-foundedness of terms relevant to the game in the abstraction.
4. An implementation of the above contributions for LIA problems.
5. The most extensive experimental comparison of infinite-state LIA realisability and synthesis tools in literature. This shows our tool substantially outperforming all others, making it the new state-of-the-art.
6. Separately, we enrich the dataset of existing benchmarks, which currently include at most weak fairness requirements, with a selection of problems incorporating strong fairness.

For the reader's convenience we present the approach informally in Sect. 3, before formalising it in detail (Sects. 4, 5, 6). Then we describe our techniques to improve its efficiency (Sect. 7), present and evaluate our tool (Sect. 8), and conclude while also discussing related and future work (Sects. 9–10). Given space constraints here, more technical details and information about the evaluation can be found in the extended version [2].

2   Background

We use the following notation throughout: for sets S and T such that $S \subseteq T$, we write $\bigwedge_T S$ for $\bigwedge S \wedge \bigwedge_{s \in T \setminus S} \neg s$. We omit set T when clear from the context. $\mathbb{B}(S)$ is the set of Boolean combinations of a set S of Boolean variables.

Linear Temporal Logic, LTL($\mathbb{AP}$), is the language over a set of propositions $\mathbb{AP}$, defined as follows,[1] where $p \in \mathbb{AP}$: $\phi \overset{\text{def}}{=} \mathbf{tt} \mid \mathbf{ff} \mid p \mid \neg\phi \mid \phi \wedge \phi \mid \phi \vee \phi \mid X\phi \mid \phi U \phi$.

For $w \in (2^{\mathbb{AP}})^\omega$, we write $w \models \phi$ or $w \in L(\phi)$, when w satisfies ϕ. A *Moore machine* is $C = \langle S, s_0, \Sigma_{in}, \Sigma_{out}, \rightarrow, out \rangle$, where S is the set of states, s_0 the initial state, Σ_{in} the set of input events, Σ_{out} the set of output events, $\rightarrow$: $S \times 2^{\Sigma_{in}} \mapsto S$ the complete deterministic transition function, and $out : S \mapsto 2^{\Sigma_{out}}$ the labelling of each state with a set of output events. For $(s, I, s') \in \rightarrow$, where $out(s) = O$ we write $s \xrightarrow{I/O} s'$.

A *Mealy machine* is $C = \langle S, s_0, \Sigma_{in}, \Sigma_{out}, \rightarrow \rangle$, where S, s_0, Σ_{in}, and Σ_{out} are as before and $\rightarrow$: $S \times 2^{\Sigma_{in}} \mapsto 2^{\Sigma_{out}} \times S$ the complete deterministic transition function. For $(s, I, O, s') \in \rightarrow$ we write $s \xrightarrow{I/O} s'$.

Unless mentioned explicitly, both Mealy and Moore machines can have an infinite number of states. A *run* of a machine C is $r = s_0, s_1, \ldots$ such that for every $i \geq 0$ we have $s_i \xrightarrow{I_i/O_i} s_{i+1}$ for some I_i and O_i. Run r *produces* the word $w = \sigma_0, \sigma_1, \ldots$, where $\sigma_i = I_i \cup O_i$. A machine C produces the word w if there is a run r producing w. Let $L(C)$ denote the set of all words produced by C.

We cast our synthesis problem into the *LTL reactive synthesis problem*, which calls for finding a Mealy machine that satisfies a given specification over input and output variables $\mathbb{E}$ and $\mathbb{C}$.

Definition 1 (LTL Synthesis). *A specification ϕ over $\mathbb{E} \cup \mathbb{C}$ is said to be* realisable *if and only if there is a Mealy machine C, with input $2^{\mathbb{E}}$ and output $2^{\mathbb{C}}$, such that for every $w \in L(C)$ we have $w \models \phi$. We call C a* controller *for ϕ.*

A specification ϕ is said to be unrealisable *if there is a Moore machine Cs, with input $2^{\mathbb{C}}$ and output $2^{\mathbb{E}}$, such that for every $w \in L(Cs)$ we have that $w \models \neg\phi$. We call Cs a* counterstrategy *for ϕ.*

The problem of synthesis is to construct C or Cs, exactly one of which exists.

Note that the duality between the existence of a strategy and counterstrategy follows from the determinacy of turn-based two-player ω-regular games [24]. We know that finite-state machines suffice for synthesis from LTL specifications [29].

To be able to represent infinite synthesis problems succinctly we consider formulas in a theory. A *theory* consists of a set of terms and predicates over these. Atomic terms are constant values ($\mathcal{C}$) or variables. Terms can be constructed with operators over other terms, with a fixed interpretation. The set $\mathcal{T}(V)$ denotes the terms of the theory, with free variables in V. For $t \in \mathcal{T}(V)$, we write t_{prev} for the term where variables v appearing in t are replaced by fresh variables v_{prev}.

---

[1] See [28] for the standard semantics.

$V = \{target : int = 0, floor : int = 0\}$
$\mathbb{E} = \{env\_inc, door\_open\}$
$\mathbb{C} = \{up, down\}$

Assumptions:

A1. $GF\,door\_open$

A2. $GF\neg door\_open$

Guarantees:

G1. $GF\,floor = target$

G2. $G(door\_open \implies (up \iff down))$

Objective:

$(A1 \wedge A2) \implies (G1 \wedge G2)$

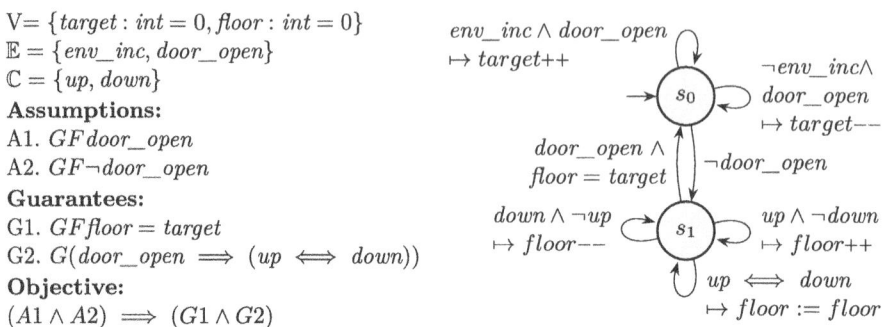

Fig. 2. Elevator example.

We use $\mathcal{ST}(V)$ to denote the set of *state predicates*, i.e., predicates over $\mathcal{T}(V)$, and $\mathcal{TR}(V)$ to denote the set of *transition predicates*, i.e., predicates over $\mathcal{T}(V \cup V_{prev})$, where $v_{prev} \in V_{prev}$ iff $v \in V$. Then, we denote by $\mathcal{Pr}(V)$ the set of all predicates $\mathcal{ST}(V) \cup \mathcal{TR}(V)$. We also define the set of updates $\mathcal{U}(V)$ of a variable set V. Each $U \in \mathcal{U}(V)$ is a function $V \mapsto \mathcal{T}(V)$.

We define the set of valuations over a set of variables V as $Val(V) = V \mapsto \mathcal{C}$, using $val \in Val(V)$ for valuations. For a valuation $val \in Val(V)$, we write $val \models s$, for $s \in \mathcal{ST}(V)$ when val is a model of s. We write $t(val)$ for t grounded on the valuation val. Given valuations $val, val' \in Val(V)$, we write $(val, val') \models t$, for $t \in \mathcal{TR}(V)$, when $val_{prev} \cup val'$ is a model of t, where $val_{prev}(v_{prev}) = val(v)$ and $dom(val_{prev}) = V_{prev}$. We say a formula (a Boolean combination of predicates) is satisfiable when there is a valuation that models it. To simplify presentation, we assume $val \not\models t$ for any val that does not give values to all the variables of t.

3   Informal Overview

We give a simple instructive LIA example (Fig. 2) to illustrate our approach. Despite its simplicity, we stress that no other existing approach can solve it (see Sect. 8): since the environment can delay progress by the controller, the resulting objectives are too rich to be expressed by deterministic Büchi automata.

On the right is an automaton representing a partial design for an elevator, our arena (see Sect. 4). A transition labelled $g \mapsto U$ is taken when the guard g holds and it performs the update U. Unmentioned variables maintain their previous value. On the left, we identify input ($\mathbb{E}$) and output ($\mathbb{C}$) Boolean variables. When guards include these variables, the environment and controller's moves can affect which transitions are possible and which one is taken. The updates determine how to change the values of other variables ($\mathbb{V}$), which could range over infinite domains. Thus, the updates of the variables in $\mathbb{V}$ are determined by the interaction between the environment and the controller. The desired controller must have a strategy such that, for every possible choice of inputs, it will set the output variables so that the resulting computation satisfies a given LTL objective, encoded on the left as $(\bigwedge_i A_i) \implies (\bigwedge_j G_j)$. LTL formulas can include quantifier-free first-order formulas over infinite-domain variables (e.g., $floor = target$). Notice that this objective includes environment fairness, making this synthesis problem impossible to encode as a deterministic Büchi game.

In our elevator, at state s_0 the environment can set a target by controlling variables in $\mathbb{E}$ to increase or decrease $target$. Once a target is set, the environment closes the elevator door ($door\_open$), and the arena transitions to s_1. At s_1, the system can force the elevator to go up or down one floor, or remain at the same floor. This is not a useful elevator: it may never reach the target floor, and it may move with the door open. We desire to control it so that the target is reached infinitely often (G1), and the latter never occurs (G2). We also assume aspects of the elevator not in our control to behave as expected, i.e., that the door is not broken, and thus it opens and closes infinitely often (A1–2).

Predicate Abstraction (Definition 5) First, we soundly abstract the arena A in terms of the predicates in the specification $(A_1 \wedge A_2) \implies (G_1 \wedge G_2)$, and the predicates, and Boolean variables of the arena (here, the states in the automaton). That is,[2] $Pr = \{floor \leq target, target \leq floor, s_0, s_1\}$. This abstraction considers all possible combinations of input and output variables and Pr, and gives a set of possible predicates holding in the next state (according to the corresponding updates). For example, consider the propositional state $p = s_1 \wedge up \wedge \neg down \wedge floor < target$. In the automaton, this activates the transition that increments $floor$. Then, satisfiability checking tells us that the successor state is either $p'_1 := s_1 \wedge floor = target$ or $p'_2 := s_1 \wedge floor < target$.

We encode the arena abstraction as an LTL formula $\alpha(A, Pr)$ of the form $init \wedge G(\bigvee_{a \in abtrans} a)$, where $abtrans$ is a set of abstract transitions (e.g., $p \wedge Xp'_1$ and $p \wedge Xp'_2$ are in $abtrans$), and $init$ is the initial state, i.e., $s_0 \wedge floor=target$.

Abstract Synthesis. From this sound abstraction, we create the abstract formula $\alpha(A, Pr) \implies \phi$ and treat predicates as fresh *input* Booleans. If this formula were realisable, a controller for it would also work concretely, but it is not: at the abstract state p, the environment can always force negation of $floor = target$.

Counterstrategy Concretisability (Definition 6). For an unrealisable abstract problem we will find an abstract counterstrategy Cs. To check whether it is spurious, we model-check if A composed with Cs violates the invariant that the predicate guesses of Cs are correct in the arena. Here, Cs admits a finite counterexample ce where the environment initially increments $target$, then moves to s_1, and the controller increments $floor$, but Cs wrongly maintains $floor < target$.

Safety Refinement (Sect. 6.1). By applying interpolation [25] on ce we discover new predicates, e.g., $target - floor \leq 1$, by which we refine the abstraction to exclude ce. If we were to continue using safety refinement, we would be attempting to enumerate the whole space, which causes a state-space explosion, given the exponential complexity of predicate abstraction, and the doubly exponential complexity of synthesis.

---

[2] LIA predicates are normalised to a form using only $\leq$; other relations are macros.

Efficient Encoding (Sect. 7). We manage state-space explosion through a binary encoding of predicates. Note each predicate on a term corresponds to an interval on the reals. For the term $t = floor - target$, $floor \leq target$ represents $t \in (-\infty, 0]$. $target \leq floor$ represents $t \in [0, \infty)$, and $floor - target \leq 1$ represents $t \in (-\infty, 1]$. These may overlap, but instead we can define formulas whose intervals partition the line $\mathbb{R}$. Here, we get formulas for each interval: $(-\infty, -1], (-1, 0], (0, 1], (1, \infty)$. Binary-encoding these reduces the complexity of abstraction and synthesis by an exponential, w.r.t. arithmetic predicates.

Liveness Refinements (Sect. 6.2). Enumeration is not enough here, given the infinite domain of the variables. Liveness refinements are necessary. Note, once Cs guesses that $floor < target$, it remains in states where $floor < target$ is true. Essentially, we discover a ce in which Cs exercises the loop while(floor ¡ target) floor := floor + 1, and the environment believes it is non-terminating. Using known methods to determine the loop is terminating, we construct a monitor for the loop in the abstraction, with extra variables and assumptions. Then a strong fairness constraint that forces the abstraction to eventually exit the loop monitor captures its termination. We term this *structural loop refinement*. Note that this is not tied to a specific region in the arena. This allows us to encode more sophisticated loops, beyond what current tools for LTL objectives can do.

With a new synthesis attempt on the refined abstraction, a fresh terminating loop is learned, while (target ¡ floor) floor := floor - 1. Refining accordingly allows us to find a controller and thus solve the problem on the next attempt.

Acceleration (Sect. 7). The described partitions of the values of a term have a natural well-founded ordering which we can exploit to identify that the controller can force the abstraction to move left or right across the intervals. Consider that if the term t is currently in the interval $(1, \infty)$, and the controller can force strict decrements of t, then the value of the t must necessarily eventually move to an interval to the left (unless we have reached the left-most interval). Thus, strict decrements force the value of t to move towards the left of the partition, while strict increments force move towards the right of the partition. Only when the environment can match these increments (decrements) with corresponding decrements (increments) then can this behaviour be prevented.

By adding LTL fairness constraints to represent the described behaviour we can immediately identify a controller, with no further refinements needed.

4   Synthesis Setting

One of our contributions is our special setting that combines arenas and LTL objectives, unlike existing LTL approaches which start immediately from LTL-modulo-theories formulas [8,14,22]. We assume a theory, with an associated set of predicates $Pr(V)$ and updates $\mathcal{U}(V)$ over a set of variables V. We also assume two disjoint sets of Boolean inputs and outputs $\mathbb{E}$ and $\mathbb{C}$, respectively controlled by the environment and the controller. Then our specifications are LTL formulas over these variables, $\phi \in \text{LTL}(\mathbb{E} \cup \mathbb{C} \cup Pr_\phi)$, where $Pr_\phi \subseteq Pr(V)$. LTL formulas talk about an *arena* whose state is captured by the value of V, and which modifies its state depending on environment and controller behaviour. Arenas are deterministic; we model (demonic) non-determinism with additional environment variables. This allows us to encode concretisability checking as invariant checking, rather than the significantly more complex CTL* model checking.

Definition 2 (Arena). *An arena A over V is a tuple $\langle V, val_0, \delta \rangle$, where V is a finite set of variables, $val_0 \in Val(V)$ is the initial valuation, and $\delta : \mathbb{B}(\mathbb{E} \cup \mathbb{C} \cup Pr(V)) \rightarrow \mathcal{U}(V)$ is a partial function with finite domain, such that for all $val \in Val(V)$ and for every $E \subseteq \mathbb{E}$ and $C \subseteq \mathbb{C}$ there is always a single $f \in dom(\delta)$ such that $(val, E \cup C) \models f$. An arena is finite when every $v \in V$ is finite.*

Notice that due to the finite domain of δ, an arena A defines a *finite* set of predicates $Pr \subseteq Pr(V)$ and a *finite* set of updates $U \subseteq \mathcal{U}(V)$ that appear in δ. We use the sets Pr and U when clear from the context.

An infinite concrete word $w \in (Val(V) \times 2^{\mathbb{E} \cup \mathbb{C}})^\omega$ is a *model* of A iff $w(0) = (val_0, E \cup C)$ (for some E and C), and for every $i \geq 0$, $w(i) = (val_i, E_i \cup C_i)$, then for the unique $f_i \in dom(\delta)$ such that $(val_i, E_i \cup C_i) \models f_i$ we have $val_{i+1} = (\delta(f_i))(val_i)$. We write $L(A)$ for the set of all models of A.

During our workflow, the words of our abstract synthesis problem may have a different domain than those of the arena. We define these as *abstract words*, and identify when they are concretisable in the arena. Then, we can define the meaning of (un)realisability modulo an arena in terms of concretisability.

Definition 3 (Abstract Words and Concretisability). *For a finite set of predicates $Pr \subseteq Pr(V)$, and a set of Boolean variables $\mathbb{E}'$, such that $\mathbb{E} \subseteq \mathbb{E}'$, an abstract word a is a word over $2^{\mathbb{E}' \cup \mathbb{C} \cup Pr}$. Abstract word a abstracts concrete word w, with letters from $Val(V) \times 2^{\mathbb{E} \cup \mathbb{C}}$, when for every i, if $a(i) = E_i \cup C_i \cup Pr_i$, then $w(i) = (val_i, (E_i \cap \mathbb{E}) \cup C_i)$ for some $Pr_i \subseteq Pr$, $val_0 \models \bigwedge_{Pr} Pr_0$, and for $i > 0$ then $(val_{i-1}, val_i) \models \bigwedge_{Pr} Pr_i$. We write $\gamma(a)$ for the set of concrete words that a abstracts. We say abstract word a is* concretisable *in an arena A when $L(A) \cap \gamma(a)$ is non-empty.*

Definition 4 (Realisability modulo an Arena). *A formula ϕ in LTL($\mathbb{E} \cup \mathbb{C} \cup Pr_\phi$) is said to be* realisable *modulo an arena A, when there is a controller as a Mealy Machine MM with input $\Sigma_{in} = 2^{\mathbb{E} \cup Pr_\phi}$ and output $\Sigma_{out} = 2^{\mathbb{C}}$ such that every abstract trace t of MM that is concretisable in A also satisfies ϕ.*

A counterstrategy *to the realisability of ϕ modulo an arena A is a Moore Machine Cs with output $\Sigma_{out} = 2^{\mathbb{E} \cup Pr_\phi}$ and input $\Sigma_{in} = 2^{\mathbb{C}}$ such that every abstract trace t of Cs is concretisable in A and violates ϕ.*

5   Abstract to Concrete Synthesis

We attack the presented synthesis problem through an abstraction-refinement loop. We soundly abstract the arena as an LTL formula that may include fresh predicates and inputs. We fix the set of predicates that appear in the objective ϕ as Pr_ϕ, and the set of predicates and inputs in the abstraction, respectively, as Pr and $\mathbb{E}'$, always such that $Pr_\phi \subseteq Pr$ and $\mathbb{E} \subseteq \mathbb{E}'$.

Definition 5 (Abstraction). *Formula $\alpha(A, \mathcal{P}r)$ in $LTL(\mathbb{E}' \cup \mathbb{C} \cup \mathcal{P}r)$ abstracts arena A if for every $w \in L(A)$ there is $a \in L(\alpha(A, \mathcal{P}r))$ such that $w \in \gamma(a)$.*

$\alpha(A, \mathcal{P}r)$ is a standard predicate abstraction [16]. Given the lack of novelty, we refer to Appendix B.1 of [2] for the full details. Note, $\alpha(A, \mathcal{P}r)$ can be non-deterministic, unlike A. Constructing it is essentially an ALLSAT problem: given a transition, we identify sets from $2^{\mathcal{P}r}$ that can be true before the transition and, for each of these, sets of $2^{\mathcal{P}r}$ that can hold after the transition. However, we construct these sets incrementally, adding predicates as we discover them; and improve on the space/time complexity with a binary encoding (Sect. 7).

Given abstraction $\alpha(A, \mathcal{P}r)$, we construct a corresponding sound LTL synthesis problem, $\alpha(A, \mathcal{P}r) \implies \phi$, giving the environment control of the predicates in $\alpha(A, \mathcal{P}r)$. We get three possible outcomes from attempting synthesis of this: (1) it is realisable, and thus the concrete problem is realisable; (2) it is unrealisable and the counterstrategy is concretisable; or (3) the counterstrategy is not concretisable. We prove theorems and technical machinery essential to allow us to determine realisability (1) and unrealisability (2). In case (3) we refine the abstraction to make the counterstrategy unviable in the new abstract problem.

Theorem 1 (Reduction to LTL Realisability). *For ϕ in $LTL(\mathbb{E} \cup \mathbb{C} \cup \mathcal{P}r_\phi)$ and an abstraction $\alpha(A, \mathcal{P}r)$ of A in $LTL(\mathbb{E}' \cup \mathbb{C} \cup \mathcal{P}r)$, if $\alpha(A, \mathcal{P}r) \implies \phi$ is realisable over inputs $\mathbb{E}' \cup \mathcal{P}r$ and outputs $\mathbb{C}$, then ϕ is realisable modulo A.*

However, an abstract counterstrategy Cs may contain unconcretisable traces, since abstractions are sound but not complete. To analyse Cs for concretisability, we define a simulation relation between states of the concrete arena and states of Cs, capturing whether each word of Cs is concretisable. Recall, a set of predicates $\mathcal{P}r$ is the union of a set of state predicates, ST (describing one state), and transition predicates, TR (relating two states), which require different treatment.

Definition 6 (Counterstrategy Concretisability). *Consider a counter-strategy as a Moore Machine $Cs = \langle S, s_0, \Sigma_{in}, \Sigma_{out}, \rightarrow, out \rangle$, and an arena A, where $\Sigma_{in} = 2^{\mathbb{C}}$ and $\Sigma_{out} = 2^{\mathbb{E}' \cup \mathcal{P}r}$.*
Concretisability is defined through the simulation relation $\preceq_A \subseteq Val \times S$:
For every valuation val that is simulated by a state s, $val \preceq_A s$, where $out(s) = E \cup ST \cup TR$, it holds that:

1. *the valuation satisfies the state predicates of s: $val \models \bigwedge ST$, and*
2. *for every possible controller output $C \subseteq \mathbb{C}$: let $val_C = \delta(val, (E \cap \mathbb{E}) \cup C)$, s_C be s.t. $s \xrightarrow{C} s_C$, and TR_C be the transition predicates in $out(s_C)$, then*
   (a) *the transition predicates of s_C are satisfied by the transition $(val, val_C) \models \bigwedge TR_C$, and*
   (b) *the valuation after the transition simulates the Cs state after the transition: $val_C \preceq_A s_C$.*

Cs *is concretisable w.r.t. A when $val_0 \preceq_A s_0$, for A's initial valuation val_0.*

With concretisability defined, we then have a method to verify whether an abstract counterstrategy is also a concrete counterstrategy.

Theorem 2 (Reduction to LTL Unrealisability). *Given arena abstraction* $\alpha(A, \mathcal{P}r)$, *if* $\alpha(A, \mathcal{P}r) \implies \phi$ *is unrealisable with a counterstrategy Cs and Cs is concretisable w.r.t. A, then ϕ is unrealisable modulo A.*

In practice, we encode counterstrategy concretisability as a model checking problem on the composition of the counterstrategy and the arena, with the required invariant that predicate values chosen by the counterstrategy hold on the arena. Conveniently, this also gives witnesses of unconcretisability as finite counterexamples (rather than infinite traces), which we use as the basis for refinement. Crucially, this depends on the choices of the environment/controller being finite, which also gives us semi-decidability of finding non-concretisability.

Proposition 1. *Counterstrategy concretisability is encodable as invariant checking, and terminates for finite problems and non-concretisable counterstrategies.*

Proposition 2. *A non concretisable counterstrategy induces a finite counterexample* $a_0, \ldots, a_k \in (2^{\mathbb{E} \cup \mathbb{C} \cup \mathcal{P}r})^*$ *and concretisability fails locally only on* a_k.

Synthesis Semi-Algorithm. Alg. 1 shows our high-level approach. Taking an arena A and an LTL formula ϕ, it maintains a set of predicates $\mathcal{P}r$ and an LTL formula ψ. When the abstract problem (in terms of $\mathcal{P}r$) is realisable, a controller is returned (line 5); otherwise, if the counterstrategy is concretisable, it is returned (line 7). If the counterstrategy is not concretisable, we refine the abstraction to exclude it (line 8), and extend $\mathcal{P}r$ with the learned predicates, and ψ with the new LTL constraints (line 9). Alg. 1 diverges unless it finds a (counter)strategy.

Algorithm 1: Synthesis algorithm based on abstraction refinement.

1 **Function** synthesise(A, ϕ):
2      $\mathcal{P}r, \psi := \mathcal{P}r_\phi, true$
3   **while** *true* **do**
4          $\phi_\alpha^A := (\alpha(A, \mathcal{P}r) \wedge \psi) \implies \phi$
5   **if** realisable($\phi_\alpha^A, \mathbb{E} \cup \mathcal{P}r, \mathbb{C}$) **then return** ($true$, strategy($\phi_\alpha^A, \mathbb{E} \cup \mathcal{P}r, \mathbb{C}$))
6          $Cs :=$ counter_strategy($\phi_\alpha^A, \mathbb{E} \cup \mathcal{P}r, \mathbb{C}$)
7   **if** concretisable(ϕ, A, Cs) **then return** ($false$, Cs)
8          $\mathcal{P}r', \psi' :=$ refinement(A, Cs)
9          $\mathcal{P}r, \psi := \mathcal{P}r \cup \mathcal{P}r', \psi \wedge \psi'$

6   Refinement

We now present the two refinements on which our iterative approach relies, based on an analysis of a discovered counterstrategy. These refinements soundly refine the abstraction with predicates and/or new LTL constraints such that similar counterexamples will not be re-encountered in the next iteration.[3]

6.1   Safety Refinement

Consider a counterstrategy Cs and a counterexample $ce = a_0, a_1, \ldots, a_k$. The transition from a_{k-1} to a_k induces a mismatch between the concrete arena state and Cs's desired predicate state. It is well known that interpolation can determine sufficient state predicates to make Cs non-viable in the fresh abstract problem; we give a brief description for the reader's convenience. Let $p_i = \bigwedge_{\mathcal{P}r}(a_i \cap \mathcal{P}r)$, with each variable v replaced by a fresh variable v_i, and each variable v_{prev} by v_{i-1}. Similarly, let g_i and u_i be respectively the corresponding symbolic transition guard and update (i.e., $\delta(g_i) = u_i$), such that all updates $v := t$ are rewritten as $v_{i+1} = t_i$, where term t_i corresponds to t with every variable v replaced by v_i.

In order to characterize the mismatch between the arena and its abstraction, we construct the following formulas. Let $f_0 = val_0 \wedge p_0 \wedge g_0 \wedge u_0$, where we abuse notation and refer to val_0 as a Boolean formula. For $1 \leq i < k$, let $f_i = p_i \wedge g_i \wedge u_i$, while $f_k = p_k$. Then $\bigwedge_{i=0}^{k} f_i$ is unsatisfiable. Following McMillan [25], we construct the corresponding set of *sequence interpolants* $I_0, \ldots, I_{k-1}$, where $f_0 \implies I_1$, $\forall 1 \leq i < k.I_i \wedge f_i \implies I_{i+1}$, $I_{k-1} \wedge f_k$ is unsatisfiable, as all the variables of I_i are shared by both f_{i-1} and f_i. From these we obtain a set of state predicates $I(ce)$ by removing the introduced indices in each I_i. Adding $I(ce)$ to the abstraction refines it to make the counterstrategy unviable.

6.2   Liveness Refinement

Relying solely on safety refinement results in non-termination for interesting problems (e.g., Fig. 2). To overcome this limitation, we propose *liveness refinement*. Our main insight is that if the counterexample exposes a spurious lasso in the counterstrategy, then we can encode its termination as a liveness property.

Lassos and Loops. A counterexample $ce = a_0, \ldots, a_k$ induces a lasso in Cs when it corresponds to a path $s_0, \ldots, s_k$ in Cs, where $s_k = s_j$ for some $0 \leq j < k$. We focus on the last such j. Here, for simplicity, we require that concretisation failed due to a wrong state predicate guess. We split the counterexample into two parts: a stem $a_0, \ldots, a_{j-1}$, and a loop $a_j, \ldots, a_{k-1}$. Let $g_j \mapsto U_j, \ldots, g_{k-1} \mapsto U_{k-1}$ be the corresponding applications of δ and let val_j be the arena state at step j.

V = *
assume val_j
while $\bigwedge(a\_j \cap \mathcal{P}r)$
    assume g_j
    V = $U_j(V)$
    ...
    assume g_{k-1}
    V = $U_{k-1}(V)$

Fig. 3. ce loop.

---

[3] We prove a progress theorem for each refinement in Appendix C of [2].

The counterexample proves that the while-program in Fig. 3 terminates (in one iteration). To strengthen the refinement, we try to weaken the loop (e.g., expand the precondition) such that it still accepts the loop part of ce while terminating. We formalise loops to be able to formalise this weakening.

Definition 7 (Loops). A loop is a tuple $l = \langle V, pre, iter\_cond, body \rangle$, where pre and iter_cond are Boolean combinations of predicates over variables V, and body is a finite sequence of pairs (g_i, U_i), where $g_i \in \mathcal{P}r(V)$ and $U_i \in \mathcal{U}(V)$.

A finite/infinite sequence of valuations $vals = val_0, val_1, \ldots$ is an execution of l, $vals \in L(l)$, iff $val_0 \models pre$, for all i such that $0 \leq i < |vals|$, where $n = |body|$, then $val_i \models g_{i \bmod n}$, $val_{i+1} = U_{i \bmod n}(val_i)$ and if $i \bmod n = 0$ then $val_i \models iter\_cond$. We say a loop is terminating if all of its executions are finite.

Definition 8 (Weakening). Loop $l_1 = \langle V_1, pre_1, ic_1, body_1 \rangle$ is weaker than $l_2 = \langle V_2, pre_2, ic_2, body_2 \rangle$ when: 1. $V_1 \subseteq V_2$; 2. $pre_2 \implies pre_1$ and $ic_2 \implies ic_1$; 3. $|body_1| = |body_2|$; 4. for $w_2 \in L(l_2)$ there is $w_1 \in L(l_1)$ such that w_2 and w_1 agree on V_1. A weakening is proper if both l_1 and l_2 terminate.

Heuristics. We attempt to find loop weakenings heuristically. In all cases we reduce *iter_cond* to focus on predicates in a_k that affect concretisability. We also remove variables from the domain of the loop that are not within the cone-of-influence [10] of *iter_cond*. We then attempt two weaker pre-conditions: (1) *true*; and (2) the predicate state before the loop is entered in the *ce*. We check these two loops, in the order above, successively for termination (using an external tool). The first loop proved terminating $(l(ce))$ is used as the basis of the refinements.

Structural Loop Refinement. We present a refinement that monitors for execution of the loop and enforces its termination.

We define some predicates useful to our definition. For each transition in the loop we define a formula that captures when it is triggered: $cond_0 \overset{\text{def}}{=} iter\_cond \wedge g_0$ and $cond_i \overset{\text{def}}{=} g_i$ for all other i. For each update U_i, we define a conjunction of transition predicates that captures when it occurs: recall U_i is of the form $v^0 := t^0, \ldots, v^j := t^j$, then we define p_i as $v^0 = t^0_{prev} \wedge \ldots \wedge v^j = t^j_{prev}$. This sets the value of variable v^k to the value of term t^k in the previous state. We further define a formula that captures the arena stuttering modulo the loop, $st \overset{\text{def}}{=} \bigwedge_{v \in V_l} v = v_{prev}$, where V_l is the set of variables of the loop. A technical detail is that we require updates in the loop $l(ce)$ to not stutter, i.e., $U(val) \neq val$ for all val. Any loop with stuttering can be reduced to one without, for the kinds of loops we consider. Thus, here $p_i \wedge st$ is contradictory, for all i.

Definition 9 (Structural Loop Refinement). Let l be a terminating loop, and $cond_i$, p_i, and st (for $0 \leq i < n$) be as defined above. Assume fresh variables corresponding to each step in the loop $inloop_0, \ldots, inloop_{n-1}$, and $inloop = inloop_0 \vee \ldots \vee inloop_{n-1}$.

The structural loop abstraction $\alpha_{loop}(A, l)$ is the conjunction of the following:

1. Initially we are not in the loop, and we can never be in multiple loop steps at the same time: $\neg inloop \wedge \bigwedge_i G(inloop_i \implies \neg \bigvee_{j \neq i}(inloop_j))$;

2. *The loop is entered when pre holds and the first transition is executed:*
$G(\neg inloop \implies ((pre \land cond_0 \land X(p_0)) \iff X(inloop_1)))$;
3. *At each step, while the step condition holds, the correct update causes the loop to step forward, stuttering leaves it in place, otherwise we exit:*

$$\bigwedge_{0 \leq i < n} G \left((inloop_i \land cond_i) \implies X \begin{pmatrix} (p_i \implies inloop_{i+1\%n}) \land \\ (st \implies inloop_i) \land \\ (\neg(st \lor p_i) \iff \neg inloop) \end{pmatrix} \right);$$

4. *At each step, if the expected step condition does not hold, we exit:*
$\bigwedge_{0 \leq i < n} G((inloop_i \land \neg cond_i) \implies X \neg inloop)$; *and*
5. *The loop always terminates, or stutters:* $GF(\neg inloop) \lor \bigvee_i FG(st_i \land inloop_i)$.

Note the fresh propositions ($inloop_i$) are controlled by the environment. The LTL formulas 1–4 monitor for the loop, exiting if a transition not in the loop occurs, and progressing or stuttering in the loop otherwise. LTL formula 5 enforces that the loop is exited infinitely often, or that the execution stutters in the loop forever. This ensures that the abstract counterstrategy is no longer viable.

7 Efficient Encoding and Acceleration

The problem we tackle is undecidable, but we rely on decidable sub-routines of varying complexity: predicate abstraction (exponential in the number of predicates) and finite synthesis (doubly exponential in the number of propositions, of which predicates are a subset). Here we present an efficient binary encoding of predicates of similar forms that (1) reduces the size of and the satisfiability checks needed to compute the abstraction from exponential to polynomial, and (2) reduces complexity of abstract synthesis from doubly to singly exponential, when restricted to predicates. Moreover, this encoding allows us to identify fairness assumptions refining the abstraction, which significantly accelerate synthesis. Computing this encoding only involves simple arithmetic, but we have not encountered previous uses of it in literature.

We collect all the known predicates over the same term, giving a finite set of predicates $P_t = \{t \bowtie c_0, ..., t \bowtie c_n\}$, where t is a term only over variables, $\bowtie \in \{<, \leq\}$ and each c_i is a value. W.l.g. we assume $t \bowtie c_i \implies t \bowtie c_{i+1}$ for all i. Thus, $t < c$ appears before any other predicate $t \bowtie c + \alpha$ for $\alpha \geq 0$. For simplicity, let us assume that t is a single variable. To enable a binary representation we find disjoint intervals representing the same constraints on variable values. Namely, replace the predicates in P_t with (1) $t \bowtie c_0$, (2) for $0 < i \leq n$ the predicate $\neg(t \bowtie c_{i-1}) \land t \bowtie c_i$, and finally, (3) $\neg(t \bowtie c_n)$. Effectively, forming a partition of the real line $\mathbb{R}$.

Let $part(P_t) = \{t \bowtie c_0, \neg(t \bowtie c_{i-1}) \land t \bowtie c_i, \neg(t \bowtie c_n) \mid 0 < i \leq n\}$. We call the left- and right-most partitions the *border* partitions since they capture the left and right intervals to infinity. The other formulas define non-intersecting bounded intervals/partitions along $\mathbb{R}$. Figure 4 illustrates these partitions: this set of formulas covers the whole line, i.e. for each point $t = c$, there is a formula f in $part(P_t)$ such that $(t = c) \models f$. Further, note how each two distinct formulas $f_1, f_2 \in part(P_t)$ are mutually exclusive. Namely, $f_1 \wedge f_2 \equiv \bot$. Given this mutual exclusivity, it is easy to construct a representation to reduce the number of binary variables in the predicate abstraction. The complexity of computing these partitions is only the complexity of sorting P_t in ascending order based on values.

In a standard predicate abstraction approach, the number of predicates is $\sum_{t \in terms} |P_t|$. With this encoding, they shrink to $\sum_{t \in terms} \lceil |log_2(|P_t| + 1)| \rceil$. Moreover, this enables a more efficient predicate abstraction computation: given we know each formula in $part(P_t)$ is mutually exclusive, we can consider each formula separately. Then, for each t instead of performing $2^{2 \times |P_t|}$ satisfiability checks we just need $(|P_t| + 1)^2$, giving a polynomial time complexity in terms of predicates, $(\prod_{t \in terms}(|P_t| + 1))^2$, instead of the exponential $2^{2 \times \sum_{t \in terms} |P_t|}$. The complexity of synthesis improves very significantly in terms of predicates, to $2^{\prod_{t \in terms} |P_t| + 1}$, instead of $2^{2^{\sum_{t \in terms} |P_t|}}$.

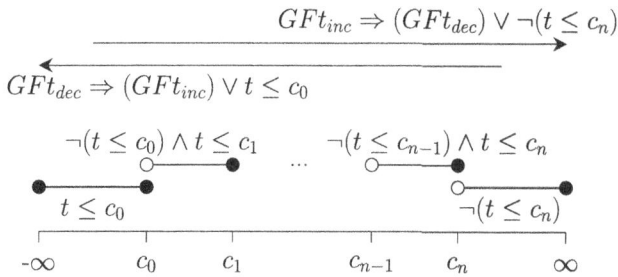

Fig. 4. Partitions for binary encoding.

Note that, to get the full view of time complexity for both abstraction and synthesis, the complexity described must be respectively multiplied by $|dom(\delta)| \times 2^{|B|}$ and $2^{2^{|B|}}$, where B is the set of Boolean propositions in the concrete problem.

As an optimisation, if both terms t and $-t$ are part of the abstraction, we transform predicates over $-t$ to predicates over t: $-t \leq c$ becomes $t \geq -c$, which becomes $\neg(t < -c)$. We note the approach described applies to both LIA and LRA, and might have applications beyond our approach.

Acceleration. The partitioning optimises the encoding of predicates extracted from the problem and learned from safety refinements. Moreover, it allows to identify liveness properties relevant to the infinite-state arena.

Consider that an abstract execution is within the leftmost partition, e.g., within $t \leq 0$. An increment in t in the arena leads to an environment choice in the abstraction of whether to stay within $t \leq 0$ or move to the next partition. Suppose the controller can repeatedly increment t with a value bounded from 0.

In the abstraction, the environment can still force an abstract execution satisfying $t \leq 0$ forever. The same is true for every partition, unless its size is smaller than the increment, e.g., a partition with one element. This abstract behaviour is not concretisable. That is, for every concrete value of t and every c, after a finite number of increments bounded from 0, the predicate $t \bowtie c$ becomes false. Similarly for any other partition. The dual is true for decrements. We note that in LIA, every increment or decrement is bounded from 0.

We encode this fact using fairness assumptions that rely on detecting increases and decreases of a term's value with transition predicates. If for a term t we identify that all changes of t in A are at least ϵ, we define the transition predicates $t_{inc} := t_{prev} \leq t - \epsilon$ and $t_{dec} := t \leq t_{prev} - \epsilon$, refining the abstraction by a memory of when transitions increase or decrease the value of t. Notice that as changes to t are at least ϵ, when both t_{dec} and t_{inc} are false t does not change. We then add the fairness assumptions: $(GFt_{dec}) \implies GF(t_{inc} \vee f_l)$ and $(GFt_{inc}) \implies GF(t_{dec} \vee f_r)$, where f_l (f_r) is t's left-(right-)most partitions.

The first (second) assumption enforces every abstract execution where t strictly decreases (increases) and does not increase (decrease), to make progress towards the left-(right-)most partition. Thus, the environment cannot block the controller from exiting a partition, if they can repeatedly force a bounded from 0 decrease (increase) without increases (decreases). For each term, we can then add these two corresponding fairness LTL assumptions to the abstraction. If the left- and right-most partitions are updated during safety refinement, we update the predicates inside these fairness assumptions with the new border partitions, ensuring we only ever have at most two such assumptions per term. In our implementation for LIA $\epsilon = 1$, and to optimise we leave out these assumptions if we cannot identify increases or decreases bounded from 0 in the arena.

8   Evaluation

We implemented this approach in a tool[4] targeting discrete synthesis problems. State-of-the-art tools are used as sub-routines: Strix [26] (LTL synthesis), nuXmv [7] (invariant checking), MathSAT [9] (interpolation and SMT checking), and CPAchecker [6] (termination checking). As a further optimisation, the tool performs also a binary encoding of the states variables of the arena, given they are mutually exclusive.

We compare our tool against 5 tools from literature raboniel [22], temos [8], rpgsolve [18], rpg-STeLA [34], and tslmt2rpg (+rpgsolve) [19]. We consider also a purely lazy version of our tool, with acceleration turned off to evaluate its utility. We do not compare against other tools fully outperformed by the rpg tools [33,35], limited to safety/reachability [3,13,27], and another we could not acquire [23]. All experiments ran on a Linux workstation equipped with 32 GiB of memory and an Intel i7-5820K CPU, under a time limit of 20 min and a memory limit of 16 GiB. We show cumulative synthesis times in Fig. 5a for tools that support synthesis, and cumulative realisability times for other tools compared with our tools' cumulative synthesis times in Fig. 5b.

---

[4] https://github.com/shaunazzopardi/sweap. An artifact for this paper is available [11].

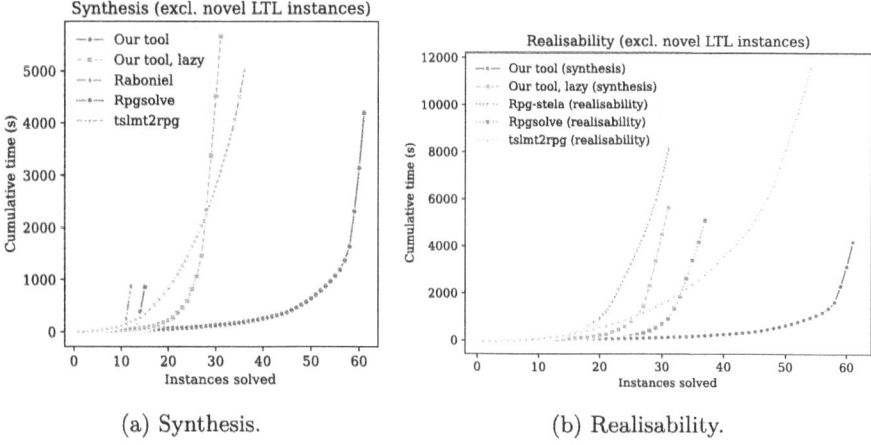

(a) Synthesis.   (b) Realisability.

Fig. 5. Time comparison.

Benchmarks. We collect 80 LIA benchmarks from the literature. Most encode practical problems, such as robotic mission control, job scheduling, sorting, or data buffering. They are defined in TSL [14] or as deterministic games, and may include arbitrary integers as input, which we equivalently encode with extra steps that let the environment set variables to any finite value (see Sect. 9). All these benchmarks consist of problems encodable as deterministic Büchi games. Some benchmarks [34] compose multiple such games together, for added difficulty. Following others, we ignore problems [8,14] that are trivial. We only introduce one novel reachability game to these benchmarks, robot-tasks,[5] that we crafted to highlight the limitations of previous approaches compared to our own. Some of the problems from [34] are not available in TSL format. We test those on neither raboniel nor temos but we expect they would both fail, as their techniques are insufficient for Büchi goals (see Sect. 9), and for tslmt2rpg we simply consider the time taken by rpgsolve on the corresponding RPG problem.

Results (comparative evaluation).[6] It is clear from Fig. 5a that the eager version of our tool solves almost double more synthesis problems than the best competitor, and faster. The lazy version is comparable to the best competitor. For realisability, Fig. 5b shows our tool with acceleration scaling and performing much better on synthesis than the other tools do on realisability. However, the lazy version is outperformed by the rpg tools. Table 1a summarises the evaluation; for each tool we report the number of solved problems (out of 81), the ones it solved in the shortest time, and those no other tool was able to solve. Our tool is the clear winner in each category. If we consider synthesis, even without acceleration we are comparable to the state of the art: our tools solve 61 (eager) and 31 (lazy) problems, while the best competitor tslmt2rpg solves 36. When

---

[5] Appendix D.1 of [2] has more details about this new benchmark.

[6] Appendix D.2 of [2] has additional experimental data, and an extended discussion.

looking closely at the behaviour on the easiest instances (see Fig. 6 in [2]), we see that our tool has an initialization overhead of a few seconds while other tools can solve simple problems in under 1 s. However, our tool scales better. We also ran our lazy tool without the binary encoding, and measured noticeably worse performances: it times out on two more problems, and takes on average 10% more time (see Fig. 7 in [2]).

Table 1. Experimental results.

(a) Comparative evaluation of Raboniel, Temos, RPGsolve, Tslmt2Rpg, Rpg-SteLa, and our Synthesis tool, with and without acceleration.

Synthesis	Rab	Tem	RPG	T2R	S_{acc}	S
solved	12	0	15	36	**61**	31
best	5	0	11	13	**43**	4
unique	0	0	1	11	**27**	0

Realisability		RPG	RSt	T2R	S_{acc}	S
solved		37	31	54	**61**	31
best		21	0	13	**37**	7
unique		0	0	**11**	9	0

(b) LTL benchmarks.

Name	U	Time (s)	
		S_{acc}	S
arbiter		**2.77**	4.90
arbiter-failure		2.04	**1.98**
elevator		**2.53**	15.92
infinite-race		**1.98**	4.38
infinite-race-u	●	–	–
infinite-race-unequal-1		**6.50**	–
infinite-race-unequal-2		–	–
reversible-lane-r		**7.39**	17.53
reversible-lane-u	●	18.70	**4.54**
rep-reach-obst-1d		**2.47**	9.04
rep-reach-obst-2d		**3.85**	38.51
rep-reach-obst-6d		–	–
robot-collect-v4		**16.51**	–
taxi-service		**39.26**	68.02
taxi-service-u	●	4.14	**3.50**

Evaluation on Novel LTL Benchmarks. We contribute 15 benchmarks with LTL objectives unencodable as deterministic Büchi objectives, i.e., they are theoretically out of scope for other tools. For sanity checking we attempted them on the other tools and validated their inability to decide these problems. We do not include them with the previous benchmarks to ensure a fairer evaluation. Three of these benchmarks could be solved by other tools if infinite-range inputs are used (arbiter, infinite-race, and infinite-race-u), but they fail since incrementing and decrementing requires environment fairness constraints.

These benchmarks involve control of cyber-physical systems such as the elevator from Fig. 2, variations thereof, a reversible traffic lane, and robotic missions, some of which are extensions of literature benchmarks. They also include strong fairness and/or let the environment delay progress for the controller.[7] Table 1b

---

[7] These benchmarks are also described in detail in Appendix D.1 of [2].

reports how both configurations of our tool handle our novel benchmarks. Column U marks unrealisable problems. The lazy approach outperforms the eager one on just 3 benchmarks out of 15. On 11 problems, acceleration enriches the first abstraction enough to lead immediately to a verdict. We note that solving infinite-race-unequal-1 requires structural refinement, as it allows infinite amount of increments and decrements, but of unequal value, while for literature benchmarks acceleration is enough.

Failure Analysis. Lastly, we discuss four limitations in our approach exposed by our experiments. Section 9 contains more detail on when and why the other tools fail. The first is inherent to synthesis: the Boolean synthesis problem may become big enough to exceed machine resources. A bespoke finite-state synthesis procedure could mitigate this, by relying on the underlying parity game rather than creating fresh problems.

The second is that some unrealisable problems admit no finite counterstrategies in our setting. robot-repair, which no tool solves, is the only such example from literature (we also designed infinite-race-u to be of this kind). Briefly, this involves two stages: a losing loop for which the controller controls exit and (after the loop) a state wherein the goal is unreachable. The environment cannot universally quantify over all predicates (since it controls them), hence no finite counterstrategy exists. But if we construct the dual problem, by swapping objectives between the environment and controller, we do find a strategy for the original environment goal. We are working on automating this dualisation.

The third is that our requirements for when to apply structural refinement may be too strong, and thus some loops go undiscovered. Instead of looking for loops solely in the counterexample prefix, one may instead consider the strongly connected components of the counterstrategy.

Lastly, there are pathological counterexamples, irrelevant to the problem, that involve the controller causing an incompatibility by going to a partition and the environment not being able to determine exactly when dec/increments should force an exit from this partition. This is the main cause of failure for our lazy approach. Modifications to concretisability checking might avoid this issue.

9   Related Work

Before discussing related synthesis approaches, we note that Balaban, Pnueli, and Zuck describe a similar CEGAR approach for infinite-state model checking [4]. From counterexamples they discover ranking functions for terminating loops, and encode their well-foundedness in the underlying fair discrete system, similar to how we encode well-foundedness during acceleration. Our structural refinement is instead more localised to specific loops. We may benefit from the more general ranking abstraction, but it is often easier to prove termination of loops through loop variants rather than ranking functions, which do not admit the same encoding. Interestingly, their approach is relatively complete, i.e. given the right ranking functions and state predicates the LTL property can be verified. We cannot say the same about our approach, given, as mentioned in the previous section, there are some unrealisable problems we cannot terminate on.

We discuss the exact differences between our setting and that of TSL synthesis [14] and RPG [18]. We then discuss infinite-state synthesis more generally.

TSL and RPG Compared to our Approach. We start by noting that, in the context of linear integer arithmetic, for every possible synthesis problem in TSL or RPG, we can effectively construct an equi-realisable problem in our setting (see Appendix E.1 of [2] for the full details). In both TSL and RPG, variables are partitioned between inputs and outputs. At each step of the game, the environment sets values for all inputs (so, choosing among potentially infinitely-many or continuously-many candidate values in one step) and the controller responds by choosing among a finite set of deterministic updates to its own variables. The environment also initialises *all* variables. Dually, in our setting, players only own Boolean variables and have only a finite set of choices. Then, infinite-range variables are updated based on the joint choice. For all three, repeating single interactions ad-infinitum leads to traces that are either checked to satisfy an LTL formula (TSL and our setting) or to satisfy safety, reachability, or repeated reachability w.r.t. certain locations in the arena/program (RPG). The restriction to finite-range updates hinders the applicability of our approach to linear real arithmetic, given the necessity of repeated uncountable choices there. However, we expect the more novel parts of our approach (liveness refinements and acceleration) to still be applicable in this richer theory. Indeed, we define acceleration in a way that it is also applicable for LRA in Sect. 7.

Infinite-state Arenas. Due to space restrictions, we refer to other work [13,18] for a general overview of existing symbolic synthesis methods, and leave out infinite-state methods restricted to decidable settings, such as pushdown games [37], Petri-net games [15], or restrictions of FO-LTL such as those mentioned in the introduction [30–32]. Such approaches tend to apply very different techniques. We instead discuss methods that take on the undecidable setting, and how they acquire/encode liveness information. We find three classes of such approaches:

Fixpoint Solving. These extend standard fixpoint approaches to symbolic game solving. GENSYS-LTL [33] uses quantifier elimination to compute the controllable predecessor of a given set, terminating only if a finite number of steps is sufficient. A similar approach limits itself to the GR(1) setting [23], showing its efficiency also in the infinite setting. rpgsolve [18] takes this further by finding so-called *acceleration lemmas*. It attempts to find linear ranking functions with invariants to prove that loops in the game terminate, and thus it may find fixpoints that GENSYS-LTL cannot. This information is however only used in a particular game region. In problems such as robot-tasks, this requires an infinite number of accelerations, leading to divergence. The reliance on identifying one location in a game where a ranking function decreases is also problematic when the choice of where to exit a region is part of the game-playing, or when the ranking needs to decrease differently based on the play's history. The latter would be required in order to scale their approach to objectives beyond Büchi and co-

Büchi. The realisability solver rpg-STeLA tries to bypass the locality limitation by using game templates to identify lemmas that can be used in multiple regions. It does well on benchmarks that were designed for it in a compositional way, but in many other cases, the extra work required to identify templates adds significant overhead. For example, it causes divergence in robot-tasks. As a bridge between program specifications in TSL and the rpg tools, tslmt2rpg [19] translates TSL specifications to RPG while adding semantic information about infinite-range variables that allows it to simplify regions in games. As for rpg-STeLA the analysis of the semantic information often causes a time overhead. Crucial here is the underlying solver, which often times out on quantifier elimination.

Abstraction. Other methods, including ours, attempt synthesis on an explicit abstraction of the problem. A failure witness may be used to refine the abstraction and make another attempt. Some of these methods target games directly [1,20,36]; others work at the level of the specification [8,14,22]. Many of these focus on refining states in the abstraction, a kind of safety refinement, as in the case of the tool raboniel [22]. As far as we know, only temos [8] adds some form of liveness information of the underlying infinite domain. It attempts to construct an abstraction of an LTL (over theories) specification by adding consistency invariants, and transitions. It also uses syntax-guided synthesis to generate sequences of updates that force a certain state change. Interestingly, it can also identify liveness constraints that abstract the effects in the limit of repeating an update u, adding constraints of the form $G(pre \land (u W post) \implies F post)$. However, it can only deal with one update of one variable at a time, and fails when the environment can delay u. Moreover, it does not engage in a CEGAR-loop, giving up if the first such abstraction is not realisable.

Constraint Solving. One may encode the synthesis problem into constrained Horn clauses (CHC), and synthesise ranking functions to prove termination of parts of a program. Consynth [5] solves general LTL and ω-regular infinite-state games with constraint solving. However, it needs a controller template: essentially a partial solution to the problem. This may require synthesising ranking functions, and (unlike our approach) makes unrealisability verdicts limited to the given template and thus not generalisable. MuVal [35] can encode realisability checking of LTL games as validity checking in a fixpoint logic that extends CHC. It also requires encoding the automaton corresponding to the LTL formula directly in the input formula, and discovers ranking functions based on templates to enforce bounded unfolding of recursive calls. Contrastingly, we do not rely on templates but can handle any argument for termination.

10   Conclusions

We have presented a specialised CEGAR approach for LTL synthesis beyond the Boolean domain. In our evaluation our implementation significantly outperforms other available synthesis tools, often synthesising a (counter-)strategy before other tools finish checking for realisability. Key to this approach are liveness refinements, which forgo the need for a large or infinite number of safety refinements. We carefully designed our framework so it can encode spuriousness checking of abstract counterstrategies as simple invariant checking, using loops in counterexamples to find liveness refinements. Another main contribution is the reduction of the complexity of predicate abstraction and synthesis by an exponential, through a binary encoding of related predicates. This also allows to identify well-foundedness constraints of the arena, which we encode in the abstraction through LTL fairness requirements.

Future Work. We believe that symbolic approaches for LTL synthesis and synthesis for LTL over structured arenas [12,17], could significantly benefit our technique. In these, determinisation for LTL properties would have to be applied only to the objective, and not to the arena abstraction. Tool support for these is not yet mature or available. For one such tool [12], we sometimes observed considerable speedup for realisability; however, it does not supply strategies.

Other directions include dealing with identified limitations (see Sect. 8), extending the tool beyond LIA, dealing with infinite inputs automatedly, and applying other methods to manage the size of predicate abstractions, e.g., [21], data-flow analysis, and implicit abstraction, and to make it more informative.

References

1. de Alfaro, L., Roy, P.: Solving games via three-valued abstraction refinement. In: Caires, L., Vasconcelos, V.T. (eds.) CONCUR 2007. LNCS, vol. 4703, pp. 74–89. Springer, Heidelberg (2007). https://doi.org/10.1007/978-3-540-74407-8_6
2. Azzopardi, S., Piterman, N., Stefano, L.D., Schneider, G.: Full LTL synthesis over infinite-state arenas (2025). https://arxiv.org/abs/2307.09776
3. Baier, C., Coenen, N., Finkbeiner, B., Funke, F., Jantsch, S., Siber, J.: Causality-based game solving. In: Silva, A., Leino, K.R.M. (eds.) CAV 2021. LNCS, vol. 12759, pp. 894–917. Springer, Cham (2021). https://doi.org/10.1007/978-3-030-81685-8_42
4. Balaban, I., Pnueli, A., Zuck, L.D.: Ranking abstraction as companion to predicate abstraction. In: Wang, F. (ed.) FORTE 2005. LNCS, vol. 3731, pp. 1–12. Springer, Heidelberg (2005). https://doi.org/10.1007/11562436_1
5. Beyene, T.A., Chaudhuri, S., Popeea, C., Rybalchenko, A.: A constraint-based approach to solving games on infinite graphs. In: 41st ACM SIGPLAN-SIGACT Symposium on Principles of Programming Languages, pp. 221–234. ACM (2014)
6. Beyer, D., Keremoglu, M.E.: Cpachecker: A tool for configurable software verification. In: Computer Aided Verification - 23rd International Conference, CAV 2011. LNCS, vol. 6806, pp. 184–190. Springer (2011). https://doi.org/10.1007/978-3-642-22110-1_16
7. Cavada, R., Cimatti, A., Dorigatti, M., Griggio, A., Mariotti, A., Micheli, A., Mover, S., Roveri, M., Tonetta, S.: The nuxmv symbolic model checker. In: Computer Aided Verification - 26th International Conference, CAV 2014. LNCS, vol. 8559, pp. 334–342. Springer (2014). https://doi.org/10.1007/978-3-319-08867-9_22

8. Choi, W., Finkbeiner, B., Piskac, R., Santolucito, M.: Can reactive synthesis and syntax-guided synthesis be friends? In: Proceedings of the 43rd ACM SIGPLAN International Conference on Programming Language Design and Implementation, pp. 229–243. PLDI 2022, Association for Computing Machinery, New York, NY, USA (2022). https://doi.org/10.1145/3519939.3523429

9. Cimatti, A., Griggio, A., Schaafsma, B.J., Sebastiani, R.: The mathsat5 SMT solver. In: Tools and Algorithms for the Construction and Analysis of Systems - 19th International Conference, TACAS 2013. LNCS, vol. 7795, pp. 93–107. Springer (2013). https://doi.org/10.1007/978-3-642-36742-7_7

10. Clarke, E.M., Grumberg, O., Peled, D.A.: Model Checking. MIT Press, London, Cambridge (1999)

11. Di Stefano, L., Azzopardi, S., Piterman, N., Schneider, G.: Software artifact for "full LTL synthesis over infinite-state arenas" (2025). https://doi.org/10.5281/zenodo.15189175

12. Ehlers, R., Khalimov, A.: Fully generalized reactivity(1) synthesis. In: Finkbeiner, B., Kovács, L. (eds.) Tools and Algorithms for the Construction and Analysis of Systems - 30th International Conference, TACAS 2024. LNCS, vol. 14570, pp. 83–102. Springer (2024). https://doi.org/10.1007/978-3-031-57246-3_6

13. Farzan, A., Kincaid, Z.: Strategy synthesis for linear arithmetic games. Proc. ACM Program. Lang. 2(POPL) (2017). https://doi.org/10.1145/3158149

14. Finkbeiner, B., Klein, F., Piskac, R., Santolucito, M.: Temporal stream logic: synthesis beyond the bools. In: Dillig, I., Tasiran, S. (eds.) CAV 2019. LNCS, vol. 11561, pp. 609–629. Springer, Cham (2019). https://doi.org/10.1007/978-3-030-25540-4_35

15. Finkbeiner, B., Olderog, E.: Ten years of petri games. In: Jansen, N., Junges, S., Kaminski, B.L., Matheja, C., Noll, T., Quatmann, T., Stoelinga, M., Volk, M. (eds.) Principles of Verification: Cycling the Probabilistic Landscape - Essays Dedicated to Joost-Pieter Katoen on the Occasion of His 60th Birthday, Part III. LNCS, vol. 15262, pp. 399–422. Springer (2025). https://doi.org/10.1007/978-3-031-75778-5_19

16. Graf, S., Saïdi, H.: Construction of abstract state graphs with PVS. In: CAV 1997. LNCS, vol. 1254, pp. 72–83. Springer (1997). https://doi.org/10.1007/3-540-63166-6_10

17. Hausmann, D., Lehaut, M., Piterman, N.: Symbolic solution of Emerson-Lei games for reactive synthesis. In: Foundations of Software Science and Computation Structures - 27th International Conference, FoSSaCS 2024. LNCS, vol. 14574, pp. 55–78. Springer (2024). https://doi.org/10.1007/978-3-031-57228-9_4

18. Heim, P., Dimitrova, R.: Solving infinite-state games via acceleration. Proc. ACM Program. Lang. 8(POPL) (2024). https://doi.org/10.1145/3632899

19. Heim, P., Dimitrova, R.: Translation of temporal logic for efficient infinite-state reactive synthesis. Proc. ACM Program. Lang. 9(POPL) (2025)

20. Henzinger, T.A., Jhala, R., Majumdar, R.: Counterexample-guided control. In: Baeten, J.C.M., Lenstra, J.K., Parrow, J., Woeginger, G.J. (eds.) ICALP 2003. LNCS, vol. 2719, pp. 886–902. Springer, Heidelberg (2003). https://doi.org/10.1007/3-540-45061-0_69

21. Henzinger, T.A., Jhala, R., Majumdar, R., Sutre, G.: Lazy abstraction. In: Conference Record of POPL 2002: The 29th SIGPLAN-SIGACT Symposium on Principles of Programming Languages, Portland, OR, USA, 16-18 January 2002, pp. 58–70. ACM (2002). https://doi.org/10.1145/503272.503279

22. Maderbacher, B., Bloem, R.: Reactive synthesis modulo theories using abstraction refinement. In: 22nd Conference on Formal Methods in Computer-Aided Design, FMCAD 2022, pp. 315–324. TU Wien Academic Press (2022). https://doi.org/10.34727/2022/isbn.978-3-85448-053-2_38

23. Maderbacher, B., Windisch, F., Bloem, R.: Synthesis from infinite-state generalized reactivity(1) specifications. In: Margaria, T., Steffen, B. (eds.) Leveraging Applications of Formal Methods, Verification and Validation. Software Engineering Methodologies - 12th International Symposium, ISoLA 2024, Crete, Greece, 27-31 October 2024, Proceedings, Part IV. LNCS, vol. 15222, pp. 281–301. Springer (2024). https://doi.org/10.1007/978-3-031-75387-9_17

24. Martin, D.A.: Borel determinacy. Ann. Math. **102**(2), 363–371 (1975). http://www.jstor.org/stable/1971035

25. McMillan, K.L.: Lazy abstraction with interpolants. In: Computer Aided Verification, 18th International Conference, CAV 2006. LNCS, vol. 4144, pp. 123–136. Springer (2006). https://doi.org/10.1007/11817963_14

26. Meyer, P.J., Sickert, S., Luttenberger, M.: Strix: explicit reactive synthesis strikes back! In: Computer Aided Verification - 30th International Conference, CAV 2018. LNCS, vol. 10981, pp. 578–586. Springer (2018). https://doi.org/10.1007/978-3-319-96145-3_31

27. Neider, D., Markgraf, O.: Learning-based synthesis of safety controllers. In: 2019 Formal Methods in Computer Aided Design (FMCAD), pp. 120–128. IEEE (2019). https://doi.org/10.23919/FMCAD.2019.8894254

28. Piterman, N., Pnueli, A.: Temporal logic and fair discrete systems. In: Handbook of Model Checking, pp. 27–73. Springer, Cham (2018). https://doi.org/10.1007/978-3-319-10575-8_2

29. Pnueli, A., Rosner, R.: On the synthesis of a reactive module. In: POPL, pp. 179–190. ACM Press (1989)

30. Rodríguez, A., Sánchez, C.: Boolean abstractions for realizability modulo theories. In: Enea, C., Lal, A. (eds.) Computer Aided Verification - 35th International Conference, CAV 2023, Paris, France, 17-22 July 2023, Proceedings, Part III. LNCS, vol. 13966, pp. 305–328. Springer (2023). https://doi.org/10.1007/978-3-031-37709-9_15

31. Rodríguez, A., Sánchez, C.: Adaptive reactive synthesis for LTL and LTLF modulo theories. In: Wooldridge, M.J., Dy, J.G., Natarajan, S. (eds.) Thirty-Eighth AAAI Conference on Artificial Intelligence, AAAI 2024, Thirty-Sixth Conference on Innovative Applications of Artificial Intelligence, IAAI 2024, Fourteenth Symposium on Educational Advances in Artificial Intelligence, EAAI 2014, 20-27 February 2024, Vancouver, Canada, pp. 10679–10686. AAAI Press (2024). https://doi.org/10.1609/AAAI.V38I9.28939

32. Rodríguez, A., Sánchez, C.: Realizability modulo theories. J. Log. Algebraic Methods Program. **140**, 100971 (2024). https://doi.org/10.1016/J.JLAMP.2024.100971

33. Samuel, S., D'Souza, D., Komondoor, R.: Symbolic fixpoint algorithms for logical LTL games. In: 2023 38th IEEE/ACM International Conference on Automated Software Engineering (ASE) pp. 698–709 (2023). https://doi.org/10.1109/ASE56229.2023.00212

34. Schmuck, A.K., Heim, P., Dimitrova, R., Nayak, S.P.: Localized attractor computations for infinite-state games. In: Gurfinkel, A., Ganesh, V. (eds.) 36th International Conference on Computer Aided Verification (CAV). LNCS, vol. 14683, pp. 135–158. Springer, Montreal, QC, Canada (2024). https://doi.org/10.1007/978-3-031-65633-0_7

35. Unno, H., Satake, Y., Terauchi, T., Koskinen, E.: Program verification via predicate constraint satisfiability modulo theories. CoRR abs/2007.03656 (2020). https://arxiv.org/abs/2007.03656
36. Walker, A., Ryzhyk, L.: Predicate abstraction for reactive synthesis. In: 2014 Formal Methods in Computer-Aided Design (FMCAD), pp. 219–226 (2014). https://doi.org/10.1109/FMCAD.2014.6987617
37. Walukiewicz, I.: Pushdown processes: games and model-checking. Inf. Comput. **164**(2), 234–263 (2001). https://doi.org/10.1006/INCO.2000.2894

Issy: A Comprehensive Tool for Specification and Synthesis of Infinite-State Reactive Systems

Philippe Heim$^{(\boxtimes)}$ and Rayna Dimitrova

CISPA Helmholtz Center for Information Security,
Saarbrücken, Germany
{philippe.heim,dimitrova}@cispa.de

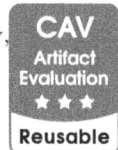

Abstract. The synthesis of infinite-state reactive systems from temporal logic specifications or infinite-state games has attracted significant attention in recent years, leading to the emergence of novel solving techniques. Most approaches are accompanied by an implementation showcasing their viability on an increasingly larger collection of benchmarks. Those implementations are –often simple– prototypes. Furthermore, differences in specification formalisms and formats make comparisons difficult, and writing specifications is a tedious and error-prone task.

To address this, we present Issy, a tool for specification, realizability, and synthesis of infinite-state reactive systems. Issy comes with an expressive specification language that allows for combining infinite-state games and temporal formulas, thus encompassing the current formalisms. The realizability checking and synthesis methods implemented in Issy build upon recently developed approaches and extend them with newly engineered efficient techniques, offering a portfolio of solving algorithms. We evaluate Issy on an extensive set of benchmarks, demonstrating its competitiveness with the state of the art. Furthermore, Issy provides tooling for a general high-level format designed to make specification easier for users. It also includes a compiler to a more machine-readable format that other tool developers can easily use, which we hope will lead to a broader adoption and advances in infinite-state reactive synthesis.

1 Introduction

Reactive systems are computational systems that constantly interact with their environment and run indefinitely. Notable examples include communication protocols and controllers for embedded systems or robots. Reactive synthesis is the problem of automatically generating correct-by-construction reactive systems from formal specifications describing the system's desired behavior. Many target applications of synthesis require the treatment of *infinite-state* models, as they operate with unbounded data such as integers. For this reason, the synthesis of reactive systems over infinite data domains has received increasing attention over the last years. In this paper, we present Issy, a comprehensive open-source tool

R. Piskac and Z. Rakamarić (Eds.): CAV 2025, LNCS 15934, pp. 298–312, 2025.
https://doi.org/10.1007/978-3-031-98685-7_14

Table 1. Supported specification type (temporal logic or games) and objectives (Safety/Reachability, Deterministic Büchi, LTL), support for infinite domains of system input and output, supported data types ($\mathbb{B}, \mathbb{Z}, \mathbb{R}$), input format.

Tool	Specification Type	SR	B	LTL	Inf Inp	Inf Out	$\mathbb{B}$	$\mathbb{Z}$	$\mathbb{R}$	Input Format
Issy	Combined games & RP-LTL	✓	✓	✓	✓	✓	✓	✓	✓	Issy, LLissy, RPG, TSL-MT
rpgsolve [7]	RPG	✓	✓	✗	✓	✗	✓	✓	✓	RPG
rpg-STeLA [22]	RPG	✓	✓	✗	✓	✗	✓	✓	✓	RPG
tslmt2rpg [9] + [7]	TSL-MT	✓	✓	✓	✓	✗	✓	✓	✓	TSL-MT var.
sweap [1]	Programs + LTL	✓	✓	✓	✗	✗	✓	✓	✗	custom format
Raboniel [13]	TSL-MT	✓	✓	✓	✓	✗	✗	✓	✓	TSL-MT var.
temos [2]	TSL-MT	✓	✓	✓	✓	✗	✓	✓	✗	TSL-MT var.
GENSYS [20]	Games	✓	✗	✗	✓	✓	✓	✓	✓	—
GENSYS-LTL [21]	Games	✓	✓	✓	✓	✓	✓	✓	✓	—
gr1mT [14]	GR(1) + data	✓	✓	✗	✓	✗	✓	✓	✓	unkown
tools in [17–19]	LTL$_T$	✓	✓	✓	✓	✓	✓	✓	✓	unkown
MuVal [24]	μCLP formulas	✓	✓	✓	✓	✓	✗	✓	✓	custom format
SIMSYNTH [4]	linear arith. games	✓	✗	✗	✓	✓	✓	✓	✓	custom format

for the specification and synthesis of infinite-state reactive systems, that builds upon recently developed approaches and newly engineered efficient techniques. Issy comes with an expressive specification language that encompasses current formalisms, thus providing a basis for the further development of synthesis tools.

Requirements for reactive systems are typically specified using *temporal logics*, such as Linear Temporal Logic (LTL) [16] in the case of finite-state systems. Alternatively, the synthesis problem can be described as a *two-player game* modelling the interaction between a system and its environment. These specification formalisms have been extended to the setting of infinite-state systems, resulting in temporal logics such as TSL-MT [5], LTL$_T$ [18], and RP-LTL [9], on the one hand, and infinite-state game models, such as reactive program games (RPGs) [7] on the other. Table 1 summarizes the types of specifications used in the main existing prototype tools for realizability and synthesis of infinite-state reactive systems, and that of our new tool Issy presented in this paper. Most of the tools fall into one of two categories: those that support temporal logic formulas (temos [2], Raboniel [13], the tools in [17–19], sweap [1], tslmt2rpg [9]) and those using directly two-player games (GENSYS [20], GENSYS-LTL [21], gr1mT [14], SIMSYNTH [4], rpgsolve [7], rpg-STeLA [22]). However, different types of requirements are more naturally modelled in one formalism or the other. For example, constraints that depend heavily of the systems' state or execution phase (such as, for instance, the available moves of a robot) are often difficult to express

Table 2. Comparison of main techniques, capabilities, technologies, availability

Tool	Technique	Unb. Loop	Synthesis	LTL Synt.	SMT	LTL to Aut	Open-Source
Issy	acceleration-based f.p. computation	✓	✓(C code)		•	•	✓
rpgsolve [7]	acceleration-based f.p. computation	✓	✓		•		✓
rpg-STeLA [22]	[7] + abstraction	✓	✗		•		✓
tslmt2rpg [9] + rpgsolve	monitor-enhanced symb. game constr.	✓	✓		•	•	✓
sweap [1]	abstraction to LTL	✓	✓	•	•		✓
Raboniel [13]	abstraction to LTL	✗	✓(Python)	•	•		✓
temos [2]	abstraction to LTL	✗	✓(several)	•	•		✓
GenSys [20]	naive f.p. comp.	✗	✓		•		✓
GenSys-LTL [21]	naive f.p. comp.	✗	✓		•	•	✓
gr1mT [14]	GR(1) f.p. comp.	✗	✓		•		✗
tool in [18]	abstraction to LTL	—	✗	•	•		✗
tool in [19]	abstraction to LTL	—	✓	•	•		✗
tool in [17]	abstraction to LTL + Skolem fun. syn.	—	✓(C code)	•	•		✗
MuVal [24]	constraint solving	✓	✗		•		✓
SimSynth [4]	constraint solving	—	✓		•		✓

in temporal logic, and result in long and complex formulas. High-level mission requirements, on the other hand, are more naturally formalized in temporal logics. Motivated by this, we developed Issy with support for a new input format that unites both specification paradigms. Often, even tools using the same specification logic have different input formats, such as for example the tools in Table 1 using TSL-MT. In contrast to the case for finite-state systems, where an established specification format, TLSF [11], exists and is used in SYNTCOMP [10], there is no such common format for infinite-state reactive systems. We envision that the Issy framework is a major step towards filling this gap. The Issy input format supports the main types of synthesis objectives, possibly infinite domains for both the input and the output variables of the specified system, and three basic data types (bool, int, and real). As Table 1 shows, the specification capabilities of Issy strictly subsume those of the existing tools.   The synthesis problem for infinite-state systems is in general undecidable. From Table 1, only [17–19] considers a decidable restriction of the problem. The others implement different incomplete techniques summarized in Table 2. One of the common approaches, used in temos, Raboniel, and sweap, is abstraction to synthesis from LTL specifications, accompanied by some form of specification refinement. Alternatives include fixpoint-based game-solving as [14, 20, 21], and constraint solving as in SIMSYNTH and MuVal, the last of which is a tool for solving first-order fixpoint constraints. In [7] we proposed a technique for solving infinite-state games that aims to address one of the limitations of prior abstraction and fixpoint-based approaches, namely, that they usually diverge on game-solving tasks that require reasoning about the unbounded iteration of strategic decisions. The core of [7] is a technique called *attractor acceleration* that employs *ranking arguments* to improve the convergence of symbolic game-solving procedures. [1] also addresses unbounded behavior, in the context of abstraction-based methods by introducing the so called liveness refinement. Column "Unb. Loop" indicates which of the techniques handle unbounded strategy loops. Further, the table indicates whether the tool performs synthesis (or only checks realizability, that is, the existence of an implementation for the specification). We also indicate the main technologies (LTL synthesis, SMT, translation of LTL to automata) used by each tool, and whether the tool is available open-source.

Issy builds on the acceleration technique in [7], but in addition to the new input format, integrates methods and ideas from our recent work [22] and [9], as well as novel techniques discussed in Sect. 4. We evaluate Issy on an extensive set of benchmarks, demonstrating its competitiveness with the state of the art.

2   The Issy Format

The Issy input format has the key advantage that it combines two modes for specification of synthesis problems for infinite-state reactive systems: temporal logic formulas, and two-player games, both over variables with infinite domains, such as integers or reals. The advantages of this mutli-paradigm specification format are two-fold. First, it allows specification designers to specify requirements in a less cumbersome way. For example, constraints that depend on the system's state, or encode behaviour in different phases, are usually easier to specify as games. On the other hand, mission specifications such that under certain assumptions the system must eventually stabilize, or that some tasks should be carried out repeatedly, are often more concisely expressed in temporal logic.

```
1 input real add   // Real-valued input variables
2 input real rem   // Input variables are global for all formulas and games.
3                  // The values of input variables are picked by the
         environment
4                  // at every step and they are not stored as part of the
         state.
5 state real load1 // Real-valued state variables
6 state real load2 // State variables are global for all formulas and games.
7 state real rem1  // They are controlled by the system, choosing the next
8 state real rem2  // values based on the current state and environment
         input.
9
10 /* Specifications consist of formulas and game specifications blocks. Those
11    blocks are interpreted conjunctively. A single formula is an implication
12    between  conjuncted assumptions and conjuncted assertions (guarantees).
         */
```

```
13 formula {
14   /* Assumption: From some time point on, the environment will always set
        the input variable add to be less than or equal to zero. */
15   assume F G [add <= 0]
16   /* Guarantee: From some point on, load1 and load2 will always be zero. */
17   assert F G ([load1 = 0] && [load2 = 0])
18 }
19
20 // Macros to make the specification easier to read
21 def balanced   = [load1 >= load2] && [load1 <= 2 * load2]
22                  ||[load2 >= load1] && [load2 <= 2 * load1]
23 def addtoone   = [load1' = load1 + add] && [load2' = load2]
24                  ||[load2' = load2 + add] && [load1' = load1]
25 def validrem   = [rem >= 0.1] && [rem <= load1 + 2/3 * load2]
26 def decrease   = [load1' = load1 - rem1'] && [rem1' + rem2' = rem]
27                  &&[load2' = load2 - 3/2 * rem2']
28
29 /* Two-player game with locations init, lbal, lrem, done and err, and
        safety winning condition for the system, requiring that err is never
        reached. */
30 game Safety from init {
31   loc init 1 // When defining locations, the type of the location w.r.t.
        the
32   loc lbal 1 // accepting condition is specified. Here, 1 means that those
33   loc lrem 1 // locations are safe. The scope of each location is the
34   loc done 1 // respective game. Different formulas and games are related
35              // via the variables, making their combination less error-
        prone.
36   loc err 0  // The location err is the only unsafe location in this game.
37
38   /* The following define the possible moves in the game via pairs of
        locations and their transition constraints over the current state and
        input variables as well as the next-state variables. A move in such a
        game works as follows. It starts in some location and assignment to
        the state variables. First, the environment chooses values for the
        input variables. Then, the system chooses the next state values and
        the next location such that the respective transition constraint is
        satisfied. */
39   from init to done with [load1 < 0] || [load2 < 0]
40   from init to lbal with [load1 >= 0] && [load2 >= 0] && keep(load1 load2)
41   // Conditions like the next one are not possible in TSL-MT.
42   from lbal to lrem with [load1' + load2' = load1 + load2]
43   from lrem to err  with !balanced
44   from lrem to done with balanced &&(!validrem ||([load1 = 0] && [load2 =
        0]))
45   from lrem to lbal with balanced && [add > 0]   && addtoone
46
47   from lrem to lrem with balanced && [add <= 0] && validrem && decrease
48   from done to done with true
49   from err  to err  with keep(load1 load2)
50 }
```

Listing 1.1. Example specification in Issy format.

Each of the two modes of specification can potentially offer opportunities for optimization of the synthesis tools processing these specifications. In [9], we showed how the translation from RP-LTL formulas to games can benefit from the high-level information present in the formula in order to simplify the game.

$\langle spec \rangle$ $::=$ $((\langle vardecl \rangle \mid \langle logicspec \rangle \mid \langle gamespec \rangle \mid \langle macro \rangle))^*$

$\langle vardecl \rangle$ $::=$ (`input' | `state') $\langle type \rangle$ $\langle identifier \rangle$

$\langle type \rangle$ $::=$ `int' | `bool' | `real'

$\langle logicspec \rangle$ $::=$ `formula' `{' $\langle logicstm \rangle$* `}'

$\langle logicstm \rangle$ $::=$ (`assert' | `assume') $\langle rpltl \rangle$

$\langle gamespec \rangle$ $::=$ `game' $\langle wincond \rangle$ `from' $\langle identifier \rangle$ `{' ( $\langle locdef \rangle$ | $\langle transdef \rangle$))* `}'

$\langle wincond \rangle$ $::=$ `Safety' | `Reachability' | `Buechi' | `CoBuechi' | `ParityMaxOdd'

$\langle locdef \rangle$ $::=$ `loc' $\langle identifier \rangle$ [$\langle nat \rangle$] [`with' $\langle formula \rangle$]

$\langle transdef \rangle$ $::=$ `from' $\langle identifier \rangle$ `to' $\langle identifier \rangle$ `with' $\langle formula \rangle$

Fig. 1. An excerpt from the Issy format. The full description is in [8].

Now, we turn to an example that illustrates and motivates the main features of the Issy format. An excerpt of the format's grammar is given in Fig. 1.

Example 1. Consider a reactive system that has to balance the loads, load1 and load2, of two components. At any point, the environment can increase the total load, via the environment-controlled input variable add. When that happens, the system has to re-balance the total load by appropriate partitioning. When the load does not increase, the system has to control the throughput of each component, state variables rem1 and rem2 respectively, in accordance with the components' speeds and the total available throughput, rem controlled by the environment. The specification of this system is given in Listing 1.1, and consists of variable declarations, a formula specification, macro definitions for better readability, and the second part of the specification given as a two-player game.

Variable declarations specify whether the variable is input controlled by the environment, or is a state variable controlled by the system. The currently supported data types are bool, int and real. The domains of variables can be further constrained in the game specifications by additional constraints.

The formula specification is a list of RP-LTL formulas, prefixed by the keywords assume and assert, denoting constraints on the environment and system respectively. They use temporal operators like LTL, but with quantifier-free first-order atoms instead of Boolean propositions. The assumption F G [add <= 0] uses the temporal operators F (eventually) and G (globally) to state that from some point on, no more load will be added by the environment. The assert statement in line 17 requires the system to ensure, under the above assumption, that both loads eventually stabilize at zero. The semantics of a formula specification is that the conjunction of the assumptions implies the conjunction of the asserts.

The possible actions of the system and the requirement to balance load1 and load2 are described by the game specification in Listing 1.1. The game has locations `init`, `lbal`, `lrem`, `done`, `err` that are local to the game, unlike variables that are global to the whole specification. The transitions between locations in the game are defined via quantifier-free formulas over input, state, and next-state variables (such as `load1'`). Nondeterminism is under the control of the system. The Issy format enables the use of macros to improve formula readability. For example, the transition in line 43 requires the system to transition from location `lrem` to the unsafe location `err` if the condition `balanced` defined by the macro in line 2 is violated. The game has a *safety* winning condition, indicated by the keyword `Safety`, and defined by the natural numbers with which the locations are labelled (0 indicates that `err` is unsafe, while all labelled 1 are safe).

A specification can contain multiple `formula` and `game` components, interpreted conjunctively. The semantics is a two-player game defined as the product of the games for the individual formulas and all game specifications. Issy requires and checks that at most one of these games has a non-safety winning condition.

The Issy specification in Example 1 shows the modelling flexibility of the format. Expressing the same requirements purely in RP-LTL or as an RPG results in a difficult to write and understand specification, making the specification process error-prone. We believe that Issy alleviates this problem to some extent, offering modularity and syntactic sugar constructs, and, most importantly, unifying the temporal logic and game formats for infinite-state reactive systems.

The issy compiler and the LLissy format. The Issy compiler, part of our synthesis framework, compiles specifications in Issy format to a low-level intermediate format called LLissy, given in the full version [8]. The compiler checks compliance with the syntax and gives informative error messages. The LLissy format is easier to parse, while retaining the ability to specify both logical formulas and games. We envision that the development of tools for translation from various high-level specification formats to the LLissy format will enable the seamless exchange of benchmarks and experimental comparison between different tools. Issy also accepts input directly in Issy format, as well as the older formats tslmt and rpg.

3   From Temporal Formulas to Games

To check the realizability of specifications and synthesize reactive programs, Issy follows the classical approach of reducing the task to solving a two-player game. To this end, it translates the specification into a symbolic synthesis game by first translating the temporal logic formulas to games, and then building their product with the rest of the specification. The construction of games from the formulas follows [9] and provides the option to build and use a *monitor* to prune/simplify the constructed game by performing first-order and temporal reasoning during game construction. More concretely, a given formula is first translated to a deterministic ω-automaton using Spot [3]. Then, monitors are constructed *on-the-fly*, building the product between the game obtained from the

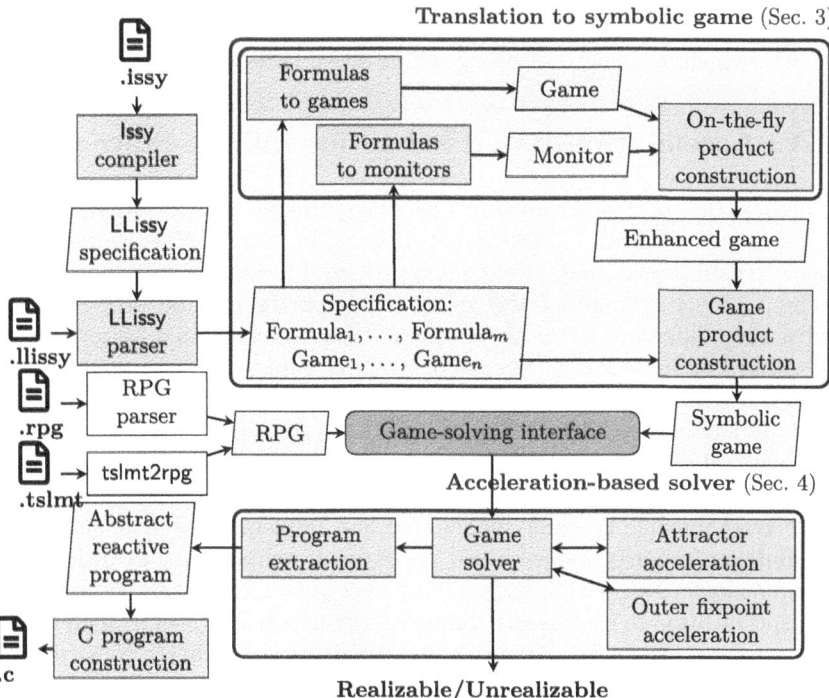

Fig. 2. Architecture of Issy. Components depicted in blue and pink are part of the tool's implementation, those depicted in white are external.

automaton and the monitor. The product with the monitor enhances the game with semantic information [9], resulting in the so-called *enhanced game*, which is potentially easier to solve. As sometimes the monitor construction causes overhead, Issy has a parameter --pruning controlling its complexity, ranging from no monitor construction (level 0), to applying powerful deduction during its construction (level 3).

The prototype tslmt2rpg [9] is restricted to the logic TSL-MT and constructs RPGs. In contrast, the translation in Issy applies to the more general logic RP-LTL, and constructs a more general form of symbolic games. In TSL-MT and RPGs, the system controls the state variables via a *fixed finite set of possible updates*, a restriction not present in RP-LTL and the respective symbolic games. For example, assertions like x' > x are not in the syntax of TSL-MT, and specifying the same behavior with updates would require a (possibly uncountable) infinite number of them. Hence, RP-LTL lifts the imbalance in TSL-MT that the environment can pick any value (from possibly infinitely many) for the inputs, but the system can only choose from a finite set of updates. Note that in RP-LTL, only state variables appear primed, not environment-controlled input variables. If a property needs to relate input values over time, input values need to be stored in state variables. Hence, inputs are not part of the state unless stored explicitly, which we believe results in an intuitive notion of state.

4   An Acceleration-Based Solver for Infinite-State Games

The architecture of Issy is shown in Fig. 2. We discussed the components translating a specification to a single synthesis game in Sect. 3. Now we present the game solver underlying Issy, focusing on the novel technical developments.

The approach behind the Issy solver builds on the method proposed in [7]. The fist main difference to the prototype rpgsolve from [7] is that rpgsolve accepts RPGs, a strictly more restricted class of symbolic games. Furthermore, the initial version of rpgsolve does not support parity winning conditions. Our Example 1 cannot be modelled as an RPG, because the system player has the power to select any real values as next-state values for the state variables. Furthermore, the specification in Example 1 translates to a parity game. Issy's solver supports a more general symbolic game model, and also implements a symbolic method for infinite-state parity games based on fixpoint computation (a lifting of the classical Zielonka's algorithm [25]). Thus, Issy is able to establish the realizability of the specification in Listing 1.1 thanks to the new techniques it implements.

The crux to this is the acceleration technique introduced in [7]. Naive fixpoint-based game-solving diverges on this example. *Attractor acceleration* [7] uses ranking arguments to establish that by iterating some strategy an unbounded number of times through some location, a player in the game can enforce reaching a set of target states. In Example 1, attractor acceleration is used within the procedure for solving the parity game to establish that (under the respective constraints on the environment) from any state satisfying the formula balanced, a state where both load1 and load2 are in the bounded interval $[\frac{3}{10}, \frac{9}{10}]$ can be enforced by the system player. This argument is formalized as what is called an *acceleration lemma* [7]. From the interval $[\frac{3}{10}, \frac{9}{10}]$, the system player can then enforce reaching in a bounded number of steps a state where load1 and load2 are zero.

We developed a novel method for generating acceleration lemmas and implemented it in Issy in addition to that from [7]. To search for acceleration lemmas, rpgsolve introduces uninterpreted predicates representing the lemmas' components, and collects SMT constraints asserting the applicability of the lemma. Thus, rpgsolve would have to discover the formula [load1 >= load2] && [load1 <= 2 * load2] || [load2 >= load1] && [load2 <= 2 * load1] as part of the acceleration lemma, which it is not able to do within a reasonable timeout. The alternative method implemented in Issy performs analysis of the game in order to generate candidate acceleration lemmas. First, it analyzes the game in order to identify variables potentially making progress in a ranking argument. For instance, variables that remain unchanged in the relevant game locations can be ruled out. Second, the new method uses the distance to the target set of states to generate ranking arguments for candidate acceleration lemmas. Finally, to search for a set of states where the respective player can enforce the decrease of the distance, it uses symbolic iteration and SMT-based formula generalization.

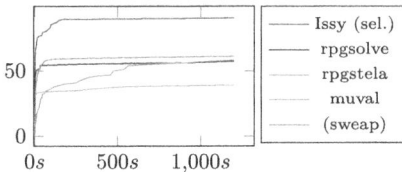 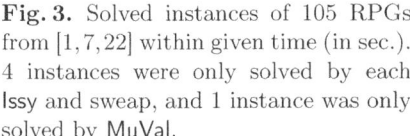

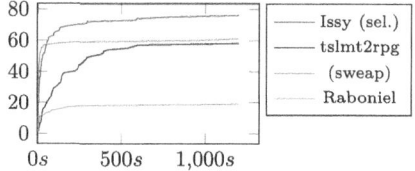

Fig. 3. Solved instances of 105 RPGs from [1,7,22] within given time (in sec.). 4 instances were only solved by each Issy and sweap, and 1 instance was only solved by MuVal.

Fig. 4. Solved instances of 94 TSL-MT from [1,9,13] within given time (in sec.). 13 instances were only solved by sweap, 2 instances were only solved by Issy, and 1 instance was only solved by Raboniel.

As demonstrated for Example 1, and more broadly by our experimental evaluation in Sect. 5, this new method for generating acceleration lemmas, which we call *geometric acceleration*, is successful in many cases challenging for rpgsolve. In Issy, geometric attractor acceleration is enabled by default, and the method can be switched using the parameter `--accel-attr`.

In addition to an alternative method for generating acceleration lemmas, the Issy solver utilizes new techniques for their localization. Building on ideas in [22], we restrict the size of the sub-games used for the acceleration lemma computation and project away variables that are not relevant in the respective subgame. Unlike [22], where this is done for pre-computing accelerations, in Issy these localization techniques are applied on-the-fly during the main game solving.

Issy also provides support for strategy synthesis and extraction of C programs for realizable specifications. The latter can be extended to other target languages, utilizing the generic data structure for reactive program representation in Issy.

Issy[1] is implemented in Haskell with focus on modularity and extensibility, including detailed documentation. Using the Haskell tool Stack, building Issy and getting its dependencies is seamless. The external tools used are Spot [3] for translation of LTL to automata, the μCLP solver MuVal [24] and the Optimal CHC solver OptPCSat [6] for the monitor construction, and z3 [15] for all SMT, formula simplification, and quantifier elimination queries.

5   Benchmarks and Evaluation

We evaluated Issy experimentally, comparing to Raboniel[2], sweap[3], MuVal[4], rpgsolve[5] and tslmt2rpg[6], thus covering all types of techniques. We did not compare to temos as past experiments [7,9] show that it is outperformed by Raboniel. The

---

[1] https://github.com/phheim/issy
[2] https://doi.org/10.5281/zenodo.7602503
[3] https://github.com/shaunazzopardi/sweap, commit: 1275a759
[4] https://github.com/hiroshi-unno/coar, commit: dc094f04
[5] https://doi.org/10.5281/zenodo.10939871
[6] https://doi.org/10.5281/zenodo.13939202

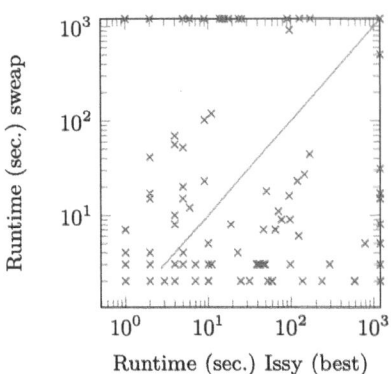

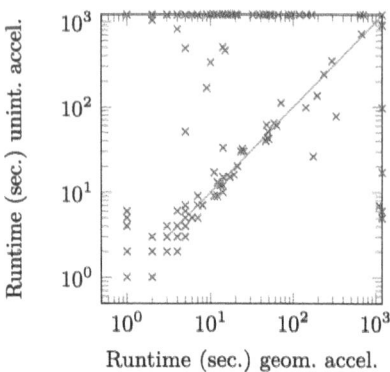

Fig. 6. Comparison of the existing and new attractor acceleration in Issy on all RPG, TSL-MT, and new Issy benchmarks. 57 instances were only solve by the new attractor acceleration and 5 instances were only solved by the existing one.

Fig. 5. Comparison of sweap and Issy on the sweap benchmarks [1], manually encoded in [1] as RPGs or TSL-MT. 23 instances were only solved by Issy and 19 instances were only solved by sweap.

other tools are either not available, unable to build, or do not accept input files. Also, we did not compare to [12] since it is restricted to safety specifications, and in [20] is mostly outperformed by GENSYS. Neither did we compare to [14] as it focuses on efficient synthesis from GR(1), not on handling unbounded behaviour, and the implementation was not available to us.

For Issy we use four configurations: with the novel geometric acceleration or the existing acceleration with uninterpreted predicates, and with or without monitor-based simplification (`--pruning 2` or 0, resp.) when applied to specifications with formulas. The later is because the effectiveness of pruning varies [9].

We used an extensive set of benchmarks[7] (contributions welcome!) containing the RPG benchmarks from [7,22] and the TSL-MT benchmarks [9,13], some of which can not be solved by existing tools. Furthermore, we included the benchmarks created by the authors of sweap [1] (in their format) as well as their manually encoded versions in the RPG and TSL-MT formats. We also created 50 new benchmarks in the new Issy format which combine formulas and games and can only be used by Issy.

We partitioned the set of benchmarks according to the type of specifications (games or temporal formulas) the tools are applicable to according to Table 1. We apply MuVal on RPGs via an automatic encoding of the games as fixpoint equations which is similar to the one in [23] and modular w.r.t. the game locations, i.e. it uses one sub-equation per location. All experiments were run on AMD EPYC processors, with one core, 4 GB of memory, and 20 min wall-clock-time for each benchmarking run.

---

[7] https://github.com/phheim/infinite-state-reactive-synthesis-benchmarks

Table 3. Benchmark instances solved by the four different `Issy` configurations.

Benchmark set	Fig. 3	Fig. 4	New Issy	hard in [7]
Total number of benchmarks	105	94	55	8
Geometric accel.	**88**	40	40	4
Uninterpreted-predicate accel.	62	32	40	2
Geometric accel. + monitor pruning	-	**72**	**42**	**5**
Uninterpreted-predicate accel. + monitor pruning	–	–	41	–

Figures 3 and 4 show the comparisons on 105 RPG and 94 TSL-MT specifications, respectively. For Issy we show the best time for *checking realizability* for each benchmark across the four different configurations. As shown in Table 3, the best time for Issy is usually with geometric acceleration. We ran sweap only on the benchmarks to which it is applicable and are available in its own format, which uses a different formalism. Therefore, we show additionally in Fig. 5 the comparison to sweap only on the set of those 148 benchmarks. We note that sweap is performing synthesis, while the results for Issy are for checking realizability, as we could not let sweap only check for realizability. The evaluation results demonstrate that Issy mostly outperforms the existing prototypes, and has matured well beyond the prototypes it stems from.

In addition to Table 3, Fig. 6 provides a detailed comparison between the new geometric and the existing uninterpreted-predicate-based acceleration methods (without pruning) on all benchmarks. It shows that geometric acceleration is effective, without making the existing acceleration method obsolete. We also ran Issy in synthesis mode (`--synt`) with geometric acceleration, especially as synthesis for uninterpreted-predicate-based acceleration is known to be hard [7]. Out of the 130 benchmarks that geometric accleration determined to be realizable, Issy could synthesize C-programs for 106 of them within the given resource bounds. This difference stems from the fact that Issy does heavy simplifications and might need to synthesize Skolem functions.

In summary, the results show Issy's competitiveness with the state of the art. Issy's comprehensive framework, together with the public collection of benchmarks provide a basis for further development of techniques and tools.

Data Availability Statement. The software generated during and analysed during the current study is available in the Zenodo repository https://doi.org/10. 5281/zenodo.15308725. A full version of this paper is available through arXiv [8].

Disclosure of Interests. The authors have no competing interests to declare that are relevant to the content of this article.

References

1. Azzopardi, S., Piterman, N., Schneider, G., Stefano, L.D.: Symbolic infinite-state LTL synthesis (2024). https://doi.org/10.48550/ARXIV.2307.09776
2. Choi, W., Finkbeiner, B., Piskac, R., Santolucito, M.: Can reactive synthesis and syntax-guided synthesis be friends? In: Jhala, R., Dillig, I. (eds.) PLDI 2022: 43rd ACM SIGPLAN International Conference on Programming Language Design and Implementation, San Diego, CA, USA, 13–17 June 2022, pp. 229–243. ACM (2022). https://doi.org/10.1145/3519939.3523429
3. Duret-Lutz, A., et al.: From spot 2.0 to spot 2.10: what's new? In: Shoham, S., Vizel, Y. (eds.) Computer Aided Verification - 34th International Conference, CAV 2022, Haifa, Israel, 7–10 August 2022, Proceedings, Part II, LNCS, vol. 13372, pp. 174–187. Springer, Cham (2022). https://doi.org/10.1007/978-3-031-13188-2_9
4. Farzan, A., Kincaid, Z.: Strategy synthesis for linear arithmetic games. Proc. ACM Program. Lang. 2(POPL), 61:1–61:30 (2018). https://doi.org/10.1145/3158149
5. Finkbeiner, B., Heim, P., Passing, N.: Temporal stream logic modulo theories. In: Bouyer, P., Schröder, L. (eds.) Foundations of Software Science and Computation Structures - 25th International Conference, FOSSACS 2022, Held as Part of the European Joint Conferences on Theory and Practice of Software, ETAPS 2022, Munich, Germany, 2–7 April 2022, Proceedings, LNCS, vol. 13242, pp. 325–346. Springer, Cham (2022). https://doi.org/10.1007/978-3-030-99253-8_17
6. Gu, Y., Tsukada, T., Unno, H.: Optimal CHC solving via termination proofs. Proc. ACM Program. Lang. 7(POPL), 604–631 (2023). https://doi.org/10.1145/3571214
7. Heim, P., Dimitrova, R.: Solving infinite-state games via acceleration. Proc. ACM Program. Lang. 8(POPL), 1696–1726 (2024). https://doi.org/10.1145/3632899
8. Heim, P., Dimitrova, R.: Issy: a comprehensive tool for specification and synthesis of infinite-state reactive systems (2025). https://doi.org/10.48550/ARXIV.2502.03013
9. Heim, P., Dimitrova, R.: Translation of temporal logic for efficient infinite-state reactive synthesis. Proc. ACM Program. Lang. 9(POPL) (2025). https://doi.org/10.1145/3704888
10. Jacobs, S., et al.: The reactive synthesis competition (SYNTCOMP): 2018–2021. CoRR abs/2206.00251 (2022). https://doi.org/10.48550/ARXIV.2206.00251
11. Jacobs, S., Pérez, G.A., Schlehuber-Caissier, P.: The temporal logic synthesis format TLSF v1.2. CoRR abs/2303.03839 (2023). https://doi.org/10.48550/ARXIV.2303.03839
12. Katis, A., et al.: Validity-guided synthesis of reactive systems from assume-guarantee contracts. In: Beyer, D., Huisman, M. (eds.) TACAS 2018, Part II. LNCS, vol. 10806, pp. 176–193. Springer, Cham (2018). https://doi.org/10.1007/978-3-319-89963-3_10
13. Maderbacher, B., Bloem, R.: Reactive synthesis modulo theories using abstraction refinement. In: Griggio, A., Rungta, N. (eds.) 22nd Formal Methods in Computer-Aided Design, FMCAD 2022, Trento, Italy, 17–21 October 2022, pp. 315–324. IEEE (2022). https://doi.org/10.34727/2022/ISBN.978-3-85448-053-2_38
14. Maderbacher, B., Windisch, F., Bloem, R.: Synthesis from infinite-state generalized reactivity(1) specifications. In: Margaria, T., Steffen, B. (eds.) Leveraging Applications of Formal Methods, Verification and Validation. Software Engineering Methodologies - 12th International Symposium, ISoLA 2024, Crete, Greece, October 27-31, 2024, Proceedings, Part IV, LNCS, vol. 15222, pp. 281–301. Springer, Cham (2024). https://doi.org/10.1007/978-3-031-75387-9_17

15. de Moura, L.M., Bjørner, N.S.: Z3: an efficient SMT solver. In: Ramakrishnan, C.R., Rehof, J. (eds.) Tools and Algorithms for the Construction and Analysis of Systems, 14th International Conference, TACAS 2008, Held as Part of the Joint European Conferences on Theory and Practice of Software, ETAPS 2008, Budapest, Hungary, March 29-April 6, 2008. Proceedings, LNCS, vol. 4963, pp. 337–340. Springer (2008). https://doi.org/10.1007/978-3-540-78800-3_24

16. Pnueli, A.: The temporal logic of programs. In: 18th Annual Symposium on Foundations of Computer Science, Providence, Rhode Island, USA, 31 October - 1 November 1977, pp. 46–57. IEEE Computer Society (1977). https://doi.org/10.1109/SFCS.1977.32

17. Rodríguez, A., Gorostiaga, F., Sánchez, C.: Predictable and performant reactive synthesis modulo theories via functional synthesis. In: Akshay, S., Niemetz, A., Sankaranarayanan, S. (eds.) Automated Technology for Verification and Analysis - 22nd International Symposium, ATVA 2024, Kyoto, Japan, October 21-25, 2024, Proceedings, Part II. Lecture Notes in Computer Science, vol. 15055, pp. 28–50. Springer (2024). https://doi.org/10.1007/978-3-031-78750-8_2

18. Rodríguez, A., Sánchez, C.: Boolean abstractions for realizability modulo theories. In: Enea, C., Lal, A. (eds.) Computer Aided Verification - 35th International Conference, CAV 2023, Paris, France, July 17-22, 2023, Proceedings, Part III. Lecture Notes in Computer Science, vol. 13966, pp. 305–328. Springer (2023). https://doi.org/10.1007/978-3-031-37709-9_15

19. Rodríguez, A., Sánchez, C.: Adaptive reactive synthesis for LTL and LTLf modulo theories. In: Wooldridge, M.J., Dy, J.G., Natarajan, S. (eds.) Thirty-Eighth AAAI Conference on Artificial Intelligence, AAAI 2024, Thirty-Sixth Conference on Innovative Applications of Artificial Intelligence, IAAI 2024, Fourteenth Symposium on Educational Advances in Artificial Intelligence, EAAI 2014, February 20-27, 2024, Vancouver, Canada. pp. 10679–10686. AAAI Press (2024). https://doi.org/10.1609/AAAI.V38I9.28939

20. Samuel, S., D'Souza, D., Komondoor, R.: Gensys: a scalable fixed-point engine for maximal controller synthesis over infinite state spaces. In: Spinellis, D., Gousios, G., Chechik, M., Penta, M.D. (eds.) ESEC/FSE '21: 29th ACM Joint European Software Engineering Conference and Symposium on the Foundations of Software Engineering, Athens, Greece, August 23-28, 2021. pp. 1585–1589. ACM (2021). https://doi.org/10.1145/3468264.3473126

21. Samuel, S., D'Souza, D., Komondoor, R.: Symbolic fixpoint algorithms for logical LTL games. In: 38th IEEE/ACM International Conference on Automated Software Engineering, ASE 2023, Luxembourg, September 11-15, 2023. pp. 698–709. IEEE (2023). https://doi.org/10.1109/ASE56229.2023.00212

22. Schmuck, A., Heim, P., Dimitrova, R., Nayak, S.P.: Localized attractor computations for infinite-state games. In: Gurfinkel, A., Ganesh, V. (eds.) Computer Aided Verification - 36th International Conference, CAV 2024, Montreal, QC, Canada, July 24-27, 2024, Proceedings, Part III. Lecture Notes in Computer Science, vol. 14683, pp. 135–158. Springer (2024). https://doi.org/10.1007/978-3-031-65633-0_7

23. Unno, H., Satake, Y., Terauchi, T., Koskinen, E.: Program verification via predicate constraint satisfiability modulo theories (2020), https://arxiv.org/abs/2007.03656

24. Unno, H., Terauchi, T., Gu, Y., Koskinen, E.: Modular primal-dual fixpoint logic solving for temporal verification. Proc. ACM Program. Lang. **7**(POPL), 2111–2140 (2023). https://doi.org/10.1145/3571265
25. Zielonka, W.: Infinite games on finitely coloured graphs with applications to automata on infinite trees. Theor. Comput. Sci. **200**(1–2), 135–183 (1998). https://doi.org/10.1016/S0304-3975(98)00009-7

Applications

On the Complexity of Checking Mixed Isolation Levels for SQL Transactions

Ahmed Bouajjani[1], Constantin Enea[2], and Enrique Román-Calvo[1]([✉])

[1] Université Paris Cité, CNRS, IRIF, Paris, France
{abou,calvo}@irif.fr

[2] LIX, École Polytechnique, CNRS and Institut Polytechnique
de Paris, Palaiseau, France
cenea@lix.polytechnique.fr

Abstract. Concurrent accesses to databases are typically grouped in transactions which define units of work that should be isolated from other concurrent computations and resilient to failures. Modern databases provide different levels of isolation for transactions that correspond to different trade-offs between consistency and throughput. Quite often, an application can use transactions with different isolation levels at the same time. In this work, we investigate the problem of testing isolation level implementations in databases, i.e., checking whether a given execution composed of multiple transactions adheres to the prescribed isolation level semantics. We particularly focus on transactions formed of SQL queries and the use of multiple isolation levels at the same time. We show that many restrictions of this problem are NP-complete and provide an algorithm which is exponential-time in the worst-case, polynomial-time in relevant cases, and practically efficient.

1 Introduction

Concurrent accesses to databases are typically grouped in transactions which define units of work that should be isolated from other concurrent computations and resilient to failures. Modern databases provide different levels of isolation for transactions with different trade-offs between consistency and throughput. The strongest isolation level, *Serializability* [21], provides the illusion that transactions are executed atomically one after another in a serial order. Serializability incurs a high cost in throughput. For performance, databases provide weaker isolation levels, e.g., *Snapshot Isolation* [6] or *Read Committed* [6].

The concurrency control protocols used in large-scale databases to implement isolation levels are difficult to build and test. For instance, the black-box testing framework Jepsen [19] found a remarkably large number of subtle problems in many production databases.

In this work, we focus on testing the isolation level implementations in databases, and more precisely, on the problem of checking whether a given execution adheres to the prescribed isolation level semantics. Inspired by scenarios

© The Author(s) 2025
R. Piskac and Z. Rakamarić (Eds.): CAV 2025, LNCS 15934, pp. 315–337, 2025.
https://doi.org/10.1007/978-3-031-98685-7_15

that arise in commercial software [22], we consider a quite generic version of the problem where transactions are formed of SQL queries and *multiple* isolation levels are used at the same time, i.e., each transaction is assigned a possibly different isolation level (the survey in [22] found that 32% of the respondents use such "heterogeneous" configurations). Previous work [7,21] studied the complexity of the problem when transactions are formed of reads and writes on a *static* set of keys (variables), and all transactions have the *same* isolation level.

As a first contribution, we introduce a formal semantics for executions with SQL transactions and a range of isolation levels, including serializability, snapshot isolation, prefix consistency, and read committed. Dealing with SQL queries is more challenging than classic reads and writes of a *static* set of keys (as assumed in previous formalizations [7,11]). SQL insert and delete queries change the set of locations at runtime and the set of locations returned by an SQL query depends on their values (the values are restricted to satisfy WHERE clauses).

We define an abstract model for executions, called *history*, where every SQL query that inspects the database (has a WHERE clause) is associated with a set of SQL queries that wrote the inspected values. This relation is called a *write-read* relation (also known as read-from). This is similar to associating reads to writes in defining memory models. We consider two classes of histories depending on the "completeness" of the write-read relation. To define a formal semantics of isolation levels, we need a complete write-read relation in the sense that for instance, an SQL select is associated with a write *for every* possible row (identified by its primary key) in the database, even if that row is *not* returned by the select because it does not satisfy the WHERE clause. Not returning a row is an observable effect that needs to be justified by the semantics. Such *full* histories can not be constructed by interacting with the database in a black-box manner (a desirable condition in testing) when only the outputs returned by queries can be observed. Therefore, we introduce the class of *client* histories where the write-read concerns only rows that are *returned* by a query. The consistency of a client history is defined as the existence of an extension of the write-read to a full history which satisfies the semantics. The semantics on full histories combines axioms from previous work [7] in a way that is directed by SQL queries that inspect the database and the isolation level of the transaction they belong to. This axiomatic semantics is validated by showing that it is satisfied by a standard operational semantics inspired by real implementations.

We study the complexity of checking if a full or client history is consistent, it satisfies the prescribed isolation levels. This problem is more complex for client histories, which record less dependencies and need to be extended to full ones.

For full histories, we show that the complexity of consistency checking matches previous results in the reads and writes model when all transactions have the same isolation level [7]: polynomial time for the so-called saturable isolation levels, and NP-complete for stronger levels like Snapshot Isolation or Serializability. The former is a new result that generalizes the work of [7] and exposes the key ideas for achieving polynomial-time complexity, while the latter is a consequence of the previous results.

We show that consistency checking becomes NP-complete for client histories even for saturable isolation levels. It remains NP-complete regardless of the expressiveness of WHERE clauses (for this stronger result we define another class of histories called *partial-observation*). The problem is NP-complete even if we bound the number of sessions. In general, transactions are organized in *sessions* [23], an abstraction of the sequence of transactions performed during the execution of an application (the counterpart of threads in shared memory). This case is interesting because it is polynomial-time in the read/write model [7].

As a counterpart to these negative results, we introduce an algorithm for checking consistency of client histories which is exponential-time in the worst case, but polynomial time in relevant cases. Given a client history as input, this algorithm combines an enumeration of extensions towards a full history with a search for a total commit order that satisfies the required axioms. The commit order represents the order in which transactions are committed in the database and it is an essential artifact for defining isolation levels. For efficiency, the algorithm uses a non-trivial enumeration of extensions that are *not* necessarily full but contain enough information to validate consistency. The search for a commit order is a non-trivial generalization of an algorithm by Biswas et al. [7] which concerned only serializability. This generalization applies to all practical isolation levels and combinations thereof. We evaluate an implementation of this algorithm on histories generated by PostgreSQL with a number of applications from BenchBase [12], e.g., the TPC-C model of a store and a model of Twitter. This evaluation shows that the algorithm is quite efficient in practice and scales well to typical workloads used in testing databases.

To summarize, we provide the first results concerning the complexity of checking the correctness of mixed isolation level implementations for SQL transactions. We introduce a formal specification for such implementations, and a first tool that can be used in testing their correctness.

2 Histories

2.1 Transactions

We model the database as a set of rows from an unbounded domain Rows. Each row is associated to a unique (primary) key from a domain Keys, given by the function key : Rows $\rightarrow$ Keys. We consider client programs accessing the database from a number of parallel sessions, each session being a sequence of transactions defined by the following grammar:

$$\iota \in \mathsf{Iso} \quad a \in \mathsf{LVars} \quad \mathsf{R} \in 2^{\mathsf{Rows}} \quad \mathsf{p} \in \mathsf{Rows} \rightarrow \{0,1\} \quad \mathsf{U} \in \mathsf{Keys} \rightarrow \mathsf{Rows}$$

$$
\begin{aligned}
\mathsf{Transaction} :: &= \mathtt{begin}(\iota); \mathsf{Body}; \mathtt{commit} \\
\mathsf{Body} :: &= \mathsf{Instr} \mid \mathsf{Instr}; \mathsf{Body} \\
\mathsf{Instr} :: &= \mathsf{InstrDB} \mid a := \mathsf{LExpr} \mid \mathtt{if}(\mathsf{LCond})\{\mathsf{Instr}\} \\
\mathsf{InstrDB} :: &= a := \mathtt{SELECT}(\mathsf{p}) \mid \mathtt{INSERT}(\mathsf{R}) \mid \mathtt{DELETE}(\mathsf{p}) \mid \mathtt{UPDATE}(\mathsf{p}, \mathsf{U}) \mid \mathtt{abort}
\end{aligned}
$$

Each transaction is delimited by `begin` and `commit` instructions. The `begin` instruction defines an isolation level ι for the current transaction. The set of isolation levels Iso we consider in this work will be defined later. The body contains standard SQL-like statements for accessing the database and standard assignments and conditionals for local computation. Local computation uses (transaction-)local variables from a set LVars. We use a, b, ... to denote local variables. Expressions and Boolean conditions over local variables are denoted with LExpr and LCond, respectively.

Concerning database accesses (sometimes called queries), we consider a simplified but representative subset of SQL: `SELECT(p)` returns the set of rows satisfying the predicate p and the result is stored in a local variable a. `INSERT(R)` inserts the set of rows R or updates them in case they already exist (this corresponds to `INSERT ON CONFLICT DO UPDATE` in PostgreSQL) , and `DELETE(p)` deletes all the rows that satisfy p. Then, `UPDATE(p, U)` updates the rows satisfying p with values given by the map U, i.e., every row r in the database that satisfies p is replaced with `U(key(r))`, and `abort` aborts the current transaction. The predicate p corresponds to a `WHERE` clause in standard SQL.

2.2 Histories

We define a model of the interaction between a program and a database called *history* which abstracts away the local computation in the program and the internal behavior of the database. A history is a set of *events* representing the database accesses in the execution grouped by transaction, along with some relations between these events which explain the output of `SELECT` instructions.

An event is a tuple $\langle e, type \rangle$ where e is an *identifier* and *type* is one of `begin`, `commit`, `abort`, `SELECT`, `INSERT`, `DELETE` and `UPDATE`. $\mathcal{E}$ denotes the set of events. For an event e of type `SELECT`, `DELETE`, or `UPDATE`, we use WHERE(e) to denote the predicate p and for an `UPDATE` event e, we use SET(e) to denote the map U.

We call `read` events the `SELECT` events that read the database to return a set of rows, and the `DELETE` and `UPDATE` events that read the database checking satisfaction of some predicate p. Similarly, we call `write` events the `INSERT`, `DELETE` and `UPDATE` events that modify the database. We also say that an event is of type `end` if it is either a `commit` or an `abort` event.

A *transaction log* (t, ι_t, E, po_t) is an identifier t, an *isolation level* identifier ι_t, and a finite set of events E along with a strict total order po_t on E, called *program order* (representing the order between instructions in the body of a transaction). The set E of events in a transaction log t is denoted by events(t). For simplicity, we may use the term *transaction* instead of transaction log.

Isolation levels differ in the values returned by read events which are not preceded by a write on the same variable in the same transaction. We denote by reads(t) the set of `read` events contained in t. Also, if t does *not* contain an `abort` event, the set of `write` events in t is denoted by writes(t). If t contains an `abort` event, then we define writes(t) to be empty. This is because the effect of aborted transactions (its set of writes) should not be visible to other transactions. The extension to sets of transaction logs is defined as usual.

To simplify the exposition we assume that for any given key $x \in$ Keys, a transaction does not modify (insert/delete/update) a row with key x more than once. Otherwise, under all isolation levels, only the last among multiple updates is observable in other transactions.

As expected, we assume that the minimal element of po_t is a begin event, if a commit or an abort event occurs, then it is maximal in po_t, and a log cannot contain both commit and abort. A transaction log without commit or abort is called *pending*. Otherwise, it is *complete*. A complete transaction log with a commit is *committed* and *aborted* otherwise.

A *history* contains a set of transaction logs (with distinct identifiers) ordered by a (partial) *session order* so that represents the order between transactions in the same session. It also includes a *write-read* relation wr which associates write events with read events. The write events associated to a read implicitly define the values observed (returned) by the read (read events do *not* include explicit values). Let T be a set of transaction logs. For every key $x \in$ Keys we consider a write-read relation $\mathsf{wr}_x \subseteq \mathsf{writes}(T) \times \mathsf{reads}(T)$. The union of wr_x for every $x \in$ Keys is denoted by wr. We extend the relations wr and wr_x to pairs of transactions by $(t_1, t_2) \in$ wr, resp., $(t_1, t_2) \in \mathsf{wr}_x$, iff there exist events w in t_1 and r in $t_2, t_2 \neq t_1$ s.t. $(w, r) \in$ wr, resp., $(w, r) \in \mathsf{wr}_x$. Analogously, we extend wr and wr_x to tuples formed of a transaction (containing a write) and a read event. We say that the transaction t_1 is *read* by the transaction t_2 when $(t_1, t_2) \in$ wr. The inverse of wr_x is defined as usual and denoted by wr_x^{-1}. We assume that wr_x^{-1} is a partial function and thus, use $\mathsf{wr}_x^{-1}(e)$ to denote the write event w such that $(w, e) \in \mathsf{wr}_x$. We also use $\mathsf{wr}_x^{-1}(e) \downarrow$ and $\mathsf{wr}_x^{-1}(e) \uparrow$ to say that there exists a write w such that $(w, e) \in \mathsf{wr}_x$ (resp. such write w does not exist).

To simplify the exposition, every history includes a distinguished transaction init preceding all the other transactions in so and inserting a row for every x. It represents the initial state and it is the only transaction that may insert as value $\dagger_x$ (indicating that initially, no row with key x is present).

Definition 1. *A history* $(T, \mathsf{so}, \mathsf{wr})$ *is a set of transaction logs* T *along with a strict partial session order* so, *and a write-read relation* $\mathsf{wr}_x \subseteq \mathsf{writes}(T) \times \mathsf{reads}(T)$ *for each* $x \in$ Keys *s.t.*

- *the inverse of* wr_x *is a partial function,*
- $\mathsf{so} \cup \mathsf{wr}$ *is acyclic (here we use the extension of* wr *to pairs of transactions),*
- *if* $(w, r) \in \mathsf{wr}_x$, *then* $\mathtt{value}_{\mathsf{wr}}(w, x) \neq \perp$, *where*

$$\mathtt{value}_{\mathsf{wr}}(w, x) = \begin{cases} r & \text{if } w = \mathtt{INSERT(R)} \land r \in R \land \textit{key}\,(r) = x \\ \dagger_x & \text{if } w = \mathtt{DELETE(p)} \land \ \mathsf{wr}_x^{-1}(w) \downarrow \\ & \quad \land \ \mathsf{p}(\mathtt{value}_{\mathsf{wr}}(\mathsf{wr}_x^{-1}(w), x)) = 1 \\ U(x) & \text{if } w = \mathtt{UPDATE(p, \ U)} \land \ \mathsf{wr}_x^{-1}(w) \downarrow \\ & \quad \land \ \mathsf{p}(\mathtt{value}_{\mathsf{wr}}(\mathsf{wr}_x^{-1}(w), x)) = 1 \\ \perp & \textit{otherwise} \end{cases}$$

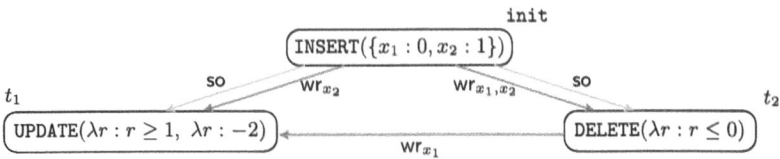

Fig. 1. An example of a history (isolation levels omitted for legibility). Arrows represent so and wr relations. Transaction `init` defines the initial state: row 0 with key x_1 and row 1 with key x_2. Transaction t_2 reads x_1 and x_2 from `init` and deletes row with key x_1 (the only row satisfying predicate $\lambda r : r \leq 0$ corresponds to key x_1). Transaction t_1 reads x_1 from t_2 and x_2 from `init`, and updates only row with key x_2 as this is the only row satisfying predicate $\lambda r : r \geq 1$.

The function wr_x^{-1} may be partial because some query may not read a key x, e.g., if the corresponding row does not satisfy the query predicate.

The function $\mathsf{value}_{\mathsf{wr}}(w, x)$ returns the row with key x written by the `write` event w. If w is an `INSERT`, it returns the inserted row with key x. If w is an `UPDATE(p, U)` event, it returns the value of U on key x if w reads a value for key x that satisfies predicate p. If w is a `DELETE(p)`, it returns the special value $\dagger_x$ if w reads a value for key x that satisfies p. This special value indicates that the database does *not* contain a row with key x. In case no condition is satisfied, $\mathsf{value}_{\mathsf{wr}}(w, x)$ returns an undefined value $\bot$. We assume that the special values $\dagger_x$ or $\bot$ do not satisfy any predicate. Note that the recursion in the definition of $\mathsf{value}_{\mathsf{wr}}(w, x)$ terminates because wr is an acyclic relation.

Figure 1 shows an example of a history. For the `UPDATE` event w in t_1, $\mathsf{value}_{\mathsf{wr}}(w, x_1) = \bot$ because this event reads x_1 from the `DELETE` event in t_2; while $\mathsf{value}_{\mathsf{wr}}(w, x_2) = -2$ as it reads x_2 from the `INSERT` event in `init`.

The set of transaction logs T in a history $h = (T, \mathsf{so}, \mathsf{wr})$ is denoted by $\mathsf{tr}(h)$ and $\mathsf{events}(h)$ is the union of $\mathsf{events}(t)$ for every $t \in T$. For a history h and an event e in h, $\mathsf{tr}(e)$ is the transaction t in h that contains e. We assume that each event belongs to only one transaction. Also, $\mathsf{writes}(h) = \bigcup_{t \in \mathsf{tr}(h)} \mathsf{writes}(t)$ and $\mathsf{reads}(h) = \bigcup_{t \in \mathsf{tr}(h)} \mathsf{reads}(t)$. We extend so to pairs of events by $(e_1, e_2) \in \mathsf{so}$ if $(\mathsf{tr}(e_1), \mathsf{tr}(e_2)) \in \mathsf{so}$. Also, $\mathsf{po} = \bigcup_{t \in T} \mathsf{po}_t$. We use $h, h_1, h_2, \dots$ to range over histories.

For a history h, we say that an event r *reads* x in h whenever $\mathsf{wr}_x^{-1}(r) \downarrow$. Also, we say that an event w *writes* x in h, denoted by w writes x, whenever $\mathsf{value}_{\mathsf{wr}}(w, x) \neq \bot$ and the transaction of w is *not* aborted. We extend the function value to transactions: $\mathsf{value}_{\mathsf{wr}}(t, x)$ equals $\mathsf{value}_{\mathsf{wr}}(w, x)$, where w is the maximal event in po_t that writes x.

2.3   Classes of Histories

We define two classes of histories: (1) *full* histories which are required to define the semantics of isolation levels and (2) *client* histories which model what is observable from interacting with a database as a black-box.

Full histories model the fact that every read query "inspects" an entire snapshot of the database in order to for instance, select rows satisfying some predicate. Roughly, full histories contain a write-read dependency for every read and key. There is an exception which concerns "local" reads. If a transaction modifies a row with key x and then reads the same row, then it must always return the value written in the transaction. This holds under all isolation levels. In such a case, there would be no write-read dependency because these dependencies model interference across different transactions. We say that a read r reads a key x *locally* if it is preceded in the same transaction by a write w that writes x.

Definition 2. *A full history* $(T, \mathsf{so}, \mathsf{wr})$ *is a history where* $\mathsf{wr}_x^{-1}(r)$ *is defined for all* x *and* r, *unless* r *reads* x *locally.*

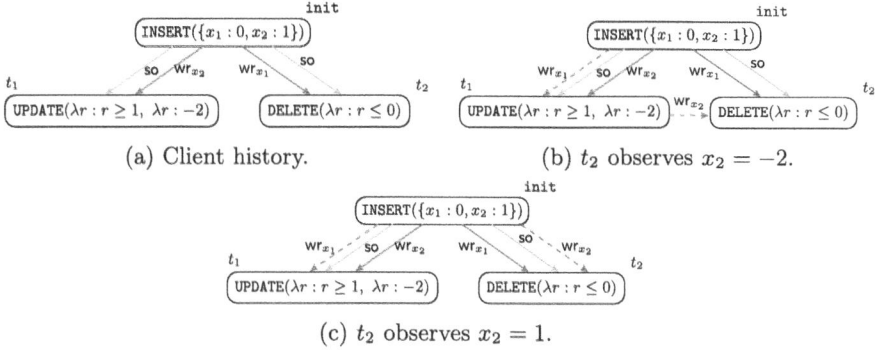

(a) Client history.   (b) t_2 observes $x_2 = -2$.

(c) t_2 observes $x_2 = 1$.

Fig. 2. Examples of a client history h and two possible extensions. The dashed edge belongs only to the extensions. The first extension is not a witness of h as t_1 writes -2 on x_2 and $\mathtt{WHERE}(t_2)(-2) = 1$.

Client histories record less write-read dependencies compared to full histories, which is formalized by the *extends* relation.

Definition 3. *A history* $\overline{h} = (T, \mathsf{so}, \overline{\mathsf{wr}})$ *extends another history* $h = (T, \mathsf{so}, \mathsf{wr})$ *if* $\mathsf{wr} \subseteq \overline{\mathsf{wr}}$. *We denote it by* $h \subseteq \overline{h}$.

Definition 4. *A client history* $h = (T, \mathsf{so}, \mathsf{wr})$ *is a history s.t. there is a full history* $\overline{h} = (T, \mathsf{so}, \overline{\mathsf{wr}})$ *with* $h \subseteq \overline{h}$, *and s.t for every* x, *if* $(w, r) \in \overline{\mathsf{wr}}_x \setminus \mathsf{wr}_x$ *then* $\mathtt{WHERE}(r)(\mathtt{value}_{\overline{\mathsf{wr}}}(w, x)) = 0$. *The history* h' *is called a witness of* h.

Compared to a witness full history, a client history may omit write-read dependencies if the written values do *not* satisfy the predicate of the read query. These values would not be observable when interacting with the database as a black-box. This includes the case when the write is a $\mathtt{DELETE}$ (recall that the special value $\dagger_x$ indicating deleted rows falsifies every predicate by convention). Figure 1 shows a full history as every query reads both x_1 and x_2. Figure 2a shows a client history: transactions t_1, t_2 does not read x_2 and x_1 resp. Figure 2b is an extension but not a witness while Fig. 2c is indeed a witness of it.

3   Axiomatic Semantics With Different Isolation Levels

We define an axiomatic semantics on histories where transactions can be assigned different isolation levels, which builds on the work of Biswas et al. [7].

3.1   Executions

An *execution* of a program is represented using a history with a set of transactions T along with a total order $\mathsf{co} \subseteq T \times T$ called *commit order*. Intuitively, the commit order represents the order in which transactions are committed in the database.

Definition 5. *An* execution $\xi = (h, \mathsf{co})$ *is a history* $h = (T, \mathsf{so}, \mathsf{wr})$ *along with a* commit order $\mathsf{co} \subseteq T \times T$, *such that transactions in the same session or that are read are necessarily committed in the same order:* $\mathsf{so} \cup \mathsf{wr} \subseteq \mathsf{co}$. ξ *is called an* execution of h.

For a transaction t, we use $t \in \xi$ to denote the fact that $t \in T$. Analogously, for an event e, we use $e \in \xi$ to denote that $e \in t$ and $t \in \xi$. The extension of a commit order to pairs of events or pairs of transactions and events is done in the obvious way.

3.2   Isolation Levels

Isolation levels enforce restrictions on the commit order in an execution that depend on the session order so and the write-read relation wr. An *isolation level* ι for a transaction t is a set of constraints called *axioms*. Intuitively, an axiom states that a read event $r \in t$ reads key x from transaction t_1 if t_1 is the latest transaction that writes x which is "visible" to r – latest refers to the commit order co. Formally, an axiom a is a predicate of the following form:

$$a(r) := \forall x, t_1, t_2. t_1 \neq t_2 \wedge (t_1, r) \in \mathsf{wr}_x \wedge t_2 \text{ writes } x \wedge \mathsf{vis}_a(t_2, r, x) \Rightarrow (t_2, t_1) \in \mathsf{co} \quad (1)$$

where r is a read event from t.

The visibility relation of a vis_a is described by a formula of the form:

$$\mathsf{vis}_a(\tau_0, \tau_{k+1}, x) : \exists \tau_1, \ldots, \tau_k. \bigwedge_{i=1}^{k+1} (\tau_{i-1}, \tau_i) \in \mathsf{Rel}_i \wedge \mathsf{WrCons}_a(\tau_0, \ldots, \tau_{k+1}, x) \quad (2)$$

with each Rel_i is defined by the grammar:

$$\mathsf{Rel}{::} = \mathsf{po} \mid \mathsf{so} \mid \mathsf{wr} \mid \mathsf{co} \mid \mathsf{Rel} \cup \mathsf{Rel} \mid \mathsf{Rel}; \mathsf{Rel} \mid \mathsf{Rel}^+ \mid \mathsf{Rel}^* \quad (3)$$

This formula states that τ_0 (which is t_2 in Eq. 1) is connected to τ_{k+1} (which is r in Eq. 1) by a path of dependencies that go through some intermediate transactions or events $\tau_1, \ldots, \tau_k$. Every relation used in such a path is described based on po, so, wr and co using union $\cup$, composition of relations ;, and transitive closure operators. Finally, extra requirements on the intermediate transactions s.t. writing a different key $y \neq x$ are encapsulated in the predicate $\mathsf{WrCons}_a(\tau_0, \ldots, \tau_k, x)$.

Each axiom a uses a specific visibility relation denoted by vis_a. $\mathsf{vis}(\iota)$ denotes the set of visibility relations used in axioms defining an isolation level ι.

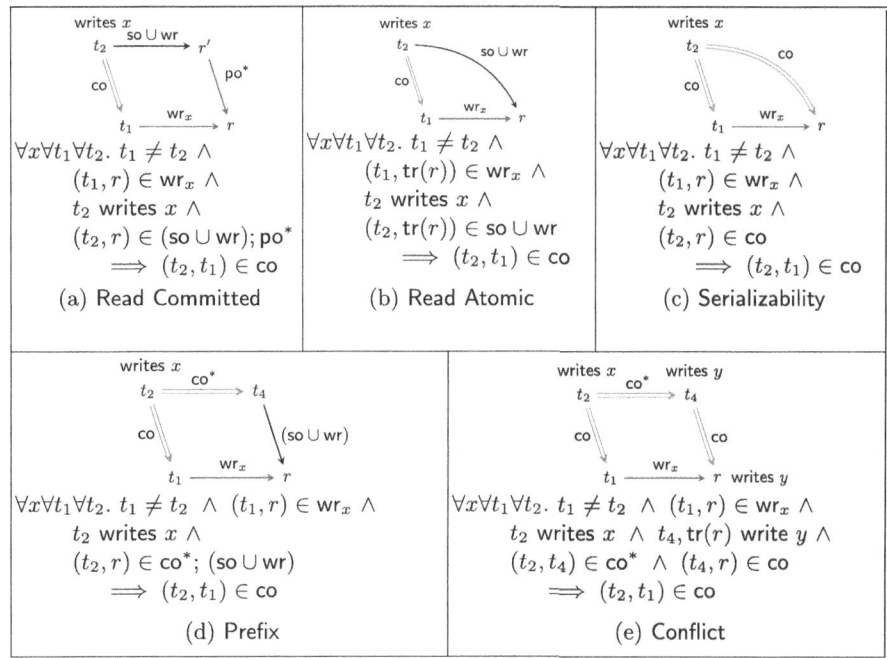

Fig. 3. Axioms defining RC, RA, SER, PC and SI isolations levels respectively. Visibility relations are "inlined" to match the definitions in [7].

Figure 3 shows two axioms which correspond to their homonymous isolation levels [7]: *Read Committed* (RC) and *Serializability* (SER). SER states that t_2 is visible to r if t_2 commits before r, while RC states that t_2 is visible to r if either $(t_2, r) \in \mathsf{so}$ or if there exists a previous event r' in $\mathsf{tr}(r)$ that reads x from t_2. Similarly, *Read Atomic* (RA) and *Prefix Consistency* (PC) are defined using their homonymous axioms while *Snapshot Isolation* (SI) is defined as a conjunction of both Prefix and Conflict.

The *isolation configuration* of a history is a mapping $\mathsf{iso}(h) : T \to \mathsf{Iso}$ associating to each transaction an isolation level identifier from a set Iso.

Whenever every transaction in a history has the same isolation level ι, the isolation configuration of that history is denoted simply by ι.

Note that SER is stronger than RC: every transaction visible to a read r according to RC is also visible to r according to SER. This means SER imposes more constraints for transaction t_1 to be read by r than RC. In general, for two isolation configurations I_1 and I_2, I_1 is *stronger than* I_2 when for every transaction t, $I_1(t)$ is stronger than $I_2(t)$ (i.e., whenever $I_1(t)$ holds in an execution ξ, $I_2(t)$ also holds in ξ). The *weaker than* relationship is defined similarly.

Given a history h with isolation configuration iso(h), h is called *consistent* when there exists an execution ξ of h such that for all transactions t in ξ, the axioms in iso(h)(t) are satisfied in ξ (the interpretation of an axiom over an execution is defined as expected). For example, let h be the full history in Fig. 2c. If both t_1, t_2's isolation are SER, then h is *not* consistent, i.e., every execution $\xi = (h, \text{co})$ violates the corresponding axioms. Assume for instance, that $(t_1, t_2) \in$ co. Then, by axiom SER, as $(\text{init}, t_2) \in \text{wr}_{x_1}$ and t_1 writes x_1, we get that $(t_1, \text{init}) \in$ co, which is impossible as $(\text{init}, t_1) \in$ so $\subseteq$ co. However, if the isolation configuration is weaker (for example iso(h)(t_2) = RC), then the history is consistent using init $<_{\text{co}} t_1 <_{\text{co}} t_2$ as commit order.

Definition 6. *A full history $h = (T, \text{so}, \text{wr})$ with isolation configuration* iso(h) *is consistent iff there is an execution ξ of h s.t. $\bigwedge_{t \in T, r \in \text{reads}(t), a \in \text{iso}(h)(t)} a(r)$ holds in ξ; ξ is called a* consistent *execution of h.*

The notion of consistency on full histories is extended to client histories.

Definition 7. *A client history $h = (T, \text{so}, \text{wr})$ with isolation configuration* iso(h) *is consistent iff there is a full history $\overline{h}$ with the same isolation configuration which is a witness of h and consistent; $\overline{h}$ is called a* consistent witness *of h.*

In general, the witness of a client history may not be consistent. In particular, there may exist several witnesses but no consistent witness.

3.3 Validation of the Semantics

To justify the axiomatic semantics defined above, we define an operational semantics inspired by real implementations and prove that every run of a program can be translated into a consistent history. Every instruction is associated with an increasing timestamp and it reads from a snapshot of the database defined according to the isolation level of the enclosing transaction. At the end of the transaction we evaluate if the transaction can be committed or not. We assume that a transaction can abort only if explicitly stated in the program. We model an optimistic approach where if a transaction cannot commit, the run blocks (modeling unexpected aborts). We focus on three of the most used isolation levels: SER, SI, RC. Other isolation levels can be handled in a similar manner. For each run ρ we extract a full history history(ρ). We show by induction that history(ρ) is consistent at every step.

Theorem 1. *For every run ρ,* history(ρ) *is consistent.*

Algorithm 1. Extending an initial pco relation with necessary ordering constraints

1: **function** SATURATE($h = (T, \text{so}, \text{wr})$, pco)   ▷ pco must be transitive.
2:    $\text{pco}_{\text{res}} \leftarrow \text{pco}$
3:    **for all** $x \in$ Keys **do**
4:       **for all** $r \in \text{reads}(h), t_2 \neq \text{tr}(r) \in T$ s.t. t_2 writes x and $t_2 \neq \text{tr}(\text{wr}_x^{-1}(r))$ **do**
5:          $t_1 \leftarrow \text{tr}(\text{wr}_x^{-1}(r))$ ▷ t_1 is well defined as h is a full history.
6:          **for all** $\text{v} \in \text{vis}(\text{iso}(h)(\text{tr}(r)))$ **do**
7:             **if** $\text{v}(t_2, r, x)$ **then**
8:                $\text{pco}_{\text{res}} \leftarrow \text{pco}_{\text{res}} \cup \{(t_2, t_1)\}$
9:    **return** pco_{res}

4 Complexity of Checking Consistency

4.1 Saturation and Boundedness

We investigate the complexity of checking if a history is consistent. Our axiomatic framework characterize isolation levels as a conjunction of axioms as in Eq. (1). However, some isolation levels impose stronger constraints than others. For studying the complexity of checking consistency, we classify them in two categories, saturable or not. An isolation level is *saturable* if its visibility relations are defined without using the co relation (i.e. the grammar in Eq. (3) omits the co relation). Otherwise, we say that the isolation level is *non-saturable*. For example, RC and RA are saturable while PC, SI and SER are not.

Definition 8. *An isolation configuration* iso(h) *is saturable if for every transaction t,* iso(h)(t) *is a saturable isolation level. Otherwise,* iso(h) *is non-saturable.*

We say an isolation configuration iso(h) is *bounded* if there exists a fixed $k \in \mathbb{N}$ s.t. for every transaction t, iso(h)(t) is defined as a conjunction of at most k axioms that contain at most k quantifiers. For example, SER employs one axiom and four quantifiers while SI employs two axioms, Prefix and Conflict, with four and five quantifiers respectively. Any isolation configuration composed with SER, SI, PC, RA and RC isolation levels is bounded. We assume in the following that isolation configurations are bounded.

Checking consistency requires computing the value$_{\text{wr}}$ function and thus, evaluating WHERE predicates. In the following, we assume that evaluating WHERE predicates on a single row requires constant time.

Algorithm 2. Checking saturable consistency

1: **function** CHECKSATURABLE($h = (T, \text{so}, \text{wr})$)
2:    **if** so $\cup$ wr is cyclic **then return** false
3:    pco $\leftarrow$ SATURATE($h, (\text{so} \cup \text{wr})^+$)
4:    **return** true if pco is acyclic, and false, otherwise

4.2   Checking Consistency of Full Histories

Algorithm 2 computes necessary and sufficient conditions for the existence of a consistent execution $\xi = (h, \text{co})$ for a history h with a saturable isolation configuration. It calls SATURATE, defined in Algorithm 1, to compute a *"partial"* commit order relation pco that includes $(\text{so} \cup \text{wr})^+$ and any other dependency between transactions that can be deduced from the isolation configuration. A consistent execution exists iff this partial commit order is acyclic. Algorithm 2 generalizes the results in [7] for full histories with heterogeneous saturable isolation configurations.

Theorem 2. *Checking consistency of full histories with bounded saturable isolation configurations can be done in polynomial time.*

For bounded non-saturable isolation configurations, checking if a history is consistent is NP-complete as an immediate consequence of the results in [7]. These previous results apply to the particular case of transactions having the same isolation level and being formed of classic read and write instructions on a fixed set of variables. The latter can be simulated by SQL queries using WHERE predicates for selecting rows based on their key being equal to some particular value. For instance, SELECT($\lambda r : \text{key(r)} = x$) simulates a read of a "variable" x.

4.3   Checking Consistency of Client Histories

We show that going from full histories to client histories, the consistency checking problem becomes NP-complete, independently of the isolation configurations. Intuitively, NP-hardness comes from keys that are not included in outputs of SQL queries. The justification for the consistency of omitting such rows can be ambiguous, e.g., multiple values written to a row may not satisfy the predicate of the WHERE clause, or multiple deletes can justify the absence of a row.

The *width* of a history width(h) is the maximum number of transactions which are pairwise incomparable w.r.t. so. In a different context, previous work [7] showed that bounding the width of a history (consider it to be a constant) is a sufficient condition for obtaining polynomial-time consistency checking algorithms. This is not true for client histories.

Theorem 3. *Checking consistency of bounded-width client histories with bounded isolation configuration stronger than RC and width(h) ≥ 3 is NP-complete.*

The proof of NP-hardness uses a reduction from 1-in-3 SAT which is inspired by the work of Gibbons and Korach [16] (Theorem 2.7) concerning sequential consistency for shared memory implementations. Our reduction is a non-trivial extension because it has to deal with any weak isolation configuration stronger than RC.

The proof of Theorem 3 relies on using non-trivial predicates in WHERE clauses. We also prove that checking consistency of client histories is NP-complete irrespectively of the complexity of these predicates. This result uses another class of histories, called *partial-observation* histories. These histories are a particular class of client histories where events read all inserted keys, irrespectively of their WHERE clauses (as if these clauses where *true*).

Definition 9. *A partial observation history* $h = (T, \text{so}, \text{wr})$ *is a client history for which there is a witness* $\overline{h} = (T, \text{so}, \overline{\text{wr}})$ *of* h, *s.t. for every* x, *if* $(w, r) \in \overline{\text{wr}}_x \setminus \text{wr}_x$, *then* w *deletes* x.

Theorem 4. *Checking consistency of partial observation histories with bounded isolation configurations stronger than* RC *is NP-complete.*

The proof of NP-hardness uses a novel reduction from 3 SAT. The main difficulty for obtaining consistent witnesses of partial observation histories is the ambiguity of which delete event is responsible for each absent row.

5   Effectively Checking Consistency of Client Histories

The result of Theorem 3 implicitly asks whether there exist conditions on the histories for which checking consistency remains polynomial as in [7]. We describe an algorithm for checking consistency of client histories and identify cases in which it runs in polynomial time.

Consider a client history $h = (T, \text{so}, \text{wr})$ which is consistent. For every consistent witness $\overline{h} = (T, \text{so}, \overline{\text{wr}})$ of h there exists a consistent execution of $\overline{h}$, $\xi = (\overline{h}, \text{co})$. The commit order co contains $(\text{so} \cup \text{wr})^+$ and any other ordering constraint derived from axioms by observing that $(\text{so} \cup \text{wr})^+ \subseteq \text{co}$. More generally, co includes all constraints generated by the least fixpoint of the function SATURATE defined in Algorithm 1 when starting from $(\text{so} \cup \text{wr})^+$ as partial commit order. This least fixpoint exists because SATURATE is monotonic. It is computed as usual by iterating SATURATE until the output does not change. We use $\text{FIX}(\lambda R : \text{SATURATE}(h, R))(\text{so} \cup \text{wr})^+$ to denote this least fixpoint. In general, such a fixpoint computation is just an under-approximation of co, and it is not enough for determining h's consistency.

The algorithm we propose, described in Algorithm 3, exploits the partial commit order pco obtained by such a fixpoint computation (line 2) for determining h's consistency. For a read r, key x, we define $1_x^r(\text{pco})$, resp., $0_x^r(\text{pco})$, to be the set of transactions that are *not* committed after $\text{tr}(r)$ and which write a value that satisfies, resp., does not satisfy, the predicate WHERE(r). The formal description of both sets can be seen in Eq. 4.

$$1_x^r(\text{pco}) = \{t \in T \mid (\text{tr}(r), t) \notin \text{pco} \ \wedge \ \text{WHERE}(r)(\text{value}_{\text{wr}}(t, x)) = 1\}$$
$$0_x^r(\text{pco}) = \{t \in T \mid (\text{tr}(r), t) \notin \text{pco} \ \wedge \ \text{WHERE}(r)(\text{value}_{\text{wr}}(t, x)) = 0\} \quad (4)$$

The set $0_x^r(\text{pco})$ can be used to identify extensions that are not witness of a history. Let us consider the client history h depicted in Fig. 4a. Observe that t_3

Algorithm 3. Checking consistency of client histories

```
 1: function CHECKCONSISTENCY(h = (T, so, wr))
 2:    let pco = FIX(λR : SATURATE(h, R))(so ∪ wr)⁺
 3:    let E_h = {(r, x) | r ∈ reads(h), x ∈ Keys.wr_x⁻¹(r) ↑ and 1_r^x(pco) ≠ ∅}
 4:    let X_h = the set of mappings that map each (r, x) ∈ E_h to a member of 0_x^r(pco)
 5:    if pco is cyclic then return false
 6:    else if there exists (r, x) ∈ E_h such that 0_x^r(pco) = ∅ then return false
 7:    else if E_h = ∅ then return EXPLORECONSISTENTPREFIXES(h, ∅)
 8:    else
 9:       for all f ∈ X_h do
10:          seen ← ∅; h' ← h ⊕_(r,x)∈E_h wr_x(f(r, x), r)
11:          if EXPLORECONSISTENTPREFIXES(h', ∅) then return true
12:       return false
```

---

is not reading x_1 and t_5 is not reading x_2. Figure 4b describes all possible full extensions $\overline{h}$ of h. An execution $\xi = (\overline{h}, \mathsf{co})$ is consistent if $(t, r) \in \overline{\mathsf{wr}}_x \backslash \mathsf{wr}_x$ implies WHERE$(r)(\mathsf{value}_{\mathsf{wr}}(t, x)) = 0$. This implies that extensions h_1, h_4, and h_7, where $(\mathsf{init}, t_5) \in \overline{\mathsf{wr}}_{x_2}$, are not witnesses of h as WHERE$(t_5)(\mathsf{value}_{\mathsf{wr}}(\mathsf{init}, x_2)) = 1$. We note that $\mathsf{init} \notin 0_{x_2}^{t_5}(\mathsf{pco}) = \{t_1\}$. Also, observe that $(t_5, t_3) \in \mathsf{wr}$; so extensions h_3, h_6 and h_9, where $(t_3, t_5) \in \overline{\mathsf{wr}}_{x_2}$, are not a witness of h. Once again, $t_3 \notin 0_{x_2}^{t_5}(\mathsf{pco})$. In general, for every read event r and key x s.t. $\mathsf{wr}_x^{-1}(r) \uparrow$, the extension of h where $(t, r) \in \overline{\mathsf{wr}}_x$, $t \notin 0_x^r(\mathsf{pco})$, is not a witness of h. In particular, if $\mathsf{wr}_x^{-1}(r) \uparrow$ but $0_x^r(\mathsf{pco}) = \emptyset$, then no witness of h can exist.

The sets $0_x^r(\mathsf{pco})$ are not sufficient to determine if a witness is a consistent witness as our previous example shows: $0_{x_1}^{t_3}(\mathsf{pco}) = \{\mathsf{init}, t_2, t_5\}$, but h_2 is not consistent. Algorithm 3, combines an enumeration of history extensions with a search for a consistent execution of each extension. The extensions are *not* necessarily full. In case $\mathsf{wr}_x^{-1}(r)$ is undefined, we use sets $1_x^r(\mathsf{pco})$ to decide whether the extension of h requires specifying $\mathsf{wr}_x^{-1}(r)$ for determining h's consistency. Algorithm 3 specifies $\mathsf{wr}_x^{-1}(r)$ only if (r, x) is a so-called *conflict*, i.e., $\mathsf{wr}_x^{-1}(r)$ is undefined and $1_x^r(\mathsf{pco}) \neq \emptyset$.

Following the example of Fig. 4, we observe that $1_{x_1}^{t_3}(\mathsf{pco}) = \emptyset$, all transactions that write on x_1 write non-negative values; but instead $1_{x_2}^{t_5}(\mathsf{pco}) = \{\mathsf{init}\}$. Intuitively, this means that if some extension h' that does not specify $\mathsf{wr}_{x_1}^{-1}(t_3)$ does not violate any axiom when using some commit order co, then we can extend h', defining $\mathsf{wr}_{x_1}^{-1}(t_3)$ as some adequate transaction, and obtain a full history $\overline{h}$ s.t. the execution $\xi = (\overline{h}, \mathsf{co})$ is consistent. On the other hand, specifying the write-read dependency of t_5 on x_2 matters. For not contradicting any axiom using co, we may require $(\mathsf{init}, t_5) \in \overline{\mathsf{wr}}_{x_2}$. However, such extension is not even a witness of h as WHERE$(\mathsf{init})(\mathsf{value}_{\mathsf{wr}}(\mathsf{init}, x_2)) = 1$. This intuition holds for the particular definitions of the isolation levels that Algorithm 3 considers.

A history is *conflict-free* if it does not have conflicts. Our previous discussion reduces the problem of checking consistency of a history to checking consistency of its conflict-free extensions. For example, the history h in Fig. 4a is not conflict-

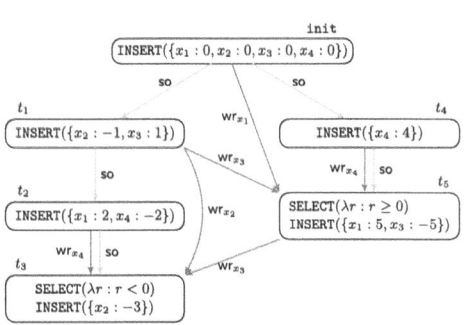

History	$\text{wr}_{x_1}^{-1}(t_3)$	$\text{wr}_{x_2}^{-1}(t_5)$
h_1	init	init
h_2	init	t_1
h_3	init	t_3
h_4	t_2	init
h_5	t_2	t_1
h_6	t_2	t_3
h_7	t_5	init
h_8	t_5	t_1
h_9	t_5	t_3

(a) A history where t_3, t_5 have **PC** and **SER** as isolation levels respectively. The isolation levels of the other transactions are unspecified.

(b) Table describing all possible full extensions of the history in Figure 4a.

History	$\text{wr}_{x_1}^{-1}(t_3)$	$\text{wr}_{x_2}^{-1}(t_5)$
h_{258}	**undef**	t_1

(c) Table describing the only conflict-free extension of Figure 4a.

Fig. 4. Comparison between conflict-free extensions and full extensions of the history h in Fig. 4a. In h, wr^{-1} is not defined for two pairs: (t_3, x_1) and (t_5, x_2); where we identify the single **SELECT** event in a transaction with its transaction. Figure 4b describes all possible full extensions of h. For example, the first extension, h_1, states that $(\text{init}, t_3) \in \text{wr}_{x_1}$ and $(\text{init}, t_5) \in \text{wr}_{x_2}$. Algorithm 3 only explore the only extension h_{258} described in Fig. 4c; where $\text{wr}_{x_1}^{-1}(t_3) \uparrow$ and $(t_1, t_5) \in \text{wr}_{x_2}$. The history h_{258} can be extended to histories h_2, h_5 and h_8.

free but the extension h_{258} defined in Fig. 4c is. Instead of checking consistency of the nine possible extensions, we only check consistency of h_{258}.

Algorithm 3 starts by checking if there is at least a conflict-free extension of h (line 6). If h is conflict-free, it directly calls Algorithm 4 (line 7); while otherwise, it iterates over conflict-free extensions of h, calling Algorithm 4 on each of them (line 11).

Algorithm 4 describes the search for the commit order of a conflict-free history h. This is a recursive enumeration of consistent prefixes of histories that backtracks when detecting inconsistency (it generalizes Algorithm 2 in [7]). A *prefix* of a history $h = (T, \text{so}, \text{wr})$ is a tuple $P = (T_P, M_P)$ where $T_P \subseteq T$ is a set of transactions and $M_P : \text{Keys} \to T_P$ is a mapping s.t. (1) so predecessors of transactions in T_P are also in T_P, i.e., $\forall t \in T_P$. $\text{so}^{-1}(t) \in T_P$ and (2) for every x, $M_P(x)$ is a so-maximal transaction in T_P that writes x (M_P records a last write for every key).

For every prefix $P = (T_P, M_P)$ of a history h and a transaction $t \in T \setminus T_P$, we say a prefix $P' = (T_{P'}, M_{P'})$ of h is an *extension* of P *using* t if $T_{P'} = T_P \cup \{t\}$ and for every key x, $M_{P'}(x)$ is t or $M_P(x)$. Algorithm 4 extensions, denoted as $P \cup \{t\}$, guarantee that for every key x, if t writes x, then $M_{P'}(x) = t$.

Extending the prefix P using t means that any transaction $t' \in T_P$ is committed before t. Algorithm 4 focuses on special extensions that lead to commit orders of consistent executions.

Table 1. Predicates relating prefixes and visibility relations where pco_t^P is defined as $pco \cup \{(t',t) \mid t' \in T_P\} \cup \{(t,t'') \mid t'' \in T \setminus (T_P \cup \{t\})\}$.

Axiom	Predicate
Serializability, Prefix, Read Atomic, Read Committed	$\nexists x \in \mathsf{Keys}$ s.t. t writes x, $wr_x^{-1}(r) \downarrow$ $v(pco_t^P)(t,r,x)$ holds in h and $wr_x^{-1}(r) \in T_P$
Conflict	$\nexists x \in \mathsf{Keys}, t' \in T_P \cup \{t\}$ s.t. t' writes x, $wr_x^{-1}(r) \downarrow$ $v(pco_t^P)(t',r,x)$ holds in h and $wr_x^{-1}(r) \neq M_P(x)$

Definition 10. *Let h be a history, $P = (T_P, M_P)$ be a prefix of h, t a transaction that is not in T_P and $P' = (T_{P'}, M_{P'})$ be an extension of P using t. The prefix P' is a* consistent extension *of P with t, denoted by $P \rhd_t P'$, if*

1. *P is pco-closed: for every transaction $t' \in T$ s.t. $(t',t) \in pco$ then $t' \in T_P$,*
2. *t does not overwrite other transactions in P: for every* read *event r outside of the prefix, i.e., $tr(r) \in T \setminus T_{P'}$ and every visibility relation $v \in vis(iso(h))(tr(r))$, the predicate $vp_v^P(t,r)$ defined in Table 1 holds in h.*

We say that a prefix is consistent if it is either the empty prefix or it is a consistent extension of a consistent prefix.

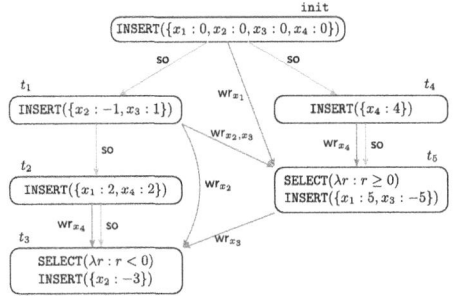

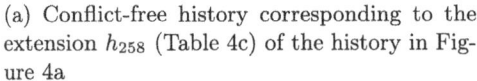

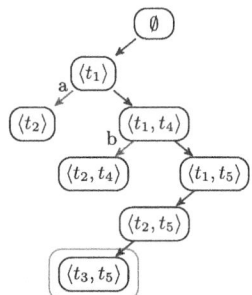

(a) Conflict-free history corresponding to the extension h_{258} (Table 4c) of the history in Figure 4a

(b) Execution of Algorithm 3 on the history in Figure 5a.

Fig. 5. Applying Algorithm 4 on the conflict-free consistent history h_{258} on the left. The right part pictures a search for valid extensions of consistent prefixes on h_{258}. Prefixes are represented by their so-maximal transactions, e.g., $\langle t_2 \rangle$ contains all transactions which are before t_2 in so, i.e., $\{init, t_1, t_2\}$. A red arrow means that the search is blocked (the prefix at the target is not a consistent extension), while a blue arrow mean that the search continues.

Figure 5b depicts the execution of Algorithm 4 on the conflict-free history Fig. 5a (history h_{258} from Fig. 4c). Blocked and effectuated calls are represented by read and blue arrows respectively. The read arrow a is due to condition 1 in Definition 10: as t_3 enforces PC, reads x_4 from t_2, and t_4 is visible to it $(\mathsf{vis}_{\mathsf{Prefix}}(t_4, t_3, x_4))$, $(t_4, t_2) \in \mathsf{pco}$; so consistent prefixes can not contain t_2 if they do not contain t_4. The read arrow b is due to condition 2: as t_5 enforces SER and it reads x_4 from t_4, consistent prefixes can not contain t_2 unless t_5 is included. When reaching prefix $\langle t_3, t_5 \rangle$, the search terminates and deduces that h is consistent. From the commit order induced by the search tree we can construct the extension of h where missing write-read dependencies are obtained by applying the axioms on such a commit order. In our case, from $\mathsf{init} <_{\mathsf{co}} t_1 <_{\mathsf{co}} t_4 <_{\mathsf{co}} t_5 <_{\mathsf{co}} t_2 <_{\mathsf{co}} t_3$, we deduce that the execution $\xi = (h_5, \mathsf{co})$ is a consistent execution of h_{258}, and hence of h; where h_5 is the history described in Fig. 4b.

For complexity optimizations, Algorithm 4 requires an isolation level-dependent equivalence relation between consistent prefixes. If there is transaction $t \in T$ s.t. $\mathsf{iso}(h)(t) = \mathsf{SI}$, prefixes $P = (T_P, M_P)$ and $P' = (T_{P'}, M_{P'})$ are *equivalent* iff they are equal (i.e. $T_P = T_{P'}, M_P = M_{P'}$). Otherwise, they are *equivalent* iff $T_P = T_{P'}$.

Algorithm 4. check consistency of conflict-free histories

1: **function** EXPLORECONSISTENTPREFIXES$(h = (T, \mathsf{so}, \mathsf{wr}), P)$
2:   **if** $|P| = |T|$ **then return** true
3:   **for all** $t \in T \setminus P$ s.t. $P \rhd_t (P \cup \{t\})$ **do**
4:     **if** $\exists P' \in$ seen s.t. $P' \equiv_{\mathsf{iso}(h)} (P \cup \{t\})$ **then continue**
5:     **else if** EXPLORECONSISTENTPREFIXES$(h, P \cup \{t\})$ **then return** true
6:     **else** seen $\leftarrow$ seen $\cup (P \cup \{t\})$
7:   **return** false

Theorem 5. *Let h be a client history whose isolation configuration is defined using* $\{\mathsf{SER}, \mathsf{SI}, \mathsf{PC}, \mathsf{RA}, \mathsf{RC}\}$. *Algorithm 3 returns* true *if and only if h is consistent.*

In general, Algorithm 3 is exponential the number of conflicts in h. The number of *conflicts* is denoted by $\#\mathsf{conf}(h)$. The number of conflicts exponent is implied by the number of mappings in X_h explored by Algorithm 3 (E_h is the set of conflicts in h). The history width and size exponents comes from the number of prefixes explored by Algorithm 4 which is $|h|^{\mathsf{width}(h)} \cdot \mathsf{width}(h)^{|\mathsf{Keys}|}$ in the worst case (prefixes can be equivalently described by a set of so-maximal transactions and a mapping associating keys to sessions).

Theorem 6. *For every client history h whose isolation configuration is composed of* $\{\mathsf{SER}, \mathsf{SI}, \mathsf{PC}, \mathsf{RA}, \mathsf{RC}\}$ *isolation levels, Algorithm 3 runs in* $\mathcal{O}(|h|^{\#\mathsf{conf}(h) + \mathsf{width}(h) + 9} \cdot \mathsf{width}(h)^{|\mathsf{Keys}|})$. *Moreover, if no transaction employs* SI *isolation level, Algorithm 3 runs in* $\mathcal{O}(|h|^{\#\mathsf{conf}(h) + \mathsf{width}(h) + 8})$.

On bounded, conflict-free histories only using $\mathsf{SER}, \mathsf{PC}, \mathsf{RA}, \mathsf{RC}$ as isolation levels, Algorithm 3 runs in polynomial time. For instance, standard reads and writes can be simulated using INSERT and SELECT with WHERE clauses that select rows based on their key being equal to some particular value. In this case, histories are

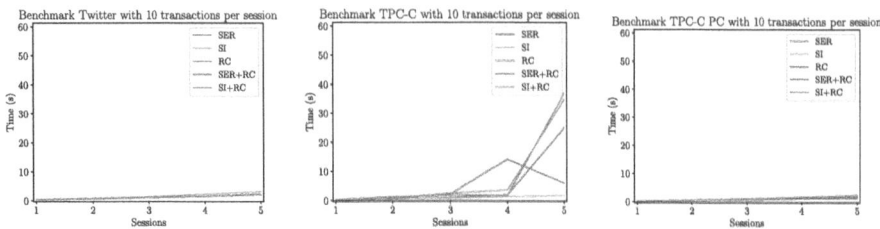

Fig. 6. Running time of Algorithm 3 while increasing the number of sessions. Each point represents the average running time of 5 random clients of such size.

conflict-less (wr would be defined for the particular key asked by the clause, and writes on other keys would not satisfy the clause). A more general setting where WHERE clauses restrict only values that are immutable during the execution (e.g., primary keys) and deletes only affect non-read rows also falls in this category.

6   Experimental Evaluation

We evaluate an implementation of CHECKCONSISTENCY in the context of the Benchbase [12] database benchmarking framework. We apply this algorithm on histories extracted from randomly generated client programs of a number of database-backed applications. We use PostgreSQL 14.10 as a database. The experiments were performed on an Apple M1 with 8 cores and 16 GB of RAM. **Implementation.** We extend the Benchbase framework with an additional package for generating histories and checking consistency. Applications from Benchbase are instrumented in order to be able to extract histories, the wr relation in particular. Our implementation is publicly available [5].

Our tool takes as input a configuration file specifying the name of the application and the isolation level of each transaction in that application. For computing the wr relation and generating client histories, we extend the database tables with an extra column WRITEID which is updated by every write instruction with a unique value. SQL queries are also modified to return whole rows instead of selected columns. To extract the wr relation for UPDATE and DELETE we add RETURNING clauses. Complex operators such as INNER JOIN are substituted by simple juxtaposed SQL queries (similarly to [8]). We map the result of each query to local structures for generating the corresponding history. Transactions aborted by the database (and not explicitly by the application) are discarded. **Benchmark.** We analyze a set of benchmarks inspired by real-world applications and evaluate them under different types of clients and isolation configurations. We focus on isolation configurations implemented in PostgreSQL, i.e. compositions of SER, SI and RC isolation levels.

In average, the ratio of SER/SI transactions is 11% for Twitter and 88% for TPC-C and TPC-C PC. These distributions are obtained via the random generation of client programs implemented in BenchBase. In general, we observe that the bottleneck is the number of possible history extensions enumerated at line 9 in Algorithm 3 and not the isolation configuration. This number is influenced by the distribution of types of transactions, e.g., for TPC-C, a bigger number of transactions creating new orders increases the number of possible full history extensions. We will clarify.

Twitter [12] models a social network that allows users to publish tweets and get their followers, tweets and tweets published by other followers. We consider five isolation configurations: SER, SI and RC and the heterogeneous SER + RC and SI + RC, where publishing a tweet is SER (resp., SI) and the rest are RC. The ratio of SER (resp. SI) transactions w.r.t. RC is 11% on average.

TPC-C [24] models an online shopping application with five types of transactions: reading the stock, creating a new order, getting its status, paying it and delivering it. We consider five isolation configurations: the homogeneous SER, SI and RC and the combinations SER + RC and SI + RC, where creating a new order and paying it have SER (respectively SI) as isolation level while the rest have RC. The ratio of SER (resp. SI) transactions w.r.t. RC is 88% on average.

TPC-C PC is a variant of the TPC-C benchmark whose histories are always conflict-free. DELETE queries are replaced by UPDATE with the aid of extra columns simulating the absence of a row. Queries whose WHERE clauses query mutable values are replaced by multiple simple instructions querying only immutable values such as unique ids and primary keys.

Experimental Results. We designed two experiments to evaluate CHECKCONSISTENCY's performance for different isolation configurations increasing the number of transactions per session (the number of sessions is fixed), the number of sessions (the number of transactions per session is fixed), resp. We use a timeout of 60 seconds per history.

The first experiment investigates the scalability of Algorithm 3 when increasing the number of sessions. For each benchmark and isolation configuration, we consider 5 histories of random clients (each history is for a different client) with an increasing number of sessions and 10 transactions per session (around 400 histories across all benchmarks). No timeouts appear with less than 4 sessions. Figure 6 shows the running time of the experiment.

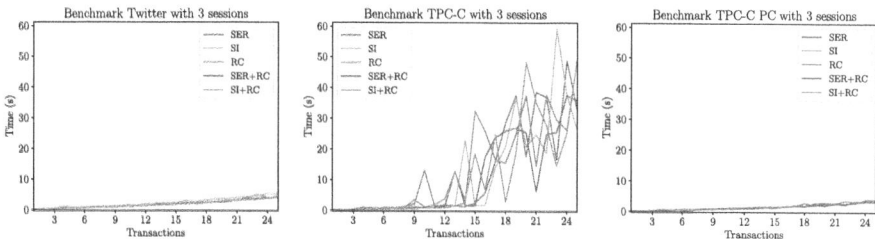

Fig. 7. Running time of Algorithm 3 increasing the number of transactions per session. We plot the average running time of 5 random clients of such size.

The second experiment investigates the scalability of Algorithm 3 when increasing the number of transactions. For each benchmark and isolation configuration, we consider 5 histories of random clients, each having 3 sessions and an increasing number of transactions per session (around 1900 histories across all benchmarks). Figure 7 shows its running time.

The runtime similarities between isolation configurations containing SI versus those without it show that in practice, the bottleneck of Algorithm 3 is the number of possible history extensions enumerated at line 11 in Algorithm 3; i.e. the number of conflicts in a history. This number is influenced by the distribution of types of transactions, e.g., for TPC-C, a bigger number of transactions creating new orders increases the number of possible full history extensions. Other isolation levels not implemented by PostgreSQL, e.g., prefix consistency PC, are expected to produce similar results.

Both experiments show that Algorithm 3 scales well for histories with a small number of writes (like Twitter) or conflicts (like TPC-C PC). In particular, Algorithm 3 is quite efficient for typical workloads needed to expose bugs in production databases which contain less than 10 transactions [7,18,20].

A third experiment compares Algorithm 3 with a baseline consisting in a naive approach where we enumerate witnesses and executions of such witnesses until consistency is determined. We consider Twitter and TPC-C as benchmarks and execute 5 histories of random clients, each having 3 sessions and an increasing number of transactions per session (around 100 histories across all benchmarks). We execute each client under RC and check the obtained histories for consistency with respect to SER.

The naive approach either times out for 35.5%, resp., 95.5% of the histories of Twitter, resp., TPC-C, or finishes in 5 s on average (max 25 s). In comparison, Algorithm 3 has no timeouts for Twitter and times out for 5.5% of the TPC-C histories; finishing in 1.5 s on average (max 12 s). Averages are computed w.r.t. non-timeout instances. The total number of executed clients is around 100. Only one TPC-C history was detected as inconsistent, which shows that the naive approach does not timeout only in the worst-case (inconsistency is a worst-case because all extensions and commit orders must be proved to be invalid).

A similar analysis on the TPC-C PC benchmark is omitted: TPC-C PC is a conflict-free variation of TPC-C with more operations per transaction. Thus, the rate of timeouts in the naive approach increases w.r.t. TPC-C, while the rate of timeouts using Algorithm 3 decreases.

Comparisons with prior work [4,7,18,20] are not possible as they do not apply to SQL (see Sect. 7 for more details).

This evaluation demonstrates that our algorithm scales well to practical testing workloads and that it outperforms brute-force search.

7   Related Work

The formalization of database isolation levels has been considered in previous work. Adya [2] has proposed axiomatic specifications for isolation levels, which however do not concern more modern isolation levels like PC or SI and which are based on low-level modeling of database snapshots. We follow the more modern approach in [7,11] which however addresses the restricted case when transactions are formed of reads and writes on a *static* set of keys (variables) and not generic SQL queries, and all the transactions in a given execution have the same isolation level. Our axiomatic model builds on axioms defined by Biswas et al. [7] which are however applied on a new model of executions that is specific to SQL queries.

The complexity of checking consistency w.r.t isolation levels has been studied in [7,21]. The work of Papadimitriou [21] shows that checking serializability is NP-complete while the work of Biswas et al. [7] provides results for the same isolation levels as in our work, but in the restricted case mentioned above.

Checking consistency in a non-transactional case, shared-memory or distributed systems, has been investigated in a number of works, e.g., [1,3,9,10,13–17]. Transactions introduce additional challenges that make these results not applicable.

Existing tools for checking consistency in the transactional case of distributed databases, e.g., [4,7,18,20] cannot handle SQL-like semantics, offering guarantees modulo their transformations to reads and writes on static sets of keys. Our results show that handling the SQL-like semantics is strictly more complex (NP-hard in most cases).

Acknowledgements. We thank the anonymous reviewers for their feedback. This work was partially supported by the Agence National de Recherche (ANR) grants "AdeCoDS" and "CENTEANES".

References

1. Abdulla, P.A., Atig, M.F., Jonsson, B., Ngo, T.P.: Optimal stateless model checking under the release-acquire semantics. Proc. ACM Program. Lang. **2**(OOPSLA), 135:1–135:29 (2018). https://doi.org/10.1145/3276505
2. Adya, A.: Weak consistency: A generalized theory and optimistic implementations for distributed transactions. Technical report, USA (1999)
3. Agarwal, P., Chatterjee, K., Pathak, S., Pavlogiannis, A., Toman, V.: Stateless model checking under a reads-value-from equivalence. In: Silva, A., Leino, K.R.M. (eds.) CAV 2021, Part I. LNCS, vol. 12759, pp. 341–366. Springer, Cham (2021). https://doi.org/10.1007/978-3-030-81685-8_16
4. Alvaro, P., Kingsbury, K.: Elle: inferring isolation anomalies from experimental observations. Proc. VLDB Endow. **14**(3), 268–280 (2020). http://www.vldb.org/pvldb/vol14/p268-alvaro.pdf. https://doi.org/10.5555/3430915.3442427
5. Bouajjani, A., Enea, C., Román-Calvo, E.: Artifact for "On the complexity of checking mixed isolation levels for SQL transactions" (2024). https://github.com/Galieve/benchbase-histories
6. Berenson, H., Bernstein, P.A., Gray, J., Melton, J., O'Neil, E.J., O'Neil, P.E.: A critique of ANSI SQL isolation levels. In: Carey, M.J., Schneider, D.A. (eds.) Proceedings of the 1995 ACM SIGMOD International Conference on Management of Data, San Jose, California, USA, 22–25 May 1995, pp. 1–10. ACM Press (1995). https://doi.org/10.1145/223784.223785

7. Biswas, R., Enea, C.: On the complexity of checking transactional consistency. Proc. ACM Program. Lang. **3**(OOPSLA), 165:1–165:28 (2019). https://doi.org/10.1145/3360591

8. Biswas, R., Kakwani, D., Vedurada, J., Enea, C., Lal, A.: MonkeyDB: effectively testing correctness under weak isolation levels. Proc. ACM Program. Lang. **5**(OOPSLA), 1–27 (2021). https://doi.org/10.1145/3485546

9. Bouajjani, A., Enea, C., Guerraoui, R., Hamza, J.: On verifying causal consistency. In: Castagna, G., Gordon, A.D. (eds.) Proceedings of the 44th ACM SIGPLAN Symposium on Principles of Programming Languages, POPL 2017, Paris, France, 18–20 January 2017, pp. 626–638. ACM (2017). https://doi.org/10.1145/3009837.3009888

10. Cantin, J.F., Lipasti, M.H., Smith, J.E.: The complexity of verifying memory coherence and consistency. IEEE Trans. Parallel Distributed Syst. **16**(7), 663–671 (2005). https://doi.org/10.1109/TPDS.2005.86

11. Cerone, A., Bernardi, G., Gotsman, A.: A framework for transactional consistency models with atomic visibility. In: Aceto, L., de Frutos-Escrig, D. (eds.) 26th International Conference on Concurrency Theory, CONCUR 2015, Madrid, Spain, 1–4 September 2015, vol. 42 of *LIPIcs*, pp. 58–71. Schloss Dagstuhl - Leibniz-Zentrum für Informatik (2015). https://doi.org/10.4230/LIPIcs.CONCUR.2015.58. https://doi.org/10.4230/LIPICS.CONCUR.2015.58

12. Difallah, D.E., Pavlo, A., Curino, C., Cudré-Mauroux, P.: OLTP-bench: an extensible testbed for benchmarking relational databases. Proc. VLDB Endow. **7**(4), 277–288 (2013). http://www.vldb.org/pvldb/vol7/p277-difallah.pdf. https://doi.org/10.14778/2732240.2732246

13. Emmi, M., Enea, C.: Sound, complete, and tractable linearizability monitoring for concurrent collections. Proc. ACM Program. Lang. **2**(POPL), 25:1–25:27 (2018). https://doi.org/10.1145/3158113

14. Furbach, F., Meyer, R., Schneider, K., Senftleben, M.: Memory-model-aware testing: a unified complexity analysis. ACM Trans. Embed. Comput. Syst. **14**(4), 63:1–63:25 (2015). https://doi.org/10.1145/2753761

15. Gibbons, P.B., Korach, E.: On testing cache-coherent shared memories. In: Snyder, L., Leiserson, C.E. (eds.) Proceedings of the 6th Annual ACM Symposium on Parallel Algorithms and Architectures, SPAA 1994, Cape May, New Jersey, USA, 27–29 June 1994, pp. 177–188. ACM (1994). https://doi.org/10.1145/181014.181328

16. Gibbons, P.B., Korach, E.: Testing shared memories. SIAM J. Comput. **26**(4), 1208–1244 (1997). https://doi.org/10.1137/S0097539794279614

17. Gontmakher, A., Polyakov, S.V., Schuster, A.: Complexity of verifying java shared memory execution. Parallel Process. Lett. **13**(4), 721–733 (2003). https://doi.org/10.1142/S0129626403001628

18. Huang, K., et al.: Efficient black-box checking of snapshot isolation in databases. Proc. VLDB Endow. **16**(6), 1264–1276 (2023). https://www.vldb.org/pvldb/vol16/p1264-wei.pdf. https://doi.org/10.14778/3583140.3583145

19. Jepsen: Distributed systems testing (2020). https://jepsen.io/

20. Liu, S., Long, G., Wei, H., Basin, D.A.: Plume: efficient and complete black-box checking of weak isolation levels. Proc. ACM Program. Lang. **8**(OOPSLA2), 876–904 (2024). https://doi.org/10.1145/3689742

21. Papadimitriou, C.H.: The serializability of concurrent database updates. J. ACM **26**(4), 631–653 (1979). https://doi.org/10.1145/322154.322158

22. Pavlo, A.: What are we doing with our lives?: Nobody cares about our concurrency control research. In: Salihoglu, S., Zhou, W., Chirkova, R., Yang, J., Suciu, D. (eds.)

Proceedings of the 2017 ACM International Conference on Management of Data, SIGMOD Conference 2017, Chicago, IL, USA, 14–19 May 2017, p. 3. ACM (2017). https://doi.org/10.1145/3035918.3056096

23. Terry, D.B., Demers, A.J., Petersen, K., Spreitzer, M., Theimer, M., Welch, B.B.: Session guarantees for weakly consistent replicated data. In: Proceedings of the Third International Conference on Parallel and Distributed Information Systems (PDIS 1994), Austin, Texas, USA, 28–30 September 1994, pp. 140–149. IEEE Computer Society (1994). https://doi.org/10.1109/PDIS.1994.331722

24. TPC: Technical report, Transaction Processing Performance Council, February 2010. http://www.tpc.org/tpc_documents_current_versions/pdf/tpc-c_v5.11.0.pdf

Data-Driven Verification of Procedural Programs with Integer Arrays

Ahmed Bouajjani[1], Wael-Amine Boutglay[1,2]($\boxtimes$), and Peter Habermehl[1]

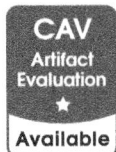

[1] Université Paris Cité, IRIF, CNRS, Paris, France
{abou,boutglay,haberm}@irif.fr
[2] Mohammed VI Polytechnic University,
Ben Guerir, Morocco

Abstract. We address the problem of verifying automatically procedural programs manipulating parametric-size arrays of integers, encoded as a constrained Horn clauses solving problem. We propose a new algorithmic method for synthesizing loop invariants and procedure pre/post-conditions represented as universally quantified first-order formulas constraining the array elements and program variables. We adopt a data-driven approach that extends the decision tree Horn-ICE framework to handle arrays. We provide a powerful learning technique based on reducing a complex classification problem of *vectors of integer arrays* to a simpler classification problem of *vectors of integers*. The obtained classifier is generalized to get universally quantified invariants and procedure pre/post-conditions. We have implemented our method and shown its efficiency and competitiveness w.r.t. state-of-the-art tools on a significant benchmark.

Keywords: Program verification · Invariant synthesis · Data-driven verification

1 Introduction

Automatic verification of procedural programs manipulating arrays is a challenging problem for which methods able to handle large classes of programs in practice are needed. Verifying that a program satisfies its specification given by a pre-condition and a post-condition amounts to synthesizing accurate loop invariants and procedure pre/post-conditions allowing to establish that every computation starting from a state satisfying the pre-condition cannot reach a state violating the post-condition. The automatic synthesis of invariants and pre/post-conditions has received a lot of interest from the community. It has been addressed using various approaches leading to the development of multiple verification methods and tools [1,17,19,30,38,39,44,47,48,51].

In this work, we address the problem of verifying procedural programs, with loops and potentially recursive procedures, manipulating integer arrays with *parametric* sizes, i.e., the sizes of arrays are considered as parameters explicitly mentioned in the program and its specification. We consider specifications

R. Piskac and Z. Rakamarić (Eds.): CAV 2025, LNCS 15934, pp. 338–363, 2025.
https://doi.org/10.1007/978-3-031-98685-7_16

written in first-order logic of arrays with linear constraints. Our contribution is to provide a new *data-driven* method for solving this verification problem. Our method generates automatically invariants and procedure pre/post-conditions of programs expressed as universally quantified formulas over arrays with integer data.

We use a learning approach for inductive invariant synthesis that consists in taking the set of all program states as the universe and considering two classes: the states reachable from the pre-condition are classified as *positive*, and those that can reach states violating the post-condition are classified as *negative*. A learner proposes a candidate invariant I to a teacher who checks that (1) the pre-condition is included in I, (2) I is included in the post-condition, and (3) I is inductive (i.e., stable under execution of program actions). If condition (1), resp. (2), is not satisfied, the teacher provides counterexamples to the learner that are positive, resp. negative. If (3) is not satisfied, the teacher cannot provide positive/negative examples, but communicates to the learner *implications* of the form $s \rightarrow s'$ meaning that if state s is included in the invariant, then state s' should be in it too. The use of such conditional classification data in the context of invariant learning (to exploit local reachability information) has been introduced in the ICE framework [33] and its instance ICE-DT [34] where invariants are generated using decision-tree learning techniques. We follow this approach. Actually, since we consider programs with procedure calls and recursion, our method is based on the Horn-ICE-DT learning schema that generalizes ICE-DT to constrained Horn clauses [28]. Horn-ICE has been applied previously to programs manipulating numerical variables, but never to procedural programs with integer arrays.

To adopt the Horn-ICE-DT schema, one needs to define a learner and a teacher. For the teacher, we use simply the Z3 [53] solver which can handle array logics [15,52,54]. Our contribution is a new decision-tree based learning method that can generate universally quantified first-order formulas on arrays with integers.

To define the learner, a crucial point is to define the space of attributes (predicates) that could be used for building the decision trees. This space depends on the type of the program states and the targeted class of invariants. For the programs we consider, states are valuations of program variables, of array bounds, and of the arrays (i.e., values stored in the arrays). Our goal is to learn invariants represented as formulas relating program variables with parametric array bounds, universally quantified index variables, and array elements at the positions given by the index variables. Then, one issue to address is, given a consistent sample of program states (i.e. no negative configuration is reachable from a positive one), to determine the number of quantified index variables that are needed for defining a classifier that separates correctly the sample. Once this number is fixed the question is what is the relevant relation that exists between program variables, index variables, and array elements. To tackle these issues, we adopt an approach that iteratively considers increasing numbers of quantifiers, and for each fixed number, reduces the learning problem from the original sample of program states (that includes array valuations) to another learning problem on a sample where elements are vectors of integers. This allows to use integer predicates for building decision trees which are then converted to universally quantified formulas corresponding to a classifier for the original problem. This reduction is nontrivial and requires to define a tight relation between the two learning problems. Roughly, given a consistent sample S of array-based data points, our method is able to determine the number n which is sufficient for its classification, and to generate a classifier for it from the classifier of another sample S'_n on integer-based data points.

The learning method we have defined allows to discover complex invariants and procedures' pre/post-conditions of programs with integer arrays that cannot be generated by existing tools for array program verification. We implemented our method and conducted experiments with a large and diverse benchmark of iterative and recursive programs, including array programs from SV-COMP. Experimental results show that, within a 300 s timeout, our tool verifies more instances than existing tools SPACER [39,43], ULTIMATE AUTOMIZER [40] FRE-QHORN [29,30], VAJRA [18], DIFFY [19], RAPID [35], PROPHIC3 [48] and MONO-CERA [4] with competitive efficiency. Moreover, our tool can verify recursive procedure programs, which are beyond the capabilities of FREQHORN, VAJRA, DIFFY, RAPID and PROPHIC3.

Related Work. Numerous techniques have been developed to infer quantified invariants, which are essential for the verification of array-manipulating programs with parametric sizes. Predicate abstraction [5,36] was extended through the use of skolem variables to support quantified reasoning [47]. Safari [2] implements lazy abstraction with interpolants [49] tailored for arrays [1]. It was augmented with acceleration techniques in Booster [3]. Abstract domains [24,38] were introduced for building abstract interpreters [23] of programs with arrays. [38] leverages existing quantifier-free domains for handling universally quantified properties. Full-program induction of [18] allows proving quantified properties within a restricted class of array programs expanded in Diffy [19] using difference invariants. Many of these approaches are limited to non-recursive programs corresponding to linear CHC. This is not a limitation for our method or for QUIC3 [39] and its integration within SPACER [43] that extends IC3/PDR [14,26] to non-linear CHC. A prior work to QUIC3 is UPDR [41] extending IC3 to infer universally quantified invariants for programs modeled using EPR.

There are many learning-based methods for invariant synthesis [7,29,33,55,56]. Several have been extended to quantified invariants [30,35]. Some of these rely on user-provided templates for invariants [9,44]. FreqHorn [29], a notable CHC solver for quantified invariants, combines data-guided syntax synthesis with range analysis, but faces limitations in handling complex iterating patterns or recursive calls (non-linearity of CHC). This is also the case for [57] tailored to the inference of weakest preconditions of linear array programs. We overcome these issues by using a fully data-driven approach and decision trees for learning successfully used in some ICE instantiations [11,34]. While ICE has been instantiated previously for learning quantified data automata [32] as invariants for linear data structures like singly-linked lists, our method instantiates the more general Horn-ICE framework [28], allowing verification of programs with arbitrary control flow structures and procedure calls. HoIce [20] is another extension of ICE to solve CHC problems. While in our work, we adopt the terminology of Horn-ICE and instantiate it, our method is also applicable within the HoIce framework. Prior instantiations of Horn-ICE were restricted to verifying numerical programs, while HoIce offers only basic support for arrays and lacks the ability to infer quantified invariants.

In [42] an algorithm that learns a formula with quantifier-alternation separating positive and negative models is given. But, similar to UPDR, it requires programs modeled using EPR. Reducing a classification problem with array values to this formalism might be possible but is not straightforward. RAPID [35] can also learn invariants with quantifier alternation, but is restricted to non-recursive programs with simple control-flow.

Alternatively, array programs can be verified without inferring quantified invariants by reducing the safety problem to one with arrays abstracted to a fixed number of variables [17,46,51,58], however the resulting program may be challenging to verify [16]. PROPHIC3 [48] mitigates this challenge by combining this abstraction technique with counterexample-guided abstraction refinement within the IC3/PDR framework. Moreover, it has the capability to reconstruct the quantified invariants for the original system. Similarly, LAMBDA [59] is designed for the verification of parametric systems and leverages IC3IA [21] as a quantifier-free model checker. MONOCERA [4] simplifies the verification problem by instrumenting the program without eliminating the arrays through abstraction. In contrast, our method preserves the original verification problem and applies reduction solely to at the level of the learner, transforming the inference of quantified invariants into a scalar classification task.

2   Overview

We demonstrate our method by applying it to the program in Fig. 1 implementing the bubble sort algorithm over an integer array a (line 4) with parametric size N (line 4)[1]. The precondition of the program is given by the `assume` statement, and its postcondition is given by the `assert` statement in line 4 (verifying whether the array a at this point is a permutation of the initial array falls outside the scope of this paper).

We start by reducing the safety verification of the program to the satisfiability of a system of constrained Horn clauses (CHC). This is achieved using the methodology described e.g. in [10,31]. For our example, the corresponding system is given below, where all free variables in each clause are implicitly universally quantified.

---

[1] We adhere to standard C semantics, which stipulate that stack-allocated variables, if uninitialized, may assume arbitrary values.

```
1   void main() {                    10    if( a[i - 1] > a[i] ) {
2     unsigned int N;                11      int tmp = a[i] ;
3     assume( N > 0 );               12      a[i] = a[i - 1] ;
4     int a[ N ];                    13      a[i - 1] = tmp ;
5     bool s = true ;                14      s = true ; }
6     while( s ) {                   15    i++ ;} }
7       s = false ;                  16   assert( ∀k₁, k₂. 0 ≤ k₁ ≤ k₂ < N
8       unsigned int i = 1 ;         17        ⟹ a[k₁] ≤ a[k₂] );}
9       while( i < N ) {
```

Fig. 1. Bubble sort over a parametric size array of integers.

$$N > 0 \wedge |a| = N \wedge s \implies I_0(N, a, s) \tag{1}$$

$$I_0(N, a, s) \wedge s \wedge \neg s' \wedge i = 1 \implies I_1(N, a, s', i) \tag{2}$$

$$I_1(N, a, s, i) \wedge i < N \wedge \neg(a[i-1] > a[i]) \wedge i' = i + 1 \implies I_1(N, a, s, i') \tag{3}$$

$$I_1(N, a, s, i) \wedge i < N \wedge a[i-1] > a[i] \wedge s' \wedge i' = i + 1$$
$$\wedge \, a' = a\{i \leftarrow a[i-1]\} \wedge a'' = a'\{i-1 \leftarrow a[i]\} \implies I_1(N, a'', s', i') \tag{4}$$

$$I_1(N, a, s, i) \wedge \neg(i < N) \implies I_0(N, a, s) \tag{5}$$

$$I_0(N, a, s) \wedge \neg s$$
$$\wedge \neg(\forall k_1, k_2. \, 0 \leq k_1 \leq k_2 < N \implies a[k_1] \leq a[k_2]) \implies \bot \tag{6}$$

The system above defines constraints on the set of uninterpreted predicates $\mathcal{P} = \{I_0, I_1\}$, where I_0 and I_1 represent the invariants of the outer loop while(s) and the nested loop while(i < N), respectively. In these constraints, $a[i]$ represents the value of the array a at index i and $a\{i \leftarrow v\}$ represents an array with the same length and elements as a, except at index i where it has the value v. The program in Fig. 1 is safe if and only if this system is satisfiable, i.e., there are interpretations for I_0 and I_1 satisfying all the clauses. As we will see below, expressing such interpretations requires using universally quantified first-order formulas.

Our method to solve CHCs like the one above is based on Horn-ICE [28] learning approach which follows the standard learning loop where a learner and a teacher interact iteratively, the learner using a sample (set of examples) to infer a candidate solution and a teacher either approving it when a solution is found, or otherwise providing counterexamples that can be used in the next learning iteration. Horn-ICE is an extension of this principle that is adapted to learning inductive invariants by using, in addition to positive and negative examples, implications that provide conditional information such as: if some states are in the invariant, then necessarily some other state must also be in the invariant. Let us describe briefly this schema. Consider a CHC system built from a program as in the example above. In each iteration, the learner generates for each uninterpreted predicate in the system an interpretation using a *data point sample* $\mathcal{S} = (X, C)$ where X is a set of data points and C a set of Horn implications over X. A *data point* $x \in X$ corresponds to a configuration of the program at some location. To each data point is assigned an uninterpreted predicate $\boldsymbol{P} \in \mathcal{P}$ (denoted by $L(x)$) and a vector of constants, one for each parameter variable of $\boldsymbol{P}$. A *Horn implication* over X is a hyper-edge (generalizing ICE's implication) of one of the following forms: (a) $\top \rightarrow x$, where $x \in X$, meaning x should satisfy the predicate $L(x)$; (b) $x_1 \wedge \cdots \wedge x_n \rightarrow x$, where $x_1, \ldots, x_n, x \in X$, i.e. if $x_1, \ldots, x_n$, respectively, satisfy $L(x_1), \ldots, L(x_n)$ then x should satisfy $L(x)$, or if x doesn't satisfy $L(x)$ at least one of the $x_1, \ldots, x_n$ should not satisfy its predicate; (c) $x_1 \wedge \cdots \wedge x_n \rightarrow \bot$, where $x_1, \ldots, x_n \in X$, i.e. at least one of the $x_1, \ldots, x_n$ should not satisfy its predicate. A data point sample $\mathcal{S} = (X, C)$ is called *consistent* if it admits a *consistent labeling* which labels each element x of X with either $\top$ or $\bot$ while satisfying all the constraints in C.

The teacher checks if the generated interpretations by the learner satisfy the CHC system and provides feedback. If a clause $\forall \vec{v}.\ \phi(\vec{v}) \implies \boldsymbol{P_j}(\vec{v})$ is violated, then a counterexample is computed which is a data point x associated with the predicate $\boldsymbol{P_j} \in \mathcal{P}$ together with a Horn implication $\top \rightarrow x$. If a clause $\forall \vec{v}_1, \ldots, \vec{v}_n.\ \boldsymbol{P_1}(\vec{v}_1) \wedge \cdots \wedge \boldsymbol{P_n}(\vec{v}_n) \wedge \phi(\vec{v}_1, \ldots, \vec{v}_n) \implies \bot$ is violated, the counterexample is data points $x_1, \ldots, x_n$ with Horn implication $x_1 \wedge \cdots \wedge x_n \rightarrow \bot$. If a clause $\forall \vec{v}_1, \ldots, \vec{v}_n, \vec{v}.\ \boldsymbol{P_1}(\vec{v}_1) \wedge \cdots \wedge \boldsymbol{P_n}(\vec{v}_n) \wedge \phi(\vec{v}_1, \ldots, \vec{v}_n, \vec{v}) \implies \boldsymbol{P_j}(\vec{v})$ is violated, the counterexample is data points $x_1, \ldots, x_n, x$ with Horn implication $x_1 \wedge \cdots \wedge x_n \rightarrow x$.

To make this schema work, one has to define a learner and a teacher, depending on the considered classes of programs and properties. In this paper, we apply this schema to handle programs with (parametric-size) arrays and properties expressed in first-order logic of arrays, which has not been done so far. For the teacher, we rely on using the Z3 [53] SMT solver which can handle different decidable fragments of array logics $[15,52,54]^2$. Z3 attempts in addition to solve queries beyond the known decidable fragments using various heuristics. Then, our main contribution consists in providing a new learning technique able to synthesize invariants/procedure summaries as universally quantified formulas over arrays. This requires addressing a number of nontrivial problems. Let us first see how the learner and the teacher interact, and what is the type of information they exchange, in the case of the bubble-sort example (Fig. 1).

In the first iteration, starting with an empty sample (with no counterexamples), the learner proposes I_0 and I_1 as true. The teacher finds this violates clause (6) and provides the counterexample $\langle I_0, N \mapsto 2, a \mapsto [1, 0], s \mapsto \bot \rangle \rightarrow \bot$, indicating that this data point must not be included in I_0's invariant (exiting the outer loop while a is not sorted). In the second iteration, the learner proposes for I_0 $\forall k_1, k_2.\ 0 \leq k_1 \leq k_2 < |a| \implies a[k_1] > 0$ and keeps true for I_1.

---

[2] In the literature arrays are typically handled using uninterpreted functions. We can easily encode parametric-size arrays like that.

The teacher identifies a violation of clause (1) and provides the counterexample $\top \to \langle I_0, N \mapsto 1, a \mapsto [0], s \mapsto \top \rangle$, indicating this configuration must be included in I_0's invariant as it is a valid initial state. After collecting more counterexamples, the learner proposes $\forall k_1, k_2.\ 0 \le k_1 \le k_2 < |a| \implies a[k_1] \le 0 \vee s$ for I_0 and true for I_1. The teacher then reports a violation of clause (5) with the implication counterexample $\langle I_1, N \mapsto 1, a \mapsto [1], i \mapsto 1, s \mapsto \bot \rangle \to \langle I_0, N \mapsto 1, a \mapsto [1], s \mapsto \bot \rangle$ indicating that if the first configuration is in I_1, the second should also be in I_0.

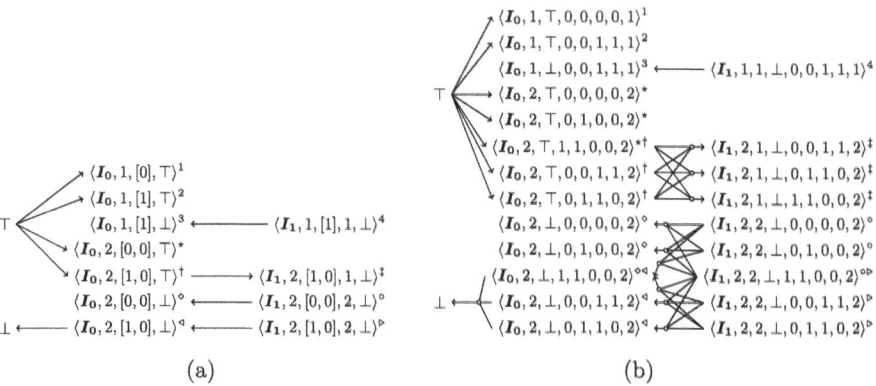

(a)   (b)

Fig. 2. (a) A data point sample during verification of bubble sort and (b) its diagram sample using 2 quantifier variables. Diagrams of (b) are derived from data points with the same superscript in (a).

Now, the question is how the learner synthesizes a candidate solution from a given consistent data point sample $\mathcal{S} = (X, C)$. The general principle is to build a formula that is a *classifier* of $\mathcal{S}$, i.e., that separates the elements of X into positive and negative ones while respecting the constraints in C (collected from counterexamples to inductiveness during the learning process). The challenge is to generate universally quantified formulas over (parametric-size) arrays from a finite set of data, and for that there are two important questions: (1) how many quantifiers are needed to express the solution? and (2) what is the mechanism to use to generate the constraints on indexed elements of arrays and program variables?

Let us keep the first question for later, and assume for the moment that the number of quantifiers is given. To address the second question, we adopt a learning mechanism based on decision-trees following the Horn-ICE-DT schema [28], which is a natural approach for generating formulas. Then, the crucial questions are what are the predicates to use as attributes to check at the nodes of these decision trees? and how to use these predicates to build a universally quantified formula? To make the space of the possible predicates easier to explore, we reduce our classification problem on array-based data points samples to another classification problem stated on integer-based data points samples that can be solved using integer constraints.

In more details, we introduce a technique called *diagramization* summarized as follows: Given a classification problem of a consistent sample S of program states including array valuations (assume that we have one array a to simplify the explanation), a fixed number n and a set V of size n of fresh index variables to be universally quantified in the classifier (called *quantifier variables*), we consider another classification problem on a sample S'_n of so-called *diagrams*. They associate values to program variables, to variables k in V, and to terms $a[k]$ (representing the element of a at position k). Elements of S'_n are vectors of integers obtained from elements of S by taking all possible projections of arrays on a fixed number of positions. The sample S'_n is obtained by considering for each array valuation in a state, all possible mappings from V to its array elements. Moreover, we transfer the classification information of S to S'_n.

At this point, a question is whether S'_n is consistent (knowing that S is consistent). Let us assume it is for the moment and come back to this issue later. Then, the learner proceeds by constructing a decision tree for S'_n using predicates on integers as attributes. In our implementation, we use predicates appearing in the program and the specification, as well as predicates generated by progressive enumeration from simple patterns in domains such as interval or octagonal constraints [50]. In fact, it is possible to determine if a given set of attributes allows to build a classifier of a given sample, and if it is does not, to generate additional attributes from the considered patterns (a sufficient set of attributes is guaranteed to be found for a consistent sample). Then, we prove that when a classifier is found for S'_n (expressed as a formula relating program variables, index variables k and corresponding terms $a[k]$), its conversion by universally quantifying over all the V variables is indeed a classifier for S (see Theorem 1).

Let us illustrate this process on our bubble-sort example. At the 10th iteration of the verification of Fig. 1, the learner has accumulated counterexamples shown in the data point sample in Fig. 2a. For simplicity, variable names are omitted; e.g., $\langle \boldsymbol{I_0}, N \mapsto 2, a \mapsto [1,0], s \mapsto \bot \rangle$ is shortened to $\langle \boldsymbol{I_0}, 2, [1,0], \bot \rangle$. As explained above, the key idea of our method is that the learner's sample can be reduced to a diagram sample, where examples consist only of scalar and boolean values. For example, for the data point $x_1 = \langle \boldsymbol{I_0}, N \mapsto 2, a \mapsto [1,0], s \mapsto \bot \rangle$, if we abstract the array a using two quantifier variables k_1 and k_2, we introduce fresh variables a_{k_1} and a_{k_2}, representing the values of a at the positions indexed by k_1 and k_2, respectively. We also introduce an additional fresh variable l_a to represent the size of the array. We explain later how the number of quantifier variables (2 in this case) is determined. In this case, x_1 is transformed into the following diagrams:

$$d_1 = \langle \boldsymbol{I_0}, N \mapsto 2, s \mapsto \bot, k_1 \mapsto 0, k_2 \mapsto 0, a_{k_1} \mapsto 1, a_{k_2} \mapsto 1, l_a \mapsto 2 \rangle$$
$$d_2 = \langle \boldsymbol{I_0}, N \mapsto 2, s \mapsto \bot, k_1 \mapsto 0, k_2 \mapsto 1, a_{k_1} \mapsto 1, a_{k_2} \mapsto 0, l_a \mapsto 2 \rangle$$
$$d_3 = \langle \boldsymbol{I_0}, N \mapsto 2, s \mapsto \bot, k_1 \mapsto 1, k_2 \mapsto 0, a_{k_1} \mapsto 0, a_{k_2} \mapsto 1, l_a \mapsto 2 \rangle$$
$$d_4 = \langle \boldsymbol{I_0}, N \mapsto 2, s \mapsto \bot, k_1 \mapsto 1, k_2 \mapsto 1, a_{k_1} \mapsto 0, a_{k_2} \mapsto 0, l_a \mapsto 2 \rangle$$

In this newly *diagramized* sample, diagrams of a positive data point must all be classified as positive. For negative data points, at least one diagram must be classified as negative. This is encoded in the diagram sample with the implication over diagrams $d_1 \wedge d_2 \wedge d_3 \wedge d_4 \to \bot$. As the data point x_1 in the original sample is negative, at least one of its four diagrams must be classified as negative. Here, d_2 is negative, as it violates the program assertion ($k_1 < k_2$ is true but not $a_{k_1} \leq a_{k_2}$). For implication counterexamples, if all diagrams of the left-hand side data point are classified as positive, then all diagrams of the right-hand side data point must also be classified as positive. Similarly, if a diagram of the right-hand side data point is classified as negative, then at least one diagram of the left-hand side data point must also be classified as negative.

Our method reduces the data point sample shown in Fig. 2a to the diagram sample shown in Fig. 2b. For brevity, variable names are again omitted, so $\langle \boldsymbol{I_0}, N \mapsto 2, s \mapsto \bot, k_1 \mapsto 0, k_2 \mapsto 1, a_{k_1} \mapsto 1, a_{k_2} \mapsto 0, l_a \mapsto 2 \rangle$ is shortened to $\langle \boldsymbol{I_0}, 2, \bot, 0, 1, 1, 0, 2 \rangle$. Notice that different data points may share some diagrams.

Then, the obtained diagram sample is classified by a decision-tree learning algorithm that produces a quantifier-free formula using attributes generated using the domain of octagonal constraints. The decision-tree learning procedure over this sample yields $s \vee a_{k_1} \leq a_{k_2}$ for $\boldsymbol{I_0}$ and $i \leq k_2 \vee a_{k_1} \leq a_{k_2}$ for $\boldsymbol{I_1}$. When universally quantified, we obtain the solution with $\forall k_1, k_2. \ 0 \leq k_1 \leq k_2 < |a| \implies a[k_1] \leq a[k_2] \vee s$ for $\boldsymbol{I_0}$ and $\forall k_1, k_2. \ 0 \leq k_1 \leq k_2 < |a| \implies a[k_1] \leq a[k_2] \vee i \leq k_2 \vee s$ for $\boldsymbol{I_1}$ that the learner proposes to the teacher.

Now, let us go back to the question whether $\mathcal{S}'$ is consistent. This question is related to another question we left pending earlier in this section which is how to determine the number of quantified variables n. In fact, it can be the case that for a consistent sample $\mathcal{S}$ and an integer n, the sample $\mathcal{S}'_n$ is not consistent as illustrated later in Example 4. This means that in this case n is not sufficient for defining a formula that classifies $\mathcal{S}$. Therefore, our learner has a loop that increments the number of quantifier variables, starting with one quantifier variable per array, until a consistent diagram sample is obtained. This is guaranteed to succeed, as stated in Theorem 2.

Finally, let us mention that when after a number of iterations between the learner and the teacher the obtained sample $\mathcal{S}$ is inconsistent, the program does not satisfy its specification.

3   Programs and Specification

Programs. In this paper, we consider C-like programs that manipulate integer-indexed arrays. Due to space constraints, we only give here an informal description of their syntax. Programs contain a designated procedure `main` serving as the entry point. Procedures (except `main`) can be recursive and may have boolean or integer parameters or pointers to stack-allocated integer-indexed arrays of integers or booleans. In the procedure body, local variables can be declared anywhere. They can be integer or boolean variables or integer-indexed arrays of integers or booleans; the size of these arrays is parametric and is equal to a linear expression over other integer variables. We allow various loop structures and conditional statements.

Specifications. Programs are specified using `assume`/`assert` statements at different program locations. We give here the language of these assumed/asserted properties. They use the variables of the program at the particular location.

For expressing the properties as well as the inferred invariants and pre/post-conditions, we use a many-sorted first-order logic with one-dimensional arrays T_A as follows. The logic T_A has the following primitive sorts: integers (Int) and booleans (B) and two sorts for *finite-size arrays*: integer arrays ($Array(Int)$) and boolean arrays ($Array(B)$). Integer constants are $\{\ldots, -1, 0, 1, \ldots\}$ and boolean constants are $\{\top, \bot\}$. Integer functions and predicates are the usual ones of Presburger logic (with the standard syntactic sugar for linear combinations and comparisons). Array constants are all finite-size arrays containing either only integer constants or only boolean constants. We write them as $[c_0, c_1, \ldots, c_k]$ for some $k \geq 0$ and $[]$ for the empty array. Furthermore, we have three functions over integer (boolean) arrays with the corresponding sorts: array read $\cdot[\cdot]$, array write $\cdot\{\cdot \leftarrow \cdot\}$ and array length $|\cdot|$. For example $a[i]$ is the i-th element of array a. We have also the equality predicate between two boolean or integer arrays.

Then, *terms*, *atoms*, *literals* and *first-order formulas* are defined in the usual way. The sort of variables used in the formulas will be always clear from the context. The *semantics* can be defined as usual. Because finite-size arrays are used, we have to define a semantics for out of bounds access. Here, instead of using an undefined value, we just say that for an array read the value of $a[i]$ is 0 (resp. $\bot$) for an integer (resp. boolean) array, if i is out of bounds. An array write $a\{i \leftarrow x\}$ has no effect if i is out of bounds.

Properties in assume/assert statements as well as in verification predicates are *parametric-size array properties*, defined as universally quantified formulas accessing an array a at indices in the range 0 to $|a| - 1$.

Definition 1 (Parametric-Size Array Property). *A parametric-size array property is a formula of the form*

$$\psi \wedge \forall \vec{Q}_{a_1}, \ldots, \vec{Q}_{a_n} . \left(\bigwedge_{i=1}^{n} \bigwedge_{k \in \vec{Q}_{a_i}} 0 \leq k < |a_i| \right) \implies \phi(\vec{Q}_{a_1}, \ldots, \vec{Q}_{a_n}) \quad (7)$$

where ψ is a quantifier free formula of T_A, the $\vec{Q}_{a_i}$ are index variables and $\phi(\vec{Q}_{a_1}, \ldots, \vec{Q}_{a_n})$ is a quantifier-free T_A formula without array writes in which all read accesses to arrays a_i are via using one variable of $\vec{Q}_{a_i}$.

To simplify the presentation we will use formulas which are syntactically not parametric-size array properties but which are equivalent to one. Notice that without further restrictions the satisfiability of parametric-size array properties is not decidable. However, one can define a decidable fragment like in [15] by restricting further ψ and the use of universally quantified index variables in ϕ.

Safety Verification. Given a program and its specification, *safety verification* consists in checking whether along all program executions, whenever all assume statements are satisfied, then also all assert statements are satisfied. It is well known that this problem amounts to invariant and procedure pre/post-condition synthesis. In the context of this work, invariants and procedure pre/post-conditions are expressed as universally quantified formulas. As explained in the overview, we reduce the safety verification of a program to the CHC satisfiability problem. Then, we define a method for learning a solution of the CHC satisfiability problem in the case of array constraints. The core of this method is the diagramization technique which is detailed in the following section.

4   Diagramization

For an uninterpreted predicate $P \in \mathcal{P}$, let $\mathcal{D}^P$ denote the set of all its variable parameters, $\mathcal{A}^P \subseteq \mathcal{D}^P$ be the set of its arrays, $\mathcal{D}_{\mathbb{B}}^P \subseteq \mathcal{D}^P$ the set of its boolean variables and $\mathcal{D}_{\mathbb{Z}}^P \subseteq \mathcal{D}^P$ the set of its integer variables.

Given a data point sample $\mathcal{S} = (X, C)$, the learner must find a classifier using quantified formulas over parametric-size arrays for $\mathcal{S}$. We begin with some definitions.

Definition 2 (Data Point Sample). *A data point sample $\mathcal{S}$ over $\mathcal{P}$ is a tuple (X, C), where X is a set of data points over $\mathcal{P}$, and C is a set of classification constraints over X, represented as Horn implications. These constraints take three forms: (1) $\top \to x$, indicating that $x \in X$ must be classified as positive; (2) $x_1 \wedge \cdots \wedge x_n \to \bot$, where $x_1, \ldots, x_n \in X$, indicating that at least one of them must be classified as negative; (3) $x_1 \wedge \cdots \wedge x_n \to x$, where $x_1, \ldots, x_n, x \in X$, meaning that $x \in X$ must be positive if all $x_1, \ldots, x_n \in X$ are positive; Conversely, if x is negative, at least one of $x_1, \ldots, x_n$ must also be negative.*

Definition 3 (Consistent labeling of a Data Point Sample). *A consistent labeling of a data point sample $\mathcal{S} = (X, C)$ is a Boolean function $\mathcal{J} \colon X \to \{\top, \bot\}$ that satisfies all the Horn implications in C. Formally, for every implication $c \in C$, we have (1) if c is of the form $\top \to x$ (where $x \in X$), then $\mathcal{J}(x) = \top$; (2) if c is of the form $x_1 \wedge \cdots \wedge x_n \to \bot$ (where $x_1, \ldots, x_n \in X$), then $\mathcal{J}(x_1) = \bot \vee \cdots \vee \mathcal{J}(x_n) = \bot$; (3) if c is of the form $x_1 \wedge \cdots \wedge x_n \to x$ (where $x_1, \ldots, x_n, d \in X$), then $\big(\mathcal{J}(x_1) = \top \wedge \cdots \wedge \mathcal{J}(x_n) = \top\big)$ implies $\mathcal{J}(x) = \top$.*

Definition 4 (Consistent Data Point Sample). *A data point sample $\mathcal{S} = (X, C)$ is said to be* consistent *if there exists a consistent labeling $\mathcal{J} \colon X \to \{\top, \bot\}$. Otherwise, $\mathcal{S}$ is* inconsistent.

Definition 5 (Classifier of a Data Point Sample). *Given a consistent data point sample $\mathcal{S} = (X, C)$, a classifier of $\mathcal{S}$ is a syntactic characterization of a labeling $\mathcal{J}$ of $\mathcal{S}$. It is defined as a mapping J that assigns each predicate $\boldsymbol{P} \in \mathcal{P}$ a formula in T_A over the variables of $\boldsymbol{P}$, and that satisfies $x \models J[L(x)]$ if and only if $\mathcal{J}(x) = \top$ for every data point $x \in X$.*

Our method consists of reducing the classification problem of $\mathcal{S}$ to another classification problem $\mathcal{S}' = (X', C')$ where we do not need quantified formula classifiers. We will first define the new data points X' and then the new Horn implications C'. Array values in the data points will be transformed into scalar values by introducing free variables representing quantifier variables, and scalar variables that take on the values of the array at the positions indicated by the quantifier variables (see Example 1 below). Then, C' is obtained by modifying C. A classifier for $\mathcal{S}'$ can then be transformed to a classifier for $\mathcal{S}$ by introducing universal quantifiers and substituting the scalar variables with array reads by quantifier variables.

Formally, for each parametric-size array $a \in \mathcal{A}^P$ of some uninterpreted predicate $\boldsymbol{P}$, we introduce a set of quantifier variables Q_a^P. For every $k \in Q_a^P$, we use a scalar variable a_k that has the same type as the elements of the array a and always has the value of a at index k. Let A^P be the set of these scalar variables, and $Q^P = \bigcup_{a \in \mathcal{A}^P} Q_a^P$. We also introduce a fresh integer variable l_a representing the size of a. Let S^P be the set of these variables. In what follows, we define the concept of a diagram.

Definition 6 (Diagram). *Let x be a data point with $L(x) = \boldsymbol{P}$. A diagram d of a data point x is associated with $\boldsymbol{P}$ and is a vector over all variables of $\boldsymbol{P}$, except the array variables, and $Q^P \cup A^P \cup S^P$, such that for all variables $v \in \mathcal{D}^P \setminus \mathcal{A}^P$, we have $d[v] = x[v]$, and for all arrays $a \in \mathcal{A}^P$, we have $d[l_a] = |x[a]|$ and for all quantifier variables $k \in Q_a^P$ of a, we have $0 \le d[k] < |x[a]|$, $d[a_k] = x[a][k]$.*

We denote with $L(d)$ the uninterpreted predicate associated with diagram d. Notice that for a data point $x \in X$, there exist multiple diagrams depending on the size of the arrays of x and the number of introduced quantifier variables for each array. To simplify, this number is the same for every array. Let $\textsc{Diagrams}^n(x)$ be the set of all diagrams of data point x using n quantifier variables per array.

Example 1. For $Q_a^{I_0} = \{k_1, k_2\}$, the diagrams of the data point $x_1 = \langle \boldsymbol{I_0}, N \mapsto 2, a \mapsto [1, 0], s \mapsto \bot \rangle$ are $Diagrams^2(x_1) = \{d_1, d_2, d_3, d_4\}$ where d_1, d_2, d_3 and d_4 were introduced in Sect. 2.

It is possible that different data points have common diagrams:

Example 2. The data point x_1 from the previous example and $x_2 = \langle \boldsymbol{I_0}, N \mapsto 2, a \mapsto [0, 0], s \mapsto \bot \rangle$ have the same diagram $\langle \boldsymbol{I_0}, N \mapsto 2, s \mapsto \bot, k_1 \mapsto 1, k_2 \mapsto 1, a_{k_1} \mapsto 0, a_{k_2} \mapsto 0, l_a \mapsto 2 \rangle$ in common.

We are now ready to define the *diagram sample* $\mathcal{S}'_n = (X', C')$ obtained from $\mathcal{S} = (X, C)$. It is parameterized by the number n of universally quantified variables used. X' will be the set containing all diagrams corresponding to data points in X and C' contains Horn implications which bring the constraint imposed on the classification between data points in X to the diagrams in X'. The intuition is that if all the diagrams associated with a data point x in $\mathcal{S}$ are classified positive by a classifier of $\mathcal{S}'_n$, then x will also be classified positive by a classifier of $\mathcal{S}$, and conversely. However, if at least one diagram of a data point x in $\mathcal{S}$ is classified negative by a classifier of $\mathcal{S}'_n$, then x will be classified negative by a classifier of $\mathcal{S}$ as well, and vice versa. These constraints are also expressed using Horn implications in C'.

Formally, the notions of diagram sample, along with labeling, consistency, and classifier, are defined analogously to those for data point samples: instead of data points, we have sets of diagrams, and implications are interpreted over diagrams rather than data points. Note, that for a classifier for a diagram sample, only formulas over the non-array variables of $\boldsymbol{P}$ and $Q^P \cup A^P \cup S^P$ are used.

We can now define the diagram sample constructed from a data point sample.

Definition 7. *Given a data point sample $\mathcal{S} = (X, C)$ and a parameter n, s.t. $|Q_a^P| = n$ for all arrays a in all predicates $\boldsymbol{P}$, we obtain a diagram sample using δ_n: $\delta_n(\mathcal{S}) = \left(\bigcup_{x \in X} \text{DIAGRAMS}^n(x), \bigcup_{c \in C} \mu_n(c) \right)$ where*

$$\mu_n(\top \to x) = \bigcup_{d \in \text{DIAGRAMS}^n(x)} \{\top \to d\}$$

$$\mu_n(x_1 \wedge \cdots \wedge x_n \to x_j) = \bigcup_{d_j \in \text{DIAGRAMS}^n(x_j)} \left\{ \bigwedge_{d \in \bigcup_{x_i \in \{x_1, \ldots, x_n\}} \text{DIAGRAMS}^n(x_i)} d \to d_j \right\}$$

$$\mu_n(x_1 \wedge \cdots \wedge x_n \to \bot) = \left\{ \bigwedge_{d \in \bigcup_{x_i \in \{x_1, \ldots, x_n\}} \text{DIAGRAMS}^n(x_i)} d \to \bot \right\}$$

Example 3. For instance, Fig. 2b shows the diagram sample derived from the data point sample in Fig. 2a.

Notice that even if the CHC system is linear, the obtained Horn implications will be nonlinear because of the presence of arrays.

Given a classifier J' for the sample $\mathcal{S}'_n := \delta_n(\mathcal{S})$ we can construct a classifier J for the data point sample $\mathcal{S}$ by quantifying the introduced quantifier variables, substituting the scalar variables with reads of the arrays with their respective quantifier variables (i.e., substituting a_k with $a[k]$), and replacing the introduced size variables with the sizes of their respective arrays (i.e., substituting l_a with $|a|$). Formally,

Definition 8. *Let J' be a classifier for $\delta_n(\mathcal{S})$, we define ξ such that for every uninterpreted predicate $\boldsymbol{P} \in \mathcal{P}$, $\xi(J')[\boldsymbol{P}] = \forall \vec{Q}_{a_1}, \ldots, \vec{Q}_{a_n}. \left(\bigwedge_{i=1}^{n} \bigwedge_{k \in \vec{Q}_{a_i}} 0 \le k < |a_i| \right) \implies J'[\boldsymbol{P}][a_k/a[k], l_a/|a|]_{a \in A^P}$ where the substitution is for all arrays of $\boldsymbol{P}$.*

We have the following theorem showing that the construction is correct allowing to obtain a classifier of the data point sample from a classifier of the diagram sample.

Theorem 1. *Let $\mathcal{S} = (X, C)$ be a consistent data point sample and let $\mathcal{S}'_n = \delta_n(\mathcal{S})$ be the corresponding diagram sample. If $\mathcal{S}'_n$ is consistent and J' is a classifier of $\mathcal{S}'_n$ then $\xi(J')$ is a classifier of $\mathcal{S}$.*

All the proofs are deferred to the full paper [12]. Notice that the existence of a classifier for $\mathcal{S}'_n$ depends on the number n of quantifier variables introduced per array. It is possible that sample $\mathcal{S}'_n$ has no classifier (because it is inconsistent), despite the existence of a classifier for $\mathcal{S}$, e.g. in the following.

Example 4. Figure 3a shows a data point sample $\mathcal{S}$, of the program in Fig. 1. It has a classifier but its corresponding diagram sample using only one quantifier per array (Fig. 3b) has no classifier (since it is inconsistent) as both $\langle \boldsymbol{I_0}, 2, \bot, 1, 0, 2 \rangle$ and $\langle \boldsymbol{I_0}, 2, \bot, 0, 1, 2 \rangle$ read as $\langle \boldsymbol{I_0}, N \mapsto 2, s \mapsto \bot, k_1 \mapsto 0, a_{k_1} \mapsto 1, l_a \mapsto 2 \rangle$, are forced to be satisfied by $\boldsymbol{I_0}$ while the implication that connects them to $\bot$ requires that at least one of them must not (In 3b, $\langle \boldsymbol{I_1}, 2, 1, \bot, 0, 0, 2 \rangle$ is read as $\langle \boldsymbol{I_1}, N \mapsto 2, i \mapsto 1, s \mapsto \bot, k_1 \mapsto 0, a_{k_1} \mapsto 0, l_a \mapsto 2 \rangle$).

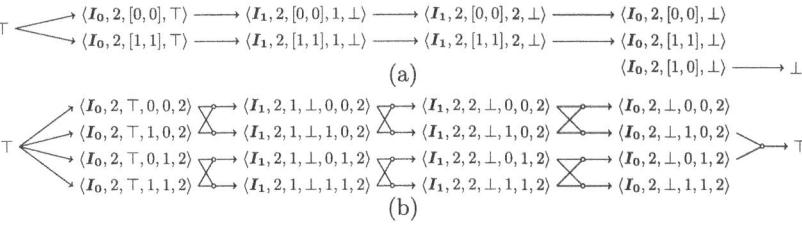

(a)

(b)

Fig. 3. (a) A data point sample which has a classifier and (b) its (non consistent) diagram sample using only one quantifier per array does not admit any classifier.

In such a situation, we increase n until the diagram sample is consistent, as the following theorem shows that there exists a sufficient number of quantifiers per array for which $\mathcal{S}'_n$ is consistent if $\mathcal{S}$ is.

Theorem 2. *Let $\mathcal{S} = (X, C)$ be a consistent data point sample. If, for every predicate $\boldsymbol{P}$ and for every array a in the domain of $\boldsymbol{P}$, we have $|Q_a^P| \geq |d[a]|$ for every diagram $d \in \textsc{Diagrams}^n(x)$ of every data point $x \in X$, then $\mathcal{S}'_n = \delta_n(\mathcal{S})$ is also consistent.*

The diagram sample size grows exponentially with respect to the number of introduced quantifier variables. This potential combinatorial explosion can be mitigated by observing that the number of diagrams in the diagram sample can be reduced by imposing a particular order on the quantifier variables of the same array $k_1, \ldots, k_n$, e.g. in example 1 we remove the third diagram. Therefore, the index guard of the property constructed using ξ is conjuncted with $k_1 \leq \cdots \leq k_n$ for the quantifier variables $k_1, \ldots, k_n$ of every array a. This is justified by $\forall k_1, k_2. \varphi(k_1, k_2)$ being equivalent to $\forall k_1, k_2. k_1 \leq k_2 \implies \varphi(k_1, k_2) \wedge \varphi(k_2, k_1)$

(can be generalized to more than 2 quantifiers). The diagram sample also depends on the size of the arrays in the data points, with a preference for arrays of smaller size. To take advantage of this, an optimization is applied by tuning the teacher to produce counterexamples with smaller arrays.

5   Decision Tree-Based Quantified Invariants Learner

Here, we present the algorithm of a decision-tree-based learner for synthesizing universally quantified properties using the diagramization primitives introduced earlier and explain how the attributes fed into the decision-tree learning algorithm are constructed.

The learner. We provide an instantiation of the learner of the Horn-ICE framework capable of synthesizing universally quantified properties in Fig. 4. The learner maintains a variable n representing the number of quantifiers to be used per array (line 1) and *Attributes* which maps predicates to a set of attributes (initialized in line 2). In each iteration, the learner is invoked with a given data point sample S and learns a solution for it starting from the current state parameters (n and *Attributes*) by constructing a diagram sample S'_n from S with n quantifiers per array (line 4). If this diagram sample is inconsistent, n is incremented until a constructed sample is consistent (loop in lines 5-6). Note that this consistency check can be performed in polynomial time since the classification constraints are expressed as Horn implications. Then, the learner checks if the attributes are sufficient to classify the sample S'. This is detected by calling SUFFICIENT (line 7). If this is not the case, more attributes are generated (line 8) until they are deemed sufficient (loop in lines 7-8). Once the diagram sample is consistent and the attributes are known to be sufficient, it learns a quantifier-free solution for S' using DECISION-TREE-HORN (line 9). Once the solution J' for S'_n is found, a solution J for S is then constructed from it and returned (line 10).

Input   : A data point sample S over predicates $\mathcal{P}$
Output: A candidate solution J of S
1 $n \leftarrow$ Initial number of quantifiers per array;
2 *Attributes* $\leftarrow$ Initial set of attributes;
3 **Proc** LEARNER.LEARN(S)
4 $\quad$ $S' \leftarrow \delta_n(S)$;
5 $\quad$ **while** $\neg CONSISTENT(S')$ **do**
6 $\quad\quad$ $|$ $n \leftarrow n + 1$; $S' \leftarrow \delta_n(S)$
7 $\quad$ **while** $\neg SUFFICIENT(Attributes, S')$ **do**
8 $\quad\quad$ $|$ *Attributes* $\leftarrow$ GENERATEATTRIBUTES(*Attributes*, S');
9 $\quad$ $J' \leftarrow$ DECISION-TREE-HORN(S', *Attributes*);
10 $\quad$ **return** $\xi(J')$;

Fig. 4. The quantified interpretations learner.

DECISION-TREE-HORN is straightforwardly adapted from Horn-ICE-DT [28] and applied on a diagram sample instead of a data point sample. If the attributes are sufficient, it constructs a quantifier-free formula for each predicate P by combining attributes in $Attributes[P]$ using the decision-tree learning algorithm. SUFFICIENT checks if the attributes are sufficient to construct classifying decisions trees for the sample by computing equivalence classes, as described in [34].

Attribute Discovery. In our approach, attributes for an uninterpreted predicate P are defined as atomic formulas over scalar variables associated with P. These variables include non-array variables appearing in the diagrams of P and variables drawn from the set $Q^P \cup A^P \cup S^P$. The attribute set for each predicate P is maintained by the mapping $Attributes$ (line 2). This set is constructed using a finite collection of attribute patterns, which fall into two broad categories:

- Enumerated patterns: These are syntactically defined templates (e.g., arithmetic constraints) that are instantiated using all possible combinations of the relevant scalar variables. Some patterns involve constants and are enumerated incrementally by increasing a bound k on the absolute values of constants. The types of constraints considered here include namely intervals ($\pm v \leq c$), upper bounds ($v_1 \leq v_2$), or octagons ($\pm v_1 \pm v_2 \leq c$) where v, v_1, v_2 range over the relevant scalar variables and $c \in \mathbb{Z}$ with $|c| \leq k$.
- Extracted patterns: These are patterns derived from the program itself, particularly from conditional and assignment statements and from specification constructs such as assume and assert statements. For example, from a program assignment like c[i] = a[i] - b[i];, we extract the pattern $v_1 = v_2 - v_3$, and instantiate it over the variable set $\mathcal{D}_{\mathbb{Z}}^P \cup Q^P \cup A^P \cup S^P$.

This dual strategy balances expressiveness and scalability: we restrict enumeration to tractable forms (interval and octagonal), while allowing more complex, potentially nonlinear constraints to be captured through pattern extraction from program logic. When the current attribute set in $Attributes$ is insufficient to classify the sample of diagrams, the function GENERATEATTRIBUTES is invoked. This function increases the constant bound k and re-instantiates the enumerated patterns with the extended constant range. Because the attribute space strictly increases with k, it follows that for a sufficiently large k, any pair of distinct diagrams can eventually be separated by an appropriate attribute.

6   Experiments

We have implemented our method in the tool TAPIS[3] (Tool for Array Program Invariant Synthesis) written in C++. It uses Clangas the frontend for parsing/type-checking admissible C programs, as well as Z3 [53] for checking satisfiability of SMT queries. Given a program, TAPIS generates the verification conditions of the program as CHCs with parametric-size arrays from its type-annotated AST. The CHC satisfiability problem is fed to the learning loop using

---

[3] An artifact that includes TAPIS and all the benchmarks is available online [13].

our learner described in Sect. 5 and Z3 as the teacher verifying the validity of the proposed solutions produced by the learner and translated to SMT queries. The teacher is tuned to find counterexamples with small array sizes. It discharges SMT queries to identify counterexamples with arrays bounded by L (initially set to 1). If no counterexample is found, the bound is removed for another check. At this point, either the formula is valid, or L is incremented, and the process repeats. Without this tuning, Z3 tends to generate counterexamples with excessively large array sizes (e.g., >1000), leading to large diagram samples during diagramization, which can cause timeouts.

We compare TAPIS with SPACER, ULTIMATE AUTOMIZER, FREQHORN, VAJRA, DIFFY, RAPID, PROPHIC3 and MONOCERA. SPACER [43] is a PDR-based CHC solver integrated in Z3 using QUIC3 [39] for universal quantifier support. UAUTOMIZER [40] is a program verification tool combining counterexample-guided abstraction refinement with trace abstraction. FREQHORN [29,30] is a syntax-guided synthesis CHC solver extended to synthesize quantified properties. VAJRA [18] implements a full-program induction technique to prove quantified properties of parametric size array-manipulating programs. DIFFY [19] improves VAJRA's full-program induction with difference invariants. RAPID [35] is a verification tool for array programs, specialized in inferring invariants with quantifier alternation using trace logic. PROPHIC3 [48] employs counterexample-guided abstraction refinement with prophecy variables to reduce array program verification to quantifier-free and array-free reasoning. PROPHIC3 is built on top of IC3IA [21]. MONOCERA [4] implements an instrumentation-based method and handles specifications involving aggregation and quantification. MONOCERA is built on top of TRICERA [27]. SPACER, FREQHORN, VAJRA, DIFFY, RAPID, PROPHIC3 and TAPIS are written in C++, while UAUTOMIZER is written in Java and MONOCERA is written in Scala.

TAPIS, UAUTOMIZER, VAJRA, DIFFY and MONOCERA support different subsets of C programs with parametric arrays. RAPID accepts programs in its own custom language. For our experimental comparisons, benchmark programs are manually translated into the language or program class accepted by each tool. SPACER and FREQHORN require CHC problems in the SMT-LIB format [6]. After generating the verification conditions of the program as CHCs, our tool exports them in SMT-LIB format for use with SPACER and FREQHORN. PROPHIC3 takes symbolic transition systems in the VMT format [22]. We use KRATOS2 [37] (and c2kratos.py) to convert C programs into the corresponding transition systems in the VMT format.

We compare the tools on two benchmark sets of 215 programs: The first set consists of all array programs from SV-COMP[4] except those involving dynamic memory, pointer arithmetic, and/or aggregations. These programs are modified by replacing fixed array sizes by parametric sizes. They are categorized into 84 safe programs and 37 unsafe ones. The first benchmark set (1) does not include recursive programs and (2) primarily consists of programs with sim-

---

[4] All C programs in the c/array-* directories of SV-Benchmarks https://gitlab.com/sosy-lab/benchmarking/sv-benchmarks.

ple iteration patterns, such as `for(i=...; i<...; i++)`. Therefore, we have constructed a second benchmark set that includes the lacking types of programs from the first set. This second benchmark, which we call *TAPIS-Bench*, includes sorting algorithms—specifically, insertion sort and quicksort, which are absent from the SV-COMP benchmark—as well as versions of SV-COMP sorting algorithms without partial annotations. Additionally, it includes other array algorithms with diverse looping patterns, such as `for(i=...; i<...; i++)`, `for(j=...; j>...; j--)`, and `for(i=..., j=...; j>i; i++, j--)`. These algorithms are implemented in both iterative and recursive versions. They are all safe and they are categorized into 49 *iterative* non-procedural programs, 37 (*rec*) (non-mutually) recursive procedures and 8 (*mut-rec*) with mutually recursive procedures. These programs are not partially annotated, and proving their safety requires synthesizing an invariant for each loop and a pre/post-condition for every procedure (except `main`). Programs with tail recursive procedures in the *rec* category have their iterative equivalents in the *iterative* category. Across the two benchmark sets, the number of procedures (including `main`) ranges from 1 to 3, while the number of loops varies between 1 and 9. The evaluation was carried out using a timeout of 300 s for each example on an 8 cores 3.2GHz CPU with 16 Go RAM.

We do not consider the CHC-COMP [25] benchmark set as they are over unbounded arrays and incompatible with our method because we require fixed-size array values in the counterexamples.

Table 1. Benchmark results.

Tool	SV-COMP		TAPIS-Bench			Total		
	safe (84)	unsafe (37)	iterative (49)	rec (37)	mut-rec (8)	safe (178)		all (215)
						iterative (133)	recursive (45)	
TAPIS	48	19	**47**	**37**	8	**95**	45	**159**
SPACER	50	30	37	14	1	87	15	132
PROPHIC3	**56**	32	30	-	-	86	-	118
MONOCERA	25	20	24	12	0	49	12	81
DIFFY	41	23	9	-	-	50	-	73
VAJRA	42	23	8	-	-	50	-	73
UAUTOMIZER	12	**34**	7	4	1	19	5	58
FREQHORN	44	2	11	-	-	55	-	57
RAPID	3	-	3	-	-	3	-	6

The results are shown in Table 1. The total columns aggregate results from SV-COMP and TAPIS-Bench. We did not include the total count of unsafe programs, as they correspond to the SV-COMP/unsafe column. The results show that overall, within the fixed timeout, among the 215 programs, TAPIS successfully solves 159 programs, surpassing SPACER by 27 programs and PROPHIC3 by 41 programs. TAPIS, despite not being specialized in proving unsafety, successfully solves 19 unsafe programs. The effectiveness of SPACER is based on its capacity to generalize the set of predecessors computed using model-based projection and interpolants. This task becomes particularly challenging in the presence of quantifiers, especially when dealing with non-linear CHC or those containing multiple uninterpreted predicates to infer. This is notably evident in the context of solving recursive programs. TAPIS solves 8 more iterative safe programs and 30 more recursive programs than SPACER. The reduction of array programs to a quantifier-free array-free problem enables PROPHIC3 to solve a significant number of safe programs. Moreover, its foundation on IC3IA, a PDR/IC3-based approach, enhances its effectiveness in solving unsafe programs, similar to SPACER, which is also built on PDR/IC3. Differently from SPACER, PROPHIC3 cannot solve programs with recursion. MONOCERA has successfully verified a total of 81 programs, including 12 recursive ones. Its effectiveness, however, strongly depends on the predefined instrumentation schema used for universal quantification. Consequently, its verification capabilities are largely confined to relatively simple array traversals, especially those in which the necessary invariants are closely aligned with the properties to be verified. Many safe programs from SV-COMP fall within the restrictive class accepted by VAJRA and DIFFY. However, these tools are limited in handling programs with different looping patterns from the *iterative* category of TAPIS-Bench. UAUTOMIZER is based on a model-checking approach and, although it can effectively solve instances with fixed-size arrays, it faces challenges in the parametric case. However, it is effective in verifying unsafe programs, solving the highest number of such cases. FREQHORN, on the other hand, only manages to solve 57 programs overall. It can not verify recursive programs as it only supports linear CHC. Additionally, FREQHORN encounters issues when handling programs with quantified preconditions/assumptions which it can not handle. The failure of FREQHORN to solve many other programs from the *iterative* category can be attributed to its range analysis. Notably, FREQHORN struggles in solving identical algorithms when implemented with different iterating patterns (like iterating from the end of the array or using two iterators simultaneously from both the beginning and end). RAPID, which specializes in inferring invariants with quantifier alternation, successfully solves only 6 programs, limited by its custom language's inability to represent programs with procedure calls or quantified preconditions. The tool's effectiveness hinges on the capability of its customized VAMPIRE [45] theorem prover to tackle the generated reasoning tasks, which pose significant challenges.

Handling parametric size arrays in program verification significantly enhances scalability compared to tools limited to fixed-size arrays. For instance, UAUTOMIZER solves the program `array-argmax-fwd` from the TAPIS-Bench with the array-size parameter N set to 2 in 83 s, and 191 s for N set to 4. However, the resolution time surpasses 36 min when N is increased to 5. Conversely, TAPIS demonstrates its efficiency by solving the same program in just 0.47 s for arbitrary N.

The benchmark sets include programs where the number of data points exceeds 300, with more than 1200 diagrams in the last iteration. These numbers can grow even larger for programs where our method timeouts. However, we do not report them explicitly, as they vary across executions due to Z3's non-determinism. TAPIS never exceeds two quantifier variables per array per predicate in the two benchmark sets. While some invariants may require only a single quantifier variable, our method occasionally necessitates more, as each quantifier variable can only be used to access a single array.

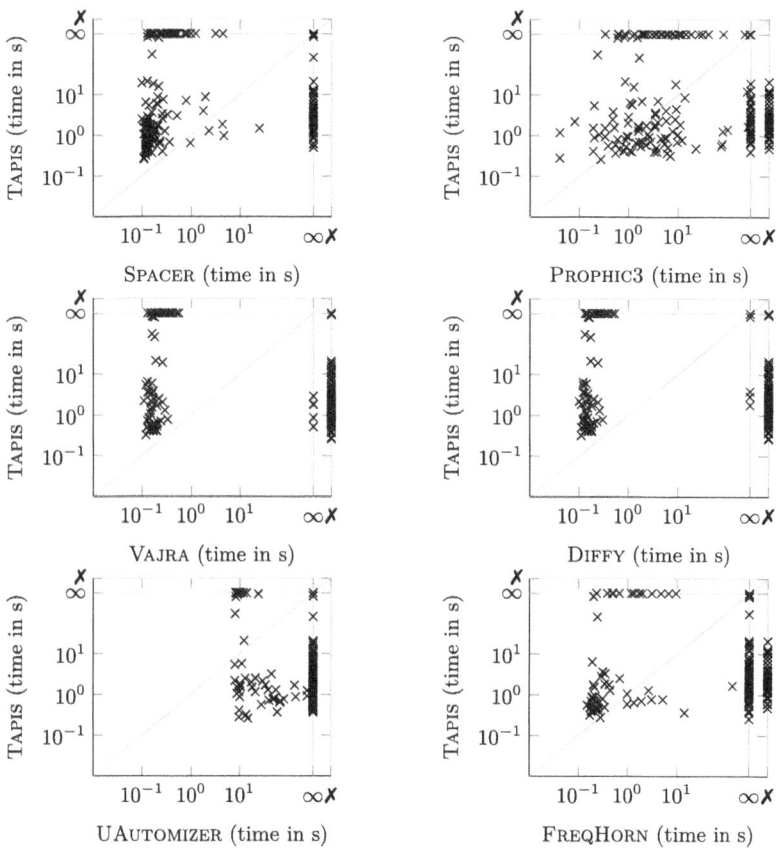

Fig. 5. Runtime of TAPIS vs. SPACER, PROPHIC3, VAJRA, DIFFY, UAUTOMIZER and FREQHORN.

The plots in Fig. 5 compare execution times of TAPIS with SPACER, PROPHIC3, VAJRA, DIFFY, UAUTOMIZER and FREQHORN. Instances at ∞ could not be solved by the tool in 300 s (timeout) and ✗ indicates instances that are not in the class of programs verifiable by the tool. They show that TAPIS has comparable execution time with PROPHIC3, FREQHORN and DIFFY, it is faster than UAUTOMIZER and is slightly slower than SPACER, VAJRA and DIFFY. Globally, the experiments show that TAPIS is able to verify a large class of programs with competitive execution times compared to the state-of-the-art.

7 Conclusion

We have proposed an efficient data-driven method for the verification of programs with arrays based on a powerful procedure for learning universally quantified loop invariants and procedure pre/post-conditions for array-manipulating programs, extending the Horn-ICE framework. The experimental results are encouraging. They show that our approach is efficient, solving globally more cases than existing tools on a significant benchmark, and that it is complementary to other approaches as it can deal with programs that could not be solved by state-of-the-art tools. For future work, several issues need to be addressed such as improving the generation of relevant attributes in decision-tree learning and handling quantifier alternation.

Acknowledgement. This work has been partially supported by ANR grant Ade-CoDS.

References

1. Alberti, F., Bruttomesso, R., Ghilardi, S., Ranise, S., Sharygina, N.: Lazy abstraction with interpolants for arrays. In: Bjørner, N., Voronkov, A. (eds.) LPAR 2012. LNCS, vol. 7180, pp. 46–61. Springer, Heidelberg (2012). https://doi.org/10.1007/978-3-642-28717-6_7
2. Alberti, F., Bruttomesso, R., Ghilardi, S., Ranise, S., Sharygina, N.: SAFARI: SMT-based abstraction for arrays with interpolants. In: Madhusudan, P., Seshia, S.A. (eds.) CAV 2012. LNCS, vol. 7358, pp. 679–685. Springer, Heidelberg (2012). https://doi.org/10.1007/978-3-642-31424-7_49
3. Alberti, F., Ghilardi, S., Sharygina, N.: Booster: an acceleration-based verification framework for array programs. In: Cassez, F., Raskin, J.-F. (eds.) ATVA 2014. LNCS, vol. 8837, pp. 18–23. Springer, Cham (2014). https://doi.org/10.1007/978-3-319-11936-6_2
4. Amilon, J., Esen, Z., Gurov, D., Lidström, C., Rümmer, P.: Automatic program instrumentation for automatic verification. In: Enea, C., Lal, A. (eds.) Computer Aided Verification - 35th International Conference, CAV 2023, Paris, France, 17-22 July 2023, Proceedings, Part III. LNCS, vol. 13966, pp. 281–304. Springer (2023). https://doi.org/10.1007/978-3-031-37709-9_14
5. Ball, T., Podelski, A., Rajamani, S.K.: Boolean and cartesian abstraction for model checking C programs. Int. J. Softw. Tools Technol. Transfer **5**(1), 49–58 (2003). https://doi.org/10.1007/s10009-002-0095-0
6. Barrett, C., Fontaine, P., Tinelli, C.: The satisfiability modulo theories library (SMT-LIB) (2016). https://smtlib.cs.uiowa.edu/
7. Barthe, G., Eilers, R., Georgiou, P., Gleiss, B., Kovács, L., Maffei, M.: Verifying Relational Properties using Trace Logic. In: Barrett, C.W., Yang, J. (eds.) 2019 Formal Methods in Computer Aided Design, FMCAD 2019, San Jose, CA, USA, 22-25 October 2019, pp. 170–178. IEEE (2019)

8. Beyer, D.: State of the Art in Software Verification and Witness Validation: SV-COMP 2024. In: Finkbeiner, B., Kovács, L. (eds.) Tools and Algorithms for the Construction and Analysis of Systems - 30th International Conference, TACAS 2024, Held as Part of the European Joint Conferences on Theory and Practice of Software, ETAPS 2024, Luxembourg City, Luxembourg, 6-11 April 2024, Proceedings, Part III. LNCS, vol. 14572, pp. 299–329. Springer (2024). https://doi.org/10.1007/978-3-031-57256-2_15

9. Beyer, D., Henzinger, T.A., Majumdar, R., Rybalchenko, A.: Invariant synthesis for combined theories. In: Cook, B., Podelski, A. (eds.) VMCAI 2007. LNCS, vol. 4349, pp. 378–394. Springer, Heidelberg (2007). https://doi.org/10.1007/978-3-540-69738-1_27

10. Bjørner, N., Gurfinkel, A., McMillan, K., Rybalchenko, A.: Horn clause solvers for program verification. In: Beklemishev, L.D., Blass, A., Dershowitz, N., Finkbeiner, B., Schulte, W. (eds.) Fields of Logic and Computation II. LNCS, vol. 9300, pp. 24–51. Springer, Cham (2015). https://doi.org/10.1007/978-3-319-23534-9_2

11. Bouajjani, A., Boutglay, W., Habermehl, P.: Data-driven Numerical Invariant Synthesis with Automatic Generation of Attributes. In: Shoham, S., Vizel, Y. (eds.) Computer Aided Verification - 34th International Conference, CAV 2022, Haifa, Israel, 7-10 August 2022, Proceedings, Part I. Lecture Notes in Computer Science, vol. 13371, pp. 282–303. Springer (2022). https://doi.org/10.1007/978-3-031-13185-1_14

12. Bouajjani, A., Boutglay, W., Habermehl, P.: Data-driven verification of procedural programs with integer arrays. CoRR abs/2505.15958 (2025)

13. Bouajjani, A., Boutglay, W.A., Habermehl, P.: Data-driven verification of procedural programs with integer arrays (Artifact) (2025). https://doi.org/10.5281/zenodo.15306371

14. Bradley, A.R.: SAT-based model checking without unrolling. In: Jhala, R., Schmidt, D. (eds.) VMCAI 2011. LNCS, vol. 6538, pp. 70–87. Springer, Heidelberg (2011). https://doi.org/10.1007/978-3-642-18275-4_7

15. Bradley, A.R., Manna, Z., Sipma, H.B.: What's decidable about arrays? In: Emerson, E.A., Namjoshi, K.S. (eds.) VMCAI 2006. LNCS, vol. 3855, pp. 427–442. Springer, Heidelberg (2005). https://doi.org/10.1007/11609773_28

16. Braine, J.: The Data-abstraction framework: abstracting unbounded data-structures in Horn clauses, the case of arrays. (La Méthode Data-abstraction: UNE technique d'abstraction de structures de données non-bornées dans des clauses de Horn, le cas des tableaux). Ph.D. thesis, University of Lyon, France (2022)

17. Braine, J., Gonnord, L., Monniaux, D.: Data abstraction: a general framework to handle program verification of data structures. In: Drăgoi, C., Mukherjee, S., Namjoshi, K. (eds.) SAS 2021. LNCS, vol. 12913, pp. 215–235. Springer, Cham (2021). https://doi.org/10.1007/978-3-030-88806-0_11

18. Chakraborty, S., Gupta, A., Unadkat, D.: Verifying array manipulating programs with full-program induction. In: TACAS 2020. LNCS, vol. 12078, pp. 22–39. Springer, Cham (2020). https://doi.org/10.1007/978-3-030-45190-5_2

19. Chakraborty, S., Gupta, A., Unadkat, D.: DIFFY: inductive reasoning of array programs using difference invariants. In: Silva, A., Leino, K. (eds.) CAV 2021. LNCS, vol. 12760, pp. 911–935. Springer, Cham (2021). https://doi.org/10.1007/978-3-030-81688-9_42

20. Champion, A., Kobayashi, N., Sato, R.: HoIce: an ICE-based non-linear horn clause solver. In: Ryu, S. (ed.) APLAS 2018. LNCS, vol. 11275, pp. 146–156. Springer, Cham (2018). https://doi.org/10.1007/978-3-030-02768-1_8

21. Cimatti, A., Griggio, A., Mover, S., Tonetta, S.: Infinite-state invariant checking with IC3 and predicate abstraction. Formal Methods Syst. Des. **49**(3), 190–218 (2016)

22. Cimatti, A., Griggio, A., Tonetta, S.: The VMT-LIB language and tools. In: Déharbe, D., Hyvärinen, A.E.J. (eds.) Proceedings of the 20th Internal Workshop on Satisfiability Modulo Theories co-located with the 11th International Joint Conference on Automated Reasoning (IJCAR 2022) part of the 8th Federated Logic Conference (FLoC 2022), Haifa, Israel, 11-12 August 2022. CEUR Workshop Proceedings, vol. 3185, pp. 80–89. CEUR-WS.org (2022)

23. Cousot, P., Cousot, R.: Abstract interpretation: a unified lattice model for static analysis of programs by construction or approximation of fixpoints. In: Graham, R.M., Harrison, M.A., Sethi, R. (eds.) Conference Record of the Fourth ACM Symposium on Principles of Programming Languages, Los Angeles, California, USA, January 1977, pp. 238–252. ACM (1977)

24. Cousot, P., Cousot, R., Logozzo, F.: A Parametric segmentation functor for fully automatic and scalable array content analysis. In: Ball, T., Sagiv, M. (eds.) Proceedings of the 38th ACM SIGPLAN-SIGACT Symposium on Principles of Programming Languages, POPL 2011, Austin, TX, USA, January 26-28, 2011, pp. 105–118. ACM (2011)

25. De Angelis, E., Vediramana Krishnan, H.G.: Competition of Solvers for Constrained Horn Clauses (CHC-COMP 2023). In: TOOLympics Challenge 2023: Updates, Results, Successes of the Formal-Methods Competitions, pp. 38–51. Springer-Verlag (2024). https://doi.org/10.1007/978-3-031-67695-6_2

26. Eén, N., Mishchenko, A., Brayton, R.K.: Efficient implementation of property directed reachability. In: Bjesse, P., Slobodová, A. (eds.) International Conference on Formal Methods in Computer-Aided Design, FMCAD 2011, Austin, TX, USA, October 30 - November 02, 2011, pp. 125–134. FMCAD Inc. (2011)

27. Esen, Z., Rümmer, P.: Tricera: Verifying C programs using the theory of heaps. In: Griggio, A., Rungta, N. (eds.) 22nd Formal Methods in Computer-Aided Design, FMCAD 2022, Trento, Italy, 17-21 October 2022, pp. 380–391. IEEE (2022)

28. Ezudheen, P., Neider, D., D'Souza, D., Garg, P., Madhusudan, P.: Horn-ICE learning for synthesizing invariants and contracts. Proc. ACM Program. Lang. **2**(OOPSLA), 131:1–131:25 (2018)

29. Fedyukovich, G., Prabhu, S., Madhukar, K., Gupta, A.: Solving constrained horn clauses using syntax and data. In: Bjørner, N.S., Gurfinkel, A. (eds.) 2018 Formal Methods in Computer Aided Design, FMCAD 2018, Austin, TX, USA, October 30 - November 2, 2018. pp. 1–9. IEEE (2018)

30. Fedyukovich, G., Prabhu, S., Madhukar, K., Gupta, A.: Quantified invariants via syntax-guided synthesis. In: Dillig, I., Tasiran, S. (eds.) CAV 2019. LNCS, vol. 11561, pp. 259–277. Springer, Cham (2019). https://doi.org/10.1007/978-3-030-25540-4_14

31. Gange, G., Navas, J.A., Schachte, P., Søndergaard, H., Stuckey, P.J.: Horn clauses as an intermediate representation for program analysis and transformation. Theory Pract. Log. Program. **15**(4–5), 526–542 (2015)

32. Garg, P., Löding, C., Madhusudan, P., Neider, D.: Learning universally quantified invariants of linear data structures. In: Sharygina, N., Veith, H. (eds.) CAV 2013. LNCS, vol. 8044, pp. 813–829. Springer, Heidelberg (2013). https://doi.org/10.1007/978-3-642-39799-8_57

33. Garg, P., Löding, C., Madhusudan, P., Neider, D.: ICE: A robust framework for learning invariants. In: Biere, A., Bloem, R. (eds.) CAV 2014. LNCS, vol. 8559, pp. 69–87. Springer, Cham (2014). https://doi.org/10.1007/978-3-319-08867-9_5

34. Garg, P., Neider, D., Madhusudan, P., Roth, D.: Learning invariants using decision trees and implication counterexamples. In: Bodík, R., Majumdar, R. (eds.) Proceedings of the 43rd Annual ACM SIGPLAN-SIGACT Symposium on Principles of Programming Languages, POPL 2016, St. Petersburg, FL, USA, 20 - 22 January 2016, pp. 499–512. ACM (2016)

35. Georgiou, P., Gleiss, B., Kovács, L.: Trace logic for inductive loop reasoning. In: 2020 Formal Methods in Computer Aided Design, FMCAD 2020, Haifa, Israel, 21-24 September 2020. pp. 255–263. IEEE (2020)

36. Graf, S., Saidi, H.: Construction of abstract state graphs with PVS. In: Grumberg, O. (ed.) CAV 1997. LNCS, vol. 1254, pp. 72–83. Springer, Heidelberg (1997). https://doi.org/10.1007/3-540-63166-6_10

37. Griggio, A., Jonáš, M.: Kratos2: An SMT-Based Model Checker for Imperative Programs. In: Enea, C., Lal, A. (eds.) Computer Aided Verification - 35th International Conference, CAV 2023, Paris, France, 17-22 July 2023, Proceedings, Part III. LNCS, vol. 13966, pp. 423–436. Springer (2023). https://doi.org/10.1007/978-3-031-37709-9_20

38. Gulwani, S., McCloskey, B., Tiwari, A.: Lifting abstract interpreters to quantified logical domains. In: Necula, G.C., Wadler, P. (eds.) Proceedings of the 35th ACM SIGPLAN-SIGACT Symposium on Principles of Programming Languages, POPL 2008, San Francisco, California, USA, 7-12 January 2008, pp. 235–246. ACM (2008)

39. Gurfinkel, A., Shoham, S., Vizel, Y.: Quantifiers on demand. In: Lahiri, S.K., Wang, C. (eds.) ATVA 2018. LNCS, vol. 11138, pp. 248–266. Springer, Cham (2018). https://doi.org/10.1007/978-3-030-01090-4_15

40. Heizmann, M., Hoenicke, J., Podelski, A.: Refinement of Trace Abstraction. In: Palsberg, J., Su, Z. (eds.) SAS 2009. LNCS, vol. 5673, pp. 69–85. Springer, Heidelberg (2009). https://doi.org/10.1007/978-3-642-03237-0_7

41. Karbyshev, A., Bjørner, N., Itzhaky, S., Rinetzky, N., Shoham, S.: Property-directed inference of universal invariants or proving their absence. In: Kroening, D., Păsăreanu, C.S. (eds.) CAV 2015. LNCS, vol. 9206, pp. 583–602. Springer, Cham (2015). https://doi.org/10.1007/978-3-319-21690-4_40

42. Koenig, J.R., Padon, O., Immerman, N., Aiken, A.: First-order quantified separators. In: Donaldson, A.F., Torlak, E. (eds.) Proceedings of the 41st ACM SIGPLAN International Conference on Programming Language Design and Implementation, PLDI 2020, London, UK, 15-20 June 2020, pp. 703–717. ACM (2020)

43. Komuravelli, A., Gurfinkel, A., Chaki, S.: SMT-based model checking for recursive programs. In: Biere, A., Bloem, R. (eds.) CAV 2014. LNCS, vol. 8559, pp. 17–34. Springer, Cham (2014). https://doi.org/10.1007/978-3-319-08867-9_2

44. Kong, S., Jung, Y., David, C., Wang, B.-Y., Yi, K.: Automatically inferring quantified loop invariants by algorithmic learning from simple templates. In: Ueda, K. (ed.) APLAS 2010. LNCS, vol. 6461, pp. 328–343. Springer, Heidelberg (2010). https://doi.org/10.1007/978-3-642-17164-2_23

45. Kovács, L., Voronkov, A.: First-order theorem proving and VAMPIRE. In: Sharygina, N., Veith, H. (eds.) CAV 2013. LNCS, vol. 8044, pp. 1–35. Springer, Heidelberg (2013). https://doi.org/10.1007/978-3-642-39799-8_1

46. Kumar, S., Sanyal, A., Venkatesh, R., Shah, P.: Property checking array programs using loop shrinking. In: Beyer, D., Huisman, M. (eds.) TACAS 2018. LNCS, vol. 10805, pp. 213–231. Springer, Cham (2018). https://doi.org/10.1007/978-3-319-89960-2_12

47. Lahiri, S.K., Bryant, R.E.: Constructing quantified invariants via predicate abstraction. In: Steffen, B., Levi, G. (eds.) VMCAI 2004. LNCS, vol. 2937, pp. 267–281. Springer, Heidelberg (2004). https://doi.org/10.1007/978-3-540-24622-0_22

48. Mann, M., Irfan, A., Griggio, A., Padon, O., Barrett, C.: Counterexample-guided prophecy for model checking modulo the theory of arrays. In: TACAS 2021. LNCS, vol. 12651, pp. 113–132. Springer, Cham (2021). https://doi.org/10.1007/978-3-030-72016-2_7

49. McMillan, K.L.: Lazy abstraction with interpolants. In: Ball, T., Jones, R.B. (eds.) CAV 2006. LNCS, vol. 4144, pp. 123–136. Springer, Heidelberg (2006). https://doi.org/10.1007/11817963_14

50. Miné, A.: The octagon abstract domain. High. Order Symb. Comput. **19**(1), 31–100 (2006)

51. Monniaux, D., Gonnord, L.: Cell morphing: from array programs to array-free horn clauses. In: Rival, X. (ed.) SAS 2016. LNCS, vol. 9837, pp. 361–382. Springer, Heidelberg (2016). https://doi.org/10.1007/978-3-662-53413-7_18

52. de Moura, L., Bjørner, N.: Deciding effectively propositional logic using DPLL and substitution sets. In: Armando, A., Baumgartner, P., Dowek, G. (eds.) IJCAR 2008. LNCS (LNAI), vol. 5195, pp. 410–425. Springer, Heidelberg (2008). https://doi.org/10.1007/978-3-540-71070-7_35

53. de Moura, L., Bjørner, N.: Z3: an efficient SMT solver. In: Ramakrishnan, C.R., Rehof, J. (eds.) TACAS 2008. LNCS, vol. 4963, pp. 337–340. Springer, Heidelberg (2008). https://doi.org/10.1007/978-3-540-78800-3_24

54. de Moura, L.M., Bjørner, N.S.: Generalized, efficient array decision procedures. In: Proceedings of 9th International Conference on Formal Methods in Computer-Aided Design, FMCAD 2009, 15-18 November 2009, Austin, Texas, USA, pp. 45–52. IEEE (2009)

55. Padhi, S., Millstein, T., Nori, A., Sharma, R.: Overfitting in synthesis: theory and practice. In: Dillig, I., Tasiran, S. (eds.) CAV 2019. LNCS, vol. 11561, pp. 315–334. Springer, Cham (2019). https://doi.org/10.1007/978-3-030-25540-4_17

56. Padhi, S., Sharma, R., Millstein, T.D.: Data-driven Precondition Inference with Learned Features. In: Krintz, C., Berger, E.D. (eds.) Proceedings of the 37th ACM SIGPLAN Conference on Programming Language Design and Implementation, PLDI 2016, Santa Barbara, CA, USA, June 13-17, 2016, pp. 42–56. ACM (2016)

57. Prabhu, S., D'Souza, D., Chakraborty, S., Venkatesh, R., Fedyukovich, G.: Weakest Precondition Inference for Non-Deterministic Linear Array Programs. In: Finkbeiner, B., Kovács, L. (eds.) Tools and Algorithms for the Construction and Analysis of Systems - 30th International Conference, TACAS 2024, Held as Part of the European Joint Conferences on Theory and Practice of Software, ETAPS 2024, Luxembourg City, Luxembourg, 6-11 April 2024, Proceedings, Part II. LNCS, vol. 14571, pp. 175–195. Springer (2024). https://doi.org/10.1007/978-3-031-57249-4_9

58. Rajkhowa, P., Lin, F.: Extending VIAP to handle array programs. In: Piskac, R., Rümmer, P. (eds.) VSTTE 2018. LNCS, vol. 11294, pp. 38–49. Springer, Cham (2018). https://doi.org/10.1007/978-3-030-03592-1_3

59. Redondi, G., Cimatti, A., Griggio, A., McMillan, K.L.: Invariant checking for SMT-based systems with quantifiers. ACM Trans. Comput. Log. **25**(4), 1–37 (2024)

Automated Parameterized Verification of a Railway Protection System with Dafny

Roberto Cavada[1], Alessandro Cimatti[1], Alberto Griggio[1],
Christian Lidström[1], Gianluca Redondi[1(✉)], Giuseppe Scaglione[2],
Matteo Tessi[2], and Dylan Trenti[1]

[1] Fondazione Bruno Kessler, Trento, Italy
{cavada,cimatti,griggio,clidstrom,gredondi,dtrenti}@fbk.eu
[2] RFI Rete Ferroviaria Italiana, Roma, Italy
{g.scaglione,m.tessi}@rfi.it

Abstract. In this paper we describe an industrial experience in the verification of the logic of a Railway Protection System (RPS). The RPS is designed within AIDA, a structured model-based design workflow and toolset. The RPS is written in a domain specific language amenable to signaling engineers, that is converted into Extended Finite State Machines (EFSM), and then into executable code. The RPS is parameterized, i.e., it can be applied, after configuration, in different operational scenarios. The logic is divided in classes, that are instantiated depending on the specific application. The verification challenge is to ensure that the required properties hold *for all possible instantiations*. We follow a verification approach based on the use of deductive methods, leveraging the Dafny framework. The AIDA environment is used to translate the RPS logic into Dafny, and also to *automatically generate* the contracts summarizing the methods implementing the guards and effects of the EFSM transitions. This approach greatly limits the need for human interaction with the underlying Dafny proof engine. In addition to domain specific optimizations, it results in an automated and efficient proof of the RPS properties.

1 Introduction

Railway infrastructure is increasingly controlled by way of software. For example, interlocking logics (IXLs) control the operation of trackside devices to create and deactivate routes within the stations while ensuring the safety and efficiency of train operations. These logics prevent conflicting train movements by coordinating the control of signals, switches, and other trackside components. The design, testing, and validation of such systems are inherently complex and require rigorous methodologies.

In this paper we describe an industrial experience in the verification of the logic of a Railway Protection System (RPS), that is intended to control the

R. Piskac and Z. Rakamarić (Eds.): CAV 2025, LNCS 15934, pp. 364–376, 2025.
https://doi.org/10.1007/978-3-031-98685-7_17

access to various areas of a railway station, hence ensuring the conditions for the safety of the workforce operating maintenance. The RPS enables remote access controls on portable devices by supporting the safe interaction with the station IXL. The RPS logic constitutes the critical core of the system and it is designed to be parameterized: it can be applied, after configuration, in different stations, operational maintenance scenarios, and protected areas.

The RPS logic has been designed within AIDA, a structured model-based design workflow and toolset [1,6]. In AIDA, a logic is written in a domain-specific language (DSL), effectively a controlled natural language amenable to signaling engineers. The DSL is automatically converted into SysML Extended Finite State Machines (EFSM), defining the interfaces of the methods and the related documentation. The SysML is in turn compiled into executable code. At instantiation time, the software is configured by filling data structures describing the class instances, the communication infrastructure and the operational context (e.g., the track layouts, the possible routes, the incompatibilities between them).

The challenge tackled in this paper is to verify that the properties required of the RPS hold *for all admissible configurations.* This objective is in sharp contrast with the seemingly easier task of verifying each instantiation independently. The reasons for this choice are twofold. First, the RPS – similarly to other railway systems under development – will be deployed on a large scale, in different stations. The development follows a *double V*-model [14], that separates the development of **generic**, i.e., parameterized, logics (corresponding to the first V, addressing domain-specific design aspects) from their instantiations and execution in specific railway stations, referred to as **configurations** (corresponding to the second V, focusing on product-specific design aspects). The verification of the parametric system is carried out as a step of the first V, hence shortening the application-specific deployment phase. Second, the instantiation of the generic application on a given configuration often results in a very large albeit finite state system, which turns out to be de facto unmanageable even for advanced verification techniques.

We base our approach on the use of deductive verification within the Dafny framework [16]. The AIDA environment is used to automatically translate the RPS logic into the Dafny language, leveraging several available high-level features (e.g., object-orientation, complex data types). The AIDA environment is also instrumented to *automatically generate the contracts* that describe the guards and effects of the EFSM transitions. Taking into account the generic nature of the application under verification, the contracts are expressed as first-order quantified statements. This approach dramatically reduces the typical burden on the verification engineer of manually writing the contracts, and greatly limits the need for human interaction with the underlying Dafny proof engine.

Overall, the approach results in an mostly automated proof of the RPS properties, and it is considered a cornerstone in verification within the company.

Related Approaches. This approach has several similarities with previous research in formal verification. In software product lines (e.g., [7,20]) the space of possible configurations is defined by a combination of discrete features, hence finite, while we deal with an infinite space of instantiations of unbounded size. Some works [20] leverage proof reuse in proving individual instantiations correct, instead of focusing on parameterized correctness of all the instantiations. Compared to some works on parameterized verification (e.g., [4]), we do not have the luxury of a highly symmetric network topology: the space of possible configurations has to be logically encoded into first-order logic. Our approach is similar to the proof-carrying code (PCC) paradigm [18]. To the best of our knowledge, however, PCC specializes on generating the correctness proof of the translation, and does not address functional properties of the generated code. Verification efforts are pervasive in the railways domain (see [9] for a survey). The Safecap project [12,13] is related, and the approach in [5,21] start from generic languages similar to the AIDA DSL. However, their focus is on the verification of the instantiated system, and not on the parameterized verification of a configurable logic for all possible instantiations.

Structure of the Paper. In Sect. 2 we present some background on Dafny. In Sect. 3 we describe the operational setting on the RPS and the AIDA framework. In Sect. 4 we describe the generated Dafny model and contracts for the RPS. In Sect. 5 we present the results of the verification. In Sect. 6 we draw some conclusions and outline the directions of future work.

2   The Dafny Framework

Dafny is a programming language and a static program verifier [16]. The Dafny language is imperative and sequential, with objective-oriented features. It also supports many modern programming language concepts, such as inductive data types, lambda expressions, and other functional programming idioms.

Dafny has integrated support for formally specifying the functional behavior of programs, most typically in the form of *method contracts*, which specify the behavior of methods in a compositional manner. As in many other specification languages (e.g., JML [8] and ACSL [2]), a method contract generally consists of a pair of *pre-* and *postconditions* (denoted by the keywords requires and ensures, respectively), as well as a *frame condition* (denoted by modifies). The precondition is an assertion that must hold at all call sites, and the postcondition must hold after the method has terminated. The frame condition specifies which memory locations are allowed to be updated by the method, facilitating the compositional verification. Other important specification constructs include *loop invariants* (which specify inductively the behavior of loops), and *block contracts* (which specify the behavior of code blocks within methods).

Furthermore, Dafny includes several ways to manually guide the proof engine. For example, code blocks within methods can be marked as *opaque*, meaning that when verifying the surrounding code, Dafny will ignore the code in the block, instead using only its (then necessary) block contract.

The Dafny verifier is a deductive verification tool, checking the correctness of implementations w.r.t. their specifications. Methods are verified compositionally, using their contracts in place of method bodies at call sites. Dafny programs are translated to the Boogie intermediate verification language [15], from which verification conditions (VCs) are generated based on the well-known *weakest precondition calculus* [10]. The VCs are then discharged using the automatic SMT-solver Z3 [17]. Correctness is reported per assertion, which includes both user-given specifications (e.g., postconditions and loop invariants), and implicit assertions arising from the data types and program structure.

While the generation and discharging of VCs is automatic, the user must supply all the necessary specifications, e.g., the contracts for all methods and the appropriate invariants for all loops. The required specifications are typically of a similar size to the implementations themselves, making this a time-consuming and labor-intensive task if done manually.

3   Operational Setting

3.1   The AIDA Framework

AIDA is a design toolset part of an integrated framework [1,3,6] that provides a comprehensive solution for modeling, testing, and generating executable implementations of railway control logics.

Railway engineers specify logics in the AIDA language, a Domain-Specific Language (DSL) specifically conceived to closely align with railway regulations and jargon. The AIDA DSL is a controlled natural language, with a well-defined syntax and semantics, with constructs to capture the structural and behavioral aspects of the logic being modeled. A logic consists of a set of classes (e.g., tracks and switches), each equipped with an Extended Finite State Machine (EFSM), characterized by a finite set of locations, local variables, and transitions, each defined via a guard and an effect. Each class is also equipped with generic lists of connected entities: for example, a route class may have lists of switches, track segments, semaphores, and so on. The guard of a transition is a Boolean combination of conditions that depend on the local state of the instance and the states of its connected entities. The effect is an imperative procedure with instructions including conditional assignments to local variables and iterations over the variables of the connected entities. The lists of connected entities remain generic during design; the DSL contains dedicated statements to support the quantification over them[1].

From the DSL, AIDA generates SysML models including state machines, class parameters and interfaces, and methods for guards and effects. From the SysML, AIDA generates executable code for the logic, both in C and in Python, and the documentation for the entire system. The process is shown in Fig. 1.

Running Example. To illustrate the design of a railway logic in AIDA, we consider a toy example involving three classes: Track, Signal, and Request. The Track

---

[1] In fact, the AIDA DSL replaces explicit quantification with syntactic sugar derived from the signaling engineers jargon.

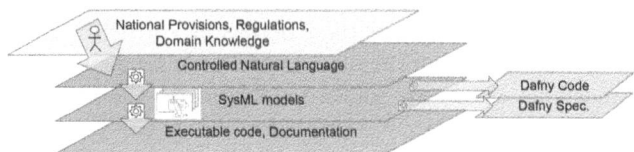

Fig. 1. Overview of the code generation process in AIDA, with extension for Dafny

class represents a railway track segment and has multiple locations, including Free and Authorize. The Signal class receives external inputs, which are stored in a variable input that can take values safe or unsafe. The Request class is used to model authorization requests and contains a boolean variable granted, which is initially set to **false**.

Each Track instance is associated with a sequence of connected Signal entities and a sequence of Request entities. A railway engineer would specify a transition for the Track class, moving it from the Free location to the Authorize location. The transition would be defined in the DSL by a guard "Check that for all Signal connected to this Track, the variable input is equal to safe", and an effect: "For all entities of Request connected to this Track, assign the variable granted to **true**".

3.2   The Railway Protection System

The Railway Protection System (RPS) logic, whose verification is the subject of this paper, is designed in the AIDA environment. The primary function of the RPS is to manage requests for accesses to the railway tracks, ensuring that maintenance operations are authorized only when a set of safety conditions are met, and to lock the protected area from movements and other hazards until it is released.

The authorization process begins when an operator submits a request to access a section of the railway for maintenance. The RPS evaluates the request by checking the logical state and various inputs from track circuits, signals, and other devices. If the system determines that the section is free – meaning no trains are detected, no conflicting requests are active, and all necessary safety conditions hold – then authorization is granted after locking the area. Otherwise, the request is denied. This process follows a structured sequence, with checks performed in a specific order according to railway regulations. To prevent unsafe operations, a minimum time interval must elapse between each step. If a timeout is reached, a request is automatically rejected.

The RPS logic consists of 12 classes, with a total of 150 variables and 238 possible transitions. The corresponding generated C code is made of about 11k LOC[2].

---

[2] Being that AIDA and the RPS are proprietary, we cannot disclose the actual RPS DSL nor the generated artifacts. Aside from being written in Italian, these descriptions are hard to interpret for non-experts.

```
method from_Free_to_Authorize_guard ()       method from_Free_to_Authorize_effect ()
returns (b : bool)                           modifies (set x | x in Auth)'granted
ensures (location = Free &&                  modifies location
    (forall c :: c in Signals               ensures location = Authorize
       ⟹ c.input = Safe)) ⟺ b {            ensures forall c :: c in CE ⟹
  b := location = Free;                         c.granted = if c in Requests
  for i:= 0 to |Signals|                         then true else old(c.granted) {
  invariant (location = Free &&                for i:= 0 to |Requests|
    (forall c :: c in Signals [.. i]         invariant forall c :: c in CE ⟹
       ⟹ c.input = Safe)) ⟺ b                  c.granted = (if c in Requests [.. i]
  {                                               then true else old(c.granted))
    if (Safe[i].input != Safe)               {
    {                                            Request[i].granted := true
      b := false; break;                      }
  } }                                         location := Authorize;
}                                           }
```

Fig. 2. Generated Dafny code for a guard and an effect of a single transition (Color figure online)

The development of the RPS was driven by a number of safety requirements, that can be expressed as quantified properties such as: *'For all instances of a railway track, if the track receives certain inputs from its connected components, then the RPS must never grant authorization'.*

4   Parameterized Verification of the RPS with Dafny

The verification of the RPS logic in Dafny is based on two phases. The first one (Sect. 4.1) is the automated generation of the Dafny code modeling the RPS implementation as well as the corresponding contracts. The second one (Sect. 4.2) is the automated contract-based verification with the Dafny prover.

4.1   Automatic Generation of Dafny Code

The code generation framework of AIDA was extended to support generation of Dafny code with embedded specifications, as shown in Fig. 1. The Dafny code generation process consists of two parallel steps: (1) generating the imperative part of the Dafny code, modeled after the existing generators, and (2) deriving the embedded contracts for the Dafny code directly from the specifications.

Generation of the Dafny Implementation. Each class in the RPS is represented by a Dafny class, which includes fields for the location, local variables, and connected entities of the class. Additionally, two methods are generated for each transition defined in the class: one for the guard and another for the effect. In both methods, checks or updates to connected entities of the class are handled through iteration. The Dafny implementations are generated from the SysML model using similar generation templates as the ones used for the C and Python code: this alignment provides a base of confidence that the Dafny code is consistent with the other existing implementations.

A transition of the running example from Sect. 3 would result in the Dafny code shown in black in Fig. 2.

Generation of the Dafny Contracts. Figure 2 also exemplifies the generation of the loop invariants (blue) and the top level contracts (red) for each method. The contracts embedded in the Dafny code are derived by mapping all the expressions that can be used in the DSL specifications into the contract language of Dafny, and then traversing the SysML model while generating the corresponding contracts. The automatic generation of embedded contracts required a significant extension to the existing toolchain.

Each method in the Dafny class is accompanied by an appropriate contract to ensure functional correctness. For guard methods, the contract is a postcondition that asserts that the boolean result aligns with the expressions in the guard. When conditions involve connected entities, the contracts include quantified expressions over the relevant sequences for validation of the conditions. Effect methods have contracts that include a frame condition, specifying which variables the method can update. The postconditions assert that these updates comply with the effect: for each variable modified by the effect, we generate a formula that states that the value after the transition is equal to an if-then-else term that captures the possible assignments. In case of connected entities, the terms are quantified over the appropriate sequences. Moreover, loop invariants are generated for both guard and effect methods to guarantee that quantified conditions are properly maintained over loops iterating over the connected entities.

The correctness of the generated contracts with respect to the implementation is checked by the Dafny verifier as part of the verification process.

```
predicate ExistanceTracksSignals ()
  reads Tracks
{
  (forall t :: (t in cfg.Tracks ⟹
    (exists s :: s in cfg.Signals && s in t.Signals )))
}

predicate NoUnsafeAccess ()
  reads Tracks
{
  (forall t :: (t in cfg.Tracks &&
    (exists s :: s in cfg.Signals && s in t.Signals && s.input = Unsafe ))
    ⟹ (forall r :: r in cfg.Requests && r in t.Requests ⟹ !r.granted ))
}
```

Fig. 3. An axiom and a safety property specified in Dafny. cfg is the object representing the (generic) configuration.

4.2   Verification of Global Properties

The properties to be proved are defined in a separate Dafny file, also containing a description of the space of possible configurations (each configuration consisting of a finite set of instances of each component type). The configuration space is defined by a set of formulae, or configuration axioms, that specify the possible configurations of the system, and which were derived via interaction with the railway experts. Figure 3 shows a configuration axiom and a property for the example system. The axiom states that all tracks in the configuration must have at least one associated signal, whereas the property requires that requests for tracks should not be granted if the input of some of the associated signals is unsafe.

First, the verification process checks that the generated Dafny code satisfies its contracts. This is done by running the Dafny verifier on the generated code. Then, the verified contracts of each method are used with the Dafny verifier to prove that the RPS satisfies global safety properties.

In order to prove that a property is an inductive invariant of the system, we prove that it is preserved by every transition of every class. The verification process focuses on individual transitions, checking one property at a time: first, we verify that the initial conditions of each class satisfy the safety properties. For this, we check with Dafny whether (the logical encoding of) the initial states imply the property. Next, for each transition, we check that the safety property is preserved by it. This is done by generating methods with preconditions asserting that the axioms and the contract of the guard hold, and that the safety property is true, before the transition. The postcondition asserts that the property remains true after the effect is applied.

In case the property is not inductive, it is possible for a verification expert to manually strengthen it and rerun the verification process.

4.3   Optimizations

Verifying quantified contracts can be challenging for the prover. Hence, we introduced two optimizations, both implemented in the code generator.

The first optimization is to introduce an opaque block around each loop. This ensures that, at the end of the loop, only the necessary quantified statements are used in the VCs when verifying the method. This enables the prover to verify each loop invariant separately, simplifying the verification in case a large amount of loops are generated in a single method.

The second optimization, called the *singleton optimization*, deals with lists of connected entities having length zero or one. This occurs because the DSL in AIDA restricts modeling connected components as sequences, forcing engineers to use those even when only a single entity was needed. In such cases, we replaced sequences with a single object of the appropriate type and modified the quantified statements to refer to the object instead of the sequence. If the list could be empty, we used a nullable type. The singleton optimization also led to a simplification of some of the safety properties.

5   Experimental Results

We ran Dafny ver. 4.9.1 on a cluster of machines with identical nodes (AMD EPYC 7413 24-Core Processor, 96 CPUs, 1.0 TB RAM). The timeout for each verification task was set to 48 h. Memory consumption was limited to 8 GB. The automatically generated Dafny code consists of 16987 lines, for a total of 409 methods, all annotated with contracts specifying their full behavior. The specifications make up 52% of the Dafny code (by character count). Due to the proprietary nature of both the tools and the underlying logic, we cannot share the artifacts used to generate the Dafny code from the railway engineers' specifications, nor the generated code itself. However, we have prepared a virtual machine containing a representative example: a simplified Dafny model that mimics key aspects of train station behavior. The VM can be accessed at https://doi.org/10.5281/zenodo.15430365.

Embedded Contracts. Table 1 summarizes the verification statistics for the contracts of the classes of the RPS. For each class, we report the total number of methods, and data w.r.t. each version of the code. In particular, we report the total times for successfully verified assertions, the total number of assertions generated (which increase with the singleton optimization in case of nullable types), the number of timeouts occurred (no errors where reported), and the number of total loops in the methods of the class (which may decrease with the singleton optimization). It might be worth noting that some classes have a large number of methods, but the verification time is low (e.g., Class 3), while other classes have a small number of methods, but the verification time is high (e.g., Class 2). The difference in time is partly explained by the complexity of the assertions: Class 2 has few but complex quantified assertions related to loops and a particularly intricate contract. Conversely, Class 3 has a larger number of simpler contracts. In general, the performance of the Dafny verifier is hard to predict. We did not encounter any dafny counterexamples in verifying the embedded contracts, as they are designed to be always correct: as already explained, they reflect the functional behavior of the EFSM transitions, and we incorporate loop invariants and assertions to guide the proof process in Dafny. In the basic encoding, we encountered timeouts in the last two classes. The introduction of opaque blocks leads to significant speed ups, but is only relevant for verifying the local contracts. The singleton optimization was applicable to 17 out of 26 lists, and the impact is also evident both on the verification of the embedded contracts and global safety properties. Breaking down the actual computation required in verification is non-trivial, due to the limited access provided by Dafny to the underlying prover. Interestingly, Dafny reports the resource consumption (RC), a deterministic metric used by Dafny to measure the amount of 'resources' used in a verification task. The average RC per verified assertion in the non-optimized version of the code is 1.12 M, compared to 629 K for the version after the singleton optimization.

Safety Properties. All 21 safety properties were successfully verified both with and without singleton optimization (the opaque blocks optimization is no longer relevant, as the embedded contracts are unchanged). The properties model the fact that certain critical locations (representing a granted authorization) cannot be reached if the inputs received from components were unsafe. The results are

Table 1. Verification statistics for embedded contracts

Class	Methods	Base				W/ Opaque				W/ Singleton			
		Time	Ass.	T/O	Loops	Time	Ass.	T/O	Loops	Time	Ass.	T/O	Loops
1	22	14 s	79	0	16	14 s	79	0	16	12 s	79	0	6
2	11	1,068 s	40	0	21	984 s	40	0	21	914 s	40	0	21
3	30	110 s	123	0	22	68 s	123	0	22	36 s	123	0	0
4	34	919 s	141	0	25	98 s	141	0	25	34 s	141	0	0
5	50	3,615 s	213	0	25	161 s	213	0	25	43 s	213	0	0
6	26	13 s	104	0	8	13 s	104	0	8	13 s	104	0	0
7	22	24 s	79	0	11	15 s	79	0	11	14 s	79	0	0
8	12	9 s	41	0	0	9 s	41	0	0	9 s	41	0	0
9	52	24 s	175	0	0	25 s	175	0	0	23 s	175	0	0
10	126	799 s	531	0	166	636 s	531	0	166	642 s	543	0	154
11	12	6,733 s	45	2	47	6,935 s	45	2	47	563 s	57	0	0
12	12	7,059 s	45	2	40	7,096 s	45	2	40	3,612 s	53	0	4

Table 2. Verification times for safety properties (non-inductive ones marked with *)

	Properties 1–7		Properties 8–14			Properties 15–21		
ID	Base	Opt.	ID	Base	Opt.	ID	Base	Opt.
1*	2,144 s	462 s	8	98 s	77 s	15	675 s	178 s
2	551 s	188 s	9	104 s	78 s	16*	1,394 s	542 s
3	7,150 s	193 s	10	101 s	68 s	17	3,278 s	189 s
4*	23,474 s	433 s	11	108 s	65 s	18	4,004 s	189 s
5	106 s	68 s	12	110 s	64 s	19*	61,265 s	547 s
6	101 s	77 s	13	110 s	63 s	20	558 s	188 s
7	101 s	77 s	14	9,385 s	180 s	21	513 s	558 s

shown in Table 2. The singleton optimization is highly effective: the average and peak RC decrease from 8.55M to 3.65M and from 1.74B to 193.7M, respectively.

Out of 21 properties, 17 were inductive. This is related to the (good) practice of 'defensive design', i.e., guards on transitions are typically strong enough to make safety properties inductive. The other 4, marked in Table 2, had to be manually strengthened with additional lemmas. In these cases, the original properties failed to be proven by Dafny, which reported a counterexample regarding a transition that could lead to the falsification of the property. From those transitions, we could identify that the locations from which such transitions were taken, were also not reachable under the same conditions appearing in the property. In other words, the critical locations were prevented from being entered under unsafe conditions by the guards of the preceeding locations. Therefore, we strengthened the properties by conjoining them with an additional lemma stating that such preceeding locations were also not reachable (under the same conditions as for the critical location). After the lemma addition, all properties were successfully verified. In conclusion, all the properties were successfully verified, and no bugs were found in the logic: we remark that the logic was in a mature state, on which debugging has been carried out already by other established methods such as interactive simulation and systematic testing.

6   Conclusion

We presented the parameterized verification of a Railway Protection System (RPS), a configurable application designed to ensure the safe access of maintenance workers to railway infrastructure,

using the Dafny framework. From the AIDA design environment, we automatically generate both the Dafny code and the corresponding contracts and annotations. The Dafny verification backend automatically proves the compliance of the code with its contracts and constructs an inductive proof of system-level properties. The ability to automatically generate a proof of the RPS properties *for all possible configurations* is considered a major result in formal verification within RFI, and promises to significantly improve the certification procedures required for the deployment in the large of such applications.

From the technical standpoint, the choice of Dafny was overall positive. The emphasis on functional properties rather than low-level implementation details has proved to be highly advantageous, allowing us to focus on expressing system behavior. On the other hand, Dafny provides users with limited debugging information and prevents direct interaction with the solver. We have also experienced some instability, as reported also in other works (e.g., [22]): for example, depending on the syntactic form of properties, verification times changed significantly.

There are two important aspects of the correctness of the approach that are outside the scope of this paper. The first is the correctness of the code generator itself, which is currently addressed through independent double generation and cross-checking. The second is that the generated Dafny code needs to be validated against the other existing code generation backends. We plan to compile the Dafny code in different languages and co-simulate it with the other executables.

In the future, we will work on extending this successful verification framework to other larger applications (e.g., full-fledged interlocking systems). To assist the verification process, we plan to develop better techniques for counterexample generation based on identifying minimal configurations sufficient to exhibit violations. Moreover, we plan to investigate slicing techniques, to reduce the size of the generated Dafny code, and approaches for automatically generating quantified inductive invariants, such as [11,19].

Disclosure of Interests. This work has been funded by project 8275061C5A, supported by RFI (Rete Ferroviaria Italiana).

References

1. Amendola, A., et al.: A model-based approach to the design, verification and deployment of railway interlocking system. In: Margaria, T., Steffen, B. (eds.) Leveraging Applications of Formal Methods, Verification and Validation: Applications, pp. 240–254. Springer International Publishing, Cham (2020)
2. Baudin, P., Filliâtre, J.C., Marché, C., Monate, B., Moy, Y., Prevosto, V.: ACSL: ANSI/ISO C Specification Language, http://frama-c.com/download/acsl.pdf
3. Becchi, A., Cimatti, A., Scaglione, G.: Testing the migration from analog to software-based railway interlocking systems. In: Gurfinkel, A., Ganesh, V. (eds.) Computer Aided Verification, pp. 219–232. Springer Nature Switzerland, Cham (2024)
4. Bloem, R., et al.: Decidability in parameterized verification. SIGACT News **47**(2), 53–64 (2016). https://doi.org/10.1145/2951860.2951873
5. Bonacchi, A., Fantechi, A., Bacherini, S., Tempestini, M.: Validation process for railway interlocking systems. Sci. Comput. Program. **128**, 2–21 (2016)
6. Cavada, R., Cimatti, A., Griggio, A., Susi, A.: A formal IDE for railways: research challenges. In: Masci, P., Bernardeschi, C., Graziani, P., Koddenbrock, M., Palmieri, M. (eds.) Software Engineering and Formal Methods. SEFM 2022 Collocated Workshops, pp. 107–115. Springer, Cham (2023)
7. Classen, A., Cordy, M., Heymans, P., Legay, A., Schobbens, P.: Formal semantics, modular specification, and symbolic verification of product-line behaviour. Sci. Comput. Program. **80**, 416–439 (2014)
8. Cok, D.R.: JML and OpenJML for Java 16. In: Proceedings of the 23rd ACM International Workshop on Formal Techniques for Java-like Programs, pp. 65–67. ACM, New York, NY, USA (2021). https://doi.org/10.1145/3464971.3468417
9. Ferrari, A., Beek, M.H.T.: Formal methods in railways: a systematic mapping study. ACM Comput. Surv. **55**(4) (2022). https://doi.org/10.1145/3520480
10. Floyd, R.W.: Assigning meanings to programs. Math. Aspects Comput. Sci. **19**, 19–32 (1967). https://doi.org/10.1007/978-94-011-1793-7_4
11. Frenkel, E., Chajed, T., Padon, O., Shoham, S.: Efficient implementation of an abstract domain of quantified first-order formulas. In: International Conference on Computer Aided Verification, pp. 86–108. Springer (2024)
12. Iliasov, A., Taylor, D., Laibinis, L., Romanovsky, A.: Formal verification of signalling programs with safecap. In: Gallina, B., Skavhaug, A., Bitsch, F. (eds.) Computer Safety, Reliability, and Security, pp. 91–106. Springer International Publishing, Cham (2018)
13. Iliasov, A., Taylor, D., Laibinis, L., Romanovsky, A.: Practical verification of railway signalling programs. IEEE Trans. Dependable Secure Comput. **20**(1), 695–707 (2023). https://doi.org/10.1109/TDSC.2022.3141555
14. Jin-hua, L., Qiong, L., Jing, L.: The w-model for testing software product lines. In: 2008 International Symposium on Computer Science and Computational Technology, vol. 1, pp. 690–693 (2008). https://api.semanticscholar.org/CorpusID: 16758610
15. Leino, K.R.M.: This is boogie 2, June 2008
16. Leino, K.R.M.: Dafny: an automatic program verifier for functional correctness. In: Clarke, E.M., Voronkov, A. (eds.) Logic for Programming, Artificial Intelligence, and Reasoning, pp. 348–370. Springer Berlin Heidelberg (2010). https://doi.org/10.1007/978-3-642-17511-4_20

17. de Moura, L., Bjørner, N.: Z3: An efficient smt solver. In: Ramakrishnan, C.R., Rehof, J. (eds.) Tools and Algorithms for the Construction and Analysis of Systems, pp. 337–340. Springer, Berlin, Heidelberg (2008). https://doi.org/10.1007/978-3-540-78800-3_24
18. Necula, G.C., Lee, P.: The design and implementation of a certifying compiler. In: PLDI, pp. 333–344. ACM (1998)
19. Redondi, G., Cimatti, A., Griggio, A., Mcmillan, K.L.: Invariant checking for smt-based systems with quantifiers. ACM Trans. Comput. Log. **25**(4), 1–37 (2024)
20. Thüm, T., Schaefer, I., Kuhlemann, M., Apel, S.: Proof composition for deductive verification of software product lines. In: ICST Workshops, pp. 270–277. IEEE Computer Society (2011)
21. Vu, L.H., Haxthausen, A.E., Peleska, J.: A domain-specific language for generic interlocking models and their properties. In: Fantechi, A., Lecomte, T., Romanovsky, A. (eds.) Reliability, Safety, and Security of Railway Systems. Modelling, Analysis, Verification, and Certification, pp. 99–115. Springer, Cham (2017)
22. Zhou, Y., Bosamiya, J., Takashima, Y., Li, J.G., Heule, M., Parno, B.: Mariposa: measuring SMT instability in automated program verification. In: Nadel, A., Rozier, K.Y. (eds.) Proceedings of the 23rd Conference on Formal Methods in Computer-Aided Design – FMCAD 2023, pp. 178–188. TU Wien Academic Press (2023)

Charon: An Analysis Framework for Rust

Son Ho[1][(✉)] , Guillaume Boisseau[2] , Lucas Franceschino[3], Yoann Prak[2],
Aymeric Fromherz[2] , and Jonathan Protzenko[4]

[1] Microsoft Azure Research, Cambridge, UK
`t-sonho@microsoft.com`
[2] Inria Paris, Paris, France
{`guillaume.boisseau,yoann.prak,`
`aymeric.fromherz`}`@inria.fr`
[3] Cryspen, Paris, France
`lucas@cryspen.com`
[4] Microsoft Azure Research, Seattle, USA
`protz@microsoft.com`

Abstract. With the explosion in popularity of the Rust programming
language, a wealth of tools have recently been developed to analyze, verify, and test Rust programs. Alas, the Rust ecosystem remains relatively
young, meaning that every one of these tools has had to re-implement
difficult, time-consuming machinery to interface with the Rust compiler
and its cargo build system, to hook into the Rust compiler's internal representation, and to expose an abstract syntax tree (AST) that is suitable
for analysis rather than optimized for efficiency.

We address this missing building block of the Rust ecosystem, and
propose Charon, an analysis framework for Rust. Charon acts as a swiss-
army knife for analyzing Rust programs, and deals with all of the tedium
above, providing clients with an AST that can serve as the foundation
of many analyses. We demonstrate the usefulness of Charon through
a series of case studies, ranging from a Rust verification framework
(Aeneas), a compiler from Rust to C (Eurydice), and a novel taint-
checker for cryptographic code. To drive the point home, we also re-
implement a popular existing analysis (Rudra), and show that it can be
replicated by leveraging the Charon framework.

Keywords: Static Analysis · Formal Verification · Rust

1 Introduction

Over the past decade, the Rust programming language has gained traction both
in academia and in industry [2,4,11,12,21,30,41], consistently ranking as the
most beloved language by developers [37,44] for the past 8 years. A large part
of this success stems from several key features of the language: Rust provides
both the high performance and low-level idioms commonly associated to C or
C++, as well as memory-safety by default thanks to its rich, borrow-based type
system. This makes Rust suitable for a wide range of applications: both Windows [42] and the Linux kernel [10] now support Rust, the latter marking the

R. Piskac and Z. Rakamarić (Eds.): CAV 2025, LNCS 15934, pp. 377–391, 2025.
https://doi.org/10.1007/978-3-031-98685-7_18

first time a language beyond C was ever approved for Linux. The safety guarantees of Rust are particularly appealing for security-critical systems: leading governments now also recommend Rust [27,43].

Of course, despite being safer than C or C++, Rust programs are not immune to bugs and vulnerabilities. Case in point, between January 1, 2024 and January 1, 2025, 137 security advisories against Rust crates were filed on RUSTSEC, a vulnerability database for the Rust ecosystem maintained by the Rust Secure Code working group. These vulnerabilities arose due to several reasons: runtime errors leading to aborted executions (`panic` in Rust, e.g., after an out-of-bounds array access), implementation or design flaws, or even memory vulnerabilities when using Rust's `unsafe` escape hatch, which allows the use of C-like, unchecked pointer operations when Rust's borrow-based type system is too restrictive.

To enforce those properties that fall outside the scope of Rust's borrow-checker, a vibrant ecosystem of static analyzers [4,26,30], model checkers [19,38] and deductive verification tools [2,3,11,12,17,18,21,25] has been proposed to reason about and analyze Rust programs. However, developing a new tool targeting Rust currently requires an important engineering effort to meaningfully and efficiently interact with the Rust compiler, `rustc`. First, Rust is a complex language, and just like many C analyses plug into `libclang`, Rust analyses need to plug into `rustc`: reimplementing a Rust frontend from scratch would be a significant undertaking. Unfortunately, the various intermediate representations (IRs) in `rustc` are optimized for speed and efficiency, not ease of consumption by analysis tools. Specifically, rather than provide a fully decorated abstract syntax tree (AST) with all available information, `rustc` instead exposes *queries* to, e.g., obtain the type of an expression only when needed. While this design allows for efficient incremental compilation, it makes life harder for tool authors, since they have to deal with additional levels of indirection, and information scattered across multiple global tables and IRs; this style of APIs requires deep knowledge of the compiler internals. Additionally, while sufficient for compilation, the information provided by the compiler sometimes needs to be expanded for analysis purposes. For instance, querying the trait solver only gives partial information about the trait instances used at a point in the code. Reconstructing this information requires additional, error-prone work from tool authors. Finally, the Rust compiler itself is not invoked in isolation; any non-trivial Rust project uses the Cargo build system, which collects dependencies, synthesizes `rustc` invocations with suitable library and include paths, and generally drives `rustc`. A realistic analysis tool must therefore hook itself onto Cargo, a non-trivial endeavor that again requires deep knowledge of Cargo and `rustc`.

To address these limitations, we present Charon, a Rust analysis framework providing an analysis-oriented interface to the Rust compiler and tooling, which allows tool authors to focus on the core of their analysis, rather than on mundane details of the Rust compiler internals. Our contributions are as follows. Through the development of a variety of tools atop `rustc`, we are of the opinion that many of MIR's design choices are unsuitable for analysis, such as: low-level pattern-matching that switches over the enumeration tag; encoding bounds-checks semantics with assertions; a precompiled representation of constants as byte arrays; and many more. Our first contribution is thus the design of ULLBC (Unstructured Low-Level Borrow Calculus) and LLBC (Low-Level Borrow Calculus), two dual views over Rust's internals that offer a control-flow graph (CFG) and an AST respectively. Both preserve the low-level MIR semantics of moves, copies, and explicit borrows and reborrows, but reconstruct constants, shallow pattern matches, and checked operations, so as to provide a semantically simple view of MIR that is suitable for further analyses. LLBC is obtained from ULLBC via a Relooper-like control-flow reconstruction [31,33]. Our second contribution is the engineering of Charon itself, and the accompanying ecosystem integration. We write a standalone, reusable infrastructure that allows a client to integrate cleanly with Cargo's build system. Furthermore, to expose clean ULLBC and LLBC representations (above), we hide away the complexity of querying the Rust compiler internals, thus offering *usable* APIs without the incidental complexity. Our third and final contribution is a series of case studies that not only informed the design of LLBC and ULLBC, but also served as an experimental validation of their wide-ranging applicability. We thus provide empirical evidence that the design choices of Charon are suitable for a wide variety of use-cases, supporting our claim that Charon is the swiss-army knife of Rust analysis.

Data-Availability. Charon is developed publicly on Github [8] and released under an open-source license; to foster reproducibility, an artifact is available online [9].

2   The Charon Framework

We now describe the architecture of both the Rust compiler and the Charon framework; Fig. 1 recaps the various steps in visual form.

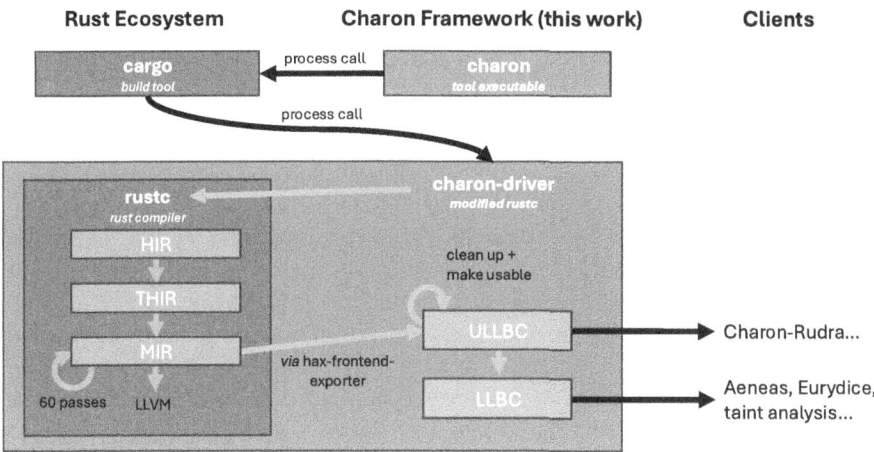

Fig. 1. Architectural diagram of the Charon framework, its relationship to the Rust compiler, and to consumers.

2.1   Background: The Rust Compiler

The Rust compiler pipeline relies on three ASTs after initial parsing: HIR ("High-level IR"), THIR ("Typed HIR"), and MIR ("Mid-level IR"). HIR is the result of expanding macros and resolving names. Then, in THIR, all type information is filled, and a first round of desugaring is performed, notably for reborrows, as well as automatic borrowing and dereferencing. At this stage, many fine points of semantics are still implicit: moves, copies, drops, control-flow of patterns, and many more, do not appear in this AST. MIR is where all these semantic details are made explicit. MIR is a CFG with a limited set of statements and terminators, making the semantics lower-level than in HIR and THIR. The Rust compiler features nearly 60 compilation passes [34] operating on the MIR AST – a standard design choice, where in practice several phases rely on different subsets of MIR. The final step, after all optimizations have been run on MIR, consists in emitting LLVM bitcode, then handing off the rest of the compilation pipeline to LLVM itself. We now review our design choices, and explain how they facilitate the task of developing analyses for Rust.

2.2   Charon Overview

As MIR explicits many fine points of semantics that make Rust hard to accurately model, it is a common starting point for verification tools [4,11,19,29], as well as compiler analyses such as borrow-checking, which were too error-prone on THIR [1,24]. In particular, moves, copies, (re)borrows, and drops, the core of Rust's semantics, are all explicit in MIR: for instance, let x = &mut y; f(x) becomes, in MIR, let x = &mut y; f(move &mut(*x)), so as to avoid invalidating x itself via a move-out. Other desugarings, e.g., for pattern-matches, which have a highly non-trivial semantics in THIR, also appear explicitly in MIR only. To allow a precise analysis of Rust programs, Charon therefore also operates on MIR.

ULLBC. From the MIR representation, Charon constructs a cleaned-up, decorated view called ULLBC. ULLBC is, like MIR, a CFG; but unlike MIR, ULLBC offers immediate contextual and semantic information (§2.4), and hides implementation-specific details (§2.5), while nevertheless exposing the entire Rust language. In particular, rather than have the user query rustc, e.g., to get type information about auxiliary data structures or to invoke the trait solver, ULLBC has all of this critical information directly attached to the CFG.

Additionally, ULLBC features several clean-up transformation passes that offer a more structured, semantic view of MIR. These passes, e.g., simplify pattern-matching operating on low-level representation to replace them with high-level, ML-style pattern matches; transform a variety of desugarings of panic! to a single, unified statement, or pack dynamic checks for integer overflows with their corresponding arithmetic operation to simplify the semantics. We envision that consumers of ULLBC ultimately will decide whether these passes are fit for them; for instance, specific consumers might want to see explicit assertions for checked operations. Should they do so, we envision a general API where they can manually choose which reconstruction passes to enable.

LLBC. Charon then applies a control-flow reconstruction algorithm on a ULLBC CFG to generate an LLBC AST that materializes structured loops and branching. In practice, we reverse-engineer `rustc`'s CFG construction, and recreate loops, conditionals, etc. out of the MIR basic blocks.

2.3   Limitations

Charon already supports a sizable subset of Rust, as evidenced by our evaluation (§3). However some less-central features are not supported, which consist of: dynamic trait dispatch (`dyn Trait`), generic associated types, trait aliases, async, and `impl`s in the return type of functions. To support analyzing crates that use such features, Charon was designed to be robust: a declaration that cannot be translated is marked as missing and the rest of the crate is translated as usual, resulting in a well-formed (if incomplete) (U)LLBC. So far, none of these missing features have impeded our case studies.

2.4   Reconstructing Compiler Information

When operating on `rustc`, retrieving information needed for program analysis is tricky for two reasons. First, instead of exposing a fully-decorated representation, `rustc` relies on (poorly documented) lazy computations to *query* the compiler internals. One thus has to skim through the code of `rustc` itself to find which auxiliary function, given a program node, may retrieve the desired information. Second, and more importantly, some information can be partial or missing.

As an example, consider a Rust trait method call; to analyze it, we first need the instance of the corresponding Rust *trait* with its proper arguments (i.e., the instantiated *impl*), and the reference to the method including its arguments (in case the method is generic). Unfortunately, the concrete trait instance is not directly available in MIR. For instance, consider the snippet of code below.

```
fn clone_vec<T>(v : &Vec<T>) -> Vec<T> where T:Clone { v.clone() }
```

When compiling this code, `rustc` needs to assess that it is legal to call the `clone` method by querying the trait solver to find an instance of `Clone` for `Vec<T>`; in our case, this instance is the standard library `Clone` implementation for `Vec<T : Clone>` (which we will call `CloneVec`), composed with the local instance `T : Clone` received as input (which we will call `CloneT`).

The trait solver only needs to assess that *there exists* such an instance. However, when analyzing this code, we might want more precise information, namely that `v.clone()` uses exactly the implementation `CloneVec` composed with `CloneT`. Unfortunately, retrieving this information from `rustc` requires several non-trivial steps. First, we need to query the trait solver; to do so, one needs to handle several complex `rustc` concepts, such as its internal representation for binders or late-bound and early-bound regions. Worse, the information given by the trait solver is partial. The solver only tells us that `v.clone()` uses `CloneVec` composed with *some* instance of `T : Clone` which can be derived from the local `where` clauses of the function, without exhibiting this derivation. Reconstructing it is a non-trivial problem in general especially as some trait instances can be implied by other trait clauses in the presence of super traits.

Another issue stems from the input parameters given to function and method calls. Consider the following snippet of code.

```
fn f<V>(x : V);
fn g<V>(x : V) { f::<V>(x); }
trait Trait<U> { fn f<V>(x : V); }
fn h<T,U,V>(x:V) where T:Trait<U> { (T as Trait<U>)::f::<V>(x) }
```

When retrieving the list of generic parameters received by the call to the *function* f in g, `rustc` gives us V. However, when querying the parameters given to the *method* call `Trait::f` in h, `rustc` concatenates the parameters of the trait instance with the parameters given to the method itself, yielding T (for the implicit `Self` parameter), U, and V, where one only expects V. This confusing behavior is error-prone; as a consequence Charon retrieves and truncates the list of parameters through the following boilerplate code, which itself relies on several (omitted) auxiliary helpers that we introduced for this purpose (in red).

```
let (gens, source) = // Is this a function or method call?
 if let Some(assoc) = tcx.opt_associated_item(id) { ... // Omitted
  match assoc.container { // Trait ``decl" or impl method call?
   AssocItemContainer::TraitContainer => { // Trait ``decl" method call
    let num_cont_gens = tcx.generics_of(cont_id).own_params.len();
    let impl_expr = self_clause_for_item(s, &assoc, gens).unwrap();
    let method_gens = &gens[num_cont_gens..];
    (method_gens.sinto(s), Some(impl_expr)) }
   AssocItemContainer::ImplContainer => { // Trait impl method call
    let cont_gens = tcx.generics_of(cont_id);
    let cont_gens = gens.truncate_to(tcx, cont_gens);
    let mut comb_trait_refs = solve_req_traits(s, cont_id, cont_gens);
    comb_trait_refs.extend(std::mem::take(&mut trait_refs));
    trait_refs = comb_trait_refs;
    (gens.sinto(s), None) } } } else {(gens.sinto(s), None)}; // Fun call
```

There are many other technicalities to consider leading to boilerplate code; for instance retrieving the trait instances alone requires more than 600 lines of code. In contrast, Charon provides the following LLBC datatype, which directly exposes all relevant trait information with the properly truncated list of parameters. The information includes support for type and trait polymorphism, at the heart of Rust's generic programming facilities, whose representation relies on a novel, abstract language of trait clauses, parent clauses, self types and trait bounds. For instance, a trait might refer to a top-level implementation but also a local where clause (e.g., T : Clone), or a trait implied by an associated type (e.g., IntoIterator contains an associated type IntoIter : Iterator<...>).

```
struct FnPtr {
  func: FunIdOrTraitMethodRef, // Function identifier
  generics: GenericArgs, }     // Generic parameters

enum FunIdOrTraitMethodRef {
  Fun(FunId),                            // Top-level function
  Trait(TraitRef, TraitItemName, ...), } // Trait method

struct TraitRef { kind: TraitRefKind, ... }
enum TraitRefKind {
  TraitImpl(TraitImplId, GenericArgs), // Top-level impl
  Clause(ClauseId),                    // Local where clause
  ItemClause(Box<TraitRefKind>, ...),  // Implied by assoc. type
```

Beyond trait resolution, Charon also reconstructs the control-flow by applying a Relooper-like algorithm, packages crates into easy-to-use structures, and optionally lifts trait associated types into type parameters while normalizing types which are known to be equal (because, e.g., of a clause T::Item = u32).

2.5 Simplifying Representations

To efficiently compile Rust projects, rustc stores program information in a variety of representations, sometimes too low-level to be directly usable for analysis purposes. In particular, in MIR, constants are already compiled, meaning that instead of a struct value, one may be simply provided with an array of bytes already laid out. For instance, let us describe the process of retrieving the high-level representation of an enumeration value which got compiled to a constant. We start from a mir::Const enumeration, over which we match, retrieving either a ty::Const if the constant is used in a type (e.g., it is used to instantiate a const generic), or a ConstValue if it doesn't. Diving further, from a ty::Const, in *one* case (there are many other cases) we get a ValTree; by using the type of the constant we learn that, as it is an abstract data type (ADT), we should call a specific rustc helper to turn it into a DestructuredConst (below), from which we can recursively reconstruct our enumeration value.

```
struct DestructuredConst<'tcx> {
  variant: Option<VariantIdx>,
  fields: &'tcx [ty::Const<'tcx>], }
```

The other cases are similarly complex, with many corner cases. In contrast, Charon provides the following unified, high-level representation for constants.

```
enum ConstantKind {
  Adt(Option<VariantId>, Vec<Constant>), ... /* Omitted */ }
struct Constant { value: ConstantKind, ty: Ty, }
```

Beyond constants, Charon also transforms other low-level representations into high-level, functional datatypes. This includes, e.g., simplifying the representation of names, reconstructing span information, removing the uses of the `Steal` datastructure which allows `rustc` to update definitions in-place through the compilation process at the cost of making some definitions unavailable if they are accessed in the wrong order, clarifying the use of binders by using an explicit and uniform treatment of parameters rather than, e.g., what `rustc` dubs "early bound" and "late bound" region variables, or simplifying trait implementations by turning default methods into regular methods.

2.6   A Primer of LLBC

In the previous sections we presented the transformations performed by Charon to make the MIR easier to consume; let us now have a quick overview of the output of Charon, focusing on LLBC. In LLBC, a crate (`TranslatedCrate`, below) contains a crate name, the content of the source files, and the declarations, where each declaration is uniquely identified (with an id of type, e.g., `TypeDeclId`). We also compute the groups of mutually recursive declarations (not shown here) that we order topologically, as it is useful both for analysis and compilation purposes.

```
struct TranslatedCrate {
  crate_name: String, files: Vector<FileId, File>,
  type_decls: Vector<TypeDeclId, TypeDecl>,
  fun_decls: Vector<FunDeclId, FunDecl>, ... /* omitted */ }
```

Function declarations and signatures are straightforward. Function declarations contain a unique identifier, metadata for the declaration name, the span and the attributes, a signature, and an optional body which is omitted if Charon encountered an error or if the function was marked with the `#[charon::opaque]` attribute. Signatures simply contain the generic parameters, the list of input types, and the output type.

```
struct FunDecl {                    struct FunSig {
  id: FunDeclId, meta: ItemMeta,      ... /* omitted */,
  signature: FunSig,                  generics: GenericParams,
  body: Result<Body, Opaque>,         inputs: Vec<Ty>,
  ... /* omitted */ }                 output: Ty, }
```

Importantly, the generic parameters (`GenericParams`) contain all the information related to the bound variables (region variables, type variables, etc.) and the `where` clauses in a simple and explicit format. This type gathers in one place information which otherwise requires querying `rustc` several times, and is uniformly used by all the definitions (functions, types, traits declarations, etc.).

```
struct GenericParams {
 regions: Vector<RegionId, RegionVar>,
 types: Vector<TypeVarId, TypeVar>,
 const_generics: Vector<ConstGenericVarId, ConstGenericVar>,
 trait_clauses: Vector<TraitClauseId, TraitClause>,   // T : Clone
 regions_outlive: Vec<RegionBinder<RegionOutlives>>,  // 'a : 'b
 types_outlive: Vec<RegionBinder<TypeOutlives>>,      // T : 'a
 trait_type_constraints: ..., }                       // T::Item = u32
```

The other definitions for types, traits, etc., all follow a similar model by containing a unique identifier, metadata (i.e., ItemMeta), generic parameters and an optional body; we omit them here. Skipping the definition of function bodies, which store the list of local variables as well as a block of statements, let us now look at the definition of LLBC statements. Statements have the expected kinds such as: assignments, function calls, returns, or loops. The Switch enumeration (not shown here) distinguishes if then elses, switches over integers, and matches over enumerations. We also preserve code spans and user comments.

```
enum StatementKind {              struct Statement {
  Assign(Place, Rvalue),            span: Span,
  Call(Call),                       kind: StatementKind,
  Abort(AbortKind), // panic        comments: Vec<String>, }
  Switch(Switch), Loop(Block),
  Return, Nop, Drop(Place),       struct Block {
  Break(usize), Continue(usize),    span: Span,
  ... /* omitted */ }               statements: Vec<Statement>, }
```

We finish this quick overview with function calls. We carefully wrote the Call structure so that all cases are grouped in one definition and are easy to distinguish. The important field is FnOperand, which covers the different cases, that is: the use of top-level functions, of trait methods, and of function pointers stored in local variables (e.g., because of the use of a anonymous functions).

```
struct Call {              struct FnPtr {
  func: FnOperand,           func: FunIdOrTraitMethodRef,
  args: Vec<Operand>,        generics: GenericArgs, }
  dest: Place, }
                           enum FunIdOrTraitMethodRef {
enum FnOperand {             Fun(FunId), // top-level function
  Regular(FnPtr),            TraitMethod(...), // trait method }
  Move(Place), }
```

When FnOperand refers to a top-level function or a trait method, it uses a FnPtr to bundle a function identifier with its generic arguments. When the FnPtr itself identifies a top-level function, it directly refers to its unique identifier, that we can use to, e.g., lookup the function definition from the TranslatedCrate shown above. When the FnPtr identifies a trait method call, it bundles a trait instance given by a `TraitRef` (see § 2.4) together with the name of the method which is actually called.

We end our overview of LLBC here. The omitted parts of the AST follow a similar logic: we attempt to factor out definitions, store as much information as we can, including metadata, and make all information explicit.

2.7   Interacting with the Rust Ecosystem

The build system of Rust, `cargo`, takes care of fetching dependencies, at the correct revision; building them recursively; and finally, invoking `rustc` on the current crate with include and library paths for all the required dependencies. To seamlessly integrate with existing Rust projects, Charon therefore directly reuses the `cargo` infrastructure.

To do so, the `charon` executable first invokes `cargo`; thanks to a special environment variable, `cargo` can be made to either call vanilla `rustc` (for dependency analysis), or our own variant of `rustc`, dubbed `charon-driver`, which we instrumented with additional hooks into the compiler. When run, `charon-driver` drives `rustc`, replacing the final compilation step to LLVM with a program analysis step, i.e., the Charon framework. From a user perspective, all these low-level implementation details are hidden, and all is needed is to call the `charon` executable from the root of the project (a.k.a. crate).

At the difference of `cargo build`, which produces an executable, calling `charon` produces a `.(u)llbc` file containing a straightforward serialization (currently in JSON) of the (U)LLBC. Any further analyses are to be performed off of those files; should the analysis itself be written in Rust, we engineered Charon so that the part that links against `rustc` lives in a separate crate from the rest (cleanups, CFG and AST representations, serialization and deserialization), avoiding the need for analysis tools to include the whole compiler toolchain.

We can also auto-generate (U)LLBC type declarations and deserializers for other languages beyond Rust; right now, we provide `charon-ml`, an OCaml library that can read back `.(u)llbc` files. OCaml is particularly-well suited to AST manipulations, and comes with convenient facilities, such as automatic visitors generation, which accelerates development of analysis tools. Adding support for a different language would only require a modicum of work.

2.8   Implementing Charon

Our toolchain is made up of two parts: the Charon codebase itself, totaling 18kLoC excluding whitespace and comments, which constructs (U)LLBC and performs additional transformation passes, and the hax-frontend-exporter crate, developed in collaboration with the hax project [6] and totaling 9kLoC, which directly consumes the output of `rustc` and performs most queries, as well as our constant simplification and custom trait resolution, which operate on both MIR and THIR, and which we believe to be useful independently of Charon as a companion to the compiler and thus package separately. The effort to write this whole project spanned 2 person-years.

3   Case Studies

Static Analyses. We implemented two static analyses on top of Charon. First, we ported Rudra, a recent static analyzer that detects potential memory safety issues in unsafe Rust programs by looking for a set of well-identified bug patterns [4], so that it uses Charon rather than directly interacting with `rustc`. The port took us one day of work, confirming in particular that ULLBC provides all the needed information; to validate the analysis, we reran our port of Rudra on versions of crates used in the original paper's evaluation. Several of these crates do not compile anymore, due to the Rust ecosystem evolving and the projects not including `.lock` files, but we were nevertheless able to analyze 6 of the most popular crates considered in the initial paper, reidentifying vulnerabilities previously discovered.

We also implemented an analyzer to detect constant-time violations in cryptographic code through a flow-, field-, and context-sensitive taint analysis operating on LLBC. We ran our analysis on implementations from several cryptographic crates, including RustCrypto [35], a port to safe Rust of the formally verified HACL* library [32,39], and an implementation of the recently standardized post-quantum ML-KEM [28] cryptographic primitive in the libcrux formally verified cryptographic library [22], totalling 88k LoC. Our taint analysis successfully shows that the considered implementations do not suffer from constant-time violations, as expected from widely-used or verified libraries, and rediscovers the KyberSlash timing attack in an earlier, unverified version of ML-KEM [5,7].

Deductive Verification. Aeneas [16,17] is a framework for verifying safe Rust programs, which works by generating models of Rust programs which are exported to a range of theorem provers. Aeneas relies on Charon to obtain the LLBC code and was the original motivation for implementing Charon; after realizing that many other tools were each reimplementing their own logic for interacting with `rustc`, we felt strongly that packaging and releasing a reusable component for this task would help current and future Rust tool authors.

Transpilation to C. Eurydice[1] is a transpiler from Rust to C whose main motivation is to allow engineers to develop new code in Rust while still being able to deliver C code for legacy reasons. It is made up of about 5000 lines of OCaml code, including whitespace and comments, and consumes Rust code via Charon, translating LLBC into C. Eurydice particularly benefits from LLBC's design: the AST is small and structured, simplifying the translation, and move and copy operations, needed to correctly match the C semantics, are explicit.

Running Charon over Charon. We mentioned earlier that Charon exposes its (U)LLBC representations in a reusable format for use in other languages; the Charon codebase itself maintains an OCaml library to manipulate this format, used in Eurydice and Aeneas. Rather than author this library manually, we instead run Charon on itself to inspect the definitions of the LLBC and ULLBC

---

[1] https://github.com/AeneasVerif/eurydice.

type definitions written in Rust, and output appropriate OCaml type definitions, visitors and deserializers to read and manipulate (U)LLBC.

Third-Party Uses of Charon. While Charon is still recent, we can already report third-party uses of the framework. The Kani model checker [19] recently added a backend that generates ULLBC so as to leverage Charon's control-flow reconstruction pass. RaRust [40] is a linear resource bound analysis for Rust which uses (an earlier version of) Charon to retrieve the LLBC of Rust programs.

4   Related Work

To the best of our knowledge, the only other project that aims to provide a view over MIR suitable for a variety of tooling is Stable-MIR [36]. Much like Charon, Stable-MIR has its own representation of important Rust constructs and features strongly-typed identifiers. Unlike Charon, Stable-MIR is not in itself a standalone `rustc` driver; it is instead closer to a toolkit to write `rustc` drivers. While it does considerably simplify the interactions with the compiler by providing appropriate methods instead of out-of-band queries and hiding away the driver details, it is by design a thin wrapper over compiler internals. As such, it does not intend to clean up or reconstruct the CFG into an AST nor does it try to simplify constants or resolve traits as we do. Both projects have similar goals however, and may fruitfully collaborate in the future.

The Charon project is collaborating with other projects that have similar needs. For instance, hax [6] and Charon share important components including their trait resolution system and simplification of constants, while Kani [19] recently added a backend that generates ULLBC so as to leverage Charon's control-flow reconstruction pass. Generally, for historical reasons, many of the existing verifiers and/or Rust-based tools maintain their own equivalent functionality, in a less general form and more tailored to their own needs. We hope for the adoption of Charon to continue and plan to formalize a roadmap, governance model, and community, to make sure more tools and clients can rely on Charon.

Beyond Rust, several efforts have proposed intermediate representations that other tools can either target or consume. Most famously, the LLVM toolchain provides a common substrate for many source languages, usable for many analyses [13–15,46]. While LLVM was initially intended as a compilation framework [20], it now includes building blocks that significantly reduce the effort needed to develop new analyses, e.g., libraries for dominators or alias analysis; we intend to provide similar features for (U)LLBC. Runtimes for managed languages like the JVM and the .NET CLR have been targeted by many languages (e.g., Scala, Clojure, F#), and have in turn created a foundation for general-purpose analyses (e.g., CLR Profiler, Abstract Interpretation for Java [23]). Similarly to Charon, Emscripten, the LLVM backend for WASM, also performs some cleanups to reconstruct structured control flow with the Relooper algorithm, so as to target the more structured semantics of WASM [45].

Acknowledgments. This work received funding from the France 2030 programs managed by the French National Research Agency under grant agreements ANR-22-PTCC-0001 and ANR-22-PETQ-0008 PQ-TLS.

References

1. Github tracking issue for bugs fixed by the MIR borrow checker or NLL. https://github.com/rust-lang/rust/issues/47366
2. Astrauskas, V., Müller, P., Poli, F., Summers, A.J.: Leveraging Rust types for modular specification and verification. In: Proceedings of the ACM SIGPLAN Conference on Object-Oriented Programming, Systems, Languages and Applications (OOPSLA) (2019)
3. Ayoun, S.É., Denis, X., Maksimović, P., Gardner, P.: A hybrid approach to semi-automated rust verification. arXiv preprint arXiv:2403.15122 (2024)
4. Bae, Y., Kim, Y., Askar, A., Lim, J., Kim, T.: Rudra: finding memory safety bugs in rust at the ecosystem scale. In: Proceedings of the ACM SIGOPS 28th Symposium on Operating Systems Principles, pp. 84–99 (2021)
5. Bernstein, D.J., et al.: KyberSlash: exploiting secret-dependent division timings in Kyber implementations. Cryptology ePrint Archive, Paper 2024/1049 (2024). https://eprint.iacr.org/2024/1049
6. Bhargavan, K., Franceschino, L., Hansen, L.L., Kiefer, F., Schneider-Bensch, J., Spitters, B.: Hax - enabling high assurance cryptographic software. RustVerify (2024). https://github.com/hacspec/hacspec.github.io/blob/master/RustVerify24.pdf
7. Bhargavan, K., Kiefer, F., Tamvada, G.: Verified ML-KEM (Kyber) in rust. https://cryspen.com/post/ml-kem-implementation/
8. Charon team: Charon github repository (2025). https://github.com/AeneasVerif/charon
9. Charon team: Charon zenodo artifact (2025). https://zenodo.org/records/15314373
10. Cook, K.: [GIT PULL] Rust introduction for v6.1-rc1. https://lore.kernel.org/lkml/202210010816.1317F2C@keescook/
11. Denis, X., Jourdan, J.H., Marché, C.: CREUSOT: a foundry for the deductive verification of rust programs. In: Riesco, A., Zhang, M. (eds.) International Conference on Formal Engineering Methods, pp. 90–105. Springer (2022). https://doi.org/10.1007/978-3-031-17244-1_6
12. Gäher, L., Sammler, M., Jung, R., Krebbers, R., Dreyer, D.: RefinedRust: a type system for high-assurance verification of Rust programs. Proc. ACM Programm. Lang. 8(PLDI), 1115–1139 (2024)
13. Grech, N., Georgiou, K., Pallister, J., Kerrison, S., Morse, J., Eder, K.: Static analysis of energy consumption for LLVM IR programs. In: Proceedings of the 18th International Workshop on Software and Compilers for Embedded Systems, pp. 12–21 (2015)
14. Gritti, F., et al.: HEAPSTER: analyzing the security of dynamic allocators for monolithic firmware images. In: Proceedings of the IEEE Symposium on Security & Privacy (S&P) (2022)
15. Gurfinkel, A., Navas, J.A.: Abstract interpretation of LLVM with a region-based memory model. In: Bloem, R., Dimitrova, R., Fan, C., Sharygina, N. (eds.) International Workshop on Numerical Software Verification, pp. 122–144. Springer (2021). https://doi.org/10.1007/978-3-030-95561-8_8

16. Ho, S., Fromherz, A., Protzenko, J.: Sound borrow-checking for rust via symbolic semantics. Proc. ACM Programm. Lang. **8**(ICFP), 426–454 (2024)
17. Ho, S., Protzenko, J.: Aeneas: rust verification by functional translation. Proc. ACM Programm. Lang. **6**(ICFP), 711–741 (2022). https://doi.org/10.1145/3547647
18. Jung, R., Jourdan, J.H., Krebbers, R., Dreyer, D.: RustBelt: securing the foundations of the Rust programming language. In: Proceedings of the ACM Symposium on Principles of Programming Languages (POPL) (2018)
19. Kani contributors: the Kani rust verified. https://github.com/model-checking/kani
20. Lattner, C., Adve, V.: LLVM: A compilation framework for lifelong program analysis & transformation. In: Proceedings of the International Symposium on Code Generation and Optimization (CGO) (2004)
21. Lattuada, A., et al.: Verus: verifying rust programs using linear ghost types. In: Proceedings of the ACM SIGPLAN Conference on Object-Oriented Programming, Systems, Languages and Applications (OOPSLA) (2023). https://doi.org/10.1145/3586037
22. libcrux contributors: libcrux - the formally verified crypto library. https://github.com/cryspen/libcrux/
23. Marx, S., Erdweg, S.: Abstract interpretation of java bytecode in sturdy. In: Proceedings of the 26th ACM International Workshop on Formal Techniques for Java-like Programs pp. 17–22 (2024)
24. Matsakis, Niko: Introducing MIR. https://blog.rust-lang.org/2016/04/19/MIR.html
25. Merigoux, D., Kiefer, F., Bhargavan, K.: HACSPEC: succinct, executable, verifiable specifications for high-assurance cryptography embedded in Rust. Technical report, Inria (2021). https://inria.hal.science/hal-03176482
26. Miri Contributors: Miri, an undefined behavior detection tool for rust. https://github.com/rust-lang/miri
27. National security agency: software memory safety (2022). https://media.defense.gov/2022/Nov/10/2003112742/-1/-1/0/CSI_SOFTWARE_MEMORY_SAFETY.PDF
28. NIST: Module-lattice-based key-encapsulation mechanism standard (2024). https://csrc.nist.gov/pubs/fips/203/final
29. Nitin, V., Mulhern, A., Arora, S., Ray, B.: Yuga: automatically detecting lifetime annotation bugs in the rust language (2023). https://arxiv.org/abs/2310.08507
30. Nitin, V., Mulhern, A., Arora, S., Ray, B.: Yuga: Automatically detecting lifetime annotation bugs in the rust language. IEEE Trans. Softw. Eng. **50**, 2602–2613 (2024)
31. Peterson, W.W., Kasami, T., Tokura, N.: On the capabilities of while, repeat, and exit statements. Commun. ACM **16**(8), 503–512 (1973)
32. Polubelova, M., et al.: HACLxN: verified generic SIMD crypto (for all your favourite platforms). In: Proceedings of the ACM Conference on Computer and Communications Security (CCS) (2020)
33. Ramsey, N.: Beyond Relooper: recursive translation of unstructured control flow to structured control flow (functional pearl). Proc. ACM Programm. Lang. **6**(ICFP), 1–22 (2022)
34. Rust compiler team: Implementors of MirPass (2024). https://doc.rust-lang.org/nightly/nightly-rustc/rustc_mir_transform/pass_manager/trait.MirPass.html#implementors
35. Rust Crypto maintainers: rust crypto - cryptographic algorithms written in pure rust. https://github.com/RustCrypto

36. Stable MIR contributors: stable MIR: define a compiler intermediate representation usable by external tools. https://github.com/rust-lang/project-stable-mir
37. StackOverflow: 2023 developer survey (2023). https://survey.stackoverflow.co/2023/#section-admired-and-desired-programming-scripting-and-markup-languages
38. Stateright Contributors: stateright, a model-checker for implementing distributed systems. https://github.com/stateright/stateright
39. The HACL* Team: a preliminary version of HACL* extracted to *safe* Rust. https://github.com/hacl-star/hacl-star/pull/918
40. The RaRust development team: Rarust (2025). https://github.com/Mepy/rarust-oopsla25
41. The register: in rust we trust: Microsoft azure CTO shuns C and C++ (2022). https://www.theregister.com/2022/09/20/rust_microsoft_c/
42. The Register: Microsoft is busy rewriting core Windows code in memory-safe Rust (2023). https://www.theregister.com/2023/04/27/microsoft_windows_rust/
43. The white house: back to the building blocks: a path toward secure and measurable software. https://www.whitehouse.gov/wp-content/uploads/2024/02/Final-ONCD-Technical-Report.pdf
44. Verdi, S.: Why rust is the most admired language among developers (2023). https://github.blog/2023-08-30-why-rust-is-the-most-admired-language-among-developers/
45. Zakai, A.: Emscripten: an LLVM-to-Javascript compiler. In: Proceedings of the ACM SIGPLAN Conference on Object-Oriented Programming, Systems, Languages and Applications (OOPSLA) (2011)
46. Zhao, J., Nagarakatte, S., Martin, M.M., Zdancewic, S.: Formalizing the LLVM intermediate representation for verified program transformations. In: Proceedings of the 39th Annual ACM SIGPLAN-SIGACT Symposium on Principles of Programming Languages, pp. 427–440 (2012)

Surfer — An Extensible Waveform Viewer

Frans Skarman[1]([📧])(ⓘ), Lucas Klemmer[2](ⓘ), Daniel Große[2](ⓘ),
Oscar Gustafsson[1](ⓘ), and Kevin Laeufer[3](ⓘ)

[1] Linköping University, Linköping, Sweden
frans.skarman@liu.se
[2] Johannes Kepler University Linz, Linz, Austria
[3] Cornell University, Ithaca, USA

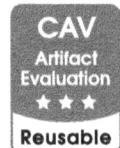

Abstract. The waveform viewer is one of the most important tools in a hardware engineer's toolbox. It is the main interface used to track down design bugs found by simulation or formal verification. In this paper, we present Surfer, a modern waveform viewer designed to integrate with the broader hardware design ecosystem. It supports translation from bit vectors to semantically meaningful values, integration with simulation and verification tools, and lays the groundwork for interactive simulation in the open-source ecosystem.

1 Introduction

The computer-aided verification community has excelled at generating ideas and tools that automatically find bugs in system designs. However, once a verification tool finds a trace that demonstrates the violation of an invariant, then the real work for the system engineer begins. They need to debug their system to understand what is going wrong and how the issue can be addressed. When the system in question is a digital hardware design for a microchip, the tool of choice for investigating the buggy behavior is the waveform viewer. A waveform viewer visualizes the signals in a circuit over time. We present Surfer, an open-source[1] waveform viewer that is designed from scratch to be easily customizable and embeddable. It has enabled new research around hardware description languages [19] and verification languages [15], been used to teach digital hardware debugging[2], and has been considered for integration in commercial hardware verification products.

A lot of engineering work goes into building a capable waveform viewer and thus, until recently, there has only been one fully-featured open-source implementation of such a tool. GTKWave [10] has been a staple in the teaching and open-source community for years. GTKWave supports many input formats and the development team has pioneered the FST format, the most-space efficient

---

[1] https://gitlab.com/surfer-project/surfer/.

[2] We are aware of classes at Cornell, MIT, UC Santa Cruz, and Johannes Kepler University Linz recommending Surfer to their students.

© The Author(s) 2025
R. Piskac and Z. Rakamarić (Eds.): CAV 2025, LNCS 15934, pp. 392–404, 2025.
https://doi.org/10.1007/978-3-031-98685-7_19

waveform format with an open specification. However, it has proven to be rather difficult to extend GTKWave beyond its current functionality, as the code base is quite old and appears to not have been written with extensibility in mind. Surfer was built from the ground up to address these issues and enable new workflows.

While existing waveform viewers excel at debugging hardware designs written in SystemVerilog or VHDL, there is no support for newer hardware languages like Chisel [3] or any of the other new languages [2,4,20,26]. These languages generally feature more advanced type systems, but none of that rich meta-data is considered when viewing signal traces in existing viewers. Without seeing the native representation of signal values, the user has a bad debugging experience. This is a significant hurdle that prevents these new languages from being adopted. Surfer addresses this problem by including an extensible translator system that can be used to decode semantically meaningful values from raw bit vectors debug traces (Sect. 2).

Besides new languages, there is also a need for a flexible waveform viewer that can be used to design new high-level debugging and analysis tools. Surfer can be easily embedded in web-applications and features a novel remote control protocol. It is also the first open-source viewer to support direct integration with a running simulator (Sect. 3). A custom waveform backend quickly loads VCD, FST or GHW files, taking advantage of modern multicore CPUs while minimizing user-facing latency and memory use and avoiding exploitable memory bugs (Sect. 4). Figure 1 shows a screenshot of the Surfer waveform viewer.

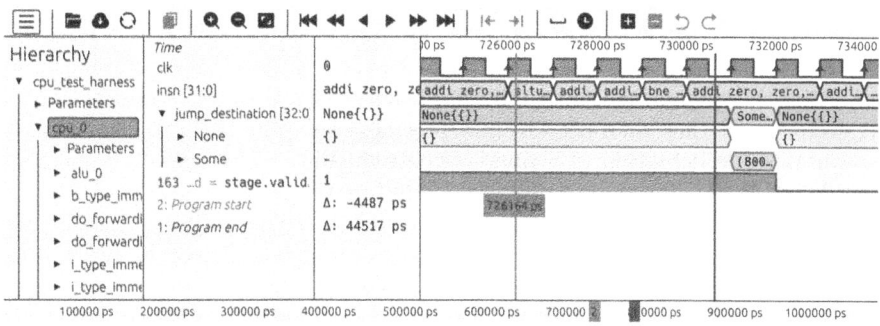

Fig. 1. A screenshot of the Surfer waveform viewer debugging a RISC-V core.

2   Extensible Translator System

An important job of a waveform viewer is to transform the raw bit vectors emitted by the simulator into semantically meaningful values. Most waveform viewers have some support for doing this for numeric values, for example allowing the user to show numbers as signed, unsigned, or hexadecimal versions. However, real-world signals often have much richer semantic meanings.

Currently, Surfer primarily deals with two sources of these semantically rich formats. The first are modern Hardware Description Language (HDLs) with more expressive type systems compared to VHDL and Verilog. Thus, effective debugging requires seeing native values directly rather than raw bit vectors. Surfer also has extensive support for decoding RISC-V, LA64, and MIPS instructions, which are commonly found in modern hardware designs. Less common formats which might be specific to a particular project can be incorporated with a custom translator written in Rust or Python.

2.1   Hardware Description Language Support

VHDL and SystemVerilog are not longer the only options available to designers when designing hardware. Chisel [3] has seen widespread adoption in industry for both design and verification [9]. VexRiscV perhaps the most commonly used soft core RISC-V is written in SpinalHDL [26], and several ASIC and FPGA designs are being developed in Amaranth [1], BlueSpec [21] and Clash [2]. In addition, there are a very large number of languages in development that have yet to see widespread adoption, including Spade [25] PipelineC, [11] Silice, [16] SUS [28], Filament [20], RHDL [4], and many others. Many of these languages include features that make traditional waveform viewers difficult to use. These languages often have more advanced type systems than Verilog. Most allow defining product types like structs or tuples. Some languages like Spade, SUS, and Clash and RHDL take this one step further and allow full algebraic data types.

Currently, most of these languages are compiled to Verilog or VHDL for synthesis and simulation, and in this process, the high-level type information is lost. After the simulation is done, the user is left with a trace that consists only of bit vectors that they then need to interpret. To exemplify this problem, Listing 2a contains the definition of a Spade type modelling commands to a memory module. A short simulation trace of a signal of this type is shown in Fig. 2b. Without knowledge of the internal representation of Spade types, this trace is very difficult to interpret, and even with such knowledge, doing the translation manually requires significant mental effort.

Surfer's translator system makes it possible for a specialized Spade translator to use type information to recover the hierarchical data from the signal. Figure 2c contains the same trace as Fig. 2b but with hierarchical translation enabled. From the root `translated` trace, the user quickly gets an overview of the full value of the signal. By expanding the individual field, it is easy to tell at a glance when commands are present, and which commands are active at different timestamps.

Translation is currently implemented for the Spade language as well as Chisel via the Tywaves [19] research project. There is also in progress work to support Clash [2] and RHDL [5] demonstrating that the translator system is extensible to support multiple different languages.

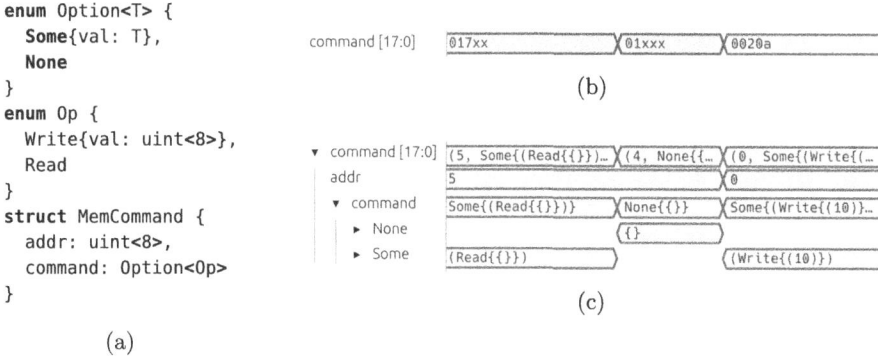

```
enum Option<T> {
  Some{val: T},
  None
}
enum Op {
  Write{val: uint<8>},
  Read
}
struct MemCommand {
  addr: uint<8>,
  command: Option<Op>
}
```

(a)

Fig. 2. Example of a Spade type (a), a trace with a raw bit vector of that type (b), and a trace with a translated version of the same signal.

2.2 Instruction Decoding

Another common source of semantically meaningful values are processor instructions. To help work with these, Surfer includes a dedicated system for decoding instructions[3]. This system lets users define the structure of their instruction set in a TOML based configuration format. Surfer ships with definitions for all officially ratified RISC-V instructions, LongArch64, and MIPS instructions and can thus translate them out of the box.

2.3 Project-Specific Python Translators

In addition to supporting translation of common formats like instructions and HDL types, Surfer also features support for user defined custom translators, allowing easy translation of project-specific signal formats. Currently, users can write simple python scripts to implement their translations. In the future, we will explore the use of plugins via WebAssembly to allow faster translators written in any language. WebAssembly being sandboxed also means that these user plugins can be distributed safely without the risk of malicious code affecting the viewer or the system it is running on.

3 Integrating Surfer with the EDA Ecosystem

The open-source EDA ecosystem has many excellent tools that do one particular job very well. However, compared to commercial EDA tools, there is significantly less integration. Most integration consists of workflow specific one-off scripts, which presents a hurdle to adopting these tools. Recently, Visual Studio Code has become a hub for more integrated HDL workflows, with plugins such as

---

[3] https://github.com/ics-jku/instruction-decoder.

YoWASP [8] and TerosHDL [27] enabling synthesis and simulation without leaving the editor. However, neither approach integrates a waveform viewer, instead relying on the user to install GTKWave manually on their local machine.

Besides Integrated Development Environment (IDEs) for developers, many online teaching tools also rely on simulation and need some sort of waveform viewer to show simulation results to students. Projects like TinyTapeout [29] require users to use locally installed waveform viewers in an otherwise fully in-browser flow, presenting a hurdle for novices. Platforms like MakerChip [22] and quicksilicon [6] have used ad-hoc waveform viewers that are built specifically for running in the web. However, since there are limited resources available for building such a tool, those end up being very basic compared to the tools used in real design work. Being able to leverage a solid waveform viewer like Surfer would make these tools more effective.

Hardware verification tools can often benefit from having an integrated waveform viewer that is powerful and easy to use. For example, Silogy [24] and LubisEDA [18] run simulations or formal checkers in cloud infrastructure and then generate a web-based report. Showing these results in an interactive waveform viewer right on the web browser is much more convenient than requiring users to download VCD files for offline viewing as it accelerates the process, and doesn't require having a waveform viewer available on the machine on which the results are viewed. A deep integration of a waveform viewer would allow users to seamlessly navigate from the textual report to the signals and time at which the problem manifests, significantly reducing setup costs for debugging.

3.1   Embedding Surfer in Web Applications and Visual Studio Code

A common thread across these three integration areas is the heavy reliance on web technology. Visual Studio Code is a Chromium-based editor, and both teaching tools and cloud compute reports are usually built on web technology. Web integration requires the tool to either be built in JavaScript, or be compiled to WebAssembly (WASM) a portable compilation target for programming languages which allows it to be run in any web-based client. Surfer is written in Rust and compiled to WASM, which allows web-integration without sacrificing performance in native builds. Besides embedding, this also allows Surfer to be used directly in a web browser without an installation.

3.2   Controlling Surfer from a Third Party Tool

Web technology solves many problems associated with *embedding* the waveform viewer into a bigger application. However, we also need to be able to *control* the viewer from the application Surfer is embedded into. In debugging and verification tools, this can be used to point the user to specific problematic signals and time stamps. As Surfer supports drawing annotations, it can also be used to show more complex things like relationships between values of different signals. Teaching tools benefit in similar ways, being able to control the viewer to highlight interesting timestamps or signals can be very beneficial.

We developed a Waveform Control Protocol (WCP) that can be used to control a waveform viewer (server) from an embedding application (client). The protocol is heavily inspired by the Language Server Protocol (LSP) which is used to build language and editor-agnostic IDEs. Like the LSP, the WCP defines a set of JSON commands and responses that a client can send to control the waveform viewer, or query it about the currently viewed signals. Being JSON-based means that the protocol can be both language, and transport agnostic. Like the LSP, the WCP can be sent over network sockets, standard IO, or in the case of web integration, by passing full JSON messages between web views. While Surfer is the first implementor of the protocol, the intention is to allow other waveform viewer-like projects to also adopt this protocol to allow broader interoperability between debugging tools.

Besides the limited but stable WCP interface, Surfer also exposes a much lower level, unstable API to integrators. The reactive architecture of Surfer, allows external programs to directly inject messages to control Surfer in a manner very similar to how Surfer reacts to mouse and keyboard commands from the user. In Surfer, the callback function that reacts to a user pressing a particular button does not directly modify program state, but instead generates a message, for example, `AddSignal(...)` . This message is added to a central queue which is processed at the end of each frame. All state changes go through this system, whether they are user interactions like adding signals, events like `WaveformDataLoaded(...)` or messages injected by external integration. This brings huge advantages for integrators because the source of these messages is irrelevant to the program, and messages can easily be serialized in a way that simple function calls cannot. This means that the messages can be injected from an integrator via any source that can communicate serialized strings such as sockets, standard input, or JavaScript. Figure 3 illustrates this architecture, which also powers Surfer's VSCode-inspired command palette and snapshot testing infrastructure.

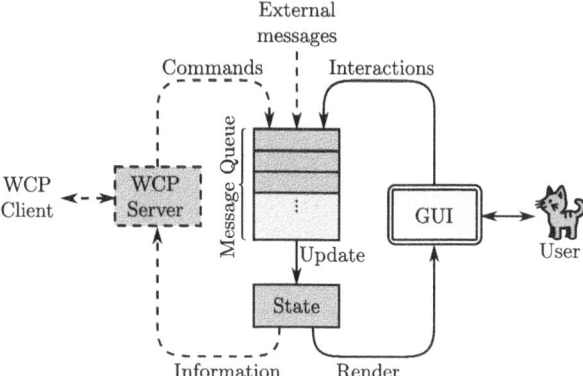

Fig. 3. The Surfer architecture. Solid lines denote the main program. Interfaces used by external integrators are dashed.

3.3   Interactive Simulation

In the open-source ecosystem, simulation is currently exclusively done in batch mode. This means that the simulator runs a test bench to completion while generating a signal trace. Only after the simulation is done, the trace is loaded into a waveform viewer for inspection. Alternatively, in an interactive workflow, the simulation is controlled through a GUI. The user can run the simulation for a few clock cycles, inspect the result right away, change some signal values and continue simulation. Previously, interactive simulation was only available with commercial tools, benefiting from tight integration between simulator and waveform viewer. In the open-source space, the user is generally free to mix and match their choice of simulator with their choice of waveform viewer, making it more difficult to support interactive simulation for the large number of possible combinations.

Instead of a tight integration between one company's simulator and viewer, the open-source approach requires standardizing a common interface. Recently, the CXXRTL Debug Server Protocol (CDSP) [7] has been introduced to support exactly this use-case. Like the WCP discussed previously, it is a JSON-based protocol that allows a client (waveform viewer) to connect to a server (simulator) to receive signal values and control the simulation. Surfer is the first waveform viewer to support this new open standard. Based on this support, we are currently integrating Surfer with the RTL-Debugger project which allows for an integrated simulation, debugging, and development environment[4].

While WCP and the CDSP are similar in implementation, their use case is quite different, which is why a both protocols are needed. CDSP is intended for communication between a simulator and a waveform viewer, with the simulator acting as the host. Through it, the waveform viewer can control the simulation, receive information about events such as failed assertions, and query the simulator for waveform data. WCP on the other hand has the waveform viewer acting as the host, and allows clients to control what the waveform viewer is currently showing. The primary use case is to allow clients integrating surfer to add signals of interest, show the user specific timestamps and draw additional information on the waveform to highlight important details. WCP also includes facilities for adding additional user interactions to the viewer, for example, allowing the user to jump to the source code location of a signal in their text editor.

3.4   Tools Integrating Surfer

We are aware of several tools that take advantage of the fact that Surfer is easy to embed and control, as described in the previous sections. The WSVA system [12] evaluates SystemVerilog Assertions on waveform traces and uses Surfer to visualize failed assertions by creating coursers pointing out the start and end of the property through the WCP interface. The WAL language runtime integrates Surfer to display results of waveform analysis programs written in

---

[4] https://github.com/amaranth-lang/rtl-debugger/pull/5.

WAL [13–15]. It uses CXXRTL Debug Protocol [7] to inject analysis results as signals into Surfer.

Several commercial and open-source projects have already integrated Surfer as part of their projects. Two commercial verification platforms LubisEDA [18] and Silogy [24] have successfully used Surfer as an embedded waveform viewer to show waveforms that reproduce errors found during verification. Currently, the products are still in the prototype phase, and have not been released to the public.

Surfer has also seen adoption in numerous teaching tools. An example of this is SonicRV[5], a tool which lets students explore how processors execute each instruction. The primary interface in it shows the current state of the processor graphically and the user can step through execution, or click on individual instructions to see how they flow through the pipeline. The Surfer integration lets the user dive deeper to see the full state of the processor using the remote control functionality. This view also allows for interacting with instructions and seeing the relevant signals and timestamps in the waveform viewer.

Since the primary means of debugging digital designs is the waveform viewer, teaching platforms that teach HDLs also need to have an integrated waveform viewer for students to see their results. Quicksilicon [6] is such a platform and now uses Surfer as the primary waveform viewer. MakerChip [22], a tool used primarily to teach the TL-Verilog language [23] also has the option of using Surfer as the waveform viewer, though they still maintain their own viewer which has integration with TL-Verilog that Surfer currently lacks. TinyTapeout [29] is an educational project that makes it straightforward to get small designs manufactured on real chips. Their workflow is fully browser-based, with the full synthesis and simulation flow being run in the cloud to let users play with chip design without installing any tools. Once the simulation is complete, users, of course, need to inspect the results if problems occurred. By using a version of Surfer that is embedded in the TinyTapeout flow, this is now possible without having to install software, reducing a hurdle to people getting their designs working and taped out.

4   A Performant Waveform Backend

Surfer displays signal traces from VCD, FST and GHW files. Our file parsing code was designed from the ground up with three important requirements in mind: (1) To keep memory consumption in check, we need to only load the signals that a user has selected. Most signals in a waveform are never displayed and should not consume unnecessary memory. (2) To improve responsiveness, the file metadata and signal names must be available as soon as possible. (3) To support re-use and embedding in various applications, Surfer needs to be able to work with untrusted input files.

To render the values of a signal, Surfer needs to be able to efficiently query the most recent value of the signal at a given time and the duration until the

---

[5] https://sonic-rv.ics.jku.at/.

Table 1. Speed and memory comparisons for a single example VCD file.

VCD file: on-disk size	2.9 GiB
GTKWave: time to load/total application memory use	16s/800 MiB
Surfer: time to load/compressed signal size (1 thread)	7.5s/74 MiB
Surfer: time to load/compressed signal size (8 threads, 4-core CPU)	2.0s/74 MiB
Surfer: average time to decompress a signal for viewing	271 µs

next change. This lookup is implemented in $O(\log_2(n))$ by performing a binary search on an array of changes sorted by the time at which the change occurs. This requires all values to be stored in a fixed size, $O(1)$-accessible, manner which takes a lot of space as it prohibits most compression schemes. To keep memory consumption in check, Surfer only stores signals that have been selected by the user in this uncompressed representation. The FST file format makes this task relatively simple, since it allows for efficient access to individual signals. VCD and GHW, on the other hand, require the complete file to be read and parsed, even if only a single signal is selected.

We developed an interesting middle ground between parsing all signals from a VCD into the uncompressed representation and reparsing the whole VCD every time a signal is added to the view. In our implementation, we parse the VCD once and then store all signals in a compressed in-memory representation, using many ideas for the FST on-disk format. When a signal is selected, it can be quickly decompressed without any file I/O. The compression rate achieved this way is high enough that this approach works, even for large VCD files. Besides allowing fast access with reduced memory usage, this intermediate storage layer also enables parallel file parsing. We can split up a single VCD file and parse each chunk on a separate CPU core. Performance results for a single example VCD are shown in Table 1.

A typical workflow for Surfer consists of the user loading a file and then browsing the signal hierarchy to select signals of interest. Thus, we first parse the header and metadata, including the signal names and hierarchy. For most input files, this can be done in much less than one second, and thus the user is presented with a signal hierarchy almost instantaneously. We continue parsing the actual signal value data in the background while the user is making their signal selection. This has allowed Surfer to avoid a loading screen.

Many of the applications described in Sect. 3.4 require running Surfer on files that were not generated by the user. Unfortunately, file parsers are notorious for containing exploitable bugs. Our parsing code exclusively uses the safe subset of Rust and therefore Surfer can be used on untrusted input files without having to worry about exploitable memory bugs. Maintaining the modular design philosophy of Surfer, our parsing library is available under the name `wellen` on GitHub[6]. It has been used outside Surfer to read waveform traces for power

---

[6] https://github.com/ekiwi/wellen.

analysis[7] and as part of the VaporView VSCode plugin [17]. There is also a python wrapper available. Thus, our focus on modularity has already paid off, enabling the community to develop new analysis and debugging tools.

4.1 Remote Servers and Continuous Integration

Simulation of large designs is often performed on dedicated compute servers rather than the developer's local computer. To view simulation results, developers traditionally have to download the whole trace file to open it up in their local waveform viewer. This transfer takes time and generates a lot of data traffic, with VCD files often measuring in the tens of gigabytes in size. Surfer offers a server mode in which it opens a waveform file on a remote machine and then allows a local instance of Surfer to access the data on demand. As soon as the local viewer receives the meta-data and signal names for the server, the user can browse them and make their selection. Once a signal is selected, the server sends the compressed value change data to the local instance for displaying. Since this feature re-uses our in-memory signal compression, it drastically reduces the amount of data sent over the network while also reducing the user-facing latency since signal data is transferred lazily.

5 Software Project

Surfer is developed as an open-source project (See footnote 1) under the EUPL license. It was created at Linköping university and has since seen several major contributions from the community. For longevity, the project is now stewarded by the FOSSi foundation. We have recently received funding from the NLnet foundation[8] to implement several highly requested features including signal grouping, drawing of analog signals, and plugin support.

6 Conclusion

Surfer is a new open-source waveform viewer that is built to be extensible and embeddable to enable new workflows in hardware design and verification. A major goal of Surfer is to integrate more high-level information from modern hardware type systems, analysis and verification tools to simplify debugging. Surfer is also the first open-source tool to support interactive simulation. Surfer has been used inside several bigger tools, primarily web-based verification and teaching platforms. We would like to invite the reader to consider what they want to build with Surfer. We like to look back at the project where an M.Sc. student was trying to work on a waveform viewer with support for Chisel types for his thesis. Building such a viewer from scratch would be impossible, but enhancing Surfer with his idea turned out to be a realistic goal [19]. Whether you want to use Surfer for teaching, or as a graphical user interface for your next verification tool, please get involved. We are happy to help you get started.

---

[7] https://github.com/antmicro/trace2power.
[8] https://nlnet.nl/.

Acknowledgements. The authors are grateful to all external contributors who have helped continuously improving Surfer. An updated list can be found in the repository, but currently these are (full name or GitLab user name):

Alejandro Tafalla	Hugo Lundin	Remi Marche
Andreas Wallner	Jacob Urbanczyk	Robin Ole Heinemann
Ben Mattes	James Connolly	Theodor Lindberg
Krusekamp	Kacper Uminski	Todd Strader
Christian Dattinger	Kaleb Barrett	Tom Verbeure
ecstrema	Lars Kadel	TopTortoise
Felix Roithmayr	Lukas Scheller	Verneri Hirvonen
Francesco Urbani	Matt Taylor	Yehowshua Immanuel
Greg Chadwick	Ondrej Ille	Øystein Hovind
Gustav Sörnäs		

This work has been partially supported by the LIT Secure and Correct Systems Lab funded by the State of Upper Austria, and by NSF award number 2426764.

References

1. Amaranth contributors: Amaranth HDL (2022). https://github.com/amaranth-lang/amaranth
2. Baaij, C.: Digital circuits in ClaSH. PhD. Thesis, University of Twente (Jan 2015). https://doi.org/10.3990/1.9789036538039
3. Bachrach, J., et al.: Chisel: constructing hardware in a Scala embedded language. In: Proc. Des. Automat. Conf. pp. 1212–1221 (Jun 2012). https://doi.org/10.1145/2228360.2228584
4. Basu, S.: Rust as a hardware description language. In: Workshop on Languages, Tools, and Techniques for Accelerator Design (2024)
5. Basu, S.: RHDL: rust as a hardware description language. In: Workshop on Languages, Tools, and Techniques for Accelerator Design (LATTE) (Apr 2025)
6. Behl, R.: QuickSilicon. https://quicksilicon.in/
7. Catherine "Whitequark": CXXRTL debug server concepts. https://cxxrtl.org/protocol.html
8. Catherine "Whitequark": YoWASP - unofficial WebAssembly-based packages for Yosys, nextpnr, and more. https://yowasp.org/
9. Dobis, A., et al.: ChiselVerify: an open-source hardware verification library for Chisel and Scala. In: Proceedings of Nordic Circuits and Systems Conference, pp. 1–7. IEEE (Oct 2021). https://doi.org/10.1109/norcas53631.2021.9599869
10. GTKWave contributors: GTKWave. https://gtkwave.sourceforge.net/
11. Kemmerer, J.: PipelineC: easy open-source hardware description between RTL and HLS. In: Proceedings of Workshop Open-Source EDA Technology (2022). https://woset-workshop.github.io/PDFs/2022/17-Kemmerer-poster.pdf

12. Klemmer, L., Große, D.: WSVA: a SystemVerilog assertion to WAL compiler. In: Workshop on Open-Source Design Automation (2024). https://ics.jku.at/files/2024OSDA_WSVA.pdf

13. Klemmer, L., Große, D.: Versatile hardware analysis techniques - from waveform-based analysis to formal verification. Springer (2025). https://doi.org/10.1007/978-3-031-83093-8

14. Klemmer, L., Große, D.: WAVING goodbye to manual waveform analysis in HDL design with WAL. IEEE Trans. Comput.-Aided Design Integr. Circuits Syst. **43**(10), 3198–3211 (2024). https://doi.org/10.1109/tcad.2024.3387312

15. Klemmer, L., Skarman, F., Gustafsson, O., Große, D.: Surfer: a waveform viewer as dynamic as RISC-V. In: RISC-V Summit Europe (Jun 2024). https://ics.jku.at/files/2024RISCVSummit_Surfer.pdf

16. Lefebvre, S.: Silice (Nov 2022). https://github.com/sylefeb/Silice/tree/5003ec72

17. Lramseyer: VaporView. https://github.com/Lramseyer/vaporview

18. Lubis EDA: Lubis EDA. https://lubis-eda.com/

19. Meloni, R., Hofstee, H.P., Al-Ars, Z.: Tywaves: a typed waveform viewer for Chisel. In: Proceedings of Nordic Circuits and Systems Conference, pp. 1–6. IEEE (Oct 2024). https://doi.org/10.1109/norcas64408.2024.10752465

20. Nigam, R., de Amorim, P.H.A., Sampson, A.: Modular hardware design with time-line types. Proc. ACM Program. Lang. (PLDI) (2023)

21. Nikhil, R.: Bluespec SystemVerilog: efficient, correct RTL from high-level speci-fications. In: Proc ACM/IEEE International Conference on Formal Methods and Models for Co-Design, pp. 69–70. IEEE (2004). https://doi.org/10.1109/memcod.2004.1459818

22. Redwood EDA: Makerchip. http://makerchip.com/

23. Redwood EDA: TL-Verilog (Oct 2022). https://web.archive.org/web/20221006080731/https://www.redwoodeda.com/tl-verilog

24. SiLogy Technologies: Silogy. https://silogy.io/

25. Skarman, F., Gustafsson, O.: Spade: an expression-based HDL with pipelines. In: Proceedings of Workshop on Open-Source Desing Automation (Apr 2023)

26. SpinalHDL contributors: SpinalHDL (2022). https://github.com/SpinalHDL/SpinalHDL

27. TerosHDL: TerosHDL - an open source toolbox for ASIC/FPGA (Oct 2024). https://terostechnology.github.io/terosHDLdoc/

28. Van Hirtum, L., Plessl, C.: Latency counting in the SUS language. In: Workshop on Languages, Tools, and Techniques for Accelerator Design (2024). https://capra.cs.cornell.edu/latte24/paper/4.pdf

29. Venn, M.: Tiny Tapeout: a shared silicon tape out platform accessible to every-one. IEEE Solid-State Circuits Mag. **16**(2), 20–29 (2024). https://doi.org/10.1109/mssc.2024.3381097

PyEuclid: A Versatile Formal Plane Geometry System in Python

Zhaoyu Li[1], Hangrui Bi[1], Jialiang Sun[1], Zenan Li[2], Kaiyu Yang[3], and Xujie Si[1(✉)]

[1] University of Toronto, Toronto, Canada
{zhaoyu,henryb,sjl,six}@cs.toronto.edu
[2] Nanjing University, Nanjing, China
lizn@smail.nju.edu.cn
[3] Meta FAIR, New York, USA
kaiyuy@meta.com

Abstract. We introduce `PyEuclid`, a unified and versatile Python-based formal system for representing and reasoning about plane geometry problems. `PyEuclid` designs a new formal language that faithfully encodes geometric information, including diagrams, and integrates two complementary components to perform geometric reasoning: (1) a deductive database with an extensive set of inference rules for geometric properties, and (2) an algebraic system for solving diverse equations involving geometric quantities. By seamlessly combining these components, `PyEuclid` enables human-like reasoning and supports generating concise reasoning steps (proofs), either fully automatically or through interactive guidance. Benchmark evaluations demonstrate that `PyEuclid` outperforms existing tools, solving a broader range of problems across both proof generation and calculation tasks. Moreover, `PyEuclid` holds significant potential for educational use and integration with advanced deep learning systems.

1 Introduction

For over two millennia, Euclid's *Elements* has stood as a cornerstone of rigorous geometric reasoning, profoundly shaping the foundations of mathematics and logic. Since the twentieth century, the emergence of computer programs and mechanical theorem proving [15,16,19,20] has driven significant progress in formalizing and enabling automated reasoning in Euclidean geometry [4,9,26,36]. These formal systems typically fall into two primary paradigms: synthetic deduction [12,14,28,33,34] and algebraic computation [7,8,10,11,13,25,29,38].

Within synthetic methods, the deductive database approach [12] employs forward chaining to systematically enumerate geometric rules and derive new facts in a database until reaching a fixed point. While effective at deducing geometric properties, this method struggles to handle the algebraic computations required for diverse problems. On the other hand, algebraic approaches such as Gröbner

---

Z. Li, H. Bi and J. Sun—These authors contributed equally to this work.

© The Author(s) 2025
R. Piskac and Z. Rakamarić (Eds.): CAV 2025, LNCS 15934, pp. 405–420, 2025.
https://doi.org/10.1007/978-3-031-98685-7_20

basis [29] and Wu's method [38] translate geometric properties into systems of polynomial equations based on point coordinates and solve them algebraically. Although powerful for proving geometric equalities, these techniques usually produce intricate proofs that are challenging for humans to interpret.

More recently, the deep-learning-augmented geometry system AlphaGeometry [35] has emerged as a notable milestone by integrating a language model [37] with a novel symbolic solver, DDAR. This system became the first to achieve silver-medal performance on International Mathematics Olympiad problems. DDAR combines a deductive database [12,41] with basic algebraic techniques for angle, ratio, and distance chasing, enabling advanced geometric reasoning. However, it has notable limitations: it cannot handle problems involving calculation and sometimes relies on numerical checks of exact point coordinates during proofs, restricting its applicability across a broader spectrum of tasks. Moreover, while some popular educational software [3,24,41] support multiple approaches to geometry theorem proving, they often apply these methods independently, limiting their generality and versatility to perform human-like geometric reasoning within a unified and cohesive framework.

Table 1. Feature comparison between `PyEuclid` and other geometry systems. A "✓" denotes full support, a "−" indicates partial support, and a "✗" signifies no support.

System	Feature						
	Proving	Calculating	Automatic	Interactive	Human-Like	Competition-Level	Coordinate-Free
JGEX [41]	✓	−	✓	✓	−	✓	−
GeoGebra [3]	✓	−	✓	✓	−	✓	✗
GCLC [24]	✓	−	✓	✗	−	✓	✗
DDAR [35]	✓	✗	✓	−	−	✓	✗
LeanEuclid [32]	✓	✗	✗	✓	✓	✗	✓
NGS [6]	✗	✓	✗	✓	✓	✗	✓
Inter-GPS [30]	✗	✓	✓	✓	✓	✗	✓
PyEuclid (Ours)	✓	✓	✓	✓	✓	✓	✓

To address these limitations, we develop `PyEuclid`, a Python-based formal system designed to represent and reason about plane geometry problems in a unified and versatile manner. Inspired by established formal systems [1,41], `PyEuclid` integrates and extends their formalization theories to encode geometric information while seamlessly integrating diagrams into the reasoning process. It supports flexible and user-friendly input formats, enabling the efficient formalization of plane geometry problems. `PyEuclid` incorporates two complementary components for geometric reasoning: (1) a novel deductive database (DD) that employs a broad range of human-like inference rules to derive new geometric properties and their corresponding algebraic equations, and (2) an advanced algebraic system (AS) that solves the system of equations, discovering new properties that complement the DD. By tightly integrating these components, `PyEuclid` provides a unified framework capable of performing both geome-

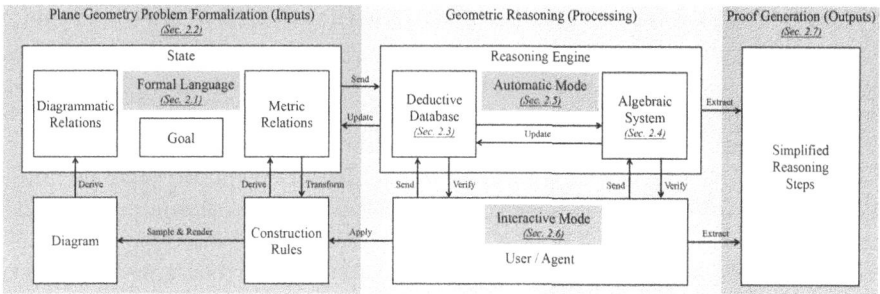

Fig. 1. An overview of the main components of PyEuclid.

try theorem proving and calculation, supporting fully automated and interactive reasoning modes to accommodate diverse user needs. After solving a problem, PyEuclid can also generate minimal, human-like reasoning steps (proofs) to enhance interpretability and verifiability. Additionally, PyEuclid provides comprehensive documentation, making it easy for users to comprehend and extend its functionality. A detailed feature comparison of PyEuclid with other plane geometry systems is presented in Table 1, showcasing its broad capabilities.

We evaluate PyEuclid on two geometry benchmarks: JGEX-AG-231 [35] for geometry theorem proving and the test set of Geometry3K [30] for geometry calculation problems. The experimental results show that PyEuclid can successfully solve more problems than existing state-of-the-art formal geometry systems in both tasks. It is also noteworthy that PyEuclid identifies various errors and inaccuracies in the human-annotated Geometry3K dataset, showcasing its robustness and accuracy in solving real-world problems.

2   Architecture

In this section, we present the design and implementation details of PyEuclid. Figure 1 shows the overview of PyEuclid's architecture and its key components. At a high level, PyEuclid supports diverse input formats (e.g., constructive or relational information, with or without diagrams) and transforms them into a unified formal representation. The reasoning engine integrates deductive and algebraic methods to perform human-like reasoning automatically or interactively with user-provided proof sketch. Upon solving a problem, PyEuclid can also generate concise reasoning steps to enhance interpretability and verifiability.

2.1   Formal Language

Drawing inspiration from established formal geometry systems [12, 41], PyEuclid is grounded in a theory where points serve as the fundamental geometric entities used to represent all other objects, including lines, circles, triangles, angles, parallelograms, and more. For instance, a line can be specified by two points it passes through, while a circle is characterized by a point as its center and a length as its radius. To accurately capture the geometric relations among these objects, PyEuclid defines 43 relations and classifies them into two categories [1]: *metric relations* and *diagrammatic relations*.

Metric relations describe quantitative geometric properties and interactions, such as "Perpendicular" or "Parallel" relations between two different lines, and "Concyclic" relations among four different points. Furthermore, PyEuclid incorporates a rich set of algebraic equations to represent relations between quantities associated with geometric objects. These quantities include measurements such as the length of a segment, the degree of an angle, or the area of a triangle. The algebraic equations cover operations like the addition and subtraction of angles or lengths, ratios of lengths, and more advanced functions, such as trigonometric functions like sine. Some metric relations can be equivalently expressed through both geometric properties and algebraic equations. For example, the statement "Perpendicular(A,B,B,C)" is equivalent to "Angle(A,B,C) = $\pi/2$".

Diagrammatic relations, on the other hand, describe topological configurations among geometric objects that can be observed directly from a diagram. Examples include "SameSide" or "OppositeSide", which define the relative positions of two different points with respect to a line, and "Between", which specifies the sequential arrangement of three collinear points.

These two categories of geometric relations align with the typical formulation of plane geometry problems: metric relations are usually explicitly stated in problem descriptions and inferred through geometric theorems, whereas diagrammatic relations are often directly extracted from diagrams without requiring additional geometric reasoning.

2.2   Problem Formalization

Given a plane geometry problem, PyEuclid formalizes it into its internal *state*, which consists of conditions and a goal. The conditions include metric and diagrammatic relations of the objects, and the *goal* represents the desired property to be proved or the quantity to be solved. This formalization process is designed to accommodate various input scenarios, which can be categorized as follows:

(1) When a geometry problem includes metric relations along with a diagram containing precise point coordinates (e.g., diagrams exported from educational geometry tools [3,24]), PyEuclid leverages a parser to automatically extract diagrammatic relations by performing numerical checking on the coordinate data.

(2) If a geometry problem specifies metric relations but the accompanying diagram either lacks coordinate information or is inaccurate, PyEuclid provides an interface for users to manually input the diagrammatic relations or adjust the automatically derived relations from the parser based on the given diagram. This ensures the formalization is consistent with the problem's intended configuration.

(3) When only metric relations are provided, `PyEuclid` generates a corresponding diagram using "ruler-and-compass construction". This process begins by translating the given metric relations into a set of geometric construction steps, incrementally building a diagram that satisfies the specified relations. The method builds upon and extends an existing set of geometric construction rules [12,35,41], where each rule is expressed in the form: "`conditions of existing points` $\Rightarrow$ `relations of the constructed point`". For instance, "`circle X A B C:` `NotCollinear(A,B,C)` $\Rightarrow$ `Length(A,X)` = `Length(B,X)` $\wedge$ `Length(B,X)` = `Length(C,X)`" specifies how to construct the circumcenter `X` of a triangle defined by points `A`, `B`, `C`. To translate metric relations into construction rules, `PyEuclid` performs an enumerative search over the rules to identify those that derive the desired metric relations, creating a sequence of feasible construction steps. Once the construction steps are determined, `PyEuclid` uses an extended visualizer [35], implemented with Matplotlib [23], to generate a diagram with precise point coordinates. From this diagram, the corresponding diagrammatic relations are derived. It is also worth noting that the generated diagram is not deterministic, as multiple points may satisfy a given construction rule at each step. Therefore, a single set of construction rules can result in multiple valid diagrammatic relations, depending on the sampled points.

(4) When explicit geometry construction steps are provided [3,12,24,35,41], `PyEuclid` directly derives both metric and diagrammatic relations by following the same approach described in case (3).

2.3 Deductive Database

Given the state of a formalized geometry problem, `PyEuclid` enables geometric reasoning by implementing a deductive database containing a wide range of inference rules to derive new geometric relations. These inference rules are expressed in the form: "`condition(s)` $\Rightarrow$ `conclusion(s)`", where the "`conclusion(s)`" represents one (or more) metric relation(s), and each "`condition`" can be either a metric or diagrammatic relation. Unlike existing deductive approaches [12,35,41] that write the inference rules based on the full angle method [11], `PyEuclid` employs more human-like inference rules, closely mirroring human reasoning processes. For example, existing systems [12,35,41] define a single inference rule for the angle relations of four concyclic points: "`cyclic A B P Q` $\Rightarrow$ `eqangle P A P B Q A Q B`", which states that if points `A`, `B`, `P`, and `Q` are concyclic, the angle between lines `PA` and `PB` is equal to the angle between lines `QA` and `QB`. In contrast, `PyEuclid` considers different cases based on diagrammatic relations among the points and introduces two inference rules: (1) "`Concyclic(A,B,P,Q)` $\wedge$ `OppositeSide(P,Q,A,B)` $\Rightarrow$ `Angle(A,P,B)` + `Angle(A,Q,B)` = π" and (2) "`Concyclic(A,B,P,Q)` $\wedge$ `SameSide(P,Q,A,B)` $\Rightarrow$ `Angle(A,P,B)` = `Angle(A,Q,B)`".

   To determine which inference rules can apply to the current problem state, `PyEuclid` encodes the geometric relations as an SAT problem using Z3 [17].

Additionally, `PyEuclid` defines an order over the points involved in each theorem, without loss of generality. This approach eliminates redundant searches caused by equivalent permutations of the same inference rule. For instance, in the case of the two rules above, the partial order "`A < B, P < Q, A < P`" is imposed, ensuring efficient enumeration of satisfying assignments. This unified framework allows users to easily extend the rule set and systematically enumerate all possible instantiated inference rules for deriving new metric relations.

Moreover, to enhance usability, `PyEuclid` classifies its inference rules into three categories: *intuitive*, *standard*, and *complex* rules. Intuitive rules consist of basic definitions of geometric theorems or simple theorems that are easily understood by humans. These rules may not always be explicitly included in proofs but provide foundational support. For example, the summation of angles rule: "`SameSide(B,D,C,A)` ∧ `SameSide(C,D,B,A)` ⇒ `Angle(B,A,C)` = `Angle(D,A,C)` + `Angle(D,A,B)`". Standard rules represent geometric theorems that typically result in linear algebraic equations involving geometric quantities. In contrast, complex rules involve theorems that lead to non-linear algebraic equations, often incorporating trigonometric functions such as sine and cosine. Users have the flexibility to select subsets of inference rules tailored to the specific problem or extend the rule set as needed. The examples of current inference rules in `PyEuclid` are provided in Appendix A.

2.4   Algebraic System

Given the algebraic equations derived from metric relations, `PyEuclid` implements an algebraic system using Sympy [31] that supports simplifying these equations and solving for specific geometric quantities whenever possible. It is important to note that the resulting algebraic equations can encompass a large set of complex relationships with diverse operations. To manage this, `PyEuclid` classifies the equations into three categories based on their quantities and operations: *angles-only*, *segments-only*, and *mixed* equations.

The angles-only equations include addition, subtraction of angle degrees, or ratios of angles equaling constants. These equations form a linear system represented as $AX = B$, where X is a vector of geometric quantities, A and B are the coefficients and constants in the equations. `PyEuclid` applies Gaussian elimination to simplify these equations and, where possible, solve for the angles. Figure 2 demonstrates an example of this process. The Segments-only equations include those involving the addition and subtraction of segment lengths, as well as ratios of lengths equaling other ratios or constants. It is straightforward to observe that equations such as "`ratio = constant`" and those involving the addition and subtraction of lengths naturally form a linear system. Additionally, equations with ratios (e.g., "`ratio = ratio`" or "`ratio = constant`") can be transformed into another linear system by rewriting them in logarithmic form.

`PyEuclid` applies Gaussian elimination sequentially to these systems, simplifying the equations and solving for the segment lengths effectively.

Lastly, for mixed or complex non-linear equations, `PyEuclid` substitutes the simplified relations derived from the three linear systems discussed earlier. If the substituted equations reduce to a single-variable equation, they can be solved directly. Additionally, `PyEuclid` supports combining the remaining complex equations into subsets where the number of equations is greater than or equal to the number of variables, allowing these subsets to be solved efficiently.

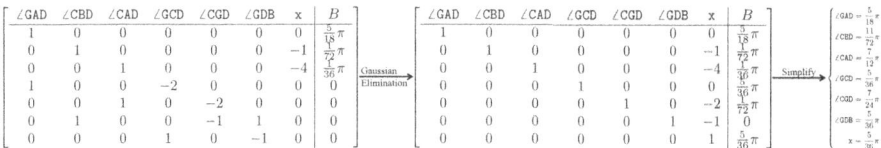

Fig. 2. An example of Gaussian elimination applied to linear equations involving angles (and unknown variable x), adapted from the Geometry3K [30] dataset. The coefficient matrix A and constant column B are combined into a matrix $[A \mid B]$ for simplification.

2.5   Automatic Mode

With the integration of the DD and AS, `PyEuclid` enables the automatic solving of formalized geometry problems in a human-like reasoning manner. In this mode, `PyEuclid` iteratively invokes the DD and AS until the solving goal is achieved. During each iteration, `PyEuclid` first applies all "intuitive" inference rules to derive straightforward conclusions, continuing until no further deductions can be made. It then applies all applicable remaining inference rules (i.e., "standard" and "complex") to the current state to infer new geometric relations and their corresponding algebraic forms. To optimize efficiency, newly derived relations are cached to prevent redundant derivations. Next, `PyEuclid` calls the AS to solve the resulting algebraic equations, deriving new metric relations that are subsequently added back to the DD for further reasoning. This iterative process mirrors human reasoning by prioritizing simpler deductions first and using newly derived facts to facilitate subsequent complex inferences and algebraic computations, which are treated as single reasoning steps. This design enhances efficiency while closely emulating a structured, human-like approach to problem-solving.

2.6   Interactive Mode

`PyEuclid` also provides an interactive interface that allows users to solve formalized plane geometry problems step-by-step. Users can first manually apply the supported construction rules to create "auxiliary" points, which may aid in solving the problem. These auxiliary constructions are incorporated into the original diagram, and the geometric relations in the state are updated accordingly.

Next, users can perform geometric reasoning by specifying the metric relations used as conditions and the conclusions derived from them. Optionally, users can provide the specific inference rules and diagrammatic relations applied as conditions, allowing PyEuclid to easily verify the reasoning steps. If no rules are specified, PyEuclid automatically invokes the DD to identify the applicable inference rules, as well as the AS to perform algebraic computations if needed, similar to the automatic mode. Once the user-provided steps are verified, PyEuclid updates the state with the newly derived relations.

2.7   Proof Generation

PyEuclid supports producing concise, human-like reasoning steps (a proof) upon solving a geometry problem. Each derived metric relation is assigned a dependency attribute that records how it was obtained. In DD, when an inference rule is applied to derive a new relation, the dependency is tagged with the metric relations used as conditions and the corresponding inference rule. In AS, specific values derived from solving mixed complex equations are tagged with their dependency on the substituted algebraic equations and the associated complex equations. For algebraic relations derived from linear systems, PyEuclid traces the minimal subset of original equations needed to derive them. This dependency traceback is modeled as an optimization problem:

$$\min \|X\|_0, \quad \text{s.t.} \quad [A \mid B]^\top X = E,$$

where $[A \mid B] \in \mathbb{R}^{m \times (n+1)}$ is the augmented coefficient matrix of the linear system (as shown in Fig. 2), $E \in \mathbb{R}^{n+1}$ represents the coefficient vector of the query relation and $X \in \mathbb{R}^m$ denotes the coefficients for each equation contributing to the query. The goal is to minimize the ℓ_0-norm of X, which counts the number of non-zero elements, thereby identifying the minimal set of equations needed. To solve this non-convex optimization problem, we reformulate it as a Mixed-Integer Linear Programming (MILP) problem. The objective function is redefined as: $\min \sum_{i=1}^m z_i$, where each binary variable z_i is associated with x_i through Big-M constraints: $-M z_i \leq x_i \leq M z_i$, with $M > 0$ as a sufficiently large constant. This reformulation converts the non-convex problem into a MILP, which PyEuclid efficiently solves using the modern solver Gurobi [21].

Starting from the goal, PyEuclid recursively traces its dependency on metric relations until all dependencies are grounded in the original problem conditions. During this traceback process, PyEuclid constructs a dependency graph, where the root represents the goal and the leaf nodes correspond to the original metric relations. Once the graph is built, PyEuclid performs a postorder traversal to systematically convert it into a sequence of reasoning steps. These steps are then formatted using a human-readable, structured output for improved interpretability. Figure 3 provides an example of the proof generation process in PyEuclid.

3 Evaluations

In this section, we evaluate PyEuclid on two established benchmarks: JGEX-AG-231 [35] for proving problems and the test set of Geometry3K [30] for calculation problems, comparing its performance against various baselines. All experiments are conducted using 30 CPU cores with a timeout of 600 s. A theorem is considered successfully proven if the solver generates a valid proof, and a calculation problem is solved if the output matches the correct solution.

Evaluation on JGEX-AG-231. JGEX-AG-231 [35] is a collection of 231 geometry theorem proving problems, ranging from textbook exercises to regional Olympiads, written by the construction rules [35,41] and a query. We implement a parser to translate these constructions and the query to our formal language and sample a diagram to perform geometric reasoning. Out of the 231 problems, PyEuclid successfully solves 202, outperforming existing systems: DD [41] (152), Wu's method [38] (173), and the previous state-of-the-art, DDAR [35] (198). Compared to DDAR, PyEuclid solves five additional problems but times out on one problem that DDAR can handle. The timeout case arises because PyEuclid represents all angles using three points, which may result in a large number of angle relations. In contrast, DDAR employs full-angle reasoning [11,12], representing angles using two lines (i.e., four points), which can lead to fewer relations and more efficient reasoning. However, PyEuclid's ability to solve the six additional problems stems from its broader inference rules and a more advanced algebraic computation system. It is also worth noting that the proofs generated by PyEuclid align more closely with human reasoning, whereas DDAR's reliance

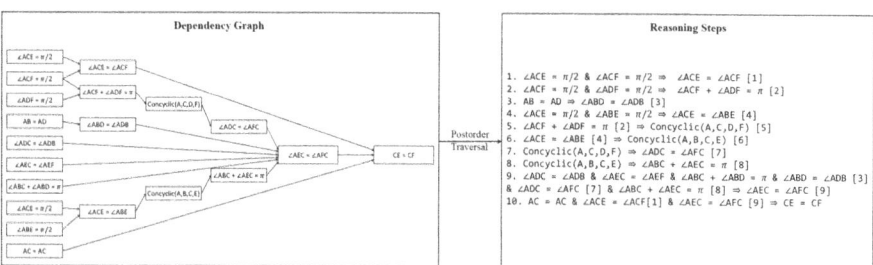

Fig. 3. An example of the dependency graph and the resulting proofs from the JGEX-AG-231 [35] dataset.

on full-angle notations can introduce ambiguities when distinguishing between equivalent and supplementary angles. Appendix B provides three examples illustrating the differences between `PyEuclid`'s proofs and those of DDAR.

Evaluation on Geometry3K. The test set of the Geometry3K [30] dataset consists of 601 SAT-style geometric calculation problems. Each problem includes a manually curated formalization in its own formal language and a diagram with rough coordinates. To process these problems, we implement a parser that translates the existing formalization into metric relations and extracts diagrammatic relations numerically from the given coordinates. We also filtered out non-calculation problems, resulting in a final set of 599 problems. We first ran `PyEuclid` on these 599 problems, successfully solving 529 of them. After manual inspection, we identified 38 "buggy" problems—21 problems containing incorrect or self-contradictory values and 17 problems with missing or incorrect relations. These benchmark issues were manually corrected. Following these corrections, `PyEuclid` successfully solved 567 out of 599 problems, achieving a state-of-the-art accuracy of 94.7%. This significantly outperforms previous symbolic solver baselines [30], which achieved an accuracy of 77.3%. Among the 32 unsolved problems, all were due to the inclusion of too many points in the problem (i.e., more than ten points). This led to an excessively large search space, preventing `PyEuclid` from reaching a conclusion within the given time limits.

4   Conclusion and Discussion

We have presented `PyEuclid`, a versatile formal plane geometry system implemented in Python. `PyEuclid` introduces a new formal language tailored for geometric problem formalization and seamlessly integrates deductive and algebraic approaches. This synergy enables human-like geometric reasoning in both automatic and interactive modes, producing concise proofs suitable for various use cases. To conclude this paper, we further discuss the current limitations of `PyEuclid` and highlight its promising potential for future applications below.

Limitations. `PyEuclid` currently lacks support for geometric inequalities, such as verifying that the sum of two sides of a triangle is greater than the third side. As a result, the system cannot handle inequality problems at this time. Additionally, the search complexity of `PyEuclid` increases substantially as the number of points in a problem grows, potentially impacting its performance on highly complex problems. Moreover, while `PyEuclid` features a powerful reasoning engine that applies a broad set of inference rules and algebraic equations in automatic mode, there remains room for further efficiency optimizations.

Applications. One potential application of `PyEuclid` lies in educational settings [2,3,22,24]. `PyEuclid` stands out for its human-like geometric reasoning and its ability to address a wide variety of plane geometry problems, encompassing both proof and calculation tasks. These problems range from basic exercises to advanced competition-level challenges, making the system versatile for learners at different skill levels. Another notable advantage of `PyEuclid` is its ability to work with imprecise diagrams, allowing students to simply specify diagrammatic relations without needing perfect diagrams. This feature aligns well with common educational scenarios where teachers or students sketch rough diagrams to illustrate problems. Furthermore, its interactive and automatic modes provide flexible learning opportunities, enabling students to engage with geometry problems in ways that suit their individual needs.

Another promising application of `PyEuclid` is its integration with deep learning models [5,6,27,30,35]. The interactive mode of `PyEuclid` acts as a bridge, allowing these models to construct auxiliary points and generate proofs. For example, large language models (LLMs) could be utilized to predict auxiliary constructions, as demonstrated by systems like AlphaGeometry [35], or to predict reasoning steps, as seen in models such as NGS [6] and Inter-GPS [30]. Moreover, a compelling future direction is to utilize `PyEuclid` to automatically solve a wide array of geometry problems, producing high-quality reasoning steps used to train and improve LLMs or vision-language models [18,40] on geometry problems. In addition, the formal language employed in `PyEuclid` is easily interpretable by both humans and LLMs, facilitating seamless translation between natural language and formal language. This feature makes `PyEuclid` particularly well-suited for autoformalization tasks [32,39], which aim to solve problems expressed in natural language. Such capabilities are highly practical in real-world scenarios, where problem descriptions are often provided in natural language, bridging the gap between human understanding and formal reasoning systems.

Acknowledgments. This work was supported, in part, by Individual Discovery Grants from the Natural Sciences and Engineering Research Council of Canada, and the Canada CIFAR AI Chair Program.

Disclosure of Interests. The authors have no competing interests to declare that are relevant to the content of this article.

A   Inferences Rules

Inference rules operate on a set of metric and diagrammatic relations, deriving new metric relations as conclusions. In `PyEuclid`, these rules are categorized into three groups: basic rules, standard rules, and complex rules. Basic rules are intuitive and often do not require explicit mention in written proofs. For instance:

- `Angle2Perp(A,B,C)`: `Angle(A,B,C)=`$\pi/2$ ⇒ `Perpendicular(A,B,B,C)`
- `MidpointRatio(A,B,C)`:`Length(A,B)=Length(A,C)` ∧ `Collinear(A,B,C)`
  ∧ `Between(A,B,C)` ⇒ `Length(B,C)/Length(A,C)=1/2`

Standard rules describe linear or log-linear relations between lengths or angles, making them suitable for theorem proving tasks. For example:

- `EqualChordPerp(A,B,P,Q)`: `Concyclic(A,B,P,Q)` ∧ `Length(A,P)=Length(B,P)` ∧ `Length(A,Q)=Length(B,Q)` ⇒ `Perpendicular(A,P,A,Q)` ∧ `Perpendicular(B,P,B,Q)`

Complex rules are used in general calculation tasks involving nonlinear or transcendental relations, such as:

- `LawOfSines(A,B,C)`: `NotCollinear(A,B,C)`
  ⇒
  `sin(Angle(A,B,C))/Length(A,C)=sin(Angle(A,C,B))/Length(A,B)=sin(Angle(B,A,C))/Length(B,C)`

B   Comparison of Proofs Between `PyEuclid` and DDAR

Note that Inter-GPS does not generate human-readable proofs but only provides final numerical results for calculation-style problems. Therefore, to better showcase the human-like reasoning of `PyEuclid`, we primarily compare its proofs with those of the previous state-of-the-art geometry proving system, DDAR.

DDAR internally uses four points to denote an angle. `Angle(A,B,C,D)` is defined as the directed included angle between the lines passing through AB and CD, which differs from the three-point angle representation commonly used by humans. When generating proofs, four-point angles are reduced to three-point angles if there is an explicit intersection. However, this formulation introduces ambiguity, as it does not distinguish between equal and supplementary angles. If we denote the intersection of AB and CD as point O, then `Angle(A,B,C,D)` could be represented as either ∠AOC or ∠AOD, which DDAR uses interchangeably. As a result, when DDAR's proof states that two angles are equal, it could mean they are either identical or that their sum is π, leading to potential inconsistencies. In contrast, `PyEuclid` exclusively uses the human-friendly three-point angle notation, eliminating such ambiguities. Below, we present three example comparisons from the JGEX-AG-231 dataset showcasing the differences between the proofs generated by `PyEuclid` and DDAR. Highlighted proof steps indicate instances where DDAR employs non-intuitive notation or incorrect reasoning, whereas all proof steps in `PyEuclid` are both human-readable and verifiably correct.

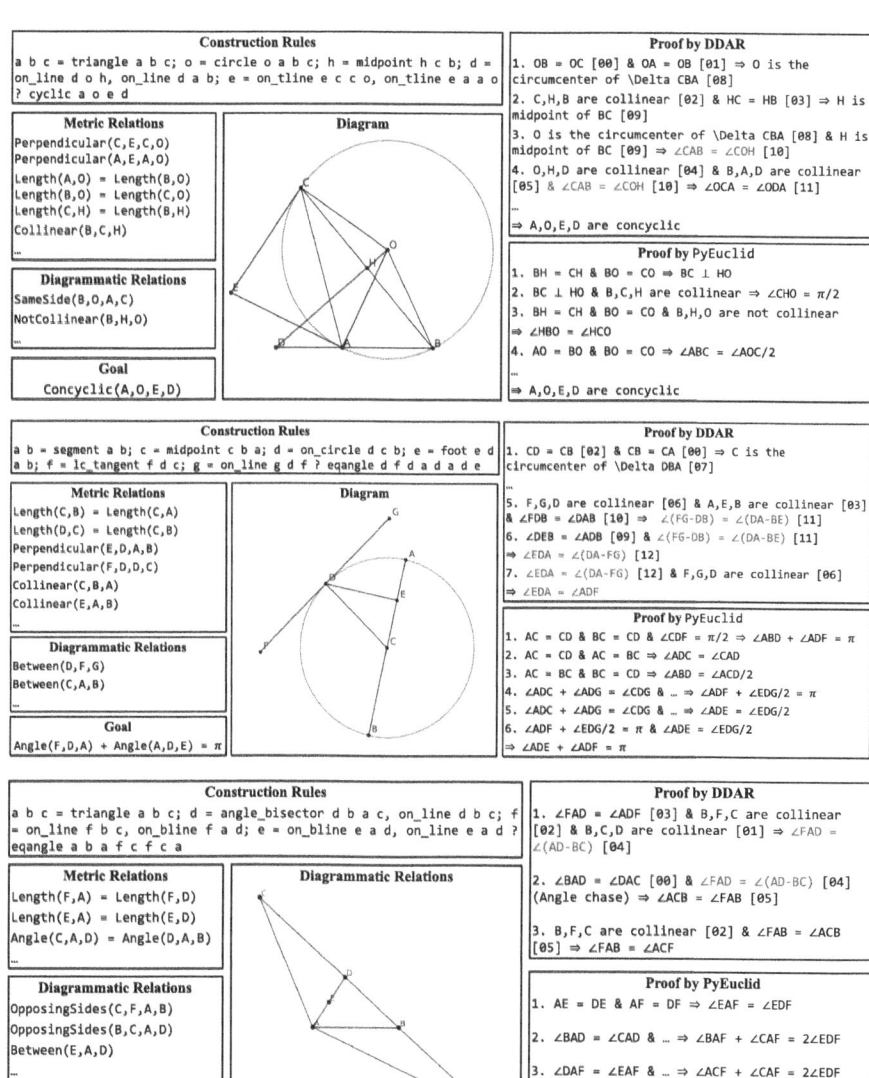

Construction Rules

a b c = triangle a b c; o = circle o a b c; h = midpoint h c b; d = on_line d o h, on_line d a b; e = on_tline e c c o, on_tline e a a o ? cyclic a o e d

Metric Relations

Perpendicular(C,E,C,O)
Perpendicular(A,E,A,O)
Length(A,O) = Length(B,O)
Length(B,O) = Length(C,O)
Length(C,H) = Length(B,H)
Collinear(B,C,H)

Diagrammatic Relations

SameSide(B,O,A,C)
NotCollinear(B,H,O)
...

Goal

Concyclic(A,O,E,D)

Proof by DDAR

1. OB = OC [00] & OA = OB [01] ⇒ O is the circumcenter of \Delta CBA [08]
2. C,H,B are collinear [02] & HC = HB [03] ⇒ H is midpoint of BC [09]
3. O is the circumcenter of \Delta CBA [08] & H is midpoint of BC [09] ⇒ ∠CAB = ∠COH [10]
4. O,H,D are collinear [04] & B,A,D are collinear [05] & ∠CAB = ∠COH [10] ⇒ ∠OCA = ∠ODA [11]
...
⇒ A,O,E,D are concyclic

Proof by PyEuclid

1. BH = CH & BO = CO ⇒ BC ⊥ HO
2. BC ⊥ HO & B,C,H are collinear ⇒ ∠CHO = π/2
3. BH = CH & BO = CO & B,H,O are not collinear ⇒ ∠HBO = ∠HCO
4. AO = BO & BO = CO ⇒ ∠ABC = ∠AOC/2
⇒ A,O,E,D are concyclic

Construction Rules

a b = segment a b; c = midpoint c b a; d = on_circle d c b; e = foot e d a b; f = lc_tangent f d c; g = on_line g d f ? eqangle d f d a d a d e

Metric Relations

Length(C,B) = Length(C,A)
Length(D,C) = Length(C,B)
Perpendicular(E,D,A,B)
Perpendicular(F,D,D,C)
Collinear(C,B,A)
Collinear(E,A,B)

Diagrammatic Relations

Between(D,F,G)
Between(C,A,B)

Goal

Angle(F,D,A) + Angle(A,D,E) = π

Proof by DDAR

1. CD = CB [02] & CB = CA [00] ⇒ C is the circumcenter of \Delta DBA [07]
...
5. F,G,D are collinear [06] & A,E,B are collinear [03] & ∠FDB = ∠DAB [10] ⇒ ∠(FG-DB) = ∠(DA-BE) [11]
6. ∠DEB = ∠ADB [09] & ∠(FG-DB) = ∠(DA-BE) [11] ⇒ ∠EDA = ∠(DA-FG) [12]
7. ∠EDA = ∠(DA-FG) [12] & F,G,D are collinear [06] ⇒ ∠EDA = ∠ADF

Proof by PyEuclid

1. AC = CD & BC = CD & ∠CDF = π/2 ⇒ ∠ABD + ∠ADF = π
2. AC = CD & AC = BC ⇒ ∠ADC = ∠CAD
3. AC = BC & BC = CD ⇒ ∠ABD = ∠ACD/2
4. ∠ADC + ∠ADG = ∠CDG & ... ⇒ ∠ADF + ∠EDG/2 = π
5. ∠ADC + ∠ADG = ∠CDG & ... ⇒ ∠ADE = ∠EDG/2
6. ∠ADF + ∠EDG/2 = π & ∠ADE = ∠EDG/2 ⇒ ∠ADE + ∠ADF = π

Construction Rules

a b c = triangle a b c; d = angle_bisector d b a c, on_line d b c; f = on_line f b c, on_bline f a d; e = on_bline e a d, on_line e a d ? eqangle a b a f c f c a

Metric Relations

Length(F,A) = Length(F,D)
Length(E,A) = Length(E,D)
Angle(C,A,D) = Angle(D,A,B)

Diagrammatic Relations

OpposingSides(C,F,A,B)
OpposingSides(B,C,A,D)
Between(E,A,D)
...

Goal

Angle(B,A,F) = Angle(A,C,F)

Proof by DDAR

1. ∠FAD = ∠ADF [03] & B,F,C are collinear [02] & B,C,D are collinear [01] ⇒ ∠FAD = ∠(AD-BC) [04]
2. ∠BAD = ∠DAC [00] & ∠FAD = ∠(AD-BC) [04] (Angle chase) ⇒ ∠ACB = ∠FAB [05]
3. B,F,C are collinear [02] & ∠FAB = ∠ACB [05] ⇒ ∠FAB = ∠ACF

Proof by PyEuclid

1. AE = DE & AF = DF ⇒ ∠EAF = ∠EDF
2. ∠BAD = ∠CAD & ... ⇒ ∠BAF + ∠CAF = 2∠EDF
3. ∠DAF = ∠EAF & ... ⇒ ∠ACF + ∠CAF = 2∠EDF
4. ∠ACF + ∠CAF = 2∠EDF & ∠BAF+ ∠CAF = 2∠EDF ⇒ ∠FAB = ∠ACF

References

1. Avigad, J., Dean, E., Mumma, J.: A formal system for euclid's elements. Rev. Symbolic Logic **2**(4), 700–768 (2009)
2. Aydogdu, M.Z., Kesan, C.: A research on geometry problem solving strategies used by elementary mathematics teacher candidates. Online Submission **4**(1), 53–62 (2014)
3. Botana, F., et al.: Automated theorem proving in geogebra: current achievements. J. Autom. Reason. **55**, 39–59 (2015)
4. Buchberger, B., Collins, G.E., Kutzler, B.: Algebraic methods for geometric reasoning. Annual Rev. Comput. Sci. **3**(1), 85–119 (1988)

5. Chen, J., et al.: Unigeo: unifying geometry logical reasoning via reformulating mathematical expression. arXiv preprint arXiv:2212.02746 (2022)
6. Chen, J., et al.: Geoqa: a geometric question answering benchmark towards multimodal numerical reasoning. arXiv preprint arXiv:2105.14517 (2021)
7. Chou, S.C., Gao, X.S., Zhang, J.Z.: Automated production of traditional proofs for constructive geometry theorems. In: [1993] Proceedings Eighth Annual IEEE Symposium on Logic in Computer Science, pp. 48–56. IEEE (1993)
8. Chou, S.C.: Mechanical geometry theorem proving. Springer (1988)
9. Chou, S.C., Gao, X.S.: Automated reasoning in geometry. Handbook Autom. Reasoning 1, 707–749 (2001)
10. Chou, S.C., Gao, X.S., Zhang, J.Z.: Automated generation of readable proofs with geometric invariants: I. multiple and shortest proof generation. J. Autom. Reasoning 17(3), 325–347 (1996)
11. Chou, S.C., Gao, X.S., Zhang, J.Z.: Automated generation of readable proofs with geometric invariants: Ii. theorem proving with full-angles. J. Autom. Reasoning 17(3), 349–370 (1996)
12. Chou, S.C., Gao, X.S., Zhang, J.Z.: A deductive database approach to automated geometry theorem proving and discovering. J. Autom. Reason. 25(3), 219–246 (2000)
13. Chou, S.C., Gao, X., Zhang, J.Z.: Machine proofs in geometry: automated production of readable proofs for geometry theorems, vol. 6. World Scientific (1994)
14. Coelho, H., Pereira, L.M.: Automated reasoning in geometry theorem proving with prolog. J. Autom. Reason. 2, 329–390 (1986)
15. Davis, M.: A computer program for Presburger's algorithm. Symbolic Comput. Automat. Reason. 1 (1957)
16. Davis, M., Putnam, H.: A computing procedure for quantification theory. J. ACM (1960)
17. de Moura, L., Bjørner, N.: Z3: an efficient SMT solver. In: Ramakrishnan, C.R., Rehof, J. (eds.) TACAS 2008. LNCS, vol. 4963, pp. 337–340. Springer, Heidelberg (2008). https://doi.org/10.1007/978-3-540-78800-3_24
18. Gao, J., et al.: G-llava: solving geometric problem with multi-modal large language model. arXiv preprint arXiv:2312.11370 (2023)
19. Gelernter, H., Hansen, J.R., Loveland, D.W.: Empirical explorations of the geometry theorem machine. In: Papers presented at the May 3-5, 1960, western joint IRE-AIEE-ACM Computer Conference, pp. 143–149 (1960)
20. Gelernter, H.L.: Realization of a geometry theorem proving machine. In: International Conference on Information Processing (1959)
21. Gurobi Optimization, LLC: Gurobi Optimizer Reference Manual (2024). https://www.gurobi.com
22. Herbst, P., Brach, C.: Proving and doing proofs in high school geometry classes: what is it that is going on for students? Cogn. Instr. 24(1), 73–122 (2006)
23. Hunter, J.D.: Matplotlib: a 2d graphics environment. Comput. Sci. Eng. 9(03), 90–95 (2007)
24. Janičić, P.: GCLC — a tool for constructive euclidean geometry and more than that. In: Iglesias, A., Takayama, N. (eds.) ICMS 2006. LNCS, vol. 4151, pp. 58–73. Springer, Heidelberg (2006). https://doi.org/10.1007/11832225_6
25. Kapur, D.: Geometry theorem proving using hilbert's nullstellensatz. In: Proceedings of the Fifth ACM Symposium on Symbolic and Algebraic Computation, pp. 202–208 (1986)

26. Kapur, D.: Automated geometric reasoning: dixon resultants, gröbner bases, and characteristic sets. In: Automated Deduction in Geometry: International Workshop on Automated Deduction in Geometry Toulouse, France, 27–29 September 1996 Selected Papers 1, pp. 1–36. Springer (1997)
27. Kazemi, M., Alvari, H., Anand, A., Wu, J., Chen, X., Soricut, R.: Geomverse: a systematic evaluation of large models for geometric reasoning. arXiv preprint arXiv:2312.12241 (2023)
28. Koedinger, K.R., Anderson, J.R.: Abstract planning and perceptual chunks: elements of expertise in geometry. Cogn. Sci. **14**(4), 511–550 (1990)
29. Kutzler, B., Stifter, S.: On the application of buchberger's algorithm to automated geometry theorem proving. J. Symb. Comput. **2**(4), 389–397 (1986)
30. Lu, P., et al.: Inter-gps: interpretable geometry problem solving with formal language and symbolic reasoning. arXiv preprint arXiv:2105.04165 (2021)
31. Meurer, A., et al.: Sympy: symbolic computing in python. PeerJ Comput. Sci. **3**, e103 (2017)
32. Murphy, L., Yang, K., Sun, J., Li, Z., Anandkumar, A., Si, X.: Autoformalizing euclidean geometry. arXiv preprint arXiv:2405.17216 (2024)
33. Nevins, A.J.: Plane geometry theorem proving using forward chaining. Artif. Intell. **6**(1), 1–23 (1975)
34. Reiter: A semantically guided deductive system for automatic theorem proving. IEEE Trans. Comput. **100**(4), 328–334 (1976)
35. Trinh, T.H., Wu, Y., Le, Q.V., He, H., Luong, T.: Solving olympiad geometry without human demonstrations. Nature **625**(7995), 476–482 (2024)
36. Wang, D.: Geometry machines: From AI to SMC. In: Calmet, J., Campbell, J.A., Pfalzgraf, J. (eds.) AISMC 1996. LNCS, vol. 1138, pp. 213–239. Springer, Heidelberg (1996). https://doi.org/10.1007/3-540-61732-9_60
37. Waswani, A., et al.: Attention is all you need. In: NIPS (2017)
38. Wen-Tsun, W.: Basic principles of mechanical theorem proving in elementary geometries. J. Autom. Reason. **2**, 221–252 (1986)
39. Wu, Y., et al.: Autoformalization with large language models. Adv. Neural. Inf. Process. Syst. **35**, 32353–32368 (2022)
40. Xia, R., et al.: Geox: Geometric problem solving through unified formalized vision-language pre-training. arXiv preprint arXiv:2412.11863 (2024)
41. Ye, Z., Chou, S.-C., Gao, X.-S.: An introduction to java geometry expert. In: Sturm, T., Zengler, C. (eds.) ADG 2008. LNCS (LNAI), vol. 6301, pp. 189–195. Springer, Heidelberg (2011). https://doi.org/10.1007/978-3-642-21046-4_10

Author Index

The manufacturer's authorised representative in the EU is Springer
Nature Customer Service Centre GmbH, Europaplatz 3, 69115 Heidelberg,
Germany. If you have any concerns regarding our products, please
contact ProductSafety@springernature.com

Printed and bound by CPI Group (UK) Ltd, Croydon, CR0 4YY

28/04/2026

02098521-0014